SELECTING AN INFERENTIAL STATISTICAL PROCEDURE

Type of design	Parametric test	Nonparametric test
One sample (when σ_X is known)	z-test (Chapter 10)	none
One sample (when σ_X is not known)	One-sample t-test (Chapter 11)	none
Two independent samples	Independent samples t-test (Chapter 12)	Mann-Whitney U, rank sums test, or one-way chi square (Chapter 15)
Two related samples	Related samples t-test (Chapter 12)	Wilcoxon test (Chapter 15)
Three or more independent samples (one factor)	Between-subjects ANOVA Post Hoc test: HSD or protected t-test (Chapter 13)	Kruskal-Wallis H or one-way chi square Post Hoc test: rank sums test (Chapter 15)
Three or more related samples (one factor)	Within-subjects ANOVA Post Hoc test: HSD or protected t-test (Appendix A)	Friedman X^2 Post Hoc test: Nemenyi's test (Chapter 15)
Two factors	Two-way between-subjects ANOVA (Chapter 14) Two-way within-subjects or mixed-design ANOVA (Appendix A)	Two-way chi square (Chapter 15)

BASIC STATISTICS FOR THE BEHAVIORAL SCIENCES

BASIC STATISTICS FOR THE BEHAVIORAL SCIENCES

Fourth Edition

GARY W. HEIMAN

Buffalo State College

HOUGHTON MIFFLIN COMPANY   **Boston**   **New York**

For my wife, Karen, the love of my life

Senior Sponsoring Editor: Kerry T. Baruth
Editorial Assistant: Nirmal Trivedi
Associate Project Editor: Christian Downey
Senior Manufacturing Coordinator: Priscilla J. Bailey
Senior Marketing Manager: Katherine Greig

Cover images: © Photodisc/Getty Images

Printed in the U.S.A.

Library of Congress Control Number: 2001133281

ISBN: 0-618-22017-8

3456789-DOW-06 05 04 03

Brief Contents

part 4

INFERENTIAL STATISTICS

Appendices

2

Statistics and the Research Process 15

part 2

DESCRIPTIVE STATISTICS: DESCRIBING SAMPLES AND POPULATIONS 39

3

Summarizing Scores Using Frequency Distributions and Percentiles 40

4

Summarizing Scores Using Measures of Central Tendency: The Mean, Median, and Mode 67

5

Summarizing Scores with Measures of Variability: Range, Variance, and Standard Deviation 95

6

Describing Data with *z*-Scores and the Normal Curve Model 127

10

Overview of Statistical Hypothesis Testing: The z-Test 239

11

Hypothesis Testing for a Single Mean or a Correlation Coefficient: The *t*-Test 269

12

Hypothesis Testing for Two-Sample Means: The *t*-Test 300

13

Hypothesis Testing for Two or More Means: The One-Way Analysis of Variance 333

14

Hypothesis Testing for Means from Two Independent Variables: The Two-Way Analysis of Variance 364

15

Chi Square and Other Nonparametric Procedures 402

APPENDICES

$\mathcal{A}$

Additional Statistical Formulas 437

$\mathcal{B}$

Statistical Tables 477

$\mathcal{C}$

Answers to Odd-Numbered Questions 497

Preface

My reasons for originally writing this book are the same as they are today. Many of the undergraduates entering my statistics course have a weak background in mathematics and some degree of "math phobia." Eventually, however, these same students must understand and perform the descriptive and inferential statistics commonly used in behavioral research. The problem is that textbooks often dwell on the remarkable things statisticians *can* do with statistics and say too little about the things researchers actually *do*. Although students can then compute an answer on demand, they do not understand why they should perform the procedure or what their answer reveals about the data. Therefore, I wanted a textbook that takes students' needs into account: a book that *explains*—clearly, patiently, and with an occasional touch of humor—the way a good teacher does.

MY OBJECTIVES

In writing this book, I pursued five objectives.

1. Take a conceptual-intuitive approach   The approach of the text is that statistics are used to make sense out of data. Each procedure is introduced using a simple study with readily understandable goals. I focus on the purpose of research as examining the relationships between variables, then present the procedures for describing and inferring such relationships, and finally return to the conceptual purpose and interpretation of the study. Throughout, I provide students with simplified ways to think about statistical concepts and to see how to translate them into practical procedures for answering practical questions.

2. Present statistics within an understandable research context   Many of the text's early examples involve simple variables and research questions taken from everyday life, so that students have an intuitive feel for the meaning of the scores and relationships discussed. In later chapters, along with students' developing statistical thinking, examples become more representative of real research. Virtually all examples and study questions involve specific variables and research questions, instead of generic data.

3. Deal directly and positively with student weaknesses in mathematics
The text presents no formulas or statistical statements without explanation. Formulas
are introduced in terms of what they accomplish, and an example of each is worked out
in a step-by-step manner. To further reduce the apparent complexity of statistics, I have
stressed the similarities among different procedures, showing how, despite slight variations in computations, they have similar components and answer similar questions.

4. Introduce new terms and concepts in an integrated way   I tie each new
concept and procedure to previous material, briefly reviewing that material before proceeding. Throughout, difficult concepts are presented in small chunks, which are then
built into a foundation and later elaborated.

5. Create a text that students will enjoy as well as learn from   To make the
text readable and engaging, I repeatedly point out the everyday usefulness of statistics,
I have included humor, at times talked directly to students, and pointed out potential
mistakes and provided tips on how to get through the course. In addition, several recur-
ring fictitious characters provide some continuity among topics, give a little "plot" to
the text, and alert students so that they learn to check that their answers make sense.
And, throughout, I have tried to convey my own excitement about statistics and
research and to dispel the notion that statistics (and statisticians) are boring.

ORGANIZATION OF THE TEXT

In Part 1, *Introduction,* Chapter 1 serves as a brief preface for the student and reviews
basic math and graphing techniques. Much of this is material that most professors present in the first class, but having it in a chapter helps to reinforce and legitimize the
information and strategies that are presented. Chapter 2 then introduces the terminology, logic, and goals of statistics within the context of behavioral research.

Chapters 3 through 6 make up Part 2, *Descriptive Statistics* (along with a discussion of
linear interpolation in Appendix A). Chapter 3 presents the common techniques for creating frequency tables and graphs, and introduces how to use the proportion of the area
under the normal curve. Chapter 4 introduces measures of central tendency, focusing on
the characteristics of the mean which later form the basis for measures of variability and
z-scores. Chapter 5 then discusses measures of variability. The chapter ends with a non-
mathematical introduction to the concept of proportion of variance accounted for,
because it fits with variance and prediction errors. The calculations for this are presented
later, in the linear regression chapter, because regression is needed to explain r^2. The
chapter dealing with z-scores (Chapter 6) is immediately after central tendency and variability so that these building blocks are fresh in students' minds when discussing z-scores.
I have included sampling distributions and computing a z-score for a sample mean here so
that students can understand these concepts without the confusion of inferential testing. In
later chapters, inferential statistics are "painlessly" introduced as essentially involving
these z-scores.

Part 3, *Describing Relationships,* consists of Chapters 7 and 8, in which correlation
and regression are introduced as descriptive procedures, with emphasis on interpreting

the correlation coefficient and the variance accounted for. (The point-biserial correlation is included to provide a bridge to measures of effect size in later chapters.) I placed these chapters before the discussion of inferential procedures because otherwise it is confusing to simultaneously introduce these procedures and their inferential tests. Substantial cautions are given, however, about the need for performing inferential procedures on correlation coefficients, and when discussed later, they are presented as a logical variation of significance testing of means.

Part 4, *Inferential Statistics,* begins with Chapter 9, which introduces probability and provides the background for hypothesis testing. The chapter picks up at the discussion of z-scores for means presented in Chapter 6, and then easily adds the notion of using the normal curve to compute probability to make decisions about the representativeness of sample means. In Chapter 10, hypothesis testing is formalized using the z-test, presenting the terminology and symbols that are used, showing how significant and nonsignificant results are interpreted, and describing Type I and Type II errors and the issue of power. Chapter 11 presents the one-sample t-test, the confidence interval for a population mean, and significance testing of correlation coefficients. Chapter 12 covers the independent- and the dependent-samples t-tests, confidence intervals used with these tests, graphing, and calculating effect size. Chapter 13 introduces the one-way, between-subjects ANOVA, including post hoc tests for equal and unequal ns, and eta squared. (The one-way within-subjects ANOVA is described in Appendix A.) Chapter 14 deals with the two-way between-subjects ANOVA, post hoc tests for main effects and for unconfounded comparisons in an interaction, as well as graphing and interpreting interactions. The two-way within-subjects ANOVA and the two-way mixed design ANOVA are also introduced, and computational formulas with examples are presented in Appendix A. Chapter 15 covers the one-way and two-way chi square, as well as the Mann-Whitney, rank sums, Wilcoxon, Kruskal-Wallis, and Friedman nonparametric tests (with appropriate post hoc tests and measures of effect size.)

The text is also designed as a reference book for students, so I've included the formulas for transforming a raw score into a percentile and vice versa, for the semi-interquartile range, for several types of confidence intervals, and for an extensive collection of nonparametric procedures. An instructor can skip the more uncommon procedures, however, without disrupting the discussion of the major procedures.

The text strives to teach students how to interpret their data—not just to report that a result is significant. Thus, I have emphasized such topics as plotting and interpreting graphs and understanding the relationships demonstrated by research. I've also included practical discussions of power and measures of effect size. These discussions occur at the end of a section or chapter so that instructors may easily skip them.

PEDAGOGICAL FORMAT AND FEATURES

A number of features are built into the book to enhance its usefulness as a tool for study and as a reference.

- Each chapter begins with a "Getting Started" section, which lists previously discussed concepts that students should review, followed by the learning goals for the chapter.

- "More Statistical Notation" sections introduce new statistical notations at the beginning of the chapter in which they are needed and, to reduce student confusion, they are introduced separately from the conceptual issues presented in the chapter.
- An opening section in each chapter titled "WHY IS IT IMPORTANT TO KNOW ABOUT . . . ?" introduces the major topic of the chapter, immediately placing it in a research context.
- Each important procedural point is emphasized by a "REMEMBER," a summary reminder set off from the text about the calculation or interpretation of a statistic.
- Computational formulas are highlighted in color throughout the text.
- Key terms are highlighted in bold, reviewed in the chapter summary, and listed in a "KEY TERMS" section at the end of the chapter. There is also an end-of-text glossary. Many mnemonics and analogies are used throughout the text to promote retention and understanding.
- Graphs and diagrams are explained in captions and fully integrated into the discussion.
- "PUTTING IT ALL TOGETHER" sections at the end of each chapter provide advice, cautions, and ways to integrate material from different chapters.
- Each "CHAPTER SUMMARY" section provides a substantive review of the material, not merely a list of the topics covered.
- A minimum of 25 conceptual and procedural questions are provided at the end of each chapter. The questions are divided into "REVIEW QUESTIONS," which require students to define terms and outline procedures, and "APPLICATION QUESTIONS," which require students to perform procedures, interpret results, and critique the procedures and conclusions of others. Odd-numbered questions have final and intermediate answers provided in Appendix C. Even-numbered questions have answers in the Instructor's Resource Manual and on a password-protected Web site.
- A Summary of Formulas is provided at the end of each chapter.
- A glossary of symbols appears on the inside back cover. Tables on the inside front cover provide guidelines for selecting from the descriptive and inferential procedures discussed in the text based on the type of data or research design employed.

NEW FEATURES IN THE FOURTH EDITION

The text was reviewed by a number of statistics instructors, both users and nonusers of the text, who have different levels of experience and who are at various types of schools. The previous edition was well received, however, and the reviewers suggested little in the way of substantial change. The general changes are

- The entire text has been extensively revised and edited to streamline the narrative.
- I also tightened the conceptual presentations and incorporated a number of new explanatory techniques.
- I added several new summary tables and charts to help students organize and remember related topics.

- The end-of-chapter questions are now separated into REVIEW QUESTIONS, which are conceptual and definitional, and APPLICATION QUESTIONS, which are computational and interpretational.
- Many of the figures were revised and relabeled.
- The design and layout of example studies are now referred to as DESIGN DIAGRAMS.
- References to "psychology" were reduced to emphasize that the text pertains to other behavioral sciences as well.

SPECIFIC CHAPTER CHANGES

- In Chapter 2 a discussion was added to better show how researchers use descriptive statistics to understand and envision the data, instead of examining every score.
- The explanation of the problem of causality in correlational and experimental research was revised in Chapters 2 and 7.
- The discussion of graphing of grouped distributions in Chapter 3 was moved to Appendix A. Also, an introduction was added that shows how the normal curve is used to model real data.
- In Chapter 4 the section on What is Central Tendency was rewritten, and the discussions of using the mean to predict and to describe scores were combined.
- Chapter 5 has extensive revisions of using the standard deviation to envision the spread in the distribution, errors in prediction, and proportion of variance accounted for. Also, the use of M and SD in professional publications was noted.
- Chapter 6 contains an expanded discussion of applying the normal curve model to real data, and a number of additional end-of-chapter problems were added.
- In Chapter 8 the discussion of the strength of the relationship and the standard error of the estimate was revised, as was the discussion of computing the proportion of variance accounted for.
- Given that most instructors de-emphasize formulas for calculating probability, the formula for the probability of equally likely events was moved from Chapter 9 to Appendix A.3, which contains the other probability formulas. Also, the explanation of how z-scores reflect the representativeness of a sample mean was revised (with new figures).
- The discussion of power and how to design a powerful study was expanded in Chapter 10. Also, the discussion of statistical hypotheses was revamped.
- Chapter 11 now contains a new summary of the steps in performing the one-sample t-test.
- In Chapter 12 deriving one-tailed hypotheses was revised, as was the computation of confidence intervals for a single mean.
- The explanations of ANOVA were revised in Chapter 13, and omega squared and the F_{max} test were deleted.
- Chapter 14 was shortened, especially when showing how to perform computations, and end-of-chapter problems that required interpolation were eliminated.

- The discussions in Chapter 15 of the two-way chi square and of procedures for ranks were extensively revised.

SUPPLEMENTARY MATERIALS

Supporting the text are several ancillaries for students and instructors:

- *Student Workbook and Study Guide*   Additional Review Questions are available in the Student Workbook and Study Guide, revised by Deborah J. Hendricks and Richard T. Walls of West Virginia University. Each chapter contains a review of objectives, terms, and formulas, a programmed review, conceptual and computational problems (with answers), and a set of multiple-choice questions similar to those in the Instructor's Resource Manual. A final chapter, called "Getting Ready for the Final Exam," facilitates student integration of the entire course. The workbook may be ordered separately, or it may be shrink-wrapped with the textbook to form a package.

- *Instructor's Resource Manual with Test Questions*   This supplement, also revised by Deborah J. Hendricks and Richard T. Walls, contains approximately 750 test items and problems, as well as suggestions for classroom activities, discussion, and use of statistical software. It also includes answers to the even-numbered end-of-chapter questions from this book. The test items are also available on computer disk for IBM and Macintosh computers.

COMPUTER APPLICATIONS

There are several ways that computers can be used with this text.

For Students

- *Using SPSS for Windows* by Dr. Charles Stangor. This is a 50-page supplement for teaching SPSS to beginning students. It is compatible with this textbook, it is easily understood, and it comes complete with data sets on disk. The supplement is available separately, or it can be shrink-wrapped with this textbook. It is very inexpensive. (At this writing, the added cost was under $3.00.)

- *ACE Tests*   Students can prepare for exams by visiting the Houghton Mifflin Web site and completing "ACE" tests free of charge. These are multiple choice tests for each chapter that are instantly graded, and then correct answers are provided. The address is http://psychology.college.hmco.com/students.

- *Answers to Even-Numbered End-of-Chapter Questions*   Students can obtain answers to all of the even-numbered end-of-chapter study questions at the Houghton Mifflin Web site. The site is password protected to preserve the answers so that others can use the even-numbered problems as graded homework. Otherwise, the password is available to instructors from a Houghton Mifflin sales representative.

For the Instructor

- *Psychology Web Site*   Some useful and innovative teaching resources can be found at Houghton Mifflin's Web site. Go to http://www.hmco.com and then click on the College Division's Psychology Page.

ACKNOWLEDGMENTS

I gratefully acknowledge the help and support of many professionals associated with Houghton Mifflin Company. In particular, I want to thank Kerry Baruth, Christian Downey, and Merrill Peterson. Finally, I want to thank Nirmal Trivedi for his professionalism and patience.

I am also grateful to the following reviewers who provided valuable feedback.

Darryl Beale, Cerritos College

Thomas Eissenberg, Virginia Commonwealth University

Jane Ellington, Austin College

Gary J. Gargano, Saint Joseph's University

Deborah J. Hendricks, West Virginia University

Agnes Hughes, Immaculata College

G. Pat Powers, Southeastern Oklahoma State University

Judith Roberts, City College of San Francisco

Hasan Ziaie, Virginia Union University

INTRODUCTION

Okay, so you're taking a course in statistics. You probably wonder what it's all about. Most students know that statistics involve math, but they don't know that studying statistics is much more interesting and educational than merely cranking out a bunch of math problems. A tour through the world of statistics will help you think, reason, and apply logic, both in your everyday life and when drawing conclusions from scientific research. You will also learn new ways of simplifying enormous complexities. And mastering a course in statistics is a real ego booster. In addition, statistics can be fun! Statistics are challenging, there is an elegance to their logic, and you can do nifty things with them. So, keep an open mind, be prepared to do a little work, and you'll be amazed by what happens. You'll find that although statistics are a little unusual, they are not incomprehensible, they do not require you to be a math wizard, and they are very relevant to the behavioral sciences.

The following two chapters provide an overview. The first chapter explains why students in the behavioral sciences need to learn statistics, and what learning statistics actually involves. The second chapter shows how statistics are used in behavioral research.

1

Approaching Statistics

GETTING STARTED

Your goals in this chapter are to learn:

- The general purpose of statistical procedures.
- An effective strategy for learning statistics.
- The basic math that's needed.

This chapter discusses some common misconceptions about statistics and considers the best way to study statistics. We also review the math and graphing techniques you'll be using.

SOME COMMONLY ASKED QUESTIONS ABOUT STATISTICS

Students repeatedly ask the following questions about statistics. The answers to these questions will teach you something about behavioral research and the use of statistics (and maybe relieve any anxiety you have).

What Are Statistics?

The word *statistics* means different things to different people. To behavioral scientists, it is typically a shortened version of the phrase *statistical procedures*, which are computations performed as part of conducting research. The answers obtained by performing some procedures are also called statistics. Thus, the word **statistics** refers both to statistical procedures and to the answers obtained from those procedures.

What Do Researchers Do with Statistics?

Researchers need statistics because they have a research question in mind, and statistics help them to answer the question. The behavioral sciences are based on empirical research. The word **empirical** means knowledge obtained through observation of events (instead of through intuition or faith). Empirical research involves measurement, and behavioral research measures behaviors. Such measurement results in numbers, or scores. The scores obtained in research are the **data.** (The word *data,* by the way, is plural, referring to more than one score, so say "the data are . . .") For example, to study intelligence, researchers measure the IQ scores of different individuals; to observe how getting rewards influences how often rats press a lever, researchers measure the rats' lever-pressing scores; or to study differences in the attitudes of married couples, researchers measure difference scores. In any study the researcher ends up with a large batch of data, which then must be made manageable and meaningful. Statistical procedures are used to *organize, summarize,* and *communicate* data and then to *conclude* what the data indicate. In essence, statistics help a researcher to make sense out of the data.

But I'm Not Interested in Research; I Just Want to Help People!

Even if you're not interested in being a researcher, you still must understand statistics so that you can comprehend other people's research. Let's say that you become a therapist or counselor, and you do not consider yourself a "scientist." You hear of a new therapy that says the way to "cure" people of some psychological problem is to scare the living daylights out of them. This sounds crazy, but what is important is the quality of the research that does or does not support this therapy. As a responsible professional, you would evaluate the research supporting this therapy before you would use it. You could not do so without understanding statistics. However, after you have studied statistics, reading and evaluating research is relatively easy.

But I Don't Know Anything about Research!

This book is written for students who have not yet studied how to conduct behavioral research. Whenever we discuss a statistical procedure, we'll also discuss simple examples of research that employ the procedure, and this should be enough to get you by. Then, later, when you study research methods, you will know the appropriate statistical procedures to use.

What if I'm Not Very Good at Statistics?

In the grand scheme of things, the application of statistics is one small, although extremely important, step in the research process. Fortunately, statisticians have already developed all of the formulas and internal workings of the statistical procedures you'll encounter, so you need be concerned only with *applying* them correctly. Also, there are not a great number of different procedures to learn, and these fancy "procedures" include such mundane things as computing an average, identifying the highest and lowest scores in the data, or describing one person's score relative to everyone else's score. Statistics are simply a tool used in the behavioral sciences, just like a wrench is a tool used in the repair of automobile engines. A mechanic need not be an expert wrencher, and a researcher need not be an expert statistician. Rather, in the same way that a mechanic must understand the correct use of wrenches to fix an engine, you must understand the correct use of statistics to understand research.

But Statistics Aren't Written in English!

There is no denying that statistics involve many strange symbols and unfamiliar terms. But the symbols and terms are simply the shorthand "code" for communicating statistical results and for simplifying statistical formulas. A major part of learning statistics is merely learning the code. Think of it this way: To understand research you must speak the language, and you are about to learn the language called statistics. Then you will be able to read, understand, and communicate statistical information using the appropriate symbols and terminology. Once you speak the language, much of the mystery surrounding statistics evaporates. In fact, before you're done, you'll understand all of the terms listed in the tables inside the front cover of this book (and all of the symbols listed inside the back cover).

What if I'm Not Very Good at Math?

Although statistics do involve math, it's simple math. You need to know only how to add, subtract, multiply, divide, square, find square roots, and draw simple graphs. What makes statistical procedures *appear* difficult is that they involve a sequence of operations (first you square the numbers, then you add them together, then you divide by another number, and so on). Working through the formulas is not difficult, but because they're written in code, it takes a little practice.

So All I Have to Do Is Learn How to Compute the Answers?

No! Don't get so carried away with formulas and calculations that you lose sight of the big picture. In the big picture, a statistical answer tells you something about data. Ultimately you want to make sense of data, and to do that, you must compute the appropriate statistic and then correctly interpret it. More than anything else, you need to learn *when* and *why* to use each procedure and how to *interpret* its answer. Be sure to put as much effort into this as you do into learning how to perform the calculations.

All Right, So How Do I Learn Statistics?

Study. Think. Practice. Think. Practice some more. The way to learn statistics is to *do* statistics. First, remember that you are learning a foreign language called statistics. Therefore, you must memorize and understand the terminology of statistics. In this book important statistical terms are printed in bold type or are preceded by such phrases as "in statistical language we say . . ." There is also a glossary of terms at the back of the book.

Second, recognize that because you do not yet speak the language, you won't learn anything by simply skimming a chapter. You must translate the terminology and symbols into a verbal description you can understand, and this takes time and effort. Also, you cannot "cram" this material. If you try, you won't learn much (and your brain will melt). Instead, work on statistics a little bit every day. Then you'll be able to digest the material in bite-sized pieces. This is the most effective—and least painful—way to learn statistics.

Finally, each new statistical concept builds on previous concepts, so be sure you understand a topic before you move on to the next one. To help you, the "GETTING STARTED" part of each chapter tells you the major concepts from preceding chapters that you'll need to already understand. And whenever we discuss a concept covered earlier, there will be a brief review of it or a reference to a previous chapter. Go back and review a topic whenever necessary. Also, every time you encounter a new formula, work through the example presented. Master the formulas and codes at each step, because they often reappear later as part of more complicated formulas.

What's with This Book?

This book takes an intuitive approach to statistical concepts. Explanations preceded by such phrases as "You can think of it as if . . ." are designed to give your mind something to grasp other than formulas and definitions. Use the examples and analogies to help you remember and understand a concept. However, statistics is a precise discipline, so pay attention to the "official" definitions as well.

The research examples tend to be very simple, and they may give you the impression that every study produces about five scores, and that all scores are nice round numbers like 2 or 5. In fact, real research typically involves many individuals, often with ugly numbers like -104.387. But if you can perform a procedure using simple numbers, you'll be able to perform it with more complex data.

This book contains several features to direct your attention to important information. Each chapter begins with a list of the major points you should learn from the chapter. (After you think you've mastered the chapter, check that you understand everything in the list.) Next, most chapters begin with a section titled "More Statistical Notation." Here you'll see the new symbols used in the chapter. Most chapters also have a section that asks "*Why is it important?*" Here you'll get an overview of the question the procedures are designed to answer and see how they are used in everyday research. Also, every so often throughout a chapter you will see statements labeled "REMEMBER." These refer to basic concepts that are especially important. The last section in each chapter is called "PUTTING IT ALL TOGETHER." It contains advice, cautions, and ways to integrate the material from different chapters.

At the end of each chapter is first a summary. Read each statement and determine whether you understand it. Then are the KEY TERMS: be sure you can define each. Next are practice problems, which will help you identify weak spots in your knowledge (think of this as a self-test before the real test). First are REVIEW QUESTIONS that test your knowledge of definitions and concepts, followed by APPLICATION QUESTIONS that test your ability to use statistics in research settings. The answers to odd-numbered problems are provided in Appendix C at the back of the book. However, do not cheat yourself by looking at the answer before you have made a serious attempt to solve the problem. Finally, for quick reference each chapter provides a list of the formulas discussed in the chapter.

REVIEW OF MATHEMATICS USED IN STATISTICS

The remainder of this chapter reviews the math used in performing statistical procedures. There are accepted systems for statistical notation, for rounding an answer, for transforming scores, and for creating graphs.

Basic Statistical Notation

Statistical notation is the standardized code for the mathematical operations performed in the formulas, for the order in which operations are performed, and for the answers we obtain.

Identifying Mathematical Operations   We write formulas in statistical notation so that we can apply them to any data. We usually use the symbol X or Y to stand for each individual score obtained in a study. When a formula says to do something to X, it means to do it to all of the scores called X. When a formula says to do something to Y, it means to do it to all of the scores called Y.

The mathematical operations we'll perform are basic ones. Addition is indicated by the plus sign and subtraction is indicated by the minus sign. We read from left to right, so $X - Y$ is read as "X minus Y." (I *said* this was basic!) This order is important, however, because $10 - 4$, for example, is $+6$, but $4 - 10$ is -6. With subtraction, pay attention to what is subtracted from what, and whether the answer is positive or negative.

We indicate division by forming a fraction, such as X/Y. The number above the dividing line is called the numerator, and the number below the line is called the denominator (the d in denominator stands for "down below"). *Always express fractions as decimals,* dividing the denominator *into* the numerator. (After all, 1/2 equals .5, not 2!)

Multiplication is indicated in one of two ways. We may place two components next to each other: XY means "multiply X times Y." Or we may indicate multiplication using parentheses: 4(2) and (4)(2) both mean "multiply 4 times 2."

The symbol X^2 means square the score, so if X is 4, X^2 is 16. Conversely, $\sqrt{X}$ means "find the square root of X," so $\sqrt{4}$ is 2. (The symbol $\sqrt{\ }$ also means "use your calculator.")

Determining the Order of Mathematical Operations   Statistical formulas often call for a series of mathematical steps. Sometimes the steps are set apart by parentheses. Parentheses mean "the quantity," so always find the quantity inside the parentheses first and then perform the operations outside of the parentheses on that quantity. For example, $(2)(4 + 3)$ indicates to multiply 2 times "the quantity 4 plus 3." So first add, which gives $(2)(7)$, and then multiply to get 14.

A square root sign also operates on "the quantity," so always compute the quantity inside the square root sign first. Thus $\sqrt{2 + 7}$ means find the square root of the quantity $2 + 7$; so $\sqrt{2 + 7}$ becomes $\sqrt{9}$, which is 3.

Most formulas are giant fractions. Pay attention to how far the dividing line is drawn, because the length of a dividing line determines the quantity that is in the numerator and the denominator. For example, you might see a formula that looks like this:

$$\frac{\frac{6}{3} + 14}{\sqrt{64}} = \frac{2 + 14}{\sqrt{64}} = \frac{16}{\sqrt{64}} = \frac{16}{8} = 2$$

The longest dividing line means you should divide the square root of 64 into the quantity in the numerator. The dividing line in the fraction in the numerator is under only the 6, so first divide 6 by 3, which is 2. Then add 14, for a total of 16. In the denominator, the square root of 64 is 8. After dividing, the final answer is 2.

If you become confused in reading a formula, remember that there is an order of precedence of mathematical operations. *Unless otherwise indicated, perform squaring or taking a square root first, then multiplication or division, and then addition or subtraction.* Thus, for $(2)(4) + 5$, multiply 2 times 4 first and then add 5. For $2^2 + 3^2$, square first, which gives $4 + 9$, which is then 13. On the other hand, $(2 + 3)^2$ is 5^2, which is 25.

Working with Formulas   We perform the operations in a formula to find an answer, and we have symbols that stand for that answer. For example, in the formula $B = AX + K$, the B stands for the numerical answer we will obtain. Get in the habit of thinking of the *symbols* as quantities. Because B stands for a number, we can discuss whether B is larger than, smaller than, or equal to some other number or symbol.

In each formula you will compute the value of the single term that is isolated on one side of the equals sign, but you will know the values of the terms on the other side of the equals sign. For the formula $B = AX + K$, say that $A = 4$, $X = 11$, and $K = 3$. Now compute B. In working any formula, the first step is to copy the formula and then rewrite it, replacing the symbols with their known values. Thus, start with

$B = AX + K$

Filling in the numbers gives

$B = 4(11) + 3$

To keep track of your calculations, rewrite the formula again after performing *one* mathematical operation. Above, multiplication takes precedence over addition, so multiply and then write the formula as

$B = 44 + 3$

After adding,

$B = 47$

For simple procedures, you may have an urge to skip rewriting the formula after each step. Don't! That's a good way to introduce errors.

Rounding

Close counts in statistics, so you must carry out calculations to the appropriate number of decimal places. Usually you must "round off" your answer. The rule is to always carry out calculations so that your *final* answer after rounding has two more decimal places than the original scores. For example, if you start with whole-number scores (e.g., 2 and 11) your final answer should contain two decimal places. But say your original scores contain one decimal place (e.g., 1.4 and 12.3). Here your final answer should contain *three* decimal places. However, *do not round off at each intermediate step in a formula; round off only at the end!* Thus, if the final answer is to contain two decimal places, you would round off your intermediate answers to at least three decimal places, and then round off the final answer to two decimal places.

To round off a calculation use the following rules:

If the number in the next decimal place is 5 or greater than 5, round up. For example, to round to two decimal places, 2.366 is rounded to 2.370, which becomes 2.37.

If the number in the next decimal place is less than 5, round down: 3.524 is rounded to 3.520, which becomes 3.52.

Recognize that we add zeroes to the right of the decimal point as a way of indicating the level of precision we are using. For example, rounding 4.996 to two decimal places produces 5, but to show we used the precision of two decimal places, we report it as 5.00.

> *REMEMBER*   Round off your final answer to two more decimal places than are in the original scores.

Transformations

Many statistical procedures are nothing more than elaborate transformations. A **transformation** is a mathematical procedure for systematically converting a set of scores into a different set of scores. Adding 5 to each score is a transformation, or converting "number correct" into "percent correct" is a transformation.

We transform data for one of two reasons. First, transformations make scores easier to work with. For example, if all of the scores contain a decimal, we might multiply every score by 10 to eliminate the decimals. Second, transformations make different kinds of scores comparable. For example, if you obtained 8 out of 10 on a statistics test and 75 out of 100 on an English test, it would be difficult to compare the two scores. However, if you transformed each grade to percent correct, you could then directly compare performance on the two tests.

In statistics, we rely heavily on transformations to proportions and percents.

Proportions   A **proportion** is a decimal number between 0 and 1 that indicates a fraction of the total. To transform a number to a proportion, simply divide the number by the total. If 4 out of 10 people pass an exam, then the proportion of people passing the exam is 4/10, which equals .4. Or, if you score 6 correct on a test out of a possible 12, the proportion you have correct is 6/12, which is .5. Conversely, to determine the number that is a certain proportion, multiply the proportion times the total. Thus, to find how many questions out of 12 you must answer correctly to get .5 correct, multiply .5 times 12, and voilà, the answer is 6.

Percents   We can also transform a proportion into a percent. A **percent** (or percentage) is a proportion multiplied by 100. Above, your proportion correct was .5, so you had (.5)(100) or 50% correct. Altogether, to transform the original test score of 6 out of 12 to a percent, first divide the score by the total to find the proportion and then multiply by 100. Thus, (6/12)(100) equals 50%.

To transform a percent back into a proportion, divide the percent by 100 (above, 50/100 equals .5). Altogether, to find the test score that corresponds to a certain percent, transform the percent to a proportion and then multiply the proportion times the total number possible. Thus, to find the score that corresponds to 50% of 12, transform 50% to the proportion .5 and then multiply .5 times 12. So, 50% of 12 is equal to (50/100)(12), which is 6.

Recognize that percents are whole numbers: Think of 50% as 50 of those things called percents. On the other hand, a decimal in a percent is a proportion of *one* percent. Thus, .2% is .2, or two-tenths, of one percent, which is .002 of the total.

Creating Graphs

One type of statistical procedure is none other than plotting graphs. In case it's been a long time since you've drawn one, recall that the horizontal line across the bottom of a graph is the *X* axis, and the vertical line at the left-hand side is the *Y* axis. The axes should be drawn so that the height of the *Y* axis is about 60 to 75% of the length of the *X* axis (see Figure 1.1). Where the two axes intersect is always labeled as a score of zero on *X* and a score of zero on *Y*. On the *X* axis, scores become larger positive scores as you move to the *right*. On the *Y* axis, scores become larger positive scores as you move *upward*.

Say that we measured the height and weight of several people. We decide to place weight on the *Y* axis and height on the *X* axis. (How to decide this is discussed later.)

FIGURE 1.1   Arrangement of the *X* and *Y* axes in a graph

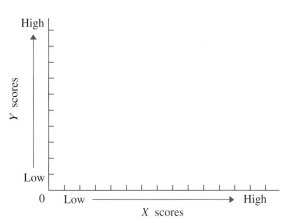

We plot the scores as shown in Figure 1.2. Notice that the lowest height score is 63, and so on the *X* axis the lowest score is 63. Whenever there is a large gap between 0 and the lowest score we are plotting, the axis is compressed using two diagonal lines (//). This indicates that we cut out the part of the *X* axis between 0 and 63 and slid the graph over closer to 0. We did the same thing to the *Y* axis, because the lowest weight is 130.

In the body of the graph we plot the scores from the table on the left. Jane is 63 inches tall and weighs 130 pounds, so we place a dot above the height of 63 and opposite the weight of 130. And so on. Each dot on the graph is called a **data point.** Notice that you read the graph by using the scores on one axis and the data points. For example, to find the weight of the person who has a height of 67, travel vertically from 67 to the data point and then horizontally back to the *Y* axis: 165 is the corresponding weight.

In later chapters you will learn when to connect the data points with lines and when to create other types of figures. Regardless of the final form of a graph, always label the *X* and *Y* axes to indicate what the scores measure (not just *X* and *Y*), and always give your graph a title indicating what it describes.

When creating a graph, make the spacing between the labels for the scores on an axis reflect the spacing between the actual scores. In Figure 1.2 the labels 64, 65, and 66 are equally spaced on the graph, because the difference between 64 and 65 is the same as the difference between 65 and 66. However, in other situations, the labels may not be equally spaced. For example, the labels 10, 20, and 40 would not be equally spaced, because the distance between these scores is not equal.

Sometimes there are so many different scores that we cannot include a label for each score. The units used in labeling each axis then determine the impression the graph gives. Say that for the previous weight scores, instead of labeling the *Y* axis in units of 10 pounds, we labeled it in units of 100 pounds as shown in Figure 1.3. This graph shows the same data as Figure 1.2, but changing the scale on the *Y* axis creates a much flatter pattern of data points. This gives the misleading impression that regardless of their height, the people all have about the same weight. However, looking at the actual

FIGURE 1.2 Plot of height and weight scores

Person	Height	Weight
Jane	63	130
Bob	64	140
Mary	65	155
Tony	66	160
Sue	67	165
Mike	68	170

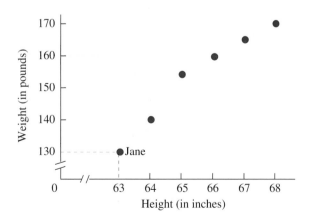

FIGURE 1.3 Plot of height and weight scores using a different scale on the *Y* axis

Height	Weight
63	130
64	140
65	155
66	160
67	165
68	170

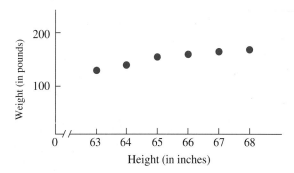

scores, you see that this is not the case. Thus, always label the axes in a way that honestly presents the data, without exaggerating or minimizing the pattern formed by the data points.

PUTTING IT ALL TOGETHER

That's all the basic math you'll need to get started. You are now ready to begin learning to use statistics. In fact, you already use statistics. If you compute your grade average, or if you ask your instructor to "curve" your grades, you are using statistics. When you understand from the nightly news that Senator Fluster is projected to win the presidential election, or when you learn from a television commercial that Brand X "significantly" reduces tooth decay, you are using statistics. You simply do not yet know the formal names for these statistics or the logic behind them. But you will.

CHAPTER SUMMARY

1. Whether or not they are active researchers, behavioral scientists rely on statistical procedures.

2. All *empirical* research is based on observation and involves some form of measurement, resulting in numbers, or scores. These scores are the *data*.

3. The term *statistics* refers to the procedures and formulas used to analyze data and to the numerical answers obtained from statistical procedures.

4. Statistical procedures are used to make sense out of data: They are used to organize, summarize, and communicate data and to draw conclusions about what the data indicate.

5. The goal in learning statistics is to know *when* to perform a particular procedure and how to *interpret* the answer.

6. Unless otherwise indicated, the order of mathematical operations is to square or find the square root first, then multiply or divide, and then add or subtract.

7. Perform mathematical operations contained within a set of parentheses first, perform operations within the square root sign prior to finding the square root, and perform operations above and below the dividing line of a fraction prior to dividing.

8. Round off the final answer in a calculation to two more decimal places than are in the original scores. If the digit in the next decimal place is equal to or greater than 5, round up; if the digit is less than 5, round down.

9. A *transformation* is a procedure for systematically converting one set of scores into a different set of scores. Transformations make scores easier to work with and make different kinds of scores comparable.

10. A *proportion* is a decimal between 0 and 1 that indicates a fraction of the total. To transform a score to a proportion, divide the score by the total. To determine the score that produces a particular proportion, multiply the proportion times the total.

11. To transform a proportion to a *percent,* multiply the proportion times 100. To transform an original score to a percent, find the proportion by dividing the score by the total and then multiply by 100. To transform a percent to a proportion, divide the percent by 100. To find the original score that corresponds to a particular percent, transform the percent to a proportion and then multiply the proportion times the total.

12. When creating a graph, draw the X and Y axes so that the height of the Y axis is 60 to 75% of the length of the X axis. Label each axis to accurately reflect the distance between scores and show how the scores change.

13. A *data point* is a dot plotted on a graph to represent a pair of X and Y scores.

KEY TERMS: Can You Define the Following?

data *3*	proportion *8*
data point *10*	statistical notation *6*
empirical *3*	statistics *2*
percent *9*	transformation *8*

REVIEW QUESTIONS

(Answers for odd-numbered problems are in Appendix C.)

1. Why do researchers need to learn statistics?
2. As someone learning statistics, what should be your goals?
3. Why should you plan on memorizing terminology and symbols in this course?
4. What does the term *statistical notation* refer to?
5. (a) To how many places should you round a final answer? (b) If you are rounding to two decimal places, what are the rules for rounding up or down?

6. (a) What is a transformation? (b) Why do we transform data?
7. If given no other information, what is the order in which to perform mathematical operations?
8. What is a percentage?
9. What is a data point?
10. A researcher measures the IQ scores of a group of college students. What four things will the researcher use statistics for?
11. What is a proportion and how is it computed?
12. How do you transform a percentage to a proportion?

APPLICATION QUESTIONS

13. (a) What proportion is 5 out of 15? (b) What proportion of 50 is 10? (c) One in a thousand equals what proportion?
14. For each of the following, to how many places will you round off your final answer? (a) When measuring the number of questions students answered correctly on a test. (b) When measuring what proportion of the total possible points students have earned in a course. (c) When counting the number of people having various blood types. (d) When measuring the number of dollar bills possessed by each person in a group.
15. Transform each answer in problem 13 to a percent.
16. The intermediate answers from some calculations based on whole-number scores are $X = 4.3467892$ and $Y = 3.3333$. We now want to find $X^2 + Y^2$. What values of X and Y do we use?
17. Round off the following numbers to two decimal places: (a) 13.7462 (b) 10.043 (c) 10.047 (d) .079 (e) 1.004
18. For $Q = (X + Y)(X^2 + Y^2)$, find the value of Q when $X = 3$ and $Y = 5$.
19. Using the formula in question 18, find Q when $X = 8$ and $Y = -2$.
20. For $X = 14$ and $Y = 4.8$, find D:

$$D = \left(\frac{X - Y}{Y}\right)\left(\sqrt{X}\right)$$

21. Using the formula in question 20, find D for $X = 9$ and $Y = -4$.
22. Of the 40 students in a gym class, 13 played volleyball, 12 ran track (4 of whom did a push-up), and the remainder were absent. (a) What proportion of the class ran track? (b) What percentage played volleyball? (c) What percentage of the runners did a push-up? (d) What proportion of the class was absent?
23. In your statistics course, there are three exams: I is worth 40 points, II is worth 35 points, and III is worth 60 points. Your professor defines a passing grade as earning 60% of the points. (a) What is the smallest score you must obtain on each exam to pass it? (b) In total you can earn 135 points in the course. How many points must you earn from the three exams *combined* to pass the course? (c) You actually earn a total of 115 points during the course. What percent of the total did you earn?
24. There are 80 students enrolled in statistics. (a) You and 11 others earned the same number of points. What percent of the class received your grade? (b) Forty

percent of the class received a grade of C. How many students received a C?
(c) Only 7.5% of the class received a D. How many students is this? (d) A student
claims that .5% of the class failed. Why is this impossible?

25. (a) How do you space the labels on the *X* or *Y* axis of a graph? (b) Why must you
be careful when selecting the amounts used as these labels?

26. Create a graph showing the data points for the following scores.

X Score	Y Score
Student's Age	Student's Test Score
20	10
25	30
35	20
45	60
25	55
40	70
45	3

2

Statistics and the Research Process

GETTING STARTED

To understand this chapter, recall the following:

- From Chapter 1, recall (1) that we use statistics to make sense out of data and (2) how to create and interpret graphs.

Your goals in this chapter are to learn:

- What a relationship is and what is meant by the "strength" of a relationship.
- How random sampling leads to representative or unrepresentative samples.
- When and why descriptive and inferential procedures are used, and what is meant by the terms *statistic* and *parameter*.
- How drawing inferences about a population of scores based on a sample of scores is actually describing how a behavior occurs in a given situation in nature.
- What the difference is between an experiment and a correlational study and how to recognize the independent variable, the conditions, and the dependent variable in an experiment.
- What the four scales of measurement are.

To understand statistics, you need to first understand the research process. Then you can see how statistics fit in. Therefore, this chapter discusses the basics of behavioral research, presents an overview of statistical procedures, and gets you started in the language of statistics.

THE LOGIC OF SCIENTIFIC RESEARCH

The goal of science is to understand the "laws of nature"—the rules that describe how the universe operates. Behavioral scientists study the laws of nature regarding the behavior of living organisms. That is, we assume there are specific influences that govern every behavior of all members of a particular group. Then, although any single study is a very small step in this process, our goal is to understand every factor that influences the behaviors of a particular group. Thus, when researchers study such things as the mating behavior of sea lions, social interactions between gorillas, or neural firing in a human's brain, they are ultimately studying the laws of nature.

There are two major components to the logic researchers use to draw conclusions about a law of nature: First, we measure the data to learn how the law operates, and then we draw conclusions about the larger group of individuals that the law applies to.

Obtaining Data by Measuring Variables

Research involves a series of translations. Nature is extremely complex, so we simplify any law by translating it into one specific influence on one specific behavior in one specific situation that we can measure. For example, we might start with the "law" that says a person must repeatedly interact with—study—a set of information in order to learn it. This is a rather global statement, however, which could apply in many situations. Therefore, we might translate it into a specific question: Does studying statistics improve your learning of them?

To complete the translation, we must decide what we mean by "studying" and how to measure it, and what we mean by "learning" and how to measure it. The factors we measure that influence behaviors—as well as the behaviors themselves—are called variables. A **variable** is anything that, when measured, can produce two or more different values. A few of the variables found in behavioral research include your age, race, gender, and intelligence; your personality type or political affiliation; how anxious, angry, or aggressive you are; how attractive you find someone; how hard you will work at a task; or how accurately you recall a situation.

Variables fall into two general categories. If a score indicates the *amount* of a variable that is present, the variable is a *quantitative* variable. A person's height, for example, is a quantitative variable. Some variables, however, cannot be measured in amounts. Instead, a score *classifies* an individual on the basis of some characteristic. Such variables are called *qualitative,* or classification, variables. A person's gender, for example, is a qualitative variable, because the "score" of male or female indicates a quality, or category.

For our study, we might measure "studying" using such variables as how much effort is put into studying or the number of times a chapter is read, but say we select the variable of the number of hours spent studying for a particular statistics test. We might measure "learning" by measuring how well statistical results can be interpreted or how quickly a specific procedure can be performed, but say we select the variable of grades on the statistics test.

As in any research, we then study a law of nature by studying the *relationship* between our variables.

Examining the Relationships Between Variables

If nature relates those mental activities we call studying to those mental activities we call learning, then different amounts of learning should occur with different amounts of studying. In other words, there should be a *relationship* between studying and learning. A **relationship** occurs when a change in one variable is accompanied by a consistent change in another variable. Because we measure scores, a relationship is a pattern in which specific scores on one variable are paired with specific scores on another variable. As the scores on one variable change, the scores on the other variable change in a consistent manner. In our example we predict the relationship in which the more you study, the higher your test grade will be.

What might this relationship look like? Say that we asked some students how long they studied for a test and their subsequent grades on the test. We might obtain the data in Table 2.1. They form a relationship, because as the scores on the variable of study time change (increase), the scores on the variable of test grades also change in a consistent fashion (also increase).[1] Further, when the scores on the study time variable do not change (for example, Jane and Bob both studied for 1 hour), the scores on the grade variable do not change either (they both received Fs). In statistics, we use the term *association* when talking about relationships. In the same way that your shadow's movements are associated with your movements, low study times are associated with low test grades and high study times are associated with high test grades.

> **REMEMBER** In a *relationship*, as the scores on one variable change, the scores on the other variable change in a consistent manner.

TABLE 2.1 Scores Showing a Relationship Between the Variables of Study Time and Test Grades

Student	Study Time in Hours	Test Grades
Jane	1	F
Bob	1	F
Sue	2	D
Tony	3	C
Sidney	3	C
Ann	4	B
Rose	4	B
Lou	5	A

[1]The data presented in this book are a work of fiction. Any resemblance to real data is purely a coincidence.

As researchers, we want to understand relationships, and a major use of statistical procedures is to examine the scores in a relationship and the pattern they form. The simplest relationships fit either the pattern "the more you X, the *more* you Y" or the pattern "the more you X, the *less* you Y." Thus, the saying "the bigger they are, the harder they fall" describes a relationship, as does that old saying "the more you practice statistics, the less difficult they are." Relationships may also form more complicated patterns where, for example, more X at first leads to more Y, but beyond a certain point even more X leads to *less* Y. For example, the more you exercise, the better you feel, but beyond a certain point more exercise leads to feeling less well, as pain and exhaustion set in.

Although the above examples involve quantitative variables, relationships can also involve qualitative variables. For example, men typically are taller than women. If you think of male and female as "scores" on the variable of gender, then this is a relationship, because as gender scores change (going from male to female), height scores consistently decrease. We can study any combination of qualitative and quantitative variables in a relationship.

Strength of a Relationship   Table 2.1 showed a perfectly consistent association between hours of study time and test grades: All those who studied the same amount received the same grade. In the real world, however, not everyone who studies the same amount of time will receive the same test grade. (Life is not fair.) A relationship can be present, however, even if there is only some *degree* of consistency, so that as the scores on one variable change, the scores on the other variable *tend* to change in a consistent fashion. For example, Table 2.2 presents a relationship between the number of hours spent studying and the number of errors made on a test. Higher study-time scores tend to be associated with lower error scores, but not every increase in study time is matched perfectly with a decrease in errors, and sometimes the same studying score produces different error scores. The degree of consistency in a particular relationship is called its strength: The **strength of a relationship** is the extent to which one value of Y is consistently associated with one and only one value of X. It is the *degree of association* between the variables. A less consistent relationship is called a *weaker* relationship.

TABLE 2.2 Scores Showing a Relationship Between Study Time and Number of Errors on Test

Student	Study Time in Hours	Number of Errors on Test
Amy	1	12
Karen	1	13
Joe	1	11
Cleo	2	11
Jack	2	10
Maria	2	9
Terry	3	9
Manny	3	10
Chris	4	9
Sam	4	8
Gary	5	7

There are two reasons that a relationship is not perfectly consistent. First, there may be extraneous external influences that are operating. For example, say that distracting noises occurred while someone studied for 1 hour, but not when someone else studied for 1 hour. Because of this, their studying might not be equally effective, resulting in different error scores paired with the same study-time score.

Second, a relationship is weaker because individual differences are operating. The term **individual differences** refers to the fact that no two individuals are identical and that differences in genetics, experience, intelligence, personality, and many other variables all influence behavior in a given situation. It is because of individual differences that a particular law of nature operates in *more or less* the same way for all members of a specific group. Thus, test performance will be influenced by a person's intelligence, aptitude, and motivation. Because students exhibit individual differences in these characteristics, they will each be influenced differently by the same amount of studying, and so will produce different error scores at the same study-time score.

Mathematically, the scores from two variables can produce a relationship having a strength anywhere from perfectly consistent association to no association. However, although perfectly consistent relationships are theoretically possible, they do not occur in real research (because there are always individual differences and extraneous variables operating). Therefore, it is never enough to merely say that you have observed a particular pattern in a relationship: you must also determine the strength of the relationship.

> **REMEMBER**   Research is concerned not only with the existence of a relationship but also with the *strength* of the relationship.

No Relationship   At the other extreme, when there is no consistent pattern between two variables, there is no relationship. For example, there is (I think) no relationship between the number of chocolate bars people consume each day and the number of times they blink each minute. If we measured the scores of individuals on these two variables, we might have the data shown in Table 2.3. Here there is no consistent change in the scores on one variable as the scores on the other variable change. Instead, the same blinking scores tend to show up at each chocolate bar score. Notice that, because there is no relationship, *differences* in the amount of chocolate consumed are not associated with consistent differences in blinking. Ultimately, when we look for a

TABLE 2.3 Scores Showing No Relationship Between Number of Chocolate Bars Consumed per Day and Number of Eye Blinks per Minute

Student	Number of Chocolate Bars Consumed per Day	Number of Eye Blinks per Minute
Mark	1	20
Ted	1	22
Ray	2	20
Denise	2	23
Maria	3	23
Irene	3	20

relationship, we look for a pattern of differences among the scores: for each different score on one variable, there should tend to be a different group of scores on the other variable.

Graphing Relationships   It is important that you be able to recognize a relationship and its strength when looking at a graph. In a graph we have the X and Y axes and we refer to a relationship as involving X and Y scores. But how do we decide which variable to call X or Y? In any study we implicitly ask this question: For a *given* score on one variable, what scores occur on the other variable? The variable you identify as the "given" is then called the X variable (plotted on the X axis), and the "other" variable is the Y variable (plotted on the Y axis). Thus, if we ask, "For a given amount of study time, what test grades occur?" then study time is the X variable and test grades is the Y variable.

Once you've identified your X and Y variables, you can describe a relationship using this general format: "Scores on the Y variable change **as a function of** changes in the X variable." So far we have discussed relationships involving "test grades as a function of study time" and "number of eye blinks as a function of amount of chocolate consumed." Likewise, if you hear of a study titled "Differences in Career Choices as a Function of Personality Type," you know that the researcher looked to see how Y scores that measure career choices changed as X scores that measure personality types changed.

> **REMEMBER**   The "given" variable in a study is designated the X variable, and we describe a relationship using the format "changes in Y *as a function of* changes in X."

To read a graph, read from left to right along the X axis and ask, "As the scores on the X axis increase, what happens to the scores on the Y axis?" Figure 2.1 shows the graphs from four sets of data.

Graph A shows the original test-grade and study-time data back in Table 2.1. Here as the X scores increase, the Y scores also increase. Further, because everyone who obtained a particular value of X obtained the same value of $Y,$ the graph shows that there is perfectly consistent association—one data point at each X.

Graph B shows test errors as a function of number of hours studied from Table 2.2. Here increasing X scores are associated with decreasing values of $Y.$ Further, because there were different *error scores* at each study-time score, on the graph there is a vertical spread of different *data points* above each X. Data points at different vertical locations correspond to different Y scores, so this shows that the relationship is not perfectly consistent.

Say that Graph C shows the relationship between Y scores reflecting different career choices and X scores reflecting different personality types. Again the pattern is that as the X scores increase, the Y scores increase. However, here the relatively large vertical array of data points above each X indicates that there is a rather wide range of different career-choice scores paired with each personality-type score, reflecting an even weaker relationship than in Graph B.

Graph D shows the eye-blink and chocolate-bar data from Table 2.3. There is no consistent pattern of change in Y scores, with more or less the same batch of data points showing up at each X. This means that essentially the same batch of Y scores is associated with each X score. Thus, as here, whenever a graph shows an essentially flat pattern, it reflects data that do not form a relationship.

FIGURE 2.1 Plots of data points from four sets of data

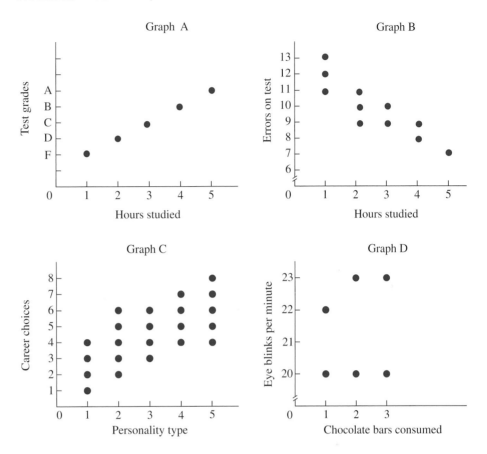

Using Relationships to Discover Laws

Now you can see how relationships form part of the logic of scientific research. The goal of science is to discover the laws of nature, and a relationship between variables is a telltale sign of a law of nature at work. Thus, if we think we have identified a law of nature, we translate it into variables we can measure. Then we conduct research to see if there is a relationship between the scores from our variables. Then we translate the relationship between the scores back into the relationship between the behaviors and events they reflect. Ultimately, then, we will have learned something about how the universe operates. For example, we observed that more hours spent studying is related to better test performance. Thus, we have evidence that, in nature, more of the mental activities we call studying do result in more of the mental activity we call learning. However, we did not observe that eye-blink scores are related to chocolate-bar scores, so we do not have evidence that, in nature, eating chocolate relates to blinking behavior. That, more or less, is the logic for interpreting scientific data.

REMEMBER   The focus of all scientific research is the study of relationships.

Drawing conclusions about a relationship, however, is only one component of the logic of research. Combined with it is the logic of *samples* and *populations*.

SAMPLES AND POPULATIONS

Recall that any law of nature applies to a specific group of individuals (all mammals, all humans, all male white rats, all four-year-old English-speaking children). The entire group to which the law applies is called a **population.** The population contains all possible members of the group, so we usually consider it to be infinitely large. Although ultimately researchers discuss the population of *individuals,* in statistics we sometimes talk of the population of *scores,* as if we have already measured the behavior of everyone in the population in a particular situation.

Of course, to measure an infinitely large population would take roughly forever! Instead, we measure a sample from the population. A **sample** is a relatively small subset of a population that is intended to represent, or stand in for, the population. It is the scores from the sample(s) that constitute our data. The individuals measured in a sample are called the **participants** or **subjects.** However, as with a population, sometimes we will discuss a sample of scores as if we have already measured the participants in a particular situation.

Notice that the definitions of a sample and a population depend on your perspective. Say that we measure the students in your statistics class on some variable. If these are the only individuals we are interested in, then we've measured the population of scores. On the other hand, if we are interested in the population of all college students studying statistics, then we've collected a sample of scores to represent that population. But if we are interested in both the population of college males studying statistics and the population of college females studying statistics, then the males in the class are one sample and the females in the class are another sample, and each represents its respective population. And, finally, one or more scores from *one* student can be a sample representing the population of all scores that the student might produce. Thus, a population is any complete group of scores that would be found in a particular situation, and a sample is a subset of those scores that we actually measure in that situation.

Drawing Inferences about a Population

The logic behind samples and populations is this: We use the scores in a sample to *infer* or to *estimate* the scores we would expect to find in the population. Essentially, we treat the observations in a sample as interchangeable with any other observations we might obtain from the population, so any sample should give scores similar to any other sample's scores. Therefore, by observing our participants, we are observing the equivalent of all other potential participants. All potential participants *are* the population. Thus, it should be true that as the scores in the sample go, so would the scores in the population go, if we could measure them. And remember that scores reflect behavior: By translating the scores in a sample into the behaviors they reflect, we can infer the behavior of the population. Thus, when the nightly news predicts who will win the presidential election based on the results of a survey, researchers are using a sample to represent a population: The scores from the sample survey (usually containing about 1200 voters) are used to infer the voting *behavior* of the population of over 50 million voters.

In the same way, if our sample of study times and test errors shows a particular relationship (as back in Table 2.2), we want to infer that a similar relationship would be found in the population. Inferring the relationship in the population means that if we could measure *every* student on our variables and then graph that data, we expect a graph that is similar to that of the sample, except that it shows the scores for the entire population.

Thus, here is how research combines the logic of relationships with that of sampling from the population. We originally hypothesized that, in nature, studying is related to learning. To determine if this is true, we must first find a relationship in our sample data where, as scores reflecting study time change, scores reflecting exam performance also change. This will provide evidence that nature seems to operate as we think. Then our goal is to draw the inference that a similar relationship would be found for *all* students in the population—that more or less for all students, higher studying scores are associated with better test performance. Then, by translating the scores back into the behaviors and events they reflect, we infer that, for all students, there is something about the mental activities that we call learning that relates to the mental activities we call studying, such that greater learning occurs with greater studying. By concluding that greater learning occurs with greater studying, we come full circle, concluding that this law of nature does operate as we originally proposed.

Thus, the ultimate goal of research is to describe the relationship found in the population, so that we can infer that as everyone's score on one variable changes, his or her score on the other variable tends to change in a particular fashion. But remember that we do not actually observe *everyone!* The potential problem is that our sample data may not be a good example of the population.

Representativeness of a Sample

For us to draw accurate conclusions about a population, a sample must be "representative" of that population. In a **representative sample,** the characteristics of the sample accurately reflect the characteristics of the population. Statistically, the characteristics of the population include such things as how often each score occurs, what the highest and lowest scores are, and what the average score is. Thus, if the average score in the population is 50, then the average score in a representative sample will be around 50. If 30% of the scores in the population are 45, then around 30% of the scores in a representative sample will be 45, and so on. To put it simply, *a representative sample accurately represents the population.*

Whether a sample is representative depends on how we select the sample. From a statistical standpoint the most important aspect of creating representative samples is random sampling.

Random Sampling   **Random sampling** is a method of selecting a sample in which all possible scores in the population have the same chance of being selected for a sample. Because we obtain scores from individuals, random sampling means that we are unbiased in choosing participants, so that all members of the population have an equal chance of being selected. To create a random sample, we select subjects based simply on the luck of the draw. We might place the names of all potential participants on slips of paper in a very large hat, stir them up, and then draw the names of those to be in our sample. Or we might use a computer to generate random numbers and select participants with corresponding social security numbers. Any way we do it, we are as unbiased as possible in selecting subjects, and we try to select from all segments of the population of interest.

A random sample *should* be representative of the population, because random sampling allows the characteristics of the population to occur in the same way in the sample. For example, say that the population of students at your college are all standing in the field, and 60% of them are female. Random sampling is analogous to blindly wandering through the field. Out of a sample of 100 people you encounter, about 60 of them should be female, because that's how often females are out there. Likewise, if 30% of the individuals in the population have a score of 45, then 30% of the participants in a random sample should have a score of 45. In this way, random sampling should produce a sample having the same characteristics as the population.

At least we *hope* it works that way!

Unrepresentative Samples   I keep saying that a random sample "should" be representative, but this is a *very* big should! Nothing forces a sample to be representative. The trouble is that whether a sample is representative is determined by which participants we select, and that is determined by random chance. Therefore, *whether a sample is representative depends on random chance*. We can, just by the luck of the draw, obtain a sample whose characteristics do not match those of the population. For example, 30% of the individuals in the population may have a score of 45, but through random sampling we might not select anyone who has this score, or we might select *only* people who have this score. Likewise, although the population average may be 50, the sample average may be something very different because of the individuals in the sample we happen to select.

> *REMEMBER*   Never automatically *assume* that a sample is representative of the population.

If samples are unrepresentative, then the entire logic of research falls apart. For example, when we select students who study for 1 hour, we might unknowingly select only poor students. If so, then their test scores will be lower than the scores of the typical student who studies for 1 hour. Or, if we select only good students who study for 2 hours, their scores will be higher than those of the typical student who studies for 2 hours. And so on. The problem is that if the sample of scores at each study time does not accurately represent the scores we'd find in the population for that study time, then the *relationship* in the sample does not accurately represent the relationship we'd find in the population: We'd find a relationship that's different from the one in our sample data, or we'd find *no* relationship! Thus, with an unrepresentative sample any evidence we think we have about a law of nature is misleading, and our conclusions are wrong.

Thus, random sampling is a double-edged sword. Usually random sampling works very well to produce a representative sample. But random sampling can backfire on us, producing a very unrepresentative sample. The trouble is we can never *know* whether a sample is representative or not. We would have to measure the entire population to see how well the sample and population matched. But if we could measure the entire population, we wouldn't need a sample to begin with. For help with this dilemma, as described in the next section, we have statistical procedures that we use to decide what inferences to draw about the relationship in the population.

USING STATISTICAL PROCEDURES TO ANALYZE DATA

Recall that statistics help us make sense out of our data, and now we can discuss exactly what "making sense" means. First, we use statistical analysis to determine whether a relationship is present. In our study-time research we want to determine whether there is a relationship between students' error scores and the amount they studied. Second, making sense of the data means describing the scores and the relationship we've found. Thus, we want to know how many errors are associated with a particular amount of study time, how consistently errors decrease, and so on. Third, if we understand a relationship, then we should be able to use a participant's score on one variable to accurately predict his or her score—and corresponding behavior—on the other variable. Thus, if we know how many hours students study, we should be able to predict the number of errors they make on the test.

> **REMEMBER** We use statistical procedures to determine if a relationship is present, describe the relationship and the scores in it, and predict the scores on one variable using the scores on the other variable.

However, we are always talking about two things: the sample data we have collected and the population of scores it represents. Therefore, we separate statistical procedures into two categories: *descriptive procedures,* which deal with samples, and *inferential procedures,* which deal with populations.

Descriptive Statistics

Because relationships are never perfectly consistent, researchers are usually confronted by many different scores that may have a relationship hidden in them. The purpose of descriptive statistics is to bring order to this chaos. **Descriptive statistics** are procedures for organizing and summarizing data so that we can communicate and describe the important characteristics of the data. (Descriptive statistics are used to describe data, so when you see *descriptive,* think *describe.*)

How do descriptive statistics work? In our study-time research back in Table 2.2, the three people who studied for 1 hour, had error scores of 11, 12, and 13. To simplify this, we can say there were *around* 11 to 13 errors. In fact, split the difference: On average, close to 12 errors are associated with 1 hour of study time. We have just used descriptive statistics: We summarized the data by reducing the results to one number (12). We communicated an important characteristic of the data by saying that the scores are around 12 (and not around 36). And we described another important characteristic of the data by saying the scores are *close* to 12 (as opposed to being spread out around 12).

Statisticians have developed descriptive procedures for answering five basic questions about the characteristics of a sample:

1. *What scores did we obtain?* To answer this question, we organize and present the scores in tables and graphs.

2. *Are the scores generally high scores or generally low scores?* We can describe the scores with one number that is the "typical" score.

3. *Are the scores very different from each other, or are they close together?* There are mathematical ways of describing "close."

4. *How does any one particular score compare to all other scores?* We have statistical transformations for comparing any score to the rest of the scores.

5. *What is the nature of the relationship we have found?* We can summarize the important characteristics of a relationship and use this information to predict scores on one variable based on scores from the other variable.

Parts 2 and 3 of this book discuss the specific descriptive procedures used to answer these five questions. When we have answered these questions, we have described the important characteristics of a sample.

Here is the essence of these descriptive statistics: By "summarizing data" they free us from having to examine every score in the data. Especially when there are many scores, hearing "close to 12" is more efficient and much easier to understand than hearing "11, 13, 12, ..." At the same time, "describing the important characteristics" of the data allows us to mentally *envision* the general pattern the data form. For example, if I say a graph of the data generally follows an upward slanting straight line, you can "see" the overall outcome of my study, without even looking at the data.

Realize, however, that there is a cost to such a summary. Even though we compute a precise mathematical answer, it will not precisely describe *every* score in the sample. (Above, not everyone who studied 1 hour scored 12.) Instead, we summarize the general tendency or trend in the scores. Less accuracy is the price we pay for a summary, so descriptive statistics always imply "around" or "more or less."

Inferential Statistics

After answering the above five questions for our sample, we want to answer the same questions for the population being represented by the sample. Thus, although technically descriptive statistics are used to describe samples, their logic is also applied to populations. Because we usually cannot measure the scores in the population, however, we must *estimate* the description of the population, based on the sample data.

But remember, we cannot automatically assume that a sample is representative of the population. Therefore, before we draw any conclusions about the relationship in the population, we must first perform inferential statistics. **Inferential statistics** are procedures for deciding whether sample data represent a particular relationship in the population. As the name implies, inferential procedures are for making *inferences* about the scores and relationship represented by a sample.

How do we do this? Recall that whether a sample is representative depends on chance, on the luck of the draw of which scores are selected for the sample. Because we understand how nature produces chance events, inferential statistics allow us to determine whether it is *likely* that the sample data are representative of a particular relationship in the population. If the sample is deemed representative, then we use the descriptive statistics computed from the sample as the basis for estimating the scores that would be found in the population. Thus, if our study-time data pass the inferential "test," then we can infer that *everyone* who studies for 1 hour will make around 12 errors, and so on.

Part 4 of this book discusses inferential statistics in great detail. Until that time, simply think of inferential procedures as ways of deciding whether the sample data are "believable": Should we believe that we would find similar data, forming a similar relationship, in the population?

> **REMEMBER** *Descriptive statistics* summarize the sample data, and *inferential statistics* are for drawing inferences about the population.

Statistics and Parameters

So that we know when we are describing a sample or a population, statisticians have created the following system. A number that describes a characteristic of a *sample* of scores is called a **statistic.** Different statistics describe different characteristics, and the symbols for the different statistics are letters from the English alphabet. On the other hand, a number that describes a characteristic of a *population* of scores is called a **parameter.** The symbols for different parameters are letters from the Greek alphabet. Thus, for example, if we compute the average for a sample of your bowling scores, we are computing a descriptive statistic. The symbol for a sample average is a letter from the English alphabet. If we then estimate the average in the population of your bowling scores, we are estimating a parameter. The symbol for a population average is a letter from the Greek alphabet.

THE CHARACTERISTICS OF A STUDY

The remainder of this book presents a number of different descriptive and inferential procedures. For a particular study, only a few of these procedures will be appropriate, and which ones you should use depends on several issues. First, your choice depends on what it is you want to know—what question about the characteristics of the sample or population do you want to answer?

Second, your choice of procedures depends on the specific research design being used. A study's **design** is the way the study is laid out: how many samples there are, how the participants are tested, and the other specifics of how a researcher goes about demonstrating a relationship. Different designs require different statistical procedures. Therefore, you must understand the characteristics of different designs. Research can be broken into two major types of designs because, essentially, there are two ways of demonstrating a relationship: *experiments* and *correlational studies.*

Experiments

In an **experiment** the researcher actively changes or manipulates one variable and then measures participants' scores on another variable to see if a relationship is *produced.* For example, say that we conduct an experiment involving the amount of time spent studying statistics and the number of errors made on a statistics test. We decide to compare 1, 2, 3, and 4 hours of study time, so we randomly select four samples of students. We have one sample study for 1 hour, administer the test, and count the number of errors each participant makes. We have another sample study for 2 hours, administer the test, and count their errors, and so on. Then we look to see if we have produced the relationship where, as we increase study time, error scores tend to decrease.

To select the statistical procedures you'll use in a particular experiment, you must first examine the components of the experiment. These components have names that you must know.

The Independent Variable An **independent variable** is the variable that is changed or manipulated by the experimenter. Implicitly, it is the variable that we think *causes* a change in the other variable. In our studying experiment we manipulate study time because we think that longer studying causes fewer errors. Thus, amount of study time is our independent variable. Or, in an experiment to determine whether eating more chocolate causes people to blink more, amount of chocolate consumed would be the independent variable, and the experimenter would manipulate the amount of chocolate a person eats. You can remember the independent variable in this way: It's the causal variable that occurs *independently* of the participants' wishes (we'll have some participants study for 4 hours whether they want to or not).

Technically, a *true* independent variable is manipulated by doing something *to* participants. However, there are many variables that an experimenter cannot change by doing something to participants. For example, you might hypothesize that growing older causes a change in some behavior. But you can't *make* some people be 20 years old and make others be 40 years old. In such situations the experimenter manipulates the variable in a different way. Here we would randomly select one sample of 20-year-olds and one sample of 40-year-olds. Similarly, if we wanted to examine whether gender was related to some behavior, we would select a sample of females and a sample of males. In our discussions we will *call* such variables independent variables, because the experimenter controls them by controlling a characteristic of the samples. Technically, though, such variables are called *quasi-independent variables.*

Thus, the experimenter is always in control of the independent variable, either by determining what is done to each sample or by determining a characteristic of the individuals in each sample. In essence, a participant's "score" on the independent variable is assigned by the experimenter. In our examples, students in the sample that studied 1 hour have a score of 1 on the study-time variable, and people in the 20-year-old sample have a score of 20 on the age variable.

Conditions of the Independent Variable   An independent variable is the *overall* variable a researcher examines; it is potentially composed of many different amounts or categories. From these the researcher selects and then tests participants under only certain *conditions* of the independent variable. A **condition** is a specific amount or category of the independent variable that creates the specific situation under which participants' scores on another variable are measured. Thus, although our independent variable is amount of study time—which could be any amount—our conditions involve only 1, 2, 3, or 4 hours of study. Likewise, if we compare the errors of males and females, then "male" and "female" are each a condition of the independent variable of gender. A condition is also known as a **level** or a **treatment:** By having participants study for 1 hour, we determine the specific "level" of studying that is present, and this is one way we "treat" the participants.

The Dependent Variable   If a relationship exists, then as we change the conditions of the independent variable, we should observe a consistent change in participants' scores on the dependent variable. The **dependent variable** is the variable that is measured under each condition of the independent variable. Scores on the dependent variable are presumably caused or influenced by the independent variable, so scores on the dependent variable *depend* on the conditions of the independent variable. In our studying experiment, the number of errors on the test is the dependent variable, because we believe that errors depend on the amount of study. Or, if we manipulate the amount of chocolate people consume and then measure their eye blinking, eye blinking is our dependent variable. Because we measure participants' scores on the dependent variable, it is also called the *dependent measure.*

> *REMEMBER*   The *independent variable* is always manipulated by the experimenter, and the *dependent variable* is always what the participant's score measures.

Drawing Conclusions from Experiments   After conducting any experiment, we need to examine the data. To do this, always create a diagram of your design. A useful way to do this for our studying experiment is shown in Design Diagram 2.1. The system we'll use is this: Each column in the diagram is a condition of the independent variable (here amount of study time) under which we tested some participants. Each number in a column is a participant's score on the dependent variable (here number of test errors).

Now we can examine the pattern in the scores. Is there a relationship here? Yes. How can we tell? Because as participants' scores on the independent variable of amount of study time increase, their scores on the dependent variable of number of test errors tend to decrease in a consistent fashion.

You can also see this relationship by plotting the data as in Figure 2.2. First, notice that in any experiment we are asking "For a *given* amount of the independent variable, what scores are found on the dependent variable?" Therefore, the independent variable is always plotted on the X axis, and the dependent variable is on the Y axis. Likewise, we ask, "Are there consistent changes in the dependent variable *as a function of* changes in the independent variable?" In Chapter 4 you'll see that we don't usually plot all of the individual data points. For now, see the relationship where as hours of study increase, the data points on the graph move lower, indicating that error scores are decreasing.

The final step, as usual, is to draw inferences about the population with respect to our variables. If the data pass the inferential test, then when our *statistic* computed from the sample data indicates that students who study for 1 hour score close to 12 errors, we will infer that if the population of college students study for 1 hour, we would find a *parameter* showing close to 12 errors. But when the statistic indicates that studying for 2 hours produces around 8 errors, we will infer a parameter indicating around 8 errors for 2 hours of study. And so on. Thus, from a statistical perspective, the goal of any experiment is to show that, in the population, there would be different scores on the dependent variable associated with each condition of the independent variable.

The Problem of Causality   Essentially, the logic a researcher uses in an experiment is this: "If I do this or that to participants in terms of one variable, it should *make* them behave in a particular way on the other variable." Therefore, when we conclude that an experiment shows a relationship in the population, we can discuss the relationship as if changing the independent variable "causes" the scores on the dependent variable to change. However, we cannot definitively *prove* that X causes Y, because it is always possible that some other hidden variable is actually the cause. In our studying experiment,

DESIGN DIAGRAM 2.1   Diagram of an Experiment Involving the Independent Variable of Number of Hours Spent Studying and the Dependent Variable of Number of Errors Made on a Statistics Test

Each column contains participants' dependent scores measured under one condition of the independent variable.

Independent Variable: Number of Hours Spent Studying

	Condition 1: 1 Hour	Condition 2: 2 Hours	Condition 3: 3 Hours	Condition 4: 4 Hours
Dependent Variable: → Number of Errors Made on a Statistics Test	13 12 11	9 8 7	7 6 5	5 3 2

for example, perhaps those participants who studied for 1 hour had headaches and the actual cause of high error scores was not lack of study time, but headaches. Or perhaps those who studied for 4 hours were more motivated, and this produced lower error scores. Or perhaps some participants cheated, or perhaps the moon was full, or who knows what! Researchers always try to eliminate these other variables, but we can never be certain that we have done so.

This is especially true when we examine a quasi-independent variable. For example, if we find that a sample of males has different scores than a sample of females, we *cannot* claim that gender caused the differences. This is because not only would the samples differ in terms of gender, but coincidentally the females would differ from the males along many other variables, including height, hair length, interests, and attitudes. Any one of these variables might actually be causing the differences in scores.

Recognize that statistics do not solve this problem. There is no statistical procedure that will *prove* that one variable causes another variable to change. Think about it: How could some formula written on a piece of paper "know" what causes certain scores to occur?

> **REMEMBER**   Statistics don't prove anything!

An experiment merely provides evidence. How the experiment was conducted and how well the experimenter controlled the variables are part of the evidence supporting a particular conclusion. Statistical results are additional evidence to support the conclusion. Such evidence helps us to *argue* for a certain point of view, but it is not "proof." There is always the possibility that we are wrong.

Correlational Studies

Not all research is an experiment. Sometimes we do not manipulate any variables and instead conduct a correlational study. In a **correlational study** we simply measure par-

FIGURE 2.2   Sample data showing the relationship between study time and errors made on a test

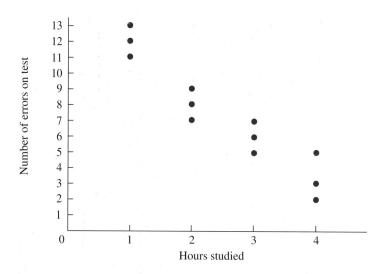

ticipants' scores on two variables and then determine whether a relationship is present. Unlike in an experiment in which the researcher actively attempts to *make* a relationship happen, in correlational designs the researcher is a more passive observer who looks to see if a relationship *exists* between the two variables. For example, originally we used a correlational approach when we simply asked a sample of students how long they studied for a test and what their test grade was. Then we determined whether a relationship was present. Likewise, we would have a correlational design if we asked people their career choices and measured their personality type, asking, "Is career choice related to personality type?"

Correlational studies have their own descriptive statistics that we use to summarize and understand the sample relationship. Then, as in experiments, the goal is to infer the relationship that would be found in the population, but for this we have specific inferential procedures for deciding whether the data represent such a relationship. Thus, our correlational study will, we hope, allow us to conclude that there is a relationship in the population so that, for all students, greater amounts of study time are associated with fewer test errors.

Again, the Problem of Causality   The statistical procedures for correlational studies also do not *prove* that changes in X cause changes in Y. In fact, the hallmark of correlational designs is that the researcher does not manipulate the variables or do anything to participants that might cause the scores to change, so we have no basis for arguing that changes in one variable cause the other to change. The logic of this design is "Do the scores on the two variables change together naturally to form a consistent pattern?" This can happen even though neither variable is the cause. At the same time, correlational designs tend to involve less control of other variables, so it is likely that many other variables are present that might be the actual cause. Therefore, we can *never* conclude that changes in one variable *cause* the other variable to change based on a correlational study. Changes in X might cause changes in Y, but we have demonstrated the relationship in such a way that we have no convincing evidence of this. All we can say is that there is a relationship between the scores on the two variables. (We'll explore this issue further in Chapter 7.)

THE CHARACTERISTICS OF THE SCORES

There is one more important issue that you must consider when deciding on the particular descriptive or inferential procedure to use in either an experiment or a correlational study. Although you always measure participants on variables, the numbers that comprise their scores can have different underlying mathematical characteristics. The particular mathematical characteristics of your scores determine which particular descriptive or inferential procedure you should use. Therefore, part of your job is to recognize the characteristics of the data that indicate which procedures are appropriate. Always pay attention to two important characteristics of the variables: the type of *measurement scale* involved and whether the scale is *continuous* or *discrete*.

The Four Types of Measurement Scales   Numbers mean different things in different contexts. The meaning of the number 1 on a license plate is different from the meaning of the number 1 in a race, which is different still from the meaning of the number 1 in a hockey score. The kind of information that scores convey depends on the *scale of measurement* that is used in measuring the variable. There are four types of measurement scales: *nominal, ordinal, interval,* and *ratio.*

With a **nominal scale,** each score does not actually indicate an amount; rather, it is used for identification. (When you see *nominal,* think *name.*) License plate numbers and the numbers on the uniforms of football players reflect a nominal scale of measurement. In research a nominal scale is used to identify the categories of a qualitative, or classification, variable. For example, we cannot perform any statistical operations on the words *male* and *female.* Therefore, we might assign each male participant a 1 and each female a 2. However, we could just as easily assign males a 2 and females a 1, or we could use any other two numbers. Because we assign the numbers arbitrarily, they do not have the mathematical properties normally associated with numbers. For example, here the number 1 does not indicate more than 0 yet less than 2 as it usually does.

Sometimes, however, a variable is measured using an **ordinal scale:** Here the scores indicate rank order, so the score of 1 means the most or least of the variable, 2 means the second most or least, and so on. (For *ordinal,* think *ordered.*) In research, ordinal scales are used, for example, to rank participants in terms of their aggressiveness, or we might have subjects rank the importance of certain attributes in their friends. Each score indicates an amount of sorts, but it is a relative amount. For example, relative to everyone else being ranked, you may be the number 1 student, but we do not know how good a student you actually are. Further, with an ordinal scale there is not an equal unit of measurement separating each score. In a race, for example, first may be only slightly ahead of second, but second may be miles ahead of third. Also, there is no number 0 in ranks (no one can be "zero-ist").

When a variable is measured using an **interval scale,** however, each score indicates an actual amount, and there is an equal unit of measurement separating each score: The difference between 2 and 3 is the same as the difference between 3 and 4. (For *interval,* think *equal* interval.) Interval scales include the number 0, but it is not a "true" zero. It does not mean zero amount; it is just another point on the scale. Because of this, you can have less than zero, so an interval scale allows negative numbers. Temperature (measured in Celsius or Fahrenheit) is an interval scale. A measurement of zero degrees does not mean that zero amount of heat is present; it means only that there is less than 1 degree and more than -1 degree. Interval scales are often used with psychological tests, such as intelligence or personality tests. Although a score of zero may be possible, it does not mean zero intelligence or zero personality.

Note that with an interval scale, it is incorrect to make "ratio statements" about the amount of a variable at one score relative to the amount at another score. For example, at first glance it seems that 4 degrees Celsius is twice as hot as 2 degrees. However, if we measure the *same* physical temperatures using the Fahrenheit scale, we have about 35 and 39 degrees, respectively. Now one temperature is not twice that of the other. (Essentially, if we don't know the true amount of a variable that is present at a score of zero, then we don't know the true amount that is present at any other score.)

Only with a **ratio scale** do the scores reflect the true amount of the variable that is present, because the scores measure an actual amount, there is an equal unit of measurement, *and* 0 truly means that zero amount of the variable is present. Therefore, ratio scales cannot include negative numbers, and only with ratio scales can we make ratio statements, such as "4 is twice as much as 2." (So for *ratio,* think *ratio!*) In research, ratio scales are used to measure such variables as the number of errors made on a test, the number of friends someone has, or the number of calories consumed in a day.

To help you remember the four scales of measurement, Table 2.4 summarizes their characteristics.

Discrete and Continuous Scales   In addition, any measurement scale may be either continuous or discrete. A **continuous scale** allows for fractional amounts; it "continues" between the whole-number amounts and so decimals make sense. The ratio variable of age is continuous because it is perfectly intelligent to say that someone is 19.6879 years old. To be continuous, a measurement must be at least theoretically continuous. For example, intelligence tests are designed to produce whole-number scores. You cannot obtain an IQ score of 95.6. But theoretically an IQ of 95.6 makes sense, so here intelligence is a theoretically continuous interval variable.

On the other hand, some variables involve a **discrete scale,** and then they can be measured only in whole-number amounts. Here decimals do not make sense. Usually, nominal and ordinal scales are discrete. In addition, some interval and ratio variables are measured using a discrete scale. For example, the number of cars someone owns and the number of children someone has are discrete ratio variables. It sounds strange when the government reports that the average family has 2.4 children and owns 1.78 cars, because these are discrete variables being treated as if they are continuous. (Imagine a .4 child driving a .78 car!)

Also, there is a special type of discrete variable. When there can be only two amounts or categories of the variable, it is a **dichotomous variable.** Pass/fail, male/female, and living/dead are examples of dichotomous variables.

> **REMEMBER**   Whether a variable is *continuous* or *discrete* and whether it is measured using a *nominal, ordinal, interval,* or *ratio* scale are factors that determine which statistical procedure to apply.

TABLE 2.4   Summary of Types of Measurement Scales

Each column describes the characteristics of the scale.

| | Type of Measurement Scale | | | |
	Nominal	*Ordinal*	*Interval*	*Ratio*
What Does the Scale Indicate?	Quality	Relative quantity	Quantity	Quantity
Is There an Equal Unit of Measurement?	No	No	Yes	Yes
Is There a True Zero?	No	No	No	Yes
How Might the Scale be Used in Research?	To identify males and females as 1 and 2	To judge who is 1st, 2nd, etc., in aggressiveness	To convey the results of intelligence and personality tests	To count the number of correct answers on a test
Additional Examples	Telephone numbers Blood type Social security numbers	Military rank Letter grades Elementary school grade	Checkbook balance Winnings/losses at gambling Individual's standing relative to class average	Weight Height Distance traveled

PUTTING IT ALL TOGETHER

The terms and logic introduced in this chapter are used throughout the scientific world. Behavioral scientists thoroughly understand such terms as relationship, independent and dependent variable, condition, and descriptive statistic. These terms are a part of their everyday vocabulary, and they think using these terms. For you to understand research and apply statistical procedures (let alone understand this book), you too must learn to think in these terms. The first step is to try to use the appropriate terminology.

As you proceed through this course, however, don't let the terminology and details obscure your ultimate purpose. Keep things in perspective by remembering the overall logic of research, which can be summarized as the following five steps:

1. Based on a hypothesized law of nature, we design either an experiment or a correlational study to measure variables and possibly observe a relationship in the sample.

2. We use descriptive statistical procedures to understand the scores and the relationship they form. The relationship in the sample data is at least one instance that provides evidence that nature works in a certain way.

3. We use inferential procedures to decide whether our sample represents the scores and relationship that we would find if we could study everyone in the population.

4. Because scores reflect behaviors and events, by describing the scores and relationship that would be found in the population, we are actually describing how the behavior of all members of a particular group operates in a particular situation.

5. Because a law of nature governs the behavior of all the members of a particular group in a particular situation, when we describe the behavior of the population, we *are* describing how a law of nature operates.

CHAPTER SUMMARY

1. A *variable* is anything that, when measured, can produce two or more different values. Variables may be *quantitative,* measuring a quantity or amount, or *qualitative,* measuring a quality or category.

2. A *relationship* occurs when a change in scores on one variable is associated with a consistent change in scores on another variable.

3. The term *individual differences* refers to the fact that no two individuals are identical.

4. Because of individual differences and external influences, relationships can have varying *strengths.*

5. The "given" variable in any study is designated the *X* variable, and we describe a relationship using the format "changes in *Y as a function of* changes in *X.*"

6. The large group of all individuals to which a relationship applies is the *population.* The subset of the population that is actually measured is the *sample,* and the individuals in a sample are the *participants* or *subjects.*

7. Usually, participants are selected using *random sampling* so that all scores in the population have the same chance of being selected.

8. Random sampling should produce a *representative sample,* meaning that the characteristics of the population are accurately reflected by the characteristics of the sample. By chance, however, a sample may be unrepresentative.

9. *Descriptive statistics* are used to organize, summarize, and describe sample data. *Inferential statistics* are for deciding whether sample data represent a relationship in the population.

10. A *statistic* is a number that describes a characteristic of a sample of scores, symbolized using a letter from the English alphabet. A statistic is used to infer or estimate the corresponding *parameter.* A parameter is a number that describes a characteristic of a population of scores, symbolized using a letter from the Greek alphabet.

11. A *research design* is the particular way in which a study is laid out.

12. In an *experiment,* the experimenter manipulates the *independent variable* and then measures participants' scores on the *dependent variable.* Each specific amount or category of the independent variable is a *condition, treatment,* or *level.*

13. In a *correlational study,* neither variable is actively manipulated. Scores on both variables are simply measured and then the relationship is described.

14. In any type of research, if a relationship is observed, it may or may not mean that changes in one variable *cause* the other variable to change.

15. The four *scales of measurement* are (1) a *nominal scale,* in which numbers name or identify a quality or characteristic; (2) an *ordinal scale,* in which numbers indicate rank order; (3) an *interval scale,* in which numbers measure a specific amount, but with no true zero; or (4) a *ratio scale,* in which numbers measure a specific amount and 0 indicates truly zero amount.

16. With a *continuous variable* decimals make sense. With a *discrete variable* decimals do not make sense. A *dichotomous variable* is a discrete variable that has only two amounts or categories.

KEY TERMS: Can You Define the Following?

as a function of *20*

condition *28*

continuous scale *33*

correlational study *30*

dependent variable *28*

descriptive statistics *25*

design *27*

dichotomous variable *33*

discrete scale *33*

experiment *27*

independent variable *27*

individual differences *19*

inferential statistics *26*

interval scale *32*

level *28*

nominal scale *32*

ordinal scale *32*

parameter *27*

participants *22*

population *22*

random sampling *23*

ratio scale *32*

relationship *17*

representative sample *23*

sample *22*	subjects *22*
statistic *26*	treatment *28*
strength of a relationship *18*	variable *16*

REVIEW QUESTIONS

(Answers for odd-numbered problems are in Appendix C.)

1. How can you recognize when a relationship exists between two variables?

2. What are the two components of the logic of research?

3. What are the two aspects of a study to consider when deciding on the particular descriptive or inferential statistics that you should employ?

4. What is the difference between an experiment and a correlational study?

5. What is the difference between the independent variable and the conditions of the independent variable?

6. In an experiment, what is the dependent variable?

7. What is random sampling?

8. (a) Why do random samples occur that are representative of the population? (b) Why do unrepresentative samples occur?

9. What are descriptive statistics used for?

10. What are inferential statistics used for?

11. (a) What is the difference between a statistic and a parameter? (b) What types of symbols are used for statistics and parameters?

12. (a) Define the four scales of measurement. (b) Rank order the scales of measurement, from the scale that provides the most precise information about the amount of a variable present to the scale that provides the least precise information.

APPLICATION QUESTIONS

13. A student, Poindexter, conducted a survey. In his sample, 83% of females employed outside the home would rather be home raising children. He concluded that "the statistical analyses prove that most working women would rather be at home." What is the problem with this conclusion?

14. In study A, a researcher gives participants various amounts of alcohol and then observes any decrease in their ability to walk. In study B, a researcher notes the various amounts of alcohol that participants drink at a party, and then observes any decrease in their ability to walk. (a) Which study is an experiment and which is a correlational study. Why? (b) Which study will be best for showing that drinking alcohol causes an impairment in walking? Why?

15. Another student, Foofy, conducts a survey of the beverage preferences of a random sample of students. She finds that most college students prefer sauerkraut juice to other beverages. What statistical argument can you give for not accepting her conclusions?

16. In each of the following experiments, identify the independent variable, the conditions of the independent variable, and the dependent variable: (a) Studying whether scores on a final exam are influenced by whether background music is soft, loud, or absent. (b) Comparing freshmen, sophomores, juniors, and seniors with respect to how much fun they have while attending college. (c) Studying whether being first-born, second-born, or third-born is related to intelligence. (d) Examining whether length of daily exposure to a sun lamp (15 minutes versus 60 minutes) accounts for differences in self-reported depression. (e) Studying whether being in a room with blue walls, green walls, red walls, or beige walls influences aggressive behavior in a group of adolescents.

17. Why can't we expect to observe a perfectly consistent relationship between variables?

18. Using the words "statistic" and "parameter," how do we describe a relationship in a population?

19. For the following data sets, which show a relationship?

Sample A		Sample B		Sample C		Sample D	
X	Y	X	Y	X	Y	X	Y
1	10	20	40	13	20	92	71
1	10	20	42	13	19	93	77
1	10	22	40	13	18	93	77
2	20	22	41	13	17	95	79
2	20	23	40	13	15	96	74
3	30	24	40	13	14	97	71
3	30	24	42	13	13	98	69

20. Which sample in problem 19 shows the strongest relationship? How do you know?

21. Which of the graphs below depict a relationship? How do you know?

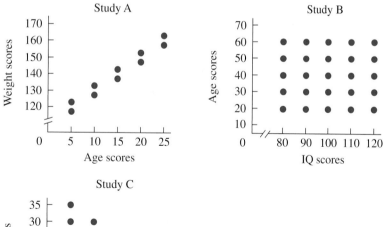

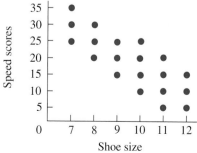

22. Which study in problem 21 demonstrates the strongest relationship? How do you know?

23. In problem 21 why is each relationship a telltale sign that a law of nature is at work?

24. (a) Poindexter says that Study A in problem 21 examines age scores as a function of weight scores. Is he correct? (b) Poindexter also claims that in Study C the researcher is asking, "For a given shoe size, what speed scores occur?" Is he correct? (c) If the studies in problem 21 were conducted as experiments, in each, which variable is the independent variable and which is the dependent variable?

25. In the chart below, identify the characteristics of each variable.

Variable	Qualitative or Quantitative	Continuous, Discrete, or Dichotomous	Type of Measurement Scale
Gender	_____	_____	_____
Academic major	_____	_____	_____
Number of minutes before and after an event	_____	_____	_____
Restaurant ratings (best, next best, etc.)	_____	_____	_____
Speed (miles per hr)	_____	_____	_____
Number of dollars in your pocket	_____	_____	_____
Position when standing in a line	_____	_____	_____
Change in weight (in lbs.)	_____	_____	_____

PART 2

DESCRIPTIVE STATISTICS: DESCRIBING SAMPLES AND POPULATIONS

So, we're off! In Chapter 2 you saw that descriptive procedures are used to answer five questions about a sample of data:

1. What scores did we obtain?
2. Are the scores generally high scores or generally low scores?
3. Are there large differences between the scores, or are there small differences between the scores?
4. How does any one particular score compare to all other scores?
5. What is the nature of the relationship we have found?

In each of the next four chapters we discuss the procedures used to answer each of the first four questions above. In Part 3 we answer the final question.

3

Summarizing Scores Using Frequency Distributions and Percentiles

GETTING STARTED

To understand this chapter, recall the following:

- From Chapter 1 recall how to calculate proportions and percents.
- From Chapter 2 recall the four types of measurement scales and the phrase "as a function of."

Your goals in this chapter are to learn:

- How simple frequency, relative frequency, cumulative frequency, and percentile are computed, and what each tells you.
- How the different types of frequency tables, bar graphs, histograms, and polygons are created.
- What normal, skewed, bimodal, and rectangular distributions are, and how to interpret them.
- How the proportion of the total area under the normal curve corresponds to the relative frequency of scores.

We call the scores we measure in a study the *raw scores:* they are raw and not yet "digestible." Descriptive statistics help us boil down the raw scores into an interpretable form. Believe it or not, one type of statistical procedure is none other than organizing scores into tables and graphs. This chapter presents some common ways to create graphs and tables.

Before we get to that, however, here are some basic symbols you'll encounter in this chapter.

MORE STATISTICAL NOTATION

By constructing a table or graph, we create a distribution. A **distribution** is the general name for any organized set of data. We organize scores so that we can see the pattern they form or, in statistical language, to see how the scores are *distributed*.

In most statistical procedures we will count how *many* scores we have. The symbol N stands for the number of scores in a set of data. (Notice that this is an *uppercase N,* and so when you see N, think *Number.*) An N of 10 means that there are 10 scores, or $N = 43$ means that there are 43 scores. In statistical terminology N is the *sample size,* indicating how big a sample is in terms of the number of scores it contains. When we have one score for each participant, N corresponds to the number of individuals in the sample, so N stands for the total number of scores, *not* the number of different scores. For example, if the 43 scores in a sample are all the same score, N still equals 43. Get in the habit of treating the symbol N as a quantity itself so that you understand such statements as "increasing N" or "this sample's N is larger than that sample's N."

We are also concerned with how often each individual score occurs in a set of data. How often a score occurs is the score's **frequency,** symbolized by the lowercase f. (Always pay attention to whether a symbol is upper- or lowercase.) Also treat f as a quantity: One score's f may be larger than another score's f, we can add the fs of different scores, and so on. As you'll see, there are several ways to describe a score's frequency, so we will combine the term frequency (and f) with other terms and symbols.

WHY IS IT IMPORTANT TO KNOW ABOUT FREQUENCY DISTRIBUTIONS?

Presenting data in a graph or table helps to answer our first question about data: What scores did we obtain? Therefore, always create a table or graph of your data. As the saying goes, "A picture is worth a thousand words," and nowhere is this more appropriate than when trying to make sense out of data. Also, a table or graph is often the most efficient way to communicate your results to others. Finally, a table or graph often makes it easier to see the relationship hidden in the data.

Before we examine the relationship between the scores of two variables, however, we first summarize the scores on each *individual* variable. Buried in any batch of scores are two important things we wish to know: Which scores occurred, and how often did each occur? As you'll see, we can answer these questions simultaneously by organizing the data in one of four ways: using each score's *simple frequency, relative frequency, cumulative frequency,* or *percentile.*

CREATING SIMPLE FREQUENCY DISTRIBUTIONS

The most common way to organize scores is to create a simple frequency distribution. A **simple frequency distribution** shows the number of times each score occurs in a set of data. The symbol for a score's **simple frequency** is simply *f.* To find *f* for a score, count how many times the score occurs. If three participants scored 6, then the frequency of 6 (its *f*) is 3. Creating a simple frequency distribution involves counting the frequency of every score in the data.

Presenting Simple Frequency in a Table

To see how to present a simple frequency distribution in a table, let's begin with the following raw scores. (These scores might measure one of the variables from a correlational study, or they may be dependent scores from an experiment.)

| 14 | 14 | 13 | 15 | 11 | 15 | 13 | 10 | 12 |
| 13 | 14 | 13 | 14 | 15 | 17 | 14 | 14 | 15 |

In this disorganized arrangement it is difficult to make sense out of these scores. Watch what happens, though, when we arrange them into the simple frequency table shown in Table 3.1. The table consists of a score column and an *f* column. The score column has the highest score in the data at the *top* of the column. Below that are all *possible* whole-number scores in decreasing order, down to the lowest score that occurred. Thus, the highest score is 17, the lowest score is 10, and although no one obtained a score of 16,

TABLE 3.1 Simple Frequency Distribution Table

The left-hand column identifies each score, and the right-hand column contains the frequency with which the score occurred.

Score	*f*
17	1
16	0
15	4
14	6
13	4
12	1
11	1
10	1

Total: $18 = N$

we still include it. Opposite each score in the f column is the score's frequency: In the sample there is one 17, zero 16s, four 15s, and so on.

Now we can easily see the frequency of each score and discern how the scores are distributed. We can also determine the combined frequency of several scores by adding together their individual fs. For example, the score of 13 has an f of 4 and the score of 14 has an f of 6, so their combined frequency is 10.

Notice that, although there are 8 scores in the score column, N is *not* 8. There are 18 scores in the original sample, so N is 18. You can see this by adding together all of the individual frequencies in the f column: The 1 person scoring 17 plus the 4 people scoring 15 and so on adds up to the 18 people in the sample. In any frequency distribution you create, be sure that the sum of the frequencies equals N. If not, you've made a mistake.

> **REMEMBER**   The sum of all individual frequencies in a sample equals N.

That's how to create a simple frequency distribution. Such a distribution is also called a *regular frequency distribution* or a plain old *frequency distribution.*

Graphing a Simple Frequency Distribution

A graph of a simple frequency distribution essentially shows the relationship between each score and the frequency with which it occurs. We ask, "For a *given* score, what is its corresponding frequency?" and then we observe changes in frequency *as a function of* changes in the scores. Therefore, we place the scores on the X axis and frequency on the Y axis.

> **REMEMBER**   A graph of a frequency distribution shows the scores on the X axis and their *frequency* on the Y axis.

Recall that a variable will involve one of four types of measurement scales—nominal, ordinal, interval, or ratio. The type of scale involved determines whether we graph a frequency distribution as a *bar graph,* a *histogram,* or a *polygon.*

Bar Graphs   Recall that in nominal data each score is a name for a category, and in ordinal data each score indicates rank order. A frequency distribution of nominal or ordinal scores is graphed by creating a bar graph. In a **bar graph** a vertical bar is centered over each score on the X axis, and *adjacent bars do not touch.*

Figure 3.1 shows two bar graphs of simple frequency distributions. The upper graph shows the nominal variable of the political affiliation of participants. The lower graph shows ordinal data involving military rank (which is a form of 1st, 2nd, and so on), and say that we counted the number of people at each rank who reenlisted during a given period. In both graphs the height of each bar corresponds to the score's frequency.

The reason we create bar graphs here is that, in both nominal and ordinal scales, no *equal unit* of measurement separates the *discrete* scores. The space between the bars indicates these facts. Recall that interval and ratio scales *do* have an equal unit of measurement between scores and are not necessarily discrete, so these scales are *not* plotted using bar graphs. Instead, we have two ways of graphing such scores, depending upon how many *different* scores the data include.

FIGURE 3.1   Simple frequency bar graphs for nominal and ordinal data

The height of each bar indicates the frequency of the corresponding score on the X axis.

Nominal Variable of Political Affiliation	
Party	**f**
Communist	1
Socialist	3
Democrat	8
Republican	6

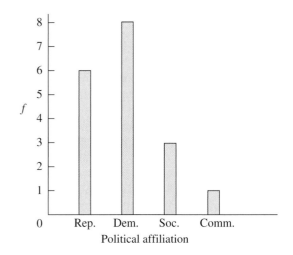

Ordinal Variable of Military Rank	
Rank	**f**
General	3
Colonel	8
Lieutenant	4
Sergeant	5

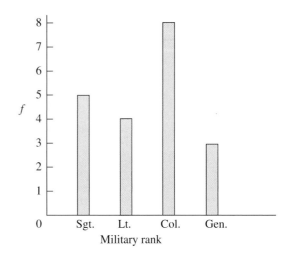

Histograms   Create a histogram when plotting a frequency distribution containing a *small number* of different interval or ratio scores. A **histogram** is similar to a bar graph except that *in a histogram adjacent bars touch.* For example, say that we measured the number of parking tickets some people received, obtaining the data in Figure 3.2. Again, the height of each bar indicates the corresponding score's frequency.

Frequency Polygons   Usually, we don't create a histogram when we have a *large number* of different scores (say if our participants had from 1 to 50 parking tickets). The 50 bars would need to be very skinny, so the graph would be difficult to read. Like

FIGURE 3.2   Histogram showing the simple frequency of parking tickets in a sample

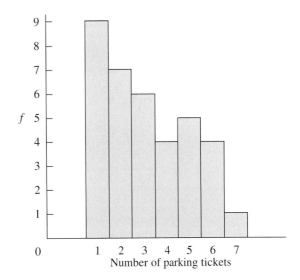

Score	f
7	1
6	4
5	5
4	4
3	6
2	7
1	9

wise, sometimes we plot more than one sample of scores on the same graph, and overlapping histograms are difficult to read. Instead, in such situations we create a frequency polygon.

To construct a **frequency polygon,** place a data point over each score on the X axis at the height on the Y axis corresponding to the appropriate frequency. Then connect the data points using *straight* lines. To illustrate this, Figure 3.3 shows the previous parking ticket data plotted as a frequency polygon.

FIGURE 3.3   Simple frequency polygon showing the frequency of parking tickets in a sample

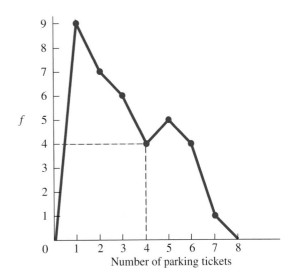

Score	f
7	1
6	4
5	5
4	4
3	6
2	7
1	9

TABLE 3.2 When to create a bar graph, histogram, or polygon

Consider the scale of measurement of scores on the X axis.

Graph	When Used?	How Produced?
Bar graph	With nominal or ordinal scores	Adjacent bars do not touch
Histogram	With small range of interval/ratio scores	Adjacent bars do touch
Polygon	With large range of interval/ratio scores	Straight lines; add points above and below actual scores

Notice that a simple frequency polygon includes on the *X* axis the next score above the highest score in the data and the next score below the lowest score (in Figure 3.3, scores of 0 and 8 are included). These added scores have a frequency of 0, so the polygon touches the *X* axis. In this way we create a complete geometric figure—a polygon—with the *X* axis as its base.

Often in statistics you must read the frequency of a score directly from the polygon. To do this, locate the score on the *X* axis and then move upward until you reach the line forming the polygon. Then, moving horizontally, locate the frequency of the score. For example, as shown by the dashed line in Figure 3.3, the score of 4 has an *f* equal to 4.

> **REMEMBER** The height of the polygon above any score corresponds to that score's *frequency*.

Table 3.2 reviews the rules for constructing bar graphs, histograms, and polygons.

TYPES OF SIMPLE FREQUENCY DISTRIBUTIONS

We have special names for common polygons that have particular shapes. Each shape comes from an idealized frequency distribution of an infinite population. By far the most important frequency distribution is the *normal distribution*. (This is the big one, folks.)

The Normal Distribution

Figure 3.4 shows the polygon of the ideal normal distribution. For reference, let's say these are test scores from the population of college students. Although specific mathematical properties define this polygon, in general it is a bell-shaped curve. But don't call it a bell curve (that's so pedestrian!). Call it a **normal curve** or a **normal distribution,** or say that the scores are *normally distributed*.

FIGURE 3.4 The ideal normal curve

Scores farther above and below the middle scores occur with progressively lower frequencies.

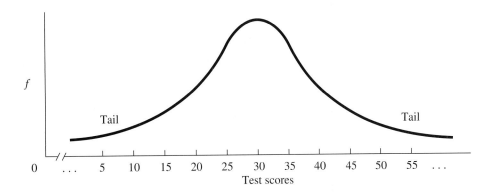

To help you interpret the normal curve (or any other polygon for that matter), imagine that you are flying in a helicopter over a parking lot. The X and Y axes are laid out on the ground, and an entire population is present (it's a very big parking lot). Those people who received a particular score stand in line in front of the marker for their score on the X axis. The lines of people are packed so tightly together that, from the air, all you see is a dark mass formed by the tops of many heads. If you painted a line that went behind the last person in line at each score, you would have the outline of the normal curve. This view is shown in Figure 3.5.

Thus, you can think of the normal curve as a solid geometric figure made up of all of the participants and their scores. When we move vertically up from any score to the height of the curve and then read off the corresponding frequency on the Y axis, it is the same as counting the number of people in line at that score. Likewise, we might, for example, read off the frequencies on the Y axis for the scores between 30 and 35 and,

FIGURE 3.5 Parking lot view of the ideal normal curve

The height of the curve above any score reflects the number of people standing at that score.

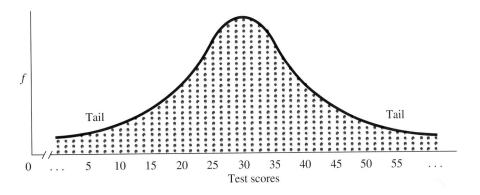

by adding them together, obtain the frequency of scores between 30 and 35. We'd get the same answer if we counted the people in line above each score and added them together. And if we add together the frequencies for all scores, we have the total number of scores (N). This is the same as counting the total number of participants standing in the parking lot.

As you can see from Figures 3.4 and 3.5, the normal distribution has the following characteristics. The score with the highest frequency is the middle score between the highest and lowest scores (the longest line of participants in the parking lot is at the score of 30). The normal curve is *symmetrical,* meaning that the left half below the middle score is a mirror image of the right half above the middle score. As we proceed away from the middle score toward the higher or lower scores, the frequencies at first decrease slightly. Farther from the middle score, however, each score's frequency decreases more drastically, with the highest and lowest scores having relatively very low frequency.

In statistics the scores that are relatively far above and below the middle score of any distribution are called the **extreme scores.** In a normal distribution the extreme scores have a relatively low frequency. In the language of statistics the far left and right portions of a normal curve containing the relatively low-frequency, extreme scores are called the **tails** of the distribution. In Figures 3.4 and 3.5 the tails are roughly below the score of 15 and above the score of 45.

The reason the normal distribution is important is because it is a very common distribution in behavioral research and statistics: On most variables most individuals score close to the middle score, with progressively fewer individuals scoring at more extreme, higher and lower scores. However, because the ideal normal curve represents a theoretical infinite population of scores, it has several characteristics that are not found with polygons created from actual data. First, with an infinite number of scores we cannot label the Y axis with specific values of f. Simply remember that the higher the curve, the higher the frequency. Second, the theoretical normal curve is a smooth curved line. There are so many different whole-number and decimal scores that we do not need to connect the data points with straight lines. The individual data points form the curved line. Finally, regardless of how extreme a score might be, theoretically it will sometimes occur. Thus, as we proceed into the tails of the distribution, the frequencies approach—but never reach—a frequency of zero, so the curve approaches but never actually touches the X axis.

Before you proceed, be sure that you are comfortable reading the normal curve. Can you see in Figure 3.4 that the most frequent scores are between 25 and 35? Do you see that a score of 15 has a relatively low frequency and a score of 45 has the same low frequency? Do you see that there are relatively few scores in the tail above 50 or in the tail below 10? Above all, you must be able to see this in your sleep:

> **REMEMBER**   On a normal distribution, the farther a score is from the central score of the distribution, the less frequently the score occurs.

Overlapping Distributions   Sometimes we have two overlapping distributions plotted on the same set of X and Y axes. For example, Figure 3.6 shows two idealized normal distributions comparing males and females on the variable of height. Generally, males tend to be taller than females, but the overlapping parts of the polygons show that some males and females are the same height and some females are taller than some

FIGURE 3.6 Overlapping distributions of male and female height

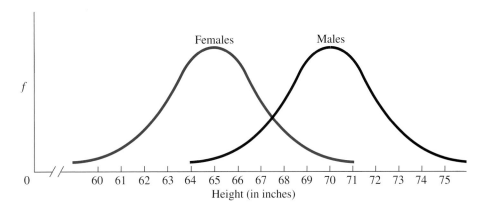

males. (If this were a parking lot full of males and females, then in the overlapping portions of the curve, members of one sex would be standing on the shoulders of those of the other sex.) When examining overlapping distributions, simply ignore one distribution when looking at the other: Count only males when looking at the male distribution and only females when looking at the female distribution. The height of each polygon at a score indicates the frequency with which the score occurred in that distribution. Thus, for example, the score of 69 inches occurs more frequently in the male distribution than in the female distribution.

Variations in the Normal Distribution   A frequency distribution may not match the shape of the previous curves exactly, but it can still meet the mathematical definition of a normal distribution. Consider the three curves in Figure 3.7. The word *kurtosis* refers to how peaked or flat—how skinny or fat—a distribution is. Curve B is generally what we think of as the ideal normal distribution, and it is called mesokurtic (*meso* means middle). Curve A is skinny relative to the ideal curve, and it is called leptokurtic (*lepto* means thin). Leptokurtic distributions occur when only a few scores around the middle score have a relatively high frequency. On the other hand, Curve C is fat relative

FIGURE 3.7 Variations of bell-shaped curves

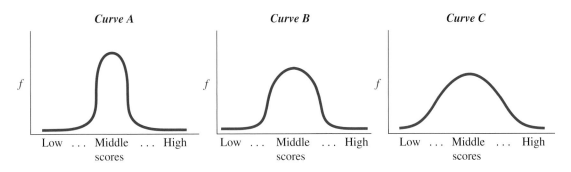

to the ideal normal curve, because there are many different scores around the middle score that each have a relatively high frequency. Such a curve is called platykurtic (*platy* means broad or flat).

These terms help to describe various normal distributions. For statistical purposes, however, as long as we have a reasonably close approximation to the normal curve, these differences in shape are not all that critical.

Other Common Frequency Polygons

Not all variables form normal distributions. When a distribution does not fit the normal curve, it is called a *nonnormal* distribution. The three most common nonnormal distributions are *skewed, bimodal,* and *rectangular* distributions.

Skewed Distributions   A skewed distribution is similar to a normal distribution except that it is not symmetrical: *A skewed distribution has only one pronounced tail.* As shown in Figure 3.8, a distribution may be either *negatively skewed* or *positively skewed*, and the skew is where the tail is.

A **negatively skewed distribution** contains extreme low scores that have a low frequency, but does not contain low-frequency, extreme high scores. The left-hand polygon in Figure 3.8 shows an idealized negatively skewed distribution. This pattern might be found, for example, by measuring the running speed of professional football players. Most would tend to run at higher speeds, but a relatively few linemen lumber in at the slower speeds. To remember that such a curve is negatively skewed, remember that the pronounced tail is over the lower scores, sloping toward zero, toward where negative scores would be.

On the other hand, a **positively skewed distribution** contains extreme high scores that have low frequency, but does not contain low-frequency, extreme low scores. The right-hand polygon in Figure 3.8 shows a positively skewed distribution. This pattern might be found, for example, if we measured participants' "reaction time" for distinguishing words that had or had not been previously seen. Usually, scores will tend to be rather low, but every once in a while a person will "fall asleep at the switch," requiring a

FIGURE 3.8   Idealized skewed distributions

The direction in which the distinctive tail slopes indicates whether the skew is positive or negative.

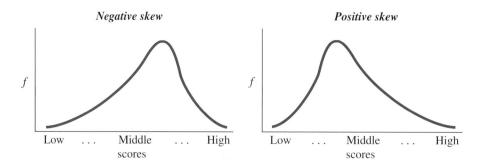

large amount of time and thus producing a high score. To remember that such a curve is positively skewed, remember that the tail slopes away from zero, toward where the higher, *positive* scores are located.

> *REMEMBER* Whether a *skewed* distribution is *negative* or *positive* corresponds to whether the distinct tail slopes toward or away from zero.

Bimodal and Rectangular Distributions   An idealized bimodal distribution is shown in the left-hand side of Figure 3.9. A **bimodal distribution** is a symmetrical distribution containing two distinct humps, each reflecting relatively high-frequency scores. At the center of each hump is one score that occurs more frequently than the surrounding scores, and technically the center scores have the same frequency. Such a distribution would occur with test scores, for example, if most students scored at 60 or 80, with fewer students failing or scoring in the 70s or 90s.

The right-hand side of Figure 3.9 shows a rectangular distribution. A **rectangular distribution** is a symmetrical distribution shaped like a rectangle. There are no discernible tails, because the extreme scores do not have relatively low frequencies. Such a distribution occurs when the frequency of all scores is the same.

On the Importance of Frequency Distributions   If you're wondering why you need to know the names of the previous ideal distributions, it's because we use descriptive statistics to describe and communicate the important characteristics of data. One very important characteristic is the shape of the frequency distribution that the data form. Thus, although I might have data containing many different scores, if, for example, I tell you they form a normal distribution, you can mentally "envision" the shape of such a distribution, and so quickly and easily understand what the scores are like: Few scores are very low or very high, with the most common, frequent scores in the middle. Recall that being able to understand a set of data without having to examine every individual score is the essence—and benefit—of using summary, descriptive statistics. Therefore, the first step when examining any data is to identify the shape of the simple frequency distribution that they form.

> *REMEMBER* The shape of the frequency distribution that scores form is an important characteristic of the data.

FIGURE 3.9   Idealized bimodal and rectangular distributions

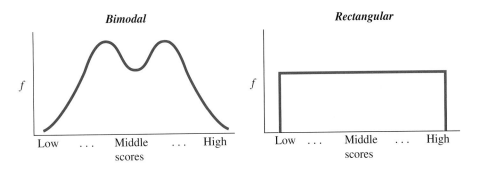

FIGURE 3.10 Simple frequency distributions of sample data with appropriate labels

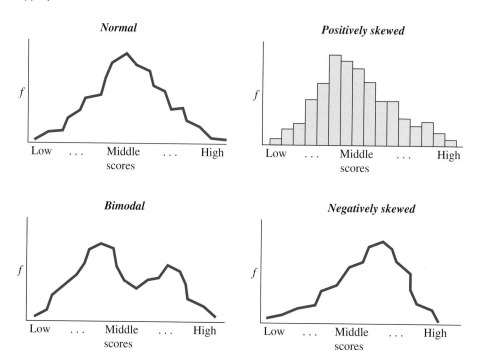

On the other hand, real-world data will form a bumpy, rough approximation to the smooth idealized curves we've discussed. Data never, for example, form a perfect normal curve. The ideal normal curve is important, because, rather than drawing a different, approximately normal curve in every study, we simplify the task by using the ideal normal curve as our "model" of any distribution that generally has this shape. This gives us one reasonably accurate way of envisioning the various, approximately normal distributions that researchers encounter. The same is true for the other common shapes we've seen.

Thus, we apply the names of the previous distributions to samples as a way of summarizing and communicating their general shape. Figure 3.10 shows several examples, as well as the corresponding labels we might use. (Notice that we even apply these names to histograms or bar graphs.) We assume that the sample represents a population that more closely fits the corresponding ideal polygon: If we measured the population, the additional scores and their corresponding frequencies would "fill in" the sample curve, smoothing it out to be closer to the ideal curve.

We will return to simple frequency distributions throughout the remainder of this book. However, counting each score's simple frequency is not the only thing we'll do.

CREATING RELATIVE FREQUENCY DISTRIBUTIONS

Another way to organize data is to transform each score's simple frequency into a relative frequency. **Relative frequency** is the proportion of N that is a score's simple frequency. Recall that a proportion is a decimal number between 0 and 1 that indicates a fraction of the total, so relative frequency indicates what fraction of the entire sample is made up by the times that one or more scores occur: we determine what proportion of N is made up by the f of particular scores. Thus, simple frequency is the *number* of times a score occurs and relative frequency is the *proportion* of time the score occurs. The symbol for relative frequency is *rel. f.*

Why compute relative frequency? We are again asking how often certain scores occurred, but relative frequency is often easier to interpret than simple frequency. For example, the finding that a score has a simple frequency of 60 is difficult to interpret, because we have no frame of reference. However, we can easily interpret that a score has a relative frequency of .20, because this means that the score's f is .20 of the total N; the score occurred .20 of the time in the sample.

Here is your first statistical formula.

THE FORMULA FOR COMPUTING A SCORE'S RELATIVE FREQUENCY IS

$$rel. f = \frac{f}{N}$$

To compute the relative frequency of a score, divide the score's frequency by N.

For example, say that in some data, out of an N of 10, the score of 7 has a simple frequency of 4. What is the relative frequency of 7? Using the formula, we have

$$rel. f = \frac{f}{N} = \frac{4}{10} = .40$$

The score of 7 has a relative frequency of .40, meaning that 7 occurred .40 of the time in the sample.

Conversely, to compute the simple frequency that corresponds to a particular relative frequency, multiply the relative frequency times N. Thus, to find the simple frequency of the score of 7 if its *rel. f* is .4 of an N of 10, multiply .4 times 10 and the answer is 4; 7 occurs four times in this sample.

Presenting Relative Frequency in a Table

A distribution based on the relative frequency of the scores is called a **relative frequency distribution.** To create a relative frequency table, first create a simple frequency table, as we did previously. Then add a third column labeled "*rel. f.*"

As an example, say that we asked a sample of mothers how many children they each have, resulting in Table 3.3. To compute *rel. f,* we need N, and here N is 20. Then the score of 1, for example, has $f = 4$, so its relative frequency is 4/20, or .20. Thus, .20 of our participants have 1 child. And so on.

We can also use the table to determine the combined relative frequency of several scores by adding the individual frequencies together. For example, a score of 1 has a relative frequency of .20, and a score of 2 has a relative frequency of .50, so together, their relative frequency is .20 + .50, or .70; mothers having 1 or 2 children compose .70 of our sample.

You may find that working with relative frequency is easier if you transform the decimals to percents. (Remember that officially relative frequency is a proportion.)

TABLE 3.3 Relative Frequency
Distribution of Number of Children

The left-hand column identifies the scores,
the middle column shows each score's
frequency, and the right-hand column shows
each score's relative frequency.

Score	f	rel. f
6	1	.05
5	0	.00
4	2	.10
3	3	.15
2	10	.50
1	4	.20
	Total: 20	1.00 = 100%

Converting relative frequency to percent gives the percent of time a score or scores occurred. To transform a proportion to a percent, multiply the proportion times 100. Above, .20 of the scores were the score of 1, so $(.20)(100) = 20\%$: 20% of the scores were 1. To transform a percent back to a relative frequency, divide the percent by 100.

To check your work, remember that the sum of all the relative frequencies in a distribution should equal 1: All scores together should constitute 100% of the sample.

> **REMEMBER** *Relative frequency* indicates the proportion of time that a score occurs in a set of data.

Graphing a Relative Frequency Distribution

As with simple frequency, we graph relative frequency with a bar graph if the scores involve a nominal or ordinal scale, and with a histogram or polygon if the scores involve an interval or ratio scale. Figure 3.11 presents examples using the data from Table 3.3. These graphs are drawn in the same way as corresponding graphs of simple frequency except that here the *Y* axis reflects relative frequency, so it is labeled in increments between 0 and 1.0.

Finding Relative Frequency Using the Normal Curve

When data form a normal distribution, an extremely important procedure is to determine relative frequency directly from the normal curve. The reason for visualizing the normal curve as the outline of a parking lot full of people is this: we can find the relative frequency of particular scores by finding the proportion of the parking lot that is occupied by people having those scores. For example, Figure 3.12 shows a normal curve with the "parking lot view." A vertical line is drawn through the middle score of 30, and so .50 of the parking lot is to the left of the line. Because the complete parking lot contains all participants, a part that is .50 of it contains 50% of the participants. (We can ignore those relatively few people who are straddling the line.) Participants are standing in the left-hand part of the lot because they received scores of 29, 28, and so

FIGURE 3.11   Examples of relative frequency distributions using the data in Table 3.3

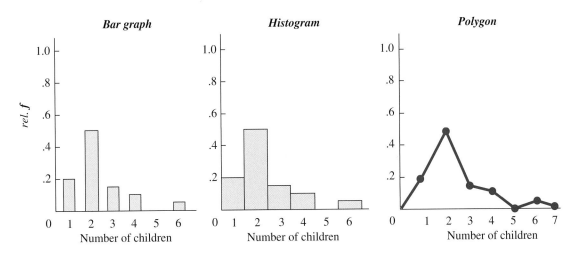

on, so in total, 50% of our participants obtained scores below 30. Thus, the scores below 30 occurred 50% of the time, so the scores below 30 have a combined relative frequency of .50.

We can do the same type of thing in any part of the curve. So, think of the normal curve as a solid geometric figure having an area under the curved line. The total space occupied by people in the parking lot is, in statistical terms, *the total area under the normal curve.* We take a vertical "slice" of the polygon above certain scores and the area of this portion of the curve is the space occupied by the people having those scores. We then compare this area to the total area to determine its **proportion of the area under the curve.** Then:

> **The proportion of the total area under the normal curve at certain scores corresponds to the relative frequency of those scores.**

FIGURE 3.12   Normal curve showing .50 of the area under the normal curve

The vertical line is through the middle score, so 50% of the distribution is to the left of the line and 50% is to the right of the line.

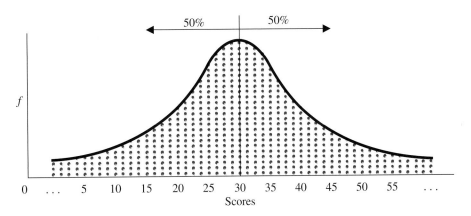

Of course, statisticians don't fly around in helicopters, eyeballing parking lots, but the same principle applies. Here's another example: Say that by using a ruler and protractor, we determine that in Figure 3.13 below, the complete normal curve—the entire polygon—occupies an area of 6 square inches on the page. This total area under the curve corresponds to the total frequency of all scores, which is *N*. Say that we also determine that the area under the curve between a score of 30 and 35 covers 2 square inches. This area is due to the frequencies of the scores found there. Therefore, the frequencies of the scores between 30 and 35 constitutes 2 out of the 6 square inches created by the frequencies of all scores, so these scores constitute two-sixths, or 33%, of the total distribution. Thus, the scores between 30 and 35 occupy 33% of the space occupied by our total *N*, so they constitute 33% of our *N*, so they occur 33% of the time and have a relative frequency of .33.

Because area corresponds to frequency, we would obtain the same answer if we used the formula for *rel. f*. First, we would add together the simple frequencies of every score between 30 and 35. Then, dividing the sum by *N*, we would again find that the relative frequency is .33. However, the advantage of computing the area under the curve is that we can get the answer without knowing the *N* or the simple frequencies of these scores. In fact, whatever the variable might be, whatever the *N* might be, and whatever the actual frequency of each score is, we know that the area these scores comprise is 33% of the total area, and that's all we need to know to determine their relative frequency. This is especially useful because, as you'll see in Chapter 6, statisticians have created a system for easily finding the area under any part of the normal curve. This means we can easily determine the relative frequency for scores in any part of a normal distribution. (No, you won't need a ruler and a protractor.) Until then, simply remember this:

> **REMEMBER** The total area under the normal curve corresponds to the times that all scores occur, so a *proportion of the total area under the curve* corresponds to the proportion of time certain scores occur, which is their relative frequency.

FIGURE 3.13 Finding the proportion of the total area under the curve

The complete curve occupies 6 square inches, with scores between 30 and 35 occupying 2 square inches.

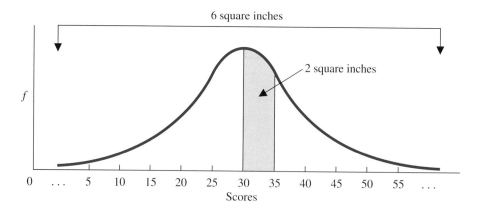

Contents

procedure is to transform cumulative frequency into a percent of the total. A **percentile** is the percent of all scores in the data that are at or below a score. While cumulative frequency indicates the number of participants who scored at or below a particular score, percentile indicates the percentage of participants who scored at or below a particular score. Thus, for example, if the score of 80 is at the 75th percentile, this means that 75% of the sample scored at or below 80.

A percentile is the *percent* of N that is a score's *cf.* A percent is computed using a *proportion,* so the first step is to transform a score's *cf* to a proportion of N: divide the score's *cf* by N. Then, multiplying the proportion times 100 converts it to a percentile. Thus, altogether,

THE FORMULA FOR FINDING THE PERCENTILE FOR A SCORE WITH A KNOWN CF IS:

$$\text{Score's Percentile} = \left(\frac{cf}{N}\right)(100)$$

Thus, if a score has a *cf* of 5 and N is 10, then it is at (5/10)(100) or the 50th percentile.

To present percentiles in a table, first create a cumulative frequency table and add a column labeled percentile. Table 3.5 shows our previous age scores. As shown, the 1 person scoring 10 or below is at (1/20)(100) or the 5th percentile. The 3 people having the score of 11 or below are at the 15th percentile. Because there are still 3 people at 12 or below, the score of 12 is also at the 15th percentile. And so on, until we arrive at the highest score which is, within rounding error, at the 100th percentile: 100% of the sample has the highest score or below.

We have additional techniques for finding the percentile for a score when we do not know its *cf* (e.g. for a score of 14.5 above), or if we seek the score at a particular percentile not found in the data (e.g. the score at the 50th percentile above.) A common way that we'll focus on is to use the area under the normal curve.

TABLE 3.5 Percentiles for Distribution of Age Scores

The right-hand column contains the percentile of each score.

Score	f	cf	Percentile
17	1	20	100
16	2	19	95
15	4	17	85
14	6	13	65
13	4	7	35
12	0	3	15
11	2	3	15
10	1	1	5

Finding Percentile Using the Area Under the Normal Curve

Percentile describes the scores that are *lower* than a particular score, and on the normal curve, lower scores are to the *left* of a particular score. Therefore, the percentile for a given score corresponds to the percent of the total area under the curve that is to the *left* of the score. For example, on the distribution in Figure 3.15, 50% of the curve is to the left of the middle score of 30. Because scores to the left of 30 are below it, 50% of the distribution is below 30 (in the parking lot, 50% of the people are standing to the left of the line and all of their scores are less than 30). Thus, the score of 30 is at the 50th percentile. Likewise, to find the percentile for a score of 20 in Figure 3.15, we would find the percent of the total area that is to the left of 20. In Chapter 6 you'll learn how to do this, but for now, say that we find that 15% of the curve is to the left of 20; then 20 is at the 15th percentile.

We can also work the other way to find the score at a given percentile. Say that we seek the score at the 85th percentile. We would measure over until 85% of the area under the curve is to the left of a certain point. If, as shown in Figure 3.15, the score of 45 is at that point, then 45 is at the 85th percentile.

Notice that we make a slight change in our definition of percentile when we use the normal curve. Technically, a percentile is the percent of scores *at* or below a certain score. However, the normal curve describes an infinite population, and so we can treat those participants scoring *at* the score as a negligible portion of the total (remember that we ignored those relatively few people who were straddling the line). Then a percentile is the percent of all scores that are *below* a certain score. Thus, in Figure 3.15, the score of 30 is at the 50th percentile, so we say that 50% of the scores are below 30 and 50% are above it.

However, if we are describing a *small* sample, we should not say that 50% of the scores are above the 50th percentile and 50% are below it. Those participants scoring *at* the 50th percentile may actually constitute a sizable portion of the sample (say, for example, 10%), so we should not ignore them. Then if we conclude that 50% are above, 50% are below, and 10% are at the score, we have the impossible total of 110%! Therefore, with small samples, percentile is calculated and defined as the percent of scores *at or below* a particular score. Because of this distinction, you should use the

FIGURE 3.15 Normal distribution showing the area under the curve to the left of selected scores

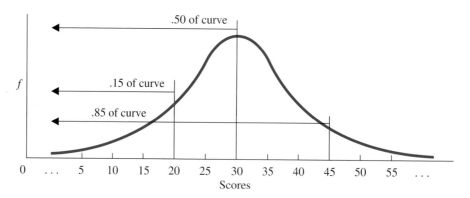

area under the normal curve to compute percentile when you have a large sample or population that also closely fits the normal curve. If instead you have a small sample or a very nonnormal distribution, the easiest approach is to directly calculate percentiles using one of the statistical computer programs that are available. The other approach is to use the formulas presented in Appendix A.1.

A WORD ABOUT GROUPED FREQUENCY DISTRIBUTIONS

A rule of thumb for any type of frequency table is that there should be between about 8 and 18 rows in the table. Fewer than 8 tends to produce a very small, often unnecessary table while more than 18 tends to produce an overly large, inefficient table. In the previous examples, we examined each score individually, creating **ungrouped distributions.** When there are too many scores to produce a manageable ungrouped distribution, we create a grouped distribution. In a **grouped distribution** different scores are combined to form small groups and then we report the total f, rel. f, or cf of each group.

For example, say that we measure 25 people and their scores span a wide range, so we create the grouped distribution shown in Table 3.6. In the score column, "0–4" contains the scores 0, 1, 2, 3, and 4, while "5–9" contains scores 5 through 9, and so on. Each group is called a *class interval,* and the number of values spanned by every class interval is called the *interval size.* Here we've used an interval size of 5, meaning that each group spans five scores.

To complete the table, find the f for each class interval by summing the individual frequencies for the scores in that interval. Thus, the scores between 0 and 4 have a total f of 7, while scores between 5 and 9 have a total f of 4. Likewise, the relative frequency of scores between 0 and 4 is .28, while for 5–9, it is .16. The cumulative frequency for each interval indicates the number of scores that are at or below the *highest* score in the interval. Thus, there are 7 scores at 4 or below, with 11 scores at 9 or below. (For details on how to create and graph a grouped distribution, consult Appendix A.1.)

TABLE 3.6 Grouped Distribution Showing *f, rel. f,* and *cf* for Each Group of Scores.

The left-hand column identifies the lowest and highest score in each class interval.

Score	f	rel. f	cf
40–44	2	.08	25
35–39	2	.08	23
30–34	0	.00	21
25–29	3	.12	21
20–24	2	.08	18
15–19	4	.16	16
10–14	1	.04	12
5– 9	4	.16	11
0– 4	7	.28	7

PUTTING IT ALL TOGETHER

All of the procedures you've learned in this chapter indicate how often certain scores occur, but each provides a slightly different perspective that allows you to interpret the data in a slightly different way. Which particular procedure you should use is determined by which provides the most useful information. However, you may not know which is the best technique for a given situation. So, use the trial-and-error method: Try everything, and then choose the technique that most accurately and efficiently summarizes the data for your purposes. Never be afraid to *explore* your data, using the techniques here or those you'll learn in future chapters.

As an aid to learning statistics, start drawing graphs. In particular, draw the normal curve. When you're working problems or taking tests, draw the normal curve and indicate where the low, middle, and high scores are located. Being able to see the frequencies of the different scores will greatly simplify your task.

CHAPTER SUMMARY

1. The number of scores in a sample is symbolized by N.

2. A *simple frequency distribution* shows the frequency of each score. The symbol for *simple frequency* is f.

3. When graphing a simple frequency distribution, if the variable involves a nominal or an ordinal scale, create a *bar graph,* in which adjacent bars do not touch. If the variable involves relatively few different interval or ratio scores, create a *histogram,* in which adjacent bars do touch. If there are many different interval or ratio scores, create a polygon, in which adjacent data points are connected with a straight line. Also include the scores above the highest score and below the lowest score.

4. In a *normal distribution* forming a *normal curve,* extreme high and low scores occur relatively infrequently, scores closer to the middle score occur more frequently, and the middle score occurs most frequently. The low-frequency, extreme low and extreme high scores are in the *tails* of the distribution.

5. A *negatively skewed distribution* is a nonsymmetrical distribution containing low-frequency, extreme low scores, but not containing low-frequency, extreme high scores. A *positively skewed distribution* is a nonsymmetrical distribution containing low-frequency, extreme high scores, but not containing low-frequency, extreme low scores.

6. A *bimodal distribution* is a symmetrical distribution containing two areas where there are relatively high-frequency scores. A *rectangular distribution* is a symmetrical distribution in which all scores have the same frequency.

7. The *relative frequency* of a score, symbolized by *rel. f,* is the proportion of time that the score occurred in a distribution. A *relative frequency distribution* is graphed in the same way as a simple frequency distribution except that the Y axis is labeled in increments between 0 and 1.0.

8. The *proportion of the total area under the normal curve* above a score or scores equals the relative frequency of the score or scores.

9. The *cumulative frequency* of a score, symbolized by *cf*, is the frequency of all scores at or below the score. A *cumulative frequency distribution* is graphed in the same way as a simple frequency polygon except that the *Y* axis is labeled "cumulative frequency" and the score above the highest score is not added.

10. *Percentile* indicates the percent of all scores at or below a given score. On the normal curve the percentile of a score is the percent of the curve to the left of the score.

11. In an *ungrouped distribution,* the *f, rel. f,* or *cf* of each individual score is reported.

12. In a *grouped distribution,* different scores are grouped together, and the total *f, rel. f,* or *cf* for each group is reported. Each group of scores is called a *class interval,* and the range of scores in the interval is called the *interval size.*

KEY TERMS: Can You Define the Following?

N   f   rel. f   cf
bar graph *43*
bimodal distribution *51*
cumulative frequency *57*
cumulative frequency distribution *57*
distribution *41*
extreme scores *48*
frequency *41*
frequency polygon *45*
grouped distribution *61*
histogram *44*
negatively skewed distribution *50*
normal curve *46*

normal distribution *46*
percentile *58*
positively skewed distribution *50*
proportion of the total area under the curve *55*
rectangular distribution *51*
relative frequency *52*
relative frequency distribution *53*
simple frequency *42*
simple frequency distribution *42*
tails *48*
ungrouped distribution *61*

REVIEW QUESTIONS

(Answers for odd-numbered problems are in Appendix C.)

1. What do each of the following symbols mean? (a) *N;* (b) *f;* (c) *rel. f;* (d) *cf.*

2. (a) What is the difference between a bar graph and a histogram? (b) With what kind of data is each used?

3. (a) What is the difference between a histogram and a polygon? (b) With what kind of data is each used?

4. (a) What is the difference between a score's simple frequency and its relative frequency? (b) What is the difference between a score's cumulative frequency and its percentile?

5. (a) What is the advantage of computing relative frequency instead of simple frequency? (b) What is the advantage of computing percentiles instead of cumulative frequency?

6. (a) What is the difference between a skewed distribution and a normal distribution? (b) What is the difference between a bimodal distribution and a normal distribution?

7. What is the difference between a positively skewed distribution and a negatively skewed distribution?

8. (a) Why must the *cf* for the highest score in a sample equal *N?* (b) Why must the sum of all *f*s from all scores in a sample equal *N?*

9. What is the difference between graphing a relationship as we did in Chapter 2 and graphing a frequency distribution?

10. What does a rectangular distribution show about the relationship between frequency and the different scores?

11. What does it mean when a score is in a tail of a normal distribution?

12. (a) How is percentile defined in a small sample? (b) How is percentile defined for a large sample or population when calculated using the normal curve?

APPLICATION QUESTIONS

13. In reading psychological research you encounter the following statements. Interpret each one. (a) "The IQ scores were approximately normally distributed." (b) "A bimodal distribution of physical agility scores was observed." (c) "The distribution of the patients' memory scores was severely negatively skewed."

14. From the data 1, 4, 5, 3, 2, 5, 7, 3, 4, 5, Poindexter created the following frequency table. What five things did he do wrong?

Score	*f*	*cf*
1	1	0
2	1	1
3	2	3
4	2	5
5	3	8
7	1	9
	N = 6	

15. The distribution of scores on your next statistics test is positively skewed. What does this indicate about the difficulty of the test?

16. (a) On a normally distributed set of exam scores, Poindexter scored at the 10th percentile, so he claims that he outperformed 90% of his class. Why is he correct or incorrect? (b) Because Foofy's score had a relative frequency of .02, she claims she had one of the highest scores on the exam. Why is she correct or incorrect?

17. What type of frequency graph should you create when counting each of the following? (a) the males and females at a college; (b) the different body weights reported in a statewide survey; (c) the number of sergeants, lieutenants, captains, and majors in an army battalion; (d) the people falling into one of eight salary ranges.

18. What is the difference between how we use the proportion of the total area under the normal curve to determine a score's relative frequency and how we use it to determine a score's percentile?

19. Interpret each of the following. (a) In a small sample you scored at the 35th percentile. (b) Your score has a *rel. f* of .40. (c) Your score is in the upper extreme scores of the normal curve. (d) Your score is in the left-hand tail of the normal curve. (e) Your score has a *cf* of 50. (f) From the normal curve, your score is at the 60th percentile.

20. Draw a normal curve and identify the approximate location of the following scores. (a) You have the most frequent score. (b) You have a low-frequency score, but the score is higher than most. (c) You have one of the lower scores, but it has a relatively high frequency. (d) Your score seldom occurred.

21. The following shows the distribution of final exam scores in a large introductory psychology class. The proportion of the total area under the curve is given for two segments.

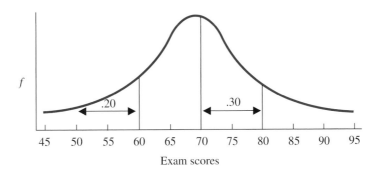

(a) Order the scores 45, 60, 70, 72, and 85 from most frequent to least frequent. (b) What is the percentile of a score of 60? (c) What proportion of the sample scored below 70? (d) What proportion scored between 60 and 70? (e) What proportion scored above 80? (f) What is the percentile of a score of 80?

22. What is the advantage and disadvantage of using grouped frequency distributions?

23. Organize the ratio scores below in a table showing simple frequency, relative frequency, and cumulative frequency.

49	52	47	52	52	47	49	47	50
51	50	49	50	50	50	53	51	49

24. (a) Draw a simple frequency polygon using the data in problem 23. (b) Draw a relative frequency histogram of this data. (c) Draw the appropriate graph showing the cumulative frequencies in these data.

25. Organize the interval scores below in a table showing simple frequency, cumulative frequency, and relative frequency.

16	11	13	12	11	16	12	16	15
16	11	13	16	12	11			

26. Using the data in problem 25, draw the appropriate graph to show (a) simple frequency (b) relative frequency (c) cumulative frequency

**SUMMARY OF
FORMULAS**

1. The formula for computing a score's relative frequency is

$$rel.\ f = \frac{f}{N}$$

where f *is the score's simple frequency and* N *is the number of scores in the sample.*

2. The formula for finding the percentile for a score with a known cf *is:*

$$\text{Score's Percentile} = \left(\frac{cf}{N}\right)(100)$$

//////// 4

Summarizing Scores Using Measures of Central Tendency: The Mean, Median, and Mode

GETTING STARTED

To understand this chapter, recall the following:

- From Chapter 2 recall the logic of "statistics" and "parameters" and the difference between an independent and a dependent variable.
- From Chapter 3 recall when to create bar graphs or polygons, how to interpret polygons, and how to calculate percentile using the area under the curve.

Your goals in this chapter are to learn:

- How measures of central tendency describe data.
- What the mean, median, or mode indicate and when each is appropriate.
- How a sample mean is used to describe both individual scores and the population of scores.
- What is meant by "deviations around the mean" and what they convey about each score's location and frequency in a normal distribution.
- How to interpret and graph the results of an experiment.

The graphs and tables discussed in Chapter 3 are a necessary part of descriptive statistics because the goal is to describe the important characteristics of the data, and the type of distribution it forms *is* one important characteristic. However, graphs and tables are not the most efficient way to summarize a distribution. Instead, we compute individual numbers—statistics—that each describe an important characteristic of the data. This chapter discusses the important characteristic called central tendency.

But first . . .

MORE STATISTICAL NOTATION

A new important symbol is Σ, the Greek capital letter S, called sigma. Sigma is used in conjunction with a symbol for scores, so you will see such notations as ΣX. In words, ΣX is pronounced **"sum of X"** and literally means to find the sum of the X scores. Thus, ΣX for the scores 5, 6, and 9, is 20, and in code we would say $\Sigma X = 20$. Notice that we do not care whether each X is a different score. If the scores are 4, 4, and 4, then $\Sigma X = 12$.

> *REMEMBER*   The symbol ΣX indicates to *sum* the X scores.

This chapter also introduces the symbol K, which stands for a constant number. This is used in transformations when we add the same number to each score or when we multiply by, divide by, or subtract a constant.

Now, on to *central tendency.*

WHY IS IT IMPORTANT TO KNOW ABOUT CENTRAL TENDENCY?

Statistics that are "measures of central tendency" are important because they answer the most basic question about data: Are the scores generally high scores or generally low scores? Why is that important? Well, after you've taken a test in your statistics course, your first question is how did you do, but your second question is how did the class as a whole do: Did everyone generally score high, low, or what? You need this information to understand both how the class performed and how you performed relative to everyone else. But it is impossible to do this by looking at the individual scores. (Imagine if your professor read them to you: 90, 63, 70, 70, 82, 87, 68 . . . .) Instead, it is much better if you know something like the class average. Likewise, in virtually all research, the first step is to shrink the data into one summary score, called a *measure of central tendency.* This is the only way to easily describe and interpret the sample as a whole.

WHAT IS CENTRAL TENDENCY?

To understand central tendency, first change your perspective of what a score indicates. Think of a score as indicating a *location* on a variable. For example, if I am 70 inches tall, don't think of my score as indicating that I have 70 inches of height. Instead, think of me as being located on the variable of height at the point marked 70 inches. Think of any variable as an infinite continuum—a straight line—and think of a score as indicating a participant's location on that line. Thus, as shown in Figure 4.1, my score locates me at the address labeled 70 inches. If my brother is 60 inches tall, then he is located at the point marked 60 on the height variable. The idea is not so much that he is 10 inches shorter than I am, but rather that we are separated by a *distance* of 10 units—in this case, 10 "inch" units. In statistics, scores are locations, and the difference between any two scores is the distance between them.

From this perspective a frequency polygon shows the location of each score. For example, Figure 4.2 shows the height scores from two samples, one containing low scores and one containing higher scores. In the parking lot view of the normal curve, participants' scores determine *where* they stand. A high score puts them on the right side of the lot, a low score puts them on the left side, and a middle score puts them in a crowd in the middle. Further, if we have two distributions containing different scores, then the *distributions* have different locations on the variable.

Now you can see that when we ask, "Are the scores generally high scores or generally low scores?" we are actually asking, "*Where* on the variable is the distribution located?" A **measure of central tendency** is a score that summarizes the location of a distribution on a variable. Listen to its name: It is the score that indicates where the *center* of the distribution *tends* to be located. Thus, it is the point on the variable *around* where most of the scores are located and provides a reasonably accurate "address" for the distribution as a whole.

Thus, in Sample A in Figure 4.2 most of the scores are in the neighborhood of 59, 60, and 61 inches, so a measure of central tendency will indicate that the distribution is located around 60 inches. In Sample B the distribution tends to be centered around 70 inches.

Notice that the above example again illustrates how to use descriptive statistics: From them you get an idea of what's in the data and can *envision* the important aspects of the distribution *without* looking at the individual scores. Thus, if a researcher told you only that one normal distribution is centered at 60 and the other is centered around 70, you could envision the information presented in Figure 4.2. Although we lose some detail, we do answer the question of whether the scores in each sample are generally high or low. You'll see other statistics that add to this mental picture of a distribution, but measures of central tendency are at the core of summarizing a distribution.

> *REMEMBER* The first step in summarizing any set of data is to compute the appropriate *measure of central tendency.*

FIGURE 4.1 Locations of individual scores on the variable of height

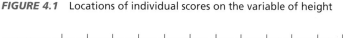
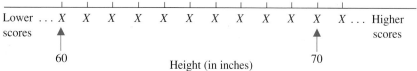

FIGURE 4.2 Two sample polygons on the variable of height

Each polygon indicates the locations of the scores and their frequencies.

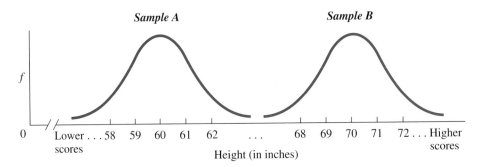

There are three common measures of central tendency. The trick is to compute the correct one so that you can *accurately* envision where most scores in the data are actually located. Which measure of central tendency you should calculate depends on two factors:

1. The scale of measurement used, so that the summary makes *sense* given the nature of the scores.
2. The shape of the frequency distribution the scores produce, so that the measure *accurately* summarizes the distribution.

In the following sections we first discuss the *mode,* then the *median,* and finally the *mean.* Then we'll see how to use these measures of central tendency to interpret experiments.

THE MODE

One way to describe where most of the scores in a distribution are located is to find the one score that occurs most frequently. The most frequently occurring score is called the **mode.** (There is no accepted symbol for the mode.) To see how the mode works, say that after collecting some test scores, we arrange them from lowest to highest and get 2, 3, 3, 4, 4, 4, 4, 5, 5, and 6. The score of 4 is the mode, because it occurs more frequently than any other score in the sample. You can see how the mode summarizes this distribution from Figure 4.3. Most of the scores are at or around 4. Notice that Figure 4.3 is roughly a normal curve, with the highest point on the curve over the mode. When a polygon has one hump, such as on the normal curve, the distribution is called **unimodal,** indicating that one score qualifies as the mode.

There may not always be a single mode in a set of data. For example, consider the scores 2, 3, 4, 5, 5, 5, 6, 7, 8, 9, 9, 9, 10, 11, and 12. Here two scores, 5 and 9, are tied for the most frequently occurring score. This sample is plotted in Figure 4.4. In Chapter 3 such a distribution was called **bimodal** because it has two modes. Describing this distribution as bimodal and identifying the two modes does summarize where most of the scores tend to be located, because most of the scores are either around 5 or around 9.

FIGURE 4.3   A unimodal distribution

The vertical line marks the highest point on the distribution, thus indicating the most frequent score, which is the mode.

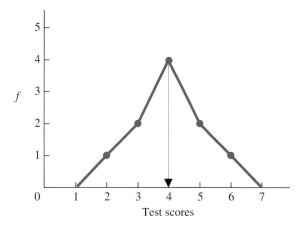

Uses of the Mode

The mode is typically used to describe central tendency when the scores reflect a nominal scale of measurement (when participants are categorized using a qualitative variable). For example, say that we asked some people their favorite flavor of ice cream, and counting the number of responses in each category produced the bar graph shown

FIGURE 4.4   A bimodal distribution

Each vertical line marks one of the two equally high points on the distribution, so each indicates the location of one of the two modes.

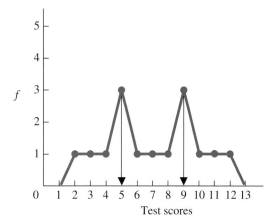

FIGURE 4.5   Bar graph showing the frequencies of preferred ice cream flavors

The mode is flavor 5, "Goopy Chocolate."

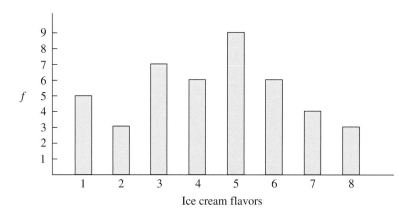

in Figure 4.5. A useful way to summarize such data would be to indicate the most frequently occurring category: Reporting that the mode was a preference for category 5, "Goopy Chocolate," is very informative.

> **REMEMBER**   The *mode* is the most frequently occurring score in the data, and is usually used to summarize nominal scores.

There are, however, two potential problems with the mode that limit its use. First, the distribution may contain many scores that are all tied at the same highest frequency. In distributions with more than two modes we fail to summarize the data. In the most extreme case we might obtain a rectangular distribution with scores such as 4, 4, 5, 5, 6, 6, 7, 7. Here either there is no mode or all scores are the mode. Either way, the mode could not be determined.

A second problem is that the mode does not take into account any scores other than the most frequent score(s), so it ignores much of the information in the data. An *accurate* summary, however, should reflect all scores so that we can accurately envision the entire distribution. For example, say we obtain the skewed distribution containing 7, 7, 7, 20, 20, 21, 22, 22, 23, and 24. The mode is 7. This gives you a misleading idea about these scores, because most of them are not *around* 7, but instead are up there in the low 20s. Thus, the mode may or may not accurately summarize where *most* scores in the distribution are located.

Because of these problems, for ordinal, interval, or ratio scores, we can usually compute a better measure of central tendency.

THE MEDIAN

Often a better measure of central tendency is the median. The **median** is simply another name for the score at the 50th percentile. Recall that 50% of a distribution is at or below the score at the 50th percentile. Thus, if the median is 10, then 50% of all scores are either at or below 10. (Note that the median will not always be one of the actual scores that occurred.) The median is typically a better measure of central tendency than the mode, because (1) only one score can be the median, and (2) the median will usually be around where most of the scores in the distribution tend to be located. The symbol for the median is usually its abbreviation, Mdn.

As you saw in Chapter 3, with a large sample or population, the 50th percentile is the score that separates the lower 50% of the distribution from the upper 50% of the distribution. For example, look at the normal curve in Graph A in Figure 4.6. Because 50% of the *area under the curve* is to the left of the line, 50% of the scores are below the score at the line. Therefore, the score at the line is the 50th percentile, so that score is the median.

In fact, the median is the score below which .50 of the area of *any* polygon is located. Thus, in the skewed distribution in Graph B of Figure 4.6, .50 of the area under the curve is to the left of the vertical line, so 50% of the scores are below the score at the line, and so the score at the line is the median.

There are several ways to calculate the median. First, when scores form a perfect normal distribution as above, the median is also the most frequent score, so it is the same score as the mode. When scores are approximately normally distributed, the median will be close to the mode.

When data are not at all normally distributed, however, there is no easy way to determine the point below which .50 of the area under the curve is located. Also, recall that using the area under the curve is not very accurate with a small sample. In these situations, you can estimate the median using the following system. Arrange the scores in order from lowest to highest. With an odd number of scores, the score in the middle position is the approximate median. For example, for the nine scores 1, 2, 3, 3, 4, 7, 9, 10, 11, the score in the middle position is the fifth score, so the median is the score of 4. On the other hand, if *N* is an even number, the average of the two scores in the middle is the approximate median. For example, for the ten scores 3, 8, 11, 11, 12, 13, 24, 35, 46,

FIGURE 4.6 Location of the median in a normal distribution (A) and in a skewed distribution (B)

The vertical line indicates the location of the median, with one-half of the distribution on each side of it.

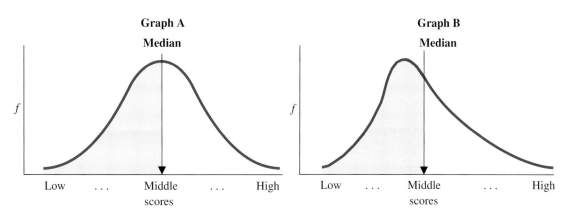

and 48 the middle scores counting from the lowest are at position 5 (the score of 12) and position 6 (the score of 13). The average of 12 and 13 is 12.5, so the median is approximately 12.5.

To precisely calculate the median, use the formula discussed in Appendix A.1. to find the score at the 50th percentile. Most computer programs employ this formula, providing the easiest solution.

Uses of the Median

The median is not used to describe nominal data: To say, for example, that 50% of our participants preferred "Goopy Chocolate" or *below* is more confusing than it is informative. On the other hand, the median is often the preferred measure of central tendency when the data are ordinal (rank-ordered) scores. For example, say that a group of students ranked how well a college professor teaches. Reporting that the professor's median ranking was 3, communicates that 50% of the students rated the professor as number 1, 2, or 3. Also, as you'll see in a later section, the median is appropriate when interval or ratio scores form a very skewed distribution.

> REMEMBER   The *median* (Mdn) is the score at the 50th percentile, and is used to summarize ordinal or highly skewed interval or ratio scores.

Computing the median still ignores some information in the data, however, because it reflects only the frequency of scores in the lower 50% of the distribution, without considering the mathematical values of these scores or considering the scores in the upper 50%. Therefore, the median is usually not our first choice for describing the central tendency of most distributions of interval or ratio scores.

THE MEAN

By far the all-time most common measure of central tendency in behavioral research is the mean. The **mean** is the score located at the mathematical center of a distribution. Although technically we call this statistic the arithmetic mean, it is what most people call the average. Compute a mean in the same way you compute an average: Add up all the scores and then divide by the number of scores you added. Unlike the mode or the median, the mean includes every score, so it does not ignore any information in the data.

Let's first compute the mean in a sample. Sample statistics use symbols from the English alphabet, and the symbol for a *sample* mean is $\overline{X}$. It is pronounced "the sample mean" (not "bar X": bar X sounds like the name of a ranch!). As with other symbols, get in the habit of thinking of $\overline{X}$ as a quantity itself, so that you understand statements such as "the size of $\overline{X}$" or "this $\overline{X}$ is larger than that $\overline{X}$."

To compute $\overline{X}$, recall that the symbol meaning "add up all the scores" is ΣX, and the symbol for the number of scores is N. Then

THE FORMULA FOR COMPUTING A SAMPLE MEAN IS

$$\overline{X} = \frac{\Sigma X}{N}$$

As an example, take the scores 3, 4, 6, and 7. Adding the scores together produces $\Sigma X = 20$, and N is 4. Thus $\overline{X} = 20/4 = 5$. Saying that the mean of these scores is 5 indicates that the mathematical center of this distribution is located at the score of 5. (As here, the mean may be a score that does not actually occur in the data.)

What is the exact mathematical center of a distribution? Think of the center of a distribution as its balance point. Thus, visualize a polygon as a teeter-totter on a playground. A score's location on the X axis corresponds to its location on the teeter-totter. The left-hand side of Figure 4.7 shows the scores 3, 4, 6, and 7 sitting on the teeter-totter, and the mean of 5 is the point that balances the distribution. The right-hand side of Figure 4.7 shows how the mean is the balance point even when the scores do not have the same frequency (the score of 1 has an f of 2). Here the mean is 4 (because $\Sigma X/N = 20/5 = 4$), and it balances the distribution.

Uses of the Mean

Computing the mean is appropriate whenever getting the "average" of the scores makes sense. Therefore, do not use the mean when describing nominal data. For example, say we are studying political affiliation, assigning a 1 to each Democrat, a 2 to Republicans, and so on. It is meaningless to say that the mean political affiliation was 2.3; the mode or percentages would be much more informative. Likewise, the median is best when describing ordinal data (because, for example, it is strange to say that, on average, runners came in 5.7th in a race). This leaves the mean to describe interval or ratio data, especially when the variable is at least theoretically continuous (decimals make sense).

In addition, however, also consider the shape of the distribution. The goal is to identify the point around which most of the scores in the distribution are located. The mean is simply the mathematical center of any distribution. Therefore, the mathematical center of the distribution must also be the point around which most of the scores are located. This will be the case when we have a *symmetrical* and *unimodal* distribution. For example, say that we are studying the intelligence of cats by timing how long it

FIGURE 4.7 The mean as the balance point of a distribution

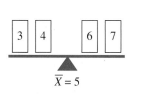

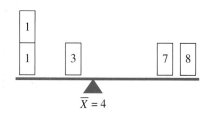

takes them to escape from a puzzling maze. The data are 5, 6, 2, 1, 3, 4, 5, 4, 3, 7, and 4 minutes, which form the roughly normal distribution shown in Figure 4.8. The mean score is 4 and here the center of the distribution is also around where the most frequently occurring scores are. Thus, the mean is appropriate here because it *is* the point *around* which *most* of the scores are located: Most of the cats did take around 4 minutes to escape.

The ultimate symmetrical distribution is the normal distribution. Therefore, always compute the mean to summarize a normal or approximately normal distribution. Notably, on a perfect normal distribution all three measures of central tendency are located at the same score. As in Figure 4.8, the mean of 4 splits the area under the curve in half, so 4 is also the median. At the same time, the middle score has the highest frequency, so 4 is also the mode.

If a distribution is only roughly normal, then the mean, median, and mode will be close to, but not exactly, the same score. You might think that in such cases any measure of central tendency would be good enough. Not true. Because the mean uses all of the information in the data, the mean is the preferred measure of central tendency. Further, most inferential statistical procedures are based on the mathematical properties of the mean. Therefore, the rule is that the mean is the preferred statistic to use with interval or ratio data unless it *clearly* provides an inaccurate description of the distribution.

> **REMEMBER**   Describe the central tendency of a normal distribution of interval or ratio scores by computing the *mean*.

The mean does *not* accurately describe a highly skewed distribution. To understand this, consider what happens to your grade average if you obtain one low grade after receiving many high grades—your average drops like a rock. The low score produces a negatively skewed distribution, and the mean gets pulled away from where most of your grades are, toward that low grade. What hurts is then telling someone your average, because it's misleading. It sounds as if all of your grades are relatively low, while only you know that you have that one zinger. For precisely this reason, we do not use the mean to summarize highly skewed distributions.

FIGURE 4.8 Location of the mean on a distribution formed by the escape times 1, 2, 3, 3, 4, 4, 4, 5, 5, 6, and 7

The vertical line indicates the location of the mean score, which is the balance point of the distribution.

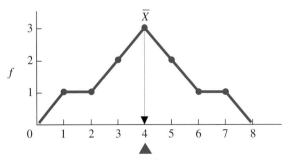

Escape times (in minutes)

FIGURE 4.9 Location of the mean on a skewed distribution formed by the time scores 1, 2, 2, 2, 3, 14

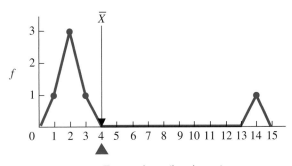

Escape times (in minutes)

The mean is pulled toward the tail of a skewed distribution because mathematically it must balance the distribution. For example, say that some other cat subjects produced the escape-time scores of 1, 2, 2, 2, 3, and 14, forming the positively skewed distribution shown above in Figure 4.9. Without the 14, the scores would form a symmetrical distribution with a mean of 2. However, because of that extreme 14, the mean is pulled away from the low scores to balance the distribution. The problem is that a measure of central tendency is supposed to describe where *most* of the scores tend to be located. But, in Figure 4.9, most scores are not around 4. As this illustrates, the mean is where the mathematical center is, *but in a skewed distribution the mathematical center is not where most of the scores tend to be.*

The solution is to use the median to summarize a very skewed distribution. Figure 4.10 shows the relative positions of the mean, median, and mode in skewed distributions. In both cases, the mean is pulled toward the extreme tail of the distribution and does not accurately summarize the distribution. The mode tends to be toward the side away from the extreme tail, so most of the distribution is not centered around the mode either. The median, however, is not thrown off by extreme scores because it does not take into account the actual values of the scores. Thus, of the three measures, the median most accurately reflects the center of a skewed distribution.

FIGURE 4.10 Measures of central tendency for skewed distributions

The vertical lines show the relative positions of the mean, median, and mode.

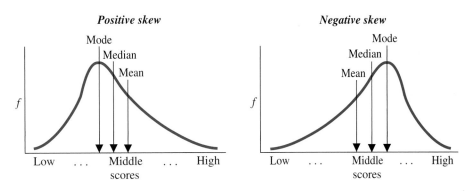

It is for the above reasons that the government uses the median to summarize such skewed distributions as that of yearly income or the price of houses. For example, the median income in the United States is around $42,000 a year. But there is a relatively small number of corporate executives, movie stars, professional athletes, and the like who make millions! Averaging in these high incomes would produce a mean at about $60,000. However, because most incomes are not located around $60,000, the median is a better summary of this distribution.

Believe it or not, we've now covered the basic measures of central tendency. In sum:

1. Use the mode with nominal data or with a distinctly bimodal distribution of any type of scores. The disadvantage is that the mode ignores information in the data and may be misleading.

2. Use the median with ordinal scores or with a very skewed distribution of interval/ratio scores. The disadvantage is that the median is based on only the lower half of a distribution.

3. Use the mean with a symmetrical, unimodal distribution of interval or ratio scores. The disadvantage is that the mean is pulled off if the distribution is skewed.

Most often the data in behavioral research are summarized using the mean. This is because most often we measure variables using interval or ratio scores that, simply because of how nature works, form a roughly normal distribution. Because the mean is used so extensively, we will delve further into its characteristics and uses in the following sections.

TRANSFORMATIONS AND THE MEAN

Recall that we perform transformations to make the scores easier to work with or to make scores from different variables comparable. The simplest transformation is to add, subtract, multiply, or divide each score by a constant. This brings up the burning question of "How do transformations affect the mean?"

If we add a constant (K) to each raw score in a sample, the new mean of the transformed scores will equal the old mean of the raw scores plus K. For example, the scores 7, 8, and 9 have a mean of 8. Adding 5 to each score produces 12, 13, and 14. The new mean is 13. The old mean of 8 plus the constant 5 also equals 13. Thus, the rule is that *new* $\overline{X}$ = *old* $\overline{X}$ + K. The same logic applies for other mathematical operations. When subtracting K from each score, *new* $\overline{X}$ = *old* $\overline{X}$ − K. When multiplying each score by K, *new* $\overline{X}$ = (*old* $\overline{X}$)K. When dividing each score by K, *new* $\overline{X}$ = (*old* $\overline{X}$)/K.

The above rules also apply to the median and to the mode. In essence, using a constant merely changes the location of each score on the variable by K points, so we also move the "address" of the distribution by the same amount.

DEVIATIONS AROUND THE MEAN

The mean is used in a number of other statistical procedures you'll see later. To understand why, you need to understand why the mean is the center score. The mean is at the center of a distribution because it is just as far from the scores above it as it is from the scores below it. That is, the *total* distance that scores in a distribution lie above the mean equals the *total* distance that scores lie below the mean.

The distance separating a score from the mean is called the score's **deviation,** indicating the amount the score "deviates" from the mean. A score's deviation is equal to the score minus the mean, or in symbols, the quantity $(X - \overline{X})$. Thus, if the sample mean is 47, a score of 50 deviates by $+3$ because $50 - 47$ is $+3$. A score of 40 deviates from the mean of 47 by -7 because $40 - 47 = -7$.

> *REMEMBER* Always subtract the mean *from* the raw score when computing a score's *deviation.*

Notice that a deviation consists of a number and a sign. A positive deviation indicates that the score is larger than the mean, and a negative deviation indicates that the score is less than the mean. The size of the deviation (regardless of its sign) indicates the distance the score lies from the mean: the *larger* the deviation, the *farther* the score is from the mean. A deviation of 0 indicates that the score equals the mean.

When we determine the deviations of all the scores in a sample, we find the *deviations around the mean.* The **sum of the deviations around the mean** is the sum of all differences between the scores and the mean. And here's why the mean is the mathematical center of a distribution:

The sum of the deviations around the mean always equals zero.

For example, the scores 3, 4, 6, and 7, have a mean of 5. The upper portion of Table 4.1 shows how to compute the deviations around the mean for these scores. The lower portion of Table 4.1 shows the deviations for the skewed distribution containing the scores 1, 2, 2, 2, 3, and 14, which has a mean of 4. In each sample, the sum of the deviations is

TABLE 4.1 Computing Deviations Around the Mean

The mean is subtracted from each score, resulting in the score's deviation.

Score	minus	Mean Score	equals	Deviation
3	−	5	=	−2
4	−	5	=	−1
6	−	5	=	+1
7	−	5	=	+2
			Sum =	0

Score	minus	Mean Score	equals	Deviation
1	−	4	=	−3
2	−	4	=	−2
2	−	4	=	−2
2	−	4	=	−2
3	−	4	=	−1
14	−	4	=	+10
			Sum =	0

zero. In fact, for *any* sample of scores, having a distribution of any shape, the sum of the deviations around the mean will equal zero. This is because the sum of the positive deviations equals the sum of the negative deviations, so the sum of all deviations is zero. In this way the mean is the center of a distribution, because in total, the mean is an equal distance from scores above and below it.

Many of the formulas you will eventually see involve something similar to finding the sum of the deviations around the mean. The statistical code for finding the sum of the deviations around the mean is $\Sigma(X - \overline{X})$. We always work inside parentheses first, so first find the deviation for each score, $(X - \overline{X})$. The Σ indicates to then find the sum of the deviations. Thus, as in the upper portion of Table 4.1, $\Sigma(X - \overline{X}) = -2 + -1 + 1 + 2$, which equals zero.

USING THE MEAN TO INTERPRET DATA

Because the sum of the deviations equals zero, the mean score is *literally* the score *around* which everyone in the sample scored, so that while some scores are above it, others are below it to the same extent. In other words, it is the one score that *more or less* describes everyone's score. Because of this, the mean is a very useful tool. As you'll see in the following sections, a sample mean is used in three ways: to predict any individual's score, to describe a score's location within a distribution, and to draw inferences about the population.

Using the Mean to Predict Scores

Recall that part of understanding the laws of nature is to predict a behavior in a particular situation, which translates into predicting the scores found in that situation. When we don't know anything else, the mean is our best prediction about the score that any individual obtains. Because the mean is the central score, it is the *typical* score, and essentially, we assume that if all the scores had been the same score, they would have been the mean score. Therefore, when in doubt, we treat all scores as if they *are* the mean, and predict that score for any individual.

For example, if your friends have a B average in college, they may not always get Bs, but you operate as if they do. If asked what you think they received in a particular course, you predict a B. For any future course, you assume your friends will continue to be B students, so you also predict B. (The logic is the same whether we are predicting past or future scores.) Likewise, if the class average on an exam is 80, we think of everyone in the class as receiving *around* 80, so out best prediction of every student's score is 80. And, because the mean typifies the participants we *did* observe, we assume it typifies any other individual we *might* have observed. Thus, we'd predict that any similar students who missed the exam would also score 80.

> *REMEMBER* Use the sample mean to predict any individual score you'd expect to find in the sample.

Not every individual score will equal the mean score, however, so our predictions will sometimes be wrong. The error in our predictions is the difference between the mean score we predict for participants and the actual scores they obtain. When predicting future scores, we expect the differences between the mean and the scores that we predict to be about the same as the differences between the mean and the scores in our sample. (In statistics, we always estimate the amount of error in predicting unknown scores based on how well we can "predict" known scores.) Thus, the amount of error in a single prediction is the difference between what we say someone got and what he or she actually got. In symbols this is the difference between someone's X and the $\overline{X}$ we predict for that person. We've already seen that $(X - \overline{X})$ is a score's deviation, so expand your perspective here: *A score's deviation indicates the amount of error we have when using the mean to predict an individual score.*

> *REMEMBER* When using the mean to predict scores, a *deviation* $(X - \overline{X})$ indicates our *error* in prediction: the difference between the $\overline{X}$ we predict for someone and the X that he or she actually gets.

If we determine the amount of error in every prediction and add them up, the total is the sum of the deviations, or $\Sigma(X - \overline{X})$. As you've seen, $\Sigma(X - \overline{X})$ always equals zero, so when using the mean to predict each score, *over the long run* our total error equals zero. This is the reason for using the mean as the predicted score: *Over the long run, it produces the minimum error in our predictions.* For example, the test scores 70, 75, 85, and 90 have a $\overline{X}$ of 80. One student, Quasimodo, scored the 70. We would estimate he scored 80, so we would be wrong by -10. But another student, Attila, scored the 90; by estimating an 80 for him, we would be off by $+10$. In the same way, our errors for the sample will cancel out so that the total error is zero. Likewise, we assume that other participants will behave similarly to Quasimodo, Attila, and the rest, so that using the mean to predict any unknown scores also results in a total error of zero.

If we used any score other than the mean, the total error would be *greater* than zero. If, for example, we described the above scores using a score of 75 or 85, the sum of the deviations would be $+20$ or -20, respectively. Having a total error of $+20$ or -20 is not as good as having a total error of zero. A total error of zero means that, over the long run, we overestimate by the same amount that we underestimate. A basic rule of statistics is that if we can't perfectly describe every score, then the next best thing is to have a number that more or less describes every score, with the same degrees of more and less. There is an old joke about two statisticians shooting targets. One hits one foot to the left of the target, and the other hits one foot to the right. "Congratulations," one says. "We got it!" Likewise, if we cannot perfectly describe every score, then we want our errors—our over- and underestimates—to balance out to zero. Only the mean provides this capability.

> *REMEMBER* Using the mean as everyone's predicted score results in a total error of zero.

Of course, this is not the whole story. Although the *total* error in predictions will equal zero, any *individual* prediction may be off by a country mile. Later chapters will discuss how to reduce these errors. For now, simply remember that *unless you have additional information about the scores,* the mean is the best score to use when predicting scores. This is because the over- and underestimates across all such predictions will cancel out to equal zero.

Using the Mean to Describe a Score's Location

Another use of the mean is to help interpret any individual score. A problem for science is that usually we do not know how to evaluate an individual score. If, for example, you score a 6 on a creativity test, we don't know whether, in nature, your score is good, bad, or indifferent. Usually, the best we can do is to evaluate the score *relative* to the rest of the sample. That is, we examine a raw score by computing the amount it deviates from the mean. The deviation communicates the score's location relative to the mean, and indirectly, relative to the rest of the distribution. For example, say that the creativity test produced the raw scores 1, 2, 3, 3, 4, 4, 4, 5, 5, 6, and 7, which form the approximately normal distribution in Figure 4.11. The *X* axis is labeled using each raw score and, underneath, its corresponding deviation score. A positive deviation indicates that the raw score is *larger* than the mean, and located to the *right* of the mean on the graph. A negative deviation indicates that the score is *less* than the mean, and falls to the *left* of the mean on the graph. The *size* of the deviation (regardless of its sign) indicates the *distance* the score is from the mean: The larger the deviation, the farther the score is above or below the mean, while a deviation of zero indicates the score is at the mean.

The deviation scores in a normal distribution also communicate the *frequencies* of the corresponding raw scores. The larger the deviation, whether positive or negative, the farther into the tail of the distribution the raw score lies, and so the less frequently the score occurs. Also, notice that the larger a deviation, the less frequently the *deviation* occurs. Above, the raw score of 7 produces the deviation of +3. Because 7 is an extreme score that occurs only once, its deviation is extreme and also occurs only once. In fact, the frequency of any score's deviation will equal the frequency of that score, so as shown in Figure 4.11, whether we label the *X* axis using raw scores or deviations, we have the same frequency polygon.

Thus, the advantage of using deviation scores to interpret raw scores is that deviation scores have a built-in frame of reference. For example, if the mean is 4, your creativity score of 6 produces a deviation of +2. By envisioning Figure 4.11, you know that a positive deviation of +2 indicates that you are above average (which with creativity is good), you know that you are to the right of and therefore above the 50th percentile (which is also good), and you know that you are out there in the direction of the

FIGURE 4.11 Frequency polygon showing deviations from the mean

The first row under the X axis indicates the original creativity scores, and the second row indicates the amounts the raw scores deviate from the mean.

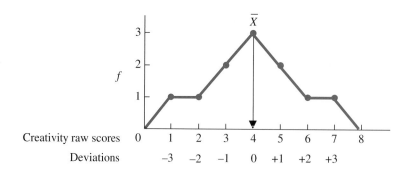

less frequent scores, where the most creative people are (so that's good, too.) Conversely, if these scores reflected the number of blunders on a test, you'd know you were out there among those who made the highest number of blunders (and that's not so good.) In either case, however, you'd have a better idea of how to interpret—*make sense of*—your score, and that is the purpose of statistics.

> *REMEMBER* A *deviation score* indicates a raw score's location and frequency relative to the rest of the distribution.

We'll elaborate on deviations around the mean in subsequent chapters. For now, remember that on the normal curve, the larger the deviation (whether positive or negative), the farther the raw score is from the mean and thus the less frequently the score and its deviation occur.

The final use of a sample mean is to estimate the corresponding population mean.

Using the Sample Mean to Describe the Population Mean

Recall that ultimately we seek to describe the population of scores we would find in a given situation. Populations are unwieldy, so we also summarize them using measures of central tendency. Here is what we want to know: If we examined the population, around which score would most of the scores be located?

Because we usually have interval or ratio scores that form at least an approximately normal distribution, we usually describe the population using the mean. The mean of a population is a *parameter,* and it is symbolized by the Greek letter μ (pronounced "mew"). Thus, to indicate that the population mean is 143, we'd say $\mu = 143$. We use the symbol μ simply to show that we're talking about a population, as opposed to a sample, but a mean is a mean, so a population mean has the same characteristics as a sample mean:

1. μ is the arithmetic average of the scores in the population.
2. μ is the score at the mathematical center of the distribution, so μ is the balance point.
3. The sum of the deviations around μ is zero.

Previously, we saw that these characteristics made the mean the best score to use when predicting any individual score in a sample and when describing a score's relative location in a sample. For the same reasons, the value of μ is the best score to use when predicting any score in the population, and as the basis for describing the relative location of any score in the population.

How do we determine the value of μ? If all the scores in the population are known, then we compute μ using the same formula that we used to compute $\overline{X}$:

$$\mu = \frac{\Sigma X}{N}$$

Usually, however, a population is infinitely large, so we cannot directly compute μ. Instead, we estimate μ based on the mean of a random sample. If, for example, a sample's mean in a particular situation is 99, then our best guess is that if we could actually compute it, the population μ in that situation would also be 99. We make such an inference because it is a population with a mean of 99 that is most likely to produce a sample with a mean of 99 to begin with. That is, a $\overline{X}$ of 99 indicates a sample with mostly scores around 99 in it. What population would be most likely to provide these scores? The population containing mostly scores around 99—where the population mean is 99. In essence, you are most likely to obtain a sample of participants who score around 99 when most individuals in the population score around 99. Thus, we assume that most scores in a sample are located where most scores in the population are located, so a sample mean should be a good estimate of μ (assuming the sample is representative).

> *REMEMBER*   The mean of a random sample $(\overline{X})$ is used to estimate the mean of the corresponding population (μ).

SUMMARIZING THE RESULTS OF AN EXPERIMENT

Now you can understand how means are used in research. We compute the mean anytime we have a sample of normally distributed scores (or compute other measures of central tendency when appropriate). Thus, if we've merely observed some participants, we compute the mean number of times they exhibit a particular behavior, or we compute the mean response in a survey. In a correlational study we compute the mean score on the X variable and the mean score on the Y variable. Based on such sample means, we can describe the typical score and predict the scores of other individuals, including those of the entire population.

We perform similar steps when summarizing the results of an experiment. For example, say that in a study of human memory, we predict that people will make more mistakes when recalling a long list of words than when recalling a short list. We conduct an overly simplistic experiment involving three conditions of the independent variable of list length. In one condition participants read a list containing 5 words and then recall it. In another condition participants read a 10-item list and recall it, and in a third condition, they read a 15-item list and recall it. For each participant, we measure the dependent variable of number of errors made in recalling the list. If the predicted relationship exists, then as the independent variable of list length increases, scores on the dependent variable of recall errors will also tend to increase.

Say we obtain the data shown in Design Diagram 4.1. It appears that there is a relationship here, because there tends to be a different and higher set of error scores associated with each condition. Most experiments involve much larger Ns, however, and with

DESIGN DIAGRAM 4.1   Errors Made by Participants Recalling a 5-, 10-, or 15-Item List

Independent variable: length of list.

Condition 1: 5-Item List	Condition 2: 10-Item List	Condition 3: 15-Item List
3	6	9
4	5	11
2	7	7

many different scores it is difficult to detect a relationship by looking at the raw scores. But that's why we have measures of central tendency: so that we can summarize the scores and at the same time simplify the relationship. Thus, your first step is *always* to compute a measure of central tendency for the scores in each condition.

Summarizing a Relationship Using Measures of Central Tendency

Recall that which measure of central tendency we compute depends on the characteristics of the scores. In an experiment the scores reflect the *dependent variable*. Therefore, compute the mean, median, or mode depending upon (1) the scale of measurement used to measure the dependent variable and (2), for interval or ratio scores, the shape of the distribution they form. In determining the shape of the distribution, ultimately we want to describe the population, so consider how the scores are distributed in the population. How do you know this? You'll never conduct research in a vacuum, and the first step will be to read about related research published in journals and books. From this, you can learn what other researchers assume about the population and how they compute central tendency.

> *REMEMBER*   The measure of central tendency to compute in an experiment is determined by the type of scale used to measure the *dependent* variable.

In our memory experiment, recall errors is a ratio variable that is assumed to form an approximately normal distribution, so we compute the mean score for each condition. In fact, because most dependent variables in behavioral research are interval or ratio variables that are normally distributed, computing the mean score for each condition is the predominant method of summarizing experiments.

We compute the mean of each condition in Design Diagram 4.1 by computing the mean in each column. These are shown in Table 4.2.

To interpret the means from any study, simply envision the scores that typically produce such a mean. In our data, for example, a normal distribution producing a mean of 3 would contain scores evenly distributed above and below 3, with most of the scores close to 3. Essentially, you envision something like the raw scores shown back in Design Diagram 4.1. Thus, we know that recalling a 5-item list resulted in one distribution located around 3 errors, but recalling a 10-item list produced a different distribution located around 6 errors, and recalling a 15-item list produced still another distribution located around 9 errors. Further, we can also use the mean score to describe the individual scores in each condition, as we did previously. In condition 1, for example, we'd predict that any participant would make about 3 errors, and we would interpret anyone's actual score by determining its deviation from the mean of 3.

TABLE 4.2   Means of Conditions in Memory Experiment

Condition 1: *5-Item List*	*Condition 2:* *10-Item List*	*Condition 3:* *15-Item List*
$\overline{X} = 3$	$\overline{X} = 6$	$\overline{X} = 9$

Recall that an experiment shows a relationship when the *scores* on the dependent variable change as we change the *conditions* of the independent variable. Because changes in the means reflect changes in the underlying raw scores, we also have a relationship when the mean scores change as a function of changes in the independent variable. The means from our memory study show a relationship, because as the conditions of the independent variable change (from 5 to 10 to 15 items in a list), the scores on the dependent variable also tend to change (from around 3, to around 6, to around 9 errors, respectively). Further, our experiment "worked" because it demonstrates that, literally, list length is a variable that makes a *difference* in individual recall scores and therefore in the mean scores. Researchers often communicate that they have found a relationship simply by saying that they have found a difference between the means. If they find no difference, they have not found a relationship. However, not all means must differ for a relationship to be present. For example, we might find that only the mean (and scores) in the 5-item condition differs from the mean (and scores) in the 15-item condition. We still have a relationship if, at least sometimes, as the conditions of the independent variable change, the dependent scores also change.

> **REMEMBER** An experiment shows a relationship when the means from two or more conditions are different.

The above logic also applies to the *median* or *mode*. For example, say that we study the dependent variable of political party affiliation, to see if it changes as a function of a person's year in college. Political parties involve nominal scores, so the mode is the appropriate measure of central tendency. We might see that freshmen most often claim to be Republican, but the mode for sophomores is Democrat, for juniors Socialist, and for seniors Communist. These data reflect a relationship because they indicate that as college level changes, political affiliation tends to change. Likewise, say we learn that the median income for freshmen is lower than the median income for sophomores, which is lower than for upperclassmen. This tells us that the location of the corresponding distribution of incomes is different for each class, so we know that the income "scores" of individuals are changing as their year in college changes.

Graphing the Results of an Experiment

Recall that when creating a graph of an experiment, the independent variable is plotted on the X axis and the dependent variable on the Y axis. Then you have two decisions to make.

Your first decision involves how to present the dependent scores. Because we want to summarize the data, usually we do *not* plot the individual scores. Rather, we plot either the mean, median, or mode of the dependent scores in each condition. Therefore, if you haven't already done it, identify the scale of measurement used to measure the dependent variable, compute the appropriate measure of central tendency in each condition, and label the Y axis accordingly. Notice that a potential for confusion is present when using the formulas. The general format of formulas is to use X to represent the scores (as when computing the mean). These formulas are used, even if you'll then plot the results on the Y axis.

Your second decision is to select the type of graph to create. You may create either a *line graph* or a *bar graph*. The type of graph you choose is determined by the characteristics of the *independent variable*.

Line Graphs   When the independent variable is an interval or a ratio variable, create a line graph. In a **line graph** adjacent data points are connected with straight lines.

For example, in our memory experiment the independent variable of list length involves a ratio scale. Therefore, we create the line graph shown on the left in Figure 4.12. First, notice that we label the X and Y axes with the specific variables (not "independent variable" and "dependent variable"). Note, too, that the label on the Y axis is "mean recall errors." The numbers on the X axis correspond to the values of the independent variable in the various conditions. Then we place a data point above the 5-item condition opposite 3 errors, indicating the mean error score for the 5-item list was 3. We also place a data point above the 10-item condition at 6 errors, and a data point above the 15-item condition at 9 errors. Finally, we connect adjacent data points with straight lines. We use straight lines with interval or ratio data because we assume that the relationship continues in a straight line between the points shown on the X axis. For example, we assume that if there had been a 6-item list, the mean error score would fall on the line connecting the means for the 5- and 10-item lists.

This graph conveys the same information as the sample means did back in Table 4.2, where each sample mean indicates a different distribution of scores for each condition. In the graph we envision these distributions as shown on the right in Figure 4.12: Each mean implies a sample of scores and their corresponding data points that occur *around*—above and below—the mean's data point. Because the vertical positions of the means change as the conditions change, we know that the raw scores also change, so there is a relationship here.

Notice that you can easily spot such a relationship, because the different means produce a line graph that is not horizontal. *On any graph, if the summary data points form a line that is not horizontal, the individual* Y *scores are changing as the* X *scores change, and so a relationship is present.* On the other hand, say that each condition had produced a mean of 5 errors. As shown on the left in Figure 4.13, this results in a horizontal (flat) line, indicating that as list length changes, the mean error score stays the

FIGURE 4.12   Line graphs showing (A) the relationship for mean errors in recall as a function of list length and (B) the data points we envision around each mean

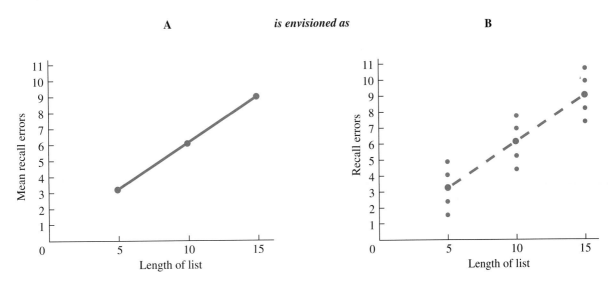

FIGURE 4.13   Line graphs showing (A) no relationship for mean errors in recall as a function of list length and (B) the data points we envision around each mean

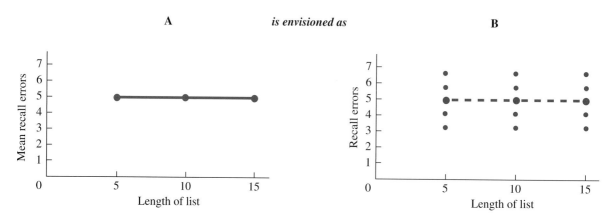

same. This implies that (as in the figure on the right) the individual scores stay the same regardless of the condition, so there is no relationship present. Thus, *on any graph, if the summary data points form a horizontal line, the individual* Y *scores do not change as the* X *scores change, and so a relationship is not present.*

Bar Graphs   When the independent variable is a nominal or an ordinal variable, we plot the results of the experiment by creating a **bar graph.** Notice that the rule here is the same as it was for frequency distributions discussed in Chapter 3: create a bar graph whenever the scores plotted along the *X* axis are nominal or ordinal scores.

For example, say that we conducted another memory experiment in which we compared the errors made by psychology majors, English majors, and physics majors. The independent variable of college major is a nominal variable, so we have the bar graph shown in Figure 4.14. The height of each bar corresponds to the mean score for the condition. The bars implicitly indicate that on the variable of college major, we arbitrarily assigned psychology a nominal score to the left of that of English, closer to zero. The bars also indicate that there is an unknown or undefined gap between categories. If, for example, we inserted the additional category of sociology between psychology and English, we could not assume that the mean for sociology majors would fall on a line running between the means for psychology and English majors.

In Figure 4.14 the tops of the bars do not form a horizontal line. This tells us there are different means and thus different scores in each condition. We can again envision that we would see individual error scores at around 8 for physics majors, around 4 for psychology majors, and around 12 for English majors. Thus, the scores change as a function of college major, so a relationship is present.

Note: In a different experiment we might have measured a nominal or an ordinal *dependent* variable. In that case we would plot the mode or median on the *Y* axis for each condition. Then, again depending on the characteristics of the independent variable, we would create either a line or bar graph. Regardless, any graph is interpreted by envisioning the individual *Y* scores that underlie the pattern formed by the summary data points that are presented.

FIGURE 4.14   Bar graph showing mean errors in recall as a function of college major

The height of each bar corresponds to the mean score for the condition.

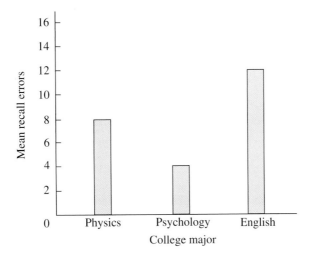

REMEMBER   The scale of measurement involved in the dependent variable determines the measure of central tendency to calculate, and the scale involved in the independent variable determines the type of graph to create.

Inferring the Relationship in the Population

So far we have summarized the results of the memory experiment in terms of the sample data. But this is only part of the story. The big question remains: Do these data reflect a law of nature? Do longer lists produce more memory errors for everyone in the population?

Recall that to make inferences about the population, we must first compute the appropriate inferential statistics. For the moment assume that our data passed the inferential test. Then we can conclude that each sample mean represents the population mean that would be found for that condition. The mean for the 5-item condition was 3, so we infer that if the population of participants recalled a 5-item list, the mean error score would be 3. In essence, we expect that everyone would have around 3 errors. Similarly, we infer that if the population recalled a 10-item list, μ would equal the condition's sample mean of 6, and if the population recalled a 15-item list, μ would be 9.

We conceptualize the above populations in the following way. Assuming that each sample mean provides a good estimate of the corresponding population mean, we know approximately *where* on the dependent variable each population of scores would be located. Further, assuming that recall errors are normally distributed in the population, we also have a good idea of the *shape* of each population distribution. Thus, we can envision the population of recall errors we would expect for each condition as the frequency polygons shown in Figure 4.15. (These are frequency distributions, with the dependent scores of memory errors on the *X* axis.) Because the distributions have different values of μ, you can see the relationship that we think exists in the population: As

FIGURE 4.15   Locations of populations of error scores as a function of list length

Each distribution contains the recall scores we would expect to find if the population were tested under each condition.

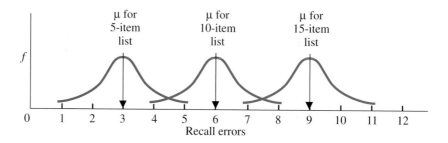

the conditions of the independent variable change, scores on the dependent variable change so that there is a different population of scores for each condition. Essentially, for every 5 items in a list, everyone's score tends to increase by about 3 errors, and so the distributions slide 3 units to the right each time, going from around 3 to around 6 to around 9. (The overlap among the distributions simply shows that some people in one condition make the same number of errors as other people in adjacent conditions.)

Remember that the population of scores reflects the behavior of everyone. If, as the independent variable changes, *everyone's* behavior changes, then we have learned about a law of nature involving that behavior. Above, everyone's recall behavior tends to change as list length changes, so we have evidence of how human memory generally works in this situation: for every 5 items in a list, errors go up by around 3. That's about all there is to it: We have basically achieved the goal of our research.

The process of arriving at the above conclusion sounds easy, because it is easy. In essence, statistical analysis of most experiments involves three steps: (1) Compute each sample mean (and other descriptive statistics) to summarize the scores and the relationship found in the experiment, (2) Perform the appropriate inferential procedure to determine whether the data are representative, and (3) Determine the location of the population of scores that you expect would be found for each condition by estimating each μ. Once you've described the expected population for each condition, you are basically finished with statistical analysis.

PUTTING IT ALL TOGETHER

As you may have noticed, the mean is *the* measure of central tendency in behavioral research. To be literate in statistics, you should understand the mode and the median, but the truly important topics in this chapter involve the mean and its characteristics, especially when applied to the normal distribution. Understand these topics, because they form the basis for virtually everything else that we will discuss.

We will eventually discuss inferential procedures, and they will tend to occupy all of your attention. However, remember that the mean (or another central tendency measure) is the basis for interpreting any study. You will always want to say something like "the participants scored around 3" in a particular condition, because then you are describing their typical *behavior* in that situation. Such a description is the goal of research, and using a measure of central tendency is *the* way to get there. Thus, regardless of what other fancy procedures we discuss, remember that to make sense out of your data, you must ultimately return to identifying *around* where the scores in each condition are located.

CHAPTER SUMMARY

1. *Measures of central tendency* summarize the location of a distribution of scores on a variable, indicating where the center of the distribution tends to be. Which measure to compute in a particular study depends on: (a) the scale used to measure the scores and (b) the shape of the distribution.

2. The *mode* is the most frequently occurring score or scores in a distribution. It is used primarily to summarize nominal data.

3. The *median,* symbolized by Mdn, is the score located at the 50th percentile. It is used primarily with ordinal data and with interval or ratio data that form a very skewed distribution.

4. The *mean* is the average score located at the mathematical center of a distribution. It is used with interval or ratio data that form a symmetrical, unimodal distribution such as the normal distribution. The symbol for a sample mean is $\overline{X}$ and the symbol for a population mean is μ.

5. Transforming raw scores by using a *constant (K),* results in a new value of the mean, median, or mode that is equal to the one that would be obtained if the transformation were performed directly on the old value.

6. The amount a score *deviates* from the mean is computed as $X - \overline{X}$. A *deviation* indicates the location of the raw score relative to the mean and relative to the distribution. In a normal distribution, the larger the deviation, the less frequently the score and the deviation occur.

7. The *sum of the deviations around the mean,* $\Sigma(X - \overline{X})$, equals zero. The mean is the best score to use when predicting any individual score, because the *total error* across all such estimates will be the sum of the deviations around the mean, which equals zero.

8. In graphing the results of an experiment, the independent variable is plotted on the X axis and the dependent variable on the Y axis. A *line graph* is created when the independent variable is measured using a ratio or an interval scale. A *bar graph* is created when the independent variable is measured using a nominal or an ordinal scale.

9. On any graph, if the summary data points form a line that is not horizontal, then the individual Y scores change as a function of changes in the X scores and a relationship is present. If the data points form a horizontal line, then the Y scores do not change as a function of changes in the X scores and a relationship is not present.

10. A random sample mean is the best estimate of the corresponding population's mean, symbolized as μ. The sample mean in each condition of an experiment is the best estimate of the μ that would be found if the population was tested under that condition.

11. When a relationship in the population is present, there will be different values of μ, implying different distributions of dependent scores, for two or more conditions of the independent variable.

KEY TERMS: Can You Define the Following?

ΣX K Mdn $\overline{X}$ $\Sigma(X - \overline{X})$ μ

bar graph *88*
bimodal distribution *70*
deviation *79*
line graph *87*
mean *74*
measure of central tendency *69*

median *72*
mode *70*
sum of the deviations around
  the mean *79*
sum of X *68*
unimodal distribution *70*

REVIEW QUESTIONS

(Answers for odd-numbered problems are in Appendix C.)

1. What does a measure of central tendency indicate?
2. What two aspects of the data determine which measure of central tendency to use?
3. What is the mode, and with what type of data is it most appropriate?
4. What is the median, and with what type of data is it most appropriate?
5. What is the mean, and with what type of data is it most appropriate?
6. Why is it best to use the mean with a normal distribution?
7. Why is it inappropriate to use the mean with a skewed distribution?
8. Which measure of central tendency is used most often in behavioral research? Why?
9. What two pieces of information about the location of a score does a deviation score convey?
10. Why do we use the mean of a sample to predict any score that might be found in that sample?

APPLICATION QUESTIONS

11. For the following data, compute (a) the mean and (b) the mode.

| 55 | 57 | 59 | 58 | 60 | 57 | 56 | 58 | 61 | 58 | 59 |

12. (a) In problem 11 what is your best estimate of the median (without computing it)? (b) Explain why you think your answer is correct. (c) Calculate the approximate median using the method described in this chapter.

13. For the data below, compute the mean.

| 18 | 16 | 19 | 20 | 18 | 19 | 23 | 54 | 20 | 16 |
| 18 | 19 | 18 | 19 | 18 | 40 | 30 | 19 | 18 | 38 |

14. (a) For the data in problem 13, what is the mode? (b) By comparing the mean and the mode, determine the shape of the distribution. How do you know this?

15. A researcher collected the following sets of data. For each, indicate the measure of central tendency she should compute: (a) the following IQ scores: 60, 72, 63, 83, 68, 74, 90, 86, 74, 80; (b) the following error scores: 10, 15, 18, 15, 14, 13, 42, 15, 12, 14, 42; (c) the following blood types: A−, A−, O, A+, AB−, A+, O, O, O, AB+; (d) the following grades: B, D, C, A, B, F, C, B, C, D, D.

16. You misplaced two of the scores in a sample, but you have the data indicated below. What should you guess the value of the missing scores to be? Why?

100   120   130   140   110   140   150   130   120   130

17. On a normal distribution of scores, four participants obtained the following deviation scores: −5, 0, +3, and +1. (a) Which person obtained the lowest raw score? How do you know? (b) Which person's raw score had the lowest frequency? How do you know? (c) Which person's raw score had the highest frequency? How do you know? (d) Which person obtained the highest raw score? How do you know?

18. In a normal distribution of scores, five participants obtained the following deviation scores: +1, −2, +5, and −10. (a) Which score reflects the highest raw score? (b) Which score reflects the lowest raw score? (c) Rank-order the deviation scores in terms of their frequency, starting with the score with the lowest frequency.

19. Foofy says a deviation of +5 is always better than a deviation of −5. Why is she correct or incorrect?

20. What is μ, and how do we usually determine its value?

21. For the following experimental results, interpret specifically the relationship between the independent and dependent variables:

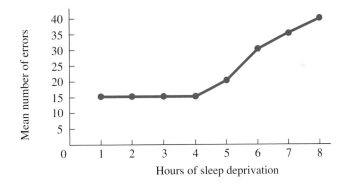

22. (a) In problem 21 give a title to the graph, using "as a function of." (b) If you participated in the study in problem 21 and had been deprived of 5 hours of sleep, how many errors do you think you would make? (c) If we tested all people in the world after 5 hours of sleep deprivation, how many errors do you think each would make? (d) What symbol stands for your prediction in part c?

23. For each of the experiments listed below, determine (1) which variable should be plotted on the *Y* axis and which on the *X* axis, (2) whether the researcher should use a line graph or a bar graph to present the data, and (3) how she should summarize scores on the dependent variable: (a) a study of income as a function of age; (b) a study of politicians' positive votes on environmental issues as a function of the presence or absence of a wildlife refuge in their political district; (c) a study of running speed as a function of carbohydrates consumed; (d) a study of rates of alcohol abuse as a function of ethnic group.

24. You hear that in Dr. Grumpyman's experiment, a line graph of scores from the Grumpy Emotionality Test slants downward as a function of increases in the amount of sunlight present on the day subjects were tested. (a) What does this tell you about the mean scores for the conditions? (b) What does this tell you about the raw scores for each condition? (c) Assuming that the samples are representative, what does this tell you about the μs? (d) What do you conclude about whether there is a relationship between emotionality and sunlight in nature?

25. You conduct a study to determine the impact that varying the amount of noise in an office has on worker productivity. You obtain the following productivity scores.

Condition 1 Low Noise	Condition 2 Medium Noise	Condition 3 Loud Noise
15	13	12
19	11	9
13	14	7
13	10	8

(a) Assuming productivity scores are normally distributed ratio scores, summarize the results of this experiment. (b) Draw the appropriate graph for these data. (c) Assuming the data are representative, draw how we would envision the populations produced by this experiment. (d) What conclusions should you draw from this experiment?

26. Assume that the data in problem 25 reflect a highly skewed interval variable. (a) Summarize these scores. (b) What conclusion would you draw from the sample data? (c) What conclusion would you draw about the populations produced by this experiment?

SUMMARY OF FORMULAS

1. *The formula for computing the sample mean is*

$$\overline{X} = \frac{\Sigma X}{N}$$

where ΣX *stands for the sum of the scores and* N *is the number of scores.*

2. *To estimate the median, arrange the scores in rank order. If* N *is an odd number, the score in the middle position is roughly the median. If* N *is an even number, the average of the two scores in the middle positions is roughly the median.*

5

Summarizing Scores with Measures of Variability: Range, Variance, and Standard Deviation

GETTING STARTED

To understand this chapter, recall the following:

- From Chapter 4, recall what the median and mean are, what $\overline{X}$ and μ stand for, what a deviation score tells you, and why the sum of the deviations around the mean is zero.

Your goals in this chapter are to learn:

- What is meant by variability.
- When the range and semi-interquartile range are used and how to interpret them.
- When the standard deviation and variance are used and how to interpret them.
- How to compute the sample variance and standard deviation, the estimated population variance and standard deviation, and the true population variance and standard deviation.
- How variance is used to measure errors in prediction, and what is meant by the proportion of variance accounted for.

So far you've learned that applying descriptive statistics involves considering the shape of the frequency distribution formed by the scores and then computing the appropriate measure of central tendency. This information simplifies the distribution and allows you to envision its general properties.

But, recall that not everyone will behave in the same way, and so there may be many, very different scores. Therefore, to have a complete description of any set of data, you must also answer the question "Are there large differences or small differences among the scores?" This chapter discusses the statistics for describing the differences among scores, which are called *measures of variability*.

First, though, here are a few new symbols and terms.

MORE STATISTICAL NOTATION

A new symbol you'll see is ΣX^2, which indicates the **sum of the squared Xs:** You first square each X and then find the sum of the squared Xs. Thus, to find ΣX^2 for the scores 2, 2, and 3, add $2^2 + 2^2 + 3^2$, which becomes $4 + 4 + 9$, which equals 17.

Learn right here to avoid confusing ΣX^2 with a similar looking, yet very different, operation symbolized by $(\Sigma X)^2$. The symbol $(\Sigma X)^2$ stands for the **squared sum of X.** Recall that you always work inside the parentheses first, so here, first find the sum of the X scores and then square that sum. Thus, to find $(\Sigma X)^2$ for the scores 2, 2, and 3, you have $(2 + 2 + 3)^2$, which is $(7)^2$, which is 49. Notice that for the same scores of 2, 2, and 3, ΣX^2 produced 17, while $(\Sigma X)^2$ produced the different answer of 49. Be careful when dealing with these terms.

> *REMEMBER* ΣX^2 indicates the *sum of squared Xs,* and $(\Sigma X)^2$ indicates the *squared sum of* X.

With this chapter we begin using *subscripts*. Pay attention to subscripts, because they are part of the symbols for certain statistics.

Finally, many statistics will have two different formulas, a *definitional formula* and a *computational formula*. A definitional formula defines a statistic. Pay attention to these formulas so you understand where the answer comes from when you compute a statistic. However, statisticians have reworked the formulas to produce computational formulas which are the formulas to use when actually computing a statistic. Trust me, computational formulas give exactly the same answers as definitional formulas, but they are much easier and faster to use.

WHY IS IT IMPORTANT TO KNOW ABOUT MEASURES OF VARIABILITY?

Computing a measure of variability is important because without it, a measure of central tendency provides an incomplete description of a distribution. The mean, for example, only indicates the central score and where the most frequent scores are. It tells us little about scores that are not at the center of the distribution and/or that occur infrequently. You can see what's missing by looking at the three samples in Table 5.1. Each has a mean of 6, so if you didn't look at the raw scores, you might think they are identical distributions. But, Sample A contains scores that differ greatly from each other and from the mean. Sample B contains scores that differ less from each other and from the mean. In Sample C there are no differences among the scores.

Thus, to completely describe a set of data, we need to know not only the central tendency but also how much the individual scores differ from each other and from the center. We obtain this information by calculating statistics called measures of variability. **Measures of variability** describe the extent to which scores in a distribution *differ* from each other. Thus, when we ask whether there are large or small differences among the scores, we are asking the statistical question "How much variability is there in the data?" When there are many, relatively large differences among the scores, the data are said to be *variable* or to contain a large amount of *variability*.

In Chapter 4 you saw that a score indicates a participant's location on a variable and that the difference between two scores is the distance that separates them. From this perspective, by telling us the extent to which scores in a distribution differ, measures of variability indicate how *spread out* the scores are. For example, Figure 5.1 shows the distances separating the scores in the previous samples. There are relatively large differences between the scores in Sample A, so this distribution is spread out. There are smaller differences between the scores in Sample B, so this distribution is not as spread out. There are no differences in Sample C, so there is no spread in this distribution. Thus, in statistical terms, we say that Sample A shows the greatest "variability."

You should always compute a measure of variability because it will describe two important and related aspects of the data. First, the opposite of variability is how *consistent* the scores are. Small variability indicates that there are not many and/or not large differences among the scores, so the scores must be rather similar and consistently close to the same value. Conversely, larger variability indicates that scores were inconsistent, often with each score very different from the next. Second, a measure of variability tells us how accurately the measure of central tendency describes the distribution. The greater the variability, the more the scores are spread out, and so the less accurately they are summarized by one central score. Conversely, the smaller the variability, the closer the scores are to each other and to the central score. Thus, by knowing the amount of variability in the above samples, we know Sample C contains consistent scores and so 6 very accurately represents it, Sample B contains less consistent scores and so 6 is not so accurate a summary, and Sample A contains very inconsistent scores and so 6 is not very close to most scores.

TABLE 5.1 Three Different Distributions Having the Same Mean Score

Sample A	Sample B	Sample C
0	8	6
2	7	6
6	6	6
10	5	6
12	4	6
$\overline{X} = 6$	$\overline{X} = 6$	$\overline{X} = 6$

FIGURE 5.1   Distance between the locations of scores in three distributions

Each arrow represents how spread out the scores in the sample are.

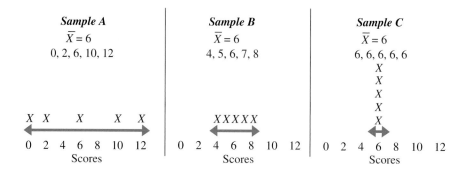

You can see the same aspect of variability in the larger distributions in Figure 5.2. Using our parking lot approach, Distribution A is rather narrow or "skinny" because there are long lines of people having the same score. These scores are all close to one another and to the mean of 50, with relatively few people standing at scores very far above or below the mean (e.g., few score at 40 or 60). Therefore, we'll find predominantly small differences among the scores, so the variability is relatively small: People tended to score rather consistently near the mean of 50.

FIGURE 5.2   Three variations of the normal curve

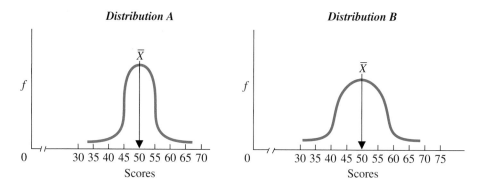

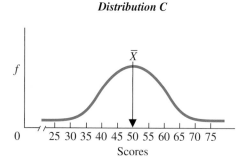

In Distribution B, however, more people obtained scores farther above and below the middle (e.g., here more people score near 40 and 60). Thus, more often we'll find larger differences, so the variability here is larger than in Distribution A because people are not so consistently scoring near the mean of 50.

Distribution C is a relatively wide or "fat" distribution. Here, longer lines of people are found even more toward the tails, with many people obtaining more extreme scores (here scores around 40 and 60 have high frequencies). Therefore, we'll find many large differences among the scores, so the variability is the largest of the three: Here, people scored rather inconsistently, frequently being way above or way below the mean of 50.

> REMEMBER *Measures of variability* indicate how spread out the scores are. While measures of central tendency indicate the *location* of a distribution, measures of variability indicate the *distances* among the scores in the distribution.

There are several ways to measure variability. Which specific measure you should compute depends on the type of data you have. The following sections discuss the three common measures of variability: the *range,* the *variance,* and the *standard deviation.*

THE RANGE

One way to describe variability is to determine how far the lowest score is from the highest score. The descriptive statistic that indicates the distance between the two most extreme scores in a distribution is called the **range.**

> *THE FORMULA FOR COMPUTING THE RANGE IS*
>
> Range = highest score − lowest score

Thus, for example, the scores back in Sample A (0, 2, 6, 10, 12) have a range of 12 − 0 = 12. The less variable scores in Sample B (4, 5, 6, 7, 8) have a range of 8 − 4 = 4. And the perfectly consistent Sample C (6, 6, 6, 6, 6) has a range of 6 − 6 = 0.

Thus, the range does communicate the spread in the data. However, the drawback to the range is that it is a rather crude measure. Because it involves only the two most extreme scores, the range is based on the least typical and often least frequent scores, while ignoring all other scores. Therefore, we usually use the range as our sole measure of variability only with nominal or ordinal data.

With nominal data, we compute the range slightly differently by counting the number of categories we're examining. If the participants in our study belong to any of 4 political parties, there is more consistency than if they belong to any of 14 parties. With ordinal data the range is the distance between the lowest and highest rank: If 100 runners finish a race spanning only the 5 positions from 1st through 5th, this is a close race with many ties; if they span 75 positions, the runners are spread out.

We also use the range when interval or ratio scores form distributions that cannot be accurately described using the other, better measures we'll discuss.

The Semi-Interquartile Range

A special version of the range is the semi-interquartile range, which is used in conjunction with the median to describe highly skewed distributions of interval or ratio scores. A *quartile* refers to a quarter of a distribution. The **semi-interquartile range** is one-half of the distance between the scores at the 25th and 75th percentiles.

THE FORMULA FOR COMPUTING THE SEMI-INTERQUARTILE RANGE IS

$$\frac{\text{Score at 75th percentile} - \text{Score at 25th percentile}}{2}$$

The first step is to determine the scores at the 25th and 75th percentiles (if need be using the formula in Appendix A). Then subtract the score at the 25th percentile from the score at the 75th percentile and divide by 2.

To see what the semi-interquartile range tells us, consider Figure 5.3. The score of 12 is at the 25th percentile and the score of 17 is at the 75th percentile. Using the above formula, the semi-interquartile range is $(17 - 12)/2$, which equals 2.5. By subtracting $17 - 12$, we determine the range across the middle 50% of the curve. But, in a skewed distribution the curve is not symmetrical around the median, so the distance between the 25th percentile and the median does not equal the distance between the 75th percentile and the median. Therefore, by dividing by 2 we calculate the average distance between the median and the scores at the 25th and 75th percentiles. Here, we have determined that the 25% of the distribution immediately below or above the median is, on average, within 2.5 points of the median. This semi-interquartile range describes the

FIGURE 5.3 Semi-interquartile range on a positively skewed distribution

Twenty-five percent of all participants scored between 12 and 14, and 25% scored between 14 and 17.

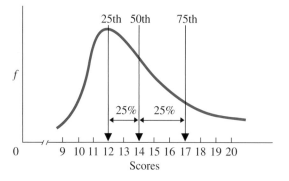

distribution more accurately than the overall range, because the semi-interquartile range describes the scores more toward the center of the distribution and does not include the lopsided tails containing extreme scores.

UNDERSTANDING THE VARIANCE AND STANDARD DEVIATION

Most of the time behavioral research involves interval or ratio scores that form a normal distribution, so the mean is the best measure of central tendency. When the mean is appropriate, we use two very similar measures of variability, called the *variance* and the *standard deviation*. These are the best measures of variability because in computing them we consider every score in the distribution.

Understand that we *use* the variance and the standard deviation to describe and communicate how different the scores are from each other. We *calculate* them, however, by measuring how much the scores differ from the mean. The mean is our reference point because it is the center of a distribution. Therefore, when the scores are spread out from each other, they are also spread out from the mean. If the scores are close to each other, they are also close to the mean.

This brings us to an important aspect of the variance and standard deviation. The mean is the point *around* which a distribution is located, and *the variance and standard deviation allow us to quantify "around."* For example, if the grades in a statistics class form a normal distribution with a mean of 80, then you know that most of the scores are around 80. But are most scores between 79 and 81 or between 60 and 100? By measuring how spread out scores are from the mean, the variance and standard deviation will define "around."

> **REMEMBER** The *variance* and *standard deviation* are two measures of variability that indicate how much the scores are spread out around the mean.

Mathematically, the *distance* between a score and the mean is the *difference* between the score and the mean. Recall from Chapter 4 that this difference is symbolized by the quantity $(X - \overline{X})$, which is the amount that a score *deviates* from the mean. Thus, a score's deviation indicates how far it is spread out from the mean. Of course, some scores will deviate from the mean by more than others, so it makes sense to compute something like the average amount the scores deviate from the mean. We could call this the "average of the deviations." The larger the average of the deviations, the greater the variability between the scores and the mean.

To compute an average, we sum the scores and divide by N. We *might* find the average of the deviations by first computing $(X - \overline{X})$ for each participant, then summing these deviations to find $\Sigma(X - \overline{X})$, and finally dividing by N, the number of deviations. Altogether, the formula for the average of the deviations[1] would be

$$\text{Average of the deviations} = \frac{\Sigma(X - \overline{X})}{N}$$

---

[1] In advanced statistics there is a very real statistic called the "average deviation." This isn't it.

We *might* compute the average of the deviations using this formula, except for a *big* problem. Recall that the sum of the deviations around the mean, $\Sigma(X - \overline{X})$, always equals zero, because the positive deviations cancel out the negative deviations. This means that the numerator in the above formula will always be zero, so the average of the deviations will always be zero. So much for the average of the deviations!

But remember our purpose here: We want a statistic *like* the average of the deviations, so that we know the average amount the scores are spread out around the mean. But, because mathematically the average of the deviations is always zero, we calculate slightly more complicated statistics called the variance and standard deviation. *Think* of them, however, as each producing a number that indicates something like the average or typical amount that the scores differ from the mean.

DESCRIBING THE SAMPLE VARIANCE

If the problem with the average of the deviations is with the positive and negative deviations, then a solution is to *square* the deviations. That is, after finding the difference between each score and the mean, we square that difference. This removes all negative deviations, so the *sum of the squared deviations* is not necessarily zero and neither is the *average squared deviation*. (As you'll see, this solution also results in statistics that have very useful characteristics.)

By finding the average squared deviation, we are computing the variance. The **sample variance** is the average of the squared deviations of scores around the sample mean. The symbol for the sample variance is S_X^2. Always include the squared sign (^{2}), because it is part of the symbol. The capital S indicates that we are describing a sample, and the subscript X indicates that it is computed for a sample of X scores.

THE DEFINITIONAL FORMULA FOR THE SAMPLE VARIANCE IS

$$S_X^2 = \frac{\Sigma(X - \overline{X})^2}{N}$$

Use this formula *only* when describing a *sample* of data (as opposed to the population).

REMEMBER   The symbol S_X^2 stands for the *sample variance*.

To see how the formula works, say that we measure the ages of some children and find they are 3, 5, 2, 6, 7, 4, and 8 years old. The mean age is 5. The computations of S_X^2 using the above formula are shown in Table 5.2. First, compute each deviation $(X - \overline{X})$ by subtracting the mean from each score. Next, as in the far right column, square each deviation to get $(X - \overline{X})^2$. Then add the squared deviations to find $\Sigma(X - \overline{X})^2$, which here is 28. The N is 7. Filling in the formula for S_X^2 gives

$$S_X^2 = \frac{\Sigma(X - \overline{X})^2}{N} = \frac{28}{7} = 4.0$$

TABLE 5.2 Calculation of Variance Using the Definitional Formula

Participant	Age Score	−	$\overline{X}$	=	$(X - \overline{X})$	$(X - \overline{X})^2$
1	2	−	5	=	−3	9
2	3	−	5	=	−2	4
3	4	−	5	=	−1	1
4	5	−	5	=	0	0
5	6	−	5	=	1	1
6	7	−	5	=	2	4
7	8	−	5	=	3	9
	$N = 7$					$\Sigma(X - \overline{X})^2 = 28$

Thus, in this sample, the variance equals 4.0. In other words, the average squared deviation of the age scores around the mean is 4.0.

Computational Formula for the Sample Variance

To simplify the preceding formula, we've replaced the symbol for the mean with its formula and then reduced the components to produce the following computational formula. Again, use this formula only when describing a *sample*.

THE COMPUTATIONAL FORMULA FOR THE SAMPLE VARIANCE IS

$$S_X^2 = \frac{\Sigma X^2 - \dfrac{(\Sigma X)^2}{N}}{N}$$

This formula says to first find the sum of the Xs, (ΣX), square that sum, and divide the squared sum by N. Then subtract that result from the sum of the squared Xs (ΣX^2). Finally, divide that quantity by N.

For example, we can arrange the previous age scores as shown in Table 5.3. The ΣX is 35. The ΣX^2 is 203, and N is 7. Putting these quantities into the computational formula, we have

$$S_X^2 = \frac{\Sigma X^2 - \dfrac{(\Sigma X)^2}{N}}{N} = \frac{203 - \dfrac{(35)^2}{7}}{7}$$

The squared sum of X is 35^2, which is 1225, so

$$S_X^2 = \frac{203 - \dfrac{1225}{7}}{7}$$

Now, 1225 divided by 7 equals 175, so

$$S_X^2 = \frac{203 - 175}{7}$$

TABLE 5.3 Calculation
of Variance Using the
Computational Formula

X Score	X^2
2	4
3	9
4	16
5	25
6	36
7	49
8	64
$\Sigma X = 35$	$\Sigma X^2 = 203$

Because 203 minus 175 equals 28, we have

$$S_X^2 = \frac{28}{7}$$

Finally, after dividing, we have

$$S_X^2 = 4.0$$

Thus, again, the sample variance for these age scores is 4.0.

Do not read any further until you understand how to work this formula!

Interpreting Variance

The good news is that the variance is a legitimate measure of variability. Ideally, though, we want the average of the deviations, and the bad news is that the variance does not make much sense as the average deviation. There are two problems. First, because the variance is the average of the *squared* deviations, it is always an unrealistically large number. To say that our age scores differ from their mean by an *average* of 4 is plain silly! Not one score actually deviates from the mean by this much, so this is certainly not the average deviation. The second problem is that variance is rather bizarre because it measures in squared units; we measured ages, so the variance indicates that the scores deviate from the mean by 4 *squared* years (whatever that means!).

Thus, it is difficult to interpret the variance as exactly like the "average" deviation. Does this mean that the variance is a waste of time? No, because variance is used extensively in the statistics we will discuss later. Also, variance does communicate the *relative* variability of scores. If someone reports that one sample has $S_X^2 = 1$ and another sample has $S_X^2 = 3$, you know that the second sample is more variable, because it has a larger average squared deviation. This tells you that the scores are relatively less consistent and less accurately described by their mean. Thus, think of variance as a number that generally communicates how variable the scores are: The larger the variance, the more the scores are spread out.

The measure of variability that more directly communicates the average deviation is the *standard deviation*.

DESCRIBING THE SAMPLE STANDARD DEVIATION

The sample variance is always an unrealistically large number because we square each deviation. To solve this problem, we take the square root of the variance. The answer is called the standard deviation. The **sample standard deviation** is the square root of the sample variance, or the square root of the average squared deviation of scores around the sample mean. (Conversely, squaring the standard deviation produces the variance.)

To create the definitional formula for the standard deviation, we simply add the square root to the previous definitional formula for variance.

> *THE DEFINITIONAL FORMULA FOR THE SAMPLE STANDARD DEVIATION IS*
>
> $$S_X = \sqrt{\frac{\Sigma(X - \overline{X})^2}{N}}$$

Notice that the symbol for the sample standard deviation is S_X, which is the square root of the symbol for the sample variance $\left(\sqrt{S_X^2} \text{ is } S_X\right)$.

REMEMBER The symbol S_X stands for the *sample standard deviation*.

To compute S_X using this formula, first compute everything inside the square root sign to get the variance: Square each score's deviation, sum the squared deviations, and then divide that sum by N. In our previous age scores the variance (S_X^2) was 4.0. Then take the square root of the variance to find the standard deviation. In this case

$$S_X = \sqrt{4.0}$$

so

$$S_X = 2.0$$

The standard deviation of the age scores is 2.0.

Computational Formula for the Sample Standard Deviation

The computational formula for the standard deviation merely adds the square root symbol to the previous computational formula for the variance.

> *THE COMPUTATIONAL FORMULA FOR THE SAMPLE STANDARD DEVIATION IS*
>
> $$S_X = \sqrt{\frac{\Sigma X^2 - \dfrac{(\Sigma X)^2}{N}}{N}}$$

This formula is used *only* when computing the *sample* standard deviation.

As an example, using those age scores back in Table 5.3, we know that ΣX is 35, ΣX^2 is 203, and N is 7. Thus:

$$S_X = \sqrt{\frac{203 - \frac{(35)^2}{7}}{7}}$$

The computations inside the square root symbol produce the variance, which is 4.0, so we have

$$S_X = \sqrt{4.0}$$

Taking the square root, we again find that the standard deviation of the age scores is

$$S_X = 2.0$$

Also be sure you can work this formula before proceeding.

Interpreting the Standard Deviation

Computing the standard deviation is as close as we come to computing the "average of the deviations." There are three related ways of interpreting this statistic. First, in our age scores, we interpret an S_X of 2.0 as indicating that the scores differ from the mean by an "average" of about 2. Some scores deviate by more and some by less, but overall the scores deviate from the mean by something like an average of 2. Further, the standard deviation measures in the same units as the raw scores, so the scores differ from the mean age by an "average" of 2 *years*.

Second, the standard deviation allows us to gauge how consistently close together the scores are and, correspondingly, how accurately they are summarized by the mean. If S_X is relatively large, then we know that a large proportion of scores are relatively far from the mean and that few scores are close to it. If S_X is smaller, then more scores are close to the mean and relatively few are far from it.

And third, the standard deviation indicates how much the scores below the mean deviate from it and how much the scores above the mean deviate from it, so the standard deviation indicates how much the scores are spread out *around* the mean. To see this, we can further summarize a distribution by describing the scores that lie at "plus one standard deviation from the mean" $(+1S_X)$ and "minus one standard deviation from the mean" $(-1S_X)$. For example, our age scores of 2, 3, 4, 5, 6, 7, 8 produced a $\overline{X} = 5.0$ and a $S_X = 2.0$. The score that is $+1S_X$ from the mean is the score at $5 + 2$, or 7. The score that is $-1S_X$ from the mean is the score at $5 - 2$, or 3. Looking at the individual scores, you can see that it is accurate to say that the majority of the scores are between 3 and 7.

> **REMEMBER** The *standard deviation* indicates the "average deviation" from the mean, the consistency in the scores, and how far scores are spread out *around* the mean.

Finally, be sure that your answer makes sense when computing S_X (and S_X^2). First, variability cannot be a negative number because you are measuring the *distance* scores are from the mean, and the formulas involve *squaring* each deviation. Second, watch for answers that don't fit the data. If, for example, your raw scores range from 0 to 50, you would expect the mean to be in the middle, around 25. Then the largest deviation is about 25 points, so the "average" deviation will be much less than 25: A S_X of 30 cannot be, and a S_X of 10 is much more likely than one of 20. It is also unlikely that S_X is something like .80: If there are only two deviations of 25, imagine how many tiny deviations it would take for the average to be only .80.

Strange answers may be correct for strange distributions, but always check whether they seem sensible. Double-check your calculations, but a rule of thumb is:

> **For any roughly normal distribution, the standard deviation should equal about one-sixth of the range.**

Applying the Standard Deviation to a Normal Distribution

There is a precise mathematical relationship between the standard deviation and the normal curve so that describing a distribution in terms of the scores that are between $-1S_X$ and $+1S_X$ is especially useful. For example, say that in the statistics class with a mean of 80, the S_X is 5. The score at $80 - 5$ (at $-1S_X$) is the score of 75, and the score at $80 + 5$ (at $+1S_X$) is the score of 85. Figure 5.4 shows about where these scores are located on a normal distribution. First, notice that there is a method for determining where the scores at $-1S_X$ and $+1S_X$ from the mean are located on any normal curve. At the scores close to the mean, the curve forms a downward convex shape ($\cap$). As you travel away from the mean, the curve changes its pattern to an upward convex shape ($\cup$). The points at which the curve changes its shape are called "inflection points." Because of the mathematical relationship between a normal curve and the standard deviation, the scores at the inflection points are always the scores that are one standard deviation away from the mean.

Now you can see how to summarize the distribution. First, saying that the mean is 80 implies that most scores are around 80. Then, finding the scores at $-1S_X$ and $+1S_X$ defines "around": Most of the scores are between 75 and 85 (in our parking lot view, this *is* where most people are standing). And here's the important part: The characteristic bell shape of the normal curve is produced when there is approximately 34% of the

FIGURE 5.4 Normal distribution showing scores at plus or minus one standard deviation

With $S_X = 5.0$, the score of 75 is at $-1S_X$ and the score of 85 is at $+1S_X$. The percentages are the approximate percentages of the scores falling into each portion of the distribution.

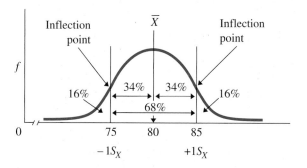

curve between the mean and the score that is at one of the inflection points, and about 16% of the curve is beyond the inflection point out into a tail. Because area under the curve translates into the frequency of scores, *about 34% of the scores in a normal distribution are between the mean and each score that is one standard deviation from the mean.* Thus, as in Figure 5.4, 34% of the scores are between 75 and 80, and 34% of the scores are between 80 and 85. Altogether, approximately 68% of the scores are always between the scores at $+1S_X$ and $-1S_X$ from the mean, so about 68% of the statistics students have scores between 75 and 85. Conversely, only about 32% of the scores are outside this range, with about 16% below 75 and 16% above 85. Thus, saying that most scores are between 75 and 85 is an accurate summary because the majority of scores (68%) are here.

> **REMEMBER**   Approximately 34% of the scores in a perfect normal distribution are between the mean and the score that is one standard deviation from the mean.

Of course, it's unlikely that the scores of a small statistics class would produce a *perfectly* normal distribution. However, recall that we use the perfect, ideal curve as a *model* for describing real data. Thus, if the statistics grades are approximately normally distributed, we'll operate as if they form a perfect normal distribution. Then we *expect* about 68% of the scores in the class to fall between 75 and 85. The closer the distribution conforms to a perfect normal curve, the closer to precisely 68% of the scores will be between 75 and 85.

Describing Different Normal Curves Using the Standard Deviation

Recall that different samples will produce variations in the normal curve. By finding the scores at $-1S_X$ and $+1S_X$ from the mean, we can envision and communicate these differences.

To interpret any S_X, envision the distribution that would typically produce it.

For example, Figure 5.5 shows those three normal curves you saw at the beginning of the chapter. But, say that without showing you the distribution, I tell you its S_X is 4.0. To obtain such an "average," the majority of the deviations must be smaller than or equal to 4, with few larger deviations. Therefore, as in the figure, you would envision something like the relatively narrow Distribution A, with the most frequent scores bunched relatively close to the mean, between the raw scores of 46 and 54 (between the scores at $-1S_X$ and $+1S_X$).

But, say that instead, I tell you that the distribution has an S_X of 7.0. This indicates that the majority of the deviations are larger—up in the neighborhood $+7$ and -7—because that's what is necessary to produce an "average" deviation of 7. Therefore, you'd envision the relatively wider Distribution B, with the frequent scores spread out over a wider range, between the scores of 43 and 57.

Finally, say that I tell you a distribution has the S_X of 12. An "average" deviation of 12 is produced when there are many deviations between $+12$ and -12. Therefore, you'd envision the very wide Distribution C, with the relatively frequent scores

FIGURE 5.5 Three variations of the normal curve

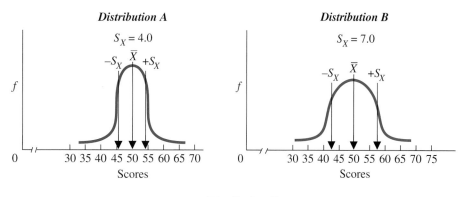

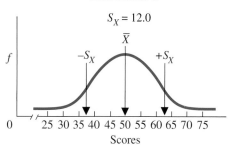

falling between about 38 and 62. Thus, a larger standard deviation (or variance) indicates a wider distribution because in a wider distribution the more extreme scores occur more frequently, producing larger deviations and a larger "average."

> **REMEMBER** The larger the value of S_X (or S_X^2), the more the scores are spread out around the mean, and the wider the distribution.

Despite differences in shape, any normal distribution will still have approximately 68% of the scores between the scores at $+1S_X$ and $-1S_X$ from the mean. A distribution containing more frequent extreme scores produces a wider distribution, so its inflection point is farther from the mean. To maintain its characteristic bell shape, however, about 34% of its area is still between the center and each inflection point (each S_X). Thus, about 34% of *any* normal distribution is between the mean and the score that is one S_X from the mean, and so about 68% of the scores are between the scores at $-1S_X$ and $+1S_X$.

In summary, then, here is how the standard deviation (and variance) add to our description of a distribution. If you know the data form a normal distribution, you can envision its general shape. If you know that the mean is 50, you know where the center of the distribution is and what the typical score is. And if you know that, for example, $S_X = 4$, you know that those participants who did not score 50 missed it by an "average" of 4 points, that the distribution is relatively narrow, and that 68% of the scores are between 46 and 54. Conversely, if you know that the $S_X = 12$, you know that those participants who did not score 50 missed it by an "average" of 12 points, that the distribution is relatively wide, and that 68% of the scores are between 38 and 62.

Mathematical Constants and the Standard Deviation

As discussed in Chapter 4, sometimes we transform scores by either adding, subtracting, multiplying, or dividing by a constant. What effect do such transformations have on the standard deviation and variance? The answer depends on whether we add (subtracting is adding a negative number) or multiply (dividing is multiplying by a fraction).

Adding a constant to all scores merely shifts the entire distribution to higher or lower scores. We do not alter the relative position of any score, so we do not alter the spread in the data. For example, take the scores 4, 5, 6, 7, and 8. The mean is 6. Now add the constant 10. The resulting scores of 14, 15, 16, 17, and 18 have a mean of 16. Before the transformation, the score of 4 was 2 points away from the mean of 6. In the transformed data, the score is now 14, but it is still 2 points away from the new mean of 16. In the same way, each score's distance from the mean is unchanged, so the standard deviation is unchanged. If the standard deviation is unchanged, the variance is also unchanged.

Multiplying by a constant, however, *does* alter the relative positions of scores, and therefore changes the variability. If we multiply the scores 4, 5, 6, 7, and 8 by 10, they become 40, 50, 60, 70, and 80. The original scores that were 1 and 2 points from the mean of 6 are now 10 and 20 points from the new mean of 60. Each transformed score produces a deviation that is 10 times the original deviation, so the new standard deviation is also 10 times greater. (Note that this rule does not apply to the variance. The new variance will equal the square of the new standard deviation.)

> *REMEMBER* Adding or subtracting a constant does not alter the variability of scores, but multiplying or dividing by a constant does alter the variability.

THE POPULATION VARIANCE AND THE POPULATION STANDARD DEVIATION

Recall that our ultimate goal is to describe the population of scores. Sometimes researchers will have access to a population of scores, and then they directly calculate the actual population variance and standard deviation. The symbol for the *true* or actual **population standard deviation** is σ_X. (The σ is the lowercase Greek letter s, or sigma.) Because the squared standard deviation is the variance, the symbol for the true **population variance** is σ_X^2. (In each case, the subscript X indicates a population of X scores.)

The definitional formulas for σ_X and σ_X^2 are similar to those we use to describe a sample:

Population Standard Deviation

$$\sigma_X = \sqrt{\frac{\Sigma(X - \mu)^2}{N}}$$

Population Variance

$$\sigma_X^2 = \frac{\Sigma(X - \mu)^2}{N}$$

The only novelty here is that we determine how far each score deviates from the population mean, μ. Otherwise the population standard deviation and variance tell us exactly the same things about the population that we saw previously for a sample: Both are ways of measuring how much, "on average," the scores differ from μ, indicating how much the scores are spread out in the population.

> *REMEMBER*   The symbols σ_X^2 and σ_X are used when describing the *true population variability.*

These symbols (and formulas) are descriptive procedures for describing the population: you are signaling that you *know* what the population standard deviation or variance is, as if the population is available to you, and you have directly calculated the actual variance and standard deviation.

However, usually the population is infinitely large and/or unavailable, so we cannot use these formulas. Instead, we make an estimate, or inference, about the population based on a sample.

Estimating the Population Variance and Population Standard Deviation

You know that our estimate of an unknown population μ is based on a sample $\overline{X}$. Now we will estimate the variability of the scores around μ. You might think that we could use the previous sample variance as our estimate of the population variance and use the sample standard deviation to estimate the population standard deviation. If, for example, the sample variance is 4, should we guess that the population variance is also 4? Nope! The sample variance and standard deviation are used *only* to describe the variability of the scores in a sample. They are *not* for estimating the corresponding population parameters.

To understand why this is true, say that we measure an entire population of scores and compute its true variance (σ_X^2). We then draw a series of random samples from the population and compute the variance of each (S_X^2). Sometimes the sample variance will equal the actual population variance, but other times the sample will not be perfectly representative of the population. Then either the sample variance will be smaller than the population variance, or the sample variance will be larger than the population variance. The problem is, that over many random samples, more often than not the sample variance will *underestimate* the population variance. The same thing happens if we perform the above operations using the standard deviation.

In statistical terminology, the formulas for S_X^2 and S_X are called the *biased estimators:* They are biased toward underestimating the true population parameters. As you saw in Chapter 4, such a bias is a problem because, if we cannot be accurate, we at least want our under- and overestimates to cancel out over the long run. (Remember the statisticians shooting targets?) With the biased estimators, the underestimates and overestimates will not cancel out to equal the true population parameter. Instead, although the sample variance (S_X^2) and sample standard deviation (S_X) accurately describe the variability of the scores in a sample, they are too often too small to serve as estimates of the true population variance and standard deviation.

Why do S^2_X and S_X produce biased population estimates? Because their formulas are not designed for estimating the population. To accurately estimate a population, we should have a *sample of random scores,* so here we need a *sample of random deviations* so that we can estimate the deviations found in the population. Yet, when we measure the variability of a sample, we use the mean as our reference point. In doing so, we encounter the restriction that the sum of the deviations, $\Sigma(X - \overline{X})$, must equal zero. Because of this, not all of the deviations in the sample are *random.* For example, say that the mean of five scores is 6, and that four of the scores are 1, 5, 7, and 9. Their deviations are -5, -1, $+1$, and $+3$, so the sum of their deviations is -2. Without even looking at the final score, we know that it must be 8, because it must have a deviation of $+2$ so that the sum of all deviations is zero. Thus, given the sample mean and the deviations of the other scores, the deviation for the score of 8 is not random; rather, it is determined by those of the other scores. Therefore, only the random deviations produced by the four scores of 1, 5, 7, and 9 reflect the variability found in the population. The same would be true for any four of the five scores. Thus, in general, out of the N scores in a sample, only $N - 1$ of them (the N of the sample minus 1) actually reflect the variability in the population.

The problem with the biased estimators (S_X and S^2_X) is that these formulas divide by N. Because we divide by too large a number, the answer tends to be too small, underestimating the variability in the population. Instead, to estimate the variability based on the scores in our sample that actually reflect variability in the population, we should divide by $N - 1$. By doing so, we compute the *unbiased* estimators of the population variance and standard deviation.

THE DEFINITIONAL FORMULAS FOR THE UNBIASED ESTIMATORS OF THE POPULATION VARIANCE AND STANDARD DEVIATION ARE

Estimated Population Variance	*Estimated Population Standard Deviation*
$$s^2_X = \frac{\Sigma(X - \overline{X})^2}{N - 1}$$	$$s_X = \sqrt{\frac{\Sigma(X - \overline{X})^2}{N - 1}}$$

Use these statistics whenever you are calculating the **estimated population standard deviation** and the **estimated population variance** based on a random sample from that population. Include all of the scores when computing the sum of the squared deviations in the numerator, *but* (and this is the big but) then divide by $N - 1$, the number of scores in the sample minus one.

Notice that the symbol for the unbiased estimator of the standard deviation is the lowercase s_X, and the symbol for the unbiased estimator of the variance is the lowercase s^2_X. To keep all of your symbols straight, remember that the symbols for the *sample* variance and standard deviation involve the capital or big *S,* and in those formulas you divide by the "big" value of N. The symbols for *estimates* of the population variance and standard deviation involve the lowercase or small *s,* and here you divide by the smaller quantity $N - 1$. Further, the *small s* is used to estimate the *small* Greek s, σ.

Finally, think of s_X^2 and s_X as the inferential variance and the inferential standard deviation, because the *only* time you use them is to infer the variance or standard deviation of the population based on a sample. Think of S_X^2 and S_X as the descriptive variance and standard deviation, because they are used to describe the sample.

> *REMEMBER* S_X^2 and S_X describe the variability in a *sample*; s_X^2 and s_X estimate the variability in the *population*.

For future reference, the quantity $N - 1$ is called the degrees of freedom. The **degrees of freedom** is the number of scores in a sample that are free to vary so that they reflect the variability in the population. The symbol for degrees of freedom is *df*, so here, $df = N - 1$.

In the final analysis you can think of $N - 1$ as simply a correction factor. Because $N - 1$ is a smaller number than N, dividing by $N - 1$ produces a slightly larger answer. Over the long run, this larger answer will prove to be a more accurate estimate of the population variability.

Computational Formulas for the Estimated Population Variance and Standard Deviation

The only difference between the computational formula for the estimated population variance and the previous formula for the sample variance is that here the final division is by $N - 1$.

> *THE COMPUTATIONAL FORMULA FOR THE ESTIMATED POPULATION VARIANCE IS*
>
> $$s_X^2 = \frac{\Sigma X^2 - \dfrac{(\Sigma X)^2}{N}}{N - 1}$$

Notice that in the numerator we still divide by N.

In the previous examples using age scores, $N = 7$ so $N - 1 = 6$, $\Sigma X^2 = 203$, and $\Sigma X = 35$. Putting these quantities into the above formula gives

$$s_X^2 = \frac{\Sigma X^2 - \dfrac{(\Sigma X)^2}{N}}{N - 1} = \frac{203 - \dfrac{(35)^2}{7}}{6}$$

Work through this formula the same way you did for the sample variance: 35^2 is 1225, and 1225 divided by 7 equals 175, so

$$s_X^2 = \frac{203 - 175}{6}$$

Now 203 minus 175 equals 28, so

$$s_X^2 = \frac{28}{6}$$

and the final answer is

$$s_X^2 = 4.67$$

This answer is slightly larger than the sample variance for these age scores, which was $S_X^2 = 4.0$. Although 4.0 accurately describes the sample, it is likely to underestimate the variance of the population: 4.67 is more likely to be the population variance. In other words, if we could compute the true population variance, we would expect σ_X^2 to be 4.67.

A standard deviation is always the square root of the corresponding variance, so the formula for the estimated population standard deviation involves merely adding the square root sign to the above formula for the variance.

THE COMPUTATIONAL FORMULA FOR THE ESTIMATED POPULATION STANDARD DEVIATION IS

$$s_X = \sqrt{\frac{\sum X^2 - \frac{(\sum X)^2}{N}}{N - 1}}$$

Above, the estimated population variance for our age scores was $s_X^2 = 4.67$. Then, s_X is $\sqrt{4.67}$, or 2.16. Thus, if we could compute the standard deviation using the entire population of scores, we would expect σ_X to be 2.16.

Interpreting the Estimated Population Variance and Standard Deviation

Interpret the estimated population variance and standard deviation in the same way as S_X^2 and S_X, except that now they describe how much we *expect* the scores to be spread out in the population, how consistent or inconsistent we *expect* the scores to be, and how accurately we *expect* the population to be summarized by μ.

Notice that, assuming a sample is representative, we have pretty much reached our ultimate goal of describing the population of scores. If we can assume that the distribution is normal, we have described its overall shape. The sample mean ($\overline{X}$) provides a good estimate of the population mean (μ). The size of s_X (or s_X^2) is our estimate of how spread out the population is—an estimate of the "average amount" that the scores deviate from μ. Further, we expect approximately 68% of the scores in the population to lie between the scores at $+1s_X$ and $-1s_X$ from μ. Then, because scores reflect behaviors, we have a good idea of how most individuals in the population behave in a given situation (which is why we conduct research in the first place).

A Brief Review

To keep track of all of the symbols, names, and formulas for the different statistics you've seen, remember that *variability* refers to the differences between scores, and that the *variance* and *standard deviation* are two methods for describing variability. In every case we are finding the difference between each score and the mean and then

FIGURE 5.6 Organizational chart of descriptive and inferential measures of variability

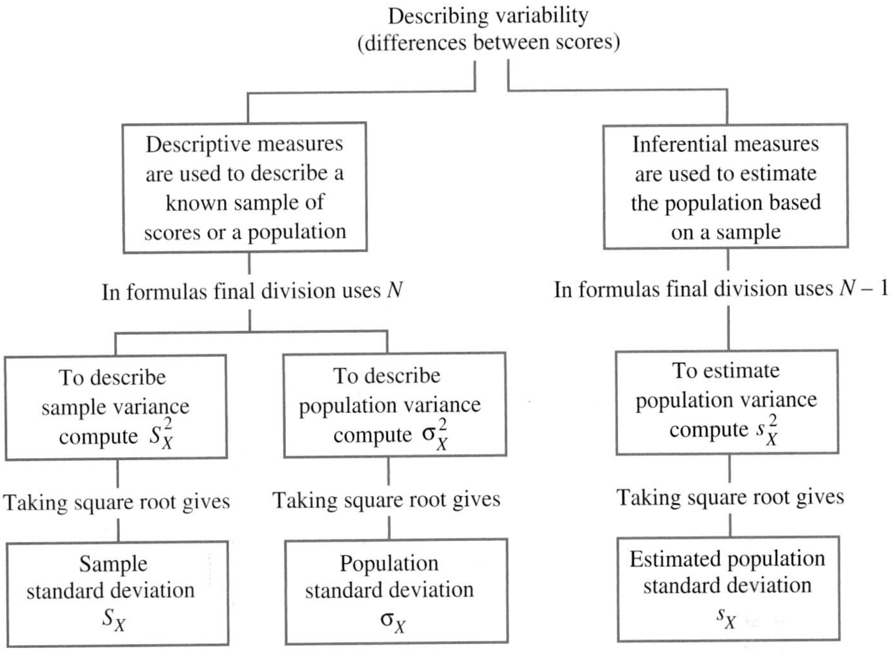

calculating something, more or less, like the average deviation. Organize your thinking about the particular measures of variability using the diagram in Figure 5.6.

Any standard deviation is merely the square root of the corresponding variance. For either measure compute the descriptive versions when the scores are available: When describing how far the scores are spread out from the sample $\overline{X}$, calculate the sample variance (S_X^2) and the sample standard deviation (S_X). When describing how far the scores are spread out from the population μ, calculate the population variance (σ_X^2) and the population standard deviation (σ_X). When the complete population of scores is unavailable, *infer* the variability of the population based on a sample by computing the *unbiased estimators:* The estimated variance (s_X^2) and the estimated standard deviation (s_X) indicate how much we *expect* the scores in the population to be spread out around μ. The difference in the formulas is that these inferential formulas require a final division by $N - 1$ instead of by N.

With these basics in hand, you are now ready to apply the variance and standard deviation to research. The following sections discuss how they are used when we predict scores, and when we summarize a study.

VARIANCE IS THE ERROR IN PREDICTIONS

In Chapter 4 you saw that the mean is the best single score to use to predict unknown scores. However, not everyone's score will be the mean score, so sometimes our predictions will be wrong. As it turns out, measures of variability also describe the amount of error we have when using the mean to make predictions.

To estimate the amount of error we have when predicting unknown scores, we determine how well we can predict the known scores in a sample: We pretend that we don't know the scores, predict them, and then see how close we came to the actual scores. For example, if that statistics class has a mean of 80, then our best guess is that any student in the class has a grade of 80. Then the amount we are wrong in a single prediction is the quantity $(X - \overline{X})$, the amount that the actual score differs, or *deviates,* from the mean. Because some predictions in a sample will contain more error than others, we summarize the error by finding the average amount that the scores deviate from the mean. As you've seen, the way to find the "average" amount that scores deviate from the mean is by computing the variance and standard deviation. Look at the formula, for example, for the sample variance:

$$S_X^2 = \frac{\Sigma(X - \overline{X})^2}{N}$$

By finding $(X - \overline{X})$ for each score, we are literally finding the difference between the score someone in the sample actually got (X), and the score we predict the person got $(\overline{X})$. Thus, this is a slightly novel way to view measures of variability: Because they measure the difference between each score and the mean, when we use the mean to predict each score, they also measure the "average" error in our predictions. The larger the variability, the larger the differences between the mean and the scores, so the larger the error we'll have when we use the mean to predict scores.

Thus, if the standard deviation in the statistics class is 5, then the scores differ from the mean by an "average" of 5 points. Therefore, if we predict the mean of 80 for everyone in the class, their actual scores will differ from the predicted score by an "average" of 5 points.

Similarly, the variance (S_X^2) indicates the average of the squared deviations from the mean, so the variance is the average "squared error" when predicting the mean score for everyone in a sample. The concept of squared errors is rather strange, which is too bad, because the proper way to describe the amount of error in our predictions is to compute the variance. In fact, the variance is sometimes called *error* or *error variance:* It is our way of measuring the average error between the predicted mean score and the actual raw scores. Thus, in that statistics class where S_X is 5, the S_X^2 is 25. This indicates that when predicting the mean as everyone's score in the sample, our "average error"—as measured by that device called variance—is about 25. Although this number is strangely large, simply remember that the larger the variance, the larger the error, and the smaller the variance, the smaller the error. To keep this in focus, consider that if every score in the statistics class was 80, the mean would be 80, and the variance would be zero. Here, predicting the mean of 80 for each student results in zero error: there is no difference between what we predict for students (the $\overline{X}$) and what they got (the Xs), and that is exactly what $S_X^2 = 0$ indicates.

> **REMEMBER** The sample variance (S_X^2) is the "average" error when we use the sample mean as the predicted score for everyone in the sample.

We can also predict scores in the population. Our best estimate of any score in the population is the population mean (μ), which we assume equals the sample mean. Thus, based on the statistics class mean of 80, we will estimate that μ is 80. Then our best prediction is that any student in the population who takes this class will receive a grade of 80. To determine the error in our predictions for the population, we use the same logic as with a sample. Here, our error in predictions equals the population variance: It describes the differences between the population mean we predict for everyone and the actual scores in the population. However, we usually cannot compute the true population variance, so instead we compute the estimated population variance (s_X^2). Thus, say that s_X^2 for the statistics class is 26.5—we expect that scores differ from μ by an "average" of about 26.5 (when measured using variance). Therefore, when we predict that other students taking this class will score at the μ of 80, we expect our squared error to be about 26.5.

> *REMEMBER*   The estimated population variance (s_X^2) is the error we expect when, based on the sample mean, we predict the population mean for anyone in the population.

SUMMARIZING RESEARCH USING MEASURES OF VARIABILITY

The standard deviation is most often reported in published psychological research because it most directly indicates how consistently close the individual scores are to the mean. Thus, the mean from a study might describe the number of times participants exhibited a particular behavior, but a small standard deviation indicates they consistently did so. Or, in a survey, the mean might describe the typical opinion held by participants, but a large standard deviation indicates substantial disagreement among them.

The same approach is used to interpret the results of an experiment. For example, in the previous chapter we examined the effect of recalling a 5-, 10-, or 15-item list. The mean summarized the dependent variable of recall scores, indicating *around* where participants in each condition scored. But for the complete picture, we should also include the standard deviation in each condition, as shown in Design Diagram 5.1.

In real research there would be many more scores per condition, and when reading about the study you would not see the individual scores. Therefore, get in the habit of using the $\overline{X}$ and S_X to envision the data that are present. Using S_X along with the $\overline{X}$ provides a better summary in three ways.

DESIGN DIAGRAM 5.1   Mean and Standard Deviation in Each Condition of Recalling 5-, 10-, or 15-Item Lists

5-Item List	10-Item List	15-Item List
3	5	9
4	5	11
2	8	7
$\overline{X} = 3$	$\overline{X} = 6$	$\overline{X} = 9$
$S_X = .82$	$S_X = 1.41$	$S_X = 1.63$

First, S_X adds to information provided by the mean. Above, the mean indicates that typically a score of 3 was observed in the 5-item condition. But from the S_X we know that, on average, scores differ above or below 3 by only .82. In the 15-item condition, however, typically participants scored at 9, and on average, varied around it by 1.63.

Second, S_X adds information when we predict individual scores. We would predict that people will score a 3 when recalling a 5-item list. Squaring the S_X of .82 gives $S_X^2 = .67$, so when the predictions in this condition are wrong, we expect to be off by about .67. Likewise, we expect scores in the 10-item list to be around 6, but on average we'll be off by an S_X^2 of 1.99 (1.41^2), and so on.

Finally, S_X and S_X^2 indicate how consistent a relationship is. Recall that the more consistent the dependent scores are in each condition of the independent variable, the *stronger* the relationship is. Because the standard deviation and variance indicate the consistency in each condition, they also communicate the strength of a relationship. To see this, say that the experiment had produced either the strong or the weak relationship shown in Design Diagram 5.2. Part A shows a perfectly consistent relationship because there is one score associated with each condition, so there is no difference or variability among the scores within each condition. This is also communicated by the fact that each S_X equals zero. In Part B, the scores within the conditions are more inconsistent and variable, so that overall this is a weaker, more inconsistent relationship. You also know this because here the values of S_X are larger.

DESIGN DIAGRAM 5.2 Mean and Standard Deviations of the Recall Experiment with a Perfectly Strong or a Weak Relationship

A. *Perfectly Strong Relationship*

5-Item List	10-Item List	15-Item List
3	6	9
3	6	9
3	6	9
$\overline{X} = 3$	$\overline{X} = 6$	$\overline{X} = 9$
$S_X = 0$	$S_X = 0$	$S_X = 0$

B. *Weaker Relationship*

5-Item List	10-Item List	15-Item List
3	6	4
5	2	10
1	10	13
$\overline{X} = 3$	$\overline{X} = 6$	$\overline{X} = 9$
$S_X = 1.63$	$S_X = 3.27$	$S_X = 3.74$

REMEMBER   Summarize an experiment by calculating the mean and standard deviation (or variance) in each condition. The smaller the variability in the conditions, the stronger the relationship.

UNDERSTANDING THE PROPORTION OF VARIANCE ACCOUNTED FOR

Because some relationships are stronger than others, you'll see that some relationships are more useful than others. Therefore, an extremely important aspect of describing the relationship found in any study is to evaluate it in terms of its scientific usefulness: How scientifically important is the relationship? What does knowing about this relationship "buy" us in terms of scientific knowledge? We began to evaluate the relationship in the previous section by looking at the values of S_X in each condition. However, this is a very subjective approach. Instead, a more objective way to evaluate a relationship is to compute the "proportion of variance accounted for" by the relationship. In this section you'll see the logic behind this procedure. (There are no calculations here, because they are part of procedures you'll encounter in Chapters 8, 12, and 13.)

In the relationships back in Design Diagram 5.2, you'll see something important: If we know what condition of list length people were tested under (their "score" on the independent variable), we have a better idea of what their dependent, recall score is. Any relationship provides information that improves the accuracy of our predictions because a particular score on one variable tends to occur with a particular score on the other variable. Therefore, if we know someone's score on one variable, we can more accurately predict his or her score on the other variable.

By using a relationship, our predictions will be more accurate, but "more accurate" than what? They will be more accurate than if we did not use the relationship to predict scores. *To evaluate a relationship, we compare our "average" prediction error when using the relationship to predict scores, to our "average" prediction error when we don't use the relationship to predict scores.*

Thus, there are two ways to divvy up the scores and calculate prediction errors. First, we'll ignore the relationship and treat all scores as if they belong to *one* sample. For example, ignoring the weak relationship between list length and recall we saw previously produces the one sample shown in Design Diagram 5.3. To predict individual scores here, we compute the overall mean for all nine scores—which is 6—and then 6 is the predicted score for everyone in the sample. Then, as usual, our "average error" in predictions is the sample variance for this group. In round numbers, here S_X^2 is about 15.

DESIGN DIAGRAM 5.3   Recall Scores, without Consideration of Their Relationship to List Length

Sample of recall scores without considering the relationship to list length.

3	6	10
6	2	4
0	10	13

Mean score = 6
Average error (S_X^2) = 15

Researchers can always measure a sample of scores, compute the mean, and use it to predict scores. Therefore, the value of S_X^2 is the largest error we are forced to accept. Because this variance is the worst that we can do, anything that improves the accuracy of predictions is measured relative to this variance. (This is the variance we will "account for.")

When we don't ignore the relationship, the scores form small subgroups in each list-length condition, as shown in Design Diagram 5.4. Now for participants in the 5-item condition we'll be more accurate by predicting the mean of their subgroup—3—as each person's score. Likewise, we'll predict the mean of 6 for those in the 10-item condition, but the mean of 9 is a better prediction for those in the 15-item condition. Later you'll see formulas for computing the prediction errors here, but think of it as finding the difference between participants' scores and the mean of their condition that we predict for them, so we calculate S_X^2 in each condition and then average them together. Here, this "average error" is about 10.

So, using this relationship to predict scores results in an average error of 10, compared to when we ignore the relationship and use the overall mean to predict scores, in which case the average error is 15.

Now we can evaluate the relationship. Is this a useful or important relationship? Yes, to the extent that with it our average error goes from 15 to 10: We are, on average, 5 points more accurate when predicting scores by using this relationship than if we don't use this relationship. However, it's difficult to know whether a 5-point improvement should be considered a large amount in nature. But recall that, ignoring the relationship and using the overall mean of the sample to predict scores produces the most error we must tolerate, so an average error of 15 is the worst we can do in this situation. Therefore, we interpret our improvement relative to this worst-case scenario: Using this relationship eliminates 5 of the 15 points of error we can have when predicting these scores. In other words, because 5 out of 15 is .33, using the relationship eliminates .33 or 33% or the error we'd have if we didn't use the relationship. Therefore, in statistical terms, we say the relationship "accounts for .33 of the variance in recall scores."

We have just calculated the proportion of variance accounted for. The **proportion of variance accounted for** is the proportion of error in our predictions when we use the overall mean to predict scores, that is eliminated when we use the relationship with

DESIGN DIAGRAM 5.4   Recall Scores, with Consideration of Their Relationship to List Length

Three subgroups of recall scores when related to list length: Each column shows the scores for that list length condition.

5 Items	10 Items	15 Items
3	6	10
6	2	4
0	10	13
$\overline{X} = 3$	$\overline{X} = 6$	$\overline{X} = 9$

Average error = 10

another variable to predict scores. In other words, the proportion of variance accounted for is the proportional improvement in predictions achieved by using a relationship to predict scores, compared to if we do not use the relationship.

> *REMEMBER* The *proportion of variance accounted for* by a relationship is the proportional improvement that results from using the relationship to predict scores, compared to not using the relationship to predict scores.

The proportion of variance accounted for indicates how useful and thus important a relationship is. The relationship in the above example is rather important because we're 33% more accurate with it than without it. Contrast this with a relationship that, say, accounts for only .03 of the variance: We're only 3% more accurate when we use this relationship than if we ignore it—or had never heard of it! Scientifically, this is not a very useful relationship, because literally, having this information does not get us very far toward accurately predicting scores.

The stronger and more consistent a relationship, the greater the proportion of variance accounted for. With a more consistent relationship, the scores in each condition are closer to each other and to their mean, so that predicting this mean for them is more accurate. Thus, the (unrealistic) perfect relationship back in Part A of Design Diagram 5.2 accounts for 1.0, or 100% of the variance in recall scores. Without the relationship, we predict the overall mean of all recall scores, and let's say the average error is 7. But using the relationship, we predict the mean of each condition for participants in that condition, and then there are *no* differences between the scores we predict for participants and the actual scores they obtained, so using the relationship results in zero error. Thus, this is an extremely useful relationship, because with it we go from 7 points of error to 0 error, eliminating 100% of the error, so we say the relationship accounts for 100% of the variance in recall scores.

Later chapters will present formulas for computing the proportion of variance accounted for, and the logic is essentially the same for both experiments and correlational studies. Determining the proportion of variance accounted for is always a very important procedure, because it is variance and variability that lead to scientific inquiry in the first place. When researchers ask, "Why does a person do this instead of that?" they are trying to predict and explain differences in scores. Because differences are measured by variance, in other words, they are trying to account for variance. Ultimately, as behavioral scientists, we want to understand the laws of nature so that we know with 100% accuracy when someone will get one score, reflecting one behavior, and when someone will get a different score, reflecting a different behavior. In statistics, this translates into accounting for 100% of the variance in scores.

PUTTING IT ALL TOGETHER

At this point the three steps to analyzing any set of data should be like a reflex for you. (1) Consider the scale of measurement used and the shape of the distribution formed by the scores. (2) Describe around where most participants scored, usually by computing the $\overline{X}$ for each group or for each condition of an experiment. (3) Describe the variability—how spread out the scores are—around each mean, usually by computing the sample standard deviation. With this information, you are largely finished with descriptive statistics, because you know the important characteristics of the sample data, and you'll be ready to draw inferences about the corresponding population. That's all there is to it.

One final note: As if you haven't seen enough symbols, research journals that follow the publication guidelines of the American Psychological Association (APA) do not use statistical symbols for the sample mean and sample standard deviation. Instead, the symbol for the sample mean is M and the symbol for the sample standard deviation is SD. (When describing the population, however, the Greek symbols μ and σ are used.) Because the standard deviation is more easily interpreted, variance is usually not reported in published reports.

CHAPTER SUMMARY

1. *Measures of variability* describe how much the scores differ from each other, or how much the distribution is spread out.

2. The *range* is the difference between the highest and the lowest score.

3. The *semi-interquartile range* is used in conjunction with the median to describe skewed distributions. It is calculated as one-half of the distance between the scores at the 25th and 75th percentiles.

4. The *variance* is used in conjunction with the mean to describe symmetrical or normal distributions of interval or ratio scores. It is the average of the squared deviations of scores around the mean.

5. The *standard deviation* is also used in conjunction with the mean to describe symmetrical or normal distributions of interval/ratio scores. It is the square root of the variance. It can be thought of as the "average" amount that scores deviate from the mean.

6. Transforming scores by adding or subtracting a constant does not alter the standard deviation. Transforming scores by multiplying or dividing by a constant alters the standard deviation by the same amount as if we had multiplied or divided the original standard deviation by the constant.

7. There are three versions of the formula for variance. S_X^2 describes how far sample scores are spread out around the $\overline{X}$, σ_X^2 describes how far the population of scores is spread out around μ, and s_X^2 is computed using sample data, but is the inferential, unbiased estimate of how far the scores in the population are spread out around μ.

8. There are three versions of the formula for the standard deviation. S_X describes how far the sample scores are spread out around $\overline{X}$, σ_X describes how far the population of scores is spread out around μ, and s_X is computed using sample data, but is the inferential, unbiased estimate of how far the scores in the population are spread out around μ.

9. The formulas for descriptive measures of variability (for S_X^2 and S_X) use N as the final denominator. The inferential formulas (for s_X^2 and s_X) use $N - 1$. The quantity $N - 1$ is the *degrees of freedom* in the sample.

10. When the mean score is predicted for everyone in the sample, the amount of error in predictions equals the sample variance (S_X^2). When we predict the population mean for everyone, the amount of error we expect in our predictions equals the estimated population variance (s_X^2).

11. When there is a relationship between two variables, knowing the scores on one variable allows us to more accurately predict the scores on the other variable. The improvement in predictions is the *proportion of variance accounted for*. It indicates the proportional improvement in predictions when using the relationship to predict scores compared to not using the relationship.

KEY TERMS: Can You Define the Following?

ΣX^2 $(\Sigma X)^2$ S_X^2 s_X^2 σ_X^2 S_X
s_X σ_X df
degrees of freedom *113*
estimated population standard deviation
   112
estimated population variance *112*
measures of variability *97*
population standard deviation *110*
population variance *110*

proportion of variance accounted for
   120
range *99*
sample standard deviation *105*
sample variance *102*
semi-interquartile range *100*
sum of squared Xs *96*
squared sum of X *96*

REVIEW QUESTIONS

(Answers for odd-numbered questions are in Appendix C.)

1. (a) In any research, what three characteristics of a distribution must the researcher describe? (b) Why is describing the variability important?
2. What do measures of variability communicate about: (a) the size of differences between the scores in a distribution; (b) how consistently the participants behaved?
3. (a) What is the range? (b) Why is it not the most accurate measure of variability? (c) When is it used as the sole measure of variability?
4. (a) What do both the variance and the standard deviation tell you about a distribution? (b) Which measure will you usually want to compute? Why?
5. (a) What is the mathematical definition of the variance? (b) Mathematically, how is a sample's variance related to its standard deviation, and vice versa?
6. (a) What do S_X, s_X, and σ_X have in common in terms of what they communicate? (b) How do they differ in terms of their use?

7. Why are your estimates of the population variance and standard deviation always larger than the corresponding values that describe a sample from that population?

8. In an experiment how does the size of S_X in each condition suggest the strength of the relationship?

9. In a condition of an experiment, a researcher obtains the following creativity scores.

3	2	1	0	7	4	8	6	9	1
6	8	6	9	4	5	0	8	7	6

In terms of creativity, interpret the variability of these data using the following: (a) the range; (b) the variance; (c) the standard deviation.

10. If you could test the entire population in question 9, what would you expect each of the following to be? (a) the typical, most common creativity score; (b) the variance; (c) the standard deviation; (d) the two scores between which about 68% of all creativity scores occur in this situation.

11. Say the sample in question 9 had an N of 1000. About how many people would you expect to score below 2? Why?

12. As part of studying the relationship between mental and physical health, you obtain the following heart rates.

73	72	67	74	78	84	79	71	76	76
79	81	75	80	78	76	78			

In terms of differences in heart rates, interpret these data using the following: (a) the range; (b) the variance; (c) the standard deviation.

13. If you could test the population in question 12, what would you expect each of the following to be? (a) the shape of the distribution; (b) the typical, most common rate; (c) the variance; (d) the standard deviation; (e) the two scores between which about 68% of all heart rates fall.

APPLICATION QUESTIONS

14. Foofy has a normal distribution of scores ranging from 2 to 9. (a) She computed the variance to be $-.06$. What should you conclude from this answer, and why? (b) She recomputes the standard deviation to be 18. What should you conclude, and why? (c) She recomputes the variance to be 1.36. What should you conclude, and why?

15. From his statistics grades, Guchi has a $\overline{X}$ of 60 and $S_X = 20$. Pluto has a $\overline{X}$ of 60 and $S_X = 5$. (a) Who is the more inconsistent student, and why? (b) Who is more accurately described as a 60 student, and why? (c) For which student can you more accurately predict the next test score, and why? (d) Who is more likely to do either extremely well or extremely poorly on the next exam?

16. You correctly compute the variance of a distribution to be $S_X^2 = 0$. What should you conclude about this distribution?

17. On a final exam the $\overline{X} = 65$ and $S_X = 6$. What score would you predict for each student, and if you're wrong, what do you expect will be the "average error" in your prediction?

18. The teacher who gave the test in question 17 found a relationship between students' scores and the amount they studied. If she uses her knowledge of each student's study time to predict the corresponding exam grade, what will happen to her average error relative to the error described in question 17?

19. If the teacher in question 18 compares the error when using study times to predict exam scores to the error when using the mean exam score to predict exam scores, what statistical information is she computing?

20. Say that the teacher in question 19 finds that the relationship between study times and exam scores accounts for .40 of the variance in exam scores. What does this mean?

21. Consider the results of this experiment.

Condition A	Condition B	Condition C
12	33	47
11	33	48
11	34	49
10	31	48

(a) What should you do to summarize the experiment? (b) These are ratio scores. Compute the appropriate descriptive statistics and summarize the relationship in the sample data. (c) Describe how consistent participants were in each condition.

22. Say that you conducted this experiment on the entire population. (a) Summarize the relationship you'd expect to observe. (b) Describe how consistently you'd expect participants to behave in each condition.

23. Looking at the individual scores in the conditions in question 21, do you expect the relationship will account for a large or small proportion of the variance in dependent scores? Why?

24. Consider these ratio scores from an experiment.

Condition 1	Condition 2	Condition 3
18	8	3
13	11	9
9	6	5

(a) What should you do to summarize the experiment? (b) Summarize the relationship in the sample data. (c) Describe how consistent participants were in each condition.

25. Say that you conducted the experiment in question 24 on the entire population. (a) Summarize the relationship you'd expect to observe. (b) Describe how consistently you'd expect participants to behave in each condition.

26. Comparing the results in questions 21 and 24, which experiment produced the stronger relationship? How do you know?

SUMMARY OF FORMULAS

1. *The formula for the range is*

$$\text{Range} = \text{Highest score} - \text{Lowest score}$$

2. *The formula for the semi-interquartile range is*

$$\frac{\text{Score at 75th percentile} - \text{Score at 25th percentile}}{2}$$

3. *The computational formula for the sample variance is*

$$S_X^2 = \frac{\sum X^2 - \dfrac{(\sum X)^2}{N}}{N}$$

4. *The computational formula for the sample standard deviation is*

$$S_X = \sqrt{\frac{\sum X^2 - \dfrac{(\sum X)^2}{N}}{N}}$$

5. *The computational formula for estimating the population variance is*

$$s_X^2 = \frac{\sum X^2 - \dfrac{(\sum X)^2}{N}}{N - 1}$$

6. *The computational formula for estimating the population standard deviation is*

$$s_X = \sqrt{\frac{\sum X^2 - \dfrac{(\sum X)^2}{N}}{N - 1}}$$

Describing Data with z-Scores and the Normal Curve Model

The techniques discussed in the preceding chapters for graphing, measuring central tendency, and measuring variability comprise the descriptive procedures used in most behavioral research. In this chapter we'll combine these procedures to answer another question about data: How does any one particular score compare to the other scores in a sample or population? We answer this question by transforming raw scores into *z-scores*.

The following sections first examine the logic of *z*-scores and discuss their simple computation. Then we will look at how *z*-scores are used, both in describing individual scores and in describing sample means.

MORE STATISTICAL NOTATION

Statistics often involve negative and positive numbers. Sometimes, however, we ignore a number's sign. The size of a number, regardless of its sign, is the *absolute value* of the number.

Also, you'll encounter the symbol $\pm$, which means "plus or minus." It describes either two numbers or the range of numbers between them. Saying "± 1," means $+1$ or -1. Saying "the scores between ± 1," means all possible scores from -1, through 0, up to and including $+1$.

WHY IS IT IMPORTANT TO KNOW ABOUT z-SCORES?

Recall that we transform scores to make scores on different variables comparable and to make scores within the same distribution easier to interpret. The "*z*-transformation" is the Rolls-Royce of transformations because with it you can compare and interpret scores from virtually *any* normal distribution of interval or ratio scores.

Why do we need to do this? Because researchers usually *don't* know how to interpret someone's raw score: Usually, you won't know whether, in the grand scheme of things in nature, a specific score should be considered high or low, good or bad, or what. Instead, the best we can do is examine a score *relative* to the other scores in the distribution, describing the score's relative standing. **Relative standing** reflects the systematic evaluation of a score relative to the sample or population in which the score occurs. The way to calculate the relative standing of a score is to transform it into a *z*-score. Then, from the *z*-score we'll know whether the individual's underlying raw score was *relatively* good, bad, or in between.

UNDERSTANDING z-SCORES

To see how *z*-scores reflect relative standing, let's say that we conduct a study at Prunepit University in which we measure the attractiveness of a sample of males. We train several judges to evaluate participants on the variable of attractiveness, and each male's score is the total number of points assigned by the judges. The attractiveness scores form the normal curve shown in Figure 6.1. We want to interpret these scores, especially those of three men: Slug, who scored 35; Binky, who scored 65; and Biff, who scored 90. Using the statistics you've learned, you already know how to interpret each score in relative terms. Let's review.

What would we say to Slug? "Bad news, Slug. Your score is to the left of the mean, so you're below average in attractiveness in this sample. What's worse, you're *way* below the mean. Down in the tail of the distribution, the height of the curve above your score is not large, indicating a low *frequency:* Not many men received this low score. Also, the proportion of the total area under the curve at your score is small, so the *relative frequency*—the proportion of all men receiving your score—is low. Finally, Slug, your *percentile* is low: A small percentage scored below your attractiveness score, while a large percentage scored above it. So, Slug, scores such as yours are relatively infrequent, and few scores are lower than yours."

What would we tell Binky? "Binky, there's good news and bad news. The good news is that your score of 65 is above the mean of 60, which is also the median, or 50th percentile: You are better-looking than more than 50% of the men in this study. The bad news is that you are not *that* far above the mean. The area under the curve at your score is relatively large, and thus the relative frequency of your score is large: The proportion of equally attractive men is large and, what's worse, a relatively large part of the distribution has higher scores."

And then there is Biff. "Yes, Biff, as you expected, you are above average in attractiveness. In fact, as you have repeatedly told everyone, you are one of the most attractive men around. The area under the curve at your score, and thus the relative frequency of your score, is quite small: only a small proportion of the men are equally attractive. Also, the area under the curve to the left of your score is relatively large, so if we cared to figure it out, we'd find that you scored at a very high percentile: A large percentage of scores are below your score, while a small percentage are above your score."

The above interpretations reflect each man's relative standing within the distribution. To do this more precisely, we calculate their *z*-scores.

FIGURE 6.1 Frequency distribution of attractiveness scores at Prunepit U

Scores for three individuals are identified on the X *axis.*

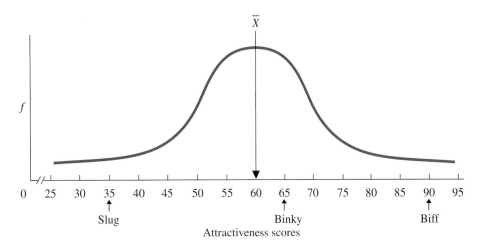

Describing a Score's Relative Location as a *z*-Score

In describing each man, we first determined his score's location relative to the mean. Therefore, to quantify a score's relative standing, we begin by measuring how far the score is above or below the mean. In other words, we compute the score's deviation, which equals $(X - \overline{X})$. Thus, for example, Biff's score of 90 deviates from the mean of 60 by $90 - 60 = +30$. The $+$ sign indicates that he is above the mean. A deviation of $+30$ *sounds* as if it might be a large deviation, but is it? As with a raw score, we don't necessarily know whether a particular deviation should be considered large or small. Therefore, we need a frame of reference. When we examine the entire distribution, we see that only a few scores deviate by as much as Biff's score, and *that* is what makes his an impressively high score. Similarly, Slug's score of 35 deviates by $35 - 60 = -25$. This, too, is impressive, because only a few scores deviate below the mean by such an amount. Thus, a score is impressive if it is far from the mean, and "far" is determined by how frequently other scores deviate from the mean by such an amount.

To interpret a score's location, then, we need a way to compare its deviation to all deviations. To do this, we need a *standard* to compare to each *deviation:* We need a *standard deviation*! As you saw in Chapter 5, calculating the standard deviation is our way of computing the "average deviation" of the scores around the mean. By comparing a score's deviation to the standard deviation, we can describe the location of an individual score in terms of this average deviation.

For example, say that for the previous attractiveness data the sample standard deviation is 10 (10 attractiveness points). Biff's deviation of $+30$ attractiveness points is equivalent to 3 standard deviations, so Biff's raw score is located 3 standard deviations above the mean. Thus, his raw score is impressive, because it is three times as far above the mean as the "average" amount that scores were above the mean.

We have simply described Biff's score in terms of its distance from the mean, measured in standard deviation units. We do the same type of thing when we convert inches to feet. In that case, the unit of measurement called a foot is defined as 12 inches, so a distance of 36 inches is equal to 3 of those units, or 3 feet. In our study the unit of measurement called a standard deviation is defined as 10 attractiveness points. Biff's deviation from the mean is 30 attractiveness points, so his raw score is a distance of 3 of those units, or 3 standard deviations, from the mean.

By transforming Biff's deviation into standard deviation units, we have performed a *z*-score transformation and computed Biff's *z*-score. A **z-score** is the distance a raw score deviates from the mean when measured in standard deviations. It is a single number that summarizes a score's relative standing: Biff's raw score deviates from the mean by an amount that is three times the "average" amount that all scores in the sample deviate from the mean.

Note that, like deviations, there are two components to a *z*-score: (1) a *z*-score will be either positive or negative, which indicates whether the raw score is above or below the mean, and (2) the absolute value of the *z*-score (ignoring the sign) indicates how *far* the score lies from the mean when measured in standard deviations. Thus, because originally his deviation was $+30$, Biff is *above* the mean by *plus* 3 standard deviations, and so his *z*-score is $+3$. If he had been below the mean by this amount, his *z*-score would have been -3.

But also note a fine distinction here: Like any actual score, a *z*-score is a *location* on the distribution. It is just that a *z*-score automatically communicates its *distance* from the mean. Thus, Biff's *z*-score of +3 is his location among all of the attractiveness scores, and we know it is a distance of 3 standard deviations from the mean. (Keep location versus distance straight.)

> **REMEMBER**   A *z-score* describes a raw score's location in terms of how far above or below the mean it is when measured in standard deviations.

Computing *z*-Scores

Above, we performed two mathematical steps in computing Biff's *z*-score. First, we found the score's deviation by subtracting the mean from the raw score. Then we divided the score's deviation by the standard deviation. The symbol for a *z*-score is *z*, so

> **THE FORMULA FOR TRANSFORMING A RAW SCORE IN A SAMPLE INTO A *z*-SCORE IS**
>
> $$z = \frac{X - \overline{X}}{S_X}$$

This is both the definitional and the computational formula for *z*. Notice that we are computing a *z*-score from a *sample* of scores, so we use the descriptive sample standard deviation, S_X (the formula in Chapter 5 with the final division by *N*, not *N* − 1). When starting from scratch with a sample of raw scores, first compute $\overline{X}$ and S_X and then substitute their values into the formula.

To find Biff's *z*-score, we substitute his raw score of 90, the $\overline{X}$ of 60, and the S_X of 10 into the formula.

$$z = \frac{X - \overline{X}}{S_X} = \frac{90 - 60}{10}$$

Find the deviation in the numerator first, and always subtract $\overline{X}$ from *X*. Rewriting the formula gives

$$z = \frac{+30}{10}$$

After dividing,

$$z = +3.00$$

Likewise, Binky's raw score of 65 produces a *z*-score of

$$z = \frac{X - \overline{X}}{S_X} = \frac{65 - 60}{10} = \frac{+5}{10} = +0.50$$

Binky's raw score is literally one-half of 1 standard deviation above the mean.

And finally, Slug's raw score is 35, so his *z* is

$$z = \frac{X - \overline{X}}{S_X} = \frac{35 - 60}{10} = \frac{-25}{10} = -2.50$$

Here, 35 minus 60 results in a deviation of *minus* 25, which, when divided by 10, results in a z-score of -2.50. Slug's raw score is 2.5 standard deviations *below* the mean. When working with z-scores, always pay close attention to the positive or negative sign.

Usually, we compute a z-score to describe the relative standing of a score in a sample, so we use the previous formula. However, we can also compute a z-score for a score in a population, if we know the population mean (μ) and the true standard deviation of the population (σ_X).

> **THE FORMULA FOR TRANSFORMING A RAW SCORE IN A POPULATION INTO A Z-SCORE IS**
>
> $$z = \frac{X - \mu}{\sigma_X}$$

This formula is identical to the previous formula except that now the answer indicates how far the raw score lies from the population mean, measured in units of the population standard deviation. (*Note:* We never compute z-scores using the estimated population standard deviation, s_X.)

Computing a Raw Score When z Is Known

Sometimes we know a z-score and want to find the corresponding raw score. For example, in the Prunepit U study, say that another student, Bucky, scored $z = +1$. What is his raw score? With $\overline{X} = 60$ and $S_X = 10$, his z-score indicates that he is 1 standard deviation above the mean or, in other words, 10 points above 60. Therefore, his raw score is 70. What did we just do? We multiplied his z-score times S_X and then added the mean.

> **THE FORMULA FOR TRANSFORMING A z-SCORE IN A SAMPLE INTO A RAW SCORE IS**
>
> $$X = (z)(S_X) + \overline{X}$$

For Bucky's z-score of $+1$, we saw

$$X = (+1)(10) + 60$$

so

$$X = +10 + 60$$

so

$$X = 70$$

To check this answer, compute the z-score for the raw score of 70. You should end up with the z-score you started with: $+1.00$.

Say that Fuzzy has a negative z-score of $z = -1.30$ (with $\overline{X} = 60$ and $S_X = 10$). Then

$$X = (-1.30)(10) + 60$$

so

$$X = -13 + 60$$

Adding a negative number is the same as subtracting its positive value, so

$$X = 47$$

Fuzzy has a raw score of 47.

The same logic applies to finding the raw score for a z that is from a population.

> **THE FORMULA FOR TRANSFORMING A z-SCORE IN A POPULATION INTO A RAW SCORE IS**
>
> $$X = (z)(\sigma_X) + \mu$$

Here, we multiply the z-score times the population standard deviation and then add μ.

After transforming a raw score or z-score, always check whether your answer makes sense. At the very least, negative z-scores must correspond to raw scores smaller than the mean, and positive z-scores must correspond to raw scores larger than the mean. Further, as you'll see, we seldom obtain z-scores greater than ± 3.00. Although they are possible, be very skeptical if you compute such a z-score, and double-check your work.

How Variability Influences z-Scores

The size of a particular z-score depends both on the amount that the raw score deviates from the mean *and* on the size of the standard deviation in the distribution. For example, Biff's deviation of $+30$ produced an impressive z-score of $+3$ because the standard deviation was 10: On "average" the scores deviated from the mean by only 10, so a deviation of $+30$ is unusually large. If, however, the data had produced a standard deviation of 30, then Biff would have a $z = (90 - 60)/30 = +1.00$. In this case Biff's score would not be as impressive because his deviation would equal the "average" deviation, indicating that his raw score is down there among the more common scores.

Thus, two factors produce a z-score having a large absolute value: (1) a large deviation from the mean and (2) a small standard deviation. A smaller deviation and/or a larger standard deviation reduces the size of the z-score.

INTERPRETING z-SCORES: THE z-DISTRIBUTION

The way to interpret the scores in a sample is to transform them all into a z-distribution. A **z-distribution** is the distribution produced by transforming a raw score distribution into z-scores. By transforming all attractiveness scores in the previous study to z-scores, we get the z-distribution shown in Figure 6.2.

FIGURE 6.2 *z*-distribution of attractiveness scores at Prunepit U

The labels on the X *axis show first the raw scores and then the z-scores.*

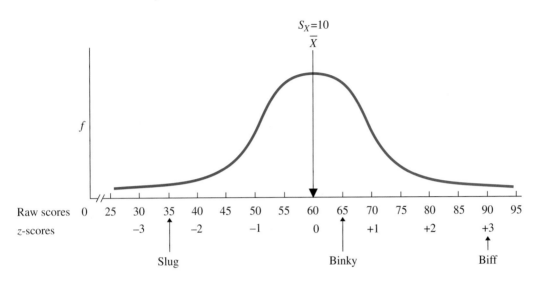

Notice the two ways the *X* axis is labeled. This shows that by creating a *z*-distribution, we have only transformed the way in which we identify each score. Saying that Biff has a *z* of +3 is merely another way to say that he has a raw score of 90. And recognize this: Because we are still looking at the same point on the distribution, Biff's *z*-score of +3 has the same frequency, relative frequency, and percentile as his raw score of 90.

The advantage of looking at *z*-scores, however, is that they directly communicate each score's relative location in the distribution. The *z*-score of 0 corresponds to the mean (here 60): A person having the mean score is zero distance from the mean. For any other score, the sign indicates the *direction* the score lies in relation to the mean. A "+" indicates that the score is above and graphed to the right of the mean. A "−" indicates that the score is below and graphed to the left of the mean. Therefore, *z*-scores become increasingly larger numbers with a positive sign as we proceed farther to the right of the mean, **AND** such larger positive *z*-scores occur less frequently. Conversely, *z*-scores become increasingly larger numbers with a negative sign as we proceed farther to the left of the mean, **AND** such larger negative *z*-scores occur less frequently. However, don't be misled by negative *z*-scores: A raw score that is farther below the mean is a *smaller* raw score, but it produces a negative *z*-score whose absolute value is *larger.* Thus, for example, a *z*-score of −2 corresponds to a *lower* raw score than a *z*-score of −1.

> **REMEMBER** The farther a raw score is from the mean, the larger its corresponding *z*-score. On a normal distribution, the larger the *z*-score, whether positive or negative, the less frequently that *z*-score and the corresponding raw score occur.

Recognize that a negative *z*-score is not automatically a bad score. For some variables, the goal is to have as low a raw score as possible (errors on a test, number of parking tickets, amount owed on a credit card bill). With these variables, larger negative *z*-scores are best, because they indicate you are farther below the mean.

Characteristics of the *z*-Distribution

The previous graph illustrates three important characteristics of any *z*-distribution.

1. A z-distribution always has the same shape as the raw score distribution. A *z*-distribution is a normal distribution only when the underlying raw score distribution is normal. Transforming a nonnormal distribution into *z*-scores will *not* make it form a normal curve.

2. The mean of any z-distribution always equals 0. The mean of the raw scores transforms into a *z*-score of 0. Or, if we compute the mean of all *z*-scores, the result is also 0: The sum of the positive and negative *z*-scores is the sum of the deviations around the mean, which is 0, so the mean *z*-score is always 0.

3. The standard deviation of any z-distribution always equals 1. One standard deviation unit for raw scores transforms into one *z*-score unit. Whether the standard deviation in the raw scores is 10 or 100, it is still the standard deviation, and the standard deviation is 1 *z*-score unit.

Because of these characteristics, all normal *z*-distributions are similar, so that a particular *z*-score will be at the same relative location on *any* distribution. Thus, for *any* variable, if $z = 0$, then the raw score equals the mean and is in the middle of the distribution. Or, for *any* variable, if *z* is $+1$, the raw score is $1S_X$ above the mean, and is still a fairly frequent score. But, on *any* variable, if a raw score produces a *z* of $+3$, it will, like Biff's, be a relatively infrequent score, located at the extreme high end. And so on: the *z*-distribution for *any* normally distributed variable will be similar to the one in Figure 6.2.

As you'll see in the following sections, these similarities provide us with three important uses for *z*-scores.

1. For comparing scores from different distributions.

2. For computing the relative frequency of scores in any distribution.

3. For describing and interpreting sample means.

USING THE *z*-DISTRIBUTION TO COMPARE DIFFERENT VARIABLES

In research, comparing a score on one variable to a score on a different variable is a problem. For example, say that Althea received a grade of 38 on a statistics quiz and a grade of 45 on an English paper. These scores reflect different kinds of tasks, assigned by different instructors using different criteria, so it's like comparing apples to oranges. To avoid this problem, we transform the raw scores from each class into *z*-scores. This gives us two *z*-distributions, each with a mean of 0, a standard deviation of 1, and a range of between about -3 and $+3$. Each *z*-score indicates an individual's relative standing in his or her respective class. Therefore, we can compare Althea's relative standing in English to her relative standing in statistics, and we are no longer comparing apples and oranges. (The *z*-transformation equates or standardizes different distributions, so *z*-scores are often referred to as **standard scores.**)

Say that for the statistics quiz, the $\overline{X}$ was 30 and the S_X was 5. We transform all grades to *z*-scores, including Althea's grade of 38, which becomes $z = +1.6$. For the English paper, the $\overline{X}$ was 40 and the S_X was 10, so Althea's grade of 45 becomes $z = +.5$. Figure 6.3 shows the locations of Althea's *z*-scores on the respective *z*-distributions. The different heights of the two curves indicate that the English class contains more students than the statistics class. Regardless, a *z*-score of $+1.6$ is farther above the mean than a *z*-score of $+.5$. Thus, in terms of her relative standing in each class, Althea did better in statistics, because she is farther above the statistics mean than she is above the English mean.

Another student, Millie, obtained raw scores that produced $z = -2$ in statistics and $z = -1$ in English. In which class did Millie do better? Her *z*-score of -1 in English is better, because it is less distance below the mean.

Of course, it would be easier to compare these two distributions if we plotted them on the same set of axes, and *z*-scores enable us to do just that.

Plotting Different *z*-Distributions on the Same Graph

Transforming the statistics and English scores into *z*-scores establishes a common variable. Therefore, to see each student's relative location in each class, we can graph both of the previous distributions on one set of axes, as shown in Figure 6.4. All normal *z*-distributions are similar, so there are only two minor differences between the curves. First, the classes have different standard deviations, so the raw scores for each class are spaced differently along the *X* axis. For example, going from a *z* of $+1$ to $+2$ corresponds to going from the raw scores of 35 to 40 in statistics, but from 50 to 60 in English. Second, the greater height of the English distribution merely reflects its larger *N*, so there is a higher *f* for each score.

FIGURE 6.3   Comparison of two distributions for statistics and English grades, showing raw scores and *z*-scores

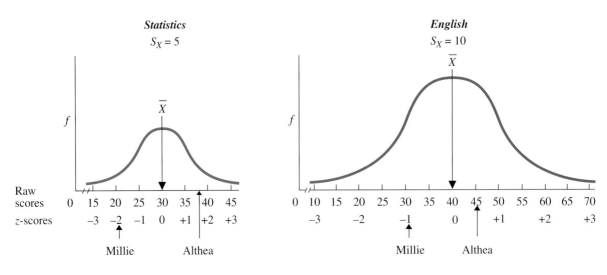

FIGURE 6.4 Comparison of distributions for statistics and English grades, plotted on the same set of axes

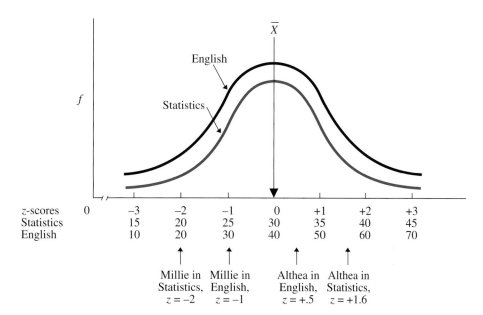

By plotting the two distributions on the same set of axes, we can easily compare any-one's scores. Thus, Althea scored better in statistics than in English, and Millie scored better in English than in statistics.

> **REMEMBER** To compare raw scores from two different variables, transform the scores into *z*-scores.

The fact that different *z*-distributions can be plotted on the same set of axes leads to our second use of the *z*-distribution: finding the relative frequency of raw scores in any normal distribution.

USING THE *z*-DISTRIBUTION TO DETERMINE THE RELATIVE FREQUENCY OF RAW SCORES

An important use of *z*-scores is that through them we can determine the relative fre-quency of specific raw scores. Recall that relative frequency is the proportion of time that a score occurs. The *z*-distribution allows you to easily compute relative frequency, from which you can also compute simple frequency and percentile.

To see how to do this, look again at the two *z*-distributions in Figure 6.4, and notice just how similar they are: Any statistics and English raw scores that produce the same *z*-score are at the *same* location on the distribution. This will be true for the *z*-scores from *any* normally distributed variable. Thus, regardless of the variable, any raw score that equals the mean score is in the same location on the *X* axis of the *z*-distribution. Or, recall that the raw scores that are $\pm 1S_X$ from the mean are always located under the "inflection points." Now you know that such scores produce *z*-scores of ± 1. Therefore, for *any* variable, scores that produce *z*-scores of ± 1 are always under the inflection points. Likewise, any other *z*-score will always be in the same relative location.

Why is this important? Because relative frequency can be computed using *the proportion of the total area under the curve*. If a particular *z*-score is always at the same location on the normal curve, then the proportion of the total area under the curve for that *z*-score is always the same. Therefore:

> **The relative frequency of a particular *z*-score will be the same on all normal *z*-distributions.**

For example, you already know that 50% of the scores on a normal curve are to the left of the mean. You also know that scores to the left of the mean produce negative *z*-scores, so in other words, the negative *z*-scores make up 50% of a distribution. Thus, the students in each class with negative *z*-scores in Figure 6.4 constitute 50% of their respective distributions. Further, 50% of a distribution corresponds to a relative frequency of .50. On *any* normal *z*-distribution, the relative frequency of the negative *z*-scores is .50.

Having determined the relative frequency of the *z*-scores, we work backwards to find the relative frequency of the corresponding raw scores. In the statistics distribution in Figure 6.4, those students having negative *z*-scores have raw scores ranging between 15 and 30, so the relative frequency of scores between 15 and 30 is .50. Likewise, in the English distribution, those students having negative *z*-scores have raw scores between 10 and 40, so the relative frequency of these scores is .50.

Similarly, recall from Chapter 5 that approximately 68% of the scores in a normal distribution fall between the scores that are $\pm 1 S_X$ from the mean (between the scores under the inflection points.) In other words, for any normal distribution, about 68% of the scores fall between the *z*-scores of $+1$ and -1. Thus, in Figure 6.4, students with *z*-scores between ± 1 constitute approximately 68% of their distributions. Having determined this, we again work backwards to the raw scores. Statistics grades between 25 and 35 constitute approximately 68% of the statistics distribution, and English grades between 30 and 50 constitute approximately 68% of the English distribution.

In the same way, you can determine the relative frequencies for any set of scores once you envision it as a *z*-distribution. For example, in a normal distribution of IQ scores (whatever the $\overline{X}$ and S_X may be), we know that those IQ scores producing negative *z*-scores have a relative frequency of .50, and about 68% of all IQ scores will fall between the two scores at the *z*-scores of ± 1. The same will be true for a distribution of running speeds, or a distribution of personality test scores, or for *any* normal distribution.

We can also use *z*-scores to determine the relative frequency of scores in any other portion of a distribution. To do so, we employ the *standard normal curve*.

The Standard Normal Curve

Because the relative frequency and location of a particular *z*-score is always the same on any normal *z*-distribution, we don't need to draw a different normal curve for every set of raw scores. Instead, we envision one standard curve that we use to represent the *z*-distribution that would result after transforming any normal raw score distribution. In fact, this curve is called the standard normal curve. The **standard normal curve** is a theoretical, perfect normal curve, which serves as a model of the perfect normal z-distribution. (Because it is a z-distribution, the mean of the standard normal curve is 0, and the standard deviation is 1.)

We use the standard normal curve to first determine the relative frequency of particular z-scores on a perfect normal curve. Then, as above, once we know the relative frequency of the z-scores, we work backwards to determine the relative frequency of the corresponding raw scores. Thus, the first step is to find the relative frequency of the z-scores. To do this, statisticians have determined the proportion of the area under various parts of the normal curve. Look at Figure 6.5. The numbers above the X axis between the vertical lines indicate the proportion of the total area between the z-scores. The number below the X axis on each arrow indicates the proportion of the total area between the mean and the z-score. (Don't worry: You won't need to memorize these proportions.)

The proportion of the total area under the curve is the same as relative frequency, so each proportion *is* the relative frequency of the z-scores located in that section of the curve. For example, .3413 of the z-scores are located between z of 0 and z of +1 on a perfect normal distribution. Or, multiplying the proportion times 100, 34.13% of all z-scores fall between a z of 0 and +1. Similarly, z-scores between +1 and +2 occur 13.59% of the time, and z-scores between +2 and +3 occur 2.15% of the time. Because the distribution is symmetrical, the same proportions occur between the mean and the corresponding negative z-scores.

To determine the relative frequency for larger areas, add together their proportions. For example, .3413 of the distribution is located between $z = -1$ and the mean, and .3413 of the distribution is between the mean and $z = +1$. Thus, a total of .6826, or 68.26%, of the distribution is located between zs of −1 and +1. (See, about 68% of the distribution really is between $\pm 1S_X$ from the mean.) We can also add together nonadjacent portions of the curve. For example, 2.28% of the distribution is in the tail of the

FIGURE 6.5   Proportions of total area under the standard normal curve

The curve is symmetrical: 50% of the scores fall below the mean, and 50% fall above the mean.

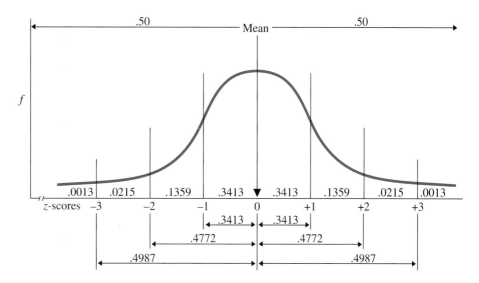

distribution beyond $z = -2$ (.0215 + .0013 = .0228). Likewise, 2.28% is beyond $z = +2$. Thus, a total of 4.56% of all scores fall in the tails beyond $z = \pm 2$.

Figure 6.5 shows why we seldom obtain *z*-scores greater than ± 3. Only .0013 of the scores are above $z = +3$ and only .0013 are below $z = -3$. In total, only .0026 (.26 of *one* percent) of the scores are beyond ± 3. However, *between* ± 3 is 99.74% of the scores (100% − .26% = 99.74%). Thus, for all practical purposes, the range of z is between ± 3. Also, now you can see why, in Chapter 5, I said that the value of S_X should equal about one-sixth of the range of the raw scores. The range of the raw scores is approximately between $z = -3$ and $z = +3$, a distance of six times the standard deviation. If the range is six times the standard deviation, then the standard deviation is one-sixth of the range.

Applying the Standard Normal Curve Model

The standard normal curve is especially useful in behavioral research, because most variables are more or less normally distributed. However, recall that we do not draw a "more or less" normal curve to conceptualize each distribution. Instead, we simplify things by using the perfect normal curve as our "model" of the actual distribution. Essentially, we assume that the actual distribution comes "close enough" to forming a perfect normal curve so that the perfect curve is a reasonably accurate description of the data. If the raw scores form close to a perfect curve, then after transforming them to *z*-scores, their *z*-distribution will also be close to a perfect normal curve. Therefore, *our model of any approximately normal z-distribution is the standard normal curve.* We then use this model and the above procedures to determine the relative frequency of scores in any part of the distribution.

Thus, to determine the relative frequency of the scores that fall between any two raw scores, first transform the raw scores into *z*-scores. Then, from the standard normal curve, determine the proportion of the total area between these *z*-scores. This proportion is the same as the relative frequency of the *z*-scores on a perfect normal curve. The relative frequency of these *z*-scores is the same as the relative frequency of their corresponding raw scores in a perfect normal distribution. Thus, the relative frequency obtained from the standard normal curve is the *expected* relative frequency of the raw scores in our data, if the data formed a perfect normal distribution.

> REMEMBER   For any approximately normal distribution, transform the raw scores to *z*-scores and use the *standard normal curve* to find the relative frequency of the scores.

For example, the original attractiveness scores from Prunepit U form an approximately normal distribution, so we can apply the standard normal curve model here. Say that Cubby has a raw score of 80, which, with $\overline{X} = 60$ and $S_X = 10$, is a *z* of +2. We can envision Cubby's location on the distribution as in Figure 6.6. We might first ask what proportion of scores are expected to fall between the mean and Cubby's score. On the standard normal curve .4772 of the total area falls between the mean ($z = 0$) and $z = +2$. Because .4772 of all *z*-scores fall between the mean and a *z* of +2, we expect .4772, or 47.72%, of all attractiveness scores at Prunepit U to fall between the mean score of 60 and Cubby's score of 80.

FIGURE 6.6 Location of Cubby's score on the *z*-distribution of attractiveness scores

Cubby's raw score of 80 is a 2-score of +2.

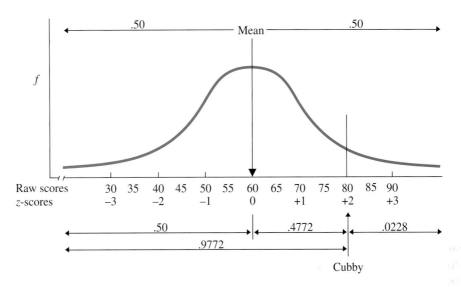

We might also ask how *many* people scored between the mean and Cubby's score. Then we would convert the above relative frequency to simple frequency by multiplying the *N* of the sample times the relative frequency. Say that the *N* at Prunepit was 1000. If we expect .4772 of all scores to fall between the mean and *z* = +2, then (.4772)(1000) = 477.2, so we expect about 477 people to have scores between the mean and Cubby's score.

Note that how accurately the expected relative frequency from the model describes our actual scores depends on three aspects of the data:

1. The closer the raw scores are to forming a normal distribution, the more accurately the model describes the data. Therefore, use the standard normal curve model *only* if you can assume that the data are at least approximately normally distributed.

2. The larger the sample *N*, the more closely the sample tends to conform to a normal curve and therefore the more accurate the model will be. The model is most accurate when applied to large samples or to populations.

3. The model is most appropriate if the raw scores are theoretically continuous scores measured using a ratio or interval scale.

The Prunepit data meet these requirements, so the expected results for Cubby should be quite accurate.

Finding Percentile Rank for a Raw Score   We can also use the standard normal curve model to determine a score's expected percentile. Recall that a percentile is the percent of all scores below—graphed to the left of—a score.

For example, to determine Cubby's percentile, look again at Figure 6.6. On a normal distribution, the mean is the median (the 50th percentile). Any positive z-score is above the mean, so Cubby's z-score of +2 is above the 50th percentile. In addition, as Figure 6.6 shows, Cubby's score is above the 47.72% of the scores that fall between the mean and his score. Thus, we add the 50% of the scores below the mean to the 47.72% of the scores between the mean and his score and, in total, 97.72% of all z-scores are below Cubby's z-score. We usually round off percentile to a whole number, so Cubby's z-score is at the 98th percentile. Likewise, Cubby's raw score of 80 is at the 98th percentile. Conversely, if 97.72% of the curve is below a z of +2, then, as in Figure 6.6, only 2.28% of the curve is above this score (100% − 97.72% = 2.28%). Thus, anyone scoring above the raw score of 80 would be in about the top 2% of scores.

On the other hand, say that Elvis obtained an attractiveness score of 40, producing a z-score of −2. You can find Elvis's percentile using Figure 6.7. A total of .0228 (2.28%) of the distribution is below (to the left of) Elvis's score. With rounding, Elvis ranks at the 2nd percentile.

Finding a Raw Score at a Given Percentile   You can also work in the opposite direction to find a raw score at a particular relative frequency or percentile. Say that we want to find the attractiveness score at the 16th percentile. Because the 16th percentile is below the 50th percentile, we are looking for a negative z-score. Consider Figure 6.8. If 16% of the scores are below the unknown score, then 34% of the scores are between it and the mean (50% − 16% = 34%). You know that 34.13% of a normal z-distribution is between z = −1 and the mean, so that leaves about 16% of the distribution to the left of this z. (Although technically, 50% − 34.13% = 15.87%). Thus, a z of −1 is at approximately the 16th percentile.

FIGURE 6.7 Location of Elvis's score on the z-distribution of attractiveness scores

Elvis is at approximately the 2nd percentile.

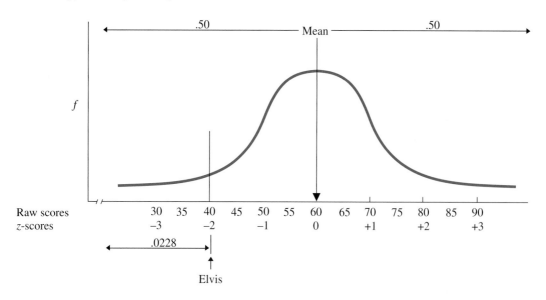

FIGURE 6.8 Proportions of the standard normal curve at approximately the 16th percentile

The 16th percentile corresponds to a z-score of about −1.0.

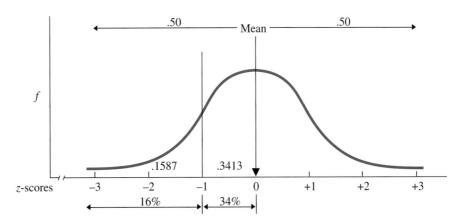

You would then use the formula $X = (z)(S_X) + \overline{X}$ to find the raw score at $z = -1$. For the attractiveness scores, $\overline{X} = 60$ and $S_X = 10$, so $X = (-1)(10) + 60 = 50$. Thus, the raw score of 50 is expected to be at approximately the 16th percentile.

Using the z-Table

So far our examples have involved whole-number z-scores, although with real data, a z-score may contain decimals. However, fractions of z-scores do *not* result in proportional divisions of the corresponding area. (The area between the mean and $z = +.5$ is *not* one-half of the area between the mean and $z = +1$.) Instead, find the proportion of the total area under the standard normal curve for any two-decimal z-score by looking in Table 1 of Appendix B. This table is called the z-*table*. A portion of the z-table is reproduced in Table 6.1.

TABLE 6.1 Sample Portion of the z-Table

A	B	C
	Area between the	Area beyond z
z	mean and z	in the tail
1.60	.4452	.0548
1.61	.4463	.0537
1.62	.4474	.0526
1.63	.4484	.0516
1.64	.4495	.0505
1.65	.4505	.0495

Say that you seek the proportions corresponding to $z = +1.63$. First locate the z in column A, labeled "z," and then move to the right. Column B, labeled "Area between the mean and z," contains the proportion of the area under the curve between the mean and the z identified in column A. Thus, .4484 of the curve (or 44.84% of all z-scores) is between the mean and the z of $+1.63$. This is shown in Figure 6.9. Column C, labeled "Area beyond z in the tail," contains the proportion of the area under the curve that is in the tail beyond the z-score in column A. Thus, .0516 of the curve (or 5.16% of all z-scores) is in the tail of the distribution beyond the z of $+1.63$ (also shown in Figure 6.9). If you get confused when using the z-table, look at the normal distribution at the top of the table. The different shaded portions and arrows indicate the part of the curve described in each column.

To work in the opposite direction to find the z-score that corresponds to a particular proportion, read the columns in the reverse order. First, find the proportion in column B or C, depending on the area you seek, and then identify the corresponding z-score in column A. For example, say that you seek the z-score corresponding to 44.84% of the curve between the mean and z. Find .4484 in column B of the table, and then, in column A, see the z-score is 1.63.

Notice that the z-table contains no positive or negative signs. Because the normal distribution is symmetrical, only the proportions for one-half of the standard normal curve are given. *You* must decide whether z is positive or negative, based on the problem you're working.

Sometimes, there will be a proportion you need that is not given in the table, or you'll need the proportion corresponding to a three-decimal z-score. In such cases, round to the nearest value in the z-table or, to compute the precise value, perform "linear interpolation" (described in Appendix A.2).

Thus, with the z-table you can answer virtually any question about the relative standing of raw scores in any part of a normal distribution. Table 6.2 summarizes the ways we have done this. Regardless of the problem you're working, always sketch the normal curve, locate the mean, and locate the portions of the curve and the z-scores or raw scores you're working with. This greatly simplifies the problem.

Using *z*-Scores to Define Psychological Attributes

The z-score transformation often forms the basis for defining a psychological attribute or characteristic. Because it is difficult to interpret the absolute value of any single raw

FIGURE 6.9 Distribution showing the area under the curve beyond $z = +1.63$ and between $z = +1.63$ and the mean

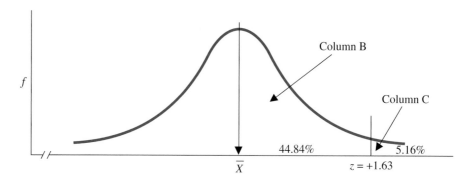

TABLE 6.2   Summary of Steps When Using the z-Tables

If You Seek	First, You Should	Then You
Relative frequency of scores between $\overline{X}$ and X	transform X to z	find its area in column B[*]
Relative frequency of scores beyond X in tail	transform X to z	find its area in column C[*]
X that marks a given rel. f between X and $\overline{X}$	Find rel. f in column B	transform its z to X
X that marks a given rel. f beyond X in tail	find rel. f in column C	transform its z to X
Percentile of an X above $\overline{X}$	transform X to z	find area in column B and add .50
Percentile of an X below $\overline{X}$	transform X to z	find area in column C

[*]To find the simple frequency of the scores, multiply rel. f times N.

score in the grand scheme of nature, it is also difficult to decide on the "cutoff" scores to use when classifying people based on their scores: What must someone do to be considered a genius? How do we define an "abnormal" personality? To answer such questions, psychologists often use a "statistical definition" based on relative standing. Essentially, this involves defining an attribute in terms of a particular z-score. For example, we might statistically define the old-fashioned term "genius" as a person with a z-score of more than +2 on an intelligence test. Because a z greater than +2 falls in about the highest 2% of the distribution, we have defined a genius as anyone with a score in the top 2% on the intelligence test. Similarly, we might define as "abnormal" any person with a z-score beyond −1.5 on a personality test. Such scores are "abnormal" in a statistical sense, because they are very infrequent in the population and are among the most extreme low raw scores.

Instructors who "curve" grades generally use the normal curve and z-scores. They assume that grades are normally distributed, so they assign letter grades based on proportions of the area under the normal curve. If the instructor defines an A student as one who is in the top 2%, then students with z-scores greater than +2 receive As. If the instructor defines B students as those in the next 13%, then students having z-scores between +1 and +2 receive Bs, and so on.

USING Z-SCORES TO DESCRIBE SAMPLE MEANS

So far we've used the standard normal curve model to describe the relative standing of any raw score. Now, using the same logic, we will determine the relative standing of an entire sample by evaluating its sample mean. This procedure is important, not only because it allows you to evaluate a sample, but also because it is the basis for inferential statistical procedures (and you will be computing some of those in the very near future).

To see how the procedure works, say that we are investigating college entrance exams and, using the Scholastic Aptitude Test (SAT), we test a random sample of 25 students at Prunepit U. Their mean score is 520. Nationally, the mean of *individual* SAT scores is 500 (and σ_X is 100), so it appears that at least some Prunepit students scored relatively high, pulling the overall mean to 520. But how do we interpret the performance of the sample as a whole? Is a sample mean of 520 impressively above average, or more mundane? By considering only our sample mean, we cannot answer this question, because we have the same problem we had when examining raw scores: Without a frame of reference, we don't know whether, in the grand scheme of things, a particular sample mean is good, bad, or in between.

The solution is to evaluate a sample mean in terms of its relative standing. Previously, we compared a particular raw score to all other possible scores that occur in this situation. (Biff's score was impressive only because most other scores in this situation were lower than his.) Now we'll compare our sample mean to the other sample means that might occur in this situation. Then we'll know whether the sample is relatively impressive or not.

The first step is to create a distribution showing all possible sample means that might occur in this situation. This distribution is called the *sampling distribution of means.*

The Sampling Distribution of Means

If the national average of SAT scores is 500, then in the population of SAT scores, the mean (μ) is 500. Because we randomly selected a sample of 25 students and obtained their SAT scores, we essentially drew a random sample of 25 scores from this population. To evaluate our sample mean, we first create a distribution showing all other possible means we might have obtained when randomly selecting a sample of 25 scores from the SAT population.

One way to do this would be to record all SAT scores from the population on slips of paper and deposit them into a very large hat. We could then hire a statistician to sample this population. So that we can see *all* possible sample means that might occur in this situation, the statistician would sample the population an infinite number of times. (She'd get very bored, so the pay would have to be good.) She would randomly select a sample with the same size *N* as ours (25), compute the sample mean, replace the scores in the hat, draw another 25 scores, compute the mean, and so on. Because the scores selected in each sample would not be identical, not all sample means would be identical. By then constructing a frequency polygon of the different values of $\overline{X}$ she obtained, the statistician would create a sampling distribution of means. The **sampling distribution of means** is the frequency distribution of all possible sample means that occur when an infinite number of samples of the same size *N* are randomly selected from one raw score population. Thus, the SAT sampling distribution of means is the infinite population of all sample means that can occur when the SAT raw score population is exhaustively sampled using our *N* of 25. It is shown in Figure 6.10. This is similar to a distribution of raw scores, with the only novelty being that here each "score" along the *X* axis is a sample mean. (Still think of the distribution as a parking lot full of people, except that now each person is the captain of a sample, having the sample's mean score and thus representing the sample.) You can see two obvious things about the sampling distribution.

FIGURE 6.10 Sampling distribution of random sample means of SAT scores

The X *axis is labeled to show the different values of* $\overline{X}$ *we obtain when we sample a population where the mean for SAT scores is 500.*

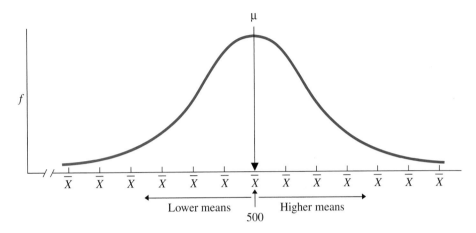

First, regardless of the shape of the raw score distribution, **a sampling distribution is always an approximately normal distribution.** This is because, most often each $\overline{X}$ will equal the raw score population mean (μ). Sometimes, however, a sample will contain a few more high scores or low scores relative to the population, so the sample mean will be close to, but slightly above or below, μ. Less frequently, the statistician will obtain rather strange samples, producing $\overline{X}$s farther above or below μ. Once in a great while, some very infrequent and unusual scores will be drawn, resulting in a sample mean that deviates greatly from μ. (The larger the N of the samples, the more closely the distribution conforms to the perfect normal curve.)

Second, **the mean of the sampling distribution always equals the mean of the underlying raw score population from which we create the sampling distribution.** The sampling distribution is the *population* of all possible means, so its mean is symbolized by μ. The μ of the sampling distribution equals the μ of the underlying raw score population, because the raw scores are balanced around a particular number (μ), so the sample means created from those scores are also balanced around that same number. Thus, above, the μ of individual SAT scores is 500, so the μ of the sampling distribution—the average sample mean—is 500. Essentially, more often than not the bored statistician will select scores around 500 in each sample, so the $\overline{X}$s will be around 500.

The story about the bored statistician is useful because it helps you to understand what a sampling distribution is. Of course, in reality, we cannot "infinitely" sample a population. However, we can create a *theoretical* sampling distribution by applying the central limit theorem. The **central limit theorem** is a statistical principle that defines the mean, the standard deviation, and the shape of a sampling distribution. From the central limit theorem, we know that the sampling distribution of means (1) forms an approximately normal distribution, (2) has a μ equal to the μ of the underlying raw score population from which the sampling distribution was created, and (3), as you'll see in a moment, has a standard deviation that is mathematically related to the standard deviation of the raw score population. Thus, based on the central limit theorem, we know that if the bored statistician did sample the population of SAT scores, she would create a sampling distribution of means like the one shown in Figure 6.10.

The importance of the central limit theorem is that we can describe the sampling distribution *without* having to actually sample the population of SAT scores. All we need to know is that the raw score population forms a normal distribution of ratio or interval scores (so that computing the mean is appropriate), that μ is 500 and σ_X is 100, and that we used an *N* of 25. Further, using the central limit theorem, we expect to produce the *same* sampling distribution from any population of raw scores having these characteristics, *regardless of what they measure.* Thus, if a personality or creativity test has a μ of 500 and a σ_X of 100, samples with an *N* of 25 would produce the identical sampling distribution as above. Likewise, by knowing the characteristics of any other raw score population, we can create the corresponding sampling distribution of means.

> REMEMBER   The central limit theorem allows us to envision the *sampling distribution of means,* which shows all of the means that would occur through exhaustive random sampling of a raw score distribution.

Why do we want to see the sampling distribution? Remember we took a small detour, but the original problem was to evaluate our Prunepit mean of 520. Once we envision the distribution in Figure 6.10, we have a *model* of the different sample means—and the frequency with which they occur—when sampling the SAT population. The different values of $\overline{X}$ occur simply because of the luck of the draw of which scores are selected for a sample. Sometimes a sample mean higher than 500 occurs because, *by chance,* the statistician randomly selected a sample of predominantly high scores. At other times she might select predominantly low scores, producing a mean below 500. And so on. Thus, the sampling distribution provides a picture of the sample means that occur due to chance when randomly sampling the SAT population. Because our original Prunepit sample was a random sample obtained by chance from this population, this picture allows us to compare our sample mean to all other sample means that occur in this situation.

To evaluate our original sample, we simply need to determine *where* a mean of 520 falls on the *X* axis of the sampling distribution in Figure 6.10 and then interpret the curve accordingly. If 520 lies close to 500, then it is a frequent, common mean when sampling SAT scores (after all, the bored statistician frequently obtained this result). But if 520 lies toward the tail of the distribution, far from 500, then it is a more infrequent and unusual sample mean (literally, such a mean seldom occurs in this situation).

The sampling distribution is a normal distribution, and you already know how to determine the location of any "score" on a normal distribution: We use—you guessed it—*z*-scores. That is, we determine how far the sample mean deviates from the mean of the sampling distribution, measured using the standard deviation of the distribution. With one number, then, the *z*-score will tell us the sample mean's relative location within the sampling distribution, and thus indicate its relative standing among all possible means that occur in this situation.

To calculate the *z*-score for a sample mean, we need one more piece of information: the "standard deviation" of the sampling distribution.

The Standard Error of the Mean

The standard deviation of the sampling distribution of means is called the **standard error of the mean.** (The term *standard deviation* was already taken.) Recall that the terms *error* and *deviation* are synonymous. Therefore, like a standard deviation, the standard error of the mean can be thought of as the "average" amount that the sample means deviate from the μ of the sampling distribution. That is, in some sampling distributions, the sample means may be very different from one another and deviate greatly from the average sample mean. At other times, the $\overline{X}$s may be very similar and deviate little from μ. The "average" amount the $\overline{X}$s deviate from their μ is the standard error of the mean.

For the moment, we'll discuss the *true* standard error of the mean, as if we had actually computed it using the entire sampling distribution. The symbol for the true standard error of the mean is $\sigma_{\overline{X}}$. The σ indicates that we are describing a population, but the subscript $\overline{X}$ indicates that we are describing a population of sample means—what we call the sampling distribution of means. The central limit theorem tells us that $\sigma_{\overline{X}}$ can be found using the following formula:

THE FORMULA FOR THE TRUE STANDARD ERROR OF THE MEAN IS

$$\sigma_{\overline{X}} = \frac{\sigma_X}{\sqrt{N}}$$

Notice that this formula involves σ_X: When we know the true standard deviation of the underlying raw score population, we will know the true "standard deviation" of the sampling distribution.

> *REMEMBER* The *standard error of the mean* ($\sigma_{\overline{X}}$) is computed using the true standard deviation of the population of raw scores (σ_X).

In the formula, the size of $\sigma_{\overline{X}}$ depends first on the size of σ_X. This is because if the raw scores are highly variable, then each time we sample the population, we're likely to get a very different set of scores, and so the various sample means will differ greatly, and so $\sigma_{\overline{X}}$ will be large. But, if the raw scores are not variable, then different samples will tend to contain the same scores, and so the means will be similar to one another (and $\sigma_{\overline{X}}$ will be small). Second, the size of $\sigma_{\overline{X}}$ depends on the size of N. With a very small N (say 2), it is easy for each sample to be different from the next, so the sample means will differ (and $\sigma_{\overline{X}}$ will be large). However, with a large N, each sample will be more representative, so that all sample means will be closer to the population mean, and so the $\sigma_{\overline{X}}$ will be small.

We can compute $\sigma_{\overline{X}}$ for the sampling distribution of SAT scores because, through record keeping, we *know* that the true standard deviation of the population of raw scores is 100. With $N = 25$, the standard error of the mean for this sampling distribution is

$$\sigma_{\overline{X}} = \frac{\sigma_X}{\sqrt{N}} = \frac{100}{\sqrt{25}}$$

The square root of 25 is 5, so

$$\sigma_{\overline{X}} = \frac{100}{5}$$

and thus

$$\sigma_{\overline{X}} = 20$$

A $\sigma_{\overline{X}}$ of 20 indicates that in the SAT sampling distribution, the individual sample means differ from the μ of 500 by an "average" of 20 points when the N of each sample is 25.

Now, at last, we can calculate a z-score for our sample mean.

Calculating a z-Score for a Sample Mean

Previously, you saw that when we know the population mean and standard deviation, the formula for transforming an individual's raw score into a z-score was

$$z = \frac{X - \mu}{\sigma_X}$$

We transform a sample mean into a z-score using a similar formula.

THE FORMULA FOR TRANSFORMING A SAMPLE MEAN INTO A z-SCORE IS

$$z = \frac{\overline{X} - \mu}{\sigma_{\overline{X}}}$$

Don't be confused by the minor difference in symbols between the preceding formulas. In both we simply find how far a score on a distribution falls from the mean of the distribution, measured in standard deviations of that distribution. With a sample mean, we find how far the sample mean is from the mean of the sampling distribution (μ), measured in standard error units ($\sigma_{\overline{X}}$).

For the sample from Prunepit U, $\overline{X} = 520$, $\mu = 500$ and $\sigma_{\overline{X}} = 20$, so we have

$$z = \frac{\overline{X} - \mu}{\sigma_{\overline{X}}} = \frac{520 - 500}{20} = \frac{+20}{20} = +1.00$$

Thus, a sample mean of 520 has a z-score of $+1$ on the SAT sampling distribution of means that occurs when N is 25.

Using the Sampling Distribution to Determine the Relative Frequency of Sample Means

Everything we said previously about a z-score for an individual score applies to a z-score for a sample mean. It makes no difference that the z-score now refers to the location of a sample mean: A z-score is a z-score! Thus, because our sample mean has a z-score of $+1$, we know that it is above the μ of the sampling distribution by an amount equal to the "average" amount that sample means deviate above μ. Therefore, we know that, although they were not stellar, our Prunepit students did outperform a substantial proportion of comparable samples. Likewise, if another sample of 25 SAT scores (say from Podunk U) produced a mean of 440, we'd know how poorly these students performed: Here, $z = (440 - 500)/20 = -3.0$, so this sample mean would be among the lowest SAT means we'd ever expect to obtain.

To obtain a more precise description of a sample mean, we can go one step further (and here's the nifty part): Because the sampling distribution of means always forms at least an approximately normal distribution, if we transformed *all* of the sample means in the sampling distribution into z-scores, we would have a roughly normal z-distribution. Recall that the standard normal curve is our model of *any* normal z-distribution. This is true even if it is a z-distribution of sample means! Therefore, as we did previously with raw scores, we can use the standard normal curve and z-tables to describe the relative frequency of sample means in any part of a sampling distribution. In fact, all of the operations we've performed using z-scores (everything that's summarized back in Table 6.2) can be done with the z-score for a sample mean.

> *REMEMBER* The standard normal curve model and the z-tables can be used with any sampling distribution, as well as with any raw score distribution.

Figure 6.11 shows the standard normal curve applied to our SAT sampling distribution. This is the same curve, with the same proportions, that we used to describe individual raw scores. Once again, the farther a score (here, a $\overline{X}$) is from the mean of the distribution (here, μ), the larger the absolute value of the z-score. The larger the z-score, the smaller the relative frequency and simple frequency of the z-score and of the corresponding sample mean. Therefore, we can use the standard normal curve (and the z-table) to determine the proportion of the area under any part of the curve. This proportion is also the expected relative frequency of the corresponding sample means in that part of the sampling distribution.

For example, the sample from Prunepit U has a z of $+1$ and, as you know, .3413, or 34.13%, of all scores fall between the mean and z of $+1$ on any normal distribution. Therefore, 34.13% of all SAT sample means are expected to fall between the μ and the sample mean at a z of $+1$. Because in our data, the μ is 500 and a z of $+1$ is at the sample mean of 520, we can also say that 34.13% of all SAT sample means are expected to

FIGURE 6.11 Proportions of the standard normal curve applied to the sampling distribution of SAT means

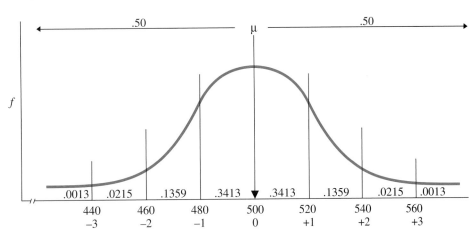

be between 500 and 520 (when N is 25). Further, by adding in the 50% of the distribution below μ, we see that about 84% of all means fall below—are to the left of—a z of $+1$. Therefore, our sample mean of 520 ranks at about the 84th percentile among all SAT sample means. Similarly, a different sample mean of 540 would have a z of $+2$ on this sampling distribution. Previously, we saw that about 2% of all z-scores are above a z of $+2$, so we expect that only about 2% of SAT sample means will be larger than 540. And finally, say that we were about to test 500 samples: 2% of 500 is $(.02)(500) = 10$, so we would expect 10 of these samples to have a $\overline{X}$ above 540.

Thus, in summary, we can use this approach to describe a sample mean from any raw score population, if we know the population's μ and σ_X. First, using the sample's N and σ_X, calculate the standard error of the mean ($\sigma_{\overline{X}}$.) Then envision the sampling distribution (or better yet, draw it) as a normal distribution with a μ equal to the μ of the underlying raw score population. Then compute the sample mean's z-score to locate the mean on the sampling distribution, and use the z-table to determine the relative frequency of such scores.

This is an especially important procedure, because eventually we'll get to inferential statistics. In the final analysis all inferential statistics involve computing something like a z-score for our sample data so that we can determine its relative frequency in a particular sampling distribution. We'll elaborate on these procedures in Chapters 9 and 10, but for now, understand that essentially, we compute z-scores and apply the standard normal curve model.

PUTTING IT ALL TOGETHER

The most important concept for you to understand is that any normal distribution of scores can be described using the standard normal curve model and z-scores. To paraphrase a famous saying, a normal distribution is a normal distribution is a normal distribution. Any normal distribution contains the same proportions of the total area under the curve between z-scores. Therefore, think z-scores! Picture a normal distribution and repeat after me: The larger the z-score, whether positive or negative, the farther the z-score and the corresponding raw score are from the mean of the distribution. The farther they are from the mean, the lower the relative frequency of the z-score and of the corresponding raw score. This is true whether the raw score is an individual's score or a sample mean.

By the way, what was Biff's percentile?

CHAPTER SUMMARY

1. The *relative standing* of a score reflects a systematic evaluation of the score relative to a sample or population. A z-*score* indicates a score's relative standing by indicating the distance the score is above or below the mean, measured in standard deviations.

2. The larger a positive z-score, the farther the raw score is above the mean. The larger the absolute value of a negative z-score, the farther the raw score is below the mean. On a normal distribution, the larger the z-score, whether positive or negative, the less frequently it—and the corresponding raw score—occurs.

3. Transforming a raw score distribution into *z*-scores produces a *z-distribution.* The *z*-distribution has the same shape as the raw score distribution, but the mean of a *z*-distribution is always 0 and the standard deviation is always 1.

4. The *standard normal curve* is a mathematically perfect normal curve that is our model of any *z*-distribution when (a) the distribution is at least roughly normally distributed and (b) the corresponding raw scores reflect an interval or ratio scale.

5. The *z-table* gives the proportion of the total area under the standard normal curve between the mean and any value of *z*. The proportion of the area under the curve is equal to the relative frequency of *z*-scores falling between the mean and *z*. This relative frequency leads to the *expected* relative frequency, simple frequency, and percentile rank of the corresponding raw scores.

6. The *sampling distribution of means* is the frequency distribution of all possible sample means that occur when an infinite number of samples of the same size *N* are randomly selected from one raw score population. Different sample means occur solely because of chance—the luck of the draw of the sample that is selected.

7. The *central limit theorem* shows that in a sampling distribution of means (a) the distribution will be approximately normal, (b) the mean of the sampling distribution of means will equal the mean of the underlying raw score population, and (c) the variability of the sample means is related to the variability of the raw scores.

8. The true *standard error of the mean* (symbolized by $\sigma_{\overline{X}}$) is the standard deviation of the sampling distribution of means. Computed when σ_X is known, $\sigma_{\overline{X}}$ indicates the average amount that the sample means deviate from the μ of the sampling distribution.

9. The location of a sample mean on the sampling distribution of means can be described by calculating a *z*-score: The distance the sample mean ($\overline{X}$) is from the mean of the distribution (μ), measured in standard error units ($\sigma_{\overline{X}}$).

10. The standard normal curve model can be applied to the sampling distribution of means. The *z*-table provides the proportion of the area under the curve for any part of the distribution. This indicates the expected relative frequency of the sample means in that part of the sampling distribution of means.

11. Biff's percentile was 99.87.

KEY TERMS: Can You Define the Following?

$\pm$ z $\sigma_{\overline{X}}$

central limit theorem *147*

relative standing *128*

sampling distribution of means *146*

standard error of the mean *148*

standard normal curve *138*

standard scores *136*

z-distribution *133*

z-score *130*

REVIEW QUESTIONS

(Answers for odd-numbered questions are in Appendix C.)

1. (a) What does a z-score indicate? (b) Why are z-scores important?
2. On what factors does the size of a z-score depend?
3. What is a z-distribution?
4. What are the three general uses of z-scores?
5. Why are z-scores referred to as standard scores?
6. Why is using z-scores and the standard normal curve model so useful?
7. (a) What is the standard normal curve model? (b) How is it applied to a set of data? (c) What three criteria should be met for the model to give an accurate description of a sample?
8. (a) What is a sampling distribution of means? (b) When is it used? (c) Why is it useful?
9. What three things does the central limit theorem tell us about the sampling distribution of means? (b) Why is this so useful?
10. What does the standard error of the mean indicate?
11. (a) What are the steps for using the standard normal curve to find a raw score's relative frequency or percentile? (b) What are the steps for finding the raw score that cuts off a specified relative frequency or percentile? (c) What are the steps for finding a sample mean's relative frequency or percentile?

APPLICATION QUESTIONS

12. In freshman English last semester, Foofy earned a 76 ($\overline{X}$ = 85, S_X = 10), and her friend Bubbles, in a different class, earned a 60 ($\overline{X}$ = 50, S_X = 4). Should Foofy be bragging about how much better she did? Why?
13. Poindexter received a grade of 55 on a biology test ($\overline{X}$ = 50) and a grade of 45 on a philosophy test ($\overline{X}$ = 50). He is considering whether to ask his two professors to curve the grades using z-scores. (a) What other information should he consider before making his request? (b) Does he want the S_X to be large or small in biology? Why? (c) Does he want the S_X to be large or small in philosophy? Why?
14. Foofy computes z-scores for a set of normally distributed exam scores. She obtains a z-score of -3.96 for 8 out of 20 of the students. What does this mean?
15. For the data   9   5   10   7   9   10   11   8   12   7   6   9, (a) Compute the z-score for the raw score of 10. (b) Compute the z-score for the raw score of 6.
16. For the data in question 15 find the raw scores that correspond to the following: (a) z = $+1.22$; (b) z = -0.48.
17. Which z-score in each of the following pairs corresponds to the smaller raw score? (a) z = $+1.0$ or z = $+2.3$; (b) z = -2.8 or z = -1.7; (c) z = $-.70$ or z = $+.20$; (d) z = 0.0 or z = -2.0.
18. For each pair in question 17, which z-score has the higher frequency?

19. In a normal distribution of scores, what proportion of all scores would you expect to fall into each of the following areas? (a) between the mean and $z = +1.89$; (b) below $z = -2.30$; (c) between $z = -1.25$ and $z = +2.75$; (d) above $z = +1.96$ and below -1.96.

20. For a distribution in which $\overline{X} = 100$, $S_X = 16$, and $N = 500$, answer the following: (a) What is the relative frequency of scores between 76 and the mean? (b) How many participants are expected to score between 76 and the mean? (c) What is the percentile of someone scoring 76? (d) How many subjects are expected to score above 76?

21. Poindexter may be classified as having a math dysfunction—and thus not have to take statistics—if he scores below the 25th percentile on a national diagnostic test. The μ of the test is 75 ($\sigma_X = 10$). Approximately what raw score is the cutoff score for him to avoid taking statistics?

22. For an IQ test we know the population $\mu = 100$ and the $\sigma_X = 16$. We are interested in creating the sampling distribution when $N = 64$. (a) What does that sampling distribution of means reflect? (b) What is the shape of the distribution of IQ means and the mean of the distribution? (c) Calculate $\sigma_{\overline{X}}$ for this distribution. (d) What is your answer in part c called, and what does it indicate?

23. A recent graduate has two job offers and must decide which to accept. The job in City A pays $27,000. The average cost of living there is $50,000, with a standard deviation of $15,000. The job in City B pays $12,000. The average cost of living there is $14,000, with a standard deviation of $1,000. Assuming salaries are normally distributed, which is the better job offer? Why?

24. A researcher obtained a sample mean of 68.4 when he gave a test to a random sample of 49 participants. For everyone who has ever taken the test, the mean is 65 (and $\sigma_X = 10$). The researcher believes that his sample mean is rather unusual. (a) How often can he expect to obtain a sample mean that is higher than 68.4? (b) Why might the researcher obtain such an unusual mean?

25. If you took 1000 random samples of 50 participants each from a population where $\mu = 19.4$ and $\sigma_X = 6.0$, how many samples would you expect to produce a mean below 18?

26. Suppose you own shares of a company's stock, the price of which has risen so that, over the past ten trading days, its mean selling price is $14.89. Over the years, the mean price of the stock has been $10.43 ($\sigma_X = 5.60). You wonder if the mean selling price over the next ten days can be expected to go higher. Should you wait to sell, or should you sell now?

27. A researcher develops a test for selecting intellectually gifted children, with a μ of 56 and a σ_X of 8. (a) What percentage of children are expected to score below 60? (b) What percentage of scores will be above 54? (c) A gifted child is defined as being in the top 20%. What is the minimum test score needed to qualify as gifted?

28. Using the test in question 27, you measure 64 children, obtaining a $\overline{X}$ of 57.28. Slug says that because this $\overline{X}$ is so close to the μ of 56, this sample could hardly be considered gifted. (a) Perform the appropriate statistical procedure to determine whether he is correct. (b) In what percentage of the top scores is this sample mean?

29. In a study you first collect these raw scores: 86   85   73   71   67   88   57   57   45   60. (a) You are about to test 200 more people. How many do you expect will score below 65? (b) How many do you expect to score above 70? (c) After collecting these additional scores, you find your expectations in parts a and b were very wrong. Why would this be?

SUMMARY OF FORMULAS

1. *The formula for transforming a raw score in a sample into a* z-*score is*

$$z = \frac{X - \overline{X}}{S_X}$$

where X is the raw score, $\overline{X}$ is the sample mean, and S_X is the sample standard deviation.

2. *The formula for transforming a* z-*score in a sample into a raw score is*

$$X = (z)(S_X) + \overline{X}$$

3. *The formula for transforming a raw score in a population into a* z-*score is*

$$z = \frac{X - \mu}{\sigma_X}$$

4. *The formula for transforming a* z-*score in a population into a raw score is*

$$X = (z)(\sigma_X) + \mu$$

5. *The formula for the true standard error of the mean is*

$$\sigma_{\overline{X}} = \frac{\sigma_X}{\sqrt{N}}$$

where σ_X is the true standard deviation of the underlying raw score population and N is the sample size.

6. *The formula for transforming a sample mean into a* z-*score on the sampling distribution of means is*

$$z = \frac{\overline{X} - \mu}{\sigma_{\overline{X}}}$$

where $\overline{X}$ is the sample mean, μ is the mean of the sampling distribution (which equals the μ of the underlying raw score population), and $\sigma_{\overline{X}}$ is the standard error of the mean.

3

DESCRIBING RELATIONSHIPS

As you know most behavioral research examines the relationships between variables. Therefore, the final question to answer with descriptive statistics is "What is the nature of the relationship we have found?" There are two major approaches to answering this question, covered in the next two chapters. Chapter 7 discusses the procedure known as *correlation,* and Chapter 8 discusses the procedure known as *linear regression.*

The topics in the upcoming chapters are different from previous topics because correlation and regression do not focus on sample means and standard deviations. Therefore, think of these chapters as a detour. After we complete the detour, we'll return to describing a sample using the mean and standard deviation. In particular, we'll return to describing the location of a sample mean on a sampling distribution of sample means, so don't forget that procedure.

7

Describing Relationships Using Correlations

GETTING STARTED

To understand this chapter, recall the following:

- From Chapter 2 recall how to graph data points and identify when a relationship is present, and what is meant by its strength.
- From Chapter 4 understand how to graph the relationship in an experiment.
- From Chapter 5 understand that greater variability indicates that scores are not close to each other.

Your goals in this chapter are to learn:

- The logic of correlational research and how it is interpreted.
- How to read and interpret a scatterplot and a regression line.
- How to identify the type and strength of a relationship.
- How to interpret a correlation coefficient.
- When to use the Pearson r, the Spearman r_s, and the point-biserial r_{pb}.
- The logic of inferring a population correlation based on a sample correlation.

Recall that in a relationship, as the scores on one variable change, there is a consistent pattern of change in the scores on the other variable. In research, in addition to demonstrating a relationship, we also want to describe and summarize the relationship. This chapter discusses the descriptive statistic for summarizing a relationship called the *correlation coefficient*. In the following sections we'll consider when such statistics are used and what they tell us. Finally, you'll see how to calculate different types of correlation coefficients. First, though, here are some new symbols.

MORE STATISTICAL NOTATION

Correlational analysis requires scores from two variables. Then, X stands for the scores on one variable, and Y stands for the scores on the other variable. Usually each pair of XY scores is from the same participant. If not, there must be a rational system for pairing the scores (e.g., pairing the scores of roommates). Because we use pairs of scores, there *must* be the same number of X and Y scores.

We use the same conventions for Y that we've previously used for X. Thus, ΣY is the sum of the Y scores, ΣY^2 is the sum of the squared Y scores, and $(\Sigma Y)^2$ is the squared sum of the Y scores. The mean of the Y scores is $\overline{Y}$ and equals $\Sigma Y/N$. The variance of a sample of Y scores is S_Y^2, and the standard deviation is S_Y. To find S_Y^2 and S_Y, use the same formulas that you used to find S_X^2 and S_X, except now plug in Y scores instead of X scores.

You will also encounter three new notations. First, $(\Sigma X)(\Sigma Y)$ indicates to first find the sum of the Xs and the sum of the Ys, and then multiply the two sums together. Second, ΣXY, called the sum of the cross products, says to first multiply each X score in a pair times its corresponding Y score and then sum all of the resulting products.

> **REMEMBER** $(\Sigma X)(\Sigma Y)$ says to multiply the sum of X times the sum of Y.
> ΣXY says to multiply each X times its paired Y and then sum the products.

Finally, D stands for the numerical *difference* between the X and Y scores in a pair, which you find by subtracting one from the other.

Now, on to the correlation coefficient.

WHY IS IT IMPORTANT TO KNOW ABOUT CORRELATION COEFFICIENTS?

Whenever we find a relationship, we then want to know its characteristics: What pattern is formed, how consistently do the scores change together, what direction do the scores change, and so on? The best—and easiest—way to answer these questions is by computing a correlation coefficient. The **correlation coefficient** is the statistic that in a single number summarizes and describes the important characteristics of a relationship. The correlation coefficient *quantifies* the pattern in a relationship, and it does so by simultaneously examining *all* pairs of X and Y scores, summarizing the entire relationship at once. No other statistic does this. Thus, the major advantage of the correlation coefficient is that it simplifies the complex relationship involving many scores into one, easily interpreted statistic. Therefore, in any research—whether in an experiment or other type of design—you should always calculate the appropriate correlation coefficient. As a starting point, however, the correlation coefficients discussed in this chapter are most commonly associated with correlational research.

UNDERSTANDING CORRELATIONAL RESEARCH

Recall that a common approach to research is the "correlational design." The term *correlation* is synonymous with *relationship,* so in a correlational design we examine the relationship—examine the correlation—between variables. (Think of the word *correlation* as meaning the shared, or "co," relationship between the variables.) The relationship can involve scores from virtually any variables, regardless of how we obtain them. Often we measure the variables using a questionnaire or by observing participants, but we may also measure responses using any of the methods used in experiments.

Experimental and correlational designs differ in terms of *how* we demonstrate the relationship. For example, typically, as people drink more coffee they become more nervous. To demonstrate this in an experiment, we would manipulate the amount of coffee consumed: We might assign some people to a condition in which they drink 1 cup, others to a condition in which they drink 2 cups, and others to one in which they drink 3 cups. By determining the conditions, we (the researchers) determine each participant's *X* score because we decide whether their "score" will be 1, 2, or 3 cups on the coffee variable. Then we would measure participants' nervousness (perhaps using some physiological device or a questionnaire) and see if more nervousness is related to more coffee.

In a correlational design, however, the researcher does *not* manipulate any variables, so here we do not determine participants' *X* scores. Rather, the scores on both variables reflect an amount or category of a variable that a participant has *already* experienced. Therefore, we simply measure the two variables and then describe the relationship that is present. Thus, we might ask participants the amount of coffee they had consumed that day and measure how nervous they were.

Recognize that computing a correlation coefficient does not create a correlational *design:* It is the absence of manipulation that creates the design. Yet, you'll often encounter correlations in correlational research, and you must be very careful when interpreting the results of such a design.

Drawing Conclusions from Correlational Research

Whenever people hear of a relationship between *X* and *Y,* they have a natural tendency to conclude that it is a *causal* relationship—that *X* causes *Y.* Thus, if we discovered that people who drink more coffee tend to be more nervous, we might want to conclude that more coffee is causing people to be more nervous. *However, the fact that there is a relationship between two variables does not mean that changes in one variable cause the changes in the other variable.* A relationship can exist even though one variable does not cause or influence the other. (Heavier people tend to be taller, but your weight does not cause your height.) Therefore, correlational research *cannot* be used to infer a causal relationship between two variables.

There are two requirements for concluding that *X* causes *Y.* First, *X* must occur before *Y.* But, in correlational research, we do not know which factor occurred first. For example, above we simply measured scores reflecting amount of coffee and nervousness. Perhaps people were first more nervous and *then* drank more coffee, so that greater nervousness may actually cause greater coffee consumption. In any correlational study it is possible that *Y* causes *X.*

The second requirement is that *X* must be the only variable that can influence *Y*. But, in correlational research, we do not control or eliminate other variables that may potentially cause scores to change. For example, in the coffee study, some of the participants may have had less sleep than others the night before testing. Perhaps the lack of sleep caused those people to be more nervous *and* to drink more coffee. In any correlational study, some other variable may cause both *X* and *Y* to change.

> *REMEMBER* In a correlational study, changes in *X* may cause changes in *Y*, changes in *Y* may cause changes in *X*, or some third variable may cause changes in both *X* and *Y*.

Thus, a correlation by itself does not indicate causality. You must also consider the research method used to demonstrate the relationship. In experiments we apply the independent variable *first* and we control other potential causal variables, so experiments provide the best evidence for drawing conclusions about the causes of a behavior. In a correlational study, however, the relationship we describe may be a *coincidence*. Sometimes the coincidental nature of the relationship is obvious. For example, there is a relationship between the number of toilets in a neighborhood and the number of crimes committed in that neighborhood: the more toilets, the more crime. Should we conclude that indoor plumbing causes crime? Of course not! Crime tends to occur more frequently in large cities, especially in crowded neighborhoods. Coincidentally, there are more indoor toilets in crowded neighborhoods in large cities.

The problem is that it is easy to be trapped by more mysterious relationships involving variables that we do not understand. For example, there is a correlation between the amount of "adult literature" (pornography) sold in a state and the incidence of rape in the state: the more pornography, the more rape. Based on this correlation, can you conclude that pornography causes rape? Not unless you also conclude that indoor plumbing causes crime! If we cannot use correlation to infer causality in one situation, we cannot use it in another. Pornography may cause rape, but, for all the reasons given above, the mere existence of this relationship is not evidence of causality.

> *REMEMBER* Never infer causality based *solely* on the existence of a correlation.

Distinguishing Characteristics of Correlational Analysis

There are four major differences between how we handle data in correlational analysis versus in an experiment. First, in our coffee experiment we would examine the mean nervousness score (the *Y* scores) for each condition of the amount of coffee consumed (the *X* scores). With correlational data, however, we typically have a rather large range of different *X* scores: People would probably report a coffee consumption beyond only 1, 2, or 3 cups. Comparing the mean nervousness scores for so many groups would be very difficult. Therefore, in correlational procedures we do not compute a mean *Y* score at each *X*. Instead, the correlation coefficient summarizes the *entire* relationship formed by all pairs of *X*-*Y* scores in the data.

A second difference is that, because we examine all pairs of *X*-*Y* scores, correlational procedures involve *one* sample:

>**In correlational analysis, N stands for the number of pairs of scores in the data.**

Third, in a correlational study, neither variable is called the independent or dependent variable, and either variable may be the X or Y variable. How do we decide? You've seen that in any relationship the X scores are the "given" scores. Thus, if we ask, "For a given amount of coffee, what are the nervousness scores?" then amount of coffee is the X variable and nervousness is the Y variable. Conversely, if we ask, "For a given nervousness score, what is the amount of coffee consumed?" then nervousness is the X variable and amount of coffee is the Y variable.

Finally, as in the next section, the data are graphed differently in correlational research. We use the individual pairs of scores to create a *scatterplot*.

Plotting Correlational Data: The Scatterplot

A **scatterplot** is a graph that shows the location of each data point formed by a pair of X-Y scores. The scatterplot in Figure 7.1 shows the data that might occur if we studied nervousness and coffee consumption. Real research typically involves a larger N, and the data points may not form such a pretty pattern. Nonetheless, a scatterplot does summarize the data somewhat. In the table, two people had scores of 1 on both coffee consumption and nervousness. On the scatterplot there is one data point for them. (As shown, some researchers circle such a data point to indicate that points are on top of each other.) In real data, many participants with a particular X score may obtain the same Y, so the number of data points may be considerably smaller than the number of pairs of raw scores.

Figure 7.1 shows that the more coffee people drink, the more nervous they tend to be: People drinking 1 cup tend to have nervousness scores around 1, those drinking 2 cups

FIGURE 7.1   Scatterplot showing nervousness as a function of coffee consumption

Each data point is created using a participant's coffee consumption as the X score and nervousness as the Y score.

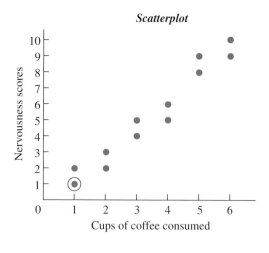

Cups of coffee: X	Nervousness scores: Y
1	1
1	1
1	2
2	2
2	3
3	4
3	5
4	5
4	6
5	8
5	9
6	9
6	10

tend to have nervousness scores around 2, and so on. Thus, the scatterplot reflects a relationship because one value or close to one value of *Y* tends to be paired with one value of *X*. As the *X* scores increase, the *Y* scores change so that a different value or values of *Y* tend to be paired with a different value of *X*.

> *REMEMBER*   When a relationship exists, a particular value of *Y* tends to be paired with one value of *X*, and a different value of *Y* tends to be paired with a different value of *X*.

Always draw the scatterplot for a set of correlational data. A scatterplot allows you to see the relationship that is present and to map out the best way to summarize it.

The shape of the scatterplot is an important indication of both the presence of a relationship and the nature of the relationship. To better see this, you can visually summarize a scatterplot by drawing a line around its outer edges. A scatterplot may have any one of a number of shapes when a relationship is present. When no relationship is present, however, the scatterplot will be either circular or elliptical, oriented so that the ellipse is parallel to the *X* axis. Thus, the scatterplots in Figure 7.2 show no relationship between coffee consumption and nervousness because as the *X* scores increase, the *Y* scores do not consistently change: No particular value of *Y* tends to be associated with a particular value of *X* and instead, virtually the same batch of *Y* scores shows up at every *X*.

The scatterplots in Figure 7.2 are further summarized by the line drawn through the center of the scatterplot. This line is called the **regression line.** (We discuss the procedure for drawing the regression line in the next chapter.) The orientation of the regression line matches the orientation of the scatterplot. Thus, when no relationship is present, the regression line is a horizontal straight line.

What the Correlation Coefficient Indicates

When a relationship is present, the scatterplot will form some shape other than a circle or a horizontal ellipse, and the regression line will not be a horizontal straight line. The

FIGURE 7.2   Scatterplots showing no relationship between coffee consumption and nervousness

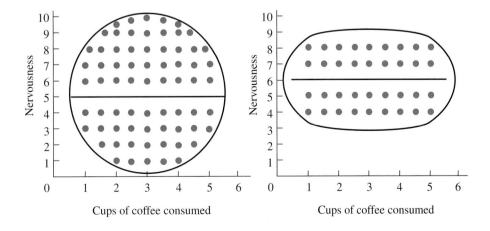

particular shape and orientation of a scatterplot reflect the characteristics of the relationship formed by the data. To summarize these characteristics, we compute the correlation coefficient. Then, as with other statistics, we can use the correlation coefficient to envision the scatterplot without actually looking at all of the individual scores. The correlation coefficient communicates two important characteristics of a relationship: *the type of relationship* and the *strength of the relationship*. The following sections discuss these characteristics.

TYPES OF RELATIONSHIPS

The **type of relationship** that is present in a set of data is determined by the overall direction in which the *Y* scores change as the *X* scores change. There are two general types of relationships: *linear* and *nonlinear* relationships.

Linear Relationships

The term *linear* means "straight line," and a linear relationship forms a pattern that follows a straight line. The scatterplots in Figure 7.3 illustrate the linear relationship between the amount of time students study and their test performance, and between the number of hours students watch television and their test performance.

Both scatterplots show a linear relationship because (1) they do not form horizontal ellipses, and (2) they are best summarized by a straight line. Any scatterplot that forms a *slanted ellipse* and has a *slanted, straight* regression line indicates that a linear relationship is present. We obtain such scatterplots because in a **linear relationship,** as the *X* scores increase, the *Y* scores tend to change in only one direction. (You read a graph from left to right and then the *X* scores increase; to prevent confusion, always begin your definition with "as the *X* scores *increase*.") Above, as students study longer, their grades tend only to increase. And, as students watch more television, their test scores tend only to decrease.

FIGURE 7.3   Scatterplots showing positive and negative linear relationships

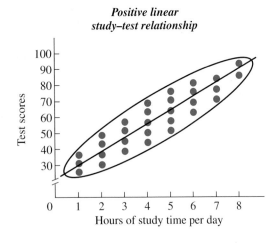

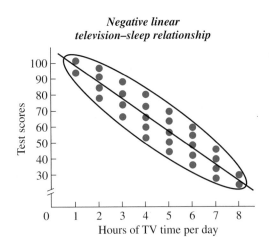

There are two subtypes of linear relationships, depending on the *direction* in which the *Y* scores change. The study–test relationship is a positive relationship. In a **positive linear relationship,** as the scores on the *X* variable increase, the scores on the *Y* variable also tend to increase. Thus, low *X* scores are paired with low *Y* scores, and high *X* scores are paired with high *Y* scores. Any relationship that fits the pattern "the more *X*, the more *Y*" is a positive linear relationship. You can remember that such relationships are called positive by remembering that as the *X* scores increase, the *Y* scores change in the direction away from zero, toward higher *positive* scores.

On the other hand, the television–test relationship is a negative relationship. In a **negative linear relationship,** as the scores on the *X* variable increase, the scores on the *Y* variable tend to decrease. Low *X* scores are paired with high *Y* scores, and high *X* scores are paired with low *Y* scores. Any relationship that fits the pattern "the more *X*, the less *Y*" is a negative linear relationship. Remember that such relationships are called negative by remembering that as the *X* scores increase, the *Y* scores change toward zero, heading toward *negative* scores.

The term *negative* does not mean that there is something wrong with a relationship. Negative relationships are no different from positive relationships *except* in terms of the direction in which the *Y* scores change as the *X* scores increase.

Nonlinear Relationships

If a relationship is not linear, then it is nonlinear. *Nonlinear* means that the data cannot be summarized by a *straight* line. Thus, another name for a nonlinear relationship is a curvilinear relationship. In a **nonlinear,** or **curvilinear, relationship,** as the *X* scores change, the *Y* scores do not tend to *only* increase or *only* decrease: At some point, the *Y* scores change their direction of change.

Nonlinear relationships come in many different shapes, but Figure 7.4 shows two common ones. In the scatterplot on the left is the relationship between a person's age and the amount of time required to move from one place to another. Very young children move slowly, but as age increases, movement time decreases. Beyond a certain age, however, the time scores change direction and begin to increase. Because of the

FIGURE 7.4 Scatterplots showing nonlinear relationships

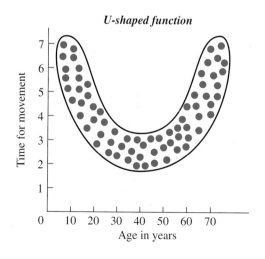
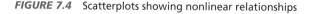
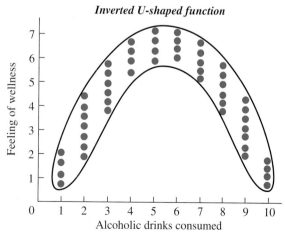

shape of the scatterplot, such a relationship is called *U-shaped*. The scatterplot on the right shows the relationship between the number of alcoholic drinks consumed and feeling well. At first, people tend to feel better as they drink, but beyond a certain point, drinking more makes them feel progressively worse. Such a scatterplot reflects an *inverted U-shaped relationship*. Curvilinear relationships may be more complex than those above, producing a wavy pattern that repeatedly changes direction.

Note that the preceding terminology is also used to describe the type of relationship found in experiments. If, as the amount of the independent variable (X) increases, the dependent scores (Y) also increase, then you have a positive relationship. If the dependent scores decrease as the independent variable (X) increases, you have a negative relationship. And if, as the independent variable (X) increases, the dependent scores change their direction of change, you have a nonlinear relationship.

How the Correlation Coefficient Describes the Type of Relationship

Behavioral research focuses primarily on linear relationships, so we'll discuss only linear correlation. How do you know whether data form a linear relationship? Make a scatterplot! If the scatterplot is best summarized by a straight line, then linear correlation is appropriate. Also, sometimes, you may want to describe the extent to which a nonlinear relationship has a linear component and somewhat fits a straight line. Here, too, linear correlation is appropriate. However, do not summarize a nonlinear relationship by computing a linear correlation coefficient. Describing a nonlinear relationship with a straight line is like putting a round peg into a square hole: The relationship won't fit the straight line very well, and the correlation coefficient won't accurately describe the relationship.

The correlation coefficient communicates two things about the type of relationship. First, because we compute a linear correlation coefficient, we communicate that we are describing a linear relationship. Second, the coefficient itself indicates whether the relationship is positive or negative. If the coefficient—the number we compute—has a minus sign in front of it, then the relationship is negative. If the coefficient does not have a minus sign, then we put a plus sign in front of it to indicate a positive relationship. Thus, a positive correlation coefficient indicates a positive linear relationship, and a negative correlation coefficient indicates a negative linear relationship.

The other characteristic of a relationship communicated by the correlation coefficient is the *strength* of the relationship.

STRENGTH OF THE RELATIONSHIP

Recall that a relationship can exhibit varying degrees of consistency, and the **strength of a relationship** is the extent to which one value of Y is consistently paired with one and only one value of X. (The strength of a relationship is also referred to as the *degree of association*.) The absolute value of the correlation coefficient (ignoring its sign) indicates the strength of the relationship. The largest value you can obtain is 1.0, and the smallest value is 0. (Thus, when we include the positive or negative sign, the correlation coefficient may be any value between -1.0 and $+1.0$.) The *larger* the absolute value of the coefficient, the *stronger* the relationship. In other words, the closer the coefficient is to ±1.0, the more consistently one value of Y is paired with one and only one value of X.

> REMEMBER A *correlation coefficient* has two components: the sign, which indicates either a positive or a negative linear relationship, and the absolute value, which indicates the strength of the relationship.

Computing the correlation coefficient is not difficult. The difficulty comes in interpreting it in terms of the strength of the relationship. Correlation coefficients do not directly measure units of "consistency." Thus, if one correlation coefficient is +.40 and another is +.80, you *cannot* conclude that +.80 describes a relationship that is twice as consistent as the one with +.40. Instead, you can evaluate any correlation coefficient by comparing it to the extreme values of 0 and ±1.0. The starting point is to know how to envision a perfect relationship.

Perfect Association

A correlation coefficient of +1.0 or −1.0 describes a perfectly consistent linear relationship. Figure 7.5 shows an example of each.

FIGURE 7.5 Data and scatterplots reflecting perfect positive and negative correlations

Perfect positive coefficient = +1.0

X	Y
1	2
1	2
1	2
3	5
3	5
3	5
5	8
5	8
5	8

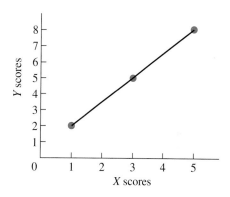

Perfect negative coefficient = −1.0

X	Y
1	8
1	8
1	8
3	5
3	5
3	5
5	2
5	2
5	2

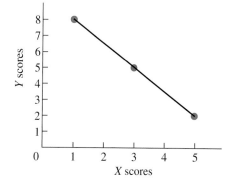

There are four ways to think about what a correlation coefficient of ±1.0 tells you about this relationship. First, it indicates that *everyone* who obtains a particular X score obtains one and only one value of Y. Every time X changes, the Y scores all change to one new value. Thus, ±1.0 indicates a one-to-one correspondence between the X and Y scores.

Second, a coefficient of ±1.0 indicates that there are no differences among the Y scores associated with a particular X. In other words, ±1.0 indicates that there is no *variability* in the Y scores at each X.

Third, a coefficient of ±1.0 ensures perfect predictability of Y scores. That is, by knowing about this relationship, if we know the X score of other individuals, we will *know* their Y score, because in this situation, only one Y score occurs with that X. (You'll see how to predict Y scores in the next chapter.)

Fourth, because there is no variability in the Y scores at each X, a coefficient of ±1.0 tells us that the data points at an X are all on top of one another. And, because it is a perfect straight-line relationship, all of the data points will lie *on* the regression line.

Intermediate Association

A correlation coefficient that does not equal ±1.0 indicates that the data form a linear relationship to only some degree. The closer the coefficient is to ±1.0, however, the closer the data come to forming a perfect relationship, and the closer the scatterplot is to forming a straight line. Therefore, the way to interpret any other value of the correlation coefficient is to compare it to ±1.0.

For example, Figure 7.6 shows data and the resulting scatterplot that produce a correlation coefficient of $+.98$. Again interpret the coefficient in four ways. First, with an absolute value less than 1.0, there is not perfectly consistent association. Not every participant obtaining a particular X obtained the same Y. However, a coefficient of $+.98$ is close to $+1.0$, so here there is "close" to perfect consistency between the X and Y scores. That is, even though there are different values of Y at the same X, the Y scores are relatively close to each other.

Second, this coefficient indicates that there are *different* Y scores associated with a single X score, so there is variability among the Y scores at each X. In Figure 7.6, participants at an X of 1 scored a Y of 1 or 2, and participants at an X of 3 scored a Y of 4 or

FIGURE 7.6   Data and scatterplot reflecting a correlation coefficient of $+.98$

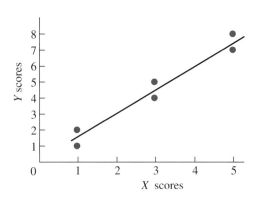

X	Y
1	1
1	2
1	2
3	4
3	5
3	5
5	7
5	8
5	8

5. However, $+.98$ is close to $+1.0$, indicating that the variability in Y scores at each X is relatively small when compared to the overall variability of all Y scores in the sample. Think of it this way: Over the entire sample, Y scores are between 1 and 8, so the overall range is 7. At each X score, however, the Ys span a range of only 1. It is this small variability in Y at each X relative to the overall variability in all Y scores that produces a correlation coefficient close to ± 1.0.

Third, when the correlation coefficient is not ± 1.0, knowing participants' X scores allows us to predict only *around* what their Y score will be. In Figure 7.6, for an X of 1 we'd predict that people score Ys around 1 or 2, while for an X of 3 we'd predict Ys around 4 or 5. There will be some error in our predictions here, but a coefficient of $+.98$ is close to $+1.0$, indicating that our predicted Y scores will be close to the actual Y scores that participants obtained and so there is relatively little error.

Fourth, because there is now variability in the Ys at each X, not all data points fall *on* the regression line: As in the scatterplot in Figure 7.6, variability in Y scores results in the vertical spread in the data points above and below the regression line at each X. However, a coefficient of $+.98$ is close to $+1.0$, so we know that the Y scores are close to, or hug, the regression line, resulting in a scatterplot that is a narrow, or skinny, ellipse. In fact, the correlation coefficient always indicates how skinny the scatterplot is. When the coefficient is ± 1.0, the scatterplot forms a straight line, which is the skinniest ellipse possible. The closer the coefficient is to ± 1.0, the skinnier the scatterplot, and vice versa.

The key to understanding the strength of any relationship is this:

> **As the variability—differences—in the Y scores at each X becomes larger, the relationship becomes weaker.**

The correlation coefficient communicates this because, as the variability in the Ys at each X becomes larger, the value of the correlation coefficient approaches 0. Figure 7.7 shows data that produce a correlation coefficient of $-.28$. The fact that this is a negative relationship has nothing to do with its strength. Rather, here the spread in the Y scores (the variability) at each X is relatively large. This does two things that are contrary to a relationship. First, instead of seeing a different Y score at *different* Xs, we see large differences among the Ys for individuals who have the *same* X. Second, there is

FIGURE 7.7 Data and scatterplot reflecting a correlation coefficient of $-.28$.

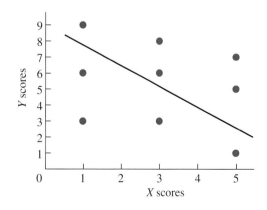

X	Y
1	9
1	6
1	3
3	8
3	6
3	3
5	7
5	5
5	1

overlap between the Y scores at the different Xs, so that instead of seeing one value of Y at one $X,$ we see the one value of Y paired with *different* values of X. Thus, the weaker the relationship, the more that the Y scores tend to change when X does not, while the Y scores tend to stay the same when X changes.

It is the variability in Y at each X that determines the consistency of a relationship, which in turn determines all of the characteristics we've examined. Thus, on a scale of 0 to ± 1.0, a coefficient of $-.28$ is not very close to ± 1.0, so we know that this relationship is not very close to forming a perfectly consistent linear relationship. Therefore, we know that (1) only barely does one value or close to one value of Y tend to be associated with one value of X, (2) the variability in the Ys at each X is almost as large as the variability of all Y scores in the data, (3) knowing participants' X scores will not produce very accurate predictions of their Y scores, and (4) the large vertical distance between the Ys at each X will produce a fat scatterplot that does not hug the regression line.

> *REMEMBER*   Greater *variability* in the Y scores at each X reduces the strength
> of a relationship and the size of the correlation coefficient.

Zero Association

The lowest possible value of the correlation coefficient is 0, indicating that no relationship is present. Figure 7.8 shows data that produce such a coefficient. A scatterplot having this shape is as far from forming a slanted straight line as possible, and a correlation coefficient of 0 is as far from ± 1.0 as possible. Therefore, we know that no values of Y tend to be consistently associated with only one value of X. Instead, the Ys found at one X are virtually the same as those found at any other X. This also means that knowing someone's X score will not in any way help us to predict the corresponding Y score. Finally, this indicates the spread in Y at any X equals the overall spread of Y in the data, producing a scatterplot that is a circle or horizontal ellipse that in no way hugs the regression line.

> *REMEMBER*   The larger a correlation coefficient (whether positive or nega-
> tive), the stronger the linear relationship, because the less the Ys are spread
> out at each X, and so the closer the data come to forming a straight line.

FIGURE 7.8   Data and scatterplot reflecting a correlation coefficient of 0.

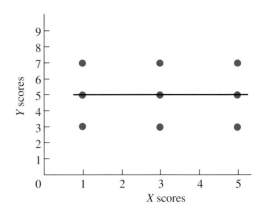

X	Y
1	3
1	5
1	7
3	3
3	5
3	7
5	3
5	5
5	7

Correlation Coefficients in Real Research

Although theoretically, a correlation coefficient may be as large as ±1.0, in real research such values do not occur. Remember that the scores reflect the behaviors of living organisms, and that, because of the influence of momentary extraneous variables and individual differences, living organisms seldom behave identically, even when in the same situation. Therefore, there will always be inconsistency in the Y scores at each X, so adjust your expectations about the relationships found in real research: Typically, we find correlation coefficients in the neighborhood of $\pm.30$ to $\pm.50$. Therefore, researchers generally consider a coefficient between 0 and $\pm.20$ to be very weak and probably negligible. Coefficients between $\pm.20$ and $\pm.40$ are common and .40 is described as moderately strong. A coefficient between $\pm.40$ to $\pm.60$ is less common, and $\pm.60$ is considered quite impressive and strong. Coefficients between $\pm.60$ to $\pm.80$ are very strong, while those beyond $\pm.80$ are extremely strong and very unlikely. A correlation equal to ±1.0 is so unlikely that, if you ever obtain one, you should assume you've made a computational error. (If you obtain a coefficient greater than ±1.0, you've definitely made an error, because ±1.0 indicates a perfect relationship, and you can't do better than that.)

COMPUTING THE CORRELATION COEFFICIENT

The following sections discuss the three most common linear correlation coefficients: the *Pearson correlation coefficient,* the *Spearman rank-order correlation coefficient,* and the *point-biserial correlation coefficient.* In each case the coefficient is a number between 0 and ±1.0, and everything you've seen previously about interpreting a correlation coefficient applies. The major difference among them is that they are calculated differently: Each is designed for different types of variables, and—as when selecting other statistical procedures—the specific coefficient you compute in a particular situation depends on the *scale of measurement* used to measure the X and Y scores.

The Pearson Correlation Coefficient

By far the most common correlation coefficient in behavioral research is the Pearson correlation coefficient. The **Pearson correlation coefficient** describes the linear relationship between two interval variables, two ratio variables, or one interval and one ratio variable. (Technically, this statistic is the *Pearson Product Moment Correlation Coefficient,* but it's usually called the Pearson correlation coefficient. It was invented by Karl Pearson.) The symbol for the Pearson correlation coefficient is the lowercase r. When you see r, think "relationship." (All of the example coefficients in the previous section were rs.)

The statistical basis for r is that it compares how consistently each value of Y is paired with each value of X in a linear fashion. In Chapter 6 you saw that we compare scores from different variables by transforming them into z-scores. Essentially, calculating r involves transforming each Y score into a z-score (call it z_Y), transforming each X score into a z-score (call it z_X), and then determining the "average" amount of correspondence between the z_Ys and the z_Xs. The Pearson correlation coefficient is defined as

$$r = \frac{\Sigma(z_X z_Y)}{N}$$

Mathematically, multiplying each z_X times the corresponding z_Y of the pair, summing the products, and then dividing by N produces the average correspondence between the pairs.

Luckily, there's an easier way to compute r. The computational formula is derived from the above formula by replacing the symbols z_X and z_Y with their formulas, and then, in each, replacing the symbols for the mean and standard deviation with their formulas. This produces a monster of a formula. After reducing it, we have the smaller monster below.

THE COMPUTATIONAL FORMULA FOR THE PEARSON CORRELATION COEFFICIENT IS

$$r = \frac{N(\Sigma XY) - (\Sigma X)(\Sigma Y)}{\sqrt{[N(\Sigma X^2) - (\Sigma X)^2][N(\Sigma Y^2) - (\Sigma Y)^2]}}$$

Here's a new example. Say that in a health study we collect scores from 10 people on the variables of the number of times they visited a doctor in the last year and the number of glasses of orange juice they drink daily. We obtain the data in Figure 7.9. We want to describe the linear relationship between juice drinking and doctor visits, so, because we have ratio scores on both variables, we compute r. Table 7.1 shows a good

FIGURE 7.9 Example showing the relationship between number of glasses of orange juice consumed daily and number of yearly doctor visits.

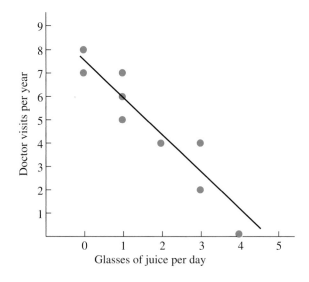

Participant	Juice Scores: X	Doctor Visits: Y
1	0	8
2	0	7
3	1	7
4	1	6
5	1	5
6	2	4
7	2	4
8	3	4
9	3	2
10	4	0

TABLE 7.1 Sample Data for Computing the r Between Orange Juice Consumed (the X variable) and Doctor Visits (the Y variable)

Participant	Glasses of Juice per Day		Doctor Visits per Year		
	X	X^2	Y	Y^2	XY
1	0	0	8	64	0
2	0	0	7	49	0
3	1	1	7	49	7
4	1	1	6	36	6
5	1	1	5	25	5
6	2	4	4	16	8
7	2	4	4	16	8
8	3	9	4	16	12
9	3	9	2	4	6
10	4	16	0	0	0
$N = 10$	$\Sigma X = 17$	$\Sigma X^2 = 45$	$\Sigma Y = 47$	$\Sigma Y^2 = 275$	$\Sigma XY = 52$
	$(\Sigma X)^2 = 289$		$(\Sigma Y)^2 = 2209$		

way to set up the data for the computational formula for r. We need to first compute ΣX, ΣX^2, $(\Sigma X)^2$, ΣY, ΣY^2, $(\Sigma Y)^2$, ΣXY, and N. First find each XY by multiplying each X times its corresponding Y, as shown in the far right-hand column in Table 7.1. Then sum the appropriate columns to get ΣX, ΣX^2, ΣY, ΣY^2, and ΣXY. Square ΣX and ΣY to get $(\Sigma X)^2$ and $(\Sigma Y)^2$.

Putting these quantities in the formula for r we get

$$r = \frac{10(52) - (17)(47)}{\sqrt{[10(45) - 289][10(275) - 2209]}}$$

To compute the numerator, multiplying 10 times 52 is 520, and 17 times 47 is 799. Rewriting the formula, we have

$$r = \frac{520 - 799}{\sqrt{[10(45) - 289][10(275) - 2209]}}$$

Complete the numerator by subtracting 799 *from* 520, which is -279. (Note the negative sign.)

To compute the denominator, first perform the operations within each bracket. In the left bracket, 10 times 45 is 450 and from that subtract 289, obtaining 161. In the right bracket, 10 times 275 is 2750 and from that subtract 2209, obtaining 541. Rewriting one more time, we have

$$r = \frac{-279}{\sqrt{[161][541]}}$$

Now multiply the quantities in the brackets together: 161 times 541 equals 87,101. After taking the square root we have

$$r = \frac{-279}{295.129}$$

Divide, and there you have it: $r = -.95$.

(*Note:* The convention among researchers is to round off a correlation coefficient to *two* decimals.)

Our r is not greater than ± 1, so our calculations *may* be correct. Also, this is a negative r, and in the scatterplot back in Figure 7.9 there is a negative relationship: As orange juice scores increase, number of doctor visits decreases. Had this been a positive relationship, r would not be negative, and we would add the $+$ sign.

Thus, we conclude that there is a negative linear relationship between juice drinking and doctor visits. On a scale of 0 to ± 1.0, where 0 is no relationship and ± 1.0 is a perfect linear relationship, this relationship is a $-.95$. Relatively speaking, this is an extremely strong linear relationship: Each amount of orange juice is associated with one relatively small range of doctor visits, and as juice scores increase, doctor visits consistently decrease. (If the correlation were this large in real life, we'd all be drinking a lot more orange juice, incorrectly thinking that this would *cause* fewer doctor visits.)

> **REMEMBER** Compute the *Pearson correlation coefficient* to describe the linear relationship between interval and/or ratio variables.

The Spearman Rank-Order Correlation Coefficient

Sometimes data involve ordinal scores (first, second, third, etc.). The **Spearman rank-order correlation coefficient** describes the linear relationship between two variables when measured by ranked scores. The symbol for the Spearman correlation coefficient is r_s. (The subscript s stands for Spearman; Charles Spearman invented this one.)

In behavioral research, ranked scores often occur because a variable is difficult to measure quantitatively. Therefore, we evaluate each participant by making qualitative judgments, and then we use these judgments to rank-order the participants. We use r_s to correlate the ranks on two such variables. Or, if we want to correlate one ranked variable with one interval or ratio variable, we transform the interval or ratio scores into ranked scores (we might rank participants with the highest interval score as 1, those with the second-highest score as 2, and so on). Either way that we obtain the ranks, r_s tells us the extent to which ranks on one variable consistently match the ranks on the other variable to form a linear relationship. If every participant has the same rank on both variables, r_s will equal $+1.0$. If every participant's rank on one variable is the opposite of his or her rank on the other variable, r_s will equal -1.0. If there is only some degree of consistent pairing of the ranks, r_s will be between 0 and ± 1.0, and if there is no consistent pairing, r_s will equal 0.

Because r_s describes the consistency with which rankings match, one use of r_s is to determine the extent to which two observers agree when they rank participants. For example, say that we ask two observers to judge how aggressively a sample of children behave while playing. Each observer assigns the rank of 1 to his or her choice for most aggressive child, 2 to the second-most aggressive child, and so on. Figure 7.10 shows the sets of ranked scores and the resulting scatterplot the two observers might produce for 9 children. In creating the scatterplot and computing r_s, we treat each observer as a variable: The scores on one variable are the rankings assigned by one observer to the children, and the scores on the other variable are the rankings assigned by the other observer. Judging from the scatterplot, it appears that there is a positive relationship here. To describe this relationship, we compute r_s.

FIGURE 7.10 Sample data for computing r_s between rankings assigned to children by observer A and observer B

Participant	Observer A: X	Observer B: Y
1	4	3
2	1	2
3	9	8
4	8	6
5	3	5
6	5	4
7	6	7
8	2	1
9	7	9

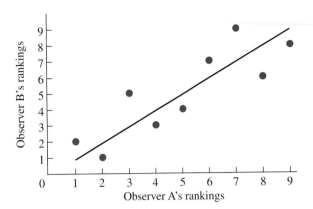

THE COMPUTATIONAL FORMULA FOR THE SPEARMAN RANK-ORDER CORRELATION COEFFICIENT IS

$$r_s = 1 - \frac{6(\Sigma D^2)}{N(N^2 - 1)}$$

N is the number of pairs of ranks, and D is the difference between the two ranks in each pair. (The formula always contains the 6 in the numerator.)

When using this formula, first arrange the data as shown in Table 7.2. For the column labeled D, you can either subtract each X from the corresponding Y or, as shown here, subtract each Y from the corresponding X. After finding the Ds, compute D^2 by squaring the difference in each pair. Finally, determine the sum of the squared differences, ΣD^2 (here ΣD^2 is 18). To compute r_s, you also need N, the number of X-Y pairs (here $N = 9$, and so $N^2 = 81$). Placing these quantities into the formula gives

TABLE 7.2 Data Arrangement for Computing r_s

Participant	Observer A: X	Observer B: Y	D	D²
1	4	3	1	1
2	1	2	−1	1
3	9	8	1	1
4	8	6	2	4
5	3	5	−2	4
6	5	4	1	1
7	6	7	−1	1
8	2	1	1	1
9	7	9	−2	4
				$\Sigma D^2 = 18$

$$r_s = 1 - \frac{6(\Sigma D^2)}{N(N^2 - 1)} = 1 - \frac{6(18)}{9(81 - 1)}$$

In the numerator, 6 times 18 is 108. In the denominator, $81 - 1$ is 80, and 9 times 80 is 720. Now

$$r_s = 1 - \frac{108}{720}$$

After dividing

$$r_s = 1 - .15$$

Subtracting yields

$$r_s = +.85$$

Thus, on a scale of 0 to ± 1.0, these rankings form a linear relationship to the extent that $r_s = +.85$. This tells us that a child receiving a particular ranking from one observer tended to receive very close to the same ranking from the other observer.

> **REMEMBER** Compute the *Spearman correlation coefficient* to describe the linear relationship between two ordinal variables.

Tied Ranks   You cannot calculate r_s until after you have dealt with any tied ranks that occur in the data. A **tied rank** occurs when two participants receive the same rank on the *same* variable (e.g., two people are tied for first on variable X). Tied ranks result in an incorrect value of r_s. Therefore, you must first resolve—correct—any tied ranks before computing r_s. As an example, say that we wish to correlate the finishing positions of the runners in two races. Table 7.3 shows such data with runners A and B tied for first place in race Y.

Resolve tied ranks using the following logic: If runners A and B had not tied for first place, then one of them would have been first and one would have been second (they were both ahead of everyone else). Therefore, *for each participant at a tied rank, assign the mean of the ranks that would have been used had there not been a tie.* The mean of 1 and 2 is 1.5, so, as in Table 7.3, runners A and B are each assigned a new Y score of 1.5. Now, in a sense, you have used up the ranks of 1 and 2, so runner C is assigned a new Y of 3. (After all, he was the third person to cross the finish line.) Like-

TABLE 7.3   Sample Data Containing Tied Ranks

Runner	Race X	Race Y		To Resolve Ties		New Y
				Tie uses up ranks		
A	4	1 }	$\cdots\rightarrow$	1 and 2,	$\cdots\rightarrow$	{ 1.5
B	3	1 }		becomes 1.5		{ 1.5
C	2	2 }	$\cdots\rightarrow$	Becomes 3rd	$\cdots\rightarrow$	{ 3
D	1	3 }	$\cdots\rightarrow$	Becomes 4th	$\cdots\rightarrow$	{ 4
.	.	.				.
.	.	.				.
.	.	.				.

wise, assign runner D the new rank of 4. If there had been additional runners, we would assign them new ranks based on what we did above. For example, if runners E, F, and G were originally tied for fourth place in race Y, they would now be tied for fifth. We would resolve this tie by assigning them each the mean of 5, 6, and 7. Then runner H would be ranked 8, and so on.

Once you have resolved all ties in the X and Y ranks, compute r_s using the new ranks and the previous formula.

The Point-Biserial Correlation Coefficient

In Chapter 12 you'll see an important use for a third type of correlation coefficient. Sometimes we want to correlate the scores from one continuous interval or ratio variable with the scores from a dichotomous variable (recall, this is a variable having only two categories). The **point-biserial correlation coefficient** describes the linear relationship between the scores from one continuous variable and one dichotomous variable. The symbol for the point-biserial correlation coefficient is r_{pb}. (The pb stands for point-biserial, and no, Mr. Point and Mr. Biserial didn't invent this one.)

As an example, say that we correlate the dichotomous variable of gender (male/female) with the interval scores from a personality test. We cannot quantify "male" and "female," so first we arbitrarily assign numbers to represent these categories: Let's use 1 to indicate male and 2 to indicate female. Think of each number as indicating whether a person scored "male" or "female." Then r_{pb} will describe how consistently certain personality test scores are paired with each gender score.

> THE COMPUTATIONAL FORMULA FOR THE POINT-BISERIAL CORRELATION COEFFICIENT IS
>
> $$r_{pb} = \left(\frac{\overline{Y}_2 - \overline{Y}_1}{S_Y}\right)\left(\sqrt{pq}\right)$$

Always call the dichotomous variable the X variable and the interval or ratio variable the Y variable. Then $\overline{Y}_1$ stands for the mean of the Y scores for one of the two groups of the dichotomous variable. (In our example, let's say that $\overline{Y}_1$ is the mean personality score for males.) The symbol $\overline{Y}_2$ stands for the mean of the Y scores for the other group. ($\overline{Y}_2$ will be the mean personality score for females.) The S_Y is the standard deviation of *all* Y scores in the data. The p stands for the proportion of the sample that is in one group of the dichotomous variable, and q stands for the proportion of the sample in the other group. (We wouldn't necessarily have an equal proportion of males and females, for example.) Each proportion is equal to the number of participants in that group divided by the total N of the study.

Say that we tested 10 people and obtained the results shown in Figure 7.11. First, compute S_Y, the standard deviation of Y. Below is the formula for the sample standard deviation, written using Ys. Substituting the data in Figure 7.11 gives

$$S_Y = \sqrt{\frac{\Sigma Y^2 - \dfrac{(\Sigma Y)^2}{N}}{N}} = \sqrt{\frac{26019 - \dfrac{(503)^2}{10}}{10}} = 8.474$$

FIGURE 7.11   Example data for computing r_{pb}

Participant	Gender: X	Test: Y	
Males			
1	1	50	
2	1	38	$\overline{Y}_1 = 45.50$
3	1	41	
4	1	53	
Females			
5	2	60	
6	2	50	
7	2	44	$\overline{Y}_2 = 53.50$
8	2	68	
9	2	53	
10	2	46	
$N = 10$		$\Sigma Y = 503$	
		$\Sigma Y^2 = 26019$	

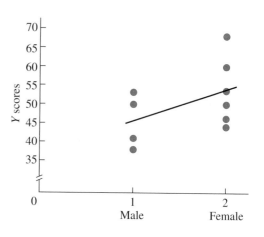

Next, the first four people scored "male," and their mean test score ($\overline{Y}_1$) is 45.50. The remaining six people scored "female," and their mean test score ($\overline{Y}_2$) is 53.50. Let's call p the proportion of the sample that scored "male," so p is 4/10, or .40. Then q is the proportion of the sample scoring "female," which is 6/10, or .60.

Filling in the formula for r_{pb} gives

$$r_{pb} = \left(\frac{\overline{Y}_2 - \overline{Y}_1}{S_Y}\right)\left(\sqrt{pq}\right) = \left(\frac{53.50 - 45.50}{8.474}\right)\left(\sqrt{(.40)(.60)}\right)$$

Subtracting 45.50 from 53.50 is 8.00, so

$$r_{pb} = \left(\frac{8.00}{8.474}\right)\left(\sqrt{(.40)(.60)}\right)$$

Dividing 8.00 by 8.474 gives .944. Also, .40 times .60 is .24, and the square root of .24 is .489. Then

$$r_{pb} = .944(.489)$$

Multiplying gives

$$r_{pb} = +.462$$

Thus, r_{pb} is +.46. We interpret this as indicating that, on a scale of 0 to ± 1.0, we have a medium-strength relationship: Somewhat close to one value of test scores tends to be associated with one gender, and test scores close to a different value tend to be associated with the other gender.

Note that in this example the dichotomous variable is a *nominal* variable, so the scores of 1 and 2 do not actually reflect more or less of the gender variable. The r_{pb} is positive only because we arbitrarily assigned a 1 to males and a 2 to females. Had we assigned females a 1 and males a 2, their locations on the X axis of the scatterplot would be reversed, and we would have a negative relationship. Likewise, the formula is $\overline{Y}_2 - \overline{Y}_1$, so above we had $53.50 - 45.50$. Had we chosen to call the female mean $\overline{Y}_1$ and the male mean $\overline{Y}_2$, we would have had $45.50 - 53.50$, which would have resulted in a negative r_{pb} of $-.46$. Thus, for any nominal variable, the absolute value of r_{pb} will accurately describe the strength of the relationship, but whether it is positive or negative depends on how you have arbitrarily arranged the data.

> *REMEMBER* Compute the *point-biserial correlation coefficient* to describe the linear relationship between an interval/ratio variable and a dichotomous variable.

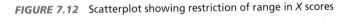

THE RESTRICTION OF RANGE PROBLEM

In collecting scores for any correlation, it is important to avoid the restriction of range problem. **Restriction of range** arises when the range between the lowest and highest scores on one or both variables is limited. This will reduce the accuracy of the correlation coefficient, producing a coefficient that is *smaller* than it would be if the range were not restricted. Here's why.

Recall that the correlation coefficient reflects the spread in Y at each X *relative* to the overall spread in all Y scores. Look at Figure 7.12. When we consider the full range of X scores, the spread in the Y scores at each X is small relative to the overall variability in Y, and the data form a narrow ellipse that hugs the regression line. Therefore, r will be relatively large, and we will correctly conclude that there is a strong relationship between these variables.

If, however, we restrict the range of X by collecting scores only between A and B in Figure 7.12, we'll have just the data in the shaded part of the scatterplot. Now the spread in Ys at each X is large relative to the overall spread in all Ys in the shaded area. This results in a scatterplot that is much more circular, and that is much worse at hugging the regression line. Therefore, a correlation coefficient using only these data will

FIGURE 7.12 Scatterplot showing restriction of range in X scores

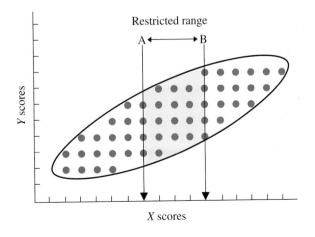

be much closer to 0, so we will conclude that this is a weak relationship. This conclusion will be wrong, however, in that, if the range had not been restricted, we would have found a much larger correlation coefficient and concluded that the relationship is stronger. (Because either variable can be the X or Y variable, restricting the range of Y has the same effect.)

> **REMEMBER** *Restricting the range* of X or Y scores leads to an underestimate of the true strength of the relationship between the variables.

How do you avoid restricting the range? Generally, restriction of range occurs when researchers are too selective when obtaining participants. Thus, if you're interested in the relationship between participants' high school grades and their subsequent salaries, don't restrict the range of grades by including only honor students: Measure all students to get the entire range of grades. Or, if you're correlating personality types with degree of emotional problems, don't restrict the study to only college students. People with severe emotional problems tend not to be in college, so we won't have their scores. Instead, include the full range of people from the general population. Likewise, any task you give participants should not be too easy (because then everyone scores in a narrow range of very high scores), nor should the task be too difficult (because then everyone obtains virtually the same low score). In all cases, the goal is to allow a wide range of scores to occur on both variables so that you have a complete description of the relationship.

CORRELATIONS IN THE POPULATION

As you know, ultimately we use a sample to describe the population we would find if we could measure it. Therefore, we use our sample correlation coefficient to estimate the correlation coefficient we would obtain if we could correlate the X and Y scores of everyone in the population. However, remember that before you can estimate a population parameter with confidence, you *must* perform inferential statistics to determine whether the sample is representative. Chapter 11 presents the inferential procedures used with correlation coefficients. If the data pass the inferential test, we assume that the correlation found in the sample is about the same as we would find in the population.

The symbol for a population correlation coefficient is ρ. This is the Greek letter rho (the Greek r). Technically, ρ is also the symbol for the population correlation coefficient when the Pearson r is used. Thus, we compute r for a random sample, which gives us an estimate of the value of ρ. However, if the data involve ranked scores, then we compute r_s and have an estimate of the population coefficient symbolized by ρ_s. If the data involve one continuous variable and one dichotomous variable, we compute r_{pb} to estimate ρ_{pb}.

A population correlation coefficient is interpreted in the same way as a sample coefficient. Thus, ρ is a number between 0 and ± 1.0, indicating either a positive or a negative linear relationship in the population. The larger the absolute value of ρ, the stronger the relationship: The more that one value of Y is associated with each X and the more closely the scatterplot for the population hugs the regression line. Interpret ρ_s and ρ_{pb} in the same way.

PUTTING IT ALL TOGETHER

It should be obvious why you should compute a correlation coefficient whenever you have a relationship to summarize. It is the one number that allows you to envision and summarize the important information in a scatterplot. For example, in our study on nervousness and the amount of coffee consumed, say that I tell you that the r in the study equals $+.50$. *Without even seeing the data,* you know there is a positive linear relationship such that as coffee consumption increases, nervousness also tends to increase. Further, because an absolute value of .50 indicates a reasonably strong relationship, you know that, given someone's coffee score, you'll have considerable accuracy in predicting his or her nervousness score. And you know that the data form a somewhat narrow, elliptical scatterplot. There is no other type of statistic that so directly summarizes a relationship. Therefore, as you'll see in later chapters, even when you conduct an experiment, always think "correlation coefficient" to describe the strength and type of relationship you've observed.

Also, be aware that correlation coefficients are tools that researchers use to check various aspects of a research design, especially the "reliability" of their measurements. The term *reliability* means "consistency." Because a correlation coefficient indicates the degree to which X and Y scores are consistently paired, we demonstrate reliability by demonstrating a relatively large correlation. For example, we used the Spearman r_s to determine how "reliably" our observers ranked the aggressiveness of children (that is, to determine what is called "interrater reliability"). Likewise, a test is reliable if the participant's scores we measured yesterday correlate positively with the same participants' scores we obtain today—if low scores today are paired with low scores from yesterday, and high scores today are paired with high scores from yesterday. Although an in-depth discussion of reliability is beyond the scope of this text, remember that when researchers describe a measurement as reliable, they mean that the measurement is consistent and, typically, that they have examined the scores in a way that produced a high positive correlation.

CHAPTER SUMMARY

1. A *relationship* exists when, as the scores on one variable change, the scores on the other variable change, so that close to one value of Y tends to be associated with one value of X. No relationship is present when, as the X scores change, the Y scores do not form a consistent pattern of change.

2. In a correlational study, the researcher does not manipulate either variable. The demonstrated relationship is not necessarily a causal relationship.

3. In a *positive linear relationship,* as the X scores increase, the Y scores tend to increase. In a *negative linear relationship,* as the X scores increase, the Y scores tend to decrease. In a *nonlinear,* or *curvilinear, relationship,* as the X scores increase, the Y scores do not only increase or only decrease.

4. A *scatterplot* is a graph that shows the location of each pair of X-Y scores in the data.

5. A scatterplot is summarized by the *regression line* drawn through it.

6. Circular or elliptical scatterplots that produce horizontal regression lines indicate no relationship. Sloping scatterplots with regression lines oriented so that as *X* increases, *Y* increases indicate a positive linear relationship. Sloping scatterplots with regression lines oriented so that as *X* increases, *Y* decreases indicate a negative linear relationship. Scatterplots producing wavy regression lines indicate curvilinear relationships.

7. A *linear correlation coefficient* describes the *type* of relationship (either positive or negative) and the *strength* of the relationship (the extent to which one value of *Y* is consistently paired with one value of *X*).

8. A smaller absolute value of the correlation coefficient indicates a weaker relationship, with greater variability in *Y* scores at each *X*, greater vertical spread in the scatterplot, and less accuracy in predicting *Y* scores based on correlated *X* scores.

9. The *Pearson correlation coefficient* (*r*) describes the linear relationship between two interval and/or ratio variables.

10. The *Spearman rank-order correlation coefficient* (r_s) describes the linear relationship between two ordinal variables.

11. The *point-biserial correlation coefficient* (r_{pb}) describes the linear relationship between scores from one continuous interval or ratio variable and one dichotomous variable.

12. The *restriction of range problem* occurs when the range of scores collected on one or both variables is limited. Then the correlation coefficient underestimates the strength of the relationship that would be found if the range were not restricted.

13. If it passes the appropriate inferential test, a sample correlation coefficient is used to estimate the corresponding population correlation coefficient: *r* estimates ρ, r_s estimates ρ_s, and r_{pb} estimates ρ_{pb}.

KEY TERMS: Can You Define the Following?

ΣXY r r_s r_{pb} ρ ρ_s ρ_{pb}
correlation coefficient *159*
curvilinear relationship *165*
linear relationship *165*
negative linear relationship *165*
nonlinear relationship *165*
Pearson correlation coefficient *171*
point-biserial correlation coefficient *177*
positive linear relationship *165*

regression line *163*
restriction of range *179*
scatterplot *162*
Spearman rank-order correlation
  coefficient *174*
strength of a relationship *166*
tied rank *176*
type of relationship *164*

REVIEW QUESTIONS

(Answers for odd-numbered questions are in Appendix C.)

1. What is the difference between an experiment and a correlational study in terms of how the researcher: (a) collects the data? (b) examines the relationship?

2. (a) You have collected data that you think show a relationship. What do you do next? (b) What is the advantage of computing a correlation coefficient? (c) What two characteristics of a linear relationship are described by a correlation coefficient?

3. What are the two reasons why you can't conclude you have demonstrated a causal relationship based on correlational research?

4. (a) When do you compute a Pearson correlation coefficient? (b) When do you compute a Spearman coefficient? (c) When do you compute a point-biserial coefficient?

5. (a) What is a scatterplot? (b) What is a regression line?

6. Why can't you obtain a correlation coefficient greater than ± 1?

7. (a) Define a positive linear relationship. (b) Define a negative linear relationship. (c) Define a curvilinear relationship.

8. As the value of r approaches ± 1.0, what does it indicate about the following? (a) the shape of the scatterplot; (b) the variability of the Y scores at each X; (c) the closeness of Y scores to the regression line; (d) the accuracy with which we can predict Y if X is known.

9. What does a correlation coefficient equal to 0 indicate about the four characteristics in question 8?

10. (a) What is the restriction of range problem? (b) What produces a restricted range? (c) How is it avoided?

11. (a) What does ρ stand for? (b) How is the value of ρ determined? (c) What does ρ tell you?

APPLICATION QUESTIONS

12. For each of the following, indicate whether it is a positive linear, negative linear, or nonlinear relationship: (a) Quality of performance (Y) increases with increased arousal (X) up to an optimal level; then quality of performance decreases with increased arousal. (b) Heavier jockeys (X) tend to win fewer horse races (Y). (c) As number of minutes of exercise increases each week (X), dieting individuals lose more pounds (Y). (d) The number of bears in an area (Y) decreases as the area becomes increasingly populated by humans (X).

13. Poindexter sees the data in question 12d and concludes, "We should stop people from moving into bear country so that we can preserve our bear population." What is the problem with Poindexter's conclusion?

14. For each of the following, give the symbol for the correlation coefficient you should compute if you measure (a) SAT scores and IQ scores; (b) taste rankings

of tea by experts and those by novices; (c) presence or absence of a head injury and scores on a vocabulary test; (d) finishing position in a race and amount of liquid consumed during the race.

15. Poindexter finds that the correlation between the X variable of number of hours studied and the Y variable of number of errors on a statistics test is $-.73$. He also finds that the correlation between the X variable of time spent taking the statistics test and the Y variable of number of errors on the test is $+.36$. He concludes that the time spent taking a test forms a stronger relationship with the number of errors than does the amount of study time. (a) Describe the relative shapes of the two scatterplots. (b) Describe the relative amount of variability in Y scores at each X in each study. (c) Describe the relative closeness of Y scores to the regression line in each study. (d) Is Poindexter correct in his conclusion? If not, what's his mistake?

16. In the correlation between orange juice consumed and number of doctor visits discussed in this chapter, does drinking more orange juice cause people to be more healthy so that they don't have to go to the doctor?

17. Foofy and Poindexter study the relationship between IQ score and high school grade average, measuring a large sample of students from PEST (the Program for Exceptionally Smart Teenagers), and compute $r = +.03$. They conclude that there is virtually no relationship between IQ and grade average. Should you agree or disagree with this conclusion? Is there a problem with their study?

18. We obtain a correlation of $+.20$ after measuring a sample of creativity test scores and intelligence test scores. (a) Can we conclude that this is similar to the relationship we'd find between all similar subjects found in nature? (b) Once we have performed the necessary procedures, what is the expected relationship between IQ and creativity? (c) Describe this relationship in terms of its consistency, its scatterplot, and whether it could be used to accurately predict creativity scores.

19. A researcher has just completed a correlational study, measuring the number of boxes of tissue purchased per week and the number of vitamin tablets consumed per week for each participant. (a) Which is the independent and the dependent variable? (b) Which variable is X? Which is Y?

20. A researcher measures the following scores for a group of people. The X variable is the number of errors on a math test, and the Y variable is the person's level of satisfaction with the performance. (a) With such ratio scores, what should the researcher conclude about this relationship? (*Hint:* Compute something!) (b) How well will he be able to predict satisfaction scores using this relationship?

Participant	Errors X	Satisfaction Y
1	9	3
2	8	2
3	4	8
4	6	5
5	7	4
6	10	2
7	5	7

21. The following data reflect whether or not someone is a college graduate (Y or N) and the score he or she obtained on a self-esteem test. To what extent is there a positive or negative linear relationship here?

Participant	College Graduate X	Self-Esteem Y
1	Y	8
2	Y	7
3	Y	12
4	Y	6
5	Y	10
6	N	2
7	N	8
8	N	6
9	N	1
10	N	9

22. In the following data the X scores reflect participants' rankings in a freshman class, and the Y scores reflect their rankings in a sophomore class. To what extent do these data form a linear relationship? (*Caution:* Think before you calculate.)

Participant	Fresh. X	Soph. Y
1	2	3
2	9	7
3	1	2
4	5	7
5	3	1
6	7	8
7	4	4
8	6	5
9	8	6

23. You want to know if a nurse's absences from work in one month (Y) can be predicted by knowing her score on a test of psychological "burnout" (X). What do you conclude from the following ratio data?

Participant	Burnout X	Absences Y
1	2	4
2	1	7
3	2	6
4	3	9
5	4	6
6	4	8
7	7	7
8	7	10
9	8	11

24. You hypothesize that students who sit toward the front of a classroom (those with a 0 on the *X* variable) perform better than those who sit toward the back of the classroom (1 on *X*) when given a brief quiz (the *Y* scores.) Do these data support your hypothesis? (Call the group with 0s group 2.)

Participant	Location X	Quiz Y
1	0	4
2	0	6
3	0	11
4	0	5
5	1	8
6	1	5
7	1	8
8	1	11
9	1	7
10	1	4

25. A researcher observes the behavior of a group of monkeys in the jungle. He determines each monkey's relative position in the dominance hierarchy of the group (with an *X* of 1 being most dominant), and also notes each monkey's relative weight (with a *Y* of 1 being the lightest). What is the relationship between dominance rankings and weight in these data?

Participant	Dominance X	Weight Y
1	1	10
2	2	8
3	5	6
4	4	7
5	9	5
6	7	3
7	3	9
8	6	4
9	8	1
10	10	2

SUMMARY OF FORMULAS

1. *The computational formula for the Pearson correlation coefficient is*

$$r = \frac{N(\Sigma XY) - (\Sigma X)(\Sigma Y)}{\sqrt{[N(\Sigma X^2) - (\Sigma X)^2][N(\Sigma Y^2) - (\Sigma Y)^2]}}$$

where X and Y stand for the scores on the X and Y variables and N is the number of pairs in the sample.

2. *The computational formula for the Spearman rank-order correlation coefficient is*

$$r_s = 1 - \frac{6(\Sigma D^2)}{N(N^2 - 1)}$$

where N is the number of pairs of ranks and D is the difference between the two ranks in each pair.

3. *The computational formula for the point-biserial correlation coefficient is*

$$r_{pb} = \left(\frac{\overline{Y}_2 - \overline{Y}_1}{S_Y}\right)\left(\sqrt{pq}\right)$$

where

$\overline{Y}_1$ is the mean of the scores on the continuous variable for one group of the dichotomous variable,

$\overline{Y}_2$ is the mean of the scores on the continuous variable for the other group of the dichotomous variable,

S_Y is the standard deviation of all of the continuous Y scores,

p is the proportion of the sample in one dichotomous group, and

q is the proportion of the sample in the other dichotomous group.

(Find p or q by dividing the number of participants in the group by N, the total number of X-Y pairs in the study.)

8

Using Linear Regression to Predict Scores

GETTING STARTED

To understand this chapter, recall the following:

- From Chapter 4 recall that without additional information, the mean is the score we predict for everyone in a sample.
- From Chapter 5 recall that when the mean is used to predict scores, the variance reflects the "average error" in predictions. Using a relationship to predict scores reduces prediction errors relative to the variance, so the relationship "accounts for variance."
- From Chapter 7 recall how to interpret r and how it describes the extent the Y scores hug the regression line.

Your goals in this chapter are to learn:

- How a regression line summarizes a scatterplot.
- How the regression equation is used to predict the Y scores at a given X.
- Which statistics measure errors in prediction when using regression.
- How the strength of the relationship determines our accuracy in predicting Y scores.
- What the proportion of variance accounted for tells us and how to compute it.

Recall that in a relationship certain Y scores are naturally paired with certain X scores. Therefore, if we know an individual's X score and the relationship between X and Y, we can predict the individual's Y score. The statistical procedure for making such predictions is called *linear regression*. In the following sections we'll examine the logic behind regression and see how to use it to predict scores. Then we'll look at ways of measuring the errors in prediction.

MORE STATISTICAL NOTATION

This chapter discusses the variance and standard deviation of the Y scores, or S_Y^2 and S_Y. The variance and standard deviation are computed here in the same ways that we computed them for the X scores. Also, recognize that, when graphed, the variability between any two Y scores is reflected by their different vertical locations along the Y axis. Therefore, the larger the values of S_Y^2 or S_Y, the more the Y scores are vertically spread out in the scatterplot.

WHY IS IT IMPORTANT TO KNOW ABOUT LINEAR REGRESSION?

A goal of research is to be able to predict when different behaviors will occur. This translates into predicting when someone has one score on a variable, and when they have a different score. We use relationships to make these predictions. It's important that you know about linear regression because it is the statistical procedure for using a relationship to predict scores. For example, the reason that students take the Scholastic Aptitude Test (SAT) when applying to some colleges is because SAT scores are somewhat positively correlated with college grades. Therefore, through regression techniques, the SAT scores of applying students are used to predict their future college performance. If the predicted grades are too low, the student is not admitted to the college. This approach is also used when people take a test when applying for a job so that the employer can predict who will be better workers, or when clinical patients are tested to identify those at risk of developing emotional problems.

> REMEMBER   The importance of *linear regression* is that it is used to predict unknown Y scores based on the X scores from a correlated variable.

UNDERSTANDING LINEAR REGRESSION

Regression procedures center around drawing the linear regression line, the summary line drawn through a scatterplot. We use regression procedures in conjunction with the Pearson correlation. While r is the *statistic* that summarizes the linear relationship, the regression line is the *line* on the scatterplot that summarizes the relationship. Always compute r first to determine whether a relationship exists. If the correlation coefficient is not 0, then perform linear regression to further summarize the relationship.

Summarizing the Scatterplot Using the Regression Line

An easy way to understand a regression line is to compare it to a line graph of an experiment. In Chapter 4 we created a line graph by plotting the mean of the Y scores for each condition—each X—and then connecting adjacent data points with straight lines. The left-hand scatterplot in Figure 8.1 shows the line graph of an experiment containing four conditions. Thus, for example, as the arrows indicate, the mean of Y at X_3 is 3. Because the mean is the central score, we assume that those participants scoring at X_3 scored *around* a Y of 3, so (1) 3 is our best single description of their scores, and (2) 3 is our best prediction for anyone else scoring at that X.

It is difficult, however, to see the *linear* (straight-line) relationship in these data, because the means do not fall on a straight line. Therefore, as in the right-hand graph in Figure 8.1, we summarize the linear relationship by drawing a regression line. Think of the regression line as a straightened-out version of the line graph: It is drawn so that it comes as close as possible to connecting the mean of Y at each X while still producing a straight line. Although not all means are on the line, the distance that some means are above the line averages out with the distance that other means are below the line. Thus, the regression line is the *best-fitting* line, because "on average" it passes through the center of the various Y means. Because each Y mean is located in the center of the corresponding Y scores, by passing through the center of the Y means, the regression line passes through the center of the Y scores. Thus, the **linear regression line** is the straight line that summarizes the linear relationship in a scatterplot by, on average, passing through the center of the Y scores at each X.

As usual, this is another descriptive procedure that allows us to summarize and envision data. Think of the regression line as reflecting the linear relationship hidden in the data. Because the actual Y scores fall above and below the line, the data only more or less fit this line. But we have no system for drawing a "more or less" linear relationship. Therefore, the regression line is how we envision what a perfect version of the linear relationship in the data would look like.

FIGURE 8.1   Comparison of a line graph and a regression line

Each data point is formed by an X-Y pair. Each asterisk (*) indicates the mean Y score at an X.

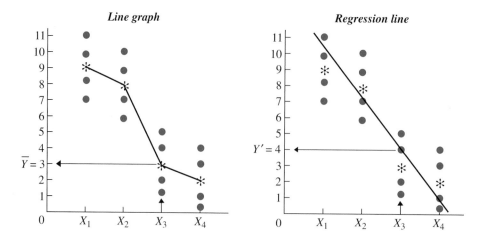

Read the regression line in the same way that you read any other graph: Travel vertically from an *X* until you intercept the regression line. Then travel horizontally until you intercept the *Y* axis. For example, as the arrows in the right-hand graph of Figure 8.1 show, the value of *Y* at X_3 is now 4. The symbol for this value is Y', pronounced "*Y* prime." Each Y' is a summary of the *Y* scores for that *X*, based on the entire linear relationship across *all X-Y* pairs in the data. Therefore, considering the entire linear relationship in Figure 8.1, those participants at X_3 scored around 4, so 4 is our best single description of their scores, and 4 is our best prediction for anyone else scoring at that *X*.

Thus, the symbol Y' stands for a **predicted *Y* score:** Each Y' is our best prediction of the *Y* scores at a corresponding *X*, based on the linear relationship that is summarized by the regression line.

Recognize that the Y' at any value of *X* is the value of *Y* falling *on* the regression line. The regression line, therefore, consists of the data points formed by pairing each possible value of *X* with its corresponding value of Y'. If you think of the line as reflecting a perfect version of the linear relationship hidden in the data, then each Y' is the *Y* score everyone would have at a particular *X* if a perfect relationship were present.

> **REMEMBER** The *linear regression line* summarizes the linear relationship in a sample, and is used to predict a participant's *Y* score—Y'—at any *X*.

Predicting Scores Using the Regression Line

Now you can see how regression techniques are used to predict unknown scores. First, we establish the relationship in a sample by computing *r*. Then, we perform the inferential procedure to determine whether the sample is representative of a relationship in the population. If it is, we use the regression line to determine the Y' for each *X*. Any Y' is the *Y* score *around* which everyone at the corresponding *X* scored in our sample. For anyone else at that *X*, we'd assume they too would score around that Y'. Therefore, we can measure the *X* scores of individuals who were not in our sample, and the corresponding Y' is our best prediction of their *Y* scores.

The emphasis on prediction in correlation and regression leads to two important terms. We'll discuss using the *X* variable to predict *Y* scores. (There are procedures out there for predicting *X* scores from *Y*.) In statistical lingo, when the *X* variable is used to predict scores, *X* is called the **predictor variable.** When the scores being predicted are on the *Y* variable, *Y* is called the **criterion variable.** Thus, when SAT scores are used to predict a student's future college grades, SAT scores are the predictor variable, and college grade average is the criterion variable. (To remember "criterion," remember that your predicted grades must meet a certain criterion for you to be admitted to the college.)

To use regression techniques, after establishing the correlation between the variables, the next step is to create the regression line. For that we use the *linear regression equation.*

THE LINEAR REGRESSION EQUATION

To draw a regression line, we don't simply eyeball the scatterplot and sketch in something that looks good. Instead, we use the linear regression equation. The **linear**

regression equation is the equation that produces the value of Y' at each X and thus defines the straight line that summarizes a relationship. When we plot the data points formed by the X-Y' pairs, and draw a line connecting them, we have the regression line. The regression equation describes two characteristics of the regression line: its *slope* and its Y *intercept.*

The **slope** is a number that indicates how slanted the regression line is and the direction in which it slants. Figure 8.2 shows examples of regression lines having different slopes. When there is no relationship, the regression line is horizontal, such as line A. Then the slope of the line is zero. A positive linear relationship produces a regression line such as lines B and C; each of these has a slope that is a positive number. Because line C is steeper, its slope is a larger positive number. A negative linear relationship, such as line D, yields a slope that is a negative number.

The **Y intercept** is the value of Y at the point where the regression line intercepts, or crosses, the Y axis. In other words, the intercept is the value of Y' when X equals 0. In Figure 8.2 line B intercepts the Y axis at +2, so the Y intercept is +2. If we extended line C, it would intercept the Y axis at a point below the X axis, so its Y intercept is a negative Y score. Because line D reflects a negative relationship, its Y intercept is the relatively high Y score of 9. Finally, line A exhibits no relationship, and its Y intercept equals +8. Notice that here the value of Y' for any value of X is always +8.

When there is no relationship, the regression line is flat and every Y' equals the Y intercept.

The regression equation works like this: The slope indicates the *direction* in which Ys change as X increases, and the *rate* at which they change. In Figure 8.2 the steeply sloped line C reflects a relatively large change in Y for each increase in X, as compared to, say, line B. The Y intercept then indicates the starting point from which the Y scores begin to change. Thus, together, the slope and intercept describe how, starting at a particular value, the Y scores change with each change in X. Then, the summary of the Y scores at each X is Y'.

FIGURE 8.2 Regression lines having different slopes and Y intercepts

Line A indicates no relationship, lines B and C indicate positive relationships having different slopes and Y intercepts, and line D indicates a negative relationship.

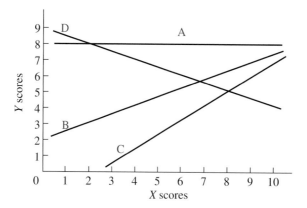

The symbol for the slope of the regression line is *b*. The symbol for the *Y* intercept is *a*. Then

---

THE LINEAR REGRESSION EQUATION IS

$$Y' = bX + a$$

This formula says that to find the value of *Y'* for a given *X*, multiply the slope (*b*) times *X* and then add the *Y* intercept (*a*).

As an example, say that a researcher has developed a paper-and-pencil test to identify workers who will be productive widget-makers. To find out whether test scores help to predict widget-making, the researcher first determines whether participants' test scores are correlated with their widget-making scores. The researcher gives the test to a small *N* of 11 people and then measures the number of widgets each makes in an hour. Figure 8.3 shows the raw scores and resulting scatterplot, with test scores as the predictor (*X*) variable and number of widgets produced per hour as the criterion (*Y*) variable.

FIGURE 8.3   Scatterplot and data for widget study

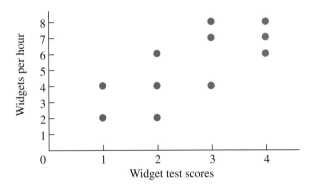

Participant	Widget Test Score: X	Widgets per Hour: Y	XY
1	1	2	2
2	1	4	4
3	2	4	8
4	2	6	12
5	2	2	4
6	3	4	12
7	3	7	21
8	3	8	24
9	4	6	24
10	4	8	32
11	4	7	28
N = 11	ΣX = 29 ΣX^2 = 89 $(\Sigma X)^2$ = 841 $\overline{X}$ = 29/11 = 2.64	ΣY = 58 ΣY^2 = 354 $(\Sigma Y)^2$ = 3364 $\overline{Y}$ = 58/11 = 5.27	ΣXY = 171

The first step is to find r:

$$r = \frac{N(\Sigma XY) - (\Sigma X)(\Sigma Y)}{\sqrt{[N(\Sigma X^2) - (\Sigma X)^2][N(\Sigma Y^2) - (\Sigma Y)^2]}}$$

so

$$r = \frac{11(171) - (29)(58)}{\sqrt{[11(89) - 841][11(354) - 3364]}}$$

The result is $r = +.736$, which rounds to $r = +.74$. This is a very strong, positive linear relationship.

To predict widget-making scores, we compute the linear regression equation. To do that, we compute the slope and the Y intercept.

Compute the slope first.

Computing the Slope

THE FORMULA FOR THE SLOPE OF THE LINEAR REGRESSION LINE IS

$$b = \frac{N(\Sigma XY) - (\Sigma X)(\Sigma Y)}{N(\Sigma X^2) - (\Sigma X)^2}$$

N is the number of pairs of scores in the sample, and X and Y are the scores in the sample. This is not a difficult formula, because we typically compute the Pearson r first. The numerator of the formula for b is the same as the numerator of the formula for r, and the denominator of the formula for b is the left-hand quantity in the denominator of the formula for r. [An alternative formula for the slope is $b = (r)(S_Y / S_X)$.]

For the widget study, substituting the appropriate values from the computations of r into the formula gives

$$b = \frac{N(\Sigma XY) - (\Sigma X)(\Sigma Y)}{N(\Sigma X^2) - (\Sigma X)^2} = \frac{11(171) - (29)(58)}{11(89) - 841}$$

After multiplying and subtracting in the numerator,

$$b = \frac{199}{11(89) - 841}$$

After completing the denominator,

$$b = \frac{199}{138} = +1.44$$

Thus, the slope of the regression line for the widget study is +1.44. This positive slope indicates a positive relationship, which fits with the positive r of +.74. Had the relationship been negative, the formula would have produced a negative slope.

We're not finished yet. Now compute the Y intercept.

Computing the *Y* Intercept

THE FORMULA FOR THE Y INTERCEPT OF THE LINEAR REGRESSION LINE IS

$$a = \overline{Y} - (b)(\overline{X})$$

First, multiply the mean of all X scores times the slope of the regression line. Then subtract that quantity from the mean of all Y scores.

For the widget study, b is +1.44, and from Figure 8.3, $\overline{Y}$ is 5.27 and $\overline{X}$ is 2.64. Filling in the above formula gives

$$a = 5.27 - (+1.44)(2.64)$$

After multiplying,

$$a = 5.27 - (+3.80) = +1.47$$

Thus, the Y intercept of the regression line for the widget study is +1.47.

We're still not finished!

Describing the Linear Regression Equation

Once you have computed the Y intercept and the slope, rewrite the regression equation, substituting the computed values for a and b. Thus, for the widget study,

$$Y' = +1.44X + 1.47$$

This is the finished regression equation that describes the linear regression line for the relationship between widget test scores and widgets-per-hour scores. Putting all of this together, the preceding computations are summarized in Table 8.1.

We're still not finished. The final step is to plot the regression line.

TABLE 8.1   Summary of Computations for the Linear Regression Equation

---

1. Compute r.

2. Compute the slope, b, where $b = \dfrac{N(\Sigma XY) - (\Sigma X)(\Sigma Y)}{N(\Sigma X^2) - (\Sigma X)^2}$

3. Compute the Y intercept, a, where $a = \overline{Y} - (b)(\overline{X})$

4. Substitute the values of a and b into the formula for the regression equation:
$$Y' = (b)(X) + a$$

Plotting the Regression Line

To plot the regression line, you need some pairs of X and Y' scores to use as data points. Therefore, choose some values of X, insert each into the finished regression equation, and calculate the value of Y' for that X. You need only two data points to draw a straight line: an X-Y' pair where X is low and an X-Y' pair where X is high. (An easy low X to use is 0, because when X equals 0, Y' equals the Y intercept.)

To see how the calculations work, we'll compute Y' for all of the X scores from the widget study (1, 2, 3, and 4). We begin with the finished regression equation:

$$Y' = +1.44X + 1.47$$

First, for $X = 1$

$$Y' = +1.44(1) + 1.47$$

Multiplying 1 times $+1.44$ and adding 1.47 yields a Y' of 2.91. Thus, people scoring 1 on the widget test are predicted to make 2.91 widgets per hour. Using the same procedure, we compute Y' for the remaining X scores. These are shown on the left in Figure 8.4.

To graph the regression line, plot the data points for the X-Y' pairs and draw the line. (Note that, as shown, published research typically does not include the scatterplot, nor is the regression line drawn through the Y intercept.)

Now we're finished. (Really.)

Using the Regression Equation to Predict Y Scores

The Y' computed for a particular X score is the predicted Y score for everyone with that X. Above, for example, people scoring an X of 1 had a predicted Y' of 2.91. Therefore, we predict that anyone else not in the sample who scores an X of 1 will also have a Y' of around 2.91. Further, we can compute Y' for any value of X that falls *within* the range of Xs in our data, even if it's a score not found in the original sample: No one scored an X of 1.5, but entering this in the regression equation yields a predicted Y score of 3.63. Do not, however, make predictions using X scores outside of the range of the original scores. Our regression equation is based only on widget test scores between 1 and 4, so

FIGURE 8.4   Regression line for widget study

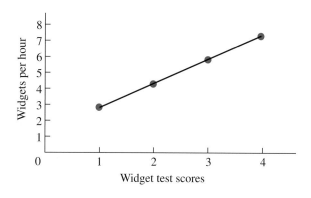

Widget Test Scores: X	Predicted Widgets per Hour: Y
1	2.91
2	4.35
3	5.79
4	7.23

we shouldn't predict a Y for an X of, for example, 6. This is because we can't be sure what the relationship is like out there at 6—maybe it's curvilinear or has a steeper slope.

That's all there is to computing the regression line and predicting scores—except for the fact that any prediction may be wrong. Therefore, the remainder of this chapter deals with errors in prediction.

ERROR WHEN THE LINEAR REGRESSION EQUATION IS USED TO PREDICT SCORES

A complete description of a relationship includes the descriptive statistics that summarize the error we have when using the relationship to predict Y scores. To describe the amount of prediction error we expect, we describe how well we can predict the actual Y scores in our sample: We pretend we don't know the scores, predict them, and then compare the predicted Y' scores to the actual Y scores. The predictions for some participants will be close to their actual Y scores while for others there may be more error, so we compute something like the average error across all predictions.

The error in a single prediction is the amount that a participant's Y score differs or *deviates* from the corresponding predicted Y' score: In symbols this is $(Y - Y')$, and it is literally the difference between the score a participant got and the score we predict he or she got. To find the average error, we find something like the average of the deviations. Therefore, we first compute Y' for everyone in the sample and subtract each Y' from its corresponding Y score. We would *like* to sum these differences, getting $\Sigma(Y - Y')$, and then find the average. But we can't. Recall that the regression line goes through the center of the scatterplot, so like a mean, the Y' scores are in the center of the scores, with Ys equally spread out above and below the Y' scores. Therefore, like a mean, the positive and negative deviations cancel out, and the sum of the deviations is always zero. Then the average error would always be zero.

To solve this problem, we *square* each deviation. The sum of the squared deviations of $Y - Y'$ is not necessarily zero, so neither is the average squared deviation. (Does this sound familiar?) When we find the average of the squared deviations, the answer is a type of variance that describes the "average" spread of the actual Y scores around—above and below—their predicted Y' scores.

Computing the Variance of the Y Scores Around Y'

The **variance of the Y scores around Y'** is the average squared difference between the actual Y scores and their corresponding predicted Y' scores. The symbol for this *sample* variance is $S_{Y'}^2$. The S^2 indicates sample variance or error, and the subscript Y' indicates that it is the error associated with using Y' to predict Y scores.

THE DEFINITIONAL FORMULA FOR THE VARIANCE OF THE Y SCORES AROUND Y' IS

$$S_{Y'}^2 = \frac{\Sigma(Y - Y')^2}{N}$$

The formula says to subtract the Y' predicted for each participant from his or her actual Y score, square each deviation, sum the squared deviations, and then divide by N. The answer is one way to measure the amount of error we have when we use a relationship and linear regression to predict Y scores.

Remember the widget study? Table 8.2 shows the X and Y scores participants obtained, as well as the Y' scores we predicted for them using the regression equation. In the column labeled $Y - Y'$, each Y' is subtracted from the corresponding Y. In the column labeled $(Y - Y')^2$, each difference is squared. Then summing the squared differences gives $\Sigma(Y - Y')^2$.

Filling in the formula for $S_{Y'}^2$,

$$S_{Y'}^2 = \frac{\Sigma(Y - Y')}{N} = \frac{22.096}{11}$$

After dividing,

$$S_{Y'}^2 = 2.009$$

With rounding,

$$S_{Y'}^2 = 2.01$$

Thus, the average squared difference between the actual Y scores and their corresponding values of Y' is 2.01. This indicates that we are "off" by something like an "average" of 2.01 when we predict participants' widgets-per-hour score (Y) based on their widget test scores (X).

> **REMEMBER**   The *variance of the* Y *scores around* Y' ($S_{Y'}^2$) is one way to describe the average error when using linear regression to predict Y scores.

TABLE 8.2   Widget Data with Computed Y' Scores

Participant	Widget Test Score: X	Widgets per Hour: Y	Predicted Widgets: Y'	Y − Y'	(Y − Y')²
1	1	2	2.91	−.91	.828
2	1	4	2.91	1.09	1.188
3	2	4	4.35	−.35	.123
4	2	6	4.35	1.65	2.723
5	2	2	4.35	−2.35	5.523
6	3	4	5.79	−1.79	3.204
7	3	7	5.79	1.21	1.464
8	3	8	5.79	2.21	4.884
9	4	6	7.23	−1.23	1.513
10	4	8	7.23	.77	.593
11	4	7	7.23	−.23	.053
$N = 11$		$\Sigma Y = 58$ $\Sigma Y^2 = 354$ $(\Sigma Y)^2 = 3364$		$\Sigma(Y - Y')^2 = 22.096$	

The reason that we use the regression procedure to predict scores is because it produces the smallest errors in prediction. First, the sum of the deviations, $\Sigma(Y - Y')$, is zero, so that over the long run, the over- and underestimates cancel out. Second, because the sum of the deviations is zero, the sum of the squared deviations is the least that it can be, and so the "average error" is the least it can be. To convey this concept, this regression technique is called the *least-squares regression method*. The phrase "sum of squared deviations" is shortened to "squares," and this method produces a sum of *squares* that is the *least* it can be. Any other method produces greater error because there are larger differences between the actual scores and the predicted scores.

Using the definitional formula for $S^2_{Y'}$ is very time consuming. However, we can replace Y' with the formulas for finding it (for finding a, b, and so on). We'll find the components for the following computational formula.

THE COMPUTATIONAL FORMULA FOR THE VARIANCE OF Y SCORES AROUND Y' IS

$$S^2_{Y'} = S^2_Y(1 - r^2)$$

This says to find the variance of all Y scores in the data (S^2_Y) and to square r. Subtract r^2 from 1 and then multiply the result times S^2_Y. The answer is $S^2_{Y'}$.

In the widget study, r was $+.736$. Using the data from Table 8.2, the S^2_Y is 4.380. Then the above formula gives

$$S^2_{Y'} = 4.380(1 - .736^2)$$

After squaring $+.736$ and subtracting the result from 1, we have

$$S^2_{Y'} = 4.380(.458)$$

so

$$S^2_{Y'} = 2.01$$

Again, the "average error" is 2.01 when predicting widget-making scores based on widget test scores.

There are, however, the usual problems when interpreting a variance like $S^2_{Y'}$. Squaring each difference between Y and Y' produces an unrealistically large number. Also, the error is measured in squared units, so our predictions above are off by 2.01 *squared* widgets. (This *must* sound familiar!) The solution is to find the square root of the variance, and the result is a type of standard deviation. Previously, however, we calculated the standard deviation by measuring the deviations of scores around the center, *mean* score. Here, we measure the deviations of scores around each center, Y' score. To distinguish the standard deviation found in regression, we call it the *standard error of the estimate*.

Computing the Standard Error of the Estimate

The **standard error of the estimate** is similar to a standard deviation of the Y scores around their Y' scores. It is the clearest way to describe the "average" error when using

Y' to predict Y scores. The symbol for the standard error of the estimate is $S_{Y'}$. (Remember, S measures the *error* in the sample, and Y' is our *estimate* of a participant's Y score.)

THE DEFINITIONAL FORMULA FOR THE STANDARD ERROR OF THE ESTIMATE IS

$$S_{Y'} = \sqrt{\frac{\Sigma(Y - Y')^2}{N}}$$

This is the same formula used previously for the variance of Y scores around Y', except with the added square root sign. Thus, to compute $S_{Y'}$, first compute $S_{Y'}^2$, and then find its square root. (Again, the basic calculation is finding the difference between participants' actual Y scores and their predicted Y' scores.)

In the widget study we computed that $S_{Y'}^2 = 2.01$. Taking the square root of this produces

$$S_{Y'} = 1.42$$

Thus, the standard error of the estimate for these data is 1.42.

To create the computational formula, we take the square root of each component of the previous computational formula for the variance of Y around Y', and have

---

THE COMPUTATIONAL FORMULA FOR THE STANDARD ERROR OF THE ESTIMATE IS

$$S_{Y'} = S_Y \sqrt{1 - r^2}$$

This says to find the square root of the quantity $1 - r^2$ and then multiply it times the standard deviation of all Y scores, (S_Y).

For the widget study, the variance in Y scores (S_Y^2) was 4.380, so taking its square root, the standard deviation of the Y scores (S_Y) is 2.093; r was $+.736$. Filling in the above formula gives

$$S_{Y'} = 2.093\sqrt{1 - .736^2}$$

Squaring $+.736$ yields .542, which subtracted from 1 gives .458. The square root of .458 is .677. Thus,

$$S_{Y'} = 2.093(.677)$$

so

$$S_{Y'} = 1.42$$

Again, the standard error of the estimate is 1.42. Because the Y scores measure widgets per hour, the standard error of the estimate is 1.42 *widgets per hour*. Therefore, we conclude that when using the regression equation to predict the number of widgets produced per hour based on a person's widget test score, we will be wrong by an "average" of about 1.42 widgets per hour.

> *REMEMBER*   The *standard error of the estimate* ($S_{Y'}$) describes the "average" error when we use Y' to predict Y scores.

It is appropriate to compute the standard error of the estimate anytime you compute a correlation coefficient, even if you do not perform regression—it's still important to know the average prediction error that using regression with your relationship would produce.

In summary, $S_{Y'}$ and $S_{Y'}^2$ indicate how much the participants' actual Y scores in a sample differ from the Y' scores we predict for them, and thus indicate the error in our predictions when we use the relationship with X to predict Y scores.

The Strength of a Relationship and Prediction Error

The strength of a relationship determines the amount of prediction error that occurs. This is because the strength of a relationship is the amount of variability—*spread*—in the Y scores at each X. For example, the left-hand scatterplot in Figure 8.5 shows a relatively strong relationship, with r close to -1. This means that there is small vertical spread in Ys at each X, so the Y scores are fairly close to the regression line, and thus close to their corresponding Y' scores. Therefore, there will be relatively small differences between the actual scores that participants obtain and the scores we predict for them, so we will have less error, and $S_{Y'}$ and $S_{Y'}^2$ will be small. Conversely, in the right-hand scatterplot is a weaker relationship (with r closer to 0), and it contains a scatterplot in which the Y scores are more spread out around the regression line. Therefore, more often, participants' actual Y scores are farther from their Y' scores, so we will have greater error, and $S_{Y'}$ and $S_{Y'}^2$ will be larger.

FIGURE 8.5   Scatterplots of strong and weak relationships

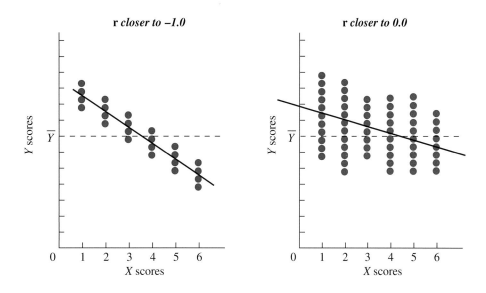

Thus, the size of $S_{Y'}$ and $S_{Y'}^2$ is *inversely* related to the size of r: The smaller the r, the larger the $S_{Y'}$ (and $S_{Y'}^2$); the larger the r, the smaller the $S_{Y'}$ (and $S_{Y'}^2$). Therefore, when we summarize a relationship with r, it not only describes the type and strength of relationship, but also indirectly tells us whether to expect large or small prediction errors when we use the relationship and regression procedures to predict scores.

> *REMEMBER*   As the strength of the relationship—and the absolute value of r increases, the actual Y scores are closer to their corresponding Y' scores, producing less prediction error and smaller values of $S_{Y'}$ and $S_{Y'}^2$.

Assumptions of Linear Regression

In order for $S_{Y'}$ and $S_{Y'}^2$ to accurately reflect the spread in Y and thus the size of the prediction errors, you must be able to make two assumptions about how the Y scores are distributed.

First, we assume homoscedasticity. **Homoscedasticity** occurs when the Y scores are spread out to the same degree at every X. The left-hand scatterplot in Figure 8.6 shows homoscedastic data for the widget study. Because the vertical spread of the Y scores around the regression line—and around each Y'—is the same at *any X*, $S_{Y'}$ will accurately describe the error in predicting Y scores at any X. Conversely, the right-hand scatterplot shows an example of heteroscedastic data. **Heteroscedasticity** occurs when the spread in Y is not equal throughout the relationship. In such cases $S_{Y'}$ will not accurately describe the "average" error for the entire relationship. In Figure 8.6, for example, $S_{Y'}$ will be much greater than the actual errors when predicting widget-making scores associated with low X scores, and much less than the error when predicting scores associated with high X scores.

Second, we assume that the Y scores at each X form an approximately normal distribution. That is, if we constructed a frequency polygon of the Y scores at each X, we

FIGURE 8.6   Illustrations of homoscedastic and heteroscedastic data

On the left, the Ys have the same spread as each X; on the right they do not.

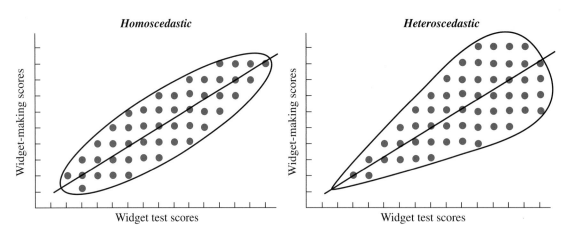

FIGURE 8.7 Scatterplot showing normal distribution of *Y* scores at each *X*

At each X, *there is a normal distribution of* Y *scores centered around* Y′.

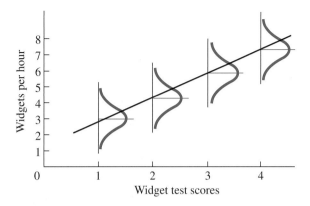

should have a normal distribution centered around *Y′*. Figure 8.7 illustrates this for the widget study. Meeting this assumption is important, because recall that in a normal distribution, approximately 68% of all scores fall between ±1 standard deviation from the mean. Because $S_{Y'}$ is like a standard deviation, if the *Y* scores are normally distributed around each *Y′*, then approximately 68% of all *Y* scores will be between $±1S_{Y'}$ from the regression line. Thus, in the widget study, $S_{Y'}$ is 1.42, so we expect approximately 68% of the actual *Y* scores to be between ±1.42 from each value of *Y′*. Therefore, we will know where over two-thirds of the actual *Y* scores at each *X* are located and thus the size of most of our errors.

You've seen that $S_{Y'}$ and $S_{Y'}^2$ reflect the size of our prediction errors when we use a relationship and regression techniques to predict *Y* scores. Therefore, we can use these statistics to evaluate how useful the relationship is in terms of how large its prediction errors will be. As you saw in Chapter 5, this evaluation process goes by the strange name of "the proportion of variance accounted for."

THE PROPORTION OF VARIANCE ACCOUNTED FOR

Recall that *the proportion of variance accounted for* is the way to evaluate the usefulness or importance of a relationship. Otherwise, we have to be subjective in our evaluation. In the widget study, for example, *r* was +.74, implying that this relationship provides reasonably accurate predictions of *Y* scores. The problem is that this is not a quantitative description of the error. The $S_{Y'}$ indicates our predictions will be off by an "average" of 1.42, or using $S_{Y'}^2$ by an "average" of 2.01, but we don't know if, in the grand scheme of things, such an error rate is large or small. The proportion of variance accounted for solves these problems, because it involves a frame of reference: We examine the errors that occur when we use the relationship to make predictions compared to the errors that occur when we don't use the relationship.

To understand this, say that the widget study produced the scatterplots in Figure 8.8. In the graph on the left we'll ignore the relationship with X and try to predict Y scores.

Without the relationship, our fall-back position is to compute the overall mean of all Y scores (Yw) and predict it as everyone's Y score.

The mean will be centered vertically among the Y scores, and we will predict this same score for everyone, regardless of their X score. Thus, it is as if we have the horizontal regression line shown in the left-hand scatterplot: At any X, we travel vertically until we reach the line, and then horizontally to obtain the corresponding predicted Y score, which in every case will be the score equal to $\bar{Y}$. (In the figure we'll predict the score of 4 for everyone.)

Our error here is the difference between the actual Y scores that participants got and the $\bar{Y}$ that we predict they got. In symbols, this error is the quantity $(Y - \bar{Y})$ for each participant. Based on this, as we saw in Chapter 5, our "average error" is the *sample variance* or S_Y^2. Thus, our error will equal whatever extent that the Y scores are vertically spread out around $\bar{Y}$.

> **REMEMBER** When we do *not* use the relationship to predict scores, our error is S_Y^2 which is computed by finding each $Y - \bar{Y}$, the difference between the Y score a participant actually obtained and the $\bar{Y}$ score we predict is obtained.

However, let's use the relationship with X to predict scores, as in the right-hand scatterplot of Figure 8.8. Here, we have the actual regression line through the center of the scatterplot: For any X score, we travel up to the line and then over to obtain the corresponding Y' score. Now out error is the difference between the actual Y scores that participants got and the Y' that we predict they got. In symbols, this is the quantity $(Y - Y')$ for each participant. Based on this, as we saw earlier in this chapter, a way to measure our "average error" is the *variance of Y scores around Y'* or $S_{Y'}^2$. Our error here will equal whatever extent that the Y scores are vertically spread out around Y'.

FIGURE 8.8 Scatterplots showing predictions when using and not using a relationship.

On the left, when a relationship is ignored, the mean of Y is always predicted; on the right, when using the relationship, the Y' scores are predicted.

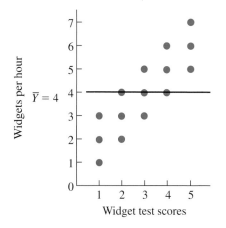
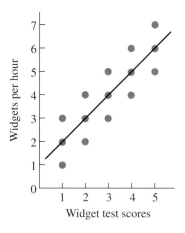

REMEMBER When we *do* use the relationship to predict scores, our error is $S_{Y'}^2$, which is computed by finding each $Y - \overline{Y}$, the difference between the Y score a participant actually obtained and the Y' we predict is obtained.

Understand two things about the prediction errors when we use a relationship. First, a relationship "tells us" the Y scores that tend to occur with an X, so we will have some idea when a particular Y score occurs. Therefore, *our error when using the relationship will always be smaller than when we don't use the relationship.* You can see this in Figure 8.8 because the data points are closer to the regression line and thus closer to their Y' scores than they are to the horizontal line that represents predicting the $\overline{Y}$.

Second, the stronger the relationship, the better off we are. You've seen that a stronger relationship produces smaller prediction errors, so a stronger relationship reduces our error even more relative to the error we'd have if we ignore the relationship. You can see this by returning to Figure 8.5 and noting that when r is larger, the actual Y scores are even closer to the regression line and to Y' than they are to the horizontal dashed line that represents predicting the $\overline{Y}$ for everyone.

To calculate the proportion of variance accounted for and evaluate a particular relationship, we compare the error produced when using the relationship (the $S_{Y'}^2$) to the error produced when not using the relationship (the S_Y^2). First, we'll accomplish this using the definitional formula.

THE DEFINITIONAL FORMULA FOR THE PROPORTION OF VARIANCE IN Y THAT IS ACCOUNTED FOR BY A LINEAR RELATIONSHIP WITH X IS

$$\text{Proportion of variance accounted for} = 1 - \left(\frac{S_{Y'}^2}{S_Y^2} \right)$$

For example, for the widget-making data back in Table 8.2, when we ignore the relationship and predict the overall mean of Y for every participant, our "average" error is the S_Y^2 of 4.38. But, when we use the relationship and predict Y' for each participant, the "average" error is the $S_{Y'}^2$ of 2.01. The formula says to first make a ratio of $S_{Y'}^2/S_Y^2$, so we have

$$\frac{S_{Y'}^2}{S_Y^2} = \frac{2.01}{4.38} = .46$$

This ratio tells us the proportion of the error we have when not using the relationship that is still present when we do use the relationship. Here, the error we have when using the relationship is .46 of the error that occurs when we don't use the relationship.

But, if the error *with* the relationship is only .46 of the error *without* the relationship, then using the relationship *eliminates* .54 of that error. As in the formula, this proportion is found by subtracting the ratio from 1. Altogether,

$$1 - \frac{2.01}{4.38} = 1 - .46 = .54$$

Thus, using this relationship eliminates .54 or 54% of the error we'd have when not using the relationship, so we are 54% more accurate with it. In other words, if we know participants' X score on the widget test and use this relationship, we are "on average" 54% closer to predicting their actual widget-making (Y) scores, than if we don't use this relationship. In statistical terms, therefore, this relationship accounts for .54 of the variance in Y scores. The **proportion of variance accounted for** is the proportion of our prediction errors when we use the mean of Y to predict Y scores that is eliminated by using the relationship with X to predict the scores. In other words, it is the proportional improvement in predictions achieved by using a relationship to predict scores, compared to if we do not use the relationship.

Understand that the term "proportion of variance accounted for" is a shortened version of "the proportion of variance in Y scores that is accounted for by the relationship with X." The variance in Y that we account for is S_Y^2, and it reflects all of the differences among the Y scores. "Accounting" for the variance means being able to predict when differences in Y scores occur. When we do not use the relationship, we cannot predict any of these differences because we continuously predict the same $\overline{Y}$ for everyone. When using the relationship, however, we predict *different* scores for different participants: We can, at least, predict a lower Y score for those who tend to score lower, a medium Y score for those scoring medium, and so on. Then, to some extent, we're closer to predicting when participants have one Y score and when they have *different* Y scores. Therefore, of all the differences in Y scores measured by S_Y^2, using the relationship helps us to predict, or "account for," some proportion of them, so we say that we account for some proportion of the variance in Y.

> **REMEMBER**   *The proportion of variance accounted for* is the proportional improvement in accuracy when using the relationship with X to predict Y scores, compared to our accuracy when using the $\overline{Y}$ to predict Y scores.

Using *r* to Compute the Proportion of Variance Accounted For

Using the above definitional formula is rather time consuming. However, we've seen that the size of r is related to the amount of error in our predictions by the formula

$$S_{Y'}^2 = S_Y^2(1 - r^2)$$

In fact, this formula contains all of the components of the previous definitional formula, so solving for the proportion of variance accounted for, we have

$$r^2 = 1 - \frac{S_{Y'}^2}{S_Y^2}$$

Because 1 minus the ratio $S_{Y'}^2/S_Y^2$ is the definitional formula for the proportion of variance accounted for, we have the following computational formula.

> *THE COMPUTATIONAL FORMULA FOR THE PROPORTION OF VARIANCE IN Y THAT IS ACCOUNTED FOR BY A LINEAR RELATIONSHIP WITH X IS*
>
> $$\text{Proportion of variance accounted for} = r^2$$

Not too tough! All you do is compute r (which you would anyway) and square it. Then you have computed the proportion of variance in Y scores that is accounted for by the relationship with X. (Yes, it took a long time to get here, but to understand r^2, you must understand $1 - S^2_{Y'}/S^2_Y$.)

Previously, we saw that in the widget study, the relationship accounted for .54 of the variance in Y scores. Because r was $+.736$, the proportion of variance accounted for is $(.736)^2$, which also is .54.

In statistical language, r^2 is called the **coefficient of determination,** which is merely another name for the proportion of variance accounted for. The proportion of variance *not* accounted for is called the **coefficient of alienation.**

> *THE COMPUTATIONAL FORMULA FOR THE PROPORTION OF VARIANCE NOT ACCOUNTED FOR IS*
>
> $$\text{Proportion of variance not accounted for} = 1 - r^2$$

Subtracting r^2 from 1 takes you back to the ratio of $S^2_{Y'}/S^2_Y$, which is the proportion of the error we have without using the relationship that still remains even when we use the relationship. In the widget study, $r^2 = .54$, so we still *cannot* account for $1 - .54$, or .46, of the variance in the Y scores.

Note that r^2 describes the proportion of variance that is accounted for by the *sample* relationship. If the r passes the inferential statistical test, we can conclude that this relationship holds for the population. Then the value of r^2 is a *rough* estimate of the proportion of variance in Y scores that is accounted for by the relationship in the population. Thus, we expect to be roughly 54% more accurate if we use the relationship and widget test scores to predict any other, unknown widget-making scores in the population.

Using the Variance Accounted For

The reason we make such a big deal out of the proportion of variance accounted for is that it is *the* statistical measure of how "important" a particular relationship is. Remember, scores reflect behavior. When we use a relationship with X to predict different Y scores, we are actually predicting differences in behavior Y. The goal of behavioral research is to understand differences in behavior. Therefore, the greater the proportion of variance accounted for by the relationship, the more accurately we can predict differences in behavior, and thus the more scientifically important and informative the relationship is.

For example, at the beginning of this discussion we wondered how to evaluate the widget-making relationship where r was $+.74$ and $S_{Y'}$ was 1.42. With r^2 equal to .54, we now know: We are .54 or 54% better off using this relationship than if we did not. And, our average prediction error of 1.42 is 54% less than we'd have without using this relationship. All in all, this is a useful and thus important relationship, and the widget test should prove valuable for identifying future successful widget makers.

This would be deemed an especially useful relationship because, in real research, we typically find rs in the neighborhood of $\pm.30$ to $\pm.50$. Squaring these translates into accounting for between only .09 and .25 of the variance. Given the complexity of nature and the behaviors of living organisms, we are unlikely to find an r that is very close to ±1.0, so we are also unlikely to find a relationship that accounts for close to 100% of the variance.

We also use r^2 when comparing different relationships to see which is more informative. Say that we find a relationship between the length of a person's hair and his or her creativity, but r is only $+.02$. Yes, this r indicates a relationship, but such a weak one is virtually useless. The fact that $r^2 = .0004$ indicates that knowing someone's hair length improves predictions about creativity by only four-hundredths of *one* percent! However, say that we also find a relationship between a person's age and his or her creativity, and here r is $-.40$. This relationship is more important, at least in a statistical sense, because $r^2 = .16$. Age is the more important variable for understanding differences in creativity because knowing participants' ages gets us 16% closer to accurately predicting their creativity. Knowing their hair length gets us only .04% closer to accurately predicting their creativity.

The logic of r^2 is applied to any relationship. For example, in the previous chapter we discussed r_s and r_{pb}. Squaring these coefficients also indicates the proportion of variance accounted for. (It is as if we performed the appropriate regression analysis, computed $S^2_{Y'}$ and S^2_Y, and so on.) Likewise, as you'll see in later chapters, we also determine the proportion of variance accounted for in experiments: We describe the proportion of variance in the dependent variable (the Y scores) accounted for by using the relationship with the independent variable (the X scores). In all cases the answer indicates how useful the relationship is.

> **REMEMBER** Computing the proportion of variance accounted for is the way to evaluate the scientific importance of a relationship.

Computing r^2 goes hand in hand with computing the other components of correlation and regression. To help you remember them all, the procedures discussed in this chapter are summarized in Table 8.3.

TABLE 8.3 Summary of Computations in Linear Regression

1. Compute r.

2. Compute the slope, b, where $b = \dfrac{N(\Sigma XY) - (\Sigma X)(\Sigma Y)}{N(\Sigma X^2) - (\Sigma X)^2}$

3. Compute the Y intercept, a, where $a = \overline{Y} - (b)(\overline{X})$

4. Substitute the values of a and b into the formula for the regression equation
   $Y' = (b)(X) + a$

5. Compute the standard error of the estimate ($S_{Y'}$) to describe the "average error" in prediction.

6. Compute r^2 to describe the proportion of variance in Y scores accounted for by the relationship.

A WORD ABOUT MULTIPLE CORRELATION AND REGRESSION

Sometimes we discover several *X* variables that each help us to more accurately predict a *Y* variable. For example, there is a positive correlation between a person's height and his or her ability to shoot baskets in basketball: The taller people are, the more baskets they tend to make. There is also a positive correlation between how much people practice basketball and their ability to shoot baskets: The more they practice, the more baskets they tend to make. Obviously, to be as accurate as possible in predicting how well people shoot baskets, we should consider both how tall they are and how much they practice. This example has two predictor variables (height and practice) that predict one criterion variable (basket shooting). When we wish to simultaneously consider *multiple predictor variables* for *one criterion variable,* we use the statistical procedures known as multiple correlation and multiple regression. Although the computations involved in these procedures are beyond the scope of this text, understand that the **multiple correlation coefficient,** called the *multiple R,* indicates the strength of the relationship between the multiple predictors taken together, and the criterion variable. The **multiple regression equation** allows us to predict someone's *Y* score by simultaneously considering his or her scores on all *X* variables. The squared multiple *R* is the proportion of variance in the *Y* variable accounted for by using the relationship with the *X* variables to predict *Y* scores.

PUTTING IT ALL TOGETHER

This and the previous chapter introduced many new symbols and concepts. However, they boil down to three major topics:

1. *The Correlation Coefficient:* The correlation coefficient communicates the *type* and *strength* of a relationship. Use it to understand the direction and consistency in the relationship and to envision its scatterplot. The larger the coefficient, the stronger the relationship—meaning that the more consistently one value of *Y* is paired with only one value of *X,* and the closer the data come to forming a perfect straight-line relationship.

2. *The Regression Equation:* The regression equation allows you to draw the regression line through the scatterplot so that you can see the linear relationship hidden in the data, and to use the relationship with *X* to predict any individual's *Y* score.

3. *Errors in Prediction:* The standard error of the estimate indicates the "average" amount your predictions will be in error when using a particular relationship. Compute the proportion of variance accounted for by squaring any correlation coefficient. This tells you how much smaller the errors in predicting *Y* scores are when you use the relationship, compared to if you do not use the relationship.

CHAPTER SUMMARY

1. *Linear regression* is the procedure for predicting unknown *Y* scores based on correlated *X* scores. It produces the *linear regression line,* which is the best-fitting straight line that summarizes a linear relationship.

2. The *linear regression equation* includes the *slope,* indicating how much and in what direction the regression line slants, and the Y *intercept,* indicating the value of Y when the line crosses the Y axis.

3. For each X the regression equation produces Y', which is the predicted Y score for that X. The regression line connects all $X - Y'$ data points.

4. The *standard error of the estimate* ($S_{Y'}$) is similar to a standard deviation of the Y scores around their respective Y' scores, and is the clearest way to describe the "average error" when using Y' to predict Y scores. The differences (and error) between Y and Y' also may be summarized by the *variance of the* Y *scores around* Y' ($S_{Y'}^2$).

5. Regression requires the assumptions that (1) the Y scores are *homoscedastic,* meaning that the spread in the Y scores around all Y' scores is the same, and (2) the Y scores at each X are normally distributed around their corresponding value of Y'.

6. The stronger the relationship, the smaller the values of $S_{Y'}$ and $S_{Y'}^2$ because then the Y scores are closer to Y' and thus the smaller the difference between Y and Y'.

7. The *proportion of variance accounted for* is the proportional improvement in accuracy that is achieved by using the relationship to predict Y scores, rather than using $\overline{Y}$ to predict scores. This *coefficient of determination* is computed by squaring the correlation coefficient.

8. The proportion of variance not accounted for—the *coefficient of alienation*—equals $1 - r^2$. This is the proportion of the prediction error that is not eliminated when Y' is the predicted score instead of $\overline{Y}$.

9. The proportion of variance accounted for indicates the statistical importance of a relationship.

10. *Multiple correlation and multiple regression* are procedures for describing the relationship when multiple predictor (X) variables are simultaneously used to predict scores on one criterion (Y) variable.

KEY TERMS: Can You Define the Following?

Y' b a $S_{Y'}^2$ $S_{Y'}$ r^2

coefficient of alienation *207*
coefficient of determination *207*
criterion variable *191*
heteroscedasticity *202*
homoscedasticity *202*
linear regression equation *192*
linear regression line *190*
multiple correlation coefficient *209*

multiple regression equation *209*
predicted Y score *191*
predictor variable *191*
proportion of variance accounted for *206*
slope *192*
standard of error of the estimate *199*
variance of the Y scores around Y' *197*
Y intercept *192*

REVIEW QUESTIONS

(Answers for odd-numbered questions are in Appendix C.)

1. What is the linear regression line?
2. What is the linear regression procedure used for?
3. What is Y', and how do you obtain it?
4. What is the general form of the linear regression equation? Identify its component symbols.
5. (a) What does the Y intercept indicate? (b) What does the slope indicate?
6. Distinguish between the *predictor variable* and the *criterion variable* in linear regression.
7. (a) What is the name for $S_{Y'}$? (b) What does $S_{Y'}$ tell you about the spread in the Y scores? (c) What does $S_{Y'}$ tell you about your errors in prediction?
8. (a) What two assumptions must you make about the data in order for the standard error of the estimate to be accurate, and what does each mean? (b) How does heteroscedasticity lead to an inaccurate description of the data?
9. How is the value of $S_{Y'}$ related to the size of r? Why?
10. When are multiple regression procedures used?
11. (a) What are the two statistical names for r^2? (b) How do you interpret r^2?

APPLICATION QUESTIONS

12. What research steps must you go through in order to use the relationship between a person's intelligence and grade average in high school, so that if you know a person's IQ score, you can more accurately predict the person's average?
13. Explain how colleges use SAT scores to predict the future grades of college-bound students.
14. (a) Explain conceptually why the proportion of variance accounted for equals 1.0 with a perfect correlation. (b) Why should you expect most relationships to account for only about 9% to 25% of the variance?
15. What do you know about a research project when you read that it employed multiple correlation and regression procedures?
16. A researcher determined that the correlation between statistics grades and scores on an admissions test to graduate school is $r = +.41$. (a) For $S_Y = 3.90$, compute the standard error of the estimate for these data. (b) If the researcher predicts the overall mean score on the admissions test for each student, using variance, on average how much error can she expect? (c) If the researcher predicts admissions test scores based on the regression equation and statistics grades, using variance, on average how much error can she expect? (d) What proportion of the error in part b remains even after using the regression equation? (e) What proportion of the error in part b is eliminated by using the regression equation? (f) What is your answer in part e called?

17. Bubbles has a statistics grade of 70, and Foofy has a grade of 98. (a) Based on the data in question 16, who is predicted to have a higher grade on the admissions test? Why? (b) Subsequently, Bubbles received the higher test score. How can this be explained?

18. Poindexter conducted a correlational study measuring participants' ability to concentrate and their ability to remember, finding $r = +.30$. He also correlated subjects' ability to visualize information and their memory ability, obtaining an $r = +.60$. He concludes that there is twice as consistent, and therefore twice as informative, a relationship between visualization and memory as there is between concentration and memory. Why do you agree or disagree?

19. (a) In question 18 what advanced statistical procedures can Poindexter employ to improve his predictions about memory ability even more? (b) Say that the resulting correlation coefficient is .67. Using the proportion of variance accounted for, explain what this means.

20. A researcher finds that variable A accounts for 15% of the variance in variable B. Another researcher finds that variable C accounts for 25% of the variance in variable B. Why is variable C scientifically more important?

21. You measure how much people are initially attracted to a person of the opposite sex and how anxious they become during their first meeting with him or her. For the following ratio data, answer the questions below.

Participant	X	Y
1	2	8
2	6	14
3	1	5
4	3	8
5	6	10
6	9	15
7	6	8
8	6	8
9	4	7
10	2	6

(a) Compute the statistic that describes the nature of the relationship formed by the data. (b) Compute the linear regression equation. (c) What anxiety score do you predict for a person who has an attraction score (X) of 9? (d) When using this relationship, what is the "average" amount of error you should expect in your predictions?

22. (a) For the relationship in question 21, what is the proportion of variance in Y that is accounted for? (b) What is the proportion of variance not accounted for? (c) Why is or is not this a valuable relationship?

23. A researcher computes an r_s of $+.20$ when correlating the rankings of students in their statistics class (X) with their rankings in terms of how studious they are (Y). Another researcher computes an r_{pb} of $-.20$ when correlating a person's gender (X) with his or her studiousness. Using the proportion of variance accounted for, interpret each result.

24. Using two questionnaires, a researcher measures how positive a person's mood is (X) and how creative he or she is (Y), obtaining the following interval scores.

Participant	X	Y
1	10	7
2	8	6
3	9	11
4	6	4
5	5	5
6	3	7
7	7	4
8	2	5
9	4	6
10	1	4

(a) Compute the statistic that summarizes this relationship. (b) What is the predicted creativity score for anyone scoring 3 on the mood questionnaire? (c) If your prediction is in error, what is the amount of error you expect to have? (d) How much smaller will your error be if you use the regression equation than if you merely use the overall mean creativity score as the predicted score for all participants?

25. Dorcas complains that it is unfair to use SAT scores to determine college admittance because she might do much better in college than predicted. (a) What statistic(s) will indicate whether her complaint is correct? (b) In reality, the positive correlation coefficient between SAT scores and college performance is not all that high. What does this tell you about how useful the SAT is for predicting college success?

SUMMARY OF FORMULAS

1. *The formula for the linear regression equation is*

$$Y' = bX + a$$

where b stands for the slope of the line, X stands for an X score, and a stands for the Y intercept.

2. *The formula for the slope of the linear regression line is*

$$b = \frac{N(\Sigma XY) - (\Sigma X)(\Sigma Y)}{N(\Sigma X^2) - (\Sigma X)^2}$$

where N is the number of pairs of scores in the sample, and X and Y are the scores in the sample.

3. *The formula for the Y intercept of the linear regression line is*

$$a = \overline{Y} - (b)(\overline{X})$$

where $\overline{Y}$ is the mean of all Y scores, b is the slope of the regression line, and $\overline{X}$ is the mean of all X scores.

4. *The computational formula for the variance of Y scores around Y' is*

$$S_{Y'}^2 = S_Y^2(1 - r^2)$$

where S_Y^2 is the variance of the Y scores in the sample.

5. *The computational formula for the standard error of the estimate is*

$$S_{Y'} = S_Y\sqrt{1 - r^2}$$

where S_Y is the standard deviation of the Y scores in the sample.

6. *The computational formula for the proportion of variance in Y that is accounted for by a linear relationship with X is*

$$\text{Coefficient of determination} = r^2$$

7. *The computational formula for the proportion of variance not accounted for is*

$$\text{Coefficient of alienation} = 1 - r^2$$

4 //////////

INFERENTIAL STATISTICS

Believe it or not, you now know the common descriptive methods used in behavioral research: In experiments we describe central tendency (usually, with the mean) and variability (usually, with the standard deviation). In correlational studies we describe the relationship (usually using the Pearson *r*) and summarize the relationship (with regression).

Now we are ready to discuss how *inferential statistics* are used in research. Inferential procedures are for deciding what we'd find if we could perform a study on the entire population. Would we find that the population has approximately the same mean as our sample? If we observe different samples that produce different means, would we find approximately the same difference between the population means? Would we find that the correlation coefficient in the population is about the same as the correlation coefficient in our sample?

The problem is that we cannot *know* what the population contains. Instead, inferential procedures are ways to make decisions about the population that are *likely* to be correct. Therefore, the first step in understanding these procedures is to understand probability. In the next chapter we discuss the concept of probability and see how it is used to make statistical decisions. Subsequent chapters then deal with the various inferential procedures used with different research designs.

9

Probability: Making Decisions about Chance Events

This chapter sets the foundation for understanding inferential procedures. Therefore, there is little in the way of how to conduct research and there are few formulas. Instead, the chapter introduces you to the wonderful world of probability. As you'll see, researchers combine their knowledge of probability with the standard normal curve model to make decisions about data. We will keep the discussion simple, because you do not need to be an expert in probability. However, you do need to understand the basic logic of chance.

MORE STATISTICAL NOTATION

In daily conversation the words *chances, odds,* and *probability* are used interchangeably. In statistics, however, they have different meanings. Odds are expressed as fractions or ratios ("The odds of winning are 1 in 2"). Chance is expressed as a percentage ("There is a 50% chance of winning"). Probability is expressed as a decimal ("The probability of winning is .50"). For inferential procedures, always express the answers you compute as probabilities.

The symbol for probability is the lowercase *p*. The probability of a particular event—such as event A—is $p(A)$, which is pronounced "*p* of A" or "the probability of A."

WHY IS IT IMPORTANT TO KNOW ABOUT PROBABILITY?

After studying the relationship in the sample, we can never "prove" what the relationship in the population will be. There will always be some uncertainty, and that's where inferential statistics and probability come in. Inferential statistics provide a system for using probability to decide whether it is likely that (1) the sample data represent a particular population, so we're confident we'd find a similar relationship in the population, or (2) the sample data do not represent the particular population, so we're unsure that we'd find the relationship in the population. To understand inferential statistics, therefore, you must first understand the logic of probability: what probability is, how to make decisions based on it, and how to use it to decide about the representativeness of samples.

THE LOGIC OF PROBABILITY

Probability is used to describe random, chance events. Such events occur when nature is being fair—when there is no bias toward one event over another (no rigged roulette wheels or loaded dice). Thus, a chance event occurs or does not occur merely because of the luck of the draw. In statistical work, probability is our way of mathematically describing how luck operates to produce an event.

But hold on! How can we describe an event that happens only by chance? By paying attention to how *often* the event occurs when chance is operating. The probability of any event is based on how often the event occurs *over the long run.* Intuitively, we use this logic all the time: If event A happens frequently over the long run, then we tend to think that it is likely to happen again, and we say that it has a high probability. If event B happens infrequently, then we tend to think that it is unlikely, and we say that it has a low probability.

When we decide that event A happens frequently, we are making a *relative* judgment. That is, we determine the event's *relative frequency:* the proportion of time that A occurs out of all events that might occur in this situation. In statistical terminology, all possible events that can occur in a given situation form the *population* of events. Thus, the **probability** of an event is equal to the event's relative frequency in the population of possible events that can occur.

> REMEMBER   The *probability* of an event equals the event's relative frequency in the population.

If a population contains all possible events that might occur, then the event or events that *do* occur make up a sample from that population. Thus, probability describes our expectation that a sample will contain a particular event when we randomly sample from a particular population. To determine this, we assume that an event's past relative frequency in the population will continue in the future. To indicate our confidence that the event will occur in any single sample, we express this relative frequency as a probability. For example, I am a rotten typist, and while typing the manuscript for this book, say that I randomly made typos 80% of the time. This means that in the population of my typing, typos occur with a relative frequency of .80. We expect the relative frequency of typos to continue at a rate of .80 in anything else I type. This expected relative frequency is expressed as a probability, so the probability is .80 that I will make a typo when I type the next woid.

Thus, a probability indicates the likelihood of an event when a particular population is randomly sampled. It is how we express our confidence that a particular event will occur. So, if event A has a relative frequency of zero in a particular situation, then the probability of event A is zero. This means that we do not expect A to occur in this situation, because it never does. But if event A has a relative frequency of .10 in this situation, then A has a probability of .10: Because it occurs only 10% of the time in the population, we expect it to occur in only 10% of our samples, so we have some—but not much—confidence that A will occur in the next sample. On the other hand, if A has a probability of .95, we are confident that it will occur: It occurs 95% of the time in the population, so we expect it in 95% of our samples. At the most extreme, event A's relative frequency can be 1: It is 100% of the population, so its probability is 1. Here, we are positive it will occur in this situation because it always does.

An event cannot happen less than 0% of the time or more than 100% of the time, so a probability can *never* be less than 0 or greater than 1. Also, all events in a population together constitute 100% of the population. This means that the relative frequencies of all events must add up to 1, so the probabilities of all events in the population must also add up to 1. Thus, if the probability of my making a typo at any moment is .80, then because $1 - .80 = .20$, the probability is .20 that any word I type will be error free.

Understand that except when p equals either 0 or 1, we are never certain that an event will or will not occur. The probability of an event is its relative frequency *over the long run* (in the population), so it is up to chance whether a particular sample contains the event. For example, even though I make typos 80% of the time, I may go for quite a while without making a typo. That 20% of the time I make no typos has to occur sometime. Thus, although the probability is .80 that I will make a typo in each word, it is only over the long run that we expect to see precisely 80% typos.

People who fail to understand that probability implies *over the long run* fall victim to the "gambler's fallacy." For example, after observing my errorless typing for a while, the fallacy is thinking that errors "must" occur now, essentially concluding that errors have become more likely. Or, say we're flipping a coin and get 7 heads in a row. The fallacy is thinking that a head is now less likely to occur, because it's already occurred too often (as if the coin says, "Hold it. That's enough heads for a while!"). The mistake of the gambler's fallacy is failing to recognize that whether an event occurs or not, its probability is not altered, because probability is determined by what happens "over the long run."

COMPUTING PROBABILITY

Computing the probability of an event is simple: We need only determine its relative frequency in the population. When we know the relative frequency of every possible event in a population, we have a probability distribution. A **probability distribution** indicates the probability of all possible events in a population.

Creating Probability Distributions

There are two ways to create a probability distribution. One way is to measure the relative frequency of every event in the population, creating an *empirical probability distribution.* Typically, however, we cannot observe the entire population, so we create the probability distribution by observing samples from the population. We assume that the relative frequency of an event in a random sample represents the relative frequency of the event in the population.

For example, say that Dr. Fraud is sometimes very cranky, and apparently his crankiness is random. We observe him on 18 days and he is cranky on 6 of them. Relative frequency equals $f/N,$ so the relative frequency of Dr. Fraud's crankiness is 6/18, or .33. We expect that he will continue to be cranky 33% of the time. Thus, the probability that he will be cranky today is $p = .33$. Conversely, he was not cranky on 12 of the 18 days, which is 12/18, or .67. Thus, $p = .67$ that he will not be cranky today. Because his cranky days plus his noncranky days constitute all possible events, we have the complete probability distribution for his crankiness.

Statistical procedures usually rely on the other way to create a probability distribution. A **theoretical probability distribution** is a theoretical model of the relative frequencies of events in a population. We devise theoretical probability distributions based on how we assume nature distributes events in the population. From such a model, we determine the expected relative frequency of each event in the population. This expected relative frequency is then the probability of each event.

For example, consider tossing a coin. On any one toss, there are two possible outcomes: a head or a tail. We assume that nature has no bias toward heads or tails, so that over the long run we will see 50% heads and 50% tails. In other words, we expect the relative frequency of heads to be .50 and the relative frequency of tails to be .50. Because relative frequency in the population *is* probability, we have a theoretical probability distribution for coin tosses: The probability of a head on any toss is $p = .50$, and the probability of a tail is $p = .50$.

Likewise, consider drawing a playing card from a deck of 52 cards. We assume that there is no bias favoring any one card, so over the long run, we expect each card to occur at a rate of once out of every 52 draws. Thus, each card has a relative frequency of 1/52, or .0192. Therefore, the probability of drawing any specific card on a single draw is $p = .0192$.

And that is the logic of probability. First, we either theoretically or empirically devise a model of how events are distributed in the population (called a *probability distribution*). The model gives the expected relative frequency of each event in the population. Then, an event's expected relative frequency equals its probability of occurring in a particular sample.

Factors Affecting the Probability of an Event

Not all random events are the same, and their characteristics influence their probability. First, events may be either independent or dependent. Two events are **independent events** when the probability of one is *not* influenced by the occurrence of the other. For example, contrary to popular belief, washing your car does *not* make it rain. These are independent events, so the probability of rain does not increase when you wash your car. On the other hand, two events are **dependent events** when the probability of one *is* influenced by the occurrence of the other. For example, whether you pass an exam usually depends on whether you study: The probability of passing increases or decreases *depending* on whether studying occurs.

The probability of an event is also affected by the type of sampling we perform. When **sampling with replacement**, any previously selected individuals or events are *replaced* back into the population before drawing additional ones. For example, say we select two playing cards. Sampling with replacement occurs if, after drawing the first card, we return it to the deck before drawing the second card. Notice that then the probabilities on the first and second draw are each based on 52 possible outcomes, and so they stay constant. On the other hand, when **sampling without replacement**, previously selected individuals or events are *not* replaced into the population before selecting again. Thus, sampling without replacement occurs if, after a card is drawn, it is discarded. Now the probability of selecting a particular card on the first draw is based on 52 possible outcomes, but the probability of selecting a card on the second draw is based on 51 outcomes. With fewer possible outcomes, the probability is slightly larger on the second draw.

The reason we discuss probability is not because we have an uncontrollable urge to flip coins and draw cards. In research the "events" we're interested in are *scores*. We usually assume that scores are independent (whether someone else scores high on a test does not influence the p that you'll score high), and sampled with replacement (the occurrence of a particular score does not diminish its frequency in the population, so its *p* remains constant). Then, as discussed in the next section, we determine the probability of a score or sample of scores by using the standard normal curve.

OBTAINING PROBABILITY FROM THE STANDARD NORMAL CURVE

In statistics we usually describe scores that we assume are normally distributed. Therefore, our "theoretical probability distribution" is based on the standard normal curve. Here's how it works.

Determining the Probability of Individual Scores

In Chapter 6 you used *z*-scores to find *the proportion of the total area under the normal curve* in any part of a distribution. This proportion corresponds to the relative frequency of the scores in that part of the population. Now, however, you know that by computing the relative frequency of scores in the population, we were also computing their *probability*.

> **The proportion of the total area under the curve for scores in any part of the distribution equals the probability of those scores.**

For example, the normal curve in Figure 9.1 provides the complete probability distribution for a set of scores. Say that we wonder what the probability is of randomly selecting a score below the mean of 59 (in the lighter shaded area in Figure 9.1). This is the same as asking about selecting a *person* who has a score below 59. To answer this, think first in terms of *z*-scores. Raw scores below the mean produce negative *z*-scores, so the question becomes "What is the probability of randomly selecting a negative *z*-score?" Negative *z*-scores constitute 50% of the area under the curve and thus have a relative frequency of .50. Therefore, the probability is .50 that we will select a negative *z*-score. Because negative *z*-scores correspond to raw scores below 59, the probability is also .50 that an individual we select will have a raw score below 59.

FIGURE 9.1   *z*-distribution showing the area for scores below the mean, and between the mean and *z* = +1

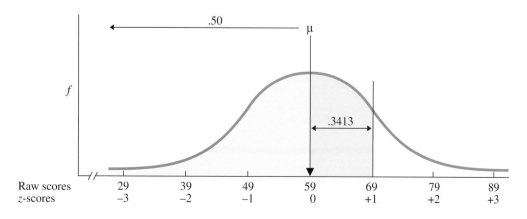

Likewise all of the techniques you learned for finding the area under the curve using z-scores and the z-tables can be used to compute probability. Let's review.

Say that we seek the probability of selecting a raw score between 59 and 69 (the dark shaded area in Figure 9.1). The formula for a z-score in the population is

$$z = \frac{X - \mu}{\sigma_X}$$

Say that the raw score of 69 has a z of +1. From column B of the z-tables in Appendix B, z-scores between the mean and a z of +1 occur .3413 of the time. Thus, the probability is .3413 of randomly selecting any one of these z-scores. Because these z-scores correspond to raw scores between 59 and 69, the probability is also .3413 that we will select a raw score between 59 and 69.

Similarly, the probability of randomly selecting a raw score between 49 and 69 is found by first converting the raw scores to z-scores: We seek the probability and thus the area between the z-scores of ±1. Doubling the .3413 above, in total, z-scores between ±1 constitute .6826 of the curve, so their probability (and that of raw scores between 49 and 69) is .6826.

Or, we can determine the probability of randomly selecting a score greater than a particular z-score. For example, what is the probability of selecting a z-score larger than +2? In Figure 9.2 this is selecting from the right-hand shaded area. Column C in the z-tables indicates that z-scores above +2 constitute .0228 of the distribution and thus occur .0228 of the time. Therefore, the probability is .0228 of randomly selecting a z-score above +2. To find the raw score at this z, we use the formula

$$X = (z)(\sigma_X) + \mu$$

This would indicate that, as in Figure 9.2, .0228 is the probability of selecting a raw score above 79.

Finally, what is the probability of selecting a score that is beyond a z of ±2? This means that we seek scores above +2 or below −2, so we seek the probability of drawing a score from either of the shaded areas in Figure 9.2. Scores beyond z = +2 constitute .0228 of the curve, and scores beyond z = −2 constitute .0228 of the curve. The word "or" indicates that we don't distinguish between the tails, so we *add* the shaded areas together. In total, .0228 + .0228, or .0456, of the curve contains scores that

FIGURE 9.2 Area under the curve beyond z = ±2.0

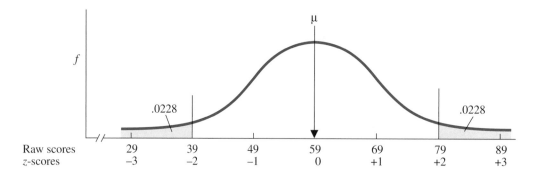

will satisfy us. Because z-scores beyond ± 2 occur .0456 of the time, the probability of selecting one of them is .0456. In Figure 9.2 a raw score of 39 corresponds to a z of -2, and a raw score of 79 corresponds to a z of $+2$. Therefore, the probability is .0456 that we will select a raw score below 39 or above 79.

> *REMEMBER* When we use the word "or" when describing events it means to add their individual probabilities together.

Determining the Probability of Sample Means

We can also use the normal curve to find the probability of sample means. In Chapter 6 we described a sample mean by examining a sampling distribution. We conceptualized the sampling distribution as the frequency distribution of all possible sample means that would result if our bored statistician randomly sampled a raw score population an infinite number of times using a particular N. A sampling distribution is also a theoretical probability distribution. Here's how it works.

In Chapter 6 we found a sample mean's location on a sampling distribution by first computing the standard error of the mean using the formula

$$\sigma_{\overline{X}} = \frac{\sigma_X}{\sqrt{N}}$$

Then we computed a z-score for the sample mean using the formula

$$z = \frac{\overline{X} - \mu}{}$$

Then, by applying the standard normal curve model, we determined the relative frequency of sample means falling above or below that z-score. Now, in the same way that we just determined the probability of raw scores, we can determine the probability of randomly selecting particular sample means.

For example, look at the sampling distribution of SAT means shown in Figure 9.3. The population mean (μ) of this distribution is 500; and when N is 25 with $\sigma_X = 100$,

FIGURE 9.3 Sampling distribution of SAT means when $N = 25$

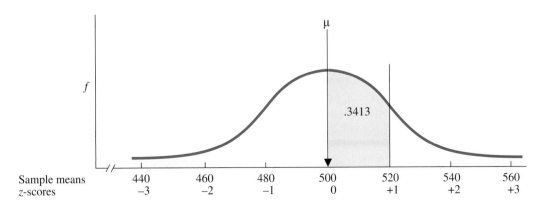

| Sample means | 440 | 460 | 480 | 500 | 520 | 540 | 560 |
| z-scores | −3 | −2 | −1 | 0 | +1 | +2 | +3 |

the standard error of the mean is 20. Say we're interested in means between 500 and 520 so, in other words, we're interested in the means having z-scores between 0 and $+1$. The relative frequency of such z-scores is .3413, so the relative frequency of the sample means that produce these z-scores is also .3413. Therefore, the probability of randomly selecting a sample mean with a z-score between 0 and $+1$ is $p = .3413$. And, therefore, the probability is .3413 that we will randomly obtain a sample mean between 500 and 520 from this population.

Think about this: Randomly selecting a sample mean is the same as randomly selecting a sample of raw scores that produce that mean. Likewise, randomly selecting a sample of raw scores is the same as randomly selecting a sample of participants and then measuring their raw scores. Therefore, the probability of selecting certain sample means is also the probability of selecting the corresponding samples that produce those means. Thus, we can rephrase our finding above: When we randomly select 25 participants from the SAT population, the probability of selecting a sample that produces a mean between 500 and 520 is .3413.

The beauty of the above procedure is that we can describe the characteristics of the sampling distribution we'd have if the bored statistician sampled *any* normally distributed raw score population. Therefore, in any experiment involving normally distributed raw scores, we can determine the probability of obtaining a particular mean.

> **REMEMBER** Determine the probability of selecting particular sample means by computing their z-score on the sampling distribution.

The above procedure forms the basis for all inferential statistics. The next step is to understand how to use probability to make decisions.

MAKING DECISIONS BASED ON PROBABILITY

To begin, let's make a decision about my typing. The probability is .80 that I'll make a typo at any moment. Should you decide that my next word will contain a typo? Yes, it's a good bet. Why? Because you are likely to win the bet. How do we know this? The probability that you've correctly decided about an event equals the probability that chance will produce the event. To see this, look at the bet over the long run: Assume that 100% of the time that you're in this situation you will bet that I'll make a typo. On 80% of the time I do make a typo, so you will be correct 80% of the time. Thus, the relative frequency of your winning the bet over the long run is .80, so the probability of winning any single bet is .80. However, I do not make typos 20% of the time, so you will lose the bet 20% of the time. Thus, the probability is .20 that you will lose any single bet. Conversely, if you bet that I will not make a typo, $p = .20$ that you'll win the bet, and $p = .80$ that you'll lose the bet.

As this illustrates, we bet in favor of high-probability events because then there is a high probability of winning the bet. We bet against low-probability events, because then, too, the probability of winning the bet is high. We use the same logic when deciding whether a sample represents a particular population.

Deciding Whether a Sample Represents a Population

Recall that in research we want to say that how a sample behaves is the way the population would behave if we could observe it. However, we can never be certain how the population would behave because there is no guarantee that the sample accurately reflects the population. In other words, we are never certain that a sample is *representative* of the population.

Back in Chapter 2 you saw that a representative sample is a mini-version of the population, having the same characteristics as the population. However, representativeness is not all or nothing. A sample can be more or less representative, having more or less of the characteristics in the population. This is because how representative a sample is depends on random *chance*—the luck of the draw of which scores are selected. By chance the sample may be somewhat different from the population from which it is selected, and thereby represent that population somewhat poorly.

Here, then, is the central problem for researchers (and the reason for inferential statistics): *When a sample is different from the population it actually represents, it has the characteristics of some* other *population and to some extent appears to represent that other population.* Thus, although a sample always represents some population, we are never sure *which* population it represents: The sample may poorly represent one population, or it may represent another population altogether.

> *REMEMBER* Any sample may poorly represent one population, or it may accurately represent a different population.

For example, say that when flipping a coin, we obtain 8 heads in a row. From this should we conclude that the coin is a "fair" coin and represents the population of fair coin tosses? Or, should we conclude that it is "rigged" and represents the population of outcomes produced by a rigged coin? If the coin is fair, then ideally we'd expect to see 4 heads and 4 tails. However, that's over the long run, and we don't really expect to see 4 heads and 4 tails on *every* set of 8 tosses. Thus, it could still be a fair coin, and we simply showed up when chance produced an unrepresentative sample of the population of fair tosses. On the other hand, if it is a rigged coin, then an odd, unlikely sequence such as 8 heads is exactly the kind of outcome we'd expect. (That's what "rigged" means!)

To make a decision here we use this logic: If there were, say, 55% heads and 45% tails, we could accept that the sample represents the population of fair coin tosses—it's close enough to the ideal 50–50 split we'd expect. Even 60% heads and 40% tails is somewhat representative of this population. Such outcomes are reasonably likely to occur when tossing a fair coin, so it's reasonable—a good bet—that chance produced these less than perfectly representative samples from the population of fair tosses.

Beyond a certain point, however, we begin to doubt that only random chance is at work. For example, obtaining 70% heads and 30% tails is rather unlikely, which literally means that chance is unlikely to produce such an unrepresentative sample from the population of fair coin tosses. And with 100% heads we begin to seriously doubt the honesty of the coin: A fair coin—and the population of fair coin tosses—is extremely unlikely to produce a sample containing 8 heads in a row. In fact, chance is so unlikely to produce this outcome that we look for some other, more feasible explanation—such as that it's a rigged coin.

Thus, to decide whether we think the coin is rigged or not, we simply need to compute the probability of getting 8 heads in a row, which turns out to be about .004. (This *p* was calculated using the *binomial expansion* in Appendix A.3.) This means that random chance and a fair coin produce such an unusual sample only about .4 of 1% of the time! It's silly to bet in favor of such an unlikely event, so we should reject the idea that our sample is a sample of—and represents—fair coin tosses. Instead, it's more sensible to conclude that the coin is rigged, because a rigged coin would be more likely to produce so many heads.

Here's another example. You obtain a mysterious paragraph of someone's typing, but you don't know whose. Is it mine? Does it represent the population of my typing? Say there are zero typos in the paragraph. It's possible that by some quirk of chance I produced such an unrepresentative sample, but it's not likely: I type errorless words only 20% of the time, so the probability that I could produce an entire errorless paragraph is extremely small. Thus, because chance is *too unlikely* to produce such a sample from the population of my typing, you should decide against this low-probability event. Instead, you should conclude that the sample represents the population of some other, competent typist where such a sample is more likely.

On the other hand, say that there are typos in 75% of the words in the paragraph. This is reasonably consistent with what you would expect if the sample represents my typing. Although you expect 80% typos from me over the long run, you should not expect precisely 80% typos in every sample. Rather, a sample with 75% errors seems likely to occur simply by chance when the population of my typing is sampled. Thus, you can accept that this paragraph somewhat poorly represents my typing.

All inferential statistics use the above logic to decide whether a sample of scores is representative of a particular population: If the sample is *likely* to occur when that population is sampled, then we decide that it *does* represent that population. If the sample is *too unlikely* to occur when that population is sampled, then we decide that the sample does *not* represent that population, and instead represents some other population.

> *REMEMBER*   The essence of inferential statistics is to decide whether a sample of scores is likely or unlikely to occur in a particular population of scores.

The next chapter puts all of this into a research context. In the final sections of this chapter, we'll examine the basics of formally deciding whether a sample represents a particular population.

Making Decisions about a Sample Mean

Say that we return to Prunepit University and obtain a random sample of SAT scores that produces a mean of 550. This is surprising because we think that students at Prunepit are terminally average. Because the ordinary national population of SAT scores has a μ of 500, we should have obtained a sample mean of 500 if our sample was perfectly representative of this population. How do we explain a sample mean of 550? On the one hand, perhaps we obtained a sample of relatively high SAT scores merely because of random chance—the luck of the draw of who was selected to be in the sample. Thus, it's possible that chance produced a less than perfectly representative sample of the population where μ is 500. On the other hand, perhaps the sample does not come from or represent the ordinary population of SAT scores: After all, these *are* Prunepit students, so they may belong to a very different population of students, having some other μ.

To decide whether our sample represents the population of SAT scores where μ is 500, we will determine the probability of obtaining a sample mean of 550 from this population. As you've seen, we determine the probability of a sample mean by computing its z-score on the sampling distribution of means. Thus, we first envision the sampling distribution showing the different means that the bored statistician would obtain if, using our N, she randomly sampled the ordinary SAT population an infinite number of times. For the Prunepit problem we envision the sampling distribution shown in Figure 9.4.

Notice, the statistician is definitely representing the SAT population where μ is 500, so whether she obtained a particular mean that was high, low, or in-between depends purely on the luck of the draw of which scores she happened to select. Therefore, think of a sampling distribution as a "picture of chance," showing how often chance produces different sample means when we sample a particular raw score population.

The next step is to calculate our sample mean's z-score to locate it on this distribution and thus determine its likelihood. For example, say that the z-score for our sample mean is at location A in Figure 9.4. Read what the frequency distribution indicates by following the dotted line: This mean has a very high frequency and thus is very *likely* when drawing a sample from the ordinary SAT population. Anytime you deal with this population, this is a mean you'd expect (because the bored statistician frequently got it). Therefore, this is exactly the kind of mean we'd expect if our Prunepit sample came from this SAT population. Thus, because our sample mean is likely to occur in the ordinary SAT population, we will accept that our sample represents it.

However, say that instead, our sample has a z-score at location B on Figure 9.4: Following the dashed line shows that this is a very infrequent mean. In this case we'd conclude that when drawing a sample from the ordinary SAT population, such a sample mean is a very *unlikely* event. Therefore, if our Prunepit sample came from this SAT population, then we would not expect this mean, because it almost never happens (the bored statistician hardly ever got it). Thus, because we have such an unlikely sample mean, we reject that the sample represents the ordinary SAT population. Instead, it makes more sense to conclude that the sample represents some other population (having some other μ), where such a sample mean would be more likely.

FIGURE 9.4 Sampling distribution of SAT means showing two possible locations of our sample mean

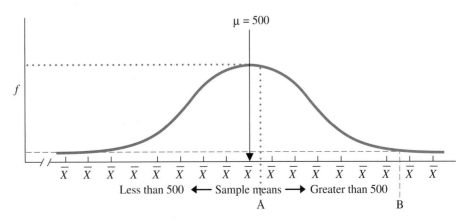

Be sure you understand the above logic. If you do, then you're ready to perform the mechanics of the procedure. Notice that we must perform two tasks: (1) Determine the probability of obtaining our sample from the SAT population, and (2) decide whether the sample is too unlikely to be representing this population. We perform both tasks simultaneously once we have *set up the sampling distribution* and determined the *critical value.*

Setting Up the Sampling Distribution

You saw above that when a sample mean is "close" to the mean of the sampling distribution (here, slightly above 500), then we accept that we have a slightly unrepresentative sample but that it still represents the underlying raw score population. (We'd make the same conclusion if the sample mean was slightly *below* 500.) However, if our sample is far enough out into the tail of the sampling distribution (not "close" to 500), we reject the idea that chance produced such an unrepresentative sample, and instead conclude that the reason our sample mean is so far from 500 is because it does not represent this raw score population. (We'd make the same conclusion if the sample mean was far into the *lower* tail of the distribution.)

But how close is close enough, and how far is far enough to make these decisions? To formalize the decision process, we do this: At some point, a sample mean is so far above or below 500 that is is unbelievable that chance produced such an unrepresentative sample. AND, any samples *beyond* this point that are further into the tail are also unbelievable. To identify this point, as shown in Figure 9.5, we literally draw a line in each tail of the distribution. In statistical terms the shaded areas beyond the lines make up the *region of rejection.* As shown, very infrequently are samples so poor at representing the SAT population that they have means lying in the region of rejection. In fact:

> **Means in the region of rejection are *so* unrepresentative of the original population that it's a better bet they represent some *other* population.**

Thus, the **region of rejection** is the part of a sampling distribution containing means that are so unlikely that we "reject" that they represent the underlying raw score population. Essentially, in the example, we "shouldn't" get a sample mean that lies in the

FIGURE 9.5 Setup of sampling distribution of means showing the region of rejection

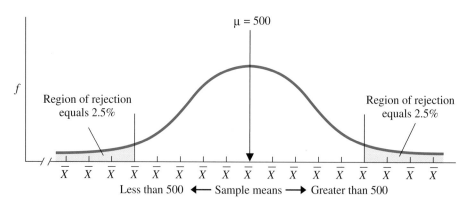

region of rejection if we're representing the ordinary SAT population, because such means almost never occur with this population. Therefore, if we do get such a mean, we probably aren't representing this population: We *reject* that the sample represents the underlying raw score population and decide that the sample represents some other population.

Conversely, if the Prunepit mean is not in the region of rejection, then it's not unlikely to be representing the ordinary SAT population. In fact, by our definition, sample means not in the region of rejection are likely to occur when this population is sampled and thus likely to represent it. In such cases we *retain* the idea that the sample is simply poorly representing this population of SAT scores.

How do we know where to draw the line that starts the region of rejection? By defining our *criterion*. The **criterion** is the probability that defines samples as too unlikely for us to accept as representing a particular population. Researchers usually use .05 as their criterion probability. Thus, by this criterion, sample means that occur *less* than 5% of the time when representing the ordinary SAT population are so unlikely that if we get such a mean, we'll reject that our sample represents this population.

The criterion we select determines the size of the region of rejection. Back in Figure 9.5 the sample means that occur 5% of the time are those that make up the extreme 5% of the sampling distribution. However, because we're talking about the means above *or* below 500 that together are a *total* of 5% of the curve, we divide 5% in half. Therefore, the extreme 2.5% of the curve in each tail of the sampling distribution will form our region of rejection.

> **REMEMBER**   The *criterion probability* that defines samples as unlikely—and also determines the size of the *region of rejection*—is usually $p = .05$.

Now the task is to determine if our sample mean falls into the region of rejection. To do this, we compare the sample's *z*-score to the *critical value*.

Identifying the Critical Value

At the spot on the sampling distribution where we draw the line to mark the beginning of the region of rejection is a specific *z*-score. Because the absolute value of *z*-scores gets larger as we go farther into the tails, if the *z*-score for our sample is larger than the *z*-score at the line, then we know that our sample mean lies *in* the region of rejection. The *z*-score at the line is called the critical value. A **critical value** marks the inner edge of the region of rejection and thus defines the value required for a sample to fall into the region of rejection. Essentially, it is the minimum *z*-score that defines a sample as too unlikely.

How do we determine the critical value? By considering our criterion. With a criterion of .05, we set up the region of rejection back in Figure 9.4 so that in each tail is the extreme 2.5% or .025 of the total area under the curve. From the *z*-table in Appendix B we see that the extreme .025 curve lies beyond the *z*-score of 1.96. Therefore, in each tail, the region of rejection begins at 1.96, so ± 1.96 is the critical value of *z*. Thus, as shown in Figure 9.6, labeling the inner edges of the region of rejection with ± 1.96 completes how you should set up the sampling distribution.

FIGURE 9.6 Setup of sampling distribution of SAT means showing region of rejection and critical values

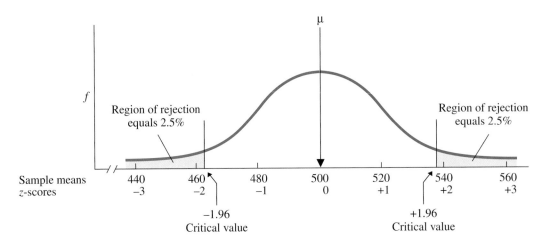

Now, we'll use Figure 9.6 to determine whether our Prunepit mean lies in the region of rejection by comparing the sample's z-score to the critical value.

A sample mean lies in the region of rejection if its z-score is *beyond* the critical value.

Thus, if our Prunepit sample mean has a z-score with an absolute value that is *larger* than ± 1.96, then the sample lies *in* the region of rejection. If the z-score is *smaller than* or *equal to* the critical value, then the sample is *not* in the region of rejection.

> REMEMBER   The *critical value* defines the minimum value of z a sample must have in order to be in the region of rejection.

Deciding if the Sample Represents the Population

Now, at long last, we can evaluate our sample mean of 550 from Prunepit U. First, we compute the sample's z-score on the sampling distribution created from the ordinary SAT population. There, $\sigma_X = 100$ and $N = 25$, so the standard error of the mean is

$$\sigma_{\overline{X}} = \frac{\sigma_X}{\sqrt{N}} = \frac{100}{\sqrt{25}} = 20$$

Then the z-score is

$$z = \frac{\overline{X} - \mu}{\sigma_{\overline{X}}} = \frac{550 - 500}{20} = +2.5$$

Think about this z-score. If the sample represents the ordinary SAT population, it's doing a very poor job of it. With a population mean of 500, a perfectly representative sample would also have a mean of 500 and thus have a z-score of 0. Good old Prunepit produced a z-score of $+2.5$!

To confirm our suspicions, compare the sample's *z*-score to the critical value of ±1.96. Locating the sample's *z*-score on the sampling distribution gives us the complete picture, which is shown in Figure 9.7. (When performing this procedure yourself, you should create the complete picture, too.) The sample's *z* of +2.5—and the underlying sample mean of 550—lies in the region of rejection. This tells us that a sample mean of 550 is among those means that we consider to be extremely unlikely to occur when someone is representing the ordinary population of SAT scores. In other words, very seldom does chance—the luck of the draw—produce such unrepresentative samples from this population, so it is not a good bet that chance produced *our* sample from this population. Therefore, we reject that our sample represents the population of SAT raw scores having a μ of 500.

Notice that we make a definitive, yes-or-no decision. Because our sample is unlikely to represent the SAT raw score population where μ is 500, we decide that no, it definitely does not represent this population.

We wrap up our conclusions in this way: If the sample doesn't represent the ordinary SAT raw score population, then it must represent some other population. For example, perhaps the Prunepit students obtained the high mean of 550 because they lied about their scores, so they may represent the population of students who lie about the SAT. Or, perhaps they are more intelligent or motivated than ordinary students, and thus represent the population of overachievers. Regardless, having rejected that the sample represents the population where μ is 500, we use the sample mean to estimate the μ of the population that the sample *does* represent. A sample having a mean of 550 is most likely to come from a population having a μ of 550. Therefore, our best guess is that the Prunepit sample represents an SAT population that, for whatever reason, has a μ of 550.

Thus, in sum, as we did with other bets, we decide against the low-probability event that the sample represents the SAT population where μ is 500, and decide in favor of the high-probability event that the sample represents a population where μ is 550.

FIGURE 9.7 Completed sampling distribution of SAT means showing location of the Prunepit U. sample relative to the critical value

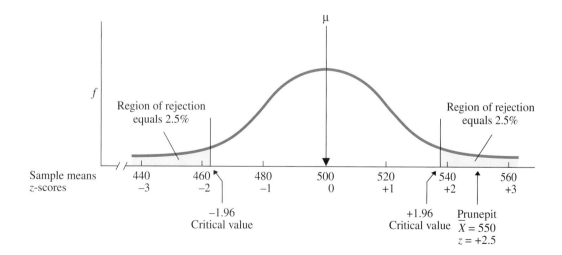

On the other hand, say that our sample mean had been 474, resulting in a *z*-score of (474 − 500)/20 = −1.30. Because −1.30 does *not* lie beyond the critical value of ±1.96, this sample mean is *not* in the region of rejection. Looking back at Figure 9.7, we see that when sampling the underlying SAT population, this sample mean is relatively frequent and thus likely. Because of this, we can accept that random chance produced a less than perfectly representative sample for us but that it probably represents the ordinary SAT population where μ is 500.

> *REMEMBER*   When a sample's *z*-score lies beyond the critical value, *reject* that the sample represents the underlying raw score population reflected by the sampling distribution. When the *z*-score does not lie beyond the critical value, *retain* the idea that the sample may represent the underlying raw score population.

Other Ways to Set Up the Sampling Distribution

Above, the region of rejection was in both tails of the distribution because we wanted to identify unrepresentative sample means that were either too far above or too far below 500. Instead, however, we can place the region of rejection in only one tail of the distribution. (In the next chapter you'll find out why you would want to do this.)

Say that we are interested only in sample means that are *less* than 500, having negative *z*-scores. Our criterion is still .05, but now we place the *entire* region of rejection in the lower, left-hand tail of the sampling distribution, as shown in Figure 9.8. **This produces a different critical value.** From the *z*-table (and using the interpolation procedures described in Appendix A.2), the extreme lower 5% of a distribution lies beyond a *z*-score of −1.645. Therefore, the *z*-score for our sample must lie beyond −1.645 for it to be in the region of rejection. If it does, we will again conclude that the sample mean is too unlikely to occur when sampling the SAT raw score population where μ = 500, so we'll reject the idea that the sample represents this population. If the *z*-score places the sample anywhere else on the sampling distribution, even far into the upper tail, we will *not* reject that the sample represents the SAT population where μ = 500.

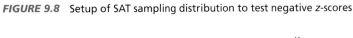

FIGURE 9.8   Setup of SAT sampling distribution to test negative *z*-scores

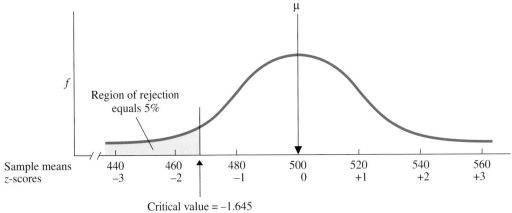

On the other hand, say that we're interested only in sample means *greater* than 500, having positive *z*-scores. Here, we place the entire region of rejection in the upper, right-hand tail of the sampling distribution, as shown in Figure 9.9. Now the critical value is *plus* 1.645, so only if our sample's *z*-score is beyond +1.645 does the sample mean lie in the region of rejection. Only then do we reject the idea that the sample represents the underlying raw score population.

On Being Wrong When We Decide about a Sample

When we rejected that we were playing with a fair coin, we might have been wrong: Maybe we obtained 8 heads in a row with a fair coin by chance. Eight heads in a row do occur sometimes, and maybe we happened to observe one of those times. After all, unlikely events are just that: They are *unlikely,* not *impossible.* Thus, it's also possible that I might type an errorless paragraph. And, it's possible that the sample mean of 550 actually represents the ordinary SAT population where μ is 500. The sampling distribution shows that sample means in the region of rejection occur when the sample *does* represent that SAT population (the statistician sometimes *does* obtain such means from this population). Maybe our Prunepit mean was one of those means.

We can also be wrong if we retain the idea that a sample represents the ordinary SAT population. Consider the most extreme case, in which we obtain a sample mean of 500! This sample certainly appears to represent the population of scores where μ is 500. Using the above procedures, we'd compute a *z*-score of 0, so we would retain this idea. But it is possible that this sample actually represents some other population. Perhaps, for example, the sample is actually a very unrepresentative sample from the population where μ is 550! Maybe, simply by the luck of the draw, our sample contains too many low scores, so that, coincidentally, it appears to represent the population where μ is 500.

Thus, regardless of which population we decide a sample represents, there is always the possibility that we've made an incorrect decision. Such errors are not likely, however, and that's why we perform inferential statistical procedures. By incorporating probability into our decision making, we are confident that *over the long run,* more often than not we will correctly identify the population that a sample represents. In the context of research, therefore, we have greater confidence that we are interpreting the data correctly.

FIGURE 9.9 Setup of SAT sampling distribution to test positive *z*-scores

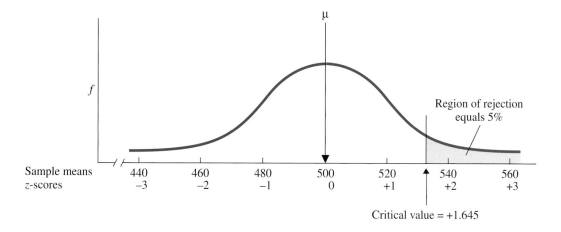

PUTTING IT ALL TOGETHER

The decision-making process discussed in this chapter is the essence of all inferential statistics. The basic question is always "Do the sample data represent a particular raw score population?" But, if a sample mean is different from the population μ we expect, then either because of chance we have a slightly unrepresentative sample of that population, or we are representing a different population. You've seen that we decide by performing the following steps:

1. Create a sampling distribution from the underlying raw score population that we think the sample may represent.

2. Select the criterion probability that defines a sample as unlikely and also defines the size of the region of rejection.

3. Based on the criterion and region of rejection, determine the critical value.

4. Compute a z-score to locate the sample mean on the sampling distribution.

5. If the z lies beyond the critical value, then the sample is in the region of rejection. Therefore, the sample is unlikely to represent the underlying raw score population, so reject that it does, and conclude that the sample represents some other population that is more likely to produce such data.

6. If the z does not lie beyond the critical value, then the sample is not in the region of rejection. Therefore, the sample is likely to represent the underlying raw score population, so retain the idea that the sample does represent this population, although somewhat poorly.

CHAPTER SUMMARY

1. *Probability,* or *p,* indicates the likelihood of an event when random chance is operating.

2. The probability of an event is equal to its relative frequency in the population.

3. The probability of correctly predicting a chance event equals the probability that the event will occur. The probability of incorrectly predicting a chance event equals the probability that the event will not occur.

4. Two events are *independent* if the probability of one event is not influenced by the occurrence of the other. Two events are *dependent* if the probability of one event *is* influenced by the occurrence of the other.

5. *Sampling with replacement* is replacing individuals or events back into the population before selecting again. *Sampling without replacement* is *not* replacing individuals or events back into the population before selecting again.

6. A *theoretical probability distribution* is a theoretical model of the relative frequencies of all possible events in a population when random chance is operating.

7. The standard normal curve model is a theoretical probability distribution that can be applied to any normal raw score distribution. Raw scores can be transformed into z-scores, and the proportion of the area under the curve is the probability of randomly selecting those z-scores. This is also the probability of selecting the corresponding raw scores.

8. A sampling distribution of means is also a theoretical probability distribution. Sample means are transformed into z-scores, and the proportion of the area under the curve is the probability of randomly selecting those z-scores. This is also the probability of selecting the corresponding sample means.

9. The probability of randomly selecting a particular sample mean is the same as the probability of randomly selecting a sample of participants whose scores produce that sample mean.

10. *The region of rejection* is located in the extreme tail or tails of a sampling distribution. Any sample mean that falls into the region of rejection is too unlikely for us to accept as representing the raw score population reflected by the sampling distribution.

11. The edge of the region of rejection closest to the mean of the sampling distribution is at the *critical value.* A sample mean falls into the region of rejection if the sample's z-score is beyond the critical value.

12. The size of the region of rejection is determined by the *criterion,* which is the probability that defines a sample as unlikely. Usually, the criterion is .05. This produces a region of rejection that constitutes the extreme .05 of the sampling distribution.

KEY TERMS: Can You Define the Following?

p	probability distribution *219*
criterion *229*	region of rejection *228*
critical value *229*	sampling with replacement *220*
dependent events *220*	sampling without replacement *220*
independent events *220*	theoretical probability distribution *219*
probability *218*	

REVIEW QUESTIONS

(Answers for odd-numbered questions are in Appendix C.)

1. (a) What does a probability convey about a random event in a sample? (b) What is the probability of a random event based on?
2. (a) What is the difference between an empirical probability distribution and a theoretical probability distribution? (b) Why is the proportion of the total area under the normal curve equal to probability?

3. (a) What is *sampling with replacement?* (b) What is *sampling without replacement?* (c) How does sampling without replacement affect the probability of events, compared to sampling with replacement?

4. (a) When are events *independent?* (b) When are they *dependent?*

5. A sample produces a mean that is different from the μ of the population that we think the sample may represent. What are the two possible reasons for this difference?

6. When testing the representativeness of a sample mean, (a) What is the *criterion?* (b) What is the *region of rejection?* (c) What is the *critical value?*

7. What does comparing the critical value to a sample's *z*-score indicate?

8. What is the difference between using both tails versus one tail of the sampling distribution in terms of (a) the size of the region of rejection? (b) the critical value?

APPLICATION QUESTIONS

9. A couple with eight daughters decides to have one more baby, because they think the next one is bound to be a boy! Is this reasoning accurate?

10. Foofy read in the newspaper that there is a .05% chance of swallowing a spider while you sleep. She subsequently developed insomnia. (a) What is the probability of swallowing a spider? (b) Why isn't her insomnia justified? (c) Why is her insomnia justified?

11. Poindexter's uncle is building a house on land that has been devastated by hurricanes 160 times in the past 200 years. Because there hasn't been a major storm there in 13 years, his uncle says this is a safe investment. His nephew argues that he is wrong, because a hurricane must be due soon. What are the fallacies in the reasoning of both men?

12. Four airplanes from different airlines have crashed in the past two weeks. This terrifies Bubbles, who must travel on a plane. Her travel agent claims that the probability of a plane crash is minuscule. Who is correctly interpreting the situation? Why?

13. For each of the following, indicate whether the first event is dependent on, or independent of, the second event: (a) Playing golf; the weather. (b) Buying new shoes; buying a new car. (c) Losing weight; eating fewer calories. (d) Winning the lottery; playing the same numbers each time.

14. What is the probability of randomly selecting a participant who scores the following? (a) $z = +2.03$ or above (b) $z = -2.8$ or above (c) z between -1.5 and $+1.5$ (d) z beyond ± 1.72

15. For a distribution in which $\overline{X} = 43$ and $S_X = 8$, what is the probability of randomly selecting the following? (a) A score of 27 or below (b) A score of 51 or above (c) A score between 42 and 44 (d) A score below 33 or above 49

16. You are shopping for a used car. Over the life of a car you like, the probability of engine trouble is .65. (a) If you conclude that the engine will malfunction, what is the probability that you are correct? What is the probability that you are

incorrect? (b) If you conclude that the engine will not malfunction, what is the probability that you are correct? What is the probability that you are incorrect? (c) Should you purchase this car? Why?

17. The mean of a population of raw scores is 18 ($\sigma_X = 12$). What is the probability of randomly selecting a sample of 30 scores having a mean above 24?

18. The mean of a population of raw scores is 50 ($\sigma_X = 18$). What is the probability of randomly selecting a sample of 40 scores having a mean below 46?

19. (a) Why do we conclude that a low-probability sample does not represent a particular population? (b) Why do we conclude that a high-probability sample does represent a particular population?

20. (a) Why is it possible that each conclusion in question 19 is wrong? (b) Why is it unlikely that we're wrong?

21. The p of obtaining 7 heads in a row with a fair coin is .008, so we reject that the coin is fair (that only chance produced this result). (a) What is the p that we are incorrect? (b) What is the p that we are correct?

22. Foofy computes the $\overline{X}$ from data that her professor says is a random sample drawn from population Q. She determines that this sample mean has a z-score of $+41$ on the sampling distribution for population Q (and she computed it correctly!). Foofy claims she has proven that this could not be a random sample from population Q. Do you agree or disagree? Why?

23. Suppose that for the data in question 17 you obtained a sample mean of 24. Using the .05 criterion with the region of rejection in both tails of the sampling distribution, should you consider the sample to be representative of the population in which $\mu = 18$? Why?

24. Suppose that for the data in question 18 you obtained a sample mean of 46. Using the .05 criterion with the region of rejection in both tails of the distribution, should you consider the sample to be representative of the population in which $\mu = 50$? Why?

25. In a study you obtain the following data representing the aggressive tendencies of some football players:

40	30	39	40	41	39	31	28	33

(a) Researchers have found that in the population of nonfootball players, μ is 30 ($\sigma_X = 5$). Using both tails of the sampling distribution, determine whether your football players represent a different population. (b) What do you conclude about the population of football players and its μ?

26. On a standard test of motor coordination, a sports psychologist found that the population of average bowlers had a mean score of 24, with a standard deviation of 6. She tested a random sample of 30 bowlers at Fred's Bowling Alley and found a sample mean of 26. A second random sample of 30 bowlers at Ethel's Bowling Alley had a mean of 18. Using the criterion of $p = .05$ and both tails of the sampling distribution, what should she conclude about each sample's representativeness of the population of average bowlers?

27. (a) In question 26, if a particular sample does not represent the population of average bowlers, what is your best estimate of the μ of the population it does represent? (b) Explain the logic behind this conclusion.

SUMMARY OF FORMULAS

1. *The formula for transforming a sample mean into a z-score on the sampling distribution of means is*

$$z = \frac{\overline{X} - \mu}{\sigma_{\overline{X}}}$$

where $\overline{X}$ is the sample mean, μ is the mean of the sampling distribution (which is also equal to the μ of the raw score distribution), and $\sigma_{\overline{X}}$ is the true standard error of the mean of the sampling distribution of means.

2. *The formula for the true standard error of the mean is*

$$\sigma_{\overline{X}} = \frac{\sigma_X}{\sqrt{N}}$$

where σ_X is the true standard deviation of the raw score population.

10

Overview of Statistical Hypothesis Testing: The *z*-Test

GETTING STARTED

To understand this chapter, recall the following:

- From Chapter 4 recall that a relationship in the population occurs when different means from the conditions of an independent variable represent different μs and thus different distributions of dependent scores.
- From Chapter 9 recall that when a sample's *z*-score falls into the region of rejection, the sample is too unlikely to accept as representing the underlying raw score population.

Your goals in this chapter are to learn:

- Why the possibility of sampling error leads to performing inferential statistical procedures.
- When experimental hypotheses lead to either a one-tailed or a two-tailed statistical test.
- How to set up a sampling distribution for one- and two-tailed tests.
- How to interpret significant and nonsignificant results.
- What Type I errors, Type II errors, and power are.

From the previous chapter you know the basics involved in all inferential statistics. In this chapter we'll put these procedures into a research context and present the statistical language and symbols used to describe them. Until further notice, we'll be talking about experiments. We'll start with the "*z*-test," but first here are some new symbols.

MORE STATISTICAL NOTATION

Five new symbols will be used in stating mathematical relationships.

1. The symbol for *greater than* is >. Reading from left to right, $A > B$ means that A is greater than B. (The large opening in ">" is always on the side of the larger quantity, and the symbol points toward the smaller quantity.)
2. The symbol for *less than* is <, so $B < A$ means that B is less than A.
3. The symbol for *greater than or equal to* is ≥, so $B \geq A$ indicates that B is greater than or equal to A.
4. The symbol for *less than or equal to* is ≤, so $B \leq A$ indicates that B is less than or equal to A.
5. The symbol for *not equal to* is ≠, so $A \neq B$ means that A is different from B.

WHY IS IT IMPORTANT TO KNOW ABOUT THE *z*-TESTS?

The *z*-test is one of the simplest inferential statistics around, so it's a good starting point for learning these procedures. Also, when reading behavioral research, you may encounter a study that employs it, so you should understand how it works. Most important, the discussion will introduce the formal system researchers use in *all* inferential procedures. Therefore, be alert to the pattern here, and understand the general steps and terminology involved, because you'll see them again and again.

THE ROLE OF INFERENTIAL STATISTICS IN RESEARCH

As you saw in the previous chapter, a random sample may be more or less representative of a population because, just by the luck of the draw, the sample may contain too many high scores or too many low scores relative to the population. Because the sample is not perfectly representative, the sample mean does not equal the population mean.

The shorthand term for communicating that chance produced an unrepresentative sample is to say that the sample reflects sampling error. **Sampling error** results when random chance produces a sample statistic (such as $\overline{X}$) that does not equal the population parameter it represents (such as μ). Because of the luck of the draw, the *sample* is in *error* to some degree in representing the population.

REMEMBER   *Sampling error* results when, by chance, the scores that are selected produce a sample statistic that is different from the population parameter it represents.

The possibility that a sample might reflect sampling error is the reason that researchers must perform inferential statistics. On the one hand, a sample mean may differ from a particular population μ because of sampling error—the sample is not perfectly representing that population. On the other hand, the difference may not be due to sampling error at all, but rather it may be due to the fact that the sample comes from, and thus represents, a different population. This creates a dilemma when we try to infer that a relationship exists in nature. Recall that in an experiment, we change the conditions of the independent variable in hopes of changing dependent scores. If the means for the conditions change, we want to infer that if we measured the entire population, we would find a different population of scores located around a different μ for each condition. But here is where sampling error comes in. Maybe the sample means for the conditions differ because of sampling error, and they are actually poorly representing the *same* population. If so, then testing everyone in the population under each condition would *not* produce a relationship: we'd find the same population of scores, having the same μ, in each condition. Or, perhaps there is a relationship in the population, but because of sampling error, it's different from the relationship in our sample data.

For example, say we compare men and women on the dependent variable of creativity. In nature, men and women don't really differ on this variable, but through sampling error—the luck of the draw—we might end up with some female participants who are more creative than our male participants or vice versa. Then sampling error will mislead us into thinking there's a relationship here, even though there really is not. Or, say that we measure the heights of some men and women and, by chance, obtain a sample of relatively short men and a sample of tall women. If we didn't already know that the population of men is taller, sampling error would mislead us into concluding that women are taller.

Thus, in any research situation, there is always the possibility we are being misled by sampling error. Therefore, we always apply inferential statistics to *every* study. **Inferential statistics** are used to decide whether sample data represent a particular relationship in the population. Using the process discussed in the previous chapter, we decide whether the samples are likely to represent populations that form a particular relationship or whether it is likely we are being misled by sampling error, and the samples actually represent populations that do not form the relationship.

The specific inferential procedure employed in a given research situation depends upon the *research design* and on the *scale of measurement* used when measuring the *dependent variable*. There are two general categories of inferential statistics: *parametric* and *nonparametric.*

Parametric statistics are procedures that require certain assumptions about the raw score populations being represented. Recall that *parameters* describe the characteristics of a population, so parametric procedures are used when we can assume the population has certain characteristics. The assumptions of a procedure are the rules for using it, so think of them as a checklist for selecting a procedure. There are specific assumptions for each parametric procedure, but two assumptions are common to them all: (1) The population of dependent scores forms a normal distribution, and (2) the scores are interval or ratio scores. Thus, parametric procedures are used when it is appropriate to calculate the mean in each condition. In this and upcoming chapters we'll focus on parametric procedures.

Nonparametric statistics are inferential procedures that do not require stringent assumptions about the populations being represented. These procedures are used with nominal or ordinal scores or with skewed interval or ratio distributions (when it is appropriate to calculate the median or mode). Chapter 15 presents nonparametric procedures.

> REMEMBER *Parametric* and *nonparametric inferential statistics* are for deciding if the data reflect a relationship in nature, or if sampling error is misleading us into thinking there is a relationship.

We use nonparametric procedures if the data clearly violate the assumptions of parametric procedures. However, we can use a parametric procedure if the data come close to meeting its assumptions. This is because parametric procedures are robust. With a **robust procedure,** if the data do not meet the assumptions of the procedure perfectly, we will have only a negligible amount of error in the inferences we draw. So, for example, if our data represent a population that is approximately normally distributed, we can still use a parametric procedure.

As you'll see, both parametric and nonparametric procedures are performed in the same way. The first step is setting up the procedure.

SETTING UP INFERENTIAL PROCEDURES

There are four steps to follow when setting up an experiment: Create the experimental hypotheses, design the experiment to test these hypotheses, translate the experimental hypotheses into statistical hypotheses, and select and set up the appropriate statistical procedure to test the statistical hypotheses.

Creating the Experimental Hypotheses

We always have some idea of how our research should turn out. This expectation is expressed in the form of two experimental hypotheses. **Experimental hypotheses** describe the predicted outcome we may or may not find in an experiment. One hypothesis states that we will demonstrate the predicted relationship (manipulating the independent variable will work as expected). The other hypothesis states that we will not demonstrate the predicted relationship (manipulating the independent variable will not work as expected).

We can predict a relationship in one of two ways. The simplest prediction is that there is some kind of relationship, but we are not sure whether scores will increase or decrease as we change the independent variable. This leads to a "two-tailed" statistical procedure. A **two-tailed test** is used when you predict that there is a relationship, but do not specifically predict the direction in which scores will change. The other, more complicated prediction not only states that there will be a relationship, but also predicts the direction in which the scores will change. This leads to a one-tailed test. A **one-tailed test** is used when you predict the specific *direction* in which scores will change. We may predict that as we change the independent variable, the dependent scores will only increase, or we may predict that they will only decrease.

REMEMBER A *two-tailed test* is used when you do not predict the direction that scores will change. A *one-tailed test* is used when you do predict the direction that scores will change.

As an example, let's first examine a study involving a two-tailed test. Say that we've discovered a substance that is related to intelligence. We are ready to test the substance with humans in an "IQ pill." The amount of the pill is our independent variable, and the person's resulting IQ is the dependent variable. Say that we believe this pill will affect IQ, but we are not sure whether it will make people smarter or dumber. Therefore, we predict a relationship such that the more of the pill a person consumes, the more his or her IQ will change. Here are our experimental hypotheses:

1. We will demonstrate that the pill works by either increasing or decreasing IQ scores.
2. We will not demonstrate that the pill works, because IQ scores will not change.

Once we know the hypothesis and prediction, we design the study.

Designing a One-Sample Experiment

Although there are many ways to design the IQ pill study, the simplest approach is as a *one-sample experiment.* We will randomly select one sample of participants and give each person, say, one pill. Then we'll give participants an IQ test. The sample will represent the population of people when they have taken one pill, and the sample $\overline{X}$ will represent that population's μ.

To demonstrate a relationship, however, we must demonstrate that *different* amounts of the pill produce *different* populations of IQ scores, having different μs. Therefore, we must compare the population represented by our sample to some other population receiving some other amount of the pill. *To perform a one-sample experiment, we must already know the population mean under some other condition of the independent variable.* One amount of the pill is zero: The IQ test we're using has been given to many people over the years who have *not* taken the pill, and let's say this population has a μ of 100. We will compare this population without the pill to the population with the pill represented by our sample. If the population without the pill has a different μ than the population with the pill, then we will have demonstrated a relationship in the population.

Creating the Statistical Hypotheses

So that we can use a statistical procedure to test our experimental hypotheses, we first translate them into *statistical hypotheses.* Essentially, the experimental hypotheses propose that either there is or is not the predicted relationship we seek. Then the **statistical hypotheses** describe the population parameters that the sample data represent if the predicted relationship does or does not exist. There are always two statistical hypotheses, the *alternative hypothesis* and the *null hypothesis.*

The Alternative Hypothesis Although you can create the hypotheses in either order, it is easier to create the alternative hypothesis first, because it corresponds to the experimental hypothesis that the experiment *does* work as predicted. The **alternative hypothesis** describes the population parameters that the sample data represent if the predicted relationship exists. The alternative hypothesis is always the hypothesis of a difference; it says that changing the independent variable produces the predicted difference in the populations.

For example, if our IQ pill works as predicted and we could test the entire population, we would find one of two outcomes. Figure 10.1 shows the populations if the pill *increases* IQ. This shows a relationship because, by changing the conditions, everyone's IQ score is increased so that the distribution moves to the right, over to the higher scores. We don't know how much scores will increase, so we do not know the value of μ with the pill. But we do know that if the pill increases IQ, then the μ of the population with the pill will be *greater* than 100, because 100 is the μ of the population without the pill.

On the other hand, Figure 10.2 shows the populations if the pill *decreases* IQ. Here, scores decrease so the distribution is moved to the left, over to the lower scores. Again, we don't know the value of μ, but if the pill decreases IQ relative to people without the pill, then the μ of the population with the pill will be *less than* 100.

The alternative hypothesis is a shorthand way of communicating all of the above. If the pill works as predicted, then the population with the pill will have a μ that is either greater than or less than 100. In other words, the population mean with the pill will *not equal* 100. The symbol for the alternative hypothesis is H_a. (The *H* stands for hypothesis, and the subscript a stands for alternative.) For the above, the alternative hypothesis is

$$H_a: \mu \neq 100$$

This H_a proposes that the sample mean produced with our pill represents a μ not equal to 100. Because we know that the μ without the pill is 100, H_a implies that there is a relationship in the population. Thus, we can interpret H_a as stating that our independent variable works as predicted.

The Null Hypothesis   The statistical hypothesis corresponding to the experimental hypothesis that the independent variable does *not* work as predicted is called the null hypothesis. The **null hypothesis** describes the population parameters that the sample data represent if the predicted relationship does *not* exist. The null hypothesis is the

FIGURE 10.1   Relationship in the population if the IQ pill increases IQ scores

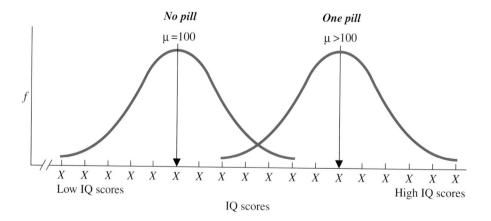

FIGURE 10.2   Relationship in the population if the IQ pill decreases IQ scores

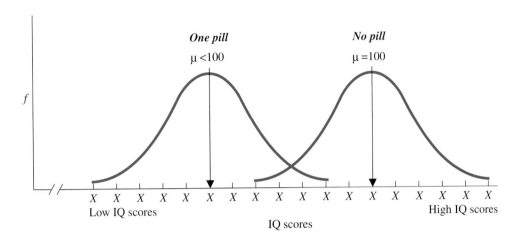

hypothesis of "no difference," saying that changing the independent variable does *not* produce the predicted difference in the population. *And, the null hypothesis maintains this position, regardless of what the sample shows:* The sample data may form the predicted relationship, but the hypothesis is that this is due to sampling error, and so the data are merely poorly representing that there is not this relationship in the population.

If the IQ pill does not work, then it would be as if the pill were not present. We already know that the population of IQ scores without the pill has a μ of 100. Therefore, if the pill does not work, then even after everyone has taken it, the population of scores will be unchanged and μ will still be 100. Thus, if we measured the population with and without the pill, we would have one population of scores, located at the μ of 100, as shown in Figure 10.3.

FIGURE 10.3   Population of scores if the IQ pill does not affect IQ scores

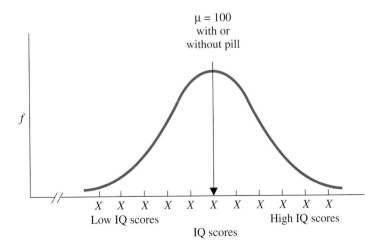

The null hypothesis is a shorthand way of communicating the above. The symbol for the null hypothesis is H_0. (The subscript is 0 because *null* means zero, as in zero relationship.) The null hypothesis for the IQ pill study is

H_0: $\mu = 100$

This hypothesis proposes that our sample actually comes from and represents the population where μ is 100. Because we know that this is the same population found without the pill, we know that H_0 implies that the predicted relationship does not exist in nature, and thus that the independent variable does not work.

> **REMEMBER**   The *alternative hypothesis* (H_a) says the sample data represent a μ that reflects the predicted relationship. The *null hypothesis* (H_0) says the sample data poorly represent the μ that's found when the predicted relationship is not present.

Here's another example: Say that we test a sample of men to see if they differ in creativity from women, who (we know) have a μ of 75 on our creativity test. Looking for *some* kind of difference is a two-tailed situation. The alternative hypothesis is that men are different from women—having a population that is different from the population of creativity scores where μ is 75. Thus, our H_a about our sample of men is that their population mean is not 75, so H_a: $\mu \neq 75$. The null hypothesis is that, regardless of how the sample of men score, their *population* of scores is the same as for women. Therefore, their mean is the same as for women, so we have H_0: $\mu = 75$.

The final step prior to collecting data is to select and set up the appropriate statistical procedure. We'll violate the order of things, however, and go directly to some data so that you can understand what it is we're setting up.

The Logic of Statistical Hypothesis Testing

The statistical hypotheses for the IQ pill study are

H_0: $\mu = 100$

H_a: $\mu \neq 100$

Remember, these are hypotheses—guesses—about the population that our sample represents. (We have no uncertainty about what happens without the pill; we *know* the μ there.) And notice that, together, H_0 and H_a include all possibilities, so one or the other must be true: Our sample represents a population having either a μ equal to or not equal to 100. We use inferential procedures to test (choose between) these hypotheses. (Inferential procedures are also called "statistical hypothesis testing.")

To begin to have evidence that nature operates as we've proposed, our sample data must turn out as predicted. (If the sample mean with the pill is 100, then it looks as though, with or without the pill, IQ stays the same, and so we'd be finished.) Instead, say that we randomly selected a sample of 36 people, gave them the pill, measured their IQ, and found that their mean score was 105. Can we conclude that the pill works?

We would *like* to say this: People who have not taken this pill have a mean IQ of 100. If the pill did not work, then the sample mean should have been 100. Therefore, a sample mean of 105 suggests that the pill does work, raising IQ scores about 5 points. If the pill does this for the sample, it should do this for the population. Therefore, we expect that a population that received the pill would have a μ of 105. Our results appear to be consistent with our alternative hypothesis, H_a: $\mu \neq 100$: If we measured everyone in the population with and without the pill, we would have the two distributions shown previously in Figure 10.1, with the population that received the pill located at the μ of 105. Conclusion: We have demonstrated a relationship such that increased amounts of the pill are associated with increased IQ scores.

But hold on! Not so fast! Remember sampling error? We just assumed that our sample is *perfectly* representative of the population it represents. But what if there was sampling error? Maybe we obtained a mean of 105 not because the pill works, but because we inaccurately represented the situation where the pill does *not* work. Maybe the pill does nothing, but by chance we happened to select participants who *already* had an above-average IQ. Thus, maybe the null hypothesis is correct: Even though it doesn't look like it, maybe our sample actually represents the population where μ is 100. Maybe we have not demonstrated that the pill works.

In fact, we can never *know* whether our pill works based on the results of one study. Whether the sample mean is 105, 1050, or 105,000, it is still possible that the null hypothesis is true: The pill doesn't work, the sample actually represents the population where μ is 100, and the sample mean is different from 100 because of sampling error.

> *REMEMBER* The null hypothesis always maintains that the sample data reflect sampling error and that there is not really the predicted relationship in the population.

Thus, we cannot automatically infer that the relationship exists in the population when our sample data show the predicted relationship, because there are always two things that can produce such data: Sampling error or a real relationship in nature. Essentially, the H_0 says that sampling error produced the sample relationship, and so we should not believe there is a corresponding relationship in nature. The H_a says that there is a relationship in nature that produced the sample relationship, so that we can believe that nature operates as the sample data suggest.

The only way to resolve this dilemma for certain would be to give the pill to the entire population and see whether μ was 100 or 105. We cannot do that. But, although we can never prove whether the null hypothesis is true, we can determine how *likely* it is to be true. That is, we can determine the probability that sampling error would produce a sample mean of 105 when the sample actually comes from the population where μ is 100. If such a mean is "too unlikely," then we'll reject H_0, rejecting that our sample poorly represents this population.

If this sounds familiar, it's because it is the procedure discussed in the previous chapter. In fact, all parametric and nonparametric statistics involve this same logic: We always test the null hypothesis by determining how likely it is for chance to produce our sample data from the population described by the null hypothesis. If the sample data are unlikely, then we conclude that the null hypothesis is the incorrect hypothesis.

The only major difference among the various inferential procedures in this book is in their calculations. Therefore, to select the correct procedure for a particular study, be sure that the experiment's design and the nature of the dependent scores fit the procedure. In statistical lingo, be sure to consider the *assumptions* of the procedure. Further, check the assumptions and select your procedures *before* you collect the data, to be sure it will be "analyzable." Otherwise, it's possible to complete a study and then find out that no statistics can be applied. The IQ pill study meets the assumptions of the parametric procedure called the *z-test*.

TESTING A MEAN WHEN σ_X IS KNOWN: THE *z*-TEST

You already know how to perform the *z*-test. The **z-test** is the procedure for computing a *z*-score for a sample mean on the sampling distribution of means that we've discussed in previous chapters. The formula for the *z*-test is the formula we used in Chapter 6 and again in Chapter 9 (and we'll see it again in a moment). The *z*-test has four assumptions:

1. We have randomly selected one sample.

2. The dependent variable is at least approximately normally distributed in the population, and involves an interval or ratio scale.

3. We *know* the mean of the population of raw scores under some other condition of the independent variable.

4. We *know* the true standard deviation of the population (σ_X) described by the null hypothesis. (It is *not* estimated using the sample.)

The *z*-test is appropriate for our IQ pill study because we have one sample of IQ scores; these scores are normally distributed, interval scores; and we know the σ_X for the population. Say that from the research literature, we know that in the population where μ is 100, the standard deviation is 15.

> *REMEMBER* The *z-test* is used only if the raw score population's σ_X is *known.*

After selecting the statistical procedure, we set up the sampling distribution.

Setting Up the Sampling Distribution for a Two-Tailed Test

In the IQ pill study, H_0 is that the pill does not work, so our sample represents the population without the pill where μ is 100 (and σ_X is 15). To test H_0, we examine the sampling distribution of means created from this raw score population. Therefore, it is as if we have again hired our (very) bored statistician. Using the N of 36 that we had in our sample, she infinitely samples the raw score population of IQ scores without the pill where μ is 100. This will produce a sampling distribution of means with a μ of 100. Notice, the μ of the sampling distribution always equals the value of μ given in the null hypothesis. Here, H_0 is $\mu = 100$, indicating that we are sampling from the raw score population where μ is 100, so the average sample mean is also 100.

> *REMEMBER* The mean of the sampling distribution always equals the value described by H_0.

You can call this sampling distribution the H_0 sampling distribution because it describes the situation *when null is true:* It describes all possible random samples from the population where μ *is* 100. Any sample mean not equal to 100 occurs *solely* because of sampling error—the luck of the draw that determined who was selected for that particular sample. Thus, for the IQ pill study, the sampling distribution shows the frequency of all $\overline{X}$s we could possibly get through sampling error when the pill doesn't work. (Always add the phrase "when null is true" to any information you get from a sampling distribution.)

Once you envision the sampling distribution, set up the statistical test in the same way as in the previous chapter: Determine the size and location of the region of rejection, and then identify the critical value. The finished distribution is shown in Figure 10.4. To get there, however, we have some new symbols and terms.

1. *Choosing alpha:* Recall from Chapter 9 that our *criterion* is the probability that defines sample means as "too unlikely" to be representing the underlying raw score population, which in turn defines the size of the region of rejection. The symbol for the criterion is α, the Greek letter **alpha.** Researchers usually set their criterion at .05, so in code they say $\alpha = .05$, meaning that the region of rejection is the extreme 5% of the curve. (Later we'll see why we might use an even smaller α.)

2. *Locating the region of rejection in the two-tailed test:* Recall that the region of rejection may include both tails or only one tail of the sampling distribution. Which arrangement to use depends on whether you have created a two-tailed or one-tailed alternative hypothesis. In our example we created a two-tailed hypothesis, predicting that the pill would work by making people either smarter or dumber, so that their $\mu \neq 100$. Thus, we'll be correct if our $\overline{X}$ is either larger than 100 or smaller than 100 and, in either case, too unlikely to represent the population in which $\mu = 100$. By including sample means that are larger or smaller than 100, we include the *two* tails of the distribution. Therefore, as shown in Figure 10.4, in a two-tailed test, part of the region of rejection is in each tail.

3. *Determining the critical value:* We'll abbreviate the critical value of z as z_{crit}. Recall that with $\alpha = .05$, the two tails together make up a total of 5% of the distribution, so the region of rejection in each tail is 2.5% of the distribution. From the z-tables, $z = 1.96$ demarcates this region, and so we complete the picture in Figure 10.4 by adding that z_{crit} is ± 1.96.

Now the test of H_0 boils down to comparing the z-score for our sample mean to the z_{crit} of ± 1.96. Therefore, it's time to compute the z-score for the sample.

FIGURE 10.4 H_0 sampling distribution of IQ means for a two-tailed test

A region of rejection is in each tail of the distribution, marked by the critical values of ± 1.96

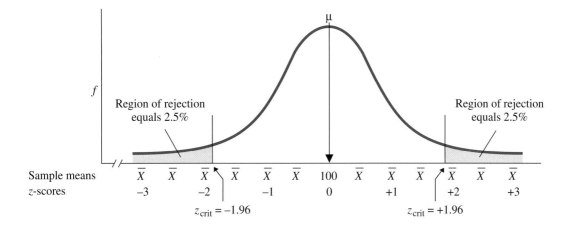

Computing z

Here is some more code. The z-score we compute is "obtained" from the data, so it is called z *obtained,* which we abbreviate as z_{obt}. You know how to compute this from previous chapters.

THE COMPUTATIONAL FORMULA FOR THE z-TEST IS

$$z_{obt} = \frac{\overline{X} - \mu}{\sigma_{\overline{X}}}$$

$\overline{X}$ is our sample mean. μ is the mean of the sampling distribution when H_0 is true (the μ of the raw score population that H_0 says the sample represents). $\sigma_{\overline{X}}$ is the standard error of the mean, which is computed as

$$\sigma_{\overline{X}} = \frac{\sigma_X}{\sqrt{N}}$$

where N is the N of the sample and σ_X is the true population standard deviation.

For the IQ pill study, the population standard deviation (σ_X) is 15, and N is 36. Thus, $\sigma_{\overline{X}}$ is

$$\sigma_{\overline{X}} = \frac{\sigma_X}{\sqrt{N}} = \frac{15}{\sqrt{36}} = \frac{15}{6} = 2.5$$

Then the z-score for our sample mean of 105 is

$$z_{obt} = \frac{\overline{X} - \mu}{\sigma_{\overline{X}}} = \frac{105 - 100}{2.5} = \frac{+5}{2.5} = +2.0$$

The final step is to interpret this z_{obt} by comparing it to z_{crit}.

INTERPRETING z

Remember that H_0 implies that our sample is simply poorly representing the raw score population where μ is 100. The H_0 sampling distribution shows how frequently—and thus how likely it is—that sampling error will produce such a sample mean when sampling from this raw score population. Therefore, if we are to believe H_0, the sampling distribution should show that a mean of 105 occurs relatively frequently and is thus likely in this situation. However, looking at the sampling distribution in Figure 10.5, we see just the opposite.

The high z_{obt} of +2.0 tells us that the bored statistician hardly ever obtained a sample mean of 105 when drawing samples that represent the population where μ is 100. This makes it difficult to believe that we obtained our sample mean by drawing it from the population where μ is 100. In fact, because a z_{obt} of +2.0 is beyond the z_{crit} of ± 1.96, our sample is in the region of rejection. Therefore, we conclude that our mean of 105 is

FIGURE 10.5 Sampling distribution of IQ means

The sample mean of 105 is located at $z_{obt} = +2.0$.

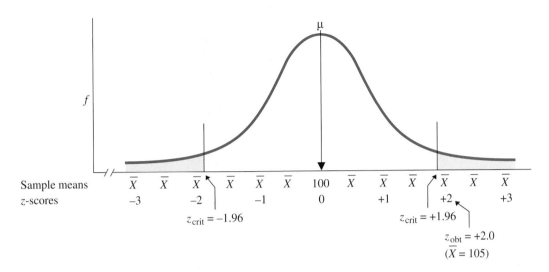

"too unlikely" to have come from and thus represent the population where $\mu = 100$, so we reject that our sample is poorly representing this population.

In statistical terms we have "rejected" the null hypothesis. If we reject H_0, then we are left with H_a, and so we "accept H_a." Here, H_a is $\mu \neq 100$, so we accept that our sample represents a population where μ is not 100. Thus, in sum, we have determined that the sample is unlikely to represent the population where μ is 100, so we conclude that it is likely to represent a population where μ is not 100.

> **REMEMBER** When a sample statistic falls beyond the critical value, the statistic lies in the region of rejection, so we *reject* H_0 *and accept* H_a.

Reporting Significant Results

The shorthand way to communicate that we have rejected H_0 and accepted H_a is to use the term *significant*. (Statistical hypothesis testing is sometimes called "significance testing.") *Significant* does *not* mean important or impressive. **Significant** indicates that our results are too unlikely to occur if the predicted relationship does not exist in the population. Therefore, we imply that the relationship found in the experiment is "believable," representing a "real" relationship found in nature, and that it was not produced by sampling error from the situation in which the relationship does not exist.

The term *significant* is used in several ways. We might say that our pill produced a "significant difference" in IQ scores. This indicates that the difference between the sample mean and the μ found without the pill is too large to accept as being due to sampling error. Or we might say that we obtained a "significant z": our sample mean has too large a z-score to accept that the sample represents the μ described by H_0. Or we can say that there is a "significant effect of the pill": The change in IQ scores reflected by the sample mean is unlikely to be caused by chance sampling error, so presumably it is the effect of—caused by—changing the conditions of the independent variable.

> REMEMBER   The term *significant* means that we have rejected the null hypothesis and believe that the data reflect a relationship found in nature.

Notice that your decision is simply either yes, reject H_0, or no, do not reject H_0. All z-scores in the region of rejection are treated the same, so one z_{obt} cannot be "more significant" than another. Likewise, there is no such thing as "very significant" or "highly significant." (That's like saying "very yes" or "highly yes.") If z_{obt} is beyond z_{crit}, regardless of how far it is beyond, you completely and fully reject H_0 and the results are simply significant, period!

But also recognize that whether a result is significant depends solely on how you define "too unlikely." *Significant* implicitly means that *given your* α and therefore the size of your region of rejection, you have decided that the data are unlikely to represent the population described by the null hypothesis. Therefore, anytime you report the results of a statistical test, you indicate the statistic computed, the obtained value, and the α used. Thus, to report our significant z_{obt} of $+2.0$, we would write

$$z = +2.0, p < .05$$

Notice that instead of indicating that α equals .05, we indicate that the probability (p) is less than .05. We'll discuss the reason for this shortly.

Interpreting Significant Results

By accepting H_a we also accept the corresponding experimental hypothesis that the independent variable works as predicted: Apparently, we've demonstrated that our IQ pill works. However, there are three very important restrictions on how far we can go in believing this claim.

First, we did not *prove* that H_0 is false. All we have "proven" is that a sample of 36 scores is *unlikely* to produce a mean of 105 if the scores come from a population where $\mu = 100$ and σ_X is 15. However, as the sampling distribution plainly shows, means of 105 *do* occur once in a while when *we are* representing this population. Maybe the pill did not work, and our sample was simply very unrepresentative. There is *always* that possibility.

Second, by accepting H_a, we accept that our sample represents a population of scores above 100. But we have not proven that it was the *pill* that produced these scores. Some other variable might have actually caused the higher IQ scores in the sample. Maybe they occurred because the participants cheated on the IQ test, or because there was something in the air that made them smarter or because there were sunspots, or who-knows-what! If we've performed a good experiment and can eliminate such factors, then we can *argue* that it is the pill that produced higher IQ scores.

Finally, assuming that the pill increased IQ scores and produced the mean of 105, then it is logical to assume that if we gave the pill to everyone in the population, the resulting μ would be 105. However, the μ is probably not *exactly* 105. Our sample may reflect (you guessed it) sampling error! That is, the sample may accurately reflect that the pill increases IQ, but it may not perfectly represent *how much* the pill increases scores. Therefore, if we gave the pill to the population, we might find a μ of 104, or

106, or *any* other value. However, a sample mean of 105 is most likely when the population μ is close to 105, so we would conclude that the μ resulting from our pill is probably *around* 105.

Bearing these qualifications in mind, we can return to the $\overline{X}$ of 105 and interpret it the way we wanted to several pages back: It looks like the pill increases IQ scores by about 5 points. But now we have much greater confidence in this conclusion, because, by knowing that the results are significant, we are confident that we are not being misled by sampling error. Therefore, we are more confident that a relationship exists in the population and that we have discovered something about how nature operates. (But stay tuned, because we could be wrong.) At this point, we would return to being behavioral researchers and interpret the results "psychologically": We translate the relationship and scores into behaviors, describing how the ingredients in the pill affect intelligence, what brain mechanisms are involved, and so on.

Retaining H_0

For the sake of illustration, let's say that the IQ pill had instead produced a sample mean of 99. Now the *z*-score for the sample is

$$z_{obt} = \frac{\overline{X} - \mu}{\sigma_{\overline{X}}} = \frac{99 - 100}{2.5} = \frac{-1.0}{2.5} = -.40$$

As usual, we interpret this z_{obt} by examining the sampling distribution, shown in Figure 10.6.

A z_{obt} of $-.40$ is *not* beyond the z_{crit} of ± 1.96, so the sample does not lie in the region of rejection. As the figure shows, when the bored statistician sampled the population with a μ of 100, she frequently obtained a mean of 99. Thus, *our* sample mean of 99 was likely to have occurred if we were representing this population. Therefore, the

FIGURE 10.6 Sampling distribution of IQ means

The sample mean of 99 has a z_{obt} of -40.

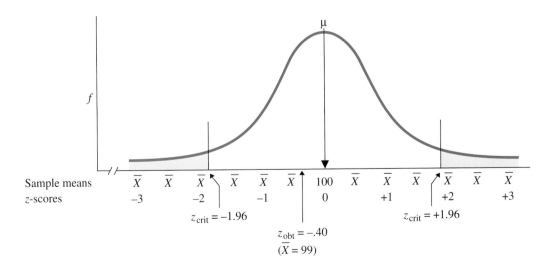

null hypothesis—that our sample is merely a poor representation of a population where μ is 100—is a reasonable hypothesis. So, we will *not* conclude that the pill works. After all, it makes no sense to claim that the pill works if the results were likely to occur *without* the pill. Likewise, we never conclude that any independent variable works if the results are likely to be due to sampling error. In such situations we say that we have "failed to reject H_0" or that we "retain H_0." Sampling error from the population where μ is 100 can explain our results just fine, thank you, so we will not reject this explanation.

The shorthand way to communicate all of this is to say that we have *nonsignificant* results. (Don't say *insignificant*.) **Nonsignificant** indicates that the results are *not* too unlikely to accept as being due to sampling error. In other words, the differences reflected by our results were likely to have occurred through chance, without there being a relationship in nature.

> **REMEMBER** *Nonsignificant* means that we failed to reject H_0 because the results are not in the region of rejection and are thus likely to occur when there is no real relationship in nature.

When a result is not significant, we again report the α level used in making the decision. Thus, to report our nonsignificant z_{obt}, we would write

$$z = -0.40, \quad p > .05$$

Notice that with nonsignificant results, we indicate that *p* is *greater* than .05.

Interpreting Nonsignificant Results

When we retain H_0, we also retain the experimental hypothesis that the independent variable does not work as predicted. However, we have not proven that it does *not* work. We have simply failed to find convincing evidence that it *does* work. The only thing we're sure of is that, if there was no relationship, sampling error *could* have produced our data. Thus, by failing to reject H_0, we *still* have two contradictory hypotheses that are both viable: (1) H_0, that the data only reflect sampling error and do not really represent a relationship, and (2) H_a, that the data do not reflect sampling error and do represent a relationship. Thus, maybe in fact the pill did not work. Or maybe the pill did work, but it changed scores so little that we weren't convinced that it works. Or maybe the pill would normally change IQ scores greatly, but we didn't see this because we have sampling error in representing the different population that would be created. We simply don't know if the pill works or not.

Therefore, when you do not reject H_0, you cannot say anything about whether the independent variable actually influences behavior or not, and you do not even begin to interpret the results "psychologically." All that you can say is that you did not find a significant difference, and thus failed to demonstrate the predicted relationship in the population.

> **REMEMBER** Nonsignificant results provide no convincing evidence—one way or the other—as to whether a relationship exists in nature.

You cannot design a study to show that no relationship exists. For example, you could not try to show that the pill does not work. At best, you'll end up retaining both H_0 and H_a, and at worst, you'll end up rejecting H_0, showing that it does work.

Summary of Statistical Hypothesis Testing

The steps and logic we've discussed are similar to all inferential procedures, so it's worthwhile to review them.

1. Create the experimental hypotheses that predict the relationship the study will or will not demonstrate.
2. Design the study to demonstrate the predicted relationship in the sample data.
3. Create the statistical hypothesis: H_0 describes the population μ that the sample mean represents if the predicted relationship does not exist. H_a describes the population μ that the $\overline{X}$ represents if the predicted relationship does exist.
4. Select the appropriate parametric or nonparametric procedure by matching the assumptions of the procedure to the study.
5. Select the value of α, which determines the size of the region of rejection.
6. Collect the data and compute the obtained z-score for the sample.
7. Set up the sampling distribution and, based on α, determine the critical value.
8. Compare the obtained value to the critical value.
9. If the obtained value lies beyond the critical value in the region of rejection, reject H_0, accept H_a, and describe the results as significant. Then describe and interpret the relationship in the population based on the sample data.
10. If the obtained value does not lie beyond the critical value in the region of rejection, do not reject H_0, and describe the results as nonsignificant. Do *not* draw any conclusions about the relationship.

THE ONE-TAILED TEST

Recall that a *one-tailed test* is used when we predict the *direction* in which scores will change. The statistical hypotheses and sampling distribution are different in a one-tailed test.

The One-Tailed Test for Increasing Scores

Say that we had developed a "smart" pill: the experimental hypotheses are (1) the pill makes people smarter by increasing IQ scores, or (2) the pill does not make people smarter.

For the statistical hypotheses, start with the alternative hypothesis: People without the pill produce a μ of 100, so if the pill works for everyone, it will *increase* the population of IQ scores, and μ will be greater than 100. Therefore, H_a: $\mu > 100$. On the other hand, if the pill does not work as predicted, either it will leave IQ scores *unchanged* or it will *decrease* them (making people dumber). Then μ will either equal 100 or be less than 100. Therefore, H_0: $\mu \leq 100$.

We will again test H_0 by testing whether the sample represents the raw score population in which μ *equals* 100. This is because if the population μ with the pill is above 100, then it is automatically above any value less than 100.

> **REMEMBER** A one-tailed null hypothesis always includes a population having a parameter equal to some value. Test H_0 by testing whether the sample data represent that population.

We again set $\alpha = .05$, but because we have a one-tailed test, the region of rejection is in only *one tail* of the sampling distribution. You can identify which tail to put it in by identifying the result you must see in order to claim that your independent variable works as predicted. To say that the smart pill works, two things must occur: First, the sample mean must be larger than 100. If not, then not even the people in your sample are smarter when given the pill. Second, the sample mean must be *significantly* larger than 100. Means that are significantly *larger* than 100 are in the region of rejection in the *upper* tail of the sampling distribution. Therefore, the entire region is in the upper tail of the distribution, as shown in Figure 10.7. (We don't place anything in the lower tail, because sample means down there indicate the same thing as means close to 100: All show that the pill doesn't work, and we're not interested in distinguishing between whether it doesn't work because it has no influence on IQ or because it makes people dumber.) Then, as in the previous chapter, the region of rejection in the upper tail of the distribution that constitutes 5% of the curve is marked by a z_{crit} of $+1.645$.

Say that after testing the pill on a sample ($N = 36$) we find $\overline{X} = 106.58$. The sampling distribution is still based on the population with $\mu = 100$ and $\sigma_X = 15$, so $\sigma_{\overline{X}} = 15/\sqrt{36} = 2.5$, and then $z_{obt} = (106.58 - 100)/2.5 = +2.63$. As shown in Figure 10.7, this z_{obt} is beyond z_{crit}, so it is in the region of rejection. Therefore, the sample mean is unlikely to be representing the population having $\mu = 100$. If the sample is unlikely to represent the population where μ is 100, then it's even more unlikely to represent a

FIGURE 10.7 Sampling distribution of IQ means for a one-tailed test of whether scores increase

The region of rejection is entirely in the upper tail.

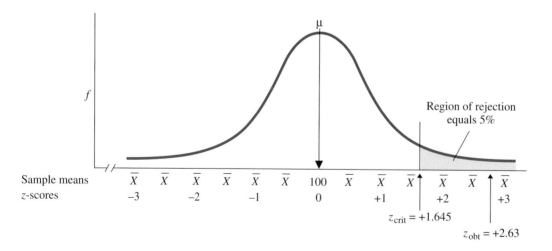

population that has a $\mu < 100$. Therefore, we reject the null hypothesis that $\mu \leq 100$, and accept the alternative hypothesis that $\mu > 100$. We conclude that the pill produces a *significant increase* in IQ scores, and estimate that with the pill, μ would equal about 106.58 (keeping in mind all of the cautions and qualifications for interpreting significant results that we discussed previously).

If z_{obt} had not been in the region of rejection, we would retain H_0, and would have no evidence as to whether the smart pill works or not.

The One-Tailed Test for Decreasing Scores

Say that, instead, we had created a pill to lower IQ scores. If the pill works, then μ would be *less than* 100, so H_a: $\mu < 100$. But, if the pill does not work as predicted, it would produce the same scores as no pill (with $\mu = 100$) or it would make people smarter (with $\mu > 100$), so H_0: $\mu \geq 100$.

We again test H_0 using the previous sampling distribution. Now, however, for us to conclude that the pill lowers IQ, our sample mean must be significantly *less* than 100. Therefore, the region of rejection is in the lower tail of the distribution, as in Figure 10.8.

With $\alpha = .05$, z_{crit} is now *minus* 1.645. If the sample produces a *negative* z_{obt} beyond -1.645 (for example, $z_{obt} = -1.69$), then we reject the H_0 that the sample mean represents a μ equal to or greater than 100, and accept the H_a that the sample represents a μ less than 100. However, if z_{obt} does not fall in the region of rejection (for example, if $z_{obt} = -1.25$), we do not reject H_0, and we have no evidence as to whether the pill works or not.

Choosing One-Tailed versus Two-Tailed Tests

One-tailed tests have a region of rejection in only one tail, so z_{obt} is significant only if it lies beyond z_{crit} *and* has the same sign as z_{crit}. This means that you could not reject H_0 if

FIGURE 10.8 Sampling distribution of IQ means for a one-tailed test of whether scores decrease

The region of rejection is entirely in the lower tail.

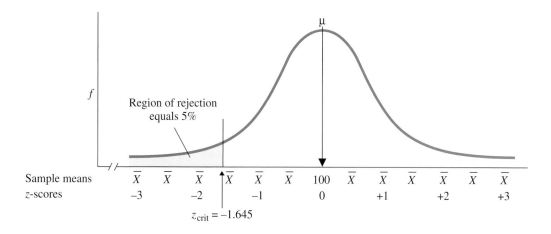

the pills worked opposite to the way you predicted they would work. You cannot move the region of rejection after the results are in order to make them significant. If the smart pill produced lowered scores, you wouldn't say, "Whoops, I meant to predict it would decrease scores." Remember, the tail you use is determined by your experimental hypothesis, and, after years of developing the theoretical and biochemical basis for a "smart pill," it would make no sense to suddenly say that the same basis leads you to predict it's a "dumb pill." Likewise, it makes no sense to switch between a one-tailed and a two-tailed test after the fact.

Therefore, use a one-tailed test *only* if you have a *convincing* reason for predicting the direction in which the independent variable will change scores. Otherwise, use a two-tailed test. This is safer because it allows you to conclude that the independent variable produced a change, even if you did not predict whether it would increase or decrease scores.

> *REMEMBER*   Use a two-tailed test unless you have a good reason for predicting the direction the scores will change.

ERRORS IN STATISTICAL DECISION MAKING

There is one other issue to consider when performing hypothesis testing, and it involves potential errors. These are not errors in our calculations, but rather errors in our decisions: Regardless of whether you conclude that the sample does or does not represent the predicted relationship, you may be wrong.

Type I Errors: Rejecting H_0 When H_0 Is True

Sometimes, the variables we investigate are *not* related in nature, and so H_0 is really true. If, when in this situation, we obtain data that cause us to reject H_0, then we make an error. A **Type I error** is defined as rejecting H_0 when H_0 is true. In practical terms, we conclude that the independent variable works when it really doesn't.

Thus, when we rejected H_0 and claimed that the pill worked, it's possible that it did not work and we made a Type I error. How could this happen? Because our sample was exactly what the sampling distribution indicated it was: a very unlikely and unrepresentative sample from the population having a μ of 100. In fact, the sample so poorly represented the situation where the pill did not work, we mistakenly thought the pill did work. *In a Type I error, there is so much sampling error that we—and our statistical procedures—are fooled into concluding that the predicted relationship exists when it really does not.*

Any time researchers discuss Type I errors, it is a *given* that H_0 is true. Think of it as being in the "Type I situation" whenever you discuss the situation in which the predicted relationship does not exist. If you *reject* H_0 in this situation, then you've made a Type I error. If you *retain* H_0 in this situation, then you've avoided a Type I error: by concluding there is no evidence that the pill works, you've made the correct decision because, in reality, the pill doesn't work.

We never know if we're making a Type I error, because only nature knows if the variables are related or not. It's still important to know about this error, however, especially because we can determine its probability. First, assume we're in the Type I situation—the null hypothesis *is* true. Then the probability of making the error is the probability of saying "reject" in this situation. This probability is determined by the size of the region of rejection, so the theoretical probability of a Type I error equals α. Here's why. For the IQ pill, for example, Figure 10.9 shows the sampling distribution when H_0 is true—when we're in the Type I situation and μ equals 100. With $\alpha = .05$, the total region of rejection is 5% of the distribution, so over the long run sample means that are in the region of rejection occur 5% of the time in this situation. In other words, *when* H_0 *is true,* sample means that cause us to *reject* H_0 occur 5% of the time. Rejecting H_0 when it is true is a Type I error. Thus, over the long run, the relative frequency of Type I errors is .05. Therefore, anytime we reject H_0, the theoretical probability that we've just made a Type I error is .05. (The same is true in a one-tailed test.)

You either will or will not make the correct decision when H_0 is true. If α is the theoretical probability of making a Type I error, then $1 - \alpha$ is the probability of avoiding a Type I error. Thus, if 5% of the time samples are in the region of rejection when H_0 is true, then 95% of the time they are not in the region of rejection when H_0 is true. Therefore, 95% of the time we will not obtain sample means that cause us to erroneously reject H_0: Anytime you retain H_0, the theoretical probability is .95 that you've avoided a Type I error.

Here is an important distinction: Although the *theoretical* probability of a Type I error equals α, the *actual* probability is slightly less than α. This is because in figuring the size of the region of rejection, we include the critical value. Yet to reject H_0, z_{obt} must be *larger* than the critical value. We cannot determine the precise area under the curve for the infinitely small point located at z_{crit}, so we can't remove it from our 5%. All that we can say is that when α is .05, any z_{obt} that is in the region of rejection is in slightly less than 5% of the curve. Because the actual area of the region of rejection is less than α, the actual probability of a Type I error is also less than α.

Thus, in each of our previous examples when we rejected H_0, the probability that we had made a Type I error was slightly less than .05. That is why we reported our significant

FIGURE 10.9 Sampling distribution of sample means showing that 5% of all sample means fall into the region of rejection when H_0 is true

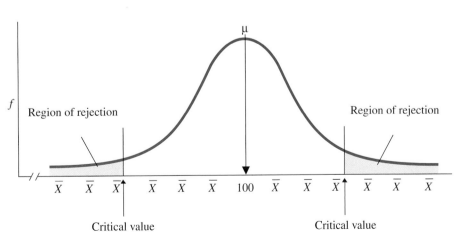

result using $p < .05$. Think of $p < .05$ as a shortened form of p(Type I error) $< .05$. This indicates that the probability is slightly less than .05 that we made a Type I error here. You must always report the probability that you have made a Type I error.

On the other hand, we reported a nonsignificant result using $p > .05$. Here, $p > .05$ communicates that the reason we did not call this result significant is because to do so would require a region greater than 5% of the curve. But then the probability of a Type I error would be greater than our α of .05, and that's unacceptable.

Typically, researchers do not use an α larger than .05 because then it is too likely that we'll conclude there's a relationship in nature when actually there isn't. This may not sound like a big deal, but the next time you fly in an airplane, consider that the designer's belief that the wings will stay on may actually be a Type I error: He's been misled by sampling error into *erroneously* thinking the wings will stay on. A 5% chance of this is scary enough—we certainly don't want more than a 5% chance that the wings will fall off. In science, we are skeptical and careful, so we make decisions like a jury: We want to be convinced "beyond a reasonable doubt" that sampling error did not produce our results, and having only a 5% chance that it did is reasonably convincing.

Type I errors are the reason a study must meet the assumptions of a statistical procedure, because if we violate the assumptions, then the true probability of a Type I error will turn out to be *larger* than our α (so it's larger than we think it is). Thus, if we severely violate a procedure's assumptions, we may think that α is .05 when in fact it is, say, .20! But recall that parametric tests are "robust." This means that we can violate the assumptions of a procedure somewhat, and the probability of a Type I error will still be close to α (it will be only, say, .051 when we've set α at .050).

Sometimes making a Type I error is so dangerous that we want to reduce its probability even further. Then we usually set alpha at .01. For example, we might make $\alpha = .01$ if the smart pill had some dangerous side effects. We would not want to expose the public to such dangers if the pill is actually worthless, so we would make it even less likely to conclude that the pill works when it really does not. When α is .01, the region of rejection is the extreme 1% of the sampling distribution, so we have a larger absolute critical value, and z_{obt} must be larger to be significant. Therefore, we will reject H_0 when it is true only 1% of the time, so the probability of making a Type I error is now $p < .01$.

Remember, however, that we use the term *significant* in an all-or-nothing fashion: A result is *not* "more" significant when $\alpha = .01$ than when $\alpha = .05$. If z_{obt} lies in the region of rejection that was used to define significant, then the result is significant, period! The *only* difference is that when $\alpha = .01$, there is a smaller probability that we've made a Type I error.

Finally, many computer programs compute the exact probability of a Type I error for a particular result. For example, we might see "$p = .02$." This indicates that the z_{obt} lies in the extreme 2% of the sampling distribution, and thus there is a .02 probability of a Type I error here. If our α is .05, then this result is significant. However, we might see "$p = .07$," which indicates that to call this result significant we'd need a region of rejection that is the extreme 7% of the sampling distribution. Because this implies an α of .07, which is greater than .05 and thus too big, this result is not significant.

> **REMEMBER**   When H_0 is true, if we reject H_0, we've made a *Type I error*. Its theoretical probability is α. Avoiding a Type I error is retaining H_0 when we're in the situation where H_0 is true, and its theoretical probability is $1 - \alpha$.

Type II Errors: Retaining H_0 When H_0 Is False

In addition to Type I errors, it is possible to make a totally different kind of error. Sometimes, the variables we investigate really *are* related in nature, and so H_0 really is false. If, when in this situation, we obtain data that cause us to retain H_0, then we make a Type II error. A **Type II error** is defined as retaining H_0 when H_0 is false (and H_a is true). With a Type II error we conclude that we have no evidence for the predicted relationship when, in fact, the relationship exists. In practical terms, here we fail to identify that the independent variable really does work.

Thus, when our sample mean of 99 caused us to retain H_0 and not claim the pill worked, it's possible that the pill did work and we made a Type II error. How could this happen? Because the sample mean of 99 was so close to 100 (the μ without the pill) that the difference could easily be explained as sampling error, so we weren't convinced there was a relationship here. Perhaps what we missed is that the pill only slightly decreases IQ, dropping everyone's score about 1 point to a μ of only 99. Or perhaps the pill would actually *increase* IQ greatly, say to a μ of 105, but we obtained an unrepresentative sample of this. Either way, *in a Type II error, the sample mean is so close to the μ described by H_0 that we—and our statistics—are fooled into concluding that the predicted relationship does not exist when it really does.*

Anytime we discuss Type II errors, it's a *given* that H_0 is false and H_a is true. That is, that we're in the "Type II situation," in which the predicted relationship does exist. If we *retain* H_0 in this situation, then we've made a Type II error. If we *reject* H_0 in this situation, then we've avoided a Type II error: We've made the correct decision by concluding that the pill works because the pill does work.

Researchers also never know when they've made a Type II error, but we can determine its probability. The computations of this are beyond the introductory level, but you should know that the symbol for the theoretical probability of a Type II error is β, the Greek letter **beta.** Whenever you retain H_0, β is the probability that you've made a Type II error. On the other hand, $1 - \beta$ is the probability of avoiding a Type II error. Thus, anytime you reject H_0, the probability is $1 - \beta$ that you've made the correct decision and rejected a false H_0.

> *REMEMBER*   A *Type II error* is retaining H_0 when H_0 is false, and its theoretical probability is β. Avoiding a Type II error is rejecting H_0 when H_0 is false, and its theoretical probability is $1 - \beta$.

Comparing Type I and Type II Errors

You probably think Type I and Type II errors are two of the most confusing inventions ever devised. So, first recognize that Type I and Type II errors are mutually exclusive: If there's a possibility you've made one type of error, then there is no chance that you've made the other type of error. Remember: In the Type I *situation, H_0* is really true (the variables are not related). In the Type II *situation H_0* is really false (the variables are related). You can't be in both situations simultaneously because variables can't be related *and* not related at the same time. Also, if you don't make one type of error, then you are *not* automatically making the other error because you might be making a correct decision. Therefore, the type of error you can *potentially* make is determined by your situation—what nature "says" about whether there is a relationship. Then, whether you actually make the error depends on whether you agree or disagree with nature.

Thus, there are actually four possible outcomes in any study. Look at Table 10.1. As in the upper row of the table, sometimes (although we never know when) H_0 is really true: Then if we reject H_0, we make a Type I error (with a $p = \alpha$). If we retain H_0, we avoid a Type I error and make the correct decision (with $p = 1 - \alpha$). But, as in the lower row of the table, sometimes (we also never know when) H_0 is really false: Then if we retain H_0, we make a Type II error (with $p = \beta$), and if we reject H_0, we avoid a Type II error and make the correct decision (with $p = 1 - \beta$).

In any experiment the results of your inferential procedure will place you in one of the *columns* of Table 10.1. If you reject H_0, then either we worry that you've made a Type I error, or you've made the correct decision and avoided a Type II error. If you retain H_0, then either we worry that you've made a Type II error, or you've made the correct decision and avoided a Type I error.

Researchers perform inferential procedures using a small α because their primary concern is to minimize the probability of Type I errors. The most serious error is to conclude that an independent variable works when really it does not, because basing scientific "facts" on what are actually Type I errors can cause untold damage. On the other hand, Type II errors are also important. In order for us to accurately learn about nature, we must avoid making Type II errors and conclude that an independent variable works when it really does.

Power

Of the various outcomes in Table 10.1, the goal of research is to reject H_0 when it is false: We conclude that the pill works, and the truth is that the pill does work. Not only have we avoided making an error, but we have learned about a relationship in nature. This ability is so important that it has a special name: **Power** is the probability that we will reject H_0 when it is false, correctly concluding that the sample data represent a relationship. When H_0 is false, we're in the Type II situation, so in other words, power is the probability of not making a Type II error, so power equals $1 - \beta$.

Power is important because, after all, why bother to conduct a study if we're unlikely to reject the null hypothesis even when there *is* a relationship present? Therefore,

TABLE 10.1 Possible Results of Rejecting or Retaining H_0

		Our Decision	
		We Reject $\mathbf{H_0}$	*We Retain* $\mathbf{H_0}$
	Type I situation: H_0 *is true* *(no relationship exists)*	We make a Type I error $(p = \alpha)$	We are correct, avoiding a Type I error $(p = 1 - \alpha)$
The truth about H_0	Type II situation: H_0 *is false* *(a relationship exists)*	We are correct, avoiding a Type II error $(p = 1 - \beta)$	We make a Type II error $(p = \beta)$

power is a concern anytime we do not reject H_0, because we wonder "Did we just miss a relationship?" For example, previously, when we did not find a significant effect of the pill, maybe the problem was that we lacked power: Maybe we were unlikely to reject H_0 *even if the pill really worked.*

To avoid this doubt, we strive to *maximize* the power of a study (maximizing the size of $1 - \beta$). Then we'll have confidence in our decision if we do ultimately retain null. Essentially, the idea is to do everything we can to insure that in case we end up in the Type II situation where there is a relationship in nature, we—and our statistics—will not miss the relationship. If we still end up retaining H_0, we know it's not for lack of trying. We're confident that if the relationship was out there, we would have found it, so it must be that the relationship is *not* out there. Therefore, we are confident in the decision to retain H_0, and, in statistical lingo we say that we're confident we have avoided a Type II error.

> *REMEMBER* We seek to maximize *power* so that if we retain H_0, we are confident we are not making a Type II error.

The time to build in power is when designing a study. We're talking about being in the Type II situation here, so it's a given that there really is a relationship in nature. We can't do anything to ensure that we're in this situation (that's up to nature), but assuming we are, then the goal is to have *significant* results. Therefore, we increase power by increasing the likelihood that our results will be significant. Results are significant if z_{obt} is larger than z_{crit}, so anything that increases the size of the obtained value relative to the critical value increases power.

We influence power first through the statistics we use. It is better to design a study so that you can use parametric procedures, because parametric procedures are more powerful than nonparametric ones: Analyzing data using a parametric test is more likely to produce significant results than analyzing the same data using a nonparametric test. Then, in case we're in the situation where H_0 is truly false, we're more likely to avoid a Type II error.

Also, a one-tailed test is more powerful than a two-tailed test. This is because the z_{crit} for a one-tailed test (1.645) is smaller than the z_{crit} for a two-tailed test (1.96). All other things being equal, your z_{obt} is more likely to be beyond 1.645, so you're more likely to have significant results. (You can reject H_0 only if z_{obt} has the same sign as z_{crit}, so you have more power *only* if you correctly predict the direction scores will change.)

In later chapters you'll see additional ways to maximize power. If you think we're rigging the decision in favor of rejecting H_0, understand that being more likely to reject H_0 when in the Type II situation doesn't mean we're more likely to reject H_0 when in the Type I situation, or vice versa. Setting α at .05 or less protects us if we end up in the situation where H_0 is true (limiting Type I errors). Maximizing power protects us if we end up in the situation where H_0 is false (limiting Type II errors). Together, these strategies minimize our errors, regardless of whether or not there's really a relationship.

> *REMEMBER* When discussing power, it is a given that H_0 is false. Power is increased by increasing the obtained value relative to the critical value so that the results are more likely to be significant.

PUTTING IT ALL TOGETHER

Essentially, the purpose of inferential statistics is to minimize the probability of making Type I and Type II errors. If we had not performed the z-test for our initial IQ pill study, we might easily have made a Type I error: We might have erroneously concluded that the pill raises IQ to around 105 when, in fact, we were being misled by sampling error. We would have no idea if this had occurred, nor even the chances that it occurred. After finding a significant result, however, we are confident that we did not make a Type I error, because the probability of doing so is less than .05. Likewise, if the results were not significant, through power we minimize the probability of a Type II error, so we are confident that we did not miss a pill that actually works.

All statistical hypothesis testing procedures follow the logic described here: H_0 is the hypothesis that says your data represent the populations you would find if the predicted relationship does not exist; H_a says that your data represent the predicted relationship. You then compute something like a z-score for the data on the sampling distribution when H_0 is true. If the z-score is larger than the critical value, it is unlikely that the results represent the populations described by H_0, so we reject H_0 and accept H_a. The results are called significant, meaning essentially that they are "believable": The relationship depicted in the sample data can be believed as existing in nature rather than being a chance pattern resulting from sampling error. That's it! That's inferential statistics (well, not quite).

CHAPTER SUMMARY

1. *Sampling error* occurs when random chance produces a sample statistic that is not equal to the population parameter it represents.

2. *Inferential statistics* are procedures for deciding whether sample data represent a particular relationship in the population.

3. *Parametric statistics* are inferential procedures that require assumptions about the parameters of the raw score populations the data represent. They are performed when it is appropriate to compute the mean.

4. *Nonparametric statistics* are inferential procedures that do not require stringent assumptions about the population parameters represented by a sample. They are performed when it is appropriate to compute the median or mode.

5. *The alternative hypothesis* (H_a) is the statistical hypothesis that describes the population μs being represented if the predicted relationship exists. H_a implies that the sample mean represents one of these μs.

6. *The null hypothesis* (H_0) is the statistical hypothesis that describes the population μs being represented if the predicted relationship does not exist. H_0 implies that the sample mean represents one of these μs.

7. A *two-tailed test* is used when we do not predict the direction in which the dependent scores will change as the independent variable changes. A *one-tailed test* is used when the direction of the relationship is predicted.

8. *Alpha (α)* is the theoretical size of the region of rejection. Typically, α equals .05.

9. The *z-test* is the parametric procedure used in a one-sample experiment if (a) the population of raw scores is normally distributed and contains interval or ratio scores, and (b) the standard deviation of the raw score population (σ_X) is *known*.

10. If z_{obt} lies beyond z_{crit}, then the corresponding sample mean lies in the region of rejection. This indicates that the mean is unlikely to occur when sampling from the population described by H_0. Therefore, we *reject H_0* and *accept H_a*. This is called a *significant* result and is taken as evidence that the predicted relationship exists in the population.

11. If z_{obt} does not lie beyond z_{crit}, then the corresponding sample mean is *not* in the region of rejection. This indicates that the mean is likely to occur when sampling the population described by H_0. Therefore, we *fail to reject*—or we *retain*—H_0. This is called a *nonsignificant* result and is taken as a failure to obtain evidence that the predicted relationship exists in the population.

12. A *Type I error* occurs when a true H_0 is rejected. The theoretical probability of a Type I error equals α. If a result is significant, the probability of a Type I error is $p < \alpha$. The theoretical probability of avoiding a Type I error by retaining a true H_0 is $1 - \alpha$.

13. A *Type II error* occurs when a false H_0 is retained. The theoretical probability of making a Type II error is β. The theoretical probability of avoiding a Type II error by rejecting a false H_0 is $1 - \beta$.

14. When we reject H_0, either we have committed a Type I error or we have avoided a Type II error. When we retain H_0, either we have committed a Type II error or we have avoided a Type I error.

15. *Power* is the probability of rejecting a false H_0, and it equals $1 - \beta$. When used appropriately, parametric procedures are more powerful than nonparametric procedures, and one-tailed tests are more powerful than two-tailed tests.

KEY TERMS: Can You Define the Following?

$\geq$ $\leq$ $\neq$ H_0 H_a α z_{crit} z_{obt} β

REVIEW QUESTIONS

(Answers for odd-numbered questions are in Appendix C.)

1. (a) What is sampling error? (b) Why does the possibility of sampling error present a problem to researchers when inferring a population μ from a sample $\overline{X}$?

2. What are inferential statistics used for?

3. (a) What does α stand for, and what two things does it determine? (b) How does the size of α affect whether a result is significant or nonsignificant?

4. What four things must a researcher do prior to collecting data for a study?

5. What are experimental hypotheses?

6. (a) What does H_0 communicate? (b) What does H_a communicate?

7. When do you use a one-tailed test? When do you use a two-tailed test?

8. (a) What does the term *significant* convey about the results of an experiment? What is a significant result in terms of: (b) when you compare the obtained and critical values? (c) whether your results lie in the region of rejection? (d) The likelihood of obtaining your sample mean when H_0 is true?

9. (a) Why should you prefer parametric procedures? (b) Why can you use parametric procedures even if you do not perfectly meet their assumptions? (c) What happens if you seriously violate the assumptions of a procedure?

10. (a) What are the advantage and disadvantage of two-tailed tests? (b) What are the advantage and disadvantage of one-tailed tests?

11. (a) What is power? (b) Why do researchers want to maximize power? (c) What result makes us worry whether we have sufficient power? (d) Why is a one-tailed test more powerful than a two-tailed test?

12. (a) Why is obtaining a significant result a goal of research? (b) Why is declaring the results significant not the final step in conducting research?

APPLICATION QUESTIONS

13. For the following experiments describe the experimental hypotheses using the independent and dependent variables: (a) Studying whether the amount of pizza consumed by college students during finals week increases relative to the rest of the semester. (b) Studying whether performing breathing exercises alters blood pressure. (c) Studying whether sensitivity to pain is affected by increased levels of hormones. (d) Studying whether frequency of dreaming while sleeping decreases as a function of more light in the room.

14. For each study in question 13, indicate whether a one- or a two-tailed test should be used, and state the H_0 and H_a. Assume that $\mu = 50$ when the amount of the independent variable is zero.

15. What is the difference between a real relationship in nature and one that results from sampling error?

16. For the following, should the researcher perform parametric or nonparametric procedures? (a) When ranking the intelligence of a group of people given a smart

pill. (b) When comparing the median income for a group of college professors to that of the national population of all incomes. (c) When comparing the mean reading speed for a sample of hearing-impaired children to the average reading speed of the population of hearing children. (d) When measuring interval scores from a personality test given to a group of emotionally troubled people, and comparing them to scores from a population of emotionally healthy people.

17. Listening to music while taking a test may be relaxing or it may be distracting. To determine which, 49 participants are tested while listening to music and they produce an $\overline{X} = 54.63$. The mean of the population of students who have taken this test without music is 50 ($\sigma_X = 12$). (a) Should we use a one-tailed or two-tailed test? Why? (b) What are our H_0 and H_a? (c) Compute z_{obt}. (d) With $\alpha = .05$, what is z_{crit}? (e) Do we have evidence of a relationship in the population? If so, describe the relationship.

18. A researcher asks whether attending a private school leads to higher or lower performance on a test of social skills. A sample of 100 students from a private school produces a mean score of 71.30 on the test, and the national mean for students from public schools is 75.62 ($\sigma_X = 28.0$). (a) Should she use a one-tailed or a two-tailed test? Why? (b) What are H_0 and H_a for this study? (c) Compute z_{obt}. (d) With $\alpha = .05$, what is z_{crit}? (e) What should the researcher conclude about this relationship in the population?

19. (a) What is the probability that in question 17 we made a Type I error? What would the error be in terms of the independent and dependent variables? (b) What is the probability that we made a Type II error? What would the error be in terms of the independent and dependent variables?

20. (a) What is the probability that the researcher in question 18 made a Type I error? What would the error be in terms of the independent and dependent variables? (b) What is the probability that the researcher made a Type II error? What would the error be in terms of the independent and dependent variables?

21. Foofy claims that using a one-tailed test is cheating because a one-tailed test produces a smaller absolute value of z_{crit}, and therefore it is easier to reject H_0 than it is with a two-tailed test. If the independent variable doesn't work, she claims, we are more likely to make a Type I error. Why is she correct or incorrect?

22. Poindexter claims that the real cheating occurs when we increase power by increasing the likelihood that results will be significant. He reasons that if we are generally more likely to reject H_0, then we are more likely to do so when H_0 is true, and therefore we are more likely to make a Type I error. Why is he correct or incorrect?

23. Bubbles reads that Study A, using a two-tailed test, found significant results: $z_{obt} = +1.97, p < .05$. She also reads about Study B, in which $z_{obt} = +14.21$, $p < .0001$. (a) She concludes that the results of Study B are way beyond the critical value used in Study A, falling into a region of rejection containing only .0001 of the sampling distribution. Why is she correct or incorrect? (b) She concludes that the results of Study B are more significant than those of Study A, both because the z_{obt} is so much larger and because α is so much smaller. Why is she correct or incorrect? (c) In terms of their conclusions, what is the difference between the two studies?

24. A researcher measures the self-esteem scores of a sample of statistics students, reasoning that their frustration with this course may lower their self-esteem relative to that of the typical college student ($\mu = 55$ and $\sigma_X = 11.35$). He obtains the following scores.

| 44 | 55 | 39 | 17 | 27 | 38 | 36 | 24 | 36 |

(a) Should he use a one-tailed or two-tailed test? Why? (b) What are H_0 and H_a for this study? (c) Compute z_{obt}. (d) With $\alpha = .05$, what is z_{crit}? (e) What should the researcher conclude about the relationship between the self-esteem of statistics students and that of other students?

25. A researcher suggests that males and females are the same when it comes to intelligence. Why is this hypothesis impossible to test?

26. Researcher A finds a significant relationship between increasing stress level and ability to concentrate. Researcher B replicates this study, but finds a nonsignificant relationship. Identify the statistical error that each researcher may have made.

27. A report indicates that Brand X toothpaste significantly reduced tooth decay relative to other brands, with $p < .44$. (a) What does "significant" indicate about the researcher's decision about Brand X? (b) What makes you suspicious of the claim that Brand X works better than other brands?

SUMMARY OF FORMULAS

1. *The computational formula for the z-test is*

$$z_{obt} = \frac{\overline{X} - \mu}{\sigma_{\overline{X}}}$$

where $\overline{X}$ is the sample mean and μ is the mean of the sampling distribution when H_0 is true (the μ of the raw score population described by H_0).

2. *The computational formula for the standard error of the mean is*

$$\sigma_{\overline{X}} = \frac{\sigma_X}{\sqrt{N}}$$

where N is the N of the sample and σ_X is the known population standard deviation.

11

Hypothesis Testing for a Single Mean or a Correlation Coefficient: The *t*-Test

GETTING STARTED

To understand this chapter, recall the following:

- From Chapter 5 recall that s_X is the *estimated* population standard deviation, that s_X^2 is the *estimated* population variance, and that both involve degrees of freedom, or *df*, which equals $N - 1$.
- From Chapter 7 recall the uses and interpretation of r, r_s, and r_{pb}.
- From Chapter 10 recall the basics of significance testing, including one- and two-tailed tests, H_0 and H_a, Type I and Type II errors, and power.

Your goals in this chapter are to learn:

- The difference between the z-test and the t-test.
- How to perform the t-test.
- What is meant by the confidence interval for μ, and how it is computed.
- How to perform significance testing of r, r_s, and r_{pb}.
- How to increase the power of t and r.

The logic of statistical hypothesis testing that you learned in the previous chapter is used in all behavioral research. The goal now is for you to learn how it is applied with different research designs. This chapter begins the process by introducing the inferential procedure called the t-*test*. This will not be difficult for you, because its calculations and interpretations are extremely similar to those of the *z*-test. Also, such terms as H_0 and H_a, significant, Type I and Type II errors, and power apply to all inferential statistics. Therefore, much of this chapter contains more of a variation on a theme than new material.

MORE STATISTICAL NOTATION

Officially the *t*-test (with a lowercase *t*) is known as Student's *t*-test (although it was developed by W. S. Gosset). The symbol for the answer we obtain from the *t*-test is t_{obt}. The symbol for the critical value of *t* is t_{crit}.

In this chapter you'll again compute s_X—the estimated population standard deviation, and s_X^2—the estimated population variance. Remember that the formula for s_X is

$$s_X = \sqrt{\frac{\Sigma X^2 - \frac{(\Sigma X)^2}{N}}{N-1}}$$

To calculate s_X^2, simply don't take the square root.

WHY IS IT IMPORTANT TO KNOW ABOUT *t*-TESTS?

It's important to know about the *t*-test because, like the *z*-test, the *t*-test is used for significance testing in a one-sample experiment. In fact, the *t*-test and the "*t*-distribution" are used more often in behavioral research. That's because with the *z*-test, a requirement was that we must *know* the true standard deviation of the raw score population (σ_X). However, usually researchers do *not* know such things about the population because they're exploring uncharted areas of behavior. ("To boldly go where no one has gone . . ." and all that.) Instead, we *estimate* σ_X by computing s_X from the sample data. Then we use the estimated population standard deviation to compute an *estimate* of the standard error of the mean. Then we compute something *like* a *z*-score to locate our sample mean on the H_0 sampling distribution. However, because we're estimating, we are not computing a *z*-score. Instead, we are computing t_{obt}. The **one-sample *t*-test** is the parametric procedure used to test the null hypothesis for a one-sample experiment when the standard deviation of the raw score population must be estimated.

> *REMEMBER* Use the *z*-test when σ_X is known; use the *t*-test when σ_X is estimated by calculating s_X.

Further, recall there's another type of one-sample study we've been ignoring, called a correlational study. As you'll see, the issue of sampling error arises here, and so you'll perform a similar procedure for hypothesis testing with a correlation coefficient. Finally, this chapter introduces the *confidence interval*, a new procedure based on *t* that is used to more precisely estimate a population μ.

SETTING UP THE *t*-TEST

To see the similarities and differences between *z* and *t,* let's examine another example of a one-sample experiment. Say that in one of those "home-and-gardening/good-housekeeper" magazines, there is a test of one's housekeeping abilities. The magazine is targeted at women, and it reports that nationally, the average test score for women is 75 (so their μ is 75), but it does not report the standard deviation. Our question is, "How do men score on this test?" To answer it, we'll give the test to a random sample of men and use their $\overline{X}$ to estimate the μ for the population of all men. Then we can compare the μ for men to the μ of 75 for the population of women. If men score differently from women, then we've found a relationship in which, as gender changes, test scores change.

As usual, we first set up the statistical test.

1. **The statistical hypotheses:** We're open-minded and look for any kind of difference, so we have a two-tailed test. If men are different than women, then the μ for men will not equal the μ for women of 75, so H_a is $\mu \neq 75$. If men are not different, then their μ will equal that of women, so H_0 is $\mu = 75$.

2. **Alpha:** We select alpha: .05 sounds good.

3. **Check the assumptions:** For the one-sample *t*-test we assume the following about the dependent variable:

   1. You have one random sample of interval or ratio scores.

   2. The raw score population forms a normal distribution.

   3. The standard deviation of the raw score population is estimated by computing s_X.

It's acceptable if the data are only somewhat normally distributed, because like all parametric tests, the *t*-test is robust—it produces minimal error even if you violate its assumptions somewhat. This is especially true if *N* is at least 30.

Based on similar research we've read about, our test scores meet these assumptions, so we proceed. For simplicity, we test 9 men. (For *power,* you should never collect so few scores.) Say the sample produces a $\overline{X} = 65.67$. Based on this, we might conclude that (as in H_a) the population of men would score around a μ of 65.67, and, because females score around a μ of 75, maybe we have demonstrated a relationship between gender and housekeeping scores. On the other hand, (as in H_0) maybe gender is not related to test scores, and we are being misled by sampling error: Maybe by chance we selected some exceptionally sloppy men for our *sample,* but men in the general population are no sloppier than women, and so the sample actually poorly represents the male population, which has a $\mu = 75$.

To test this null hypothesis, we'll use the same logic we've used previously: H_0 says that the men's mean represents a population where μ is 75. By computing t_{obt}, we'll locate our sample mean on the sampling distribution of means that occur when representing this population. If t_{obt} is beyond t_{crit}, our sample mean lies in the region of rejection, so we'll reject the idea that the sample is merely poorly representing this population.

The only novelty here is that t_{obt} is calculated differently and t_{crit} comes from the *t*-distribution.

CALCULATING THE ONE-SAMPLE *t*-TEST

The computation of t_{obt} consists of three steps that parallel the three steps in the *z*-test, as shown in Table 11.1. (Follow along.) The first step in the *z*-test was to find the true standard deviation (σ_X) of the raw score population. For the *t*-test, we compute the estimated standard deviation (s_X) using the sample data and the formula reviewed at the beginning of this chapter.

The second step of the *z*-test was to compute the true standard error of the mean ($\sigma_{\bar{X}}$) by dividing σ_X by $\sqrt{N}$. For the *t*-test, we compute the *estimated* standard error of the mean by dividing s_X by $\sqrt{N}$.

THE DEFINITIONAL FORMULA FOR THE ESTIMATED STANDARD ERROR OF THE MEAN IS

$$s_{\bar{X}} = \frac{s_X}{\sqrt{N}}$$

Again we are finding the standard deviation of the sampling distribution of means. But, because it involves s_X, the **estimated standard error of the mean** is an estimate of the standard deviation of the sampling distribution of means. Notice, the symbol here is $s_{\bar{X}}$. (The s stands for an estimate of the population, and the subscript $\bar{X}$ indicates that it is for a population of means.)

The third step in the *z*-test was to compute z_{obt} using the formula $z = (\bar{X} - \mu)/\sigma_{\bar{X}}$. The final step in the *t*-test is to compute t_{obt}.

THE DEFINITIONAL FORMULA FOR THE ONE-SAMPLE t-*TEST IS*

$$t_{obt} = \frac{\bar{X} - \mu}{s_{\bar{X}}}$$

$\bar{X}$ is the sample mean, μ is the mean of the H_0 sampling distribution (which equals the value of μ described in the null hypothesis), and $s_{\bar{X}}$ is the estimated standard error of the mean.

The only difference here is that z_{obt} indicated the distance our mean was from the μ of the sampling distribution, measured in units called the standard error of the mean; t_{obt} measures this distance in estimated standard error units.

TABLE 11.1 Comparison of the Steps in Computing the *z*-Test and *t*-Test

Steps	*z-Test*	*t-Test*
1. Variability of raw scores	true σ_X	estimated s_X
2. Standard error of the mean	$\sigma_{\overline{X}} = \dfrac{\sigma_X}{\sqrt{N}}$	$s_{\overline{X}} = \dfrac{s_X}{\sqrt{N}}$
3. Locate $\overline{X}$ on sampling distribution	$z_{\text{obt}} = \dfrac{\overline{X} - \mu}{\sigma_{\overline{X}}}$	$t_{\text{obt}} = \dfrac{\overline{X} - \mu}{s_{\overline{X}}}$

Computational Formulas for the One-Sample *t*-Test

You can compute t_{obt} using the three steps above, or you can use one of the following computational formulas. First, if we replace the symbol $s_{\overline{X}}$ with the formula for computing it, we have

$$t_{\text{obt}} = \frac{\overline{X} - \mu}{\dfrac{s_X}{\sqrt{N}}}$$

To shorten the computations, you can avoid taking the square root when computing s_X. Instead, we replace the standard deviation with the estimated variance (s_X^2) and then take the square root of the entire denominator. Thus,

THE COMPUTATIONAL FORMULAS FOR THE ONE-SAMPLE t-TEST ARE

$$t_{\text{obt}} = \frac{\overline{X} - \mu}{\sqrt{\dfrac{s_X^2}{N}}} \quad \text{and} \quad t_{\text{obt}} = \frac{\overline{X} - \mu}{\sqrt{(s_X^2)\left(\dfrac{1}{N}\right)}}$$

You can use either of these formulas. The formula on the left computes $s_{\overline{X}}$ by first dividing s_X^2 by N and then finding the square root. Dividing by N is the same as multiplying by $1/N$, so the formula on the right computes $s_{\overline{X}}$ by first multiplying s_X^2 times the quantity $1/N$ and then finding the square root.

For our housekeeping study, say that we obtained the data in Table 11.2. First, compute s_X^2. Substituting the data into the formula gives

$$s_X^2 = \frac{\Sigma X^2 - \dfrac{(\Sigma X)^2}{N}}{N - 1} = \frac{39289 - \dfrac{349281}{9}}{9 - 1} = 60.00$$

Thus, the estimated variance of the population of housekeeping scores is 60.

TABLE 11.2   Test Scores of Nine Males

Subject	*Grades* (X)	X^2
1	50	2500
2	75	5625
3	65	4225
4	72	5184
5	68	4624
6	65	4225
7	73	5329
8	59	3481
9	64	4096
$N = 9$	$\Sigma X = $ 591	$\Sigma X^2 = 39289$
	$(\Sigma X)^2 = 349281$	
	$\overline{X} = $ 65.67	

Now compute t_{obt} for the mean of 65.67 when the population μ is 75, s_X^2 is 60, and N is 9. Filling in a computational formula, we have

$$t_{obt} = \frac{\overline{X} - \mu}{\sqrt{(s_X^2)\left(\dfrac{1}{N}\right)}} = \frac{65.67 - 75}{\sqrt{(60)\left(\dfrac{1}{9}\right)}}$$

In the denominator, 1/9 is .11, which multiplied times 60 is 6.667. So

$$t_{obt} = \frac{65.67 - 75}{\sqrt{6.667}} = \frac{-9.33}{2.582} = -3.61$$

The square root of 6.667 is 2.582, so the estimated standard error of the mean ($s_{\overline{X}}$) is 2.582. Dividing -9.33 by 2.582 gives the t_{obt} of -3.61.

Thus, our sample mean produced a t_{obt} of -3.61 on the sampling distribution of means in which $\mu = 75$. The question is, "Is this t_{obt} significant?" To answer this, the final step is to compare t_{obt} to the appropriate t_{crit}, and for that we examine the *t*-distribution.

The *t*-Distribution

In previous chapters we described the sampling distribution of means using *z*-scores because the *z*-distribution is the appropriate model of the sampling distribution when σ_X is known. Now the *t*-distribution is our model when σ_X is estimated. Think of the *t*-distribution in the following way. One last time we hire our by now *very* bored statistician. She infinitely draws samples of the same size N from the raw score population described by H_0. For each sample she computes $\overline{X}$, s_X, and t_{obt}. She then plots the frequency distribution of the different means, labeling the X axis with the corresponding values of t_{obt} as well. Thus, the **t-distribution** is the distribution of all possible values of t computed for random sample means selected from the raw score population described by H_0.

FIGURE 11.1 Example of a *t*-distribution of random sample means

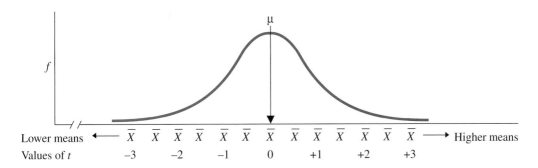

You can envision the *t*-distribution as in Figure 11.1. As with *z*-scores, a sample mean equal to μ has a *t* equal to zero. Means greater than μ have positive values of *t*, and means less than μ have negative values of *t*. The larger the absolute value of t_{obt}, the farther it and the corresponding sample mean are into the tail of the distribution. Therefore, the larger the *t*, the lower the mean's relative frequency and thus the lower its probability.

The t_{obt} locates our sample mean on this model, telling us the probability of obtaining such a mean when H_0 is true. If t_{obt} places our mean close to the center of the distribution, then it is a frequent and likely mean: It is likely to occur when, as in our example, men and women belong to the same population. But, if t_{obt} places our sample mean far into a tail of the distribution, then it is an infrequent and thus unlikely mean: It is unlikely to occur if men and women belong to the same population. To determine if our mean is far enough into a tail, we find t_{crit} and create the region of rejection.

But there is one important novelty here: There are actually *many* versions of the *t*-distribution, each having a slightly different shape. The shape of a particular distribution depends on the size of *N* that is used when creating it. If the statistician uses a small *N*, the *t*-distribution will be only a rough approximation to the standard normal curve. This is because the samples will often contain large sampling error, so often s_X will be very different from σ_X, and this inconsistency produces a *t*-distribution that is roughly normal. Larger samples, however, will tend to accurately represent the population, so each time s_X will be close to the true value of σ_X. As with the *z*-test, using the true value of σ_X produces a sampling distribution that conforms to a true normal distribution. In between, as sample size increases, each *t*-distribution will be a successively closer approximation to the true normal curve.

The fact that there are differently shaped *t*-distributions is important for one reason: When we set up the region of rejection, we want it to contain precisely that portion of the curve defined by our α. If $\alpha = .05$, then we want to mark off precisely the extreme 5% of the curve. On distributions that are shaped differently, we mark off that 5% at different locations. Because the location of the region of rejection is marked off by the critical value, *with differently shaped* t-*distributions we will have different critical values.* For example, Figure 11.2 shows the two-tailed region of rejection in two *t*-distributions. Notice the size of the (blue) region of rejection in a tail of Distribution A. Say that this is the extreme 5% of Distribution A and is beyond the t_{crit} of ± 2.5.

FIGURE 11.2 Comparison of two *t*-distributions based on different sample *N*s

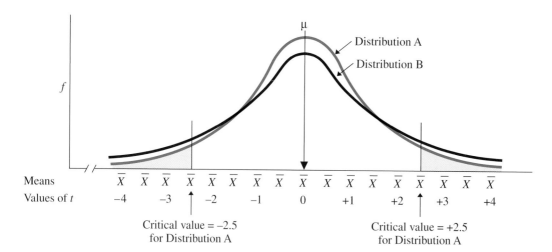

However, if we also use ±2.5 as t_{crit} on Distribution B, the region of rejection is larger, containing *more* than 5% of the distribution. Conversely, the t_{crit} marking off 5% of Distribution B will mark off *less* than 5% of Distribution A. (The same problem exists for a one-tailed test.)

This issue is important because not only is α the size of the region of rejection, it is also the probability of a Type I error. Unless we use the appropriate t_{crit}, the actual probability of a Type I error will not equal our α (and that's not supposed to happen!). Thus, there is only one version of the *t*-distribution to use when testing a particular t_{obt}: the one that the bored statistician would create by using the *same N* as in our sample.

The Degrees of Freedom

To be precise, it's not *N* that determines the appropriate *t*-distribution for a study. Instead, it's *N* − 1, what we call the degrees of freedom, or *df*. Because we compute s_X using *N* − 1, it is *df* that determines how consistently s_X estimates the true σ_X. Therefore, the larger the *df*, the closer the *t*-distribution is to forming a normal curve.

It does not take a tremendously large *df*, however, to produce a truly normal *t*-distribution. When *df* is greater than 120, the *t*-distribution is virtually identical to the standard normal curve, and *t* is the same as *z*. It's when the *df* is between 1 and 120 that there are differently shaped *t*-distributions having different critical values. Therefore, when our *df* is between 1 and 120, we use the *df* to first identify the appropriate sampling distribution for our study. The t_{crit} on that distribution will accurately mark off the region of rejection so that the probability of a Type I error equals α.

> *REMEMBER* The appropriate t_{crit} for the one-sample *t*-test comes from the *t*-distribution that has *df* equal to *N* − 1, where *N* is the number of scores in our sample.

Using the *t*-Tables

We obtain the appropriate value of t_{crit} from Table 2 in Appendix B, entitled "Critical Values of *t*." Take a look at these "*t*-tables." You'll find separate tables for two-tailed and one-tailed tests. In each, locate the appropriate column under your α (either .05 or .01). Then find the value of t_{crit} in the row opposite the *df* for your sample. For example, in the housekeeping study, *N* is 9, so *df* is $N - 1 = 8$. For a two-tailed test with α = .05 and *df* = 8, t_{crit} is ±2.306.

The table contains no positive or negative signs. In a two-tailed test you add the "±," and in a one-tailed test you supply the appropriate "+" or "−." Also, the table uses the symbol for infinity (∞) for *df* greater than 120. This means that when *df* is greater than 120, using the estimated population standard deviation is virtually the same as using the true population standard deviation. Therefore, the *t*-distribution matches the standard normal curve, and the critical values are those of the *z*-test.

INTERPRETING THE *t*-TEST

Once you've calculated t_{obt} and identified t_{crit}, you can make a decision about your results. Remember the housekeeping study? We must decide whether or not the men's mean of 65.67 represents the same population of scores that women have. Our t_{obt} is −3.61, and the two-tailed t_{crit} is ±2.306, producing the sampling distribution in Figure 11.3. Remember, this can be interpreted as showing the frequency of all means that occur by chance when H_0 is true—here, when men are the same as women, both having a population in which μ = 75. But, our t_{obt} lies beyond t_{crit}, so the results are significant: Our $\overline{X}$ of 65.67 is so unlikely to occur if our mean had been representing the population in which μ is 75, that we reject that we were representing this population—

FIGURE 11.3 Two-tailed *t*-distribution for *df* = 8 when H_0 is true and μ = 75

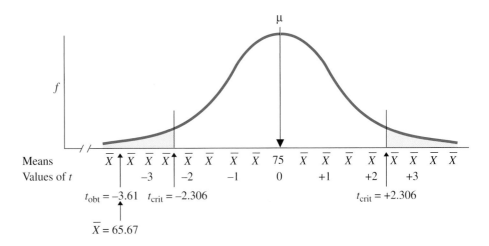

we reject H_0. Then the issue of Type I errors and the rules for interpreting significant results are the same as in the previous chapter. We report the results as

$$t(8) = -3.61, p < .05$$

This communicates four things: We performed the t-test, we had 8 degrees of freedom, the t_{obt} is -3.61, and we judged the t and the underlying $\overline{X}$ to be significant, with the probability less than .05 that we've made a Type I error (rejected a true H_0). [In fact, from the t-tables, when α is .01, t_{crit} is ± 3.355, and so our t_{obt} would be significant if we had used this α. Therefore, instead of saying $p < .05$, we gain more information by reporting that $p < .01$, because then we know that the probability of a Type I error is not in the neighborhood of .04, .03, or .02.]

By rejecting that μ equals 75, we accept the alternative hypothesis that the sample represents a population that is different from that of women, with a μ not equal to 75. To be more precise, because the sample mean for men is 65.67, our best estimate is that the population μ for men is around 65.67. Thus, we expect one population of scores for men located at around 65.67 and a different population for women located at 75. We conclude that the results demonstrate a relationship in the population between the independent variable (gender) and the dependent variable (test scores). Then we return to being a researcher and interpret the relationship in psychological or sociological terms. What do the scores and relationship tell you about the underlying behaviors and their causes? Are men really more ignorant about housekeeping than women, and if so, why? Or, do men merely pretend to be ignorant, and if so, why? And so on.

Of course, if t_{obt} had not fallen beyond t_{crit} (for example, if $t_{obt} = +1.32$), then it would not lie in the region of rejection and we would not reject H_0. We would conclude that the sample was likely to represent the population in which μ is 75, so we would have no evidence for a relationship between gender and test scores. Then the issue of Type II errors and the rules for interpreting nonsignificant results are the same as in the previous chapter. We report this nonsignificant result as $t(8) = +1.32, p > .05$.

One-Tailed Hypotheses in the One-Sample t-Test

We would perform a one-tailed test if, for example, we had predicted that men score *higher* than women. Then H_a would be that the sample represents a population μ greater than 75 ($H_a: \mu > 75$). H_0 would be that the sample represents a μ less than or equal to 75 ($H_0: \mu \leq 75$). Then we find the one-tailed t_{crit} from the t-tables for our df and α. To decide which tail of the sampling distribution to put the region of rejection in, determine what's needed to support H_a. Here, for the sample to represent a population of higher scores, the $\overline{X}$ must be *greater* than 75 and be *significant*. As shown in the left-hand graph in Figure 11.4, such means are in the upper tail, so this is where we place the region of rejection and t_{crit} is positive.

We'd also perform a one-tailed test if we had predicted that men score *lower* than women, using the sampling distribution on the right in Figure 11.4. Now H_a is that μ is less than 75, and H_0 is that μ is greater than or equal to 75. Because we seek a $\overline{X}$ that is *significant* and *lower* than 75, the region of rejection is in the lower tail, and t_{crit} is negative.

In either case, calculate t_{obt} using the previous formulas. If the absolute value of t_{obt} is larger than t_{crit} and has the same sign, then the $\overline{X}$ is unlikely to be representing a μ described by H_0. Therefore, reject H_0, accept H_a, and the results are significant.

FIGURE 11.4 H_0 sampling distribution of t for a one-tailed test

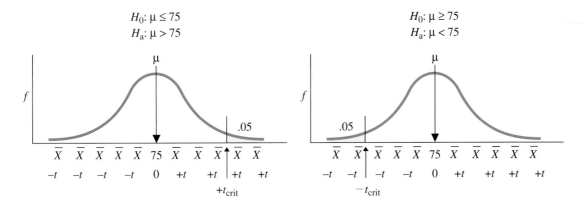

Some Help When Using the *t*-Tables

If you peruse the *t*-tables (a little light reading), you will *not* find a critical value for every *df* between 1 and 120. When the *df* of your sample does not appear in the table, there are two approaches you can take.

First, remember that all you need to know is whether or not t_{obt} lies in the region of rejection. Often you can determine this by examining the critical values for the *df* above and below the *df* of your sample. For example, say that we perform a one-tailed *t*-test at $\alpha = .05$ with 49 *df*. The *t*-tables give t_{crit} for 40 *df* (+1.684) and for 60 *df* (+1.671). Because 49 *df* lies between 40 *df* and 60 *df*, the critical value we seek lies between +1.671 and +1.684. It's a good idea to draw a picture of this, as in Figure 11.5.

FIGURE 11.5 One *t*-distribution showing the location of three values of t_{crit}

The t_{crit} of +1.684 is for 40 df (dashed line), the t_{crit} of +1.671 is for 60 df (dotted line), and the t_{crit} for 49 df (solid line) is between them.

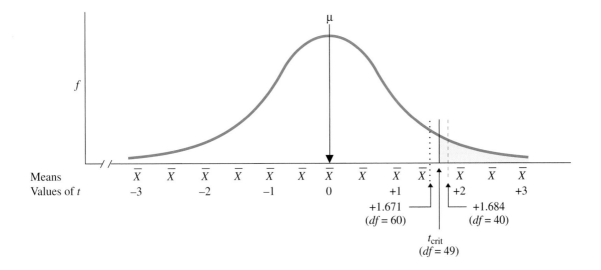

Our actual region of rejection starts at a point in between these two critical values. Therefore, if t_{obt} lies beyond the t_{crit} of $+1.684$, then it is in our region of rejection for 49 *df*, and so it is significant. On the other hand, if t_{obt} is *not* beyond the t_{crit} of $+1.671$, then it is not in the region of rejection we'd have for 49 *df*, and so it won't be significant. In the same way, you can evaluate any obtained value that falls *outside* of the bracketing critical values given in the tables.

The second approach is used if t_{obt} falls *between* the bracketing values of t_{crit} in the table. Then perform the interpolation procedure described in Appendix A.2.

ESTIMATING THE POPULATION μ BY COMPUTING A CONFIDENCE INTERVAL

As you've seen, after rejecting H_0, we estimate the population μ that the sample mean represents. There are two ways to estimate μ.

The first way is to use **point estimation,** in which we describe a point on the variable at which the population μ is expected to fall. Earlier we estimated that the μ of the population of men is located on the variable of housekeeping scores at the *point* identified as 65.67. However, if we actually tested the entire population, μ would probably not be *exactly* 65.67. The problem with point estimation is that it is extremely vulnerable to sampling error. Our sample of men probably does not *perfectly* represent the population of men, so we can say only that the μ for men is probably *around* 65.67.

The other, better way to estimate a μ is to include the possibility of sampling error and perform interval estimation. With **interval estimation,** we specify an interval—a range of values—within which we expect the population parameter to fall. You often encounter such intervals in real life, and they are usually phrased in terms of "plus or minus" some amount (called the **margin of error**). For example, when the evening news reports that a sample survey showed that 45% of the voters support the President, the margin of error may be plus or minus 3%. This means that the pollsters have created an interval around 45%. They expect that if they could ask the *entire* population, the result would be within $\pm3\%$ of 45%: They believe that between 42% and 48% of all voters in the population would actually support the President.

We perform interval estimation by creating a confidence interval. Confidence intervals can be used to describe various population parameters, but the most common is the confidence interval for a single μ. The **confidence interval for a single μ** describes an interval containing values of μ, any one of which our sample mean is likely to represent. Thus, instead of saying that our sample of men represents a μ *around* 65.67, a confidence interval is the way to statistically define "around." Thus, we'll identify those values of μ above and below 65.67 that the sample mean is likely to represent as shown here:

$$\underbrace{\mu_{low} \cdots \mu \ \mu \ \mu \ \mu \ 65.67 \ \mu \ \mu \ \mu \ \mu \cdots \mu_{high}}$$

values of μ, one of which is likely to be
represented by our sample mean

The μ_{low} is the lowest value of μ that our sample mean is likely to represent, and μ_{high} is the highest value of μ that the mean is likely to represent. When we compute these two values, we have the confidence interval.

When is a sample mean likely to represent a particular μ? It depends on sampling error. For example, intuitively we know that sampling error is unlikely to produce a sample mean of 65.67 if μ is, say, 500. In other words, 65.67 is significantly different from 500. But sampling error *is* likely to produce a sample mean of 65.67 if, for example, μ is 65 or 66. In other words, 65.67 is not significantly different from these μs. Thus, a sample mean is likely to represent a particular μ if the mean is *not* significantly different from that μ. The logic behind a confidence interval is to compute the highest and lowest values of μ that are not significantly different from the sample mean. All μs between these two values are also not significantly different from the sample mean, so the mean is likely to represent one of them.

> **REMEMBER**   A *confidence interval* describes the highest and lowest values of μ that are not significantly different from our sample mean, and thus contains values that the mean is likely to represent.

Understand that we usually compute a confidence interval only after finding a significant t_{obt}. If the original t-test in the housekeeping study had not been significant, we would not know whether or not men have a different population than women, so it would make no sense to try to describe the μ of this population. However, given our significant results, we can compute the confidence interval.

Computing the Confidence Interval for a Single μ

Because the t-test was appropriate for significance testing of the sample mean, it also forms the basis for the confidence interval. Here's what's behind the formula for the confidence interval: We seek the highest and lowest values of μ that are not significantly different from the sample mean. For a sample mean to differ significantly from μ, its t_{obt} must be beyond t_{crit}. Therefore, the most a sample mean can differ from μ and still not be significant is when its t_{obt} *equals* t_{crit}. We can state this using the formula for the t-test:

$$t_{\text{obt}} = \frac{\overline{X} - \mu}{s_{\overline{X}}} = t_{\text{crit}}$$

To find the largest and smallest values of μ that do not differ significantly from our sample mean, we simply determine the values of μ that we can put into this formula. Because we are describing values above and below the sample mean, we use the two-tailed value of t_{crit}. Then we find the value of μ that produces a $-t_{\text{obt}}$ equal to $-t_{\text{crit}}$. Rearranging the above formula, we have

$$\mu = (s_{\overline{X}})(+t_{\text{crit}}) + \overline{X}$$

We also want the value of μ that produces a $+t_{\text{obt}}$ equal to $+t_{\text{crit}}$, which is

$$\mu = (s_{\overline{X}})(-t_{\text{crit}}) + \overline{X}$$

The sample mean represents a μ *between* these two values, so we put the above formulas together into one formula.

> *THE COMPUTATIONAL FORMULA FOR THE CONFIDENCE INTERVAL FOR A SINGLE μ IS*
>
> $$(s_{\overline{X}})(-t_{\text{crit}}) + \overline{X} \leq \mu \leq (s_{\overline{X}})(+t_{\text{crit}}) + \overline{X}$$

The symbol μ stands for the unknown value represented by the sample mean. The $\overline{X}$ and $s_{\overline{X}}$ are computed from your data. Find the two-tailed value of t_{crit} in the *t*-tables at your α for $df = N - 1$, where N is the sample N.

> REMEMBER   Use the *two-tailed* critical value when computing a confidence interval even if you performed a one-tailed *t*-test.

For our housekeeping study, the men's $\overline{X}$ was 65.67 and $s_{\overline{X}} = 2.582$. The two-tailed t_{crit} for $df = 8$ and $\alpha = .05$ is ± 2.306. Filling in the formula, we have

$$(2.582)(-2.306) + 65.67 \leq \mu \leq (2.582)(+2.306) + 65.67$$

After multiplying 2.582 times -2.306 and $+2.306$ we have

$$-5.954 + 65.67 \leq \mu \leq +5.954 + 65.67$$

The formula at this point tells us that our men's mean represents a μ of 65.67, plus or minus 5.954.

After adding ± 5.954 to 65.67, we have

$$59.72 \leq \mu \leq 71.62$$

This is the finished confidence interval. Returning to our previous diagram, we replace the symbols μ_{low} and μ_{high} with the numbers 59.72 and 71.62, respectively.

$$59.72 \ldots \mu \; \mu \; \mu \; \mu \; 65.67 \; \mu \; \mu \; \mu \; \mu \ldots 71.62$$

values of μ, one of which is likely to be
represented by our sample mean

As shown, our men's sample mean probably represents a μ around 65.67, meaning that μ is greater than or equal to 59.72, but less than or equal to 71.62.

Confidence Intervals and the Size of Alpha

Why is this called a "confidence" interval? We defined this interval using $\alpha = .05$, so .05 is the theoretical probability of making a Type I error. Thus, 5% of the time the interval will be in error and will not contain the μ represented by our $\overline{X}$. However, recall that $1 - \alpha$ is the probability of avoiding a Type I error. Thus, $1 - .05$, or 95%, of the time the interval *will* contain the μ represented by our $\overline{X}$. Therefore, the probability is .95 that the interval contains the μ. Recall that probability is our way of expressing our confidence in an event. Thus, we have created the "95% confidence interval": We are 95% confident that the interval between 59.72 and 71.62 contains the μ represented by our sample mean.

The smaller the α, the greater our confidence. Had we set α at .01, with $df = 8$, t_{crit} is ± 3.355, and so our 99% confidence interval would have been $57.01 \leq \mu \leq 74.33$. This "99% confidence interval" spans a wider range than did the 95% confidence interval. That's because a wider interval is needed to have greater confidence that it contains the μ we seek. (Think of a confidence interval as a fishing net. The larger the net, the more confident we are that we'll catch the μ that's actually being represented.) However, the problem is that a wider range is also less precise in identifying the value of μ being represented. Usually, we compromise between sufficient confidence and sufficient precision by creating the 95% confidence interval.

Thus, we conclude our one-sample t-test by saying, with 95% confidence, that our sample of men represents a μ between 59.72 and 71.62. Because the center of the interval is at 65.67, we still communicate that μ is *around* 65.67, but we have much more information than if we merely said that μ is somewhere around 65.67. Therefore, anytime you are describing the μ represented by a sample mean, you should compute a confidence interval.[1]

Summary of the One-Sample t-Test

All of the preceding procedures boil down to the following steps:

1. Check that the experiment meets the assumptions of the t-test.

2. Create either the two-tailed or one-tailed H_0 and H_a.

3. From the sample data compute s_X^2 (or s_X), then compute $s_{\bar{X}}$, and then compute t_{obt}.

4. For the df in the study $(N - 1)$ find the appropriate t_{crit}.

5. If t_{obt} is beyond t_{crit}, reject H_0; the results are significant; interpret the relationship "psychologically."

6. If t_{obt} is not beyond t_{crit}, the results are not significant.

7. For significant results, use the two-tailed t_{crit} to compute the confidence interval for the μ represented by your $\bar{X}$.

SIGNIFICANCE TESTS FOR CORRELATION COEFFICIENTS

It's time to shift mental gears and consider that other type of one-sample study—a correlational study in which we compute a correlation coefficient. Here's a new example: Say that we had chosen to examine the relationship between a man's age and his housekeeping score in a correlational design. We measure the test scores and the ages of a sample of 25 men, and determine that the Pearson correlation coefficient is appropriate. Say that, using the formula from Chapter 7, we compute an $r = -.45$, indicating that the older a man, the lower his housekeeping score.

---

[1]You can also compute a confidence interval when performing the z-test. Use the formula above, except use the critical values from the z-tables in Appendix B. If $\alpha = .05$, then $z_{crit} = \pm 1.96$. If $\alpha = .01$, then $z_{crit} = \pm 2.575$.

Remember, though, that this correlation coefficient describes the relationship in the *sample*. Ultimately, we want to describe the relationship in the population. Therefore, we use the sample coefficient to estimate the population correlation we'd expect to find if we computed the correlation for the entire population. Recall that the population correlation coefficient is called rho, and for the Pearson coefficient its symbol is ρ. Thus, in our study we might estimate that ρ would equal $-.45$ if we measured the entire population of men.

But hold on, there's a problem here: That's right, sampling error. The problem of sampling error applies to *all* statistics. Here the idea is that because of the luck of the draw of who was selected for the sample, their scores happened to produce this correlation, but in reality, there is either no relationship or a different relationship in the population. So, here we go again! For any correlation coefficient you compute, you must determine whether it is significant.

> *REMEMBER* Never accept that a sample correlation coefficient reflects a real relationship in nature unless it is significant.

Statistical Hypotheses for the Correlation Coefficient

As usual, you should create the experimental and statistical hypotheses before collecting the data, and you can perform either a one-tailed or a two-tailed test. Use a two-tailed test if you do not predict the direction of the relationship. For example, let's say we're unsure whether, as men age, they produce higher scores or lower scores. This is a two-tailed situation because we're predicting either a positive *or* a negative correlation. Then the other hypothesis is that the study will not demonstrate any kind of relationship.

This latter hypothesis translates into the null hypothesis because H_0 always implies that the predicted relationship does not exist. If there is not a positive or negative correlation, then there is zero correlation. Most of the time, behavioral researchers test a null hypothesis involving zero correlation in the population. Therefore, in this book,

> *THE TWO-TAILED NULL HYPOTHESIS FOR TESTING OF A CORRELATION COEFFICIENT IS ALWAYS*
>
> $$H_0: \rho = 0$$

H_0 implies that the sample *r* represents a ρ equal to zero. If *r* does not equal zero, it's because of sampling error. You can understand this by looking at the hypothetical scatterplot in Figure 11.6. Assume this shows the population of *X* and *Y* scores when H_0 is true: There is no relationship, and so ρ is 0. Recall, however, that a slanting elliptical scatterplot reflects an *r* not equal to zero. The null hypothesis implies that, by chance, we selected an elliptical sample scatterplot from this circular population plot. Thus, our H_0 says that age and housekeeping scores are not really related, but the scores in our sample happen to pair up so that it looks as though they're related.

FIGURE 11.6 Scatterplot of a population for which $\rho = 0$, as described by H_0

Any r is a result of sampling error when selecting a sample from this scatterplot.

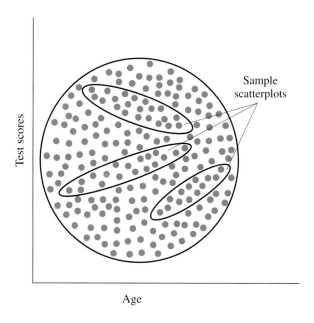

On the other hand, the alternative hypothesis always implies that the predicted relationship does occur. If we predict that there is either a positive or a negative relationship, we predict that ρ does *not* equal zero.

> **THE TWO-TAILED ALTERNATIVE HYPOTHESIS FOR TESTING OF A CORRELATION COEFFICIENT IS ALWAYS**
>
> $$H_a : \rho \neq 0$$

H_a implies that r represents a population that produces a ρ that is not zero and thus there is this relationship in nature. Essentially, H_a says that the population's scatterplot would be similar to the sample's scatterplot.

As usual, we test H_0, so here we test whether the sample correlation represents a ρ of zero. If r is unlikely to be representing $\rho = 0$, then we reject H_0 and accept the H_a that the sample represents a population in which $\rho \neq 0$.

Recall from Chapter 7 that there are three types of correlation coefficients: the Pearson r; the Spearman r_s; and the point-biserial r_{pb}. The logic and format of the above statistical hypotheses are the same regardless of which coefficient you compute (merely change the subscripts). The following sections discuss the particulars of statistical hypothesis testing for each type of coefficient.

THE SIGNIFICANCE TEST FOR THE PEARSON *r*

As usual, the first step is to make sure the study meets the assumptions of the statistical procedure. The Pearson correlation coefficient involves three assumptions:

1. There is a random sample of *X-Y* pairs, and each variable is an interval or ratio variable.

2. The *Y* scores and the *X* scores each represent a normal distribution. Further, they represent a *bivariate* normal distribution. This means that the *Y* scores at each value of *X* form a normal distribution and that the *X* scores at each value of *Y* form a normal distribution. (If *N* is larger than 25, however, violating this assumption is of little consequence.)

3. The null hypothesis is that the population correlation is zero. (When your H_0 is that ρ is some other value, a procedure different than the following is used.)

Our housekeeping and age scores meet these assumptions, so we set α at .05 and test *r*. To do that, we examine the sampling distribution.

The Sampling Distribution of *r*   The sampling distribution of *r* shows the values of *r* that occur when we randomly sample the population in which ρ is 0. The bored statistician quit! But by now you could create the sampling distribution yourself. Using the same *N* as in our study, you would select an infinite number of samples of *X-Y* pairs from the population where ρ = 0 (as if you pulled each sample from the circular scatterplot back in Figure 11.6). Each time you would compute *r*. If you then plotted the frequency of the various values of *r*, you would have the sampling distribution of *r*. The **sampling distribution of a correlation coefficient** is a frequency distribution showing all possible values of the coefficient that can occur when samples of size *N* are drawn from a population in which ρ is zero. Such a sampling distribution is shown in Figure 11.7.

FIGURE 11.7   Distribution of random sample *r*s when ρ = 0

It is an approximately normal distribution, with values of r *plotted along the X axis.*

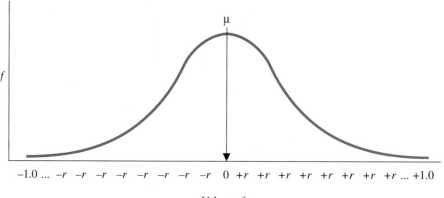

Values of *r*

The only novelty here is that instead of showing different sample means along the *X* axis, it shows different values of *r*. When $\rho = 0$, the most frequent sample *r* is also 0, so the mean of the sampling distribution—the average *r*—is 0. Because of sampling error, however, sometimes *r* will not equal zero. Sometimes, by luck, we'll obtain a positive *r*, and sometimes we'll obtain a negative *r*. When this happens, most often the *r* will be relatively small, and these are the high-frequency values that are close to 0 in Figure 11.7. But, less frequently, we'll obtain a larger *r*, and these are the values that fall more into the tails of Figure 11.7. Thus, the larger the *r* (whether positive or negative), the less likely it is to occur when the sample represents a population in which $\rho = 0$.

To test H_0, we simply determine where on this distribution our *r* lies. To do so, we could perform a variation of the *t*-test, but luckily that is not necessary. Instead, the value of *r* directly communicates its location on the sampling distribution. The mean of the sampling distribution is always 0, so, for example, our *r* of $-.45$ is a distance of .45 below the mean. Therefore, we test H_0 simply by examining the value of the obtained *r*. The symbol for an obtained *r* is r_{obt}. To determine whether r_{obt} lies in the region of rejection, we compare it to the critical value of *r*, which is symbolized as r_{crit}.

As with the *t*-distribution, the shape of the sampling distribution of *r* is slightly different for each *df*, so there is a different value of r_{crit} for each *df*. Table 3 in Appendix B gives the critical values of the Pearson correlation coefficient. *But,* here's a new one: With the Pearson correlation coefficient, the degrees of freedom equals $N - 2$, where *N* is the number of *pairs* of scores in the sample. (Recall that *df* is a "correction factor" when drawing inferences about a population. Different statistics require a different correction factor, so the *df* will change.)

> *REMEMBER*   For the Pearson *r*, the degrees of freedom equals $N - 2$, where
> *N* is the number of pairs of scores.

To find r_{crit}, enter Table 3 in Appendix B for either a one- or a two-tailed test at the appropriate α and *df*. For the housekeeping correlation, *N* was 25, so $df = 23$, and so, for a two-tailed test with $\alpha = .05$, r_{crit} is $\pm.396$. Armed with this information, we set up the sampling distribution as in Figure 11.8. An r_{obt} of $-.45$ is beyond the r_{crit} of $\pm.396$, so it is in the region of rejection. As usual, this means that the results are significant. Look at the low frequency that the sampling distribution shows for such an *r*. This *r* is so unlikely to occur, if we had been representing the population where ρ is 0, that we reject the H_0 that we were representing this population. We conclude that the r_{obt} is "significantly different from 0."

Interpreting a Significant *r*   The rules for interpreting a significant result here are the same as before. In particular, α is again the theoretical probability of a Type I error. Here, a Type I error is rejecting the H_0 that there is zero correlation in the population, when in fact there *is* zero correlation in the population. As Figure 11.8 shows, with $\alpha = .05$, when H_0 is true, we'll obtain *r*s that cause us to reject H_0 a total of 5% of the time. Therefore, the probability that we made a Type I error this time is slightly less than .05. We report this significant r_{obt} as

$$r(23) = -.45, p < .05$$

Note the *df* in parentheses.

FIGURE 11.8 H_0 sampling distribution of r when H_0: $\rho = 0$

For the two-tailed test, there is a region of rejection for positive values of r_{obt} *and for negative values of* r_{obt}.

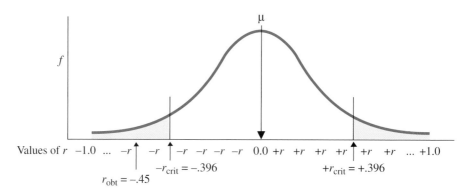

Remember that rejecting H_0 does not prove anything. In particular, this was a correlational study, so we have not proven that changes in age *cause* test scores to change. In fact, we have not even proven that there is a relationship in nature (we may have made a Type I error). Instead, we are simply more confident that the r_{obt} does not merely reflect some quirk of sampling error, and that instead, it represents a "real" relationship in nature.

Because the sample r_{obt} is $-.45$, our best estimate is that in the population, ρ equals $-.45$. However, recognizing that the sample may contain sampling error, we expect that ρ is probably *around* $-.45$. (We could more precisely describe this ρ by computing a confidence interval for the values of ρ that r_{obt} is likely to represent. Confidence intervals for ρ, however, are computed using a very different procedure from the one discussed previously.)

In Chapter 8 you saw that we further describe a relationship by computing the regression equation and the proportion of variance accounted for. However, do this only when r_{obt} is significant! Only then are we confident that we're describing a "real" relationship. Thus, for the housekeeping study, we would now compute the linear regression equation for predicting test scores if we know a man's age. We would also compute r^2, which is $-.45^2$ or .20. Recall, this is the *proportion of variance* in the sample's Y scores that is *accounted for* by the relationship with X. Here, an r^2 of .20 tells us that we are 20% more accurate when we use the relationship with age to predict housekeeping scores than when we do not use the relationship.

Remember that it is r^2 and not "significance" that determines how important a relationship is. The term *significant* indicates only that the relationship is unlikely to be a fluke of chance. The r^2 indicates the importance of a relationship because the larger it is, the more that knowing participants' X scores improves our accuracy in predicting and understanding differences in their Y scores—differences in their *behavior*—and so the larger the r^2, the greater the importance of the relationship.

Thus, a relationship must be significant to be even potentially important (because it must first be believable). But, a significant relationship is not necessarily important. For example, an r_{obt} of $+.10$ might be significant, but this is not a statistically important relationship: $+.10^2$ is only .01, so this relationship accounts for only 1% of the variance, and so is virtually useless in explaining differences in *Y* scores. (We're only 1% better off with it than without it.) Thus, although this relationship is unlikely to occur through sampling error, it is also an unimportant relationship.

After describing the relationship, as usual the final step is to interpret it psychologically. For example, perhaps our above correlation coefficient reflects socialization processes, with older men scoring lower on the housekeeping test because they come from generations in which wives typically did the housekeeping, while men were the "breadwinners."

Of course, if r_{obt} does not lie beyond r_{crit}, then you would retain H_0 and conclude that the sample may represent a population where $\rho = 0$. As usual, you have not proven that there is no relationship in the population—you have simply failed to convincingly demonstrate that there *is* one. Therefore, make no claims about the relationship that may or may not exist, and do not compute the regression equation or r^2. Report nonsignificant results as above, except that $p > .05$.

One-Tailed Tests of *r*   If we had predicted only a positive correlation or only a negative correlation, then we would have performed a one-tailed test.

THE ONE-TAILED HYPOTHESES FOR TESTING A CORRELATION COEFFICIENT ARE

Predicting positive correlation	*Predicting negative correlation*
H_0: $\rho \leq 0$	H_0: $\rho \geq 0$
H_a: $\rho > 0$	H_a: $\rho < 0$

Test each H_0 by again testing whether the sample represents a population in which there is zero relationship—so again examine the sampling distribution for $\rho = 0$. From the *r*-tables in Appendix B find the one-tailed critical value for *df* and α, and set up one of the sampling distributions shown in Figure 11.9. When predicting a positive correlation, use the left-hand distribution: r_{obt} is significant if it is positive and falls beyond the

FIGURE 11.9 H_0 sampling distribution of *r* where $\rho = 0$ for one-tailed test

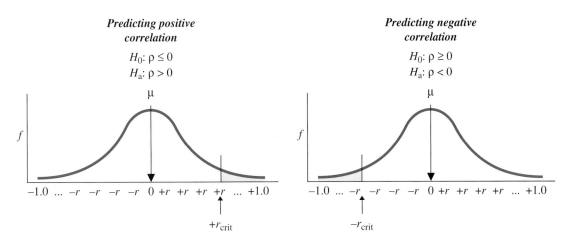

positive r_{crit}. When predicting a negative correlation, use the right-hand distribution: r_{obt} is significant if it is negative and falls beyond the negative r_{crit}.

If r_{obt} is not beyond the appropriate r_{crit}, then r_{obt} is not significant, and the study has failed to demonstrate the predicted relationship.

Testing the Spearman r_s and the Point-Biserial r_{pb}

We perform a similar procedure when testing the Spearman correlation coefficient (r_s) or the point-biserial correlation coefficient (r_{pb}). These correlations describe *sample* relationships, but—that's right—perhaps they merely reflect sampling error. Perhaps if we computed the correlation in the population, we'd find that the r_s actually represents a population correlation, symbolized by ρ_s, that is 0. Likewise, perhaps the r_{pb} actually represents a population correlation, symbolized by ρ_{pb}, that is 0. Therefore, before you can conclude that these correlations represent a relationship in nature, you must perform the appropriate hypothesis testing.

To test each sample correlation coefficient, perform the following steps:

1. Set alpha: how about .05?
2. Consider the assumptions of the test. The r_s requires a random sample of pairs of *ranked* (ordinal) scores. The r_{pb} requires scores from one dichotomous variable and one interval or ratio variable. (*Note:* Because of the data involved and the lack of parametric assumptions, r_s and r_{pb} are technically nonparametric procedures.)
3. Create the statistical hypotheses. You can test the one- or two-tailed hypotheses we saw previously with ρ, except use the symbols ρ_s or ρ_{pb}.

The only new aspect of testing r_s or r_{pb} is in their respective sampling distributions.

Testing r_s   To test r_s, we use a new family of sampling distributions and a different table of critical values. Table 4 in Appendix B, entitled "Critical Values of the Spearman Rank-Order Correlation Coefficient," contains the critical values for one- and two-tailed tests of r_s. Obtain critical values as in previous tables, except here use *N, not* degrees of freedom.

> REMEMBER   The critical value of r_s is obtained using *N*, the number of pairs of scores in the sample.

Here's an example. In Chapter 7 we correlated the aggressiveness rankings given to 9 children by two observers and found that $r_s = +.85$. We assumed the observers' rankings would agree, predicting a positive correlation. Therefore, we have a one-tailed test with the hypotheses H_0: $\rho_s \leq 0$ and H_a: $\rho_s > 0$. From Table 4 in Appendix B, with $\alpha = .05$ and $N = 9$, the one-tailed critical value is $+.600$, producing the sampling distribution shown in Figure 11.10.

Because an r_s of $+.85$ is beyond the critical value of $+.600$, we reject H_0. Our r_s is significantly different from zero, and we estimate that ρ_s in the population of such rankings is around $+.85$. The results are reported as

FIGURE 11.10 One-tailed H_0 sampling distribution of values of r_s when H_0 is $\rho_s = 0$

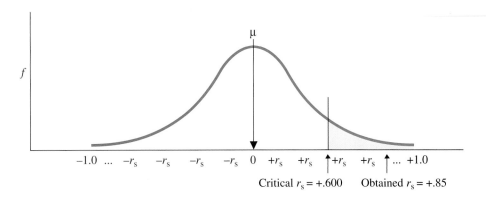

$$r_s(9) = +.85, \; p < .05$$

Note that the *N* of the sample is given in parentheses.

Now we would compute the squared r_s and interpret the results in terms of the behaviors being reflected. (With different predictions, we might have performed the other one-tailed test or a two-tailed test.)

Testing r_{pb}　　Test r_{pb} using the same logic as above. The sampling distributions of r_{pb} are identical to the distributions for the Pearson *r,* so critical values of r_{pb} are obtained from Table 3 in Appendix B. Again the degrees of freedom equals $N - 2$.

> *REMEMBER*　　Critical values of r_{pb} are in the *r*-tables in Appendix B, for *df* equal to $N - 2$, where *N* is the number of pairs of scores.

As an example, in Chapter 7 we computed an r_{pb} of $+.46$ for 10 participants using the dichotomous variable of gender (male or female) and the continuous variable of scores from a personality test. Say we perform a two-tailed test with the hypotheses H_0: $\rho_{pb} = 0$ and H_a: $\rho_{pb} \neq 0$. From Table 3 in Appendix B with $\alpha = .05$ and $df = 8$, the critical value is $\pm.632$, producing the sampling distribution shown in Figure 11.11. The r_{pb} of $+.46$ is not beyond the critical value, so we do not reject H_0, and the correlation is not significantly different from zero. The results are reported as

$$r_{pb}(8) = +.46, \; p > .05$$

Again, note the *df* in parentheses.

In a different study, predicting only a positive or negative correlation would lead to a one-tailed test. Remember, though, as discussed in Chapter 7, *we* determine whether r_{pb} is positive or negative by how we arrange the dichotomous variable, so be sure your one-tailed predictions match your arrangement.

FIGURE 11.11 H_0 sampling distribution of r_{pb} when H_0 is $\rho_{pb} = 0$

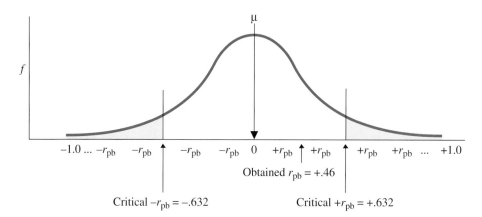

Summary of Testing a Correlation Coefficient

All of the preceding procedures boil down to the following steps:

1. Check that the study meets the assumptions of r, r_s, or r_{pb}.
2. Create either the two-tailed or one-tailed H_0 and H_a.
3. From the sample data compute the correlation coefficient.
4. Obtain the critical value from Appendix B:
    a. The critical value for r or r_{pb} is in Table 3, using $df = N - 2$.
    b. The critical value for r_s is in Table 4, using $df = N$.
5. If the obtained coefficient is beyond the critical value, the results are significant. If the coefficient is not beyond the critical value, the results are not significant.
6. For significant results compute the proportion of variance accounted for by squaring the obtained coefficient, and for r compute the linear regression equation.

MAXIMIZING THE POWER OF A STATISTICAL TEST

Recall that *power* is the probability of *not* committing a Type II error. We're talking about those times when H_0 really is false, and so the error here is retaining H_0. Instead, we should reject H_0. Therefore, power is a concern whenever we retain H_0 because we want to be confident that our statistics did not lead to the wrong decision and that we did not miss a relationship in nature. If we're talking about those times we should reject the null hypothesis, then maximizing power boils down to maximizing the probability that the results will be significant. If we've maximized the likelihood of finding significant results, but they still turn out to be nonsignificant, then we can confidently accept that we did not miss a real relationship that was present.

To do this, researchers make various decisions about how to conduct a study, each of which translates into maximizing the absolute size of the obtained statistic relative to the critical value. The larger the obtained value, the more likely it is to fall beyond the critical value, and thus the more likely it is to be significant.[2] The following sections discuss how to maximize power in the *t*-test and in correlations.

Maximizing the Power of the *t*-Test

Here, we maximize power by maximizing the size of t_{obt} relative to t_{crit}. Look at the formula

$$t_{\text{obt}} = \frac{\overline{X} - \mu}{\frac{s_X}{\sqrt{N}}}$$

There are three aspects of a study that increase power.

1. *Larger differences produced by changing the independent variable increase power.* In the housekeeping study, the greater the difference between the sample mean for men and the μ for women, the greater the power. In the formula a larger difference between $\overline{X}$ and μ produces a larger numerator, and dividing into a larger numerator results in a larger t_{obt}. Therefore, when designing a study, try to select conditions that are substantially different from one another, to produce a big difference in dependent scores between the conditions.

2. *Smaller variability in the raw scores increases power.* The *t*-test measures the difference between $\overline{X}$ and μ relative to the standard error of the mean ($s_{\overline{X}}$). The standard error equals the denominator of the above formula, and is influenced by the variability of the raw scores. Here, the smaller the standard deviation (s_X), the smaller the denominator. Then, dividing by a smaller denominator produces a larger t_{obt}. Therefore, when conducting research, try to measure participants in a consistent way that minimizes the variability of scores within each condition.

3. *A larger N increases power.* The size of N influences the results in two ways. First, in the formula, dividing s_X by a larger $\sqrt{N}$ produces a smaller denominator, which results in a larger t_{obt}. Second, a larger N produces larger df, which produces a smaller t_{crit}. The smaller the t_{crit}, the more likely that t_{obt} lies beyond it, so the more likely that t_{obt} is significant. Therefore, in research, try to test as large an N as possible.

Notice, however, that this is for *small* samples. Generally, an N of 30 is needed for minimal power, and increasing N up to 121 adds substantially to it. However, an N of, say, 500 is not substantially more powerful than an N of, say, 450.

> *REMEMBER*   Increase power in an experiment by maximizing differences in dependent scores *between* conditions, minimizing differences among scores *within* conditions, and testing a larger N.

---

[2]More advanced textbooks give computational procedures for determining the amount of power that is present in a given study.

Maximizing the Power of a Correlation Coefficient

We attempt to maximize the power of a correlational study by trying to maximize the size of the correlation coefficient. A larger coefficient is more likely to be beyond the critical value (significant), and so we are less likely to miss that a real relationship is present.

Three components increase the size and thus power of a correlation coefficient.

1. *Avoiding a restricted range increases power.* Recall from Chapter 7 that *restriction of range* results from a small range of scores on the *X* or *Y* variable. This produces a sample correlation coefficient that is smaller than it would be without a restricted range. Therefore, to maximize the size of your correlation coefficient, try to measure the full range of possible *X* and *Y* scores.

2. *Minimizing the variability of the* Y *scores at each* X *increases power.* Recall that the smaller the variability in *Y* scores at each *X*, the stronger the relationship and thus the larger the correlation coefficient. Ideally, the goal is a perfectly consistent relationship. Therefore, try to test participants in a consistent fashion to minimize the variability in *Y* scores at each *X*.

3. *Increasing N increases power.* With a larger *N* and thus a larger *df*, the critical value is smaller, and thus a given coefficient is more likely to be significant.

> *REMEMBER* Increase power in a correlation coefficient by avoiding a restricted range, minimizing the variability in *Y* scores, and increasing N.

PUTTING IT ALL TOGETHER

In one sense I hope that you found this chapter rather boring—not because it *is* boring, but because, for each statistic, we performed virtually the same operations. In testing *any* statistic, we ultimately do and say the same things. In all cases, if the obtained statistic is out there far enough in the sampling distribution, it is too unlikely for us to accept as representing the H_0 situation, so we reject H_0. Any H_0 implies that the sample does not represent the predicted relationship, so rejecting H_0 increases our confidence that the data *do* represent the predicted relationship. We're especially confident because the probability is less than α that we've made an error in this decision. If we fail to reject H_0, then hopefully we have sufficient power, so that we're unlikely to have made an error here, too. These are the fundamentals of *all* inferential statistics.

CHAPTER SUMMARY

1. The t-*test* is for testing one sample mean when (a) there is one random sample of interval or ratio data, (b) the raw score population is a normal distribution, and (c) the standard deviation of the raw score population is estimated by computing s_X from the sample data.

2. In the *t*-test compute the *estimated standard error of the mean* ($s_{\bar{X}}$), which is an estimate of the standard deviation of the sampling distribution.

3. A t-*distribution* is a theoretical sampling distribution of all possible values of t when a raw score population is infinitely sampled using a particular N. The appropriate t-distribution to use in a study is the one identified by $N - 1$ degrees of freedom (df).

4. In *point estimation* a μ is assumed to be at a point on the variable equal to $\overline{X}$. Because the sample probably contains sampling error, a point estimate is likely to be incorrect. In *interval estimation* a μ is assumed to lie within a specified interval. Interval estimation is performed by computing a *confidence interval*.

5. The *confidence interval for a single μ* describes a range of μs, any one of which the sample mean is likely to represent. The interval contains the highest and lowest values of μ that are not significantly different from the sample mean. Our confidence that the interval contains the μ equals $(1 - \alpha)100$.

6. The *sampling distribution of a correlation coefficient* is a frequency distribution showing all possible values of the coefficient that occur when samples of size N are drawn from a population in which the correlation coefficient is zero.

7. Significance testing of the *Pearson* r assumes that (a) we have a random sample of pairs of scores from two interval or ratio variables and (b) the Y scores are normally distributed at each X, and the X scores are normally distributed at each Y.

8. Significance testing of the *Spearman* r_s assumes a random sample of pairs of ordinal scores.

9. Significance testing of the *point-biserial* r_{pb} assumes a random sample of pairs of scores from one dichotomous variable and one interval or ratio variable.

10. Only when a correlation coefficient is significant is it appropriate to compute the linear regression equation and the proportion of variance accounted for.

11. Maximize the power of the t-test by (a) creating large differences between the conditions of the independent variable, (b) minimizing the variability of the dependent scores within each condition, and (c) increasing the N of small samples.

12. Maximize the power of a correlation coefficient by (a) avoiding a restricted range, (b) minimizing the variability in Y at each X, and (c) increasing the N of small samples.

KEY TERMS: Can You Define the Following?

t_{obt} t_{crit} $s_{\overline{X}}$ df H_0 H_a r_{obt} r_{crit}

confidence interval for a single μ *280*

estimated standard error of the mean *272*

interval estimation *280*

margin of error *280*

one-sample *t*-test *270*

point estimation *280*

sampling distribution of a correlation coefficient *286*

t-distribution *274*

REVIEW QUESTIONS

(Answers for odd-numbered questions are in Appendix C.)

1. A scientist has conducted a one-sample experiment. (a) What two parametric procedures are available to her? (b) What is the deciding factor for selecting between them? (c) What are the other assumptions of the *t*-test?

2. In this chapter you learned about five different statistical procedures (plus power). List them.

3. (a) What is the difference between $s_{\bar{X}}$ and $\sigma_{\bar{X}}$? (b) How is their use the same?

4. (a) Why are there different values of t_{crit} when samples have different Ns? (b) What must you compute in order to find t_{crit}?

5. (a) Summarize the steps involved in analyzing a Pearson correlational study.

6. Summarize the steps involved in analyzing the results of a one-sample experiment.

7. What is the final step in examining the data in any study?

8. Say you have a sample mean of 44 in a study. (a) Estimate the corresponding μ using point estimation. (b) What does a confidence interval computed for this μ tell you? (c) Why is computing a confidence interval better than using a point estimate?

9. (a) What is power? (b) What outcome should cause you to worry about having sufficient power? (c) Why? (d) At what stage do you build in power?

10. (a) What are the three aspects of maximizing the power of a *t*-test? (b) What are the three aspects of maximizing the power of a correlation coefficient?

APPLICATION QUESTIONS

11. You wish to determine whether this textbook is beneficial or detrimental to students learning statistics. On a national statistics exam $\mu = 68.5$ for students who have used other textbooks. A random sample of students who have used this book has the following scores:

64	69	92	77	71	99	82	74	69	88

    (a) What are H_0 and H_a for this study? (b) Compute t_{obt}. (c) With $\alpha = .05$, what is t_{crit}? (d) What do you conclude about the use of this book? (e) Compute the confidence interval for μ.

12. A researcher predicts that smoking cigarettes decreases a person's sense of smell. On a standard test of olfactory sensitivity, the μ for nonsmokers is 18.4. By giving this test to a random sample of people who smoke a pack a day, the researcher obtains the following scores:

16	14	19	17	16	18	17	15	18	19	12	14

    (a) What are H_0 and H_a for this study? (b) Compute t_{obt}. (c) With $\alpha = .05$, what is t_{crit}? (d) What should the researcher conclude about this relationship? (e) Compute the confidence interval for μ.

13. Foofy conducts a study to determine if hearing an argument in favor of an issue alters participants' attitudes toward the issue one way or the other. She presents a 30-second speech in favor of an issue to 8 people. In a national survey the mean attitude score toward this issue was $\mu = 50$. She obtains the following scores:

| 10 | 33 | 86 | 55 | 67 | 60 | 44 | 71 |

(a) What are H_0 and H_a? (b) What is the value of t_{obt}? (c) With $\alpha = .05$, what is the value of t_{crit}? (d) What are the statistical results? (e) If appropriate, compute the confidence interval for μ. (f) Using the preceding statistics, what conclusions should Foofy draw about the relationship between such arguments and their impact on attitudes?

14. For the study in question 13, (a) What statistical principle should Foofy be concerned with? (b) Identify three problems with her study from a statistical perspective. (c) Why would correcting the problems identified in part b improve her study?

15. Poindexter examined the relationship between the quality of sneakers worn by volleyball players and their average number of points scored per game. Studying 20 people who owned sneakers of good to excellent quality, he computed $r = +.41$. Without further ado, he immediately claimed to have support for the notion that better-quality sneakers are related to better performance on a somewhat consistent basis. He then computed r^2 and the regression equation. Do you agree or disagree with his approach? Why?

16. Eventually, for the study in question 15, Poindexter reported that $r(18) = +.41$, $p > .05$. (a) What should he conclude about this relationship? (b) What other computations should he perform to describe the relationship in these data? (c) What statistical principle should he be concerned with? (d) What aspects of the study can he improve? (e) What will correcting the things from part d do to his results?

17. A scientist suspects that as a person's stress level changes, so does the amount of his or her impulse buying. He collects data from 72 people and obtains an r of $+.38$. (1) What are H_0 and H_a? (b) With $\alpha = .05$, what is r_{crit}? (c) Report these results using the correct format. (d) What conclusions should he draw? (e) What other calculations should be performed to describe the relationship in these data?

18. Foofy conducts a correlational study examining the relationship between an individual's physical strength and his or her college grade point average. Using a computer, she computes the correlation for a sample of 2000 people and obtains $r(1998) = +.08, p < .0001$. She claims she has uncovered a useful tool for predicting which college applicants are likely to succeed academically. Do you agree or disagree? Why?

19. A researcher investigates the relationship between handedness and strength of personality. She tests 42 people, assigning left-handers a score of 1 and right-handers a score of 2. She obtains a correlation coefficient of $+.33$ between handedness and scores on a personality test. (a) Which type of correlation coefficient did she compute? (b) What are H_0 and H_a? (c) With $\alpha = .05$, what is the critical value? (d) What should the researcher conclude about the strength of the relationship in the population? What should she conclude about the direction of the relationship in the population? (e) Are the results of this study relatively useful?

20. A newspaper article claims that for all U.S. colleges, the academic rank of a college is negatively related to the rank of its football team. You examine the accuracy of this claim. From a sample of 28 colleges, you obtain a correlation coefficient of $-.32$. (a) Which type of correlation coefficient did you compute? (b) What are H_0 and H_a? (c) With $\alpha = .05$, what is the critical value? (d) What are the statistical results? (e) What should you conclude about the accuracy of the newspaper claim for all colleges in the United States? (f) In predicting a particular school's academic ranking in your sample, how important is it that you look at the school's football ranking?

21. A researcher proposes that a person's sense of humor is related to his or her math ability. He measures participants' math skills and how funny they find three puns. He tests 10 math majors and finds a nonsignificant r. (a) What characteristic of his participants may account for this result? (b) What problem with the humor test may account for this result? (c) What other obvious improvement in power can the researcher achieve?

22. While reading a published research report, you encounter the following statements. For each, identify the N, the procedure performed and the outcome, the relationship, and the type of error possibly being made. (a) "When we examined the perceptual skills data, the mean of 55 for the sample of adolescents differed significantly from the population mean of 70 for adults, $t(45) = 3.76$, $p < .01$." (b) "The correlation between personality type and emotionality, however, was not significantly different from zero, with $r(25) = +.42, p > .05$."

23. You wish to compute the 95% confidence interval for a sample with a df of 80. Using interpolation, determine the t_{crit} you should use.

24. Poindexter performed a two-tailed experiment in which $N = 20$. He couldn't find his t-tables, but somehow he remembered the t_{crit} at $df = 10$. He decided to compare his t_{obt} to this t_{crit}. Why is this a correct or incorrect approach? (*Hint:* Consider whether t_{obt} turns out to be significant or nonsignificant at this t_{crit}.)

25. (a) Why must a relationship be significant in order to be important? (b) Why can a relationship be significant and still be unimportant?

///////// **SUMMARY OF FORMULAS**

1. *The definitional formula for the one-sample* t-*test is*

$$t_{obt} = \frac{\overline{X} - \mu}{s_{\overline{X}}}$$

where the value of $s_{\overline{X}}$ is computed as

$$s_{\overline{X}} = \frac{s_X}{\sqrt{N}}$$

and s_X is computed as

$$s_X = \sqrt{\frac{\Sigma X^2 - \frac{(\Sigma X)^2}{N}}{N-1}}$$

2. *The computational formulas for the one-sample t-test are*

$$t_{obt} = \frac{\overline{X} - \mu}{\sqrt{\frac{s_{\overline{X}}^2}{N}}} \quad \text{and} \quad t_{obt} = \frac{\overline{X} - \mu}{\sqrt{(s_{\overline{X}}^2)\left(\frac{1}{N}\right)}}$$

where $s_{\overline{X}}^2$ is the estimated variance computed for the sample.
Values of t_{crit} *are found in Table 2 of Appendix B, "Critical Values of* t,*" for* df $=$ N $-$ 1.

3. *The computational formula for a confidence interval for a single* μ *is*

$$(s_{\overline{X}})(-t_{crit}) + \overline{X} < \mu < (s_{\overline{X}})(+t_{crit}) + \overline{X}$$

where t_{crit} is the two-tailed value for $df = N - 1$ and $\overline{X}$ and $s_{\overline{X}}$ are computed using the sample data.

4. *To test the significance of a correlation coefficient, compare the obtained correlation coefficient to the critical value. The number of pairs of scores in the sample is* N. *Critical values are found in Appendix B as follows:*

Correlation Coefficient	*Critical Values*	**df**
r	Table 3: r-tables	$df = N - 2$
r_s	Table 4: r_s-tables	$df = N$
r_{pb}	Table 3: r-tables	$df = N - 2$

Hypothesis Testing for Two Sample Means: The *t*-Test

To understand this chapter, recall the following:

- From Chapter 4 recall how to graph experimental results.
- From Chapters 5 and 8 recall how to conceptualize the proportion of variance accounted for.
- From Chapter 7 understand the point-biserial correlation coefficient (r_{pb}).
- Remember what you've learned about inferential statistics.

Your goals in this chapter are to learn:

- The logic of a two-sample experiment.
- The difference between independent samples and related samples.
- How to perform the independent-samples and related-samples *t*-tests.
- How to compute a confidence interval for the difference between two μs and for the μ of difference scores.
- How r_{pb}^2 is used to describe effect size in a two-sample experiment.

This chapter presents the major parametric procedures used when an experiment involves *two* samples. These procedures center around the two-sample *t*-test. As the name implies, this test is similar to the one-sample *t*-test you saw in Chapter 11, except that the characteristics of a two-sample design require that we use slightly different formulas. In addition, we'll discuss procedures for more completely describing a significant relationship.

MORE STATISTICAL NOTATION

It is time to pay close attention to subscripts. We will compute the means of two samples, identifying one as $\overline{X}_1$ and the other as $\overline{X}_2$. Likewise, we will compute an estimate of the population variance represented by each sample, identifying one as s_1^2 and the other as s_2^2.

And here's a new one: So far the uppercase N has stood for the number of scores in a sample. Actually, N indicates the total number of scores in the *study*, but with only one sample, N was also the number of scores in the sample. However, now we'll be discussing experiments with two samples, so the lowercase n with a subscript stands for the number of scores in each sample. Thus, n_1 is the number of scores in Sample 1, and n_2 is the number of scores in Sample 2. N is the total number of scores in the experiment, so adding the ns together equals N.

REMEMBER N stands for the total number of scores in an experiment; n stands for the number of scores in a condition.

WHY IS IT IMPORTANT TO KNOW ABOUT THE TWO-SAMPLE *t*-TEST?

To perform the one-sample experiment discussed in previous chapters, we must already know the value of μ for a population under one condition of the independent variable. However, because researchers explore new behaviors and variables, they usually do not know any values of μ ahead of time. Instead, the simplest alternative is to conduct a two-sample experiment: We measure participants' scores under two conditions of the independent variable, then determine if they reflect a relationship. It's important for you to understand this procedure because a two-sample experiment is a fairly common design. You are likely to use two-sample *t*-tests in your own research, and you will encounter them when reading the research of others.

UNDERSTANDING THE TWO-SAMPLE EXPERIMENT

In a two-sample experiment we measure participants' scores under two conditions of the independent variable. Condition 1 produces sample mean $\overline{X}_1$ that represents μ_1, the μ we would find if we tested everyone in the population under Condition 1. Condition

2 produces sample mean $\overline{X}_2$ that represents μ_2, the μ we would find if we tested everyone in the population under Condition 2. A possible outcome from such an experiment is shown in Figure 12.1. If each sample mean represents a different population for each condition, then the experiment has demonstrated a relationship in nature: As we change the conditions of the independent variable, the scores in the population change in a consistent fashion.

However, there's the usual problem of sampling error. Even though we may have different sample means, the independent variable may not really work, and the relationship may not really exist in the population. It's possible that, if we tested the entire population, we might actually find the *same* population of scores under both conditions of the independent variable. In Figure 12.1, for example, we might find only the lower or upper distribution, or we might find one in the middle. Then the conditions of the independent variable literally would not make a difference in the population, and there would be only one value of μ: call it μ_1 or μ_2, it wouldn't matter because it's the *same* μ. Thus, it is possible that our different sample means poorly represent the same population μ and that we are being misled by sampling error. Therefore, before we make any conclusions about the experiment, we must determine whether the difference between the sample means is likely to merely reflect sampling error.

The parametric statistical procedure for determining whether the results of a two-sample experiment are significant is the two-sample *t*-test. However, there are two distinctly different ways to create the two samples, so there are two very different versions of the *t*-test: One is called the "independent-samples *t*-test" and the other is the "related-samples *t*-test."

> REMEMBER   There are two ways to calculate the two-sample *t*-test, using either the *independent-samples* t-*test* or the *related-samples* t-*test*.

First, we will discuss the independent samples *t*-test.

FIGURE 12.1   Relationship in the population in a two-sample experiment

As the conditions change, the population tends to change in a consistent fashion.

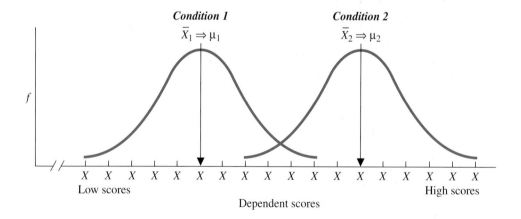

THE INDEPENDENT-SAMPLES *t*-TEST

The **independent-samples *t*-test** is the parametric procedure used for significance testing of two sample means from **independent samples.** Two samples are independent when we randomly select and assign a participant to a sample, without regard to who else has been selected for either sample. Then the scores are independent events, which, as in Chapter 9, means that the probability of a particular score occurring in one sample is not influenced by the scores that occur in the other sample. In practice, you can recognize that samples are independent by the *absence* of anything fancy used to create them: We don't do anything like matching up participants between the conditions or testing the same participants in both conditions. Instead, we simply have one random sample of participants in one condition, and another, separate and "independent" sample in the other condition.

Here is a study that calls for the independent-samples *t*-test. We propose that people who witness a crime or other event will recall the event differently when they are hypnotized. We'll create two samples of participants who watch a videotape of a supposed robbery. Later, one group will be hypnotized and then answer 30 questions about the event. The other group will answer the questions without being hypnotized. Thus, the conditions of the independent variable are the presence or absence of hypnosis, and the dependent variable is the number of times information is correctly recalled. You can envision this design as shown in Design Diagram 12.1. Recall scores are normally distributed ratio scores, so we compute the mean of each condition, summing vertically in each column. If the means differ, we'll have evidence of a relationship where, as amount of hypnosis changes, recall scores also change.

By now you know the routine: (1) Check the assumptions of the statistical procedure and create the statistical hypotheses, (2) set up and perform the statistical test, and (3) if the results are significant, describe and interpret the relationship.

DESIGN DIAGRAM 12.1   Diagram of Hypnosis Study using an Independent-Samples Design

The independent variable is amount of hypnosis, and the dependent variable is recall.

	No Hypnosis	*Hypnosis*
Recall Scores →	*X*	*X*
	X	*X*
	X	*X*
	X	*X*
	X	*X*
	$\overline{X}$	$\overline{X}$

Assumptions of the Independent-Samples *t*-Test

In addition to requiring independent samples, this *t*-test also requires:

1. The dependent scores measure an interval or ratio variable.

2. The populations of raw scores form normal distributions. (If each sample *n* is greater than 30, the populations need only form roughly normal distributions.)

3. And here's a new one: The populations have homogeneous variance. **Homogeneity of variance** means that the variance (σ_X^2) of all populations being represented are equal.

4. It is not required that each condition have the same *n*, but the *n*s should not be massively unequal—a difference in the neighborhood of 10 to 20 is best. (The more the *n*s differ from each other, the more important it is to have homogeneity of variance.)

For the moment, let's say that from reading the research literature, we find that the hypnosis study meets these assumptions.

Now for the statistical hypotheses.

Statistical Hypotheses for the Independent-Samples *t*-Test

Depending on your experimental hypotheses, you may have a one- or a two-tailed test. For now, say that we don't specifically predict the *direction* of the difference that hypnosis will make between the two conditions, so we have a two-tailed test: We merely predict that the samples will be different, representing different populations that have different μs.

First, the alternative hypothesis. Because we do not predict which of the two μs will be larger, the predicted relationship exists if one population mean (μ_1) is larger or smaller than the other (μ_2); that is, μ_1 should not equal μ_2. We could state the alternative hypothesis as H_a: $\mu_1 \neq \mu_2$, but there is a better way. If the two μs are not equal, then their *difference* does not equal zero. Thus, the two-tailed alternative hypothesis for our study is

$$H_a: \mu_1 - \mu_2 \neq 0$$

H_a implies that the means from our two conditions each represent a different population of recall scores, having a different μ.

Of course, there's our old nemesis, the null hypothesis. Perhaps there is no relationship, so if we tested everyone under the two conditions, we would find the same population and μ. In other words, μ_1 *equals* μ_2. We could state this as H_0: $\mu_1 = \mu_2$, but, again, there is a better way. If the two μs are equal, then their *difference* is zero. Thus, our two-tailed null hypothesis is

$$H_0: \mu_1 - \mu_2 = 0$$

H_0 implies that both sample means represent the same population of recall scores, having the same μ. If the sample means differ, it's because of sampling error in representing that one μ.

Notice that we derived these hypotheses without specifying the value of either μ. Therefore, the above hypotheses are the two-tailed hypotheses for *any* independent-samples *t*-test when we are testing if there is no relationship in the population, regardless of the dependent variable being measured.

As usual, we test the null hypothesis, and to do that we examine the sampling distribution.

The Sampling Distribution for the Independent-Samples *t*-Test

To understand the sampling distribution here, let's say that, in our study, we find a mean recall score of 20 in the no-hypnosis condition, and a mean of 23 in the hypnosis condition. We can summarize these results by looking at the *difference* between the means: Changing from no hypnosis to hypnosis results in a difference in mean recall of 3 points. We always test H_0 by finding the probability of obtaining our results when there is not a relationship, so here we will determine the probability of obtaining a *difference* of 3 between two $\overline{X}$s when they both actually represent the same μ.

> *REMEMBER* The independent-samples *t*-test determines the probability of obtaining our *difference* between $\overline{X}$s when H_0 is true.

You can think of the sampling distribution as follows. Using the same *n*s as in our study, we select *two* random samples from *one* raw score population. (Just like H_0 says happened in our study.) We compute the two sample means and arbitrarily subtract one from the other. The result is the *difference between the means,* which we symbolize by $\overline{X}_1 - \overline{X}_2$. We do this an infinite number of times and plot a frequency distribution of these differences. We then have the **sampling distribution of differences between means,** which is the distribution of all possible differences between two means when they are drawn from the raw score population described by H_0. You can envision this sampling distribution as shown in Figure 12.2. This is just like any other sampling

FIGURE 12.2 Sampling distribution of differences between means when H_0: $\mu_1 - \mu_2 = 0$

The X axis has two labels: Each $\overline{X}_1 - \overline{X}_2$ *symbolizes the difference between two sample means; when labeled as* t, *a larger* ±t *indicates a larger difference between means that is less likely when* H_0 *is true.*

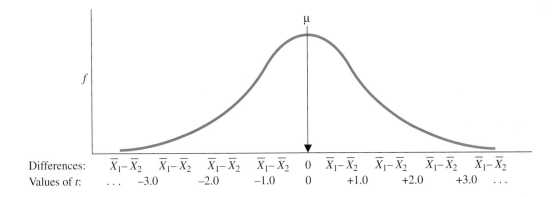

distribution except that along the X axis are the *differences* between two sample means, each labeled $\overline{X}_1 - \overline{X}_2$. As usual, the mean of the sampling distribution is stated in H_0, and here it is zero. The mean is zero because, most often, both sample means will equal the μ of the population of raw scores, so the difference between them will be zero. However, sometimes by chance both sample means will not equal μ or each other. Depending on whether $\overline{X}_1$ or $\overline{X}_2$ is larger, the difference will be positive or negative. Small negative or positive differences occur frequently when H_0 is true, but larger ones do not. Therefore, the larger the absolute difference between the means, the farther into either tail of the distribution the difference falls.

To test H_0, we determine where on this sampling distribution the difference between our sample means lies. To do so, we compute a new version of t_{obt}. As shown in Figure 12.2, the larger the absolute value of $\pm t_{obt}$, the farther into the tail of the distribution the difference between our means lies, and so the less likely this difference is to occur when H_0 is true.

Computing the Independent-Samples *t*-Test

In the previous chapter you computed t_{obt} by performing three steps: (1) estimating the variance of the raw score population, (2) computing the estimated standard error of the sampling distribution, and (3) computing t_{obt}. You complete the same three steps to perform the two-sample *t*-test.

Estimating the Population Variance   First, calculate s_X^2 for *each* condition, using the formula:

$$s_X^2 = \frac{\Sigma X^2 - \dfrac{(\Sigma X)^2}{n}}{n - 1}$$

Each time, use the Xs from only one condition, and n is the number of scores in that condition.

Each s_X^2 estimates the population variance, but each may contain sampling error. (Because of this, if s_1^2 does not equal s_2^2, we have not necessarily violated the assumption of homogeneity of variance in the population.) Therefore, to obtain the best estimate, we'll compute a weighted average of the two values of s_X^2. Each variance is weighted based on the size of *df* in the sample. The weighted average of the sample variances is called the **pooled variance,** and its symbol is s_{pool}^2.

THE COMPUTATIONAL FORMULA FOR THE POOLED VARIANCE IS

$$s_{pool}^2 = \frac{(n_1 - 1)s_1^2 + (n_2 - 1)s_2^2}{(n_1 - 1) + (n_2 - 1)}$$

This formula says to multiply the s_X^2 from each sample times $n - 1$ for that sample, then add the results together and divide by the sum of $(n_1 - 1) + (n_2 - 1)$.

For example, say that the hypnosis study produced the results shown in Table 12.1. Let's label the hypnosis condition Sample 1, so it produces $\overline{X}_1$, s_1^2, and n_1. The no-hypnosis condition produces $\overline{X}_2$, s_2^2, and n_2. Filling in the above formula, we have

$$s_{\text{pool}}^2 = \frac{(17-1)9.0 + (15-1)7.5}{(17-1) + (15-1)}$$

In the numerator, 16 times 9 is 144, and 14 times 7.5 is 105. In the denominator, 16 plus 14 is 30, so

$$s_{\text{pool}}^2 = \frac{144 + 105}{30} = \frac{249}{30} = 8.30$$

Thus, we estimate that the variance of any of the populations of recall scores represented by our samples is 8.30.

Computing the Standard Error of the Difference   Recall that the variability in the raw score population determines the variability of the sampling distribution, so now we use s_{pool}^2 to compute the standard error of the sampling distribution. The standard error for differences between means is called the standard error of the difference. The **standard error of the difference** is the estimated standard deviation of the sampling distribution of differences between the means, indicating how spread out the differences are when the distribution is created using samples having our *n* and our value of s_{pool}^2. The symbol for the standard error of the difference is $s_{\overline{X}_1 - \overline{X}_2}$. (The subscript indicates that we are dealing with differences between pairs of means.)

In the previous chapter, in the one-sample *t*-test a formula for the standard error of the mean was

$$s_{\overline{X}} = \sqrt{(s_X^2)\left(\frac{1}{N}\right)}$$

Now the formula for the standard error of the difference is very similar.

THE DEFINITIONAL FORMULA FOR THE STANDARD ERROR OF THE DIFFERENCE IS

$$s_{\overline{X}_1 - \overline{X}_2} = \sqrt{(s_{\text{pool}}^2)\left(\frac{1}{n_1} + \frac{1}{n_2}\right)}$$

TABLE 12.1   Data from the Hypnosis Study

	Sample 1: Hypnosis	Sample 2: No Hypnosis
Mean details recalled	$\overline{X}_1 = 23$	$\overline{X}_2 = 20$
Number of subjects	$n_1 = 17$	$n_2 = 15$
Estimated variance	$s_1^2 = 9.0$	$s_2^2 = 7.5$

To compute $s_{\bar{X}_1 - \bar{X}_2}$, first reduce the fractions $1/n_1$ and $1/n_2$ to decimals; then add them together and multiply the sum times s^2_{pool}. Then find the square root.

For the hypnosis study, s^2_{pool} is 8.30, n_1 is 17, and n_2 is 15. Filling in the above formula gives

$$s_{\bar{X}_1 - \bar{X}_2} = \sqrt{8.3\left(\frac{1}{17} + \frac{1}{15}\right)}$$

Since 1/17 is .059 and 1/15 is .067, their sum is .126. Then

$$s_{\bar{X}_1 - \bar{X}_2} = \sqrt{8.3(.126)} = \sqrt{1.046} = 1.023$$

Thus, the standard error of the difference ($s_{\bar{X}_1 - \bar{X}_2}$) equals 1.023.

Computing *t* for Two Independent Samples   In previous chapters we found how far the result of the study ($\bar{X}$) was from the mean of the H_0 sampling distribution (μ), measured in standard error units. In general, this formula is

$$t_{\text{obt}} = \frac{(\text{Result of the study}) - (\text{Mean of } H_0 \text{ sampling distribution})}{\text{Standard error}}$$

Now we perform the same computation, but here the "result of the study" is the *difference* between the two sample means. So in place of "result of the study" we put $\bar{X}_1 - \bar{X}_2$. Also, now the mean of the H_0 sampling distribution is the *difference* between μ_1 and μ_2 described by H_0. Thus, we replace "mean of H_0 sampling distribution" with $\mu_1 - \mu_2$. Finally, we replace "standard error" with $s_{\bar{X}_1 - \bar{X}_2}$. Putting this all together, we have

THE DEFINITIONAL FORMULA FOR THE INDEPENDENT-SAMPLES t-TEST IS

$$t_{\text{obt}} = \frac{(\bar{X}_1 - \bar{X}_2) - (\mu_1 - \mu_2)}{s_{\bar{X}_1 - \bar{X}_2}}$$

Here, $\bar{X}_1$ and $\bar{X}_2$ are the sample means, $s_{\bar{X}_1 - \bar{X}_2}$ is computed as shown previously, and the value of $\mu_1 - \mu_2$ is the difference specified by the null hypothesis. The reason for writing H_0 as $\mu_1 - \mu_2 = 0$ is so that it indicates the value of $\mu_1 - \mu_2$ to put in this formula. (Later this becomes important when $\mu_1 - \mu_2$ is not zero.)

For the hypnosis study, our sample means were 23 and 20, the difference between μ_1 and μ_2 is 0, and $s_{\bar{X}_1 - \bar{X}_2}$ is 1.023. Putting these values into the above formula gives

$$t_{\text{obt}} = \frac{(23 - 20) - 0}{1.023}$$

Then

$$t_{\text{obt}} = \frac{(+3.0) - 0}{1.023} = \frac{+3.0}{1.023} = +2.93$$

Our t_{obt} is $+2.93$. Thus, the difference of $+3.0$ between our sample means is located at something like a *z*-score of $+2.93$ on the sampling distribution of differences when H_0 is true and both samples represent the same population.

Computational Formulas for the Independent-Samples *t*-Test   We can save a little paper by combining some of the previous steps.

First, in the formula for $s_{\bar{X}_1 - \bar{X}_2}$, the symbol for s_{pool}^2 is replaced by the formula for s_{pool}^2. Then,

---

THE COMPUTATIONAL FORMULA FOR THE STANDARD ERROR OF THE DIFFERENCE IS

$$s_{\bar{X}_1 - \bar{X}_2} = \sqrt{\left[\frac{(n_1 - 1)s_1^2 + (n_2 - 1)s_2^2}{(n_1 - 1) + (n_2 - 1)}\right]\left[\frac{1}{n_1} + \frac{1}{n_2}\right]}$$

In the left-hand brackets we compute s_{pool}^2, and by multiplying it times the right-hand bracket and then taking the square root, we have $s_{\bar{X}_1 - \bar{X}_2}$.

We can also combine the steps of computing s_{pool}^2, $s_{\bar{X}_1 - \bar{X}_2}$, and t_{obt} into one formula if the symbol for the standard error ($s_{\bar{X}_1 - \bar{X}_2}$) is replaced by its above computational formula.

THE COMPUTATIONAL FORMULA FOR THE INDEPENDENT-SAMPLES t-TEST IS

$$t_{obt} = \frac{(\bar{X}_1 - \bar{X}_2) - (\mu_1 - \mu_2)}{\sqrt{\left[\frac{(n_1 - 1)s_1^2 + (n_2 - 1)s_2^2}{(n_1 - 1) + (n_2 - 1)}\right]\left[\frac{1}{n_1} + \frac{1}{n_2}\right]}}$$

For the hypnosis study we have

$$t_{obt} = \frac{(23 - 20) - 0}{\sqrt{\left[\frac{(17 - 1)9.0 + (15 - 1)7.5}{(17 - 1) + (15 - 1)}\right]\left[\frac{1}{17} - \frac{1}{15}\right]}}$$

which becomes

$$t_{obt} = \frac{+3.0}{\sqrt{(8.3)(.126)}} = \frac{+3.0}{1.023} = +2.93$$

And again, $t_{obt} = +2.93$.

Interpreting t_{obt} in the Independent-Samples *t*-Test

To determine if t_{obt} is significant, compare it to t_{crit}, which is found in the *t*-tables (Table 2 in Appendix B). As usual, obtain t_{crit} using degrees of freedom, but with two samples, the *df* are computed differently: Now the degrees of freedom equals $(n_1 - 1) + (n_2 - 1)$.

> **REMEMBER**   Critical values of *t* for the independent-samples *t*-test are found for $df = (n_1 - 1) + (n_2 - 1)$.

Another way of expressing this *df* is $(n_1 + n_2) - 2$.

For the hypnosis study, $n_1 = 17$ and $n_2 = 15$, so *df* equals $(17 - 1) + (15 - 1)$, which is 30. With alpha at .05, the two-tailed t_{crit} is ±2.042. Figure 12.3 locates these values on the sampling distribution of differences.

The interpretation here is the same as for previous inferential tests: H_0 says that the difference between our sample means is merely a poor representation of no difference in the population. But, looking at the sampling distribution, you see that you'll hardly ever get a difference of +3.0 when your two samples represent no difference in the population. Therefore, because t_{obt} is in the region of rejection, we reject H_0 and conclude that our difference of +3.0 is unlikely to be representing zero difference in the population. In other words, the difference between our means is significantly different from zero. We communicate this result as

$$t(30) = +2.93, \; p < .05$$

As usual, *df* is in parentheses, and because $\alpha = .05$, the probability is less than .05 that we've made a Type I error (rejected a true H_0).

We can now accept the alternative hypothesis that the difference between our sample means represents a difference between μs that is *not* zero. Now we work backwards to the individual populations of scores: Saying that the difference between the means is significantly different from zero is the same as saying that the two means differ significantly *from each other.* Here, the mean for hypnosis (23) is larger than the mean for no hypnosis (20), so, we can conclude that increasing the amount of hypnosis leads to significantly higher recall scores.

FIGURE 12.3 H_0 sampling distribution of differences between means when $\mu_1 - \mu_2 = 0$

The t_{obt} *shows the location of a difference of +3.0*

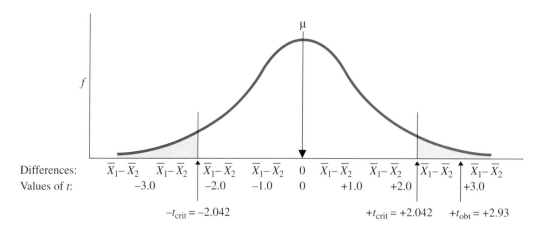

If t_{obt} was not beyond t_{crit}, we would not reject H_0, and we would not have evidence of a relationship between hypnosis and recall.

Because we did find a significant result, as usual the next step is to describe and interpret the relationship. First, you know from the previous chapter that we could compute a confidence interval for the μ that is represented by each sample mean. That is, looking at only one condition at a time, (using only one $s_{\overline{X}}^2$ and $\overline{X}$ and computing a new standard error and t_{crit}), we'd know the range of values of μ likely to be represented by our hypnosis condition. Then we'd compute the range of μs likely to be represented by the no-hypnosis condition.

However, there is also another way to describe the populations represented by our samples—by creating a *confidence interval for the difference between the μs.*

Confidence Interval for the Difference Between Two μs

The **confidence interval for the difference between two μs** describes a range of *differences* between two μs, any one of which is likely to be represented by the *difference* between our two sample means. For example, above we found a difference of $+3.0$ between the sample means $(\overline{X}_1 - \overline{X}_2)$, so if we could examine the corresponding μ_1 and μ_2, we'd expect that their difference, $\mu_1 - \mu_2$, would be *around* $+3.0$. The confidence interval contains the highest and lowest values of $\mu_1 - \mu_2$ around $+3.0$ that the difference between our sample means is likely to represent.

THE FORMULA FOR THE CONFIDENCE INTERVAL FOR THE DIFFERENCE BETWEEN TWO μs IS

$$(s_{\overline{X}_1 - \overline{X}_2})(-t_{crit}) + (\overline{X}_1 - \overline{X}_2) \leq \mu_1 - \mu_2 \leq (s_{\overline{X}_1 - \overline{X}_2})(+t_{crit}) + (\overline{X}_1 - \overline{X}_2)$$

Here, $\mu_1 - \mu_2$ stands for the unknown difference we are estimating. The t_{crit} is the *two-tailed* value found for the appropriate α at $df = (n_1 - 1) + (n_2 - 1)$. The values of $s_{\overline{X}_1 - \overline{X}_2}$ and $(\overline{X}_1 - \overline{X}_2)$ are computed in the *t*-test from the sample data.

In the hypnosis study, the two-tailed t_{crit} for $df = 30$ and $\alpha = .05$ is ± 2.042, $s_{\overline{X}_1 - \overline{X}_2}$ is 1.023, and $\overline{X}_1 - \overline{X}_2$ is $+3.0$. Filling in the formula gives

$$(1.023)(-2.042) + (+3.0) \leq \mu_1 - \mu_2 \leq (1.023)(+2.042) + (+3.0)$$

Multiplying 1.02 times ± 2.042 gives

$$-2.089 + (+3.0) \leq \mu_1 - \mu_2 \leq +2.089 + (+3.0)$$

So, finally,

$$.911 \leq \mu_1 - \mu_2 \leq 5.089$$

Because $\alpha = .05$, this is the 95% confidence interval: We are 95% confident that the interval between .911 and 5.089 contains the difference we'd find between the μs for no hypnosis and hypnosis. In essence, if someone asked us how big a difference hypnosis makes for everyone when recalling information in our study, we'd be 95% confident that the difference is, on average, between about .91 and 5.09 correct answers.

ADDITIONAL ASPECTS OF THE INDEPENDENT-SAMPLES *t*-TEST

We're not completely finished with the hypnosis study yet because there is more to do to understand the relationship. We'll examine these things after we've looked at the other kind of two-sample *t*-test. But first, the following describes two variations in how the independent-samples *t*-test is performed.

Performing One-Tailed Tests on Independent Samples

We could have conducted the hypnosis study using a one-tailed test if we had predicted the direction of the difference between the two conditions. Say that we predicted a positive relationship such that the greater the degree of hypnosis, the higher the recall scores. Everything discussed above applies here, but beware: One-tailed tests can produce serious confusion! This is because you *arbitrarily* call one mean $\overline{X}_1$ and one $\overline{X}_2$ and then subtract $\overline{X}_1 - \overline{X}_2$. How you assign the subscripts determines whether you find a positive or a negative difference, and thus whether t_{obt} is positive or negative. As you know, the sign of t_{obt} is very important in a one-tailed test.

To prevent confusion, use more meaningful subscripts than 1 and 2. For example, you could use the subscript h for the hypnosis condition and n for the no-hypnosis condition. Then follow these steps:

1. Decide which $\overline{X}$ and corresponding μ is expected to be larger. (Say we think the μ for hypnosis (μ_h) is larger.)

2. Arbitrarily decide which condition to subtract from the other. (Say we'll subtract no-hypnosis *from* hypnosis.)

3. Decide whether the difference will be positive or negative. (Subtracting the smaller μ_n from the larger μ_h should produce a positive difference, *greater* than zero.)

4. Create H_a and H_0 to match this prediction. (Our H_a is that $\mu_h - \mu_n > 0$; H_0 is that $\mu_h - \mu_n \leq 0$.)

5. Locate the region of rejection based on your predictions and subtraction. (Our $\overline{X}_h - \overline{X}_n$ should produce a positive difference and these are in the right-hand tail of the sampling distribution, so place the region of rejection here and t_{crit} is positive.)

6. Complete the *t*-test as above, using the previous formulas for t_{obt}. But! Subtract the $\overline{X}$s in the same way the μs are subtracted! (We used $\mu_h - \mu_n$, so we'd compute $\overline{X}_h - \overline{X}_n$.) If you subtract the $\overline{X}$s opposite to how you subtract the μs, the sign of t_{obt} will be opposite to that of t_{crit}, and the results can never be significant.

The confusion arises because, while *still predicting a larger* μ_h, we could have reversed H_a, saying $\mu_n - \mu_h < 0$. Here, subtracting the larger μ_h from the smaller μ_n should produce a difference less than zero, and subtracting the sample means this way should produce a negative t_{obt}. Now the region of rejection is in the negative tail of the distribution, and t_{crit} is negative.

Testing Hypotheses about Nonzero Differences

So far, we've tested null hypotheses that say the independent variable produces no difference in the population. However, you can also test hypotheses that the variable does not change an *existing* difference. Here's a new example. Say that on a test of flying ability, the population of Navy pilots differs from the population of Marine pilots by 10 points. However, recently the Navy developed a new training method for its pilots. To test this method, we randomly select a sample of Navy pilots and compare them to a sample of Marine pilots. We are testing whether the samples represent populations that still differ by 10 points. In a two-tailed test the null hypothesis is that the difference between Navy and Marine pilots is still 10, or H_0: $\mu_1 - \mu_2 = 10$. The alternative hypothesis is that the training program has an effect, so the difference is not 10, or H_a: $\mu_1 - \mu_2 \neq 10$.

In the *t*-test we would do everything as above, except that wherever the quantity $\mu_1 - \mu_2$ was zero, now $\mu_1 - \mu_2$ is 10. Thus, we have a sampling distribution of differences created when the μs of the two populations differ by 10, so the mean of the sampling distribution is 10. Comparing t_{obt} to t_{crit} indicates whether the difference between our sample means is significantly different from 10. If it is, then we conclude that with the training, the populations of Navy and Marine pilots no longer differ by 10, but rather by the difference represented by our samples.

Power and the Independent-Samples *t*-Test

Remember *power*—the probability of rejecting H_0 when it is false? Having sufficient power is important anytime results are not significant (because maybe H_0 should have been rejected). Therefore, we try to maximize power by maximizing the size of t_{obt} relative to t_{crit} so that we're more likely to have significant results. As you saw in the previous chapter, there are three ways to maximize power through the way you design a study, each of which also impacts on the formula for the independent-samples t_{obt}.

1. *Maximize the difference produced by the two conditions.* Select two very different conditions of your independent variable, so that they are likely to produce a large difference in dependent scores. This produces a larger value of $(\overline{X}_1 - \overline{X}_2)$, producing a larger numerator in the formula, so t_{obt} will be larger.

2. *Minimize the variability of the raw scores.* Conduct the study as consistently as possible, eliminating anything that might produce differences in scores *within* a condition. This minimizes each s_X^2, so s_{pool}^2 is smaller, and then in the denominator of the *t*-test, $s_{\overline{X}_1 - \overline{X}_2}$ is smaller. A smaller denominator produces a larger t_{obt}.

3. *Maximize the sample* ns. The larger your n_1 and n_2, the larger the t_{obt}. In addition, larger *n*s give a larger *df,* resulting in a smaller t_{crit}.

THE RELATED-SAMPLES *t*-TEST

Now we will discuss the other version of the *t*-test for two samples. The **related-samples *t*-test** is the parametric procedure used with two sample means from two related samples. **Related samples** occur when we pair each score in one sample with a particular score in the other sample. There are two types of research designs that produce related samples: *matched-samples designs* and *repeated-measures designs.*

In a **matched-samples design,** the researcher matches each participant in one condition with a participant in the other condition. We do this so that we have more comparable participants in the conditions. For example, say that we want to measure how well people shoot baskets when using either a standard basketball or a new type of basketball (one with handles.) Ideally, we want the people in both samples to be the same height. If, by the luck of random sampling, one condition contained taller people than the other, then differences in shooting baskets could be due to the differences in height instead of the different balls. We can create two samples containing people who are the same height by forming matching pairs of people who are the same height and then assigning a member of the pair to each condition. Thus, if we randomly select two participants who are six feet tall, one will be randomly assigned to one condition and the other to the other condition. Likewise, a four-foot person in one condition is matched with a four-footer in the other condition, and so on. Now any differences in basket shooting between the two samples cannot be due to differences in height, because the same heights are present in both samples. In the same way, we might match participants using any relevant variable (such as weight, age, or physical ability), or we might use natural pairs to match participants (such as roommates, husband-and-wife teams, or identical twins).

The ultimate form of matching is to match each participant with himself or herself. This is the other, more common, way of producing related samples, called repeated measures. In a **repeated-measures design,** each participant is tested under all conditions of the independent variable. For example, we might first test people when they use the standard basketball, and then measure the same people again when they use the new basketball. (Although we have one sample of participants, we have two samples of scores.) Then, any differences in basket shooting between the samples cannot be due to differences in height or to any other attribute of the participants.

What makes matched and repeated-measures samples *related* is the fact that each score in one sample is related to the paired score in the other sample. Related samples are also called *dependent samples*. As in Chapter 9, two events are dependent when the probability of one event is influenced by the occurrence of the other event. Related samples are dependent because the probability that a score in a pair is a particular value is influenced by the paired score. For example, if a four-foot-tall male scored close to 0 in one sample, the probability is high that the matching four-footer also scored close to 0. This is not the case with independent samples: In the hypnosis study, whether someone scores 0 in the no-hypnosis condition will not influence the probability of anyone scoring 0 in the hypnosis condition.

We cannot use the independent-samples *t*-test in such situations because its sampling distribution describes the probability of a particular difference between two means from *independent* samples. With related samples we must compute this probability differently, so we create the sampling distribution differently and we compute t_{obt} differently.

Assumptions of the Related-Samples *t*-Test

Except for requiring related samples, the assumptions of the related-samples *t*-test are the same as those for the independent-samples *t*-test: (1) The dependent variable involves an interval or ratio scale, and it is normally distributed, (2) the variance of the raw score populations must be estimated, and (3) the populations being represented have homogeneous variance. Because related samples form pairs of scores, the *n* in the two samples must be equal.

If the data meet the assumptions, then it's onward and upward: (1) Create the statistical hypotheses, (2) set up and perform the statistical test, and (3) if the results are significant, describe and interpret the relationship.

The Logic of Hypotheses Testing in the Related-Samples *t*-Test

Let's say we are interested in phobias (irrational fears of objects or events). We have a new therapy we want to test on spider-phobics—people who are overly frightened by spiders. From the local phobia club, we randomly select the very unpowerful *N* of five spider-phobics, and test our therapy using repeated measures of two conditions: before therapy and after therapy. Before therapy we measure each person's fear response to a picture of a spider, measuring heart rate, breathing rate, perspiration, etc., and then compute a "fear" score between 0 (no fear) and 20 (holy terror!). After providing the therapy, we again measure the person's fear response to the picture. (Anytime you have a before-and-after, or *pretest/posttest* design such as this, use the related-samples *t*-test.)

We expect to demonstrate that the therapy will decrease participants' fear of spiders, so we have a one-tailed test. Then, say we obtained the data in Design Diagram 12.2. Sure enough, the mean phobia score before therapy (in the left column) is 14.80, and the mean after therapy is 11.20, so it looks as if therapy reduced fear scores by an average of 14.80 − 11.20 = 3.6 points. But, on the other hand, maybe therapy does nothing; maybe this difference is solely the result of sampling error from the *one* population of fear scores we'd have with or without therapy.

So far, this is similar to an independent-samples *t*-test. However, instead of comparing the sample means directly to determine if they differ significantly, we must first transform the data. Then we test our hypotheses using these transformed scores.

We transform the raw scores by finding each *difference score:* the difference between the two raw scores in a pair. The symbol for a difference score is *D*. Table 12.2 shows how to find the difference scores in the phobia study. First, we arbitrarily subtract each participant's after-therapy score from his or her before-therapy score. (You could subtract the before scores from the after scores, but subtract all scores in the same way. If this were a matched-samples design, we'd subtract the scores in each pair of matched participants.)

DESIGN DIAGRAM 12.2 Fear Scores in the Before-Therapy and After-Therapy Conditions in a Related-Samples Design

Each participant is tested in both conditions.

Participant	*Before Therapy*	*After Therapy*
1 (Foofy)	11	8
2 (Biff)	16	11
3 (Millie)	20	15
4 (Attila)	17	11
5 (Slug)	10	11
	$\overline{X} = 14.80$	$\overline{X} = 11.20$

TABLE 12.2   Finding the Difference Scores in the Phobia Study

Each D = Before-After

Participant	Before Therapy	−	After Therapy	=	D	D²
1	11	−	8	=	+3	9
2	16	−	11	=	+5	25
3	20	−	15	=	+5	25
4	17	−	11	=	+6	36
5	10	−	11	=	−1	1
					$\Sigma D = +18$	$\Sigma D^2 = 96$
$N = 5$					$\overline{D} = +3.6$	

Next, the sample of difference scores is summarized by computing the *mean differ-ence*. The symbol for the mean difference is $\overline{D}$. Add the positive and negative differ-ences to find the sum of the differences, symbolized by ΣD. Then divide by *N*, the number of difference scores. For the phobia data, the mean difference ($\overline{D}$) equals 18/5, which is +3.6. This indicates that the before scores were, on average, 3.6 points higher than the after scores. (As in the far right-hand column of Table 12.2, later we'll need to square each difference and then find the sum, finding ΣD^2.)

Now here's the strange part: Forget about the before and after scores for the moment, and consider only the difference scores. From a statistical standpoint, we have *one* sam-ple mean ($\overline{D}$) from *one* random sample of (difference) scores. As you saw in the previ-ous chapter, with one sample mean, we perform the one-sample *t*-test! The fact that we have difference scores in no way violates this procedure, so we will create our statisti-cal hypotheses and then test them in virtually the same way we did with the one-sample *t*-test.

> REMEMBER   The *related-samples* t-*test* is performed by conducting the one-sample *t*-test on the difference scores.

Statistical Hypotheses for the Related-Samples *t*-Test

Now we can create the statistical hypotheses. Our sample of difference scores repre-sents the population of difference scores that would result if we could measure the pop-ulation of raw scores under each condition and then subtract the scores in one population from the corresponding scores in the other population. The population of difference scores has some μ that we identify as μ_D. To create the statistical hypothe-ses, we determine the predicted values of μ_D in H_0 and H_a.

In the phobia study, we predict that the population of scores after therapy will con-tain lower fear scores than the population of scores before therapy. If we subtract the lower after-scores from the higher before-scores, as we did in our sample, then we should have a population of difference scores containing positive numbers. The result-ing μ_D should also be a positive number. Our alternative hypothesis always implies that the predicted relationship exists, so here

H_a: $\mu_D > 0$

H_a implies that our sample represents a population of differences having a μ_D greater than zero, and thus that after-therapy scores are lower than before-therapy scores in the population.

On the other hand, there are two ways we can fail to demonstrate the predicted relationship. First, the therapy may do nothing to fear scores, so that the population of before-scores contains the same scores as the population of after-scores. If we subtract the after-scores from the before-scores, the population of difference scores will have a μ_D of zero. Note that not every difference need equal zero. Because of random physiological or psychological fluctuations, not all participants will produce the same fear score on two observations, and thus their difference scores may not be zero. On average, however, the positive and negative differences should cancel out to produce a μ_D of zero. Second, the therapy may increase fear scores. If so, then subtracting larger after-scores from smaller before-scores produces a population of difference scores consisting of negative numbers, with a μ_D that is less than zero. Thus, given the way we are subtracting to produce difference scores, our null hypothesis is

$$H_0: \mu_D \leq 0$$

H_0 implies that our sample represents such a population, and thus that the predicted relationship between therapy and fear does not exist.

As usual, we test H_0 by testing whether our sample mean is likely to represent the μ described by H_0, which here is that μ_D is zero. To do so, we examine the sampling distribution of means, which here is the sampling distribution of $\overline{D}$. This is the frequency distribution of the different values of $\overline{D}$ that occur when H_0 is true. Then we locate our $\overline{D}$ on this sampling distribution by computing t_{obt}.

Computing the Related-Samples *t*-Test

Computing t_{obt} here is identical to computing the one-sample *t*-test discussed in Chapter 11—only the symbols have been changed from X to D. To compute the t_{obt} for related samples, perform the following three steps.

First, find s_D^2, which is the estimated variance of the population of difference scores.

THE FORMULA FOR s_D^2 IS

$$s_D^2 = \frac{\Sigma D^2 - \dfrac{(\Sigma D)^2}{N}}{N - 1}$$

Using the data from the phobia study in Table 12.2, we have

$$s_D^2 = \frac{\Sigma D^2 - \dfrac{(\Sigma D)^2}{N}}{N - 1} = \frac{96 - \dfrac{(18)^2}{5}}{4} = 7.80$$

Second, find $s_{\overline{D}}$. This is the **standard error of the mean difference,** or the "standard deviation" of the sampling distribution of $\overline{D}$. (Just as $s_{\overline{X}}$ was the standard deviation of the sampling distribution when we called the mean $\overline{X}$.)

THE FORMULA FOR THE STANDARD ERROR OF THE MEAN DIFFERENCE IS

$$s_{\bar{D}} = \sqrt{(s_D^2)\left(\frac{1}{N}\right)}$$

For the phobia study, $s_D^2 = 7.80$, and $N = 5$, so

$$s_{\bar{D}} = \sqrt{(s_D^2)\left(\frac{1}{N}\right)} = \sqrt{(7.80)\left(\frac{1}{5}\right)} = \sqrt{1.56} = 1.25$$

Third, find t_{obt}.

THE DEFINITIONAL FORMULA FOR THE RELATED-SAMPLES t-TEST IS

$$t_{obt} = \frac{\bar{D} - \mu_D}{s_{\bar{D}}}$$

For the phobia study, $\bar{D}$ is $+3.6$, $s_{\bar{D}}$ is 1.25, and H_0 says that μ_D equals 0. Filling in the formula, we have

$$t_{obt} = \frac{\bar{D} - \mu_D}{s_{\bar{D}}} = \frac{+3.6 - 0}{1.25} = +2.88$$

This tells us that our $\bar{D}$ is located at a t_{obt} of $+2.88$ on the sampling distribution of $\bar{D}$ when H_0 is true.

Computational Formula for the Related-Samples *t*-Test   We can combine the above steps of computing $s_{\bar{D}}$ and t_{obt} into one formula.

THE COMPUTATIONAL FORMULA FOR THE RELATED-SAMPLES t-TEST IS

$$t_{obt} = \frac{\bar{D} - \mu_D}{\sqrt{(s_D^2)\left(\frac{1}{N}\right)}}$$

The numerator is the same as in the definitional formula. The denominator contains the formula for the standard error of the mean difference instead of its symbol.

Interpreting the Related-Samples *t*-Test

We interpret t_{obt} by comparing it to t_{crit}. Find t_{crit} in the *t*-tables (Table 2 in Appendix B) for $df = N - 1$, where N is the number of difference scores. For the phobia study, with $\alpha = .05$ and $df = 4$, the one-tailed value of t_{crit} is $+2.132$. The t_{crit} is positive because we predicted that therapy would *decrease* fear. When we subtract the (hopefully) smaller after-scores from the larger before-scores, we should obtain a positive value of $\overline{D}$, producing a positive t_{obt}. Therefore, as in Figure 12.4, the region of rejection is in the upper tail, and t_{crit} is positive.

This sampling distribution shows the values of $\overline{D}$ that occur when H_0 is true and we *are* sampling from a population of differences having an average difference (μ_D) of 0. For the phobia study it essentially shows all values of $\overline{D}$ we'd get because of chance fluctuations in participants' before- and after-scores when H_0 is true and the therapy really does not work. The values that are farther above or below 0 are less frequent and thus less likely to occur when H_0 is true. Our t_{obt} is in the region of rejection, so our $\overline{D}$ of $+3.6$ is unlikely to be representing the population where $\mu_D \leq 0$. Therefore, the results are significant, and we report them as

$$t_{\text{obt}}(4) = +2.88, \ p < .05$$

By rejecting H_0, we can accept H_a and conclude the sample represents a μ_D of around $+3.6$. Because the difference between the conditions is significantly different from zero, the original means for these conditions also differ significantly from each other: The mean of the before-scores (14.80) differs significantly from the mean of the after-scores (11.20). Thus, we conclude that the sample data represent a relationship in the population. At this point, as usual, you focus on interpreting the relationship, explaining how and why the therapy decreases fear. (If t_{obt} had not been beyond t_{crit}, we would not reject H_0 and we'd have no evidence that the therapy reduces fear.)

Based on the sample means, our best estimate is that, in the population, before therapy the μ would be *around* 14.80 and after therapy the μ would be *around* 11.20. It would be nice to more precisely define "around" by computing a confidence interval for each μ as in the previous chapter. However, we cannot do that, because that procedure assumes that each mean comes from an *independent* sample and these don't. We can, however, compute a *confidence interval for* μ_D.

FIGURE 12.4 One-Tailed Sampling Distribution of $\overline{D}$s When $\mu_D = 0$

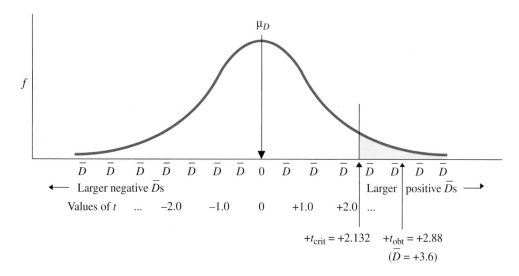

Computing the Confidence Interval for μ_D

Our sample of difference scores has a $\overline{D}$ of $+3.6$, so it probably represents a population of difference scores having a μ_D of *around* $+3.6$. To define "around" here, we compute the confidence interval for μ_D. The **confidence interval for μ_D** describes a range of values of μ_D, one of which our sample mean is likely to represent. The interval is defined by the highest and lowest values of μ_D that are not significantly different from $\overline{D}$.

> *THE COMPUTATIONAL FORMULA FOR THE CONFIDENCE INTERVAL FOR μ_D IS*
>
> $$(s_{\overline{D}})(-t_{\text{crit}}) + \overline{D} \leq \mu_D \leq (s_{\overline{D}})(+t_{\text{crit}}) + \overline{D}$$

This is the same formula used in the one-sample *t*-test, except that the symbol $\overline{X}$ has been replaced by $\overline{D}$. The t_{crit} is the *two-tailed* value for $df = N - 1$, where N is the number of difference scores, $s_{\overline{D}}$ is the standard error of the mean difference computed in the *t*-test, and $\overline{D}$ is the mean of the difference scores.

In the phobia study, $s_{\overline{D}} = 1.25$, and $\overline{D} = +3.6$, and with $\alpha = .05$ and $df = 4$, t_{crit} is ± 2.776. Filling in the formula gives

$$(1.25)(-2.776) + 3.6 \leq \mu_D \leq (1.25)(+2.776) + 3.6$$

which becomes

$$0.13 \leq \mu_D \leq 7.07$$

Thus, we are 95% confident that our sample mean of $+3.6$ represents a population μ_D within this interval. In other words, if we performed this study on the entire population, we would expect the average difference in before- and after-scores to be between 0.13 and 7.07.

Testing Other Hypotheses with the Related-Samples *t*-Test

In the phobia study we could have subtracted the predicted larger before-scores from the predicted smaller after-scores. Then the one-tailed hypotheses would be reversed. If the therapy did not work as predicted, we would expect a $\overline{D}$ of zero or greater, so H_0: $\mu_D \geq 0$. If the therapy worked, we would expect a negative $\overline{D}$, representing a μ_D less than zero, and we'd have H_a: $\mu_D < 0$. To keep things straight, always decide (1) which group should have larger scores, (2) which group you'll subtract from which, and (3) whether the difference should be positive (giving H_a: $\mu_D > 0$) or negative (giving H_a: $\mu_D < 0$).

In a different study that did not predict the direction of the difference between the two conditions, we'd use a two-tailed test. If the populations of raw scores do not differ, then μ_D is zero, so H_0: $\mu_D = 0$. If the populations of raw scores differ, then μ_D is not zero, so H_a: $\mu_D \neq 0$.

Finally, you can also test an H_0 that the populations differ by some amount other than zero. For example, previously we discussed the study of Navy and Marine pilots who differed by 10 points in flying ability. Suppose we perform a related-samples study by matching each Navy pilot with a Marine pilot who has had the same amount of flying experience. The null hypothesis is that the two samples still represent populations that differ by 10. When we subtract the two populations, the population of differences has a μ_D equal to 10, so H_0 is $\mu_D = 10$. The alternative hypothesis is that there is a new difference between the two raw score populations so that the difference is not 10, so H_a: $\mu_D \neq 10$.

In any of the above situations, select t_{crit} and calculate t_{obt} using the same procedure as in the phobia study.

Power and the Related-Samples *t*-Test

Power applies to all statistical tests, and essentially, you maximize power in the same ways every time. As with the independent-samples *t*-test, you maximize the power of a related-samples *t*-test by (1) maximizing the differences in scores *between* the conditions (producing a larger $\overline{D}$); (2) minimizing the variability of the scores *within* each condition (producing a smaller s_D and $s_{\overline{D}}$), and (3) maximizing the size of N (the number of difference scores). Each of these strategies produces a larger t_{obt} relative to t_{crit}, so you're more likely to have significant results when H_0 is false.

Recognize that a related-samples design is intrinsically more powerful than an independent-samples design, because related samples result in less variability among the scores. For example, say that we (incorrectly) reanalyzed the phobia study, pretending we had independent samples. The variability of the raw fear scores would be larger than the variability of the difference scores because we eliminate some of the variability in the raw scores by transforming them to Ds. For example, Table 12.3 presents the scores of Participants 2 and 3. Although there is variability in their before-scores and in their after-scores, there is no variability in their difference scores. Reducing variability in scores produces a larger t_{obt}, so the t_{obt} for related samples will be larger than the t_{obt} for independent samples. Thus, by choosing a related samples design when it's appropriate, you increase power.

DESCRIBING THE RELATIONSHIP IN A TWO-SAMPLE EXPERIMENT

By now you understand how to determine whether results are significant. However, in either *t*-test, the fact that t_{obt} is significant is not the end of the story. If you stop after hypothesis testing, then you've found a relationship, but you have not described it. It's like saying, "I've computed a correlation coefficient, but I'm not telling what it is."

TABLE 12.3   Scores of Participants 2 and 3 from Phobia Study

Participant	Before Therapy	−	After Therapy	=	Difference D
2	16		11		+5
3	20		15		+5

Therefore, you're not finished until you've fully described the relationship. Your focus should always be on the means from each condition so that you understand the behavior by summarizing the typical score—and typical behavior—found in each condition. Also, pay attention to the *direction* of the difference between the means because this tells you the direction that scores—and the behaviors—change as you change the independent variable. And, confidence intervals allow you to generalize your findings, describing the range of typical scores—and typical behaviors—you expect in the population (in nature).

In addition, as in the following sections, you should also *graph* the relationship and compute the *effect size.*

Graphing the Results of a Two-Sample Experiment

As you know, we graph experimental results by plotting the mean of each condition on the *Y* axis and the conditions of the independent variable on the *X* axis. Thus, we would plot the results of the hypnosis study and the results of the phobia study as shown in Figure 12.5. (Note that for the phobia study, the mean of the original fear scores from the before and after conditions are plotted, and not the *D*s.) In research publications such a simple graph would not be included—the reader is expected to visualize it from a report of the means. However, when you conduct research, always create a graph for yourself because it helps you to understand your results.

Interpret the graph and the relationship by, in essence, applying *correlational* statistics. We performed the *t*-test because it's the most powerful way to test H_0 in a two-sample experiment. However, recall that the advantage of correlational procedures is that they summarize the type and strength of a relationship. Thus, look at these graphs as showing the relationship between participants' *Y* scores (their dependent scores) and their *X* score (their condition on the independent variable).

First, the hypnosis line graph shows a positive relationship, and the phobia graph shows a negative relationship, so we know the *types* of relationships present. Now envision the scatterplot that the data would form. In the hypnosis graph, for example, the individual data points would be above and below the mean of 20 in the no-hypnosis

FIGURE 12.5 Line graphs of the results of the hypnosis study and the phobia study

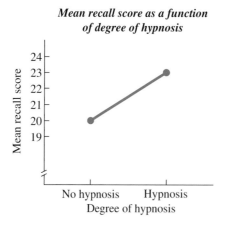

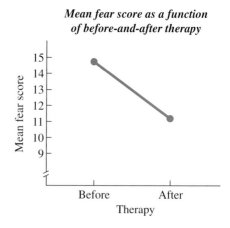

condition and "around" the mean of 23 in the hypnosis condition. Also, recall that the *regression line* is the line that summarizes a scatterplot by running through its center. With only two conditions, the line graph connecting the means of the two conditions *is* the regression line we'd find. Then using it, we predict the mean scores of 20 or 23, respectively, for any other people we might test under these hypnosis conditions.

> *REMEMBER* Whenever the results of an experiment are significant, think in terms of correlational procedures to describe and interpret the relationship.

What's missing, of course, is the *strength* of the relationship. Therefore, the next step is to think in terms of a correlation coefficient.

Describing the Strength of the Relationship in a Two-Sample Experiment Using r_{pb}

The *point-biserial correlation coefficient* (r_{pb}) is the appropriate coefficient for describing a parametric two-sample experiment. This is because r_{pb} is used with one dichotomous X variable (that is, consisting of two categories) and one continuous interval or ratio Y variable. In a two-sample experiment, the conditions of the independent variable are a dichotomous X variable and scores on the dependent variable are a continuous interval or ratio Y variable.

You could compute r_{pb} using the formula in Chapter 7, but instead you can compute it using t_{obt}.

THE FORMULA FOR COMPUTING r_{pb} FROM t_{obt} IS

$$r_{pb} = \sqrt{\frac{(t_{obt})^2}{(t_{obt})^2 + df}}$$

This formula can be used for either independent or related samples. *But:*

For independent samples, $df = (n_1 - 1) + (n_2 - 1)$, where n is the number of scores in a sample.

For related samples, $df = N - 1$, where N is the number of difference scores.

In the hypnosis study, $t_{obt} = +2.94$ with $df = 30$, so

$$r_{pb} = \sqrt{\frac{(2.94)^2}{(2.94)^2 + 30}} = \sqrt{\frac{8.64}{8.64 + 30}} = \sqrt{\frac{8.64}{38.64}} = \sqrt{.224} = .47$$

Thus, the relationship between recall scores and degree of hypnosis can be summarized as $r_{pb} = +.47$. For the phobia study $t_{obt} = +2.88$ and $df = 4$, so the relationship between fear scores and before or after therapy can be summarized as $r_{pb} = -.82$. Notice that the final step in the formula is to find the square root, so the answer will always be positive. Depending on the data, *you* decide whether r_{pb} is positive or negative. Back in Figure 12.5 the hypnosis study produced a positive relationship, so its r_{pb} is positive, but the phobia study produced a negative relationship, so its r_{pb} is negative.

In each study, the coefficient describes how consistently participants scored at or close to the mean score in their condition, and thus whether you should envision a "skinny" or "fat" scatterplot. Thus, although both describe significant relationships, the larger r_{pb} for the phobia study indicates that there we demonstrated a stronger, more consistent relationship than in the hypnosis study.

Recall, however, that a problem with a correlation coefficient is that it can be difficult to interpret, because we can only subjectively evaluate it relative to 0 and ±1. Instead, the most direct way to evaluate a relationship is to square the correlation coefficient, computing *the proportion of variance accounted for.* In experiments, when we do that we compute "effect size."

Describing Effect Size in a Two-Sample Experiment

To compute the proportion of variance accounted for in a two-sample experiment, square r_{pb} (simply don't find the square root in the formula). The answer is interpreted in the same way that it was interpreted back in Chapter 8. Essentially, r_{pb}^2 indicates how much more accurately we can predict dependent (Y) scores when we know the condition under which participants were tested, compared to when we are unaware of the relationship and instead predict the overall mean of all Y scores for everyone in the study. For the hypnosis study, squaring r_{pb} gives $(.47)^2$, or .22. Thus, on average we are 22% closer to predicting participants' actual recall scores when we predict the mean score of each hypnosis condition for them, compared to when we predict the overall mean of the experiment. Likewise, in the phobia study, $r_{pb}^2 = (.82)^2$, or .67, so we can account for 67% of the variance in fear scores by knowing whether or not participants have undergone the therapy.

> REMEMBER In a two-sample experiment, r_{pb}^2 equals the proportion of the variance accounted for.

In an experiment, the proportion of variance accounted for goes by a different name: It is called the "effect size." This is because when an experiment demonstrates a significant relationship, our explanation is that the independent variable has an *effect* on the dependent variable, "causing" scores on the dependent variable to change. (The word "cause" is in quotes, because, remember, we never *prove* that changing the independent variable causes the scores to change. Thus, we "explain" the variability in our recall data, for example, as being caused by changing the conditions of hypnosis, and how consistently hypnosis does this is its effect size. The **effect size** indicates how consistently differences in dependent scores are "caused" by changing the independent variable. The larger the effect size, the more consistently the scores in each condition are located at or close to the mean for that condition, so the more consistent is the influence of the independent variable.

The greater the effect size, the more that knowing the condition of the independent variable improves our accuracy in describing and predicting participants' dependent scores, and so the greater the scientific importance of the relationship. For example, we found that only 22% of the differences in recall scores were accounted for by hypnosis. We assume that everything has a cause, so there must be *other* variables that are causing the unaccounted-for differences in recall scores (perhaps IQ, memory ability, or motivation play a role). Regardless, the amount of hypnosis is only somewhat important in determining someone's recall score in this study. A larger effect size, however, would indicate that the scores are *more* similar within each condition. Then the independent variable *alone* would play a greater role in determining each person's score, and so the variable would be more important.

> *REMEMBER*   *Effect size* indicates how big of a role changing the conditions of the independent variable plays in determining differences in dependent scores.

Effect size is important because it's the way to determine whether a relationship is important or much ado about nothing. In fact, the American Psychological Association now requests that all published research include a measure of effect size.[1] Because effect size has not always been reported, great elaborate experiments have often been performed to study what are actually very minor variables. Therefore, compute effect size whenever you have significant results, so you'll know whether your variable is worth studying.

However, although a large effect size indicates an important relationship in a statistical sense, it does not indicate importance in a practical sense: Statistics will never tell you if you have performed a silly study. In the real world, our conclusion that memory was improved by hypnosis has little practical importance: To improve my memory, I should walk around under hypnosis all day? Statistical importance addresses a different issue: If you want to understand how nature works when it comes to hypnosis and memory, *then* this relationship is relevant and important. It is relevant because the results were significant, so we are confident that it is a relationship found in nature. It is important to the extent that hypnosis has an influence on memory that accounts for 22% of the differences in recall scores.

PUTTING IT ALL TOGETHER

Remember that one of your goals in this course has been to learn when to use different statistical procedures. The obvious answer here is that you've learned two procedures that are used in a two-sample experiment. Perform the independent-samples t-test if you've created independent samples and the related- (dependent-) samples t-test if you've created related (dependent) samples. You can simplify their calculations if you look at them as in Table 12.4.

In both procedures first estimate the variability of the underlying raw score populations. Then compute the standard error of the sampling distribution found when H_0 is true. Then locate the experiment's results on that sampling distribution by computing t_{obt}. If t_{obt} is significant, you can believe you have found a relationship and are not being misled by sampling error. Then compute the appropriate confidence interval, graph the results, and compute r_{pb}^2. Then interpret the relationship in terms of the underlying behaviors that it reflects. If t_{obt} is not significant, consider whether you have sufficient power.

---

[1]See the fifth edition of the *Publication Manual of the American Psychological Association,* 2001, published by the American Psychological Association, Washington, D.C.

TABLE 12.4 Comparison of the Steps in Computing the Independent- and Related-Samples *t*-Test

Steps	Independent Samples	Related Samples
1. Variability of raw scores	s^2_{pool}	s^2_D
2. Standard error	$s_{\bar{X}_1 - \bar{X}_2} = \sqrt{s^2_{pool}\left(\dfrac{1}{n_1} + \dfrac{1}{n_2}\right)}$	$s_{\bar{D}} = \sqrt{s^2_D\left(\dfrac{1}{N}\right)}$
3. t_{obt}	$t_{obt} = \dfrac{(\bar{X}_1 - \bar{X}_2) - (\mu_1 - \mu_2)}{s_{\bar{X}_1 - \bar{X}_2}}$	$t_{obt} = \dfrac{\bar{D} - \mu_D}{s_{\bar{D}}}$

CHAPTER SUMMARY

1. Two samples are *independent* when participants are randomly selected for a sample without regard to who else has been selected for either sample, and each participant is in only one condition.

2. The *independent-samples* t-*test* assumes that (a) two independent samples of scores measure an interval or ratio variable, (b) the populations represented by each sample form a normal distribution, and (c) the populations have homogeneous variance.

3. *Homogeneity of variance* means that the value of σ^2_X in the populations being represented are equal.

4. A significant t_{obt} from the independent-samples *t*-test indicates that the difference between $\bar{X}_1$ and $\bar{X}_2$ is unlikely to represent the difference between μ_1 and μ_2 described by H_0. Therefore, the results are assumed to represent the predicted relationship in the population.

5. The *confidence interval for* $\mu_1 - \mu_2$ contains a range of differences between two μs, one of which is likely to be represented by the difference between our two sample means.

6. Two samples are *related* when each score in one sample is paired with a particular score in the other sample. Scores are paired either by *matching* each participant in one condition with someone in the other condition or by *repeated measures* of the same participants under both conditions.

7. The *related-samples* t-*test* is a one-sample *t*-test performed on the difference scores. A significant t_{obt} indicates that the mean of the difference scores ($\bar{D}$) is significantly different from the μ_D described by H_0. Then the means of the raw scores in each condition also differ significantly.

8. The *confidence interval for* μ_D contains a range of values of μ_D, any one of which is likely to be represented by the sample's $\bar{D}$.

9. The power of either two-sample *t*-test increases with (a) larger differences in scores *between* the conditions, (b) smaller variability of scores *within* each condition, and (c) larger ns. The related-samples t-test is more powerful than the independent-samples t-test.

10. The strength of a significant relationship between the independent and dependent variables in a two-sample experiment is described by computing the *point-biserial correlation coefficient*, (r_{pb}).

11. The *squared point-biserial coefficient* (r_{pb}^2) measures the proportion of variance in the dependent scores that is accounted for by changing the conditions of the independent variable. The proportion of variance accounted for in an experiment is called the *effect size*. The larger the effect size, the closer the scores in a condition are to each other and to the mean of the condition, so (1) the greater the role of the independent variable in determining scores, and (2) the greater our accuracy in predicting scores (and understanding the behavior) when using the relationship.

KEY TERMS: Can You Define the Following?

n N s_{pool}^2 $s_{\bar{X}_1 - \bar{X}_2}$ $\bar{D}$ s_D^2 $s_{\bar{D}}$ r_{pb}^2

confidence interval for $\mu_1 - \mu_2$ *311*
confidence interval for μ_D *320*
effect size *324*
homogeneity of variance *304*
independent samples *303*
independent-samples *t*-test *303*
matched-samples design *313*
pooled variance *306*

related samples *313*
related-samples *t*-test *313*
repeated-measures design *314*
sampling distribution of differences
  between the means *305*
standard error of the difference *307*
standard error of the mean difference
  317

REVIEW QUESTIONS

(Answers for odd-numbered questions are in Appendix C.)

1. A scientist has conducted a two-sample experiment. (a) What two parametric procedures are available to him? (b) What is the deciding factor for selecting between them?

2. (a) How do you create independent samples? (b) What are the two ways to create related samples? (c) What other assumptions must be met before using the two-sample *t*-test?

3. All other things being equal, should you create a related-samples or an independent-samples design? Why?

4. What is homogeneity of variance?

5. (a) What is $s_{\bar{X}_1 - \bar{X}_2}$? (b) What is $s_{\bar{D}}$? (c) What's the difference between n and N?

6. (a) What does effect size indicate? (b) How is it computed in a two-sample experiment?

7. What does the confidence interval for μ_D indicate?

8. What does a confidence interval for the difference between two μs indicate?

9. In this chapter you learned five different statistical procedures. What are they?

10. (a) What is the final step when completing an experiment? (b) Why is r_{pb}^2 useful at this stage?

11. Foofy obtained a statistically significant two-sample t_{obt}. What three things should she do to complete her analysis?

APPLICATION QUESTIONS

12. For each of the following, which type of *t*-test is required? (a) An investigation of the effects of a new memory-enhancing drug on the memory of Alzheimer's patients, testing a group of patients before and after administration of the drug. (b) An investigation of the effects of alcohol on motor coordination, comparing one group of participants given a moderate dose of alcohol to the population μ for people given no alcohol. (c) An investigation of whether males and females rate the persuasiveness of an argument delivered by a female speaker differently. (d) The study described in part c, but with the added requirement that for each male of a particular age, there is a female of the same age.

13. In an experiment a researcher seeks to demonstrate a relationship between hot or cold baths and the amount of relaxation they produce. He obtains the following relaxation scores from two independent samples.

Sample 1 (hot): $\overline{X} = 43$, $s_X^2 = 22.79$, $n = 15$
Sample 2 (cold): $\overline{X} = 39$, $s_X^2 = 24.6$, $n = 15$

(a) What are H_0 and H_a? (b) Compute t_{obt}. (c) With $\alpha = .05$, what is t_{crit}? (d) What should the researcher conclude about this relationship? (e) Compute the confidence interval for the difference between the μs. (f) How big of an effect does bath temperature have on relaxation? (g) Describe how you would graph these results.

14. A researcher investigates whether a period of time feels longer or shorter when people are bored compared to when they are not bored. Using independent samples, the researcher obtains the following estimates of the time period (in minutes):

Sample 1 (bored): $\overline{X} = 14.5$, $s_X^2 = 10.22$, $n = 28$
Sample 2 (not bored): $\overline{X} = 9.0$, $s_X^2 = 14.6$, $n = 34$

(a) What are H_0 and H_a? (b) Compute t_{obt}. (c) With $\alpha = .05$, what is t_{crit}? (d) What should the researcher conclude about this relationship? (e) Compute the confidence interval for the difference between the μs. (f) How important is boredom in determining how quickly time seems to pass?

15. Foofy predicts that students who use a computer program that corrects spelling errors will receive higher grades on a term paper. She uses an independent-samples design in which Group A uses a spelling checker and Group B does not. She tests H_0: $\mu_A - \mu_B \leq 0$ and H_a: $\mu_A - \mu_B > 0$. She obtains a negative value of t_{obt}. (a) What should she conclude about this study? (b) Say that her sample means actually support her predictions. What miscalculation is she likely to have made?

16. To increase the power of the hypnosis study discussed in this chapter, how could you design the study to (a) Maximize the difference in the recall scores between the conditions? (b) Minimize the variability in the scores? (c) What else should you do?

17. A researcher asks whether people will score higher or lower on a questionnaire measuring their well-being when they are exposed to lots of sunshine compared to when they're not exposed to much sunshine. A sample of 8 people is first measured after low levels of sunshine exposure and then again after high levels of exposure. The researcher collects the following well-being scores:

Low:	14	13	17	15	18	17	14	16
High:	18	12	20	19	22	19	19	16

(a) Subtracting low from high, what are H_0 and H_a? (b) Compute the appropriate t-test. (c) With $\alpha = .05$, report your results in the correct format. (d) Compute the appropriate confidence interval. (e) What is the predicted well-being score for someone tested under low sunshine? Under high sunshine? (f) On average, how much more accurate are these predictions than if you did not know how much sunshine people experience? (g) What should the researcher conclude about these results?

18. A researcher investigates whether classical background music is more or less soothing to air-traffic controllers than more modern background music. He plays a classical selection to one group and a modern selection to another. At the end of the day, he gives each person an irritability questionnaire and obtains the following data:

Sample A (classical): $n = 6, \overline{X} = 14.69, s_X^2 = 8.4$
Sample B (modern): $n = 6, \overline{X} = 17.21, s_X^2 = 11.6$

After computing the independent samples t-test, he finds $t_{obt} = +1.38$. (a) With $\alpha = .05$, report the statistical results. (b) What should the researcher conclude about these results? (c) What other statistics should be computed? (d) What statistical flaw is likely in the experiment? (e) What could the researcher do to improve the experiment? (f) What effect might this have?

19. A researcher investigates whether children exhibit a higher number of aggressive acts after watching a violent television show. The number of aggressive acts for the same 10 participants before and after watching the show are as follows:

Sample 1 (After)	*Sample 2 (Before)*
5	4
6	6
4	3
4	2
7	4
3	1
2	0
1	0
4	5
3	2

(a) Subtracting before-scores from after-scores, what are H_0 and H_a? (b) Compute t_{obt}. (c) With $\alpha = .05$, what is t_{crit}? (d) What should the researcher conclude about this relationship? (e) Compute the appropriate confidence interval. (f) If you want to understand children's aggression, how important is it to consider whether they watch violent television shows?

20. You investigate whether the older or younger male in pairs of brothers tends to be more extroverted. You obtain the following extroversion scores:

Sample 1 (Younger)	Sample 2 (Older)
10	18
11	17
18	19
12	16
15	15
13	19
19	13
15	20

(a) What are H_0 and H_a? (b) Compute t_{obt}. (c) With $\alpha = .05$, what is t_{crit}? (d) What should you conclude about this relationship? (e) Is this a scientifically informative relationship?

21. A rather dim student proposes testing the conditions of "male" and "female" using a repeated-measures design. What's wrong with this idea?

22. What three aspects of the phobia study discussed in this chapter would you address to increase its power?

23. An experimenter investigated the effects of sensitivity training on a policeman's effectiveness at resolving domestic disputes (comparing independent samples of policemen who had or had not completed the training). The dependent variable was participants' ability to successfully resolve a simulated domestic dispute. The following success scores were obtained:

No Course	Course
11	13
14	16
10	14
12	17
8	11
15	14
12	15
13	18
9	12
11	11

(a) Should a one-tailed or a two-tailed test be used? (b) What are H_0 and H_a? (c) Subtracting the $\overline{X}$ for course from the $\overline{X}$ for no course, compute t_{obt} and determine whether it is significant. (d) Compute the confidence interval for the difference between the μs. (e) What conclusions can the experimenter draw from these results? (f) Compute the effect size and interpret it.

24. When reading a research article, you encounter the following statements. For each, identify the *N*, the design, the statistical procedure performed and the result, the relationship, and if a Type I or Type II error is possibly being made. (a) "The *t*-test indicated a significant difference between the mean for men (5.4) and for women (9.3), with $t(58) = 7.93$, $p < .01$. Unfortunately, the effect size here was only .08." (b) "The *t*-test indicated that participants' weights after three weeks of dieting were significantly reduced relative to the pretest measure, with $t(40) = 3.56$, $p < .05$, and $r_{pb}^2 = .16$."

25. If the results of question 23 are not significant, what four things can the researcher consider to increase power?

SUMMARY OF FORMULAS

1. *The computational formula for the independent-samples* t-*test is*

$$t_{obt} = \frac{(\overline{X}_1 - \overline{X}_2) - (\mu_1 - \mu_2)}{\sqrt{\left[\dfrac{(n_1 - 1)s_1^2 + (n_2 - 1)s_2^2}{(n_1 - 1) + (n_2 - 1)}\right]\left[\dfrac{1}{n_1} + \dfrac{1}{n_2}\right]}}$$

Values of t_{crit} are found in Table 2 in Appendix B for $df = (n_1 - 1) + (n_2 - 1)$. $(\overline{X}_1 - \overline{X}_2)$ is the difference between the sample means, $(\mu_1 - \mu_2)$ is the difference described in H_0, s_1^2 and n_1 are from one sample, and s_2^2 and n_2 are from the other sample. Values of s_1^2 and s_2^2 are found using the formula

$$s_X^2 = \frac{\Sigma X^2 - \dfrac{(\Sigma X)^2}{n}}{n - 1}$$

2. *The formula for the confidence interval for the difference between two* μs *is*

$$(s_{\overline{X}_1 - \overline{X}_2})(-t_{crit}) + (\overline{X}_1 - \overline{X}_2) \le \mu_1 - \mu_2 \le (s_{\overline{X}_1 - \overline{X}_2})(+t_{crit}) + (\overline{X}_1 - \overline{X}_2)$$

where t_{crit} is the two-tailed value for $df = (n_1 + n_2) - 2$, $(\overline{X}_1 - \overline{X}_2)$ is the difference between the sample means, and $s_{\overline{X}_1 - \overline{X}_2}$ is the standard error of the difference found using the formula

$$s_{\overline{X}_1 - \overline{X}_2} = \sqrt{\left[\frac{(n_1 - 1)s_1^2 + (n_2 - 1)s_2^2}{(n_1 - 1) + (n_2 - 1)}\right]\left[\frac{1}{n_1} + \frac{1}{n_2}\right]}$$

3. *The computational formula for the related-samples* t-*test is*

$$t_{\text{obt}} = \frac{\bar{D} - \mu_D}{\sqrt{(s_D^2)\left(\dfrac{1}{N}\right)}}$$

Values of t_{crit} are found in Table 2 in Appendix B for $df = N - 1$, where N is the number of difference scores. $\bar{D}$ is the mean of the difference scores, μ_D is the value described by H_0, and s_D^2 is the variance of the difference scores, found using the formula

$$s_D^2 = \frac{\Sigma D^2 - \dfrac{(\Sigma D)^2}{N}}{N - 1}$$

where D is each difference score and N is the number of difference scores.

4. *The formula for the confidence interval for* μ_{D} *is*

$$(s_{\bar{D}})(-t_{\text{crit}}) + \bar{D} \le \mu_D \le (s_{\bar{D}})(+t_{\text{crit}}) + \bar{D}$$

t_{crit} is the two-tailed value for $df = N - 1$, where N is the number of difference scores, and $s_{\bar{D}}$ is the standard error of the mean difference, found using the formula

$$s_{\bar{D}} = \sqrt{(s_D^2)\left(\frac{1}{N}\right)}$$

where s_D^2 is the variance of the difference scores and N is the number of difference scores.

5. *The formula for computing* r_{pb} *from* t_{obt} *is*

$$r_{\text{pb}} = \sqrt{\frac{(t_{\text{obt}})^2}{(t_{\text{obt}})^2 + df}}$$

With independent samples, $df = (n_1 - 1) + (n_2 - 1)$, where each n is the number of scores in a sample.

With related samples, $df = N - 1$, where N is the number of difference scores.

6. *The proportion of variance accounted for* in a two-sample experiment equals the squared value of r_{pb} or r_{pb}^2.

Hypothesis Testing for Two or More Means: The One-Way Analysis of Variance

---

GETTING STARTED

To understand this chapter, recall the following:

- From Chapter 5 recall that variance measures the differences between scores by measuring their distance from the mean.
- From Chapter 10 recall why we limit the probability of a Type I error to .05.
- From Chapter 12 recall that we "pool" the sample variances to estimate the variance in the population.
- And also from Chapter 12 recall what effect size is and why it is important.

Your goals in this chapter are to learn:

- The terminology of analysis of variance.
- Why we compute F_{obt} and then post hoc tests.
- Why F_{obt} should equal 1 if H_0 is true, and why F_{obt} is greater than 1 if H_0 is false.
- When to compute *Fisher's protected* t-*test* or *Tukey's HSD*.
- How *eta squared* describes effect size.

You may have noticed that each new procedure we discuss involves a more complex experiment than the previous one. In Chapter 12 you saw how to analyze an experiment involving two conditions of an independent variable. Now we'll discuss experiments involving more than two conditions. The parametric procedure used in such experiments is called *analysis of variance.*

MORE STATISTICAL NOTATION

The analysis of variance has its own language that is also commonly used in research publications:

1. Analysis of variance is abbreviated as **ANOVA.**
2. An independent variable is called a **factor.**
3. Each condition of the independent variable is also called a **level** or a **treatment,** and differences produced by the independent variable are a **treatment effect.**
4. The symbol for the number of levels in a factor is **k.**

WHY IS IT IMPORTANT TO KNOW ABOUT ANOVA?

It is important to know about analysis of variance because it is *the* most common inferential statistical procedure used to analyze experiments. Why? Because there are actually many versions of ANOVA, so it can be used with many different experimental designs: It can be applied to an experiment involving independent samples or related samples, to an independent variable involving any number of conditions, and to a study involving any number of independent variables. Such complex designs are common because, first, the hypotheses of the study may require comparing more than two conditions of an independent variable. Second, researchers often add more conditions because after all the time and effort involved in creating two conditions, little more is needed to test additional conditions, and thus to learn even more about a behavior (which *is* the purpose of research). Therefore, you'll often encounter the ANOVA when conducting your own research or when reading that of others.

AN OVERVIEW OF ANOVA

Because there are a number of versions of ANOVA to use, depending on the design of a study, we have important terms for distinguishing among them. First, a **one-way ANOVA** is performed when only one independent variable is tested in the experiment (a "two-way" ANOVA is used with two independent variables, and so on). Further, when an independent variable is studied using independent samples in all conditions, it is called a **between-subjects factor** and involves using the formulas from a **between-subjects ANOVA.** When a factor is studied using related (dependent) samples in all levels, it is called a **within-subjects factor** and involves a different set of formulas called a **within-subjects ANOVA.** We'll begin by discussing the one-way, between-subjects ANOVA.

As an example, let's examine how well people perform a task, depending on how difficult they believe the task will be (the "perceived difficulty" of the task). We'll randomly select three samples containing the unpowerful n of 5 participants each and provide them with the same easy 10 math problems. However, to influence their perceptions, we will tell participants in Level 1 that the problems are easy, in Level 2 that the problems are of medium difficulty, and in Level 3 that the problems are difficult. Thus, we have three levels of the factor of perceived difficulty. Our dependent variable is the number of problems that participants then correctly solve within an allotted time. If participants are tested under only one condition, and we do not match them, then this is a one-way, between-subjects design.

A good way to diagram a one-way ANOVA is shown in Design Diagram 13.1. Each column is a level of the factor, containing the scores of participants tested under that condition (here symbolized by X). The symbol n stands for the number of scores in a condition, so here $n = 5$ per level. The mean of each level is the mean of the scores from that condition (that column). We again identify the n and $\overline{X}$ for each level using a subscript, and because there are three levels in this factor, $k = 3$. (Notice that the general format is to label the factor as factor A, with levels A_1, A_2, A_3, and so on.) The total number of scores in the experiment is N, and here $N = 15$. Further, the overall mean of all scores in the experiment is the mean of all 15 scores.

As with all experiments, the purpose here is to demonstrate a relationship between the independent variable and the dependent variable. The only novelty is that now we have three samples of scores. Ideally, we'll find a different mean for each condition, suggesting that if we tested the entire population under each level of difficulty, we would find three different populations of scores located at three different μs. But there's the usual problem: Differences between the means may reflect sampling error, so that actually we would find the same population of scores, having the same μ, for all levels of difficulty. Therefore, as usual, before we can conclude that a relationship

DESIGN DIAGRAM 13.1 Diagram of a Study Having Three Levels of One Factor

Each column represents a condition of the independent variable.

Factor A: Independent Variable of Perceived Difficulty

Level A_1: Easy	Level A_2: Medium	Level A_3: Difficult	← Conditions $k = 3$
X	X	X	
X	X	X	
X	X	X	
X	X	X	
X	X	X	
$\overline{X}_1$	$\overline{X}_2$	$\overline{X}_3$	Overall $\overline{X}$
$n_1 = 5$	$n_2 = 5$	$n_3 = 5$	$N = 15$

exists, we must eliminate the idea that the differences between our sample means reflect sampling error in representing that no relationship exists. The **analysis of variance** is the parametric procedure for determining whether significant differences occur in an experiment containing two or more sample means. Thus, when you have only two conditions of the independent variable, you can use either a two-sample t-test or the ANOVA: You'll reach exactly the same conclusions with either procedure, and both have the same probability of making Type I and Type II errors. However, you *must* use ANOVA when you have more than two conditions of an independent variable (or more than one independent variable).

How ANOVA Controls the Experiment-Wise Error Rate

You might think that we could use the independent-samples t-test to determine whether there are significant differences among the three means above. That is, we might perform "multiple t-tests," testing whether $\overline{X}_1$ differs from $\overline{X}_2$, then whether $\overline{X}_2$ differs from $\overline{X}_3$, and finally whether $\overline{X}_1$ differs from $\overline{X}_3$. However, we cannot use this approach because of the resulting probability of making a Type I error (rejecting a true H_0). We distinguish between making a Type I error *when comparing a pair of means,* and making a Type I error *somewhere* in the experiment. With $\alpha = .05$, the probability of a Type I error in a *single* t-test is .05. But here, we can make a Type I error when comparing $\overline{X}_1$ to $\overline{X}_2$, $\overline{X}_2$ to $\overline{X}_3$, or $\overline{X}_1$ to $\overline{X}_3$. The *overall* probability of making a Type I error *somewhere* in the experiment is called the **experiment-wise error rate.**

We can use the t-test when comparing only two means in an experiment because with only one comparison, the experiment-wise error rate equals α. But with more than two means in the experiment, multiple t-tests result in an experiment-wise error rate that is much larger than the α we have selected. Because of the importance of avoiding Type I errors, we do not want the error rate to be larger than we think it is, and it should never be larger than .05. Therefore, we perform ANOVA. With it, we can compare the means from all levels of the factor simultaneously, and the experiment-wise error rate will equal the alpha we've chosen.

> REMEMBER   The reason for performing ANOVA is that it keeps the *experiment-wise error rate* equal to α.

As with any other statistical test, you proceed here by checking the assumptions, setting up the test, and then performing it.

Assumptions of the One-Way, Between-Subjects ANOVA

In a one-way, between-subjects ANOVA, the experiment has only one independent variable, and all of the conditions contain independent samples. We assume that

1. Each condition contains a random sample of interval or ratio scores.
2. The population represented in each condition forms a normal distribution.
3. The variances of all populations represented are homogeneous.

Although the number of participants in each condition (n) need not be equal, violations of the assumptions are less serious when all ns are equal. Also, certain procedures are *much* easier to perform with equal ns.

If the study meets the assumptions of ANOVA, we set alpha (usually at .05) and create the statistical hypotheses.

Statistical Hypotheses in ANOVA

ANOVA tests only two-tailed hypotheses. The null hypothesis is that there are no differences between the populations represented by the conditions. Thus, for our perceived difficulty study with the three levels of easy, medium, and difficult, we have

$$H_0: \mu_1 = \mu_2 = \mu_3$$

In general, when we perform ANOVA on a factor with k levels, the null hypothesis is

$$H_0: \mu_1 = \mu_2 = \cdots = \mu_k$$

The "$\ldots = \mu_k$" indicates that there are as many μs as there are levels.

You might think that the alternative hypothesis would be $\mu_1 \neq \mu_2 \neq \mu_3$. However, a study may demonstrate differences between *some* but not *all* conditions. Perhaps our data represent a difference between μ_1 and μ_2, but not between μ_1 and μ_3, or perhaps only μ_2 and μ_3 differ. To communicate this idea, the alternative hypothesis is

$$H_a: \text{not all } \mu \text{s are equal}$$

H_a implies that there is a relationship in the population involving at least two of the conditions: The population mean represented by one of the level means is different from the population mean represented by at least one other mean.

As usual, we test H_0, so ANOVA always tests whether all sample means represent the same population mean.

The Order of Operations in ANOVA: The *F* Statistic and Post Hoc Comparisons

The statistic that forms the basis for ANOVA is *F*. Thus, we first compute *F* to determine whether any of the means represent different μs. The *F* we calculate is F_{obt}, which we compare to the critical value, F_{crit}.

When F_{obt} is not significant, it indicates that there are no significant differences between the means of any of the levels and that all means are likely to represent the same μ. When this occurs, the experiment has failed to demonstrate a relationship, we are finished with the statistical analyses, and it's back to the drawing board.

When F_{obt} is significant, it indicates only that *somewhere* among the means *at least two* of them differ significantly. The problem is that F_{obt} does not indicate *which* specific means differ significantly, and perhaps more than two means are different, or maybe all of them are. Thus, if F_{obt} for the perceived difficulty study is significant, then there are one or more significant differences somewhere among the means of the easy, medium, and difficult levels, but we won't know where they are.

To understand the relationship between our variables, we must determine which specific levels differ significantly. Therefore, we perform a second statistical procedure, called *post hoc comparisons*. **Post hoc comparisons** are like *t*-tests, in which we compare all possible *pairs* of level means from a factor, one pair at a time, to determine which means differ significantly. Thus, for the difficulty study we'll compare the means from easy and medium, from easy and difficult, and from medium and difficult. Only then will we know which means differ significantly from each other.

Note that you perform post hoc comparisons *only* when F_{obt} is significant. Finding a significant F_{obt} and then performing post hoc comparisons ensures that the total experiment-wise probability of a Type I error among all comparisons will actually equal whatever alpha you have selected.

> **REMEMBER** If F_{obt} is significant, then perform *post hoc comparisons* to determine which specific means differ significantly.

There is one exception to this rule. When there are only two levels in the factor, the significant difference indicated by F_{obt} must be between the only two means in the study, so it is unnecessary to perform post hoc comparisons.

The first step is to compute F_{obt}. Therefore, the following sections present the statistical basis for ANOVA and the logic of its computation.

COMPONENTS OF THE ANOVA

Analysis of variance does just that: It analyzes variance. Recall that computing variance is simply a way to measure the *differences* between scores. (As you read the following, keep saying to yourself: "Variance is differences.") ANOVA involves partitioning the variance. That is, we take the total variability of the scores in an experiment and break it up, or partition it, in terms of its sources. There are two potential sources of variance. First, scores may differ from each other even when participants are in the same condition. We call this variability the **variance within groups.** Second, scores may differ from each other because they are from different conditions. We call this variability the **variance between groups.** Thus, in a one-way ANOVA, we partition the variance as shown in this diagram:

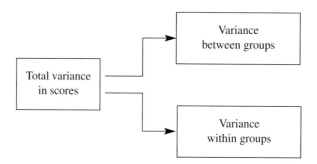

Using the sample data, we compute estimates of the value that each of these variances would have in the population. But we do not *call* each an estimated variance. Instead, we call each a *mean square.* This is a shortened name for *mean squared deviation,* which is what you actually calculate when computing variance. The symbol for a mean square is *MS.* Because we estimate the variance within groups and the variance between groups, we compute two mean squares: the *mean square within groups* and the *mean square between groups.*

The Mean Square Within Groups

The **mean square within groups** is an estimate of the variability in scores as measured by differences *within* the conditions of an experiment. The symbol for the mean square within groups is MS_{wn}. The word *within* says it all: Think of MS_{wn} as the "average variability" of the scores within each condition around the mean of that condition. You can conceptualize the computation of MS_{wn} as shown in Table 13.1: First, we find the variance in level 1 (finding how much the scores in level 1 differ from $\overline{X}_1$), then we find the variance of scores in level 2 around $\overline{X}_2$, and then we find the variance of scores in level 3 around $\overline{X}_3$. Then we "pool"—average together—the variances, just like we did in the independent-samples *t*-test. Thus, the MS_{wn} is the "average" variability of the scores in each condition around the mean of that condition.

We compare the scores in each condition with the mean for that condition, so MS_{wn} reflects the inherent variability among scores that arises from individual differences or other influences when participants are all treated the same. You saw in Chapter 5 that the variance (σ_X^2) is also called error. Thus, MS_{wn} estimates the **error variance,** which here is symbolized by σ_{error}^2. (MS_{wn} is also known as the *error term.*) In symbols,

Sample	*Estimates*	*Population*
MS_{wn}	$\rightarrow$	σ_{error}^2

The MS_{wn} is an estimate of the error variance found in any of the populations represented by a condition. Thus, for example, an MS_{wn} equal to 4 indicates that we estimate the variance of the scores in any of the populations represented by our conditions to be 4.

> *REMEMBER*   The MS_{wn} is an estimate of the *error variance,* the inherent variability within any population represented by the conditions.

The Mean Square Between Groups

The other variance computed in ANOVA is the mean square between groups. Here, the word *between* says it all. The **mean square between groups** is an estimate of the differences in scores that occur *between* the levels in a factor. The mean square between

TABLE 13.1   How to Conceptualize the Computation of MS_{wn}

Here, we find the difference between each score in a condition and the mean of that condition.

TABLE 13.2 How to Conceptualize the Computation of MS_{bn}

Here, we find the difference between the mean of each condition and the overall mean of the study.

Factor A

Level A_1:	*Level A_2:*	*Level A_3:*
X	X	X
X	X	X
X	X	X
X	X	X
X	X	X
$\overline{X}_1$	$\overline{X}_2$	$\overline{X}_3$	Overall $\overline{X}$

groups is symbolized by MS_{bn}. You can conceptualize the computation of MS_{bn} as shown in Table 13.2. Here, we determine how much the mean of each level deviates from the overall mean of all scores in the experiment. In the same way that the deviations of raw scores around their mean describe how different the scores are from each other, the deviations of the sample means around the overall mean indicate how different the sample means are from each other. *Thus,* MS_{bn} *is our way of measuring how much the means of our levels differ from each other.*

The key to understanding ANOVA is understanding what MS_{bn} represents when H_0 is true and when it is false. First, when H_0 is true, the scores in all conditions come from the same population. When we sample the population, not every score will equal μ or each other, so we'll obtain different means. Simply by chance, we get one batch of scores that differs from another batch. But! Differences between the means here have the same cause as differences among the individual scores *within* each condition: the inherent variability—σ^2_{error}—in the population. If the raw scores are naturally close to each other, then we'll get similar scores in each sample, so the means will be similar. If the raw scores are highly variable, then we'll get very different scores in each sample, so the means will also be highly variable. Thus, *the differences between the means will be the same size as the differences among individual scores.* Therefore, when H_0 is true, MS_{bn} estimates the population's variability among the individual scores—σ^2_{error}—just like MS_{wn} does.

Here's a more familiar example: Consider the population of someone's college grades—mine, for instance. You could estimate the variability of my grades by taking samples—say, my freshman year and my junior year—and, for each, finding how much my individual scores differ from my mean for that year: This is variability *within groups* of my scores. Or, you could compute my mean as a freshman and my mean as a junior, and see how much these means differ from my overall college grade average: This is variability *between groups* of my scores.

These grades all belong to the one population of me, so both approaches will give the *same* answer. Say I consistently scored at or close to C. Then my individual grades within any year will be close to my C average for the year, and my grade average for each year will be close to my overall mean of C. Likewise, if I was an inconsistent student, then my individual grades would be inconsistent *within* any year, and to the same extent, I'd be inconsistent *between* years. Thus, whether you look within or between the years, you'll find the same degree of my inconsistency—my inherent variability.

In the same way, when H_0 is true, then all scores in the experiment come from the same population. To whatever extent the scores are inherently variable, then the individual scores will be inconsistent *within* each group, and *to the same extent,* there will be that inconsistency *between* the groups. Thus, when we calculate MS_{bn} and MS_{wn}, they both estimate the one value of σ^2_{error}, so they should be *equal*. So, if MS_{wn} is 4, then MS_{bn} should also be 4, with both indicating that the inherent variability in the population (σ^2_{error}) is 4.

> *REMEMBER* When H_0 is true, MS_{bn} estimates the population's variability among the individual scores—the σ^2_{error}—just like MS_{wn} does, and so MS_{bn} should equal MS_{wn}.

Now consider when H_0 is false and the means of the levels come from different populations. Now there are two things that determine the value of MS_{bn}. First, scores from any two conditions differ because we have a *treatment effect:* Changing the conditions produces different populations of scores having different μs. Differences due to treatment effect are called treatment variance, which is symbolized as σ^2_{treat}. **Treatment variance** reflects differences between scores that occur because the scores are from different populations. We estimate these differences using the differences between the means of our levels, which we determine when calculating MS_{bn}. Therefore, MS_{bn} contains an estimate of the treatment variance (σ^2_{treat}).

The second influence on MS_{bn} when H_0 is false is the same as when H_0 is true: To some extent, differences between our means reflect the inherent variability among the scores. This is because a sample won't be perfectly representative. The more inherently variable the scores in the population are, the more likely we are to get a batch of different, unrepresentative scores in the sample, so the more the $\overline{X}$ will differ from μ. This will happen in each population created in each condition. Then the $\overline{X}$s differ from each other, not only because they come from different populations, but also because each $\overline{X}$ differs from its μ. Thus, MS_{bn} will reflect the differences between the μs for the conditions, as well as the difference between each $\overline{X}$ and its μ resulting from the inherent variability in the scores.

The same thing can be seen in my grades. Say that after my sophomore year, I grew up and became a B+ student. Therefore, my junior and senior grades belong to a *different population* than my earlier grades. If you compare my freshman and junior means to my overall college mean, there will be differences having two causes. First, one mean differs from any other mean because I'm still not perfectly consistent, so my yearly means differ from each other for the same reason my individual grades differ—my inherent error variance. In addition, however, growing up produced a new population of grades, so my freshman and junior means also differ because of this treatment variance. Thus, the differences between my freshman and junior means will reflect my inherent inconsistency (σ^2_{error}) plus differences due to growing up (σ^2_{treat}).

So, when H_0 is false, MS_{bn} contains error variance *plus* treatment variance. In symbols, this is

Sample	*Estimates*	*Population*
MS_{bn}	$\rightarrow$	$\sigma^2_{error} + \sigma^2_{treat}$

The σ^2_{error} component is again the same value as estimated by MS_{wn}. But with the added σ^2_{treat} component, MS_{bn} will now be *larger* than MS_{wn}. Thus, for example, say that MS_{wn} equals 4 and MS_{bn} equals 10. Think of MS_{bn} as indicating that, in addition to an error variance of 4, there is an "average difference" of 6 between the populations.

> **REMEMBER** If H_0 is false, then MS_{bn} contains error variance (σ^2_{error}), which measures differences *within* each population, and treatment variance (σ^2_{treat}), which measures differences *between* the populations.

On the other hand, the variability of scores *within* a condition remains the same regardless of whether H_0 is true or false. That is, we assume homogeneity of variance, regardless of whether all conditions represent the same or different populations. (If you look at the variability within my freshman year and within my junior year, this can only reflect my inherent inconsistency for that particular year, so each still reflects only my σ^2_{error}, regardless of whether I grew up not.) Thus, MS_{wn} is the same size, reflecting only that same σ^2_{error}, regardless of whether H_0 is true.

Comparing the Mean Squares: The Logic of the *F*-Ratio

We're not all that interested in the actual values of MS_{bn} and MS_{wn}. Instead, we are interested in their ratio, called the *F*-ratio. The **F-ratio** equals the mean square between groups divided by the mean square within groups.

THE COMPUTATIONAL FORMULA FOR THE F-RATIO IS

$$F_{obt} = \frac{MS_{bn}}{MS_{wn}}$$

MS_{bn} is always on top!

You can conceptualize the *F*-ratio as representing this:

$$\begin{array}{ccc} \textit{Sample} & \textit{Estimates} & \textit{Population} \\ F_{obt} = \dfrac{MS_{bn}}{MS_{wn}} & \begin{array}{c}\rightarrow \\ \rightarrow\end{array} & \dfrac{\sigma^2_{error} + \sigma^2_{treat}}{\sigma^2_{error}} \end{array}$$

The MS_{bn} represents the inherent differences between scores in any population (σ^2_{error}) *plus* whatever differences there are between the populations represented by the conditions (σ^2_{treat}). This value is divided by the MS_{wn}, which is only an estimate of the error variance in the populations (σ^2_{error}).

Now you can understand what the *F*-ratio indicates about the null hypothesis. If H_0 is true and all conditions represent the same population, then there are zero differences due to treatment. Then MS_{bn} contains solely σ^2_{error}, and the σ^2_{treat} component equals zero. In symbols, when H_0 is true,

$$\begin{array}{ccc} \textit{Sample} & \textit{Estimates} & \textit{Population} \\ F_{obt} = \dfrac{MS_{bn}}{MS_{wn}} & \begin{array}{c}\rightarrow \\ \rightarrow\end{array} & \dfrac{\sigma^2_{error} + 0}{\sigma^2_{error}} = \dfrac{\sigma^2_{error}}{\sigma^2_{error}} = 1 \end{array}$$

Both mean squares are merely estimates of the one value of σ^2_{error}. Therefore, the mean square between groups should *equal* the mean square within groups. When two numbers are equal, their ratio equals 1.

When H_0 is true and all conditions represent one population, the F-ratio should equal 1.

On the other hand, if H_a is true, then at least two conditions represent different populations, and there are differences between at least two means that are due to treatment. Therefore, when H_a is true, the σ^2_{treat} component of MS_{bn} does not equal zero, so

$$\begin{array}{ccc} \textbf{\textit{Sample}} & \textbf{\textit{Estimates}} & \textbf{\textit{Population}} \\[4pt] F_{obt} = \dfrac{MS_{bn}}{MS_{wn}} & \begin{array}{c}\rightarrow \\ \rightarrow\end{array} & \dfrac{\sigma^2_{error} + \text{some amount of } \sigma^2_{treat}}{\sigma^2_{error}} = F > 1 \end{array}$$

Here MS_{bn} contains error variance *plus* some amount of treatment variance, so MS_{bn} will be *larger* than MS_{wn}, which contains only error variance. Placing a larger number in the numerator of the F-ratio produces an F_{obt} greater than 1.

When H_a is true, MS_{bn} is larger than MS_{wn}, and F_{obt} is greater than 1.

The larger the differences between our conditions, the larger the σ^2_{treat} component, and thus the larger MS_{bn} will be. However, the size of MS_{wn} remains constant. Therefore, the larger the differences between the means, the larger the F_{obt} will be.

Regardless of whether we have a positive, negative, or curvilinear relationship, MS_{bn} will simply be larger than MS_{wn}, so that F_{obt} is greater than 1. (This is why we have only two-tailed hypotheses in ANOVA.) An F_{obt} between 0 and 1 is possible, but it occurs when MS_{wn} is larger than MS_{bn}. This can occur only when there is zero treatment component in MS_{bn}, and MS_{bn} and/or MS_{wn} are inaccurate estimates of σ^2_{error}. F_{obt} cannot be less than zero, because the mean squares are variances, which cannot be negative numbers.

Thus, on the one hand, F_{obt} should equal 1 if the means from the levels represent the same μ. On the other hand, F_{obt} should be greater than 1 if the means represent two or more different μs. But hold on! There is another reason F_{obt} might be greater than 1, and that is (here we go again) sampling error! When H_0 is true, F_{obt} "should" equal 1 *if* the mean squares are perfectly representative. But what if they're not representative? Perhaps H_0 is true so there is only one population of scores present, but by chance, the scores we obtain produce differences between groups that are larger than the differences within groups. This will produce an MS_{bn} that is larger than MS_{wn}, so F_{obt} will be larger than 1 simply because of sampling error.

This all boils down to the same old problem of significance testing. An F_{obt} greater than 1 may accurately reflect the situation in which two or more conditions represent different populations (and there really is a treatment effect). Or, because of sampling error, an F_{obt} greater than 1 may inaccurately reflect the situation in which all conditions represent the same population (and there only *appears* to be a treatment effect). Therefore, whenever we obtain an F_{obt} greater than 1, we determine the probability of obtaining such an F_{obt} when H_0 is true. To do this, we examine the F-distribution.

The *F*-Distribution

The **F-distribution** is the sampling distribution showing the various values of F that occur when H_0 is true and all conditions represent one population. We could create a sampling distribution in the following way: Using the same number of levels (k) and the same ns as in our study, we randomly sample *one* raw score population repeatedly. Each time, we compute MS_{bn}, MS_{wn}, and F_{obt}. After doing this an infinite number of times, we plot the various values of F_{obt}. The resulting distribution can be envisioned as in Figure 13.1. This is more or less the same old H_0 sampling distribution, except now the X axis shows the values of F that occur when H_0 is true and all levels represent the same population. The F-distribution is skewed, because there is no limit to how large F_{obt} can be, but it cannot be less than zero. The mean of the distribution is 1 because, most often, MS_{bn} will equal MS_{wn} and F will equal 1. We are concerned with the right-hand tail, which shows that sometimes the means are unrepresentative and by chance produce an F that is greater than 1. As shown, however, the larger the F, the less frequent and thus the less likely it is to occur when H_0 is true.

The F_{obt} can reflect a relationship in the population only when it is greater than 1, so the entire region of rejection is in the upper tail of the F-distribution. If F_{obt} is larger than F_{crit}, then F_{obt}—and the differences between the level means that produced it—is unlikely to occur when H_0 is true. Therefore, we reject H_0 and have a significant F_{obt}.

Degrees of Freedom and the Critical Value

Like the t-distribution, the F-distribution consists of a family of curves, each having a slightly different shape, depending on the degrees of freedom. However, there are *two* values of df that determine the shape of each F-distribution: the df used when computing the mean square between groups and the df used when computing the mean square within groups. The symbol for the df between groups is df_{bn}, and the symbol for the df within groups is df_{wn}.

To obtain F_{crit}, turn to Table 5 in Appendix B, entitled "Critical Values of F." Across the top of these "F-tables," the columns are labeled "df between groups," and along the left-hand side, the rows are labeled "df within groups." Locate the appropriate column and row using the dfs from your study. The critical values in dark type are for $\alpha = .05$, and those in light type are for $\alpha = .01$. For example, say we eventually determine that $df_{bn} = 2$ and $df_{wn} = 12$. Then for $\alpha = .05$, the F_{crit} is 3.88. Be careful to keep your "withins" and "betweens" straight: $df_{bn} = 2$ and $df_{wn} = 12$ is very different from $df_{bn} = 12$ and $df_{wn} = 2$.

FIGURE 13.1 Sampling distribution of F when H_0 is true

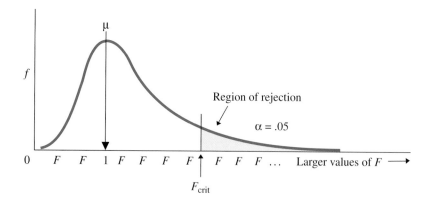

Don't be overwhelmed by the details of ANOVA. Buried in here is the simple idea that the larger the differences between the means for the conditions of the independent variable, the larger the MS_{bn} and thus the larger the F_{obt}. If the F_{obt} is larger than F_{crit}, then our conditions are unlikely to be representing the same population. Therefore, we reject H_0 and conclude that the data represent a relationship.

COMPUTING THE *F*-RATIO

The computations require one more new term. When we computed the estimated variance in Chapter 5, the quantity $\Sigma(X - \overline{X})^2$ was called the sum of the squared deviations. In ANOVA, this is shortened to the **sum of squares.** The symbol for the sum of squares is *SS*.

In the numerator of the formula for variance, we replace the sum of the squared deviations with *SS*:

$$s_X^2 = \frac{\Sigma(X - \overline{X})^2}{n - 1} = \frac{SS}{df} = MS$$

In the denominator, $n - 1$ is called the degrees of freedom, so we replace $n - 1$ with *df*. Because variance is called a mean square, the fraction formed by the sum of squares (*SS*) divided by the degrees of freedom (*df*) is the general formula for a mean square.

Adding subscripts, we will compute the mean square between groups (MS_{bn}) by computing the sum of squares between groups (SS_{bn}) and dividing by the degrees of freedom between groups (df_{bn}). Likewise, we will compute the mean square within groups (MS_{wn}) by computing the sum of squares within groups (SS_{wn}) and dividing by the degrees of freedom within groups (df_{wn}). Once we have MS_{bn} and MS_{wn}, we compute F_{obt}.

If all this strikes you as the most confusing thing ever devised, you'll find an ANOVA summary table very helpful. Here is the general format of the summary table for a one-way ANOVA:

Summary Table of One-Way ANOVA

Source	*Sum of Squares*	**df**	*Mean Square*	**F**
Between	SS_{bn}	df_{bn}	MS_{bn}	F_{obt}
Within	SS_{wn}	df_{wn}	MS_{wn}	
Total	SS_{tot}	df_{tot}		

The source column identifies each source of variation, either between or within groups. Along the way, we also look at another source, the "Total." In place of the word "Between," you can use the name of the independent variable. Also, in place of the word "Within," you will sometimes see "Error." Eventually we'll fill in the values in the other columns, producing F_{obt}.

Computational Formulas for the One-Way Between-Subjects ANOVA

Say that we actually performed the perceived difficulty study discussed earlier: We told three samples of five participants each that some math problems were easy, of medium difficulty, or difficult, and we measured the number of problems they correctly solved. The data are presented in Table 13.3.

As shown in the table, the first step in performing ANOVA is to compute ΣX, ΣX^2, and $\overline{X}$ for each level. Adding the ΣX from each level gives the total ΣX, and adding the ΣX^2 from each level gives the total ΣX^2. Then, as shown in the following sections, there are four steps in the computations, finding: (1) the sum of squares, (2) the degrees of freedom, (3) the mean squares, and (4) F_{obt}. So that you don't get lost, fill in the ANOVA summary table as you complete each step. (There *will* be a test later.)

Computing the Sums of Squares   The first task is to compute the sum of squares. Do this in three steps.

Step 1: Compute the total sum of squares (SS_{tot}).

THE COMPUTATIONAL FORMULA FOR THE TOTAL SUM OF SQUARES IS

$$SS_{tot} = \Sigma X^2_{tot} - \left(\frac{(\Sigma X_{tot})^2}{N} \right)$$

Here, we treat the entire experiment as if it were one big sample. Thus, ΣX_{tot} is the sum of all Xs, and ΣX^2_{tot} is the sum of all squared Xs. N is the total N in the study.

TABLE 13.3   Data from Perceived Difficulty Experiment

	Factor A: Perceived Difficulty		
Level A_1: *Easy*	*Level A_2:* *Medium*	*Level A_3:* *Difficult*	
9	4	1	
12	6	3	
4	8	4	
8	2	5	
7	10	2	*Totals*
$\Sigma X = 40$	$\Sigma X = 30$	$\Sigma X = 15$	$\Sigma X = 85$
$\Sigma X^2 = 354$	$\Sigma X^2 = 220$	$\Sigma X^2 = 55$	$\Sigma X^2 = 629$
$n_1 = 5$	$n_2 = 5$	$n_3 = 5$	$N = 15$
$\overline{X}_1 = 8$	$\overline{X}_2 = 6$	$\overline{X}_3 = 3$	$k = 3$

Using the data from Table 13.3, $\Sigma X^2_{tot} = 629$, $\Sigma X_{tot} = 85$, and $N = 15$, so

$$SS_{tot} = 629 - \frac{(85)^2}{15}$$

$$SS_{tot} = 629 - \frac{7225}{15}$$

$$SS_{tot} = 629 - 481.67$$

Thus, $SS_{tot} = 147.33$.

Step 2 Compute the sum of squares between groups (SS_{bn}).

THE COMPUTATIONAL FORMULA FOR THE SUM OF SQUARES BETWEEN GROUPS IS

$$SS_{bn} = \Sigma\left(\frac{(\text{Sum of scores in the column})^2}{n \text{ of scores in the column}}\right) - \left(\frac{(\Sigma X_{tot})^2}{N}\right)$$

Back in Table 13.3, each column represents a level of the factor. Thus, find the ΣX for a level, square the ΣX, and then divide by the n in that level. After doing this for all levels, add the results together and subtract the quantity $(\Sigma X_{tot})^2/N$. Thus, we have

$$SS_{bn} = \left(\frac{(40)^2}{5} + \frac{(30)^2}{5} + \frac{(15)^2}{5}\right) - \left(\frac{(85)^2}{15}\right)$$

so

$$SS_{bn} = (320 + 180 + 45) - 481.67$$

and

$$SS_{bn} = 545 - 481.67$$

So, $SS_{bn} = 63.33$.

Step 3 Compute the sum of squares within groups (SS_{wn}).

We use a shortcut to compute SS_{wn}. Mathematically, SS_{tot} equals SS_{bn} plus SS_{wn}. Therefore, the total minus the between leaves the within.

THE COMPUTATIONAL FORMULA FOR THE SUM OF SQUARES WITHIN GROUPS IS

$$SS_{wn} = SS_{tot} - SS_{bn}$$

Above, SS_{tot} is 147.33 and SS_{bn} is 63.33, so

$$SS_{wn} = 147.33 - 63.33 = 84.00$$

Thus, $SS_{wn} = 84.00$.

Filling in the first column of the ANOVA summary table, we have

Source	Sum of Squares	df	Mean Square	F
Between	63.33	df_{bn}	MS_{bn}	F_{obt}
Within	84.00	df_{wn}	MS_{wn}	
Total	147.33	df_{tot}		

As a double check, make sure that the total equals the between plus the within. Here, $63.33 + 84.00 = 147.33$.

Now compute the degrees of freedom.

Computing the Degrees of Freedom   Compute df_{bn}, df_{wn}, and df_{tot}. Again, there are three steps.

1. *The degrees of freedom between groups equals* k − *1,* where *k* is the number of levels in the factor. In the example, there are three levels of perceived difficulty (easy, medium, and difficult), so $k = 3$. Thus, $df_{bn} = 2$.

2. *The degrees of freedom within groups equals* N − k, where *N* is the total *N* in the experiment and *k* is the number of levels in the factor. In the example, *N* is 15 and *k* is 3, so $df_{wn} = 15 − 3 = 12$.

3. *The degrees of freedom total equals* N − *1,* where *N* is the total *N* in the experiment. In the example, *N* is 15, so $df_{tot} = 15 − 1 = 14$.

The df_{tot} equals the sum of the df_{bn} plus the df_{wn}. Thus, to check our work, $df_{bn} + df_{wn} = 2 + 12$, which equals 14, the df_{tot}.

Adding the *df* to the summary table, it looks like this:

Source	Sum of Squares	df	Mean Square	F
Between	63.33	2	MS_{bn}	F_{obt}
Within	84.00	12	MS_{wn}	
Total	147.33	14		

Now find each mean square.

Computing the Mean Squares   You can work directly from the summary table to compute the mean squares. Any mean square equals the appropriate sum of squares divided by the corresponding *df*. Thus,

THE COMPUTATIONAL FORMULA FOR THE MEAN SQUARE BETWEEN GROUPS IS

$$MS_{bn} = \frac{SS_{bn}}{df_{bn}}$$

From the summary table we see that

$$MS_{bn} = \frac{63.33}{2} = 31.67$$

so MS_{bn} is 31.67.

> **THE CO'MPUTATIONAL FORMULA FOR THE MEAN SQUARE WITHIN GROUPS IS**
>
> $$MS_{wn} = \frac{SS_{wn}}{df_{wn}}$$

For the example,

$$MS_{wn} = \frac{84}{12} = 7.00$$

so MS_{wn} is 7.00.

Do *not* compute the mean square for SS_{tot} because it has no use.

Now in the summary table we have

Source	*Sum of Squares*	**df**	*Mean Square*	**F**
Between	63.33	2	31.67	F_{obt}
Within	84.00	12	7.00	
Total	147.33	14		

Computing the *F* Finally, compute F_{obt}.

> **THE COMPUTATIONAL FORMULA FOR F IS**
>
> $$F_{obt} = \frac{MS_{bn}}{MS_{wn}}$$

In our example, MS_{bn} is 31.67 and MS_{wn} is 7.00, so

$$F_{obt} = \frac{MS_{bn}}{MS_{wn}} = \frac{31.67}{7.00} = 4.52$$

Thus, F_{obt} is 4.52.

Now the completed ANOVA summary table is

Source	*Sum of Squares*	**df**	*Mean Square*	**F**
Between	63.33	2	31.67	4.52
Within	84.00	12	7.00	
Total	147.33	14		

The F_{obt} is always placed in the row labeled "Between."

Interpreting F_{obt} in a One-Way ANOVA

To interpret F_{obt}, we must have F_{crit}, so turn to Table 5 in Appendix B. To enter the table, we need df_{bn} and df_{wn}. The values we use are those used in computing F_{obt} (in the summary table). In the example, df_{bn} is 2 and df_{wn} is 12. With $\alpha = .05$, F_{crit} is 3.88.

Thus, F_{obt} is 4.52 and F_{crit} is 3.88. Lo and behold, as shown in Figure 13.2, F_{obt} is significant. The null hypothesis says that the differences between the means of our levels are due to sampling error and that all means poorly represent one population mean. However, our F_{obt} is out there in the region of rejection, telling us that such differences between $\bar{X}$s hardly ever happen when H_0 is true. Because F_{obt} is larger than F_{crit}, we reject H_0, concluding that our different level means are unlikely to represent one population μ. Thus, we conclude that the F_{obt} is significant and that the factor of perceived difficulty produces a significant difference in mean performance scores. Report the results as

$$F(2, 12) = 4.52, p < .05$$

In the parentheses we report df_{bn} and then df_{wn}. As usual, because $\alpha = .05$, the probability that we have made a Type I error is $p < .05$.

Of course, had F_{obt} been less than F_{crit}, then the corresponding differences between our means would *not* be unlikely to occur when H_0 is true, so we would not reject H_0.

Because we rejected H_0 and accepted H_a, we return to the means from the levels of our factor:

Perceived Difficulty

Easy	Medium	Difficult
$\bar{X}_1 = 8$	$\bar{X}_2 = 6$	$\bar{X}_3 = 3$

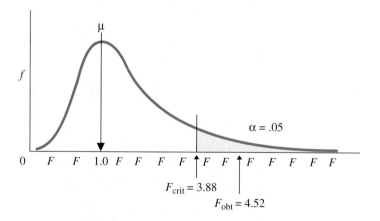

FIGURE 13.2 Sampling distribution of F when H_0 is true for $df_{bn} = 2$ and $df_{wn} = 12$

We are confident that these means represent a relationship in the population, in which increasing perceived difficulty is associated with fewer problems solved. However, we do not know whether *every* increase in difficulty produces a significant drop in performance. Remember: A significant F_{obt} merely indicates that there is *at least* one significant difference somewhere between these means. Now we must determine which specific means differ significantly, and to do that, we perform post hoc comparisons.

PERFORMING POST HOC COMPARISONS

Statisticians have developed a variety of post hoc procedures, which differ in how likely they are to produce Type I or Type II errors. We'll discuss two procedures that have acceptably low error rates.[1] Depending on whether or not your *n*s are equal, perform either *Fisher's protected* t-*test* or *Tukey's* HSD *test*.

Fisher's Protected *t*-Test

Perform **Fisher's protected *t*-test** when the *n*s in the levels of the factor are not equal.

THE COMPUTATIONAL FORMULA FOR FISHER'S PROTECTED t-*TEST IS*

$$t_{obt} = \frac{\overline{X}_1 - \overline{X}_2}{\sqrt{MS_{wn}\left(\frac{1}{n_1} + \frac{1}{n_2}\right)}}$$

This is basically the formula for the independent-samples *t*-test, except that MS_{wn} has replaced the pooled variance (s_{pool}^2) computed in the *t*-test. We are testing H_0: $\mu_1 - \mu_2 = 0$, where $\overline{X}_1$ and $\overline{X}_2$ are the means for any two levels of the factor and n_1 and n_2 are the corresponding *n*s in those levels. The t_{crit} is the two-tailed value found in Table 2 of Appendix B. For *df*, use the df_{wn} you had when computing F_{obt}.

It is not incorrect to perform the protected *t*-test even when all *n*s are equal. Thus, for example, we can compare the mean from our easy level (8.0) to the mean from our difficult level (3.0). Each *n* is 5, and from the ANOVA, MS_{wn} is 7.0. Filling in the formula gives

$$t_{obt} = \frac{8.0 - 3.0}{\sqrt{7.0\left(\frac{1}{5} + \frac{1}{5}\right)}}$$

Then

$$t_{obt} = \frac{+5.0}{\sqrt{7.0(.4)}} = \frac{+5.0}{\sqrt{2.8}} = \frac{+5.0}{1.67} = +2.99$$

[1]Carmer, S. G., and Swanson, M. R. (1973). An evaluation of ten multiple comparison procedures by Monte Carlo methods. *Journal of the American Statistical Association, 68,* pp. 66–74.

Then compare t_{obt} to the two-tailed value of t_{crit} found in the t-tables. For our study, with $\alpha = .05$ and $df_{wn} = 12$, t_{crit} is ± 2.179. Because the t_{obt} of $+2.99$ is beyond the t_{crit} of ± 2.179, the means from the easy and difficult levels differ significantly.

To complete these comparisons, perform the protected t-test on all possible pairs of means in the factor. Thus, after comparing the means from easy and difficult, we would test the means from easy and medium and then the means from medium and difficult. When you are finished, the experiment-wise error rate will be "protected," so that the probability of a Type I error for all of these comparisons together is $p < .05$.

If a factor contains many levels, then the protected t-test becomes very tedious. If you think there *must* be an easier way, you're right.

Tukey's *HSD* Multiple Comparisons Test

Perform the **Tukey *HSD* multiple comparisons test** when the ns in all levels of the factor are equal. The *HSD* is a rearrangement of the t-test that computes the minimum difference between two means that is required for the means to differ significantly (*HSD* stands for the Honestly Significant Difference). There are four steps to performing the *HSD* test.

Step 1 Find q_k. Using the appropriate value of q_k in the computations is what protects the experiment-wise error for the number of means being compared. Find the value of q_k in Table 6 in Appendix B, entitled "Values of Studentized Range Statistic." In the table, locate the column labeled with the k corresponding to the number of means in your factor. Next, find the row labeled with the df_{wn} used to compute your F_{obt}. Then find the value of q_k for the appropriate α. For our study above, $k = 3$, $df_{wn} = 12$, and $\alpha = .05$, so $q_k = 3.77$.

Step 2 Compute the *HSD*.

> *THE COMPUTATIONAL FORMULA FOR TUKEY'S* HSD *TEST IS*
>
> $$HSD = (q_k)\left(\sqrt{\frac{MS_{wn}}{n}}\right)$$

MS_{wn} is the denominator from your significant F-ratio, and n is the number of scores in each level of the factor.

In the example, MS_{wn} was 7.0 and n was 5, so

$$HSD = (q_k)\left(\sqrt{\frac{MS_{wn}}{n}}\right) = (3.77)\left(\sqrt{\frac{7.0}{5}}\right) = 4.46$$

Thus, *HSD* is 4.46.

Step 3 Determine the differences between each pair of means. Simply subtract each mean from every other mean. Ignore whether differences are positive or negative (this is a two-tailed test of the H_0 that $\mu_1 - \mu_2 = 0$).

The differences for the perceived difficulty study can be diagramed as shown below:

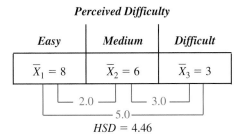

On the line connecting any two levels is the absolute difference between their means.

Step 4 Compare each difference to the *HSD*. If the absolute difference between two means is *greater than* the *HSD,* then these means differ significantly. (It's as if you performed a *t*-test on these means and t_{obt} was significant.) If the absolute difference between two means is less than or equal to the *HSD,* then it is *not* a significant difference (and would not produce a significant t_{obt}).

Above, the *HSD* was 4.46. The means from the easy level (8) and the difficult level (3) differ by more than 4.46, so they differ significantly. The mean from the medium level (6), however, differs from the other means by less than 4.46, so it does not differ significantly from them.

Thus, our final conclusion about this study is that we demonstrated a relationship between performance scores and perceived difficulty, but only for the easy and difficult conditions. If these two conditions were given to the population, we would expect to find two different populations of scores, having two different μs. We cannot say anything about whether the medium level would produce a different population, however, because we failed to find that it produced a significant difference. Finally, as usual, we would now interpret the results in terms of the behaviors being studied, explaining why this manipulation worked as it did.

SUMMARY OF STEPS IN PERFORMING A ONE-WAY ANOVA

It's been a long haul, but here is everything we do when performing a one-way ANOVA:

1. The null hypothesis is H_0: $\mu_1 = \mu_2 = \ldots = \mu_k$, and the alternative hypothesis is H_a: not all μs are equal. Choose alpha, check the assumptions, and collect the data.

2. First, compute the sum of squares between groups (SS_{bn}) and the sum of squares within groups (SS_{wn}). Then compute the degrees of freedom between groups (df_{bn}) and the degrees of freedom within groups (df_{wn}). Dividing the SS_{bn} by df_{bn} gives the mean square between groups (MS_{bn}). Dividing the SS_{wn} by the df_{wn} gives the mean square within groups (MS_{wn}). Finally, dividing the MS_{bn} by the MS_{wn} gives the F_{obt}.

3. Find F_{crit} in Appendix B, Table 5, using df_{bn} and df_{wn}. If H_0 is true, F_{obt} "should" equal 1. The larger the value of F_{obt}, the less likely it is that H_0 is true. If F_{obt} is larger than F_{crit}, then F_{obt} is significant, indicating that the means in at least two conditions differ significantly.

4. If F_{obt} is significant and there are more than two levels of the factor, determine which levels differ significantly by performing post hoc comparisons. Perform the protected t-test if the ns in all levels of the factor are not equal, or perform the *HSD* test if all ns are equal.

If you followed all of that, then congratulations, you're getting *good* at this stuff. Of course, all of this merely determines whether there is a relationship. Now you must describe that relationship.

DESCRIBING THE RELATIONSHIP IN A ONE-WAY ANOVA

As in previous chapters you are not finished when you have demonstrated a significant relationship. Ultimately, you must understand the relationship, and for help, you should describe the relationship by: (1) computing a confidence interval for each μ, (2) graphing the relationship, and (3) computing the effect size.

The Confidence Interval for Each Population μ

In our example the mean from the easy condition was 8.0, so we expect that the population mean represented by this condition would be "around" 8. As usual, to more clearly define "around," we compute a confidence interval for the μ represented by the sample mean. This is the same confidence interval for μ that was discussed in Chapter 11, except that here it is computed using the components of ANOVA.

THE COMPUTATIONAL FORMULA FOR THE CONFIDENCE INTERVAL FOR A SINGLE μ IS

$$\left(\sqrt{\frac{MS_{wn}}{n}}\right)(-t_{crit}) + \overline{X} \leq \mu \leq \left(\sqrt{\frac{MS_{wn}}{n}}\right)(+t_{crit}) + \overline{X}$$

The value of t_{crit} is the two-tailed value found in the t-tables using the appropriate α and using df_{wn} from the ANOVA as the df. MS_{wn} is also from the ANOVA, and $\overline{X}$ and n are from the level we are describing.

For example, in the easy condition, $\overline{X} = 8.0$, $MS_{wn} = 7.0$, $df_{wn} = 12$, and $n = 5$. The two-tailed t_{crit} (at $df = 12$ and $\alpha = .05$) is ± 2.179. Placing these values into the above formula gives

$$\left(\sqrt{\frac{7.0}{5}}\right)(-2.179) + 8.0 \leq \mu \leq \left(\sqrt{\frac{7.0}{5}}\right)(+2.179) + 8.0$$

This becomes

$$(-2.578) + 8.0 \leq \mu \leq (+2.578) + 8.0$$

and finally,

$$5.42 \leq \mu \leq 10.58$$

Because $\alpha = .05$, this is the 95% confidence interval: If we were to test the entire population under our easy condition, we are 95% confident that the population mean would fall between 5.42 and 10.58.

Follow the same procedure to describe the μ from any other *significant* level of the factor.

Graphing the Results in ANOVA

As usual, graph your results by placing the dependent variable on the Y axis and the independent variable on the X axis. Then plot the mean for each condition. Figure 13.3 shows the line graph for the perceived difficulty study. Note that we include the medium level of difficulty, even though it did not produce significant differences.

As usual, the line graph summarizes the relationship that is present, and here it indicates a largely negative linear relationship. Now we need to describe the strength of the relationship.

Eta Squared: The Proportion of Variance Accounted For

Remember that by saying only that a relationship is significant, it's like saying "I've found a correlation, but I'm not telling what it is." Therefore, first think *correlation coefficient* to describe the strength of the relationship between your independent and dependent variables. However, here you compute a new correlation coefficient called eta (pronounced "ay-tah"). **Eta** is entirely analogous to r_{pb} (ranging between 0 and 1) except that eta can be used to describe any linear or nonlinear relationship containing two or more levels of a factor.

FIGURE 13.3 Mean number of problems correctly solved as a function of perceived difficulty

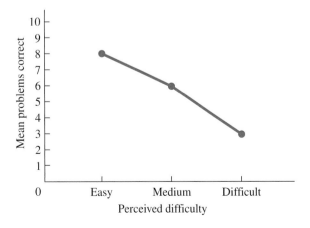

But remember that to get to the heart of describing a relationship, you should think *squared correlation coefficient.* This is the *effect size* of the independent variable—the proportion of variance in dependent scores that is associated with changing the conditions. With ANOVA, effect size is computed by squaring eta: **eta squared** indicates the proportion of variance in the dependent variable that is accounted for by changing the levels of a factor. The symbol for eta squared is η^2.

THE COMPUTATIONAL FORMULA FOR ETA SQUARED IS

$$\eta^2 = \frac{SS_{bn}}{SS_{tot}}$$

Both SS_{bn} and SS_{tot} are computed in the ANOVA. The SS_{bn} reflects the differences between the conditions. The SS_{tot} reflects the total differences between all scores in the experiment. Then η^2 reflects the proportion of all differences in scores that are associated with the different conditions.

For example, for the perceived difficulty study, SS_{bn} was 63.33 and SS_{tot} was 147.33. So,

$$\eta^2 = \frac{SS_{bn}}{SS_{tot}} = \frac{63.33}{147.33} = .43$$

This is interpreted in the same way that we previously interpreted r_{pb}^2. The larger the value of η^2, the more consistently the factor "caused" participants to have a particular score in a particular condition, and thus the more scientifically important the factor is for explaining and predicting differences in the underlying behavior. Thus, an η^2 of .43 indicates that we are .43, or 43%, more accurate at predicting participants' scores when we predict for them the mean of the difficulty level they were tested under, rather than using the overall mean of the study. In other words, 43% of all differences in these scores are accounted for ("caused") by changing the levels of perceived difficulty. Because 43% is a substantial amount, this factor is important in determining participants' performance, so it is important for scientific study.

Eta squared can be used with either equal or unequal *n*s. However, eta squared is a *descriptive* statistic that only describes the effect size in the *sample* data. It is a very rough *estimate* of the proportion of the variance in the population that would be accounted for by our relationship.

OTHER CONSIDERATIONS WHEN USING ANOVA

Before we leave the one-way ANOVA, there are two additional topics to briefly consider: the *within-subjects ANOVA* and *power.*

The Within-Subjects ANOVA

Recall that sometimes we conduct research that requires related samples, and then we perform the *within-subjects* ANOVA. This occurs when we match each participant in one condition with a participant in every other condition or, more commonly, when we repeatedly measure the same group of participants under all the levels of a factor. A within-subjects F_{obt} is conceptually identical to the F_{obt} discussed in this chapter (as are post hoc tests, η^2, and so on), except that the calculations are slightly different. The computational formulas for a one-way, within-subjects ANOVA are presented in Appendix A.4. These computations are similar to those you'll see in the next chapter, so you'll understand them better if you read that chapter first.

Power and ANOVA

Recall that we always want to maximize *power,* the probability of rejecting H_0 when it is false. Here, we do this by maximizing the size of F_{obt}. Looking at the *F*-ratio,

$$F_{obt} = \frac{MS_{bn}}{MS_{wn}}$$

you'll see that anything that increases the size of the numerator or decreases the size of the denominator produces a larger F_{obt}. As in previous chapters you increase the power of an ANOVA through three aspects of your design: (1) Maximize the size of the differences *between* the means, which increases the size of MS_{bn}. Do this by selecting very different levels of the factor that will produce large differences in the dependent behavior: If each condition is a very different situation from the next, then each is likely to produce a very different mean score. (2) Minimize the variability of scores *within* the conditions, which minimizes the size of MS_{wn}. Do this by testing participants very consistently in each condition: The more similar the situation is for all participants within a condition, the more similar (less variable) their scores will be. (3) Maximize the size of n in each condition, which maximizes df_{wn}. This produces a smaller value of MS_{wn} and a smaller F_{crit}. Any of the above will increase the probability that F_{obt} is significant, thereby increasing power. The same considerations increase the power of post hoc comparisons.

PUTTING IT ALL TOGETHER

Be sure that you are comfortable with the logic and terminology of this chapter. When all is said and done, the *F*-ratio is a convoluted way of measuring the differences between the means of our conditions and then fitting those differences to a sampling distribution. The larger the F_{obt}, the less likely that the means are representing the same μ. A significant F_{obt} indicates that the means are unlikely to represent one population mean. Once you determine that F_{obt} is significant, then determine which sample means actually differ significantly and describe the relationship they form. That's all there is to it.

There is, however, one other type of procedure that you should be aware of. Everything in our discussions so far has involved *one* dependent variable, and the statistics we've performed are called *univariate statistics.* We can, however, measure participants on two or more dependent variables in one experiment. Statistics for multiple dependent variables are called *multivariate statistics.* These include the multivariate *t*-test and the multivariate analysis of variance (MANOVA). Even though these are very complex procedures, the basic logic still holds: The larger the t_{obt} or F_{obt}, the less likely it is that the samples represent the same population. But to discuss multivariates further would require another book, so we'll leave it at that.

CHAPTER SUMMARY

1. The general terms used previously and their corresponding ANOVA terms are shown in this table:

General Term	=	ANOVA Term
independent variable	=	factor
condition	=	level
sum of squared deviations	=	sum of squares (SS)
variance (s_X^2)	=	mean square (MS)
effect of independent variable	=	treatment effect

2. A *one-way* analysis of variance tests for significant differences between the means from two or more levels of a factor. In a *between-subjects* factor, each condition involves an independent sample. In a *within-subjects* factor, the conditions involve related samples, either by matching different participants or by repeatedly measuring the same participants in all conditions.

3. The *experiment-wise error rate* is the probability that a Type I error will occur in an experiment. ANOVA is used instead of multiple *t*-tests because ANOVA keeps the experiment-wise error rate equal to α.

4. The *assumptions of the one-way, between-subjects ANOVA* are (a) the scores in each condition are independent random samples, (b) each sample represents a normally distributed population of interval or ratio scores, and (c) all populations have homogeneous (equal) variance.

5. ANOVA tests two-tailed hypotheses. H_0 is that the mean from every condition represents the same population mean. H_a is that the means from at least two conditions represent different population means.

6. The *mean square within groups* (MS_{wn}), estimates the *error variance,* the inherent variability among scores *within* each population. The *mean square between groups* (MS_{bn}), estimates the error variance plus the treatment variance. The *treatment variance* reflects differences in the populations produced by the conditions of the independent variable.

7. F_{obt} is computed using the F-*ratio,* which equals the mean square between groups divided by the mean square within groups.

8. F_{obt} may be greater than 1 because either (a) there is no treatment effect, but the sample means are not perfectly representative of this, or (b) two or more sample means represent different population means.

9. The F-*distribution* is the sampling distribution of all possible values of F_{obt} when H_0 is true.

10. The larger the F_{obt}, the less likely it is that the means from all levels represent the same μ. If F_{obt} is significant, then the different level means are unlikely to represent the same population mean.

11. If F_{obt} is significant and there are more than two levels, perform *post hoc comparisons* to determine which means differ significantly. When the *ns* are *not* equal, perform *Fisher's protected* t-*test* on each pair of means. If all *ns* are equal, perform *Tukey's HSD test.*

12. *Eta squared* (η^2) describes the *effect size*—the *proportion of variance* in dependent scores accounted for by the levels of the independent variable.

13. The *power* of ANOVA increases by increasing differences between the level means, decreasing the variability of scores within each condition, and increasing the *n* of small samples.

KEY TERMS: Can You Define the Following?

k F_{obt} F_{crit} MS_{wn} σ^2_{error} MS_{bn}
σ^2_{treat} df_{bn} df_{wn} η^2 SS_{bn} SS_{wn}
HSD
analysis of variance *336*
ANOVA *334*
between-subjects ANOVA *334*
between-subjects factor *334*
error variance *339*
eta *355*
eta squared *356*
experiment-wise error rate *336*
factor *334*
F-distribution *343*
Fisher's protected *t*-test *351*
F-ratio *342*

level *334*
mean square between groups *339*
mean square within groups *339*
one-way ANOVA *334*
post hoc comparisons *337*
sum of squares *345*
treatment *334*
treatment effect *334*
treatment variance *341*
Tukey's *HSD* multiple comparisons test
  352
variance between groups *338*
variance within groups *338*
within-subjects ANOVA *335*
within-subjects factor *335*

REVIEW QUESTIONS

(Answers for odd-numbered questions are in Appendix C.)

1. What does each of the following terms mean? (a) ANOVA (b) one-way design (c) factor (d) level (e) treatment (f) between subjects (g) within subjects

2. (a) What is the difference between *n* and *N?* (b) What does *k* stand for?

3. What are two reasons for conducting a study with more than two levels of a factor?

4. (a) What are error variance and treatment variance? (b) What are the two types of mean squares, and what does each one estimate?

5. (a) What is the experiment-wise error rate? (b) Why does ANOVA solve the problem with the experiment-wise error rate created by multiple *t*-tests?

6. Summarize the steps involved in analyzing an experiment when $k > 2$.

7. (a) When is it necessary to perform post hoc comparisons? Why? (b) When is it unnecessary to perform post hoc comparisons? Why?

8. When do you use each of the two types of post hoc tests discussed in this chapter?

9. (a) What do η^2 and r_{pb}^2 have in common? (b) How do they differ?

10. (a) Why should F_{obt} equal 1 if the data represent the H_0 situation? (b) Why is F_{obt} greater than 1 when the data represent the H_a situation? (c) What does a significant F_{obt} indicate about differences between the levels of a factor?

11. A research article reports the results of a "multivariate" analysis. What does this term communicate about the study?

APPLICATION QUESTIONS

12. A researcher conducts an experiment in which scores are measured under two conditions of an independent variable. (a) How will the researcher know whether to perform a parametric or nonparametric procedure? (b) Which two parametric procedures are available to her? (c) If the researcher conducts an experiment with three levels of the independent variable, which two versions of a parametric procedure are available to her? (d) How does she choose between them?

13. (a) In a study comparing the effects of four conditions of the independent variable, what is H_0 for the ANOVA? (b) What is H_a in the same study? (c) Describe in words what H_0 and H_a say for this study.

14. (a) In the perceived difficulty study discussed in this chapter, how could you increase power? (b) How do these strategies affect the size of F_{obt} and thus increase power? (c) What does this do to post hoc tests?

15. (a) Poindexter computes an F_{obt} of .63. How should this be interpreted? (b) He computes another F_{obt} of -1.7. How should this be interpreted?

16. Foofy obtained a significant F_{obt} from an experiment with five levels. She concludes that she's demonstrated a relationship in which changing each condition of the independent variable results in a significant change in the dependent variable. (a) Is she correct? Why or why not? (b) What must she now do?

17. (a) Why must the relationship in a one-way ANOVA be significant in order to be potentially important? (b) What does "significant" tell you about the relationship? (c) Why can the relationship be significant yet unimportant?

18. You read in a research report that the between-subjects factor of participants' salary produced significant differences in judgments of self-esteem. (a) What does this tell you about the design? (b) What does it tell you about the results?

19. A research article reports that a new diet led to a significant decrease in weight for a group of participants. (a) What does this tell you about the design? (b) What do we call this design?

20. A researcher investigated the number of viral infections people contract as a function of the amount of stress they experienced during a six-month period. She obtained the following data:

Amount of Stress

Negligible Stress	Minimal Stress	Moderate Stress	Severe Stress
2	4	6	5
1	3	5	7
4	2	7	8
1	3	5	4

(a) What are H_0 and H_a? (b) Compute F_{obt} and complete the ANOVA summary table. (c) With $\alpha = .05$, what is F_{crit}? (d) Report your statistical results. (e) Perform the appropriate post hoc comparisons. (f) What do you conclude about this study? (g) Describe the effect size and interpret it. (h) Estimate the value of μ that is likely to be found in the severe stress condition.

21. Here are data from an experiment studying the effect of age on creativity scores:

Age 4	Age 6	Age 8	Age 10
3	9	9	7
5	11	12	7
7	14	9	6
4	10	8	4
3	10	9	5

(a) Compute F_{obt} and create an ANOVA summary table. (b) With $\alpha = .05$ what do you conclude about F_{obt}? (c) Perform the appropriate post hoc comparisons. What should you conclude about this relationship? (d) Statistically, how important is the relationship in this study? (e) Describe how you would graph these results.

22. In a study in which $k = 3$, $n = 21$, $\overline{X}_1 = 45.3$, $\overline{X}_2 = 16.9$, and $\overline{X}_3 = 8.2$, you compute the following sums of squares:

Source	Sum of Squares	df	Mean Square	F
Between	147.32	_____	_____	_____
Within	862.99	_____	_____	
Total	1010.31	_____		

(a) Complete the ANOVA summary table. (b) With $\alpha = .05$ what do you conclude about F_{obt}? (c) Perform the appropriate post hoc comparisons. What do you conclude about this relationship? (d) What is the effect size in this study, and what does this tell you about the influence of the independent variable?

23. In this chapter we saw how to perform five statistical procedures. What are they?

24. A researcher investigated the effect of volume of background noise on participants' accuracy rates while performing a boring task. He tested three groups of randomly selected students and obtained the following means and sums of squares:

	Low Volume	Moderate Volume	High Volume
$\overline{X}$	61.5	65.5	48.25
n	4	5	7

Source	Sum of Squares	df	Mean Square	F
Between groups	652.16	___	___	___
Within groups	612.75	___	___	
Total	1264.92	___		

(a) Complete the ANOVA (b) At $\alpha = .05$, what is F_{crit}? (c) Report the statistical results in the proper format. (d) Perform the appropriate post hoc tests. (e) What do you conclude about this study? (f) Compute the effect size and interpret it.

⁄⁄⁄⁄⁄⁄⁄⁄ SUMMARY OF FORMULAS

1. *The format for the summary table for a one-way ANOVA is*

Summary Table of One-Way ANOVA

Source	Sum of Squares	df	Mean Square	F
Between	SS_{bn}	df_{bn}	MS_{bn}	F_{obt}
Within	SS_{wn}	df_{wn}	MS_{wn}	
Total	SS_{tot}	df_{tot}		

2. Computing the sum of squares,

  a. *The computational formula for* SS_{tot} *is*

$$SS_{tot} = \Sigma X^2{}_{tot} - \left(\frac{(\Sigma X_{tot})^2}{N} \right)$$

All scores in the experiment are included, and N is the total number of scores.

  b. *The computational formula for* SS_{bn} *is*

$$SS_{bn} = \Sigma \left(\frac{(\text{Sum of scores in the column})^2}{n \text{ of scores in the column}} \right) - \left(\frac{(\Sigma X_{tot})^2}{N} \right)$$

where each column contains the scores from one level of the factor.

  c. *The computational formula for* SS_{wn} *is*

$$SS_{wn} = SS_{tot} - SS_{bn}$$

3. Computing the mean square,

   a. *The computational formula for* MS_{bn} *is*

   $$MS_{bn} = \frac{SS_{bn}}{df_{bn}}$$

   with $df_{bn} = k - 1$, where k is the number of levels in the factor.

   b. *The computational formula for* MS_{wn} *is*

   $$MS_{wn} = \frac{SS_{wn}}{df_{wn}}$$

   with $df_{wn} = N - k$, where N is the total N of the study and k is the number of levels in the factor.

4. *The computational formula for the* F-*ratio is*

   $$F_{obt} = \frac{MS_{bn}}{MS_{wn}}$$

   Critical values of F are found in Table 5 in Appendix B for df_{bn} and df_{wn}.

5. *The computational formula for the protected* t-*test is*

   $$t_{obt} = \frac{\overline{X}_1 - \overline{X}_2}{\sqrt{MS_{wn}\left(\frac{1}{n_1} + \frac{1}{n_2}\right)}}$$

   Values of t_{crit} are the two-tailed values found in the t-tables for $df = df_{wn} = N - k$.

6. *The computational formula for the* HSD *is*

   $$HSD = (q_k)\left(\sqrt{\frac{MS_{wn}}{n}}\right)$$

   Values of q_k are found in Table 6 for df_{wn} and k, where k equals the number of levels of the factor.

7. *The computational formula for computing the confidence interval for a single* μ, *using the results of a between-subjects ANOVA, is*

   $$\left(\sqrt{\frac{MS_{wn}}{n}}\right)(-t_{crit}) + \overline{X} \leq \mu \leq \left(\sqrt{\frac{MS_{wn}}{n}}\right)(+t_{crit}) + \overline{X}$$

   $\overline{X}$ and n are from the level being described, and t_{crit} is the two-tailed value of t_{crit} at the appropriate α for df_{wn}.

8. *The computational formula for eta squared is*

   $$\eta^2 = \frac{SS_{bn}}{SS_{tot}}$$

Hypothesis Testing for Means from Two Independent Variables: The Two-Way Analysis of Variance

GETTING STARTED

To understand this chapter, recall the following:

- From Chapter 13 understand the terms *factor* and *level*, how to calculate F, what a significant F indicates, when to perform post hoc tests, and what η^2 indicates.

Your goals in this chapter are to learn:

- What a two-way factorial ANOVA is.
- How to collapse across a factor to find main effect means.
- How to calculate the cell means for the interaction.
- How the Fs in a two-way ANOVA are computed.
- What a significant main effect indicates.
- What a significant interaction indicates.
- How to perform post hoc tests, compute η^2, and draw the graph for each effect.
- How to interpret the results of a two-way experiment.

In the previous chapter you saw that ANOVA simultaneously tests for significant differences between all means from *one* factor. In this chapter we'll expand the experiment to involve two factors, which we analyze using a two-way ANOVA. This is like the ANOVA of the previous chapter, except that here we compute several values of F_{obt}. Therefore, be forewarned that the procedure is rather involved (although it is more tedious than it is difficult). As you read the chapter, don't be concerned about memorizing all of the specific formulas. Rather, understand the overall logic.

MORE STATISTICAL NOTATION

As with all experiments, the purpose of a two-factor experiment is to determine whether there's a relationship between the independent variable and dependent variables. The only difference from previous experiments is that in a **two-way design** there are two independent variables—two factors. Such designs are analyzed by performing a two-way ANOVA. The **two-way ANOVA** is the parametric inferential procedure performed when an experiment contains two independent variables. Recognize, however, that as with previous procedures, there are again different formulas, depending on whether the study involves independent or related (dependent) samples. For now, we'll discuss the design in which *both* independent variables are tested using *independent* samples, in which case we perform the **two-way, between-subjects ANOVA.**

Each of the two factors may contain any number of levels, so we have a code for describing a specific design. The generic format is to call one independent variable factor A and the other independent variable factor B. To describe a particular ANOVA, we use the number of levels in each factor. If, for example, factor A has two levels and factor B has two levels, we have a two-by-two ANOVA, which is written as 2×2. Or if one factor has four levels and the other factor has three levels, we have a 4×3 ANOVA, and so on.

WHY IS IT IMPORTANT TO KNOW ABOUT THE TWO-WAY ANOVA?

The two-way ANOVA can be applied to a variety of two-factor experiments. Why do we study two factors in one experiment? First, a two-factor design tells us everything about the influence of each factor that we would learn if it were the only independent variable. But we can also study something that we'd otherwise miss—the *interaction effect.* For now, think of an interaction effect as the influence of combining the levels from the two factors. Interactions are important because, in nature, often there are many variables present that influence a behavior. By manipulating more than one factor in an experiment, we can examine the influence of such combined variables on a behavior. Thus, the primary reason for conducting a study with two (or more) factors is to observe the interaction between them.

A second reason for multifactor studies is that once you've created a design for studying one independent variable, often only a minimum of additional effort is required to study additional factors. Thus, multifactor studies are an efficient and cost-effective way of determining the effects of—and interactions among—several independent variables. Therefore, it's important to know about two-way ANOVAs because you'll often encounter them in behavioral research.

UNDERSTANDING THE TWO-WAY DESIGN

The key to understanding the two-way ANOVA is to understand a two-way design. As an example, say that we are again interested in the effects of a "smart pill" on a person's IQ. We'll call the number of smart pills given to participants factor A, and test two levels (1 or 2 pills), after which we'll measure participants' IQ scores. The design of this factor is shown in Design Diagram 14.1. Each column represents a level of factor A and, within a column, each X represents a participant's IQ score. Averaging the scores in each column yields the mean IQ for each pill level, showing the effect of factor A: how the typical IQ score changes as we increase dosage.

Say that we're also interested in studying the influence of a person's age on IQ. We'll call age factor B, and test two levels (10- and 20-year-olds). You can envision this design as illustrated in Design Diagram 14.2. The only novelty here is that the two conditions are arranged horizontally, so that each *row* represents a different level of the factor. Here, averaging the scores in each row yields the mean IQ for each age level, showing the effect of factor B: how the typical IQ score changes with increasing age.

To create a two-way design, we would *simultaneously* manipulate both the participants' age and the number of pills they receive. A good way to visualize this 2×2 design is in Design Diagram 14.3. Each column is still a level of factor A (number of pills). Each row is still a level of factor B (age). But now we have a new term: Each small square produced by a particular combination of a level of factor A with a level of factor B is called a **cell.** In this design there are four cells, each containing a sample of

DESIGN DIAGRAM 14.1   Diagram of Factor of Number of Smart Pills

Each column represents a condition of the independent variable of number of pills. Each X represents a participant's IQ score, and each X̄ is the mean for that level of factor A.

Factor A: Number of Pills

Level A_1: One Pill	Level A_2: Two Pills
X	X
X	X
X	X
X	X
X	X
X	X
X	X
$\overline{X}$	$\overline{X}$

DESIGN DIAGRAM 14.2   Diagram of Factor of Age

Each row represents a level of age. Each X represents a participant's score, and each $\overline{X}$ represents the mean IQ score in that level.

Factor B: Age	Level B_1: 10-Year-Olds	X X X X X X	$\overline{X}$
	Level B_2: 20-Year-Olds	X X X X X X	$\overline{X}$

participants who are one age and are given one amount of the pill. For example, the highlighted cell contains scores from a sample of 20-year-olds who receive one pill.

Using the general code, we identify the levels of factor A as A_1 and A_2 and the levels of factor B as B_1 and B_2. Then we identify each cell using the levels of the two factors. For example, the cell formed by combining level 1 of factor A and level 1 of factor B is cell A_1B_1. We can identify the mean and *n* from each cell in the same way, so, for example, in cell A_1B_1 we have $\overline{X}_{A_1B_1}$.

One final consideration: Combining all levels of one factor with all levels of the other factor produces a **complete factorial design.** Design Diagram 14.3 shows a complete factorial, because all levels of drug dose are combined with all age levels. On the other hand, in an **incomplete factorial design,** not all levels of the two factors are combined. For example, if we had not collected data for 20-year-olds given one smart pill, we would have an incomplete factorial design. Incomplete factorial designs require elaborate procedures not discussed here.

If the sample in every *cell* is an independent sample, then we analyze such a design using the *two-way, between-subjects ANOVA.*

DESIGN DIAGRAM 14.3   Two-Way Design for Studying the Factors of Number of Smart Pills and Participant's Age

		Factor A: Number of Pills		
		Level A_1: 1 Pill	Level A_2: 2 Pills	
Factor B: Age	Level B_1: 10-Year-Olds	X X X $\overline{X}_{A_1B_1}$	X X X $\overline{X}_{A_2B_1}$	}← Scores
	Level B_2: 20-Year-Olds	X X X $\overline{X}_{A_1B_2}$	X X X $\overline{X}_{A_2B_2}$	}←

↑___ One of the four cells

OVERVIEW OF THE TWO-WAY, BETWEEN-SUBJECTS ANOVA

Regardless of whether we are talking about each separate factor or their interaction, we want to conclude that if we tested the entire population under the various conditions, we'd find different populations of scores located at different μs. But there is the usual problem: Differences between the sample means may simply reflect sampling error, so we might actually find the same population, having the same μ for all conditions. Therefore, once again we must eliminate the idea that the differences between the sample means merely reflect sampling error. To do this, we perform ANOVA. As usual, first set alpha (usually $\alpha = .05$) and then check the assumptions.

Assumptions of the Two-Way, Between-Subjects ANOVA

Perform the two-way, between-subjects ANOVA when you have a complete factorial design and

1. All cells contain independent samples.
2. The dependent variable measures interval or ratio scores that are approximately normally distributed.
3. The populations have homogeneous variance (all have equal σ_X^2).

Logic of the Two-Way ANOVA

Enough about smart pills. Here's a semi-fascinating idea for a new study. Have you ever noticed that television commercials are much louder than the programs themselves? Advertisers seem to believe that increased volume creates increased viewer attention which makes the commercial more persuasive. To test whether louder messages are more persuasive, we'll play a recording of an advertising message to participants at each of three volumes. Volume is measured in decibels, but to simplify things we'll call the three levels of volume soft, medium, and loud. Say that we're also interested in the differences between how males and females are persuaded, so our other factor is the gender of the listener. Therefore, we have a two-factor experiment involving three levels of volume and two levels of gender. We'll test all conditions with independent samples, so we have a 3×2 between-subjects, factorial ANOVA. The dependent variable indicates how persuasive a person believes the message to be on a scale of 0 (not at all) to 25 (totally convincing).

We collect the scores and organize them as in Design Diagram 14.4. For simplicity we have a distinctly unpowerful *N:* Nine men and nine women were randomly selected, and then three men and three women were randomly assigned to hear the message at each volume, so there are three persuasiveness scores per cell.

But now what? How do we make sense out of it all? We want to determine the effect on persuasiveness scores when we change (1) the levels of the volume factor, (2) the levels of the gender factor, and (3) the interaction of volume and gender. For each, we want to determine whether the effect is significant. Because we want to view each of these effects separately, we'll view the means from each separately, in a way very similar to that of a *one-way ANOVA!* You already understand a one-way ANOVA, so the rest of this chapter is simply a guide for computing the various *F*s.

DESIGN DIAGRAM 14.4   A 3 × 2 Design for the Factors of Volume and Gender

Factor A: Volume

		Level A$_1$: *Soft*	*Level A$_2$:* *Medium*	*Level A$_3$:* *Loud*
	Level B$_1$: *Male*	9 4 11	8 12 13	18 17 15
Factor B: *Gender*				
	Level B$_2$: *Female*	2 6 4	9 10 17	6 8 4

$N = 18$

In a nutshell, here is where we're going:

Any two-way ANOVA breaks down into finding the two *main effects* and the *interaction effect*.

Main Effects

The **main effect** of a factor is the effect that changing the levels of that factor has on dependent scores while ignoring all other factors in the study. In the persuasiveness study, to find the main effect of factor A (volume), we simply ignore the levels of factor B (gender). Literally erase the horizontal line that separates the rows of males and females above in Design Diagram 14.4, and treat the experiment as if it were this:

Factor A: Volume

Level A$_1$: *Soft*	*Level A$_2$:* *Medium*	*Level A$_3$:* *Loud*	
9 4 11 2 6 4	8 12 13 9 10 17	18 17 15 6 8 4	$k_A = 3$
$\overline{X}_{A_1} = 6$ $n_{A_1} = 6$	$\overline{X}_{A_2} = 11.5$ $n_{A_2} = 6$	$\overline{X}_{A_3} = 11.33$ $n_{A_3} = 6$	

We ignore whether there are males or females in each condition, so we simply have six participants tested under each volume (in each column). Then we have one factor, with three means from the three levels of volume. Thus, k_A—the number of levels in factor A—is 3, with $n = 6$ in each level.

In statistical terminology, we have *collapsed* across the factor of gender. **Collapsing** across a factor means averaging together all scores from all levels of that factor. When we collapse across one factor, we have the *main effect means* for the remaining factor. Thus, collapsing across gender above produces the main effect means for the three levels of volume, $\overline{X}_{A1} = 6$, $\overline{X}_{A2} = 11.5$, and $\overline{X}_{A3} = 11.33$.

> *REMEMBER* When we examine the *main effect of factor A*, we look at the overall mean of each level of A, examining the column means.

After collapsing across factor B, we then essentially perform a one-way ANOVA to find the main effect of factor A. Here, we ask, "Do these main effect means represent different μs that would be found if we tested the entire population under each of these three volumes?" To answer this question, first create the statistical hypotheses. The null hypothesis is

$$H_0: \mu_{A1} = \mu_{A2} = \mu_{A3}$$

In our study this says that changing volume has no effect, so the main effect means from the levels of volume represent the same population of persuasiveness scores. If we reject H_0, then we will accept the alternative hypothesis, which is

$$H_a: \text{not all } \mu_A \text{ are equal}$$

For our study this says that at least two main effect means from the volume factor represent different populations of persuasiveness scores, having different μs.

To test H_0, we compute an F_{obt} called F_A. If F_A is significant, it indicates that at least two main effect means from factor A differ significantly. Then we describe this relationship by graphing the main effect means, performing post hoc comparisons to determine which of the means differ significantly, and determining the proportion of variance in dependent scores that is accounted for by changing the levels of factor A.

After analyzing the main effect of factor A, we move on to the main effect of factor B. Now we collapse across factor A (volume), so erase the vertical lines separating the levels of volume back in Design Diagram 14.4, producing this:

Factor B: Gender	***Level B_1:* Male**	9 8 18 4 12 17 11 13 15	$\overline{X}_{B_1} = 11.89$ $n_{B_1} = 9$		$k_B = 2$
	***Level B_2:* Female**	2 9 6 6 10 8 4 17 4	$\overline{X}_{B_2} = 7.33$ $n_{B_2} = 9$		

We simply have the persuasiveness scores of males and females, ignoring the fact that some of each heard the message at different volumes. Now there is one factor with two levels, and we treat this as a one-way ANOVA to see if there are significant differences between the main effect means for males ($\overline{X}_{B_1} = 11.89$) and females ($\overline{X}_{B_2} = 7.33$). Notice that with two levels of factor B (gender), k_B is 2 and the n of each level is 9. For factor A, however, k_A was 3 and n was 6.

REMEMBER When we examine the *main effect of factor B,* we look at the overall mean for each level of B, examining the row means.

To test the main effect of B, the null hypothesis is

$$H_0: \mu_{B1} = \mu_{B2}$$

In our study this says that the mean for males represents the same μ as the mean for females. The alternative hypothesis is

$$H_a: \text{not all } \mu_B \text{ are equal}$$

In our study this says that the means for males and females represent different populations of persuasiveness scores, having different μs.

To test H_0 for factor B, we compute a separate F_{obt}, called F_B. If F_B is significant, then at least two of the main effect means for factor B differ significantly. Then we graph the main effect means for factor B, perform the post hoc comparisons, and compute the proportion of variance accounted for by factor B.

Interaction Effects

After you've examined the individual main effects of factors A and B, you examine their interaction. The interaction of two factors is called a two-way interaction. A **two-way interaction effect** results from combining the levels of factor A with the levels of factor B. In our example the interaction effect is the effect that each volume has when combined with each gender. An interaction is identified as A × B. Here, factor A has 3 levels and factor B has 2 levels, so it is a 3 × 2 (say "3 by 2") interaction.

Because an interaction examines the influence of combining the levels of the factors, we do not collapse across, or ignore, either factor. Instead, we treat each *cell* in the study as a level of the interaction and compare the cell means.

REMEMBER When you look for the interaction effect, you compare the cell means. When you look for a main effect, you compare the level means.

In our study we start with the three scores in each of the six cells back in Design Diagram 14.4, so $k_{A \times B}$ is 6 and n is 3. Then, the cell means for the interaction between volume and gender is shown in Design Diagram 14.5.

DESIGN DIAGRAM 14.5 The Volume by Gender Interaction

		Factor A: Volume		
		Soft	*Medium*	*Loud*
Factor B: Gender	*Male*	$\bar{X} = 8$	$\bar{X} = 11$	$\bar{X} = 16.67$
	Female	$\bar{X} = 4$	$\bar{X} = 12$	$\bar{X} = 6$

$$k = 6$$
$$n = 3$$

However, examining an interaction is not as simple as saying that the cell means are significantly different. Instead, we test the extent to which the cell means differ *after* removing those differences that are attributable to the main effects of factors A and B. Thus, consistent differences between scores that are not due to changing factor A or factor B alone are due to changing the combination of A and B.

Interpreting an interaction is difficult, because both independent variables are changing, as well as the dependent scores. To simplify the process, look at the influence of changing the levels of factor A under *one* level of factor B. Then see if this effect of factor A is *different* when you look at the other level of factor B. For example, here is the first row of the previous diagram, showing the relationship between volume and scores for the males. What happens? As volume increases, mean persuasiveness scores also increase, in an apparently positive, linear relationship.

Factor A: Volume

	Soft	Medium	Loud
B_1: male	$\overline{X} = 8$	$\overline{X} = 11$	$\overline{X} = 16.67$

But now look at the relationship between volume and persuasiveness scores for the females.

Factor A: Volume

	Soft	Medium	Loud
B_2: female	$\overline{X} = 4$	$\overline{X} = 12$	$\overline{X} = 6$

Here, there is a nonlinear relationship: As volume increases, mean persuasiveness scores first increase but then decrease.

Thus, there is a different relationship between volume and persuasiveness scores for each gender level. An **interaction effect** is present when the relationship between one factor and the dependent scores changes with, or depends on, the level of the other factor that is present. (Thus, whether increasing the volume always increases scores *depends* on whether we're talking about males or females.) In other words, there's an interaction effect when the influence of changing one factor is not the same for each level of the other factor. (Increasing volume does not have the same effect for males as it does for females.)

You can also see the interaction by looking at the difference between males and females at each level of volume. Sometimes the males score higher, sometimes the females do; it *depends* on which level of volume we're talking about.

Conversely, an interaction effect would not be present if the cell means formed the *same* pattern for males and females. For example, say the cell means had been as follows.

Factor A: Volume

	Soft	Medium	Loud
Factor B: Gender **Male**	$\overline{X} = 5$	$\overline{X} = 10$	$\overline{X} = 15$
Female	$\overline{X} = 20$	$\overline{X} = 25$	$\overline{X} = 30$

Here, increasing the volume increases scores by about 5 points, *regardless* of whether it's for males or females. (Or, females always score higher, regardless of volume.) Thus, an interaction effect is not present when the influence of changing the levels of one factor does not depend on which level of the other variable we are talking about. Or, in other words, there's no interaction when there is the same relationship between the scores and one factor for each level of the other factor.

> REMEMBER *A two-way interaction effect* indicates that the influence that one factor has on scores depends on which level of the other factor is present.

As with other effects, the data may appear to show an interaction, but this may be an illusion created by sampling error. Therefore, we determine whether there is a *significant* interaction effect. To write the H_0 and H_a in symbols is complicated[1], but in words, H_0 is that the cell means do not represent an interaction effect in the population, and H_a is that at least some of the cell means do represent an interaction effect in the population.

To test H_0, we compute another F_{obt}, called $F_{A \times B}$. If $F_{A \times B}$ is significant, it indicates that at least two of the cell means differ significantly in a way that produces an interaction effect. Then, as always, we graph the interaction, perform post hoc comparisons to determine which cell means differ significantly, and compute the proportion of variance accounted for by the interaction.

Overview of the Computations of the Two-Way ANOVA

As you've seen, in a two-way ANOVA you compute three Fs: one for the main effect of factor A, one for the main effect of factor B, and one for the interaction of A × B. The logic and calculations for each of these are the same as in the one-way ANOVA because any F_{obt} is the ratio formed by dividing the mean square between groups (MS_{bn}) by the mean square within groups (MS_{wn}).

As usual, MS_{wn} is the variance within groups; in a two-way ANOVA it is computed by computing the "average" variability in the *cells*. Any differences among the scores are due to the inherent variability of scores, so MS_{wn} is an estimate of the error variance in the population. This is our *one* estimate of the error variance used as the denominator in computing all three F ratios.

---

[1]Technically, H_0 says that differences between scores due to A at one level of B equal the differences between scores due to A at the other level of B. Thus, we have H_0: $\mu_{A_1B_1} - \mu_{A_2B_1} = \mu_{A_1B_2} - \mu_{A_2B_2} = \mu_{A_2B_1} - \mu_{A_3B_1} = \mu_{A_2B_2} - \mu_{A_3B_2}$. H_a is that not all differences are equal.

The variance between groups is measured by computing the MS_{bn}. This indicates the differences between the means, as an estimate of the treatment variance plus the error variance in the population. Thus, as usual, each F contains the following:

Sample	Estimates	Population

$$F_{obt} = \quad \frac{MS_{bn}}{MS_{wn}} \qquad \begin{array}{c}\rightarrow\\\rightarrow\end{array} \qquad \frac{\sigma^2_{error} + \sigma^2_{treat}}{\sigma^2_{error}}$$

However, because we have two factors and the interaction, we have three sources of between-groups variance: (1) variance between groups due to factor A, (2) variance between groups due to factor B, and (3) variance between groups due to the interaction. We compute a separate mean square for each of these as an estimate of the treatment variance each produces. Thus, to examine the main effect of factor A (volume), we compute the sum of squares between groups for factor A (called SS_A), and then, after dividing by the degrees of freedom for factor A (called df_A), we have the mean square between groups for factor A (called MS_A.) Next, to examine the main effect of factor B (gender), we compute the sum of squares between groups for factor B (SS_B) and then, dividing by the degrees of freedom between groups for factor B (df_B), we have the mean square between groups for factor B (called MS_B). For the interaction we compute the sum of squares between groups for A $\times$ B ($SS_{A\times B}$) and, after dividing by the degrees of freedom ($df_{A\times B}$), we have the mean square between groups for the interaction ($MS_{A\times B}$).

Also, we compute MS_{wn} by computing SS_{wn} and then dividing by df_{wn}.

The summary table in Table 14.1 shows the preceding components. Then, to complete the ANOVA, for factor A divide MS_A by MS_{wn} to produce F_A. For factor B, divide MS_B by MS_{wn} to produce F_B. For the interaction, divide $MS_{A\times B}$ by MS_{wn} to produce $F_{A\times B}$.

Each F_{obt} is tested in the same way as in the previous chapter. F_{obt} may be larger than 1 because (1) H_0 is true but we have sampling error, or (2) H_0 is false and at least two means represent a relationship in the population. The larger the value of F_{obt}, the less likely it is that H_0 is true. If an F_{obt} is larger than F_{crit}, then it is significant and we reject the corresponding H_0.

TABLE 14.1   Summary Table of Two-Way ANOVA

Source	Sum of Squares	/	df	=	Mean Square	F
Between						
Factor A (volume)	SS_A		df_A		MS_A	F_A
Factor B (gender)	SS_B		df_B		MS_B	F_B
Interaction (vol $\times$ gen)	$SS_{A\times B}$		$df_{A\times B}$		$MS_{A\times B}$	$F_{A\times B}$
Within	SS_{wn}		df_{wn}		MS_{wn}	
Total	SS_{tot}		df_{tot}			

COMPUTING THE TWO-WAY ANOVA

Having a computer perform the calculations is the best way to perform this ANOVA. Regardless, your first step is to organize the data in each cell. Table 14.2 shows our persuasiveness scores for the factors of volume and gender, as well as the various components you must compute.

First, compute ΣX and ΣX^2 for each cell and note the n of each cell. Thus, for example, in the male–soft cell, $\Sigma X = 4 + 9 + 11 = 24$, $\Sigma X^2 = 4^2 + 9^2 + 11^2 = 218$, and $n = 3$. Also, compute the mean for each cell (for the male–soft cell, $\overline{X} = 24/3 = 8$). These are the means tested in the interaction.

Now collapse across factor B (gender) and look only at the three volumes. Compute ΣX vertically for each column: The ΣX in a column is the sum of the ΣXs from the cells in that column (e.g., for soft, $\Sigma X = 24 + 12$). Note the n in each column (here, $n = 6$) and compute the sample mean for each column (e.g., $\overline{X}_{soft} = 6$). These are the means tested in the main effect of factor A.

Now collapse across factor A (volume) and look only at males versus females. Compute ΣX horizontally for each row: The ΣX in a row equals the sum of the ΣXs from the cells in that row (for males, $\Sigma X = 24 + 33 + 50 = 107$). Note the n in each row (here, $n = 9$) and compute the sample mean for each row (e.g., $\overline{X}_{male} = 11.89$). These are the means tested in the main effect of factor B.

TABLE 14.2 Summary of Data for 3 × 2 ANOVA

		Factor A: Volume			
		A_1: Soft	A_2: Medium	A_3: Loud	
Factor B: Gender	B_1: Male	4 9 11 $\overline{X} = 8$ $\Sigma X = 24$ $\Sigma X^2 = 218$ $n = 3$	8 12 13 $\overline{X} = 11$ $\Sigma X = 33$ $\Sigma X^2 = 377$ $n = 3$	18 17 15 $\overline{X} = 16.67$ $\Sigma X = 50$ $\Sigma X^2 = 838$ $n = 3$	$\overline{X}_{male} = 11.89$ $\Sigma X = 107$ $n = 9$
	B_2: Female	2 6 4 $\overline{X} = 4$ $\Sigma X = 12$ $\Sigma X^2 = 56$ $n = 3$	9 10 17 $\overline{X} = 12$ $\Sigma X = 36$ $\Sigma X^2 = 470$ $n = 3$	6 8 4 $\overline{X} = 6$ $\Sigma X = 18$ $\Sigma X^2 = 116$ $n = 3$	$\overline{X}_{fem} = 7.33$ $\Sigma X = 66$ $n = 9$
		$\overline{X}_{soft} = 6$ $\Sigma X = 36$ $n = 6$	$\overline{X}_{med} = 11.5$ $\Sigma X = 69$ $n = 6$	$\overline{X}_{loud} = 11.33$ $\Sigma X = 68$ $n = 6$	$\Sigma X_{tot} = 173$ $\Sigma X_{tot}^2 = 2075$ $N = 18$

Finally, compute the total sum of squares (called ΣX_{tot}), by adding the ΣX from the three levels of factor A (the three column sums), so $\Sigma X_{tot} = 36 + 69 + 68 = 173$. (Or you can add the ΣX from the two levels of factor B.) Also, find the total ΣX^2 (called ΣX_{tot}^2) by adding the ΣX^2 from each cell, so $\Sigma X_{tot}^2 = 218 + 377 + 838 + 56 + 470 + 116 = 2075$. Note that the total N is 18.

As you'll see in the following sections, you use the above computations to first compute the sums of squares, then the degrees of freedom, then the mean squares, and finally the Fs. To keep track of your computations and prevent brain strain, fill in the ANOVA summary table as you go along.

Computing the Sums of Squares

First, compute the sums of squares.

Step 1 Compute the total sum of squares.

THE COMPUTATIONAL FORMULA FOR THE TOTAL SUM OF SQUARES IS

$$SS_{tot} = \Sigma X_{tot}^2 - \left(\frac{(\Sigma X_{tot})^2}{N} \right)$$

This says to divide $(\Sigma X_{tot})^2$ by N and then subtract the answer from ΣX_{tot}^2.

From Table 14.2, $\Sigma X_{tot} = 173$, $\Sigma X_{tot}^2 = 2075$, and $N = 18$. Filling in the formula gives

$$SS_{tot} = 2075 - \left(\frac{(173)^2}{18} \right)$$

so

$$SS_{tot} = 2075 - 1662.72$$

so

$$SS_{tot} = 412.28$$

Note that the quantity $(\Sigma X_{tot})^2/N$ above is also used when computing other sums of squares. It is called the *correction* (here the correction equals 1662.72).

Step 2 Compute the sum of squares for factor A. As in the diagrams here, always have factor A form your *columns*.

THE COMPUTATIONAL FORMULA FOR THE SUM OF SQUARES BETWEEN GROUPS FOR COLUMN FACTOR A IS

$$SS_A = \Sigma \left(\frac{(\text{Sum of scores in the column})^2}{n \text{ of scores in the column}} \right) - \left(\frac{(\Sigma X_{tot})^2}{N} \right)$$

This says to square the ΣX in each column of factor A and divide by the n in the column. Then add the answers together and subtract the correction.

From Table 14.2, the three columns produced sums of 36, 69, and 68, and n was 6. Filling in the above formula gives

$$SS_A = \left(\frac{(36)^2}{6} + \frac{(69)^2}{6} + \frac{(68)^2}{6}\right) - \left(\frac{(173)^2}{18}\right)$$

$$SS_A = (216 + 793.5 + 770.67) - 1662.72$$

$$SS_A = 1780.17 - 1662.72$$

so

$$SS_A = 117.45$$

Step 3 Compute the sum of squares between groups for factor B. In your diagram the levels of factor B should form the *rows*.

THE COMPUTATIONAL FORMULA FOR THE SUM OF SQUARES BETWEEN GROUPS FOR ROW FACTOR B IS

$$SS_B = \Sigma\left(\frac{(\text{Sum of scores in the row})^2}{n \text{ of scores in the row}}\right) - \left(\frac{(\Sigma X_{tot})^2}{N}\right)$$

This says to square the ΣX for each level of factor B and divide by the n in the level. Then add the answers and subtract the correction.

In Table 14.2, the two rows produced sums of 107 and 66, and n was 9. Filling in the formula gives

$$SS_B = \left(\frac{(107)^2}{9} + \frac{(66)^2}{9}\right) - 1662.72$$

$$SS_B = 1756.11 - 1662.72$$

so

$$SS_B = 93.39$$

Step 4 Compute the sum of squares between groups for the interaction. First, compute something called the overall sum of squares between groups, identified as SS_{bn}.

THE COMPUTATIONAL FORMULA FOR THE OVERALL SUM OF SQUARES BETWEEN GROUPS IS

$$SS_{bn} = \Sigma\left(\frac{(\text{Sum of scores in the cell})^2}{n \text{ of scores in the cell}}\right) - \left(\frac{(\Sigma X_{tot})^2}{N}\right)$$

Find $(\Sigma X)^2$ for each cell and divide by the n of the cell. Then add the answers together and subtract the correction.

From Table 14.2,

$$SS_{bn} = \left(\frac{(24)^2}{3} + \frac{(33)^2}{3} + \frac{(50)^2}{3} + \frac{(12)^2}{3} + \frac{(36)^2}{3} + \frac{(18)^2}{3} \right) - 1662.72$$

$$SS_{bn} = 1976.33 - 1662.72$$

so

$$SS_{bn} = 313.61$$

The SS_{bn} equals the sum of squares for factor A plus the sum of squares for factor B plus the sum of squares for the interaction. Therefore, to find $SS_{A \times B}$, subtract the sum of squares for both main effects (in steps 2 and 3) from the overall SS_{bn}. Thus,

THE COMPUTATIONAL FORMULA FOR THE SUM OF SQUARES BETWEEN GROUPS FOR THE INTERACTION IS

$$SS_{A \times B} = SS_{bn} - SS_A - SS_B$$

In our example we've computed $SS_{bn} = 313.61$, $SS_A = 117.45$, and $SS_B = 93.39$, so

$$SS_{A \times B} = 313.61 - 117.45 - 93.39$$

so

$$SS_{A \times B} = 102.77$$

Step 5 Compute the sum of squares within groups. The sum of squares within groups plus the overall sum of squares between groups equals the total sum of squares. Therefore, subtract the overall SS_{bn} in step 4 from the SS_{tot} in step 1 to obtain the SS_{wn}.

THE COMPUTATIONAL FORMULA FOR THE SUM OF SQUARES WITHIN GROUPS IS

$$SS_{wn} = SS_{tot} - SS_{bn}$$

Above, we calculated $SS_{tot} = 412.28$ and $SS_{bn} = 313.61$, so

$$SS_{wn} = 412.28 - 313.61$$

so

$$SS_{wn} = 98.67$$

All of the previous sums of squares are shown in the ANOVA summary table in Table 14.3. Notice that we do not include the overall SS_{bn}.

Now determine the various values of *df*.

TABLE 14.3 Summary Table of Two-Way ANOVA showing the Sums of Squares

Source	Sum of Squares	df	Mean Square	F
Between				
Factor A (volume)	117.45	df_A	MS_A	F_A
Factor B (gender)	93.39	df_B	MS_B	F_B
Interaction (vol × gen)	102.77	$df_{A\times B}$	$MS_{A\times B}$	$F_{A\times B}$
Within	98.67	df_{wn}	MS_{wn}	
Total	412.28	df_{tot}		

Computing the Degrees of Freedom

1. *The degrees of freedom between groups for factor A is* $k_A - 1$, *where* k_A *is the* number of levels in factor A. (In our example, k_A is the three levels of volume, so $df_A = 2$.)

2. *The degrees of freedom between groups for factor B is* $k_B - 1$, *where* k_B *is the* number of levels in factor B. (In our example, k_B is the two levels of gender, so $df_B = 1$.)

3. *The degrees of freedom between groups for the interaction is the* df *for factor A multiplied times the* df *for factor B.* (In our example, $df_A = 2$ and $df_B = 1$, so $df_{A\times B} = 2$.)

4. *The degrees of freedom within groups equals* $N - k_{A\times B}$, *where* N *is the total* N of the study and $k_{A\times B}$ is the number of cells in the study. (In our example, N is 18 and we have six cells, so $df_{wn} = 18 - 6 = 12$.)

5. *The degrees of freedom total equals* $N - 1$. Use this to check your previous calculations, because the sum of the above *df*s should equal df_{tot}. (In our example $df_{tot} = 17$.)

Place each *df* in the ANOVA summary table as shown in Table 14.4. Perform the remainder of the computations by working directly from this summary table. Next we go on to the mean squares.

Computing the Mean Squares

Any mean square equals the appropriate sum of squares divided by the appropriate *df*. Therefore, for factor A,

THE COMPUTATIONAL FORMULA FOR THE MEAN SQUARE BETWEEN GROUPS FOR FACTOR A IS

$$MS_A = \frac{SS_A}{df_A}$$

TABLE 14.4   Summary Table of Two-Way ANOVA with *df* and Sums of Squares

Source	Sum of Squares	df	Mean Square	F
Between				
Factor A (volume)	117.45	2	MS_A	F_A
Factor B (gender)	93.39	1	MS_B	F_B
Interaction (vol × gen)	102.77	2	$MS_{A \times B}$	$F_{A \times B}$
Within	98.67	12	MS_{wn}	
Total	412.28	17		

In our example, from Table 14.4 we find

$$MS_A = \frac{117.45}{2} = 58.73$$

THE COMPUTATIONAL FORMULA FOR THE MEAN SQUARE BETWEEN GROUPS FOR FACTOR B IS

$$MS_B = \frac{SS_B}{df_B}$$

In our example,

$$MS_B = \frac{93.39}{1} = 93.39$$

THE COMPUTATIONAL FORMULA FOR THE MEAN SQUARE BETWEEN GROUPS FOR THE INTERACTION IS

$$MS_{A \times B} = \frac{SS_{A \times B}}{df_{A \times B}}$$

Thus, we have

$$MS_{A \times B} = \frac{102.77}{2} = 51.39$$

THE COMPUTATIONAL FORMULA FOR THE MEAN SQUARE WITHIN GROUPS IS

$$MS_{wn} = \frac{SS_{wn}}{df_{wn}}$$

Thus, we have

$$MS_{wn} = \frac{98.67}{12} = 8.22$$

Putting the above values into the summary table gives Table 14.5.

Now, finally, compute the Fs.

Computing F

Any F equals the MS_{bn} divided by the MS_{wn}. Therefore,

> **THE COMPUTATIONAL FORMULA FOR F_A FOR THE MAIN EFFECT OF FACTOR A IS**
>
> $$F_A = \frac{MS_A}{MS_{wn}}$$

In our example, from Table 14.5 we have

$$F_A = \frac{58.73}{8.22} = 7.14$$

> **THE COMPUTATIONAL FORMULA FOR F_B FOR THE MAIN EFFECT OF FACTOR B IS**
>
> $$F_B = \frac{MS_B}{MS_{wn}}$$

Thus, we have

$$F_B = \frac{93.39}{8.22} = 11.36$$

TABLE 14.5 Summary Table of Two-Way ANOVA Showing the Mean Squares, *df*, and Sums of Squares

Source	Sum of Squares	df	Mean Square	F
Between				
Factor A (volume)	117.45	2	58.73	F_A
Factor B (gender)	93.39	1	93.39	F_B
Interaction (vol × gen)	102.77	2	51.39	$F_{A \times B}$
Within	98.67	12	8.22	
Total	412.28	17		

THE COMPUTATIONAL FORMULA FOR $F_{A \times B}$ FOR THE INTERACTION EFFECT IS

$$F_{A \times B} = \frac{MS_{A \times B}}{MS_{wn}}$$

Thus, we have

$$F_{A \times B} = \frac{51.39}{8.22} = 6.25$$

And now the finished summary table is in Table 14.6.

Interpreting Each *F*

Once you have completed the summary table, determine whether each F_{obt} is significant by comparing it to the appropriate F_{crit}. To find each F_{crit} in the *F*-tables (Table 5 in Appendix B), use the df_{bn} and the df_{wn} used in computing each F_{obt}.

1. To find F_{crit} for testing F_A, use df_A as the *df* between groups and df_{wn}. In our example, $df_A = 2$ and $df_{wn} = 12$. So, for $\alpha = .05$, the F_{crit} is 3.88.
2. To find F_{crit} for testing F_B, use df_B as the *df* between groups and df_{wn}. In our example, $df_B = 1$ and $df_{wn} = 12$. So, at $\alpha = .05$, the F_{crit} is 4.75.
3. To find F_{crit} for the interaction, use $df_{A \times B}$ as the *df* between groups and df_{wn}. In our example, $df_{A \times B} = 2$ and $df_{wn} = 12$. Thus, at $\alpha = .05$, the F_{crit} is 3.88.

Note that because factors A and B have different *df* between groups, they have different critical values.

> REMEMBER   Each F_{crit} will be different if the degrees of freedom between groups are different.

Thus, we end up comparing the F_{obt} from our ANOVA summary table with F_{crit} as follows:

TABLE 14.6   Completed Summary Table of Two-Way ANOVA

Source	Sum of Squares	df	Mean Square	F
Between				
Factor A (volume)	117.45	2	58.73	7.14
Factor B (gender)	93.39	1	93.39	11.36
Interaction (vol × gen)	102.77	2	51.39	6.25
Within	98.67	12	8.22	
Total	412.28	17		

	F_{obt}	F_{crit}
Main effect of volume (A)	7.14	3.88
Main effect of gender (B)	11.36	4.75
Interaction (A × B)	6.25	3.88

By now you can do this with your eyes closed: Imagine a sampling distribution with a region of rejection and F_{crit} in the positive tail. (If you can't imagine this, look back in Chapter 13 at Figure 13.1.) First, our F_A of 7.14 is larger than the F_{crit}, so F_A lies in the region of rejection. Therefore, we conclude that differences between the means for the levels of factor A are significant: Changing the volume of a message produced significant differences in persuasiveness scores. Report this result as

$$F(2, 12) = 7.14, p < .05$$

Likewise, the F_B of 11.36 is significant, so we conclude that the males and females in this study represent different populations of scores. Report this result as

$$F(1, 12) = 11.36, p < .05$$

Finally, the $F_{A×B}$ of 6.25 is significant, so we conclude that combining the levels of the factors produces means that represent an interaction effect in the population: The effect that changing the volume has in the population *depends* on whether it is a population of males or a population of females. Or, we can say that the difference between the male and female populations we'd see *depends* on whether a message is played at soft, medium, or loud volume. Report this result as

$$F(2, 12) = 6.25, p < .05$$

Note: It is just a coincidence of your particular data which Fs will be significant. Whether any one F_{obt} is significant does not influence whether any other F_{obt} is significant. Therefore, any combination of the main effects and/or the interaction may or may not be significant.

At this point we have completed the ANOVA. However, we are a long way from being finished with the analysis. Because each significant F_{obt} indicates only that a difference exists *somewhere* among the corresponding means, the next step is to examine those means.

INTERPRETING THE TWO-WAY EXPERIMENT

To understand and interpret the results of a two-way ANOVA, you should examine the means from each significant main effect and interaction by graphing them and performing post hoc comparisons.

Graphing Main Effects

As usual, plot the dependent variable along the Y axis and the levels of a factor along the X axis. To graph the main effect of factor A, plot the main effect means from each level of factor A. (Our column means were these: for low volume, $\overline{X} = 6$; for medium, $\overline{X} = 11.5$; and for loud, $\overline{X} = 11.33$.) To graph the main effect of factor B, separately plot the main effect means from each level of factor B (Our row means were these: for males, $\overline{X} = 11.89$; for females, $\overline{X} = 7.33$.) Figure 14.1 shows the resulting graphs of our main effects. Note that volume is measured in decibels, so the X axis of the volume factor should be labeled in decibels. Also, note that the graph for gender is a bar graph because this independent variable is measured using a *nominal* scale.

Such simple graphs probably would not appear in a publication, but they help you to see the pattern formed by the means. The right-hand graph shows the obvious fact that males scored higher than females. In the left-hand graph, the slanting line between soft and medium volume suggests a large (possibly significant) difference between these levels. However, the line between medium and loud volume is close to horizontal, so there may not be a significant difference here. To specifically determine which means differ significantly, we perform post hoc comparisons. But first, let's graph the interaction.

Graphing the Interaction Effect

An interaction can be a beast to interpret, so always graph it! To do so, plot all *cell means* on a *single* graph. As usual, place the dependent variable along the Y axis. Then place the levels of one factor along the X axis. You'll show the second factor by drawing a separate line connecting the means for each level of that factor. Therefore, place the factor with the most levels on the X axis so that there are as few lines as possible. Thus, for the persuasiveness study, label the X axis with the three volume levels. Then plot the cell means. As in any graph, you're showing the relationship between the X variable and the Y variable, but here you're showing the relationship between volume and persuasiveness scores first for males, and then for females. Thus, approach this in the same way that we examined the means back in Design Diagram 14.5. There you first looked at the relationship between volume and persuasiveness scores for males:

FIGURE 14.1   Graphs showing main effects of volume and gender

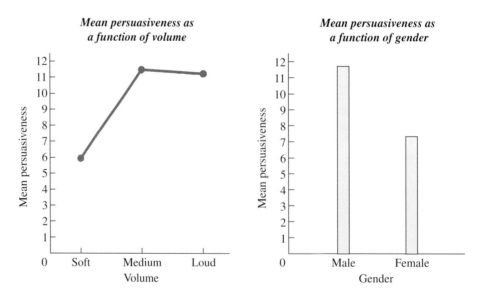

	Soft	Medium	Loud
Male	$\overline{X} = 8$	$\overline{X} = 11$	$\overline{X} = 16.67$

To graph this relationship, plot these three means and connect the adjacent data points with straight lines. Then look at the relationship between volume and scores for females:

	Soft	Medium	Loud
Female	$\overline{X} = 4$	$\overline{X} = 12$	$\overline{X} = 6$

Plot these three means and connect the adjacent data points with straight lines.

The resulting graph is shown in Figure 14.2. Notice: Always provide a key to identify each line.

The way to read the graph is to look at one line at a time. For males (the dashed line), as volume increases, mean persuasiveness scores increase. However, for females (the solid line), as volume increases, persuasiveness scores first increase but then decrease. Thus, there is a positive linear relationship for males and a nonlinear relationship for females. Therefore, the graph also shows an interaction effect by showing that the effect that increasing volume has on persuasiveness scores *depends* on whether the participants are male or female.

FIGURE 14.2   Graph of cell means, showing the interaction of volume and gender

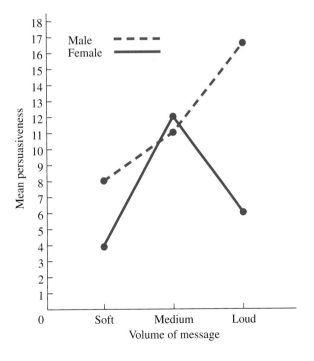

Note one final aspect of an interaction. An interaction can produce an infinite variety of different graphs, but when *an interaction effect is present, it produces lines that are not parallel.* Remember that each line summarizes the relationship, and that a line that is shaped or oriented differently from another line indicates a *different* relationship. Therefore, when the lines for the interaction are not parallel, each line depicts a *different* relationship. This indicates that the relationship between *X* and *Y* changes depending on the level of the second factor, so that an interaction effect is present. Conversely, when an interaction effect is not present, the lines will be essentially parallel, with each line depicting essentially the same relationship. To see this distinction, say that our data had produced one of the two graphs in Figure 14.3. On the left is the ultimate in non-parallel lines. Here, as the levels of A change, the mean scores either increase or decrease, depending on the level of B we're talking about, so an interaction is present. However, on the right the lines are parallel. Here, as the levels of A change, the scores increase, regardless of which level of factor B we examine. Therefore, this graph does not depict an interaction effect. (The fact that, *overall,* the scores are higher in B_1 than in B_2 is the main effect of—difference due to—factor B.)

Think of significance testing of the interaction $F_{A \times B}$ as testing whether the lines are significantly different from parallel. When an interaction is not significant, the lines on the graph are not significantly different from parallel, so they may represent parallel lines that would be found if we graphed the means of the populations. When an interaction is significant, somewhere in the graph the lines *do* differ significantly from parallel. Therefore, if we could graph the means of the populations, the lines probably would not be parallel, and there would be an interaction effect in the population.

> **REMEMBER** An *interaction effect* is present when its graph produces lines that are *not* parallel.

Of course, we don't know which of these cell means actually differ significantly, because we haven't performed the post hoc comparisons yet.

Performing Post Hoc Comparisons

As usual, you perform post hoc comparisons on any *significant* F_{obt}. If there are unequal *n*s among the levels of a factor, perform Fisher's protected *t*-test (as in Chapter

FIGURE 14.3 Two graphs showing when an interaction is and is not present

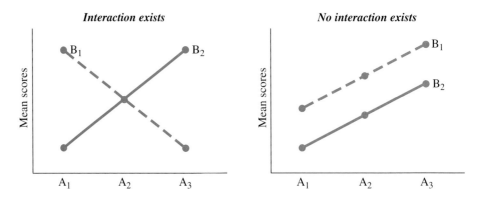

13). If the *n*s in all levels are equal, perform Tukey's *HSD* procedure. However, recognize that Tukey's procedure is computed differently for an interaction than for a main effect.

Performing Tukey's *HSD* for Main Effects   Perform post hoc comparisons on the means for the levels from each significant main effect, as if it were a one-way ANOVA.
  Recall that the computational formula for the HSD is

$$HSD = (q_k)\left(\sqrt{\frac{MS_{wn}}{n}}\right)$$

where MS_{wn} is the denominator of the F_{obt}, q_k is found in Table 6 of Appendix B for df_{wn} and k (where k is the number of levels in the factor), and n is the number of scores in a level. *But*, be careful here: For each factor there may be a different value of n and $k!$ In our persuasiveness study, *six* scores went into each mean for a level of volume, but *nine* scores went into each mean for a level of gender. *The n is always the number of scores used to compute each mean you are comparing* right now! Also, because q_k depends on k, when factors have a different k, they have different values of q_k.

  REMEMBER   Compute a different *HSD* for each significant main effect when their ks or ns are different.

  In the persuasiveness study the volume factor has three main effect means, and the n of each mean is 6. In the ANOVA, $MS_{wn} = 8.22$. With $\alpha = .05$, $k = 3$, and $df_{wn} = 12$; from Table 6, the $q_k = 3.77$. Placing these values in the above formula gives

$$HSD = (q_k)\left(\sqrt{\frac{MS_{wn}}{n}}\right) = (3.77)\left(\sqrt{\frac{8.22}{6}}\right) = 4.41$$

Thus, the *HSD* for factor A is 4.41.
  We can diagram the differences between the factor A means as

Factor A: Volume

A_1: Soft	A_2: Medium	A_3: Loud
$\overline{X} = 6$	$\overline{X} = 11.5$	$\overline{X} = 11.33$

5.50   0.17

5.33

HSD = 4.41

In the middle of each line connecting two means is the absolute difference between them. The mean for soft differs from the means for medium and loud by more than the *HSD* of 4.41. Thus, soft produces a significant difference from the other volumes. But, the means for medium and loud differ by *less* than 4.41, so these conditions do *not* differ significantly.

When a factor contains only two levels (like our gender factor), then you do not perform post hoc comparisons (it must be that the mean for males differs significantly from the mean for females). If, however, there were more than two levels in a significant factor B, you would compute the appropriate *HSD* for the *n* and *k* in that factor and compare these main effect means as we did above.

Performing Tukey's *HSD* for the Interaction   The post hoc comparisons on a significant interaction involve the *cell means*. However, we do *not* compare every cell mean to every other cell mean. Look at the interaction means in Table 14.7. We would not, for example, compare the mean for males at loud volume to the mean for females at soft volume. This is because, if the means do differ significantly, we would not know what caused the difference because the two cells differ in terms of both gender *and* volume. Therefore, we would have a confused, or confounded, comparison. A **confounded comparison** occurs when two cells differ along more than one factor. When performing post hoc comparisons on an interaction, we perform only **unconfounded comparisons,** in which two cells differ along only one factor. Therefore, compare only cell means within the same column, because these differences result from factor B. Compare means within the same row because these differences result from factor A. Do not, however, make any diagonal comparisons, because these are confounded comparisons.

With equal *n*s in all cells, you can examine the interaction using a slight variation of the Tukey *HSD*.[2] Previously, we found q_k in Table 6 using *k*, the number of means being compared. To compute the *HSD* for an interaction, you must first determine the *adjusted k*. This value "adjusts" for the actual number of unconfounded comparisons you will make out of all possible comparisons you might make. Obtain the *adjusted k* from Table 14.8 (or at the beginning of Table 6 of Appendix B). In the left-hand column, locate the design of your study. Do not be concerned about the order of the numbers. We called our persuasiveness study a 3 × 2 design, so look at the row labeled "2 × 3." Reading across that row, as a double check confirm that the middle column contains the total number of cell means in the interaction (we have 6). In the right-hand column is the *adjusted k* (for our study it is 5).

TABLE 14.7   Summary of Interaction Means for Persuasiveness Study

Horizontal and vertical lines between two cells show unconfounded comparisons; diagonal lines show confounded comparisons.

Factor A: Volume

		A_1: Soft	A_2: Medium	A_3: Loud
Factor B: Gender	B_1: Male	$\overline{X} = 8$	$\overline{X} = 11$	$\overline{X} = 16.67$
	B_2: Female	$\overline{X} = 4$	$\overline{X} = 12$	$\overline{X} = 6$

[2]Adapted from Cicchetti D.V. 1972, Extension of Multiple Range Tests to Interaction Tables in the Analysis of Variance, *Psychological Bulletin, 77,* 405–408.

TABLE 14.8   Values of Adjusted *k*

Design of Study	*Number of Cell Means in Study*	*Adjusted Value of* **k**
2 × 2	4	3
2 × 3	6	5
2 × 4	8	6
3 × 3	9	7
3 × 4	12	8
4 × 4	16	10
4 × 5	20	12

The *adjusted k* is the value of *k* to use to obtain q_k from Table 6. Thus, for the persuasiveness study, with $\alpha = .05$, $df_{wn} = 12$, and $k = 5$, the $q_k = 4.51$. Now compute the *HSD* using the same formula used previously. Our MS_{wn} is 8.22, but in each cell are 3 scores, so the *n* in each mean that we're comparing right now is 3. So

$$HSD = (q_k)\left(\sqrt{\frac{MS_{wn}}{n}}\right) = (4.51)\left(\sqrt{\frac{8.22}{3}}\right) = 7.47$$

Thus, the *HSD* for the interaction is 7.47.

Now determine the differences between all cell means *within* each column and *within* each row. To see these differences, arrange them as shown in Table 14.9. On the line connecting any two cells is the absolute difference between their means. Any difference between two means that is larger than the HSD is a significant difference. There are only three significant differences here: (1) between the mean for females at the soft volume and the mean for females at the medium volume, (2) between the mean for males at the soft volume and the mean for males at the loud volume, and (3) between the mean for males at the loud volume and the mean for females at the loud volume.

TABLE 14.9   Table of the Interaction Cells Showing the Differences Between Unconfounded Means

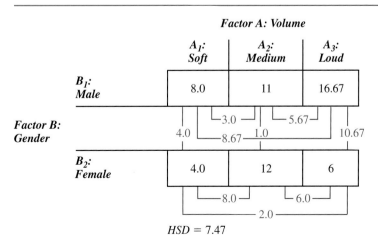

$HSD = 7.47$

Interpreting the Overall Results of the Experiment

There is no *one* way to interpret all experiments because each experiment indicates something different. The goal is to come up with a complete, honest, and simplified description of the results. To do that, look at the significant differences between means (from the post hoc comparisons) for all significant main effects and interaction effects.

All of the differences found in the persuasiveness study are summarized in Table 14.10. Outside of the diagram are the main effect means. Each line connecting two means indicates that they differ significantly. Inside the diagram, each line connecting two cell means indicates a significant difference within the interaction.

Usually, the interpretation of a two-way study rests with the interaction, even when main effects are significant. This is because usually the conclusions about significant main effects must be qualified (or are downright untrue) because of the interaction. For example, there is a significant difference between the main effect means of males and females. You might be tempted to conclude that males score higher than females. However, looking at the cell means of the interaction, we see that gender differences *depend* on volume: Only in the loud condition is there a significant difference between males and females. (This difference is so large that it produced an overall mean for males that is larger than the overall mean for females.) Therefore, because the interaction contradicts the pattern suggested by the main effect, we *cannot* make an overall, general conclusion about differences between males and females.

Likewise, we cannot make an overall conclusion about the main effect of volume, which showed that soft volume was significantly different from both the medium and loud volumes. The interaction indicates that increasing the volume from soft to medium actually produced a significant difference *only* for females, while increasing the volume from soft to loud produced a significant difference *only* for males.

Thus, as above, usually you cannot draw any conclusions about significant main effects when the interaction is significant. After all, the interaction indicates that the influence of one factor *depends* on the levels of the other factor and vice versa, so you should not turn around and act like either factor has a consistent overall effect. Therefore, the interpretation is limited to the interaction. When the interaction is not significant, then focus on any significant main effects. (For completeness, however, always perform the entire ANOVA, and report the results for all main effects and the interaction.)

TABLE 14.10 Summary of Significant Differences in the Persuasiveness Study

Each line connects two means that differ significantly.

		Factor A: Volume			
		Level A_1: *Soft*	**Level A_2:** *Medium*	**Level A_3:** *Loud*	
Factor B: **Gender**	**Level B_1:** *Male*	8.0	11	16.67	$\overline{X} = 11.89$
	Level B_2: *Female*	4.0	12	6	$\overline{X} = 7.33$
		$\overline{X}_{\text{soft}} = 6$	$\overline{X}_{\text{med}} = 11.5$	$\overline{X}_{\text{loud}} = 11.33$	

REMEMBER The primary interpretation of a two-way ANOVA rests on the interpretation of the significant interaction.

Thus, we conclude that increasing the volume of a message beyond soft does tend to increase persuasiveness scores in the population, but this increase occurs for females with medium volume and for males with loud volume. Further, we conclude that differences in persuasiveness scores occur between males and females in the population, but only if the volume of the message is loud.

Remember experiment-wise error, the probability of a Type I error somewhere in our conclusions? Well, after all of the above shenanigans, for all of these conclusions together, the probability of a Type I error is still $p < .05$. Also, remember power—the probability of not making a Type II error? All that was said in previous chapters about power applies to the two-way ANOVA as well. Thus, for any differences that are not significant, we must be concerned about whether we have maximized power by maximizing the differences between means, minimizing the variability within each cell, and having a large enough n.

As usual, after finding significant results, you would now turn to interpreting them in terms of the behaviors they reflect. For help you would further describe the relationship by computing effect size and confidence intervals.

Describing the Effect Size: Eta Squared

Recall that whenever you demonstrate a significant relationship, you should think *squared correlation coefficient* to describe the relationship. Therefore, in the two-way ANOVA, you again compute eta squared (η^2) to describe effect size—the proportion of variance in dependent scores that is accounted for by a relationship. Compute a separate eta squared for each *significant* main and interaction effect. The formula for eta squared is

$$\eta^2 = \frac{\text{Sum of squares between groups for the effect}}{SS_{tot}}$$

To compute each eta squared, divide the SS_{tot} into the sum of squares for the factor, either SS_A, SS_B, or $SS_{A \times B}$. For our example, for factor A (volume), SS_A was 117.45 and SS_{tot} was 412.28. Therefore, the eta squared for factor A (η^2_A) is

$$\eta^2_A = \frac{SS_A}{SS_{tot}} = \frac{117.45}{412.28} = .28$$

Thus, if we predict participants' scores using the main effect mean of the volume condition they were tested under, we can account for 28% of the total variance in persuasiveness scores. Following the same procedure for the gender factor, SS_B is 93.39, so η^2_B is .23: Predicting the mean of a gender condition for male and female participants, respectively, will account for an additional 23% of the variance in scores. Finally, for the interaction, $SS_{A \times B}$ is 102.77, so $\eta^2_{A \times B}$ is .25: By using the mean of the cell to predict a participant's score, we can account for an additional 25% of the variance.

Recall that the greater the effect size, the more important the manipulation is in determining participants' scores. Because each of the above effects has about the same size, they are all of equal importance in understanding differences in persuasiveness scores in this experiment. However, suppose that one effect accounted for only 1% of the total variance. Such a small η^2 indicates that this relationship is very inconsistent. Therefore, it is not a very useful or informative relationship, and we are better served by emphasizing the other, larger significant effects. In essence, if eta squared indicates that an effect was not a big deal in the experiment, then we should not make a big deal out of it when interpreting the experiment.

The effect size is especially important to consider when dealing with interactions. The one exception to the rule of always focusing on the significant interaction is when it has a very small effect size. If the interaction's effect is small (say, only .02), then although the interaction contradicts the pattern in a main effect, it is only slightly and inconsistently contradictory. In such cases you may focus your interpretation on any significant main effects that had a more substantial effect size.

Confidence Intervals for a Single μ

You can compute the confidence interval for the μ that is represented by a main effect mean or by a cell mean. Use the formula presented in the previous chapter, which was

$$\left(\sqrt{\frac{MS_{wn}}{n}}\right)(-t_{crit}) + \overline{X} \le \mu \le \left(\sqrt{\frac{MS_{wn}}{n}}\right)(+t_{crit}) + \overline{X}$$

where t_{crit} is the two-tailed value at the appropriate α with $df = df_{wn}$, MS_{wn} is from the ANOVA, $\overline{X}$ is the mean for the level or cell you are describing, and n is the number of scores that the mean is based on.

SUMMARY OF THE STEPS IN PERFORMING A TWO-WAY ANOVA

The following summarizes the steps in a two-way ANOVA:

1. Design the experiment, check the assumptions, and collect the data.

2. Compute the sums of squares between groups for each main effect and for the interaction, and compute the sum of squares within groups. Dividing each sum of squares by the appropriate *df* produces each mean square. Dividing each mean square between groups by the mean square within groups produces each F_{obt}.

3. Find F_{crit} in Table 5 of Appendix B, using the *df* between groups for each factor or interaction and the df_{wn}. If an F_{obt} is larger than F_{crit}, then there is a significant difference between two or more means from that factor or interaction.

4. Graph the main effects by plotting the level means of a factor, with the dependent variable on the *Y* axis and the levels of the factor on the *X* axis. Graph the interaction by plotting the cell means: Label the *X* axis with the levels of one factor, and in the body of the graph use a separate line to connect the cell means from each level of the other factor.

5. Perform post hoc comparisons for each significant main effect or interaction.

6. Compute eta squared to describe the proportion of variance in dependent scores accounted for by each significant main effect or interaction.

7. Based on the significant main and/or interaction effects and their values of η^2, develop an overall conclusion regarding the relationships formed by the specific means from cells and levels that differ significantly.

8. Compute the confidence interval for the value of μ represented by the mean in any relevant level or cell.

Congratulations, you are getting *very* good at this stuff.

WITHIN-SUBJECTS AND MIXED DESIGNS

Recall that sometimes an experiment involves *related samples* either because we've *repeatedly measured* the same participants under all conditions of a factor, or *matched* different participants. When you have two factors that both involve related samples, you perform a different version of the two-way ANOVA. The **two-way, within-subjects ANOVA** is performed when both factors are tested using related (dependent) samples. On the other hand, sometimes we "mix" a design, with one factor a within-subjects factor (involving related samples) and the other factor a between-subjects factor (involving independent samples). Perform the **two-way, mixed-design ANOVA** when the design involves one within-subjects factor and one between-subjects factor.

The formulas for these ANOVAs (with example data for each) are presented in Appendix A.5 and A.6. Although these calculations are slightly different than in the between-subjects ANOVA, the logic and interpretation are the same. Collapsing across factor B, we examine the main effect means for factor A. Collapsing across factor A, we examine the main effect means for factor B. Then without collapsing, we examine the interaction between the two factors, comparing the cell means. For any significant F_{obt}, we perform post hoc tests if needed, compute η^2 and confidence intervals, and graph the effect.

PUTTING IT ALL TOGETHER

Technically, there is no limit to the number of factors you can have in an ANOVA. There is, however, a practical limit to how many factors we can *interpret,* especially when dealing with an interaction. Say that we added a third factor to the persuasiveness study—the sex of the speaker of the message. This would produce a three-way (3 × 2 × 2) ANOVA in which we compute an F_{obt} for the main effect of each factor: A (volume), B (participant gender) and C (speaker gender). We'd also have an F_{obt} for each of three, two-way interactions (A × B, A × C, and B × C). In addition, we'd have an F_{obt} for a three-way interaction (A × B × C)! If it's significant, it indicates that the interaction between volume and gender changes, depending on the sex of the speaker.

If this sounds very complicated, it's because it *is* very complicated. To graph a 3 × 2 × 2 interaction, you would have at least four lines on *one* graph! Three-way interactions are very difficult to interpret, and interactions containing four or more factors are practically impossible to interpret. Therefore, unless you have a very good reason for including many factors in one study, it is best to limit yourself to two or, at most, three factors. You may not learn about many variables at once, but what you do learn you will understand.

CHAPTER SUMMARY

1. In a two-way, between-subjects ANOVA there are two independent variables, and all of the conditions of both factors contain independent samples. In a *complete factorial design,* each level of one factor is combined with all levels of the other factor. Each *cell* is formed by a particular combination of a level from each factor.

2. The ANOVA examines the *main effect* of manipulating each independent variable alone by comparing the overall means from the levels of the factor. The ANOVA also examines the *interaction effect* of manipulating both variables simultaneously by comparing the cell means.

3. The main effect means for a factor are obtained by *collapsing* across (combining the scores from) the levels of the other factor.

4. The *assumptions* of the two-way, between-subjects ANOVA are that (a) each cell is a random independent sample of interval or ratio scores, (b) the populations represented are normally distributed, and (c) the variances of all populations are homogeneous.

5. Perform a two-way ANOVA by computing an F_{obt} for each main effect and for the interaction.

6. A significant F_{obt} for a main effect indicates that at least two main effect means from the factor represent significant differences in scores.

7. A significant F_{obt} for an interaction indicates that the effect of changing the levels of one factor *depends* on which level of the other factor you examine. Therefore, the relationship between one factor and the dependent variable changes as the levels of the other factor change. When graphed, an interaction produces *nonparallel lines.*

8. Perform *post hoc comparisons* on each significant effect having more than two levels to determine which specific means differ significantly. Post hoc comparisons on the interaction are performed for *unconfounded* comparisons only. The means from two cells are unconfounded if the cells differ along only one factor. Two means are *confounded* if the cells differ along more than one factor.

9. Conclusions from a two-way ANOVA are based on the significant main and interaction effects and which level or cell means differ significantly. Usually, conclusions about the main effects are contradicted when the interaction is significant.

10. *Eta squared* describes the effect size of each significant main effect and interaction. A confidence interval can be computed for the μ represented by any $\overline{X}$ in the study.

11. A *two-way, within-subjects ANOVA* is used when both factors involve related samples, either from matched groups or from repeatedly measuring the same participants in all conditions.

12. A *two-way, mixed-design ANOVA* is used when one factor is tested using independent samples and one factor is tested using related samples.

KEY TERMS: Can You Define the Following?

F_A F_B $F_{A\times B}$ SS_A df_A
MS_A SS_B df_B MS_B $SS_{A\times B}$
$df_{A\times B}$ $MS_{A\times B}$
cell *366*
collapsing *370*
complete factorial design *367*
confounded comparison *388*
incomplete factorial design *367*
interaction effect *372*

main effect *369*
two-way ANOVA *365*
two-way, between-subjects ANOVA
   365
two-way design *365*
two-way interaction effect *371*
two-way, mixed-design ANOVA *393*
two-way, within-subjects ANOVA *393*
unconfounded comparisons *388*

REVIEW QUESTIONS

(Answers for odd-numbered questions are in Appendix C.)

1. (a) A researcher will conduct a study involving one independent variable. What are the two types of parametric procedures available to her? (b) She next will conduct a study involving two independent variables. What are the three versions of the parametric procedure available to her? (c) In part b what aspect of her design determines which version she should perform?

2. Identify the following terms (a) Two-way design (b) Complete factorial (c) Cell (d) Two-way between-subjects design

3. What are the two reasons for conducting two-factor experiments?

4. Which type of ANOVA is used in a two-way design when: (a) both factors are tested using independent samples? (b) one factor involves independent samples and one factor involves related (dependent) samples? (c) both factors involve related samples?

5. (a) What is the difference between a main effect mean and a cell mean? (b) A significant main effect indicates what about your study? (c) A significant interaction effect indicates what about your study?

6. Why do we usually base the interpretation of a two-way design on the interaction effect when it is significant?

7. (a) What is a confounded comparison, and when does it occur? (b) What is an unconfounded comparison, and when does it occur? (c) Why don't we perform post hoc tests on confounded comparisons?

8. What does it mean to collapse across a factor?

9. For a 2 × 2 ANOVA describe the following in words. (a) The statistical hypotheses for factor A. (b) The statistical hypotheses for factor B. (c) The statistical hypotheses for A × B.

10. Explain how each main effect and the interaction in a two-way ANOVA are similar to a one-way ANOVA.

APPLICATION QUESTIONS

11. Why is it wise to limit a multifactor experiment to two or three factors?

12. (a) When is it appropriate to compute the effect size in a two-way ANOVA? (b) For each effect, what does the effect size tell you?

13. (a) How can you increase the power of a two-way ANOVA? (b) Doing so will increase the power of F_{obt} and what other procedure?

14. A student hears that a 2×3 design was conducted and concludes that six factors were examined. Is this conclusion correct? Why or why not?

15. Below are the cell means of three experiments. For each experiment, compute the main effect means and indicate whether there appears to be an effect of A, B, and/or A × B.

Study 1	A_1	A_2
B_1	2	4
B_2	12	14

Study 2	A_1	A_2
B_1	10	5
B_2	5	10

Study 3	A_1	A_2
B_1	8	14
B_2	8	2

16. In question 15, if you label the X axis with factor A and graph the cell means, what pattern will we see for each interaction?

17. After performing a 3×4 ANOVA with equal ns, you find that all Fs are significant. What other procedures should you perform?

18. A 2×2 studies participants' frustration levels when solving problems as a function of the difficulty of the problem and whether they are math or logic problems. Logic problems produce significantly more frustration than math problems, that greater difficulty leads to significantly greater frustration, but that difficult math problems produce significantly greater frustration than more difficult logic problems, but the reverse is true for easy problems. In the ANOVA performed for this study, what effects are significant?

19. In question 18 say instead that the researcher found no difference between math and logic problems, that frustration significantly increases with greater difficulty, and that this is true for both math and logic problems. In the ANOVA performed for this study, what effects are significant?

20. In an experiment you measure the popularity of two brands of soft drinks (factor A), and for each brand you test males and females (factor B). The following table shows the main effect and cell means from the study:

	Factor A		
	Level A_1: Brand X	Level A_2: Brand Y	
Factor B — Level B_1: Males	14	23	18.5
Level B_2: Females	25	12	18.5
	19.5	17.5	

(a) Describe the graph of the interaction means when factor A is on the X axis. (b) Does there appear to be an interaction effect? Why? (c) Why will a significant interaction prohibit you from making conclusions based on the main effects?

21. A researcher examines performance on an eye–hand coordination task as a function of three levels of reward and three levels of practice, obtaining the following cell means.

		Low	Medium	High
			Reward	
		Low	*Medium*	*High*
Practice	*Low*	4	10	7
	Medium	5	5	14
	High	15	15	15

(a) What are the main effect means for reward, and what do they indicate about this factor? (b) What are the main effect means for practice, and what do they indicate? (c) Is an interaction effect likely? (d) How would you perform unconfounded post hoc comparisons of the cell means?

22. (a) In question 21 why does the interaction contradict your conclusions about the effect of reward? (b) Why does the interaction contradict your conclusions about practice?

23. In question 21 the researcher reports that the effect size of reward is .14, that the effect size of practice is .31, and that the interaction accounts for .01 of the variance. What does each value indicate about the influence of these effects?

24. Given the results in question 23, how would this change your interpretation of the study in question 21?

25. A study compared the performance of males and females tested by either a male or a female experimenter. Here are the data:

		Factor A: Participants	
		Level A_1: Males	*Level A_2:* Females
	Level B_1: Male Experimenter	6 11 9 10 9	8 14 17 16 19
Factor B: Experimenter			
	Level B_2: Female Experimenter	8 10 9 7 10	4 6 5 5 7

(a) Using $\alpha = .05$, perform an ANOVA and complete the summary table. (b) Compute the main effect means and interaction means. (c) Perform the appropriate post hoc comparisons. (d) What do you conclude about the relationships this study demonstrates? (e) Compute the effect size where appropriate.

26. You conduct an experiment involving two levels of self-confidence (A_1 is low, and A_2 is high) and examine participants' anxiety scores after they speak to one of four groups of differing sizes (B_1 through B_4 represent speaking to a small, medium, large, or extremely large group, respectively). You compute the following sums of squares ($n = 4$ and $N = 32$):

Source	Sum of Squares	df	Mean Square	F
Between				
Factor A	8.42	_____	_____	_____
Factor B	76.79	_____	_____	_____
Interaction	23.71	_____	_____	_____
Within	110.72	_____	_____	
Total	219.64	_____		

(a) Complete the ANOVA summary table. (b) With $\alpha = .05$, what do you conclude about each F_{obt}? (c) Compute the appropriate values of *HSD*. (d) For the levels of factor B, the means are $\overline{X}_1 = 18.36$, $\overline{X}_2 = 20.02$, $\overline{X}_3 = 24.6$, and $\overline{X}_4 = 28.3$. What should you conclude about the main effect of B? (e) How important is the size of the audience in determining a person's anxiety score? How important is the person's self-confidence?

SUMMARY OF FORMULAS

The general format for the summary table for a two-way, between-subjects ANOVA is

Summary Table of Two-Way ANOVA

Source	Sum of Squares	df	Mean Square	F
Between				
Factor A	SS_A	df_A	MS_A	F_A
Factor B	SS_B	df_B	MS_B	F_B
Interaction	$SS_{A \times B}$	$df_{A \times B}$	$MS_{A \times B}$	$F_{A \times B}$
Within	SS_{wn}	df_{wn}	MS_{wn}	
Total	SS_{tot}	df_{tot}		

1. Computing the sums of squares,
   a. *The computational formula for the sum of squares total is*

   $$SS_{tot} = \Sigma X_{tot}^2 - \left(\frac{(\Sigma X_{tot})^2}{N} \right)$$

b. *The computational formula for the sum of squares between groups for the column factor A is*

$$SS_A = \Sigma\left(\frac{(\text{Sum of scores in the column})^2}{n \text{ of scores in the column}}\right) - \left(\frac{(\Sigma X_{\text{tot}})^2}{N}\right)$$

c. *The computational formula for the sum of squares between groups for the row factor B is*

$$SS_B = \Sigma\left(\frac{(\text{Sum of scores in the row})^2}{n \text{ of scores in the row}}\right) - \left(\frac{(\Sigma X_{\text{tot}})^2}{N}\right)$$

d. *The computational formula for the sum of squares between groups for the interaction is*

$$SS_{A\times B} = SS_{\text{bn}} - SS_A - SS_B$$

where SS_{bn} is found using the formula

$$SS_{\text{bn}} = \Sigma\left(\frac{(\text{Sum of scores in the cell})^2}{n \text{ of scores in the cell}}\right) - \left(\frac{(\Sigma X_{\text{tot}})^2}{N}\right)$$

e. *The computational formula for the sum of squares within groups is*

$$SS_{\text{wn}} = SS_{\text{tot}} - SS_{\text{bn}}$$

2. Computing the degrees of freedom,
   a. The degrees of freedom between groups for factor A (df_A) equals $k_A - 1$, where k_A is the number of levels in factor A.
   b. The degrees of freedom between groups for factor B (df_B) equals $k_B - 1$, where k_B is the number of levels in factor B.
   c. The degrees of freedom between groups for the interaction $(df_{A\times B})$ equals df_A multiplied times df_B.
   d. The degrees of freedom within groups (df_{wn}) equals $N - k_{A\times B}$, where N is the total N of the study and $k_{A\times B}$ is the total number of cells in the study.

3. Computing the mean square,
   a. *The formula for MS_A is*

   $$MS_A = \frac{SS_A}{df_A}$$

   b. *The formula for MS_B is*

   $$MS_B = \frac{SS_B}{df_B}$$

   c. *The formula for $MS_{A\times B}$ is*

   $$MS_{A\times B} = \frac{SS_{A\times B}}{df_{A\times B}}$$

   d. *The formula for MS_{wn} is*

   $$MS_{\text{wn}} = \frac{SS_{\text{wn}}}{df_{\text{wn}}}$$

4. Computing F_{obt},

a. *The formula for F_A is*

$$F_A = \frac{MS_A}{MS_{wn}}$$

b. *The formula for F_B is*

$$F_B = \frac{MS_B}{MS_{wn}}$$

c. *The formula for $F_{A \times B}$ is*

$$F_{A \times B} = \frac{MS_{A \times B}}{MS_{wn}}$$

5. The critical values of F are found in Table 5 of Appendix B.

a. To find F_{crit} to test F_A, use df_A and df_{wn}.

b. To find F_{crit} to test F_B, use df_B and df_{wn}.

c. To find F_{crit} to test $F_{A \times B}$, use $df_{A \times B}$ and df_{wn}.

6. Performing Tukey's *HSD* post hoc comparisons

a. *For a significant main effect, the computational formula for the HSD is*

$$HSD = (q_k)\left(\sqrt{\frac{MS_{wn}}{n}}\right)$$

where q_k is found in Table 6 for k equal to the number of levels in the factor, MS_{wn} is from the ANOVA, and n is the number of scores used to compute each mean in the factor. Any two means that differ by an amount that is greater than the *HSD* are significantly different.

b. *For a significant interaction, the HSD is computed as follows.*

(1) Enter the following table for the design (or number of cells), and obtain the adjusted value of k.

Values of Adjusted k

Design of Study	Number of Cell Means in Study	Adjusted Value of k
2 × 2	4	3
2 × 3	6	5
2 × 4	8	6
3 × 3	9	7
3 × 4	12	8
4 × 4	16	10
4 × 5	20	12

(2) Enter Table 6 using the *adjusted k* and df_{wn} to find the value of q_k.

(3) Compute the *HSD* as in step 6a.

(4) Any two unconfounded cell means that differ by an amount that is greater than the *HSD* are significantly different.

7. *The computational formula for eta squared is*

$$\eta^2 = \frac{\text{Sum of squares between groups for the factor}}{SS_{\text{tot}}}$$

When η^2 is computed for factor A, factor B, or the A $\times$ B interaction, the "sum of squares between groups for the effect" is SS_A, SS_B, or $SS_{A \times B}$, respectively.

8. *The computational formula for computing the confidence interval for a single μ is*

$$\left(\sqrt{\frac{MS_{\text{wn}}}{n}}\right)(-t_{\text{crit}}) + \overline{X} \leq \mu \leq \left(\sqrt{\frac{MS_{\text{wn}}}{n}}\right)(+t_{\text{crit}}) + \overline{X}$$

where t_{crit} is the two-tailed value at the appropriate α with $df = df_{\text{wn}}$, MS_{wn} is from the ANOVA, and $\overline{X}$ and n are from the level or cell being described.

15

Chi Square and Other Nonparametric Procedures

GETTING STARTED

To understand this chapter, recall the following:

- From Chapter 2 recall the four types of measurement scales (nominal, ordinal, interval, and ratio).
- From Chapter 12 remember the types of designs that call for either the independent-samples t-test or the related-samples t-test.
- From Chapter 13 recall the one-way ANOVA, post hoc tests, and eta squared.

Your goals in this chapter are to learn:

- When to use nonparametric statistics.
- The logic and use of the one-way chi square.
- The logic and use of the two-way chi square.
- The nonparametric procedures corresponding to the independent-samples and related-samples t-test, and to the between-subjects and within-subjects ANOVA.

Recall that there are two categories of inferential statistics, parametric and nonparametric. Now we'll turn to **nonparametric statistics.** Don't despair, however, because the designs and logic you'll see here are very similar to those of previous statistics: Nonparametric procedures are still inferential statistics for deciding whether the differences between samples accurately represent differences in populations. Therefore, H_0 and H_a, sampling distributions, Type I and Type II errors, alpha levels, critical values, and maximizing power all apply.

WHY IS IT IMPORTANT TO KNOW ABOUT NONPARAMETRIC PROCEDURES?

Previous parametric procedures have required that dependent scores reflect an interval or ratio scale, that the scores are normally distributed, and that the population variances are homogeneous. It is better to design a study that allows you to use parametric procedures, because they are more powerful than nonparametric procedures. However, sometimes researchers don't obtain data that fit parametric procedures. Some dependent variables are nominal variables (e.g., whether someone is male or female). Sometimes we can measure a dependent variable only by assigning ordinal scores (e.g., judging this participant as showing the most of the variable, this one second-most, and so on). And sometimes a variable involves an interval or ratio scale, but the populations are severely skewed and/or do not have homogeneous variance.

Parametric procedures are *robust,* meaning that they will tolerate *some* violation of the assumptions. But, if the data severely violate the rules, then the result is to *increase* the probability of a Type I error. Recall that the whole purpose of inferential statistics is to limit rejecting H_0 when it's true, but here the actual probability of a Type I error will be unacceptably *larger* than the alpha level you've set.

Instead, turn to nonparametric procedures. Nonparametric procedures do not assume a normal distribution or homogeneous variance, and the data may be nominal or ordinal. And with such data, the probability of a Type I error will still equal your alpha. Therefore, it is important to know about nonparametric procedures, because you may use them in your own research, and you will definitely encounter them when reading the research of others.

> *REMEMBER* Use *nonparametric statistics* when dependent scores form very nonnormal distributions, when the population variance is not homogeneous, or when scores are measured using ordinal or nominal scales.

In the following sections we'll first discuss the most common nonparametric procedure, called *chi square.* Then we'll discuss the nonparametric procedures that are analogous to *t*-tests and ANOVAs, except that they are used with *rank-ordered scores.*

CHI SQUARE PROCEDURES

Chi square procedures are used when participants are measured using a nominal variable. With nominal variables, we do not measure an amount, but rather we indicate the *category* that a participant falls into. Thus, we have nominal variables when counting how many individuals answer yes, no, or maybe to a question; how many claim to vote Republican, Democratic, or Socialist; how many say that they were or were not abused children; and so on. In each case, we count the number, or *frequency,* of participants falling in each category.

The next step is to determine what the data represent. For example, we might find that out of 100 people, 40 say yes to a question and 60 say no. These numbers indicate how the *frequencies are distributed* across the categories of yes/no. As usual, we want to draw inferences about the population: Can we infer that if we asked the entire population this question, 40% of the population would say yes and 60% would say no? Or would the frequencies be distributed in a different manner? To make inferences about the frequencies in the population, we perform the chi square (pronounced "kigh square"). The **chi square procedure** is the nonparametric inferential procedure for testing whether the frequencies in each category in sample data represent specified frequencies in the population.

> *REMEMBER*   Whenever you count the number of participants that fall in different categories, use the *chi square procedure* for significance testing.

The symbol for the chi square statistic is χ^2. Theoretically, there is no limit to the number of categories—levels—you may have in a variable and no limit to the number of variables you may have. Therefore, we describe a chi square design in the same way we described ANOVAs: When a study has only one variable, use the *one-way chi square;* when a study has two variables, use the *two-way chi square;* and so on.

ONE-WAY CHI SQUARE: THE GOODNESS OF FIT TEST

The **one-way chi square** is used when data consist of the frequencies with which participants belong to the different categories of *one* variable. As usual, we're examining a relationship, but here it's the relationship between the different categories and the frequency with which participants fall in each. We ask, "As the categories change, do the frequencies with which participants fall in the categories also change?"

Here is an example study that calls for a one-way chi square. Being right-handed or left-handed is apparently related to brain organization, and many of history's great geniuses were left-handed. To explore the relationship between the frequencies of left- and right-handedness in geniuses, say that, using an IQ test, we select a sample of 50 geniuses. Then we ask them whether they are left- or right-handed (ambidextrous is not an option). The total numbers of left- and right-handers are the frequencies in the two categories. The results are shown here:

Handedness

Left-Handers	Right-Handers
$f_o = 10$	$f_o = 40$

$$k = 2$$
$$N = \text{total } f_o = 50$$

Each column contains the frequency with which participants are in that category. We call this value the **observed frequency,** symbolized by f_o. The sum of the f_os from all categories equals N, the total number of participants in the study. Notice that k stands for the number of categories, or levels, and here $k = 2$.

The above results seem pretty straightforward: 10 of the 50 geniuses (20%) are left-handers, and 40 of them (80%) are right-handers. Therefore, we might argue that the same distribution of 20% left-handers and 80% right-handers would occur in the population of geniuses. But, there is the usual problem: sampling error. Maybe, by luck, the people in our sample are unrepresentative, so in the population of all geniuses, we would not find this distribution of right- and left-handers. Maybe our results poorly represent some *other* distribution. As usual, this is the null hypothesis, implying that we are being misled by sampling error.

What is that "other distribution" of frequencies that the sample poorly represents? To answer this, we create a *model* of the distribution of the frequencies we expect to find in the population when H_0 is true. Recall that H_0 always implies that our study failed to demonstrate the predicted relationship. Therefore, the H_0 model describes the distribution of frequencies in the population if there is not the predicted relationship.

It is for this reason that the one-way chi square procedure is also called the "Goodness of Fit Test." Essentially, the one-way χ^2 tests how "good" the "fit" is between your data and the H_0 model. Thus, the **goodness of fit test** is another way of asking whether sample data are likely to represent the distribution of frequencies in the population as described by H_0.

Creating the Statistical Hypotheses for the One-Way Chi Square

Usually, researchers test the H_0 that there is no difference among the frequencies in the categories in the population, meaning that there is no relationship in the population. For the handedness study, say that, for the moment, we ignore that there are generally more right-handers than left-handers in the world. Therefore, if there is no relationship in the population, then our H_0 model is that the frequencies of left- and right-handed geniuses in the population are equal. There is no conventional way to write this in symbols, so simply write

H_0: all frequencies in the population are equal

This implies that if the observed frequencies (f_o) in the sample are not equal, it's because of sampling error.

The alternative hypothesis always implies that the study did demonstrate the predicted relationship, so

H_a: not all frequencies in the population are equal

For our handedness study, H_a implies that the observed frequencies represent different frequencies of left- and right-handers in the population of geniuses.

We can test only whether the sample frequencies are different from those described by H_0, so the one-way χ^2 tests *only* two-tailed hypotheses.

Computing the Expected Frequencies for the One-Way Chi Square

To compute the χ^2 statistic, we translate the H_0 model into the expected frequency for each category. The **expected frequency** is the frequency we expect in a category if the sample data perfectly represent the distribution of frequencies in the population described by the null hypothesis. The symbol for an expected frequency is f_e. Our H_0 is that the frequencies of left- and right-handedness are equal. If the sample perfectly represents this, then out of our 50 participants, 25 should be right-handed and 25 should be left-handed. Thus, the expected frequency in each category is $f_e = 25$.

For future reference, notice that f_e is actually based on a probability. If the frequencies in the population are equal, then the probability of someone's being left-handed equals the probability of someone's being right-handed. With only two possible categories, the probability of someone falling into either category is .5. Recall that probability is the same as relative frequency, so we expect .5 of all geniuses to be left-handed and .5 of all geniuses to be right-handed. Therefore, out of the 50 geniuses in our study, we expect to have .5 or 25 of them in each category. *Thus, the expected frequency in a category is equal to the probability of someone's falling into that category multiplied times the N of the study.*

When H_0 is that the frequencies in the categories are equal, the f_e will be the same in all categories, and there's a shortcut for computing it:

THE COMPUTATIONAL FORMULA FOR EACH EXPECTED FREQUENCY WHEN TESTING AN H_0 OF NO DIFFERENCE IS

$$f_e \text{ in each category} = \frac{N}{k}$$

Thus, in the handedness study, with an N of 50 and $k = 2$,

$$f_e \text{ in each category} = \frac{50}{2} = 25$$

(*Note:* Sometimes f_e may contain a decimal. For example, if we included a third category, ambidextrous, then $k = 3$, and each f_e would be 16.67.)

As in any statistical test, you must check that the study meets the assumptions of the test.

Assumptions of the One-Way Chi Square

The one-way χ^2 has five assumptions:

1. Participants are categorized along one variable having two or more categories, counting the frequency (the number) in each category.

2. Each participant can be in only one category (i.e., you cannot have repeated measures).

3. Category membership is *independent:* The fact that an individual is in a category does not influence the probability that another participant will be in any category.

4. The computations include the responses of *all* participants in the study (i.e., you would not count only the number of right-handers. In a different study, if you counted the number of people who agreed with a statement, you would also include the second category of those who disagreed).

5. So that the data meet certain theoretical rules, the f_e in any category should be at least 5.

Computing χ^2

If the sample perfectly represents the situation when H_0 is true, then each f_o "should" equal its corresponding f_e. If not, H_0 says the difference is due to sampling error. But, the greater the difference between the observed and expected frequency, the less likely it is that sampling error will produce such a difference, so the less likely it is that H_0 is true.

The χ^2 measures the differences between f_o and f_e in all categories in a study. We compute an obtained χ^2, which we'll call χ^2_{obt}.

THE COMPUTATIONAL FORMULA FOR CHI SQUARE IS

$$\chi^2_{obt} = \Sigma\left(\frac{(f_o - f_e)^2}{f_e}\right)$$

This says to find the difference between f_o and f_e in each category, square that difference, and then divide it by the f_e for that category. After doing this for all categories, sum the quantities, and the answer is χ^2_{obt}. (*Note:* Because each difference is squared, χ^2 can never be a negative number.)

For the handedness study we have these frequencies:

Handedness

Left-Handers	Right-Handers
$f_o = 10$ $f_e = 25$	$f_o = 40$ $f_e = 25$

Filling in the formula gives

$$\chi^2_{obt} = \Sigma\left(\frac{(f_o - f_e)^2}{f_e}\right) = \left(\frac{(10 - 25)^2}{25}\right) + \left(\frac{(40 - 25)^2}{25}\right)$$

After subtracting,

$$\chi^2_{obt} = \left(\frac{(-15)^2}{25}\right) + \left(\frac{(15)^2}{25}\right)$$

Squaring then gives

$$\chi^2_{obt} = \left(\frac{225}{25}\right) + \left(\frac{225}{25}\right)$$

After dividing,

$$\chi_{obt}^2 = 9 + 9 = 18.0$$

so

$$\chi_{obt}^2 = 18.0$$

Interpreting χ^2

We interpret χ_{obt}^2 by determining its location on the sampling distribution when H_0 is true. The sampling distribution of χ^2 contains all possible values of χ^2 when H_0 is true (the observed frequencies represent the model described by H_0). Thus, for the handedness study, the χ^2-distribution is the distribution of all possible values of χ^2 when there are two categories and the frequencies in the two categories in the population are equal. You can envision the χ^2-distribution as shown in Figure 15.1.

Even though the χ^2-distribution is not at all normal, it is used in the same way as previous sampling distributions. When the data perfectly represent the H_0 model so that each f_o equals its f_e, χ^2 is zero. However, sometimes by chance, the observed frequencies differ from the expected frequencies, producing a χ^2 greater than zero. The larger the χ^2, the larger the differences and then the less likely they are to occur when H_0 is true.

With chi square we again have two-tailed hypotheses but one region of rejection. If χ_{obt}^2 is larger than the critical value, then it is in the region of rejection: It occurs less than 5% of the time when H_0 is true. Then χ^2 is significant: The observed frequencies are unlikely to represent the distribution of frequencies in the population described by H_0.

To determine if χ_{obt}^2 is significant, compare it to the critical value, symbolized by χ_{crit}^2. As with previous statistics, the χ^2-distribution changes shape as the degrees of freedom change, so to find the appropriate value of χ_{crit}^2, you must first have the degrees of freedom.

FIGURE 15.1 Sampling distribution of χ^2 when H_0 is true

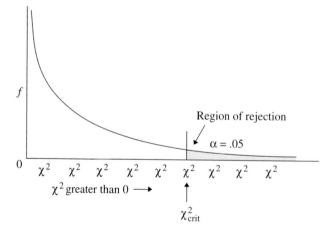

> *THE DEGREES OF FREEDOM IN A ONE-WAY CHI SQUARE EQUAL*
>
> $df = k - 1$

where k is the number of categories.

Find the critical value of χ^2 in Table 7 in Appendix B, entitled "Critical Values of Chi Square." For the handedness study, $k = 2$, so $df = 1$, and with $\alpha = .05$, the $\chi^2_{crit} = 3.84$. Our χ^2_{obt} of 18.0 is larger than this χ^2_{crit}, so the results are significant: We reject the H_0 that each f_o represents an equal frequency in the population, and report the results as

$$\chi^2(1) = 18.0, p < .05$$

Notice the df in parentheses.

We then accept the H_a that the sample represents frequencies in the population that are not equal. In fact, as in our samples, we would expect to find about 20% left-handers and 80% right-handers in the population of geniuses. We conclude that we have evidence of a relationship between the categories of handedness and the frequency with which geniuses fall in each. Then, as usual, we interpret the relationship, here attempting to explain what aspects of being left-handed and being a genius are related.

If χ^2_{obt} had not been significant, we would have failed to reject H_0 and would have no evidence—one way or the other—regarding how handedness is distributed among geniuses.

Other Uses of the Goodness of Fit Test

Instead of testing an H_0 that the frequencies in all categories are distributed equally, we can also test other H_0 models, which say that the frequencies are distributed in some other way. For example, we should not have ignored the fact that only about 10% of the general population is left-handed. The better test is to determine whether the distribution of handedness in our sample of geniuses fits this model of the distribution of handedness in the general population. The null hypothesis is now H_0: 10% left-handed, 90% right-handed. For simplicity, we can write H_a as: not H_0, implying that our data represent a population of geniuses that is not 10% left-handed and 90% right-handed.

As usual, each f_e is based on H_0. Accordingly, left-handed geniuses should occur 10% of the time, so for our 50 geniuses 10% is 5, so the $f_e = 5$. Right-handed geniuses should occur 90% of the time, and 90% of 50 is 45, so for right-handers the $f_e = 45$.

We should *not* perform two χ^2 procedures on the same data, but for the sake of illustration, we'll compare the previous handedness data and our new expected frequencies. We have

Handedness

Left-Handers	*Right-Handers*
$f_o = 10$ $f_e = 5$	$f_o = 40$ $f_e = 45$

$$k = 2$$
$$\text{Total } f_o = 50$$

Using the same formula we used previously, we have

$$\chi^2_{obt} = \Sigma\left(\frac{(f_o - f_e)^2}{f_e}\right) = \left(\frac{(10 - 5)^2}{5}\right) + \left(\frac{(40 - 45)^2}{45}\right)$$

Notice that the value of f_e is different in each fraction. Working through the formula gives

$$\chi^2_{obt} = 5.0 + .56$$

so

$$\chi^2_{obt} = 5.56$$

With $\alpha = .05$ and $k = 2$, the critical value of χ^2 is again 3.84. Because the χ^2_{obt} of 5.56 is larger than χ^2_{crit}, we reject H_0 and conclude that the observed frequencies are significantly different from what we would expect if handedness in the population of geniuses was distributed as it is in the general population. Instead, our best guess is that the population of geniuses is distributed as in our sample data, with 20% left-handers and 80% right-handers.

Additional Procedures in a One-Way Chi Square

As usual, a graph is a useful way to summarize the data, especially if there are more than two categories. Label the Y axis with the frequencies and the X axis with the categories, and then plot the f_o in each category. Figure 15.2 shows the results of the handedness study. Handedness is a nominal variable, and recall that when the X variable is nominal, you should create a *bar graph*.

Unlike ANOVA, the one-way chi square is not followed by post hoc comparisons. A significant χ^2_{obt} indicates that, across all categories, the frequencies are significantly different. Then use the observed frequency in each category to estimate the frequencies that would be found in the population. Also, there is no measure of effect size.

THE TWO-WAY CHI SQUARE: THE TEST OF INDEPENDENCE

The **two-way chi square** procedure is used when you count the frequency of category membership along *two* variables. This is similar to the complete factorial design you

FIGURE 15.2   Frequencies of left- and right-handed geniuses

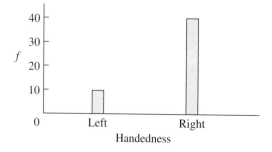

saw in the previous chapter. Depending on the number of categories in each variable, the design can be a 2×2, 2×3, 4×3, and so on. The procedure for computing χ^2 is the same regardless of the design. The assumptions of the two-way chi square are the same as for the one-way chi square.

Logic of the Two-Way Chi Square

Here is a study that calls for a two-way chi square. At one time, psychologists claimed there were two personality types: Type A and Type B. The Type A personality tends to be a very pressured, hostile individual who never seems to have enough time. The Type B personality tends not to be so time pressured, and is more relaxed and mellow. A controversy developed over whether people with Type A personalities are less healthy, especially when it comes to the big one—having heart attacks. Say that we enter this controversy by randomly selecting a sample of 80 people. Using the appropriate personality test, we determine how many are Type A and how many Type B. We then count the frequency with which Type A and Type B subjects have had heart attacks. We must also count the frequency with which Type A and Type B subjects have *not* had heart attacks (see item 4 in "Assumptions of the One-Way Chi Square"). Therefore, we have two categorical variables: personality type (A or B) and health (heart attack or no heart attack). Design Diagram 15.1 shows the layout of this study.

Although this looks like a two-way ANOVA, it is not analyzed like one. Instead of testing for main effects, *the two-way χ^2 procedure tests only what is essentially the interaction.* Recall that with an interaction, the influence of one variable *depends* on the other. The two-way χ^2 is also called the **test of independence** because it tests whether the frequency of participants falling into each category of one variable is independent of the frequency of their falling into each category on the other variable. Thus, our study will test whether the frequencies of having or not having a heart attack are independent of the frequencies of being Type A or Type B.

To understand "independence," Table 15.1 shows the data we'd get for our 80 participants if category membership on our variables was perfectly independent. Here, the frequency of having or not having a heart attack does not depend on the frequency of being Type A or Type B. Another way to view the two-way χ^2 is as a test of whether a

DESIGN DIAGRAM 15.1   A Two-Way Chi Square design Comparing Participants' Personality Type and Health

		Personality Type	
		Type A	*Type B*
Health	*Heart Attack*	f_o	f_o
	No Heart Attack	f_o	f_o

TABLE 15.1   An Example of Observed Frequencies When Personality Type and Heart Attacks Are Perfectly Independent

		Personality Type	
		Type A	Type B
Health	Heart Attack	$f_o = 20$	$f_o = 20$
	No Heart Attack	$f_o = 20$	$f_o = 20$

correlation exists between the two variables. When variables are independent, there is no correlation, and using the categories from one variable is no help in predicting the frequencies for the other variable. In Table 15.1 knowing if people are Type A or Type B does not help to predict if they do or do not have heart attacks (and the categories of heart attack and no heart attack do not help in predicting personality type).

On the other hand, Table 15.2 shows an example if category membership on the two variables was totally dependent. Here, the frequency of a heart attack or no heart attack *depends* on personality type. Likewise, a perfect correlation exists because whether people are Type A or Type B is a perfect predictor of whether or not they have had a heart attack (and vice versa).

Now say that the actual frequencies from our 80 participants are those shown in Table 15.3. There is a *degree* of dependence here because a heart attack tends to be the more frequent response for Type A personalities, while no heart attack is more frequent for Type B personalities. Therefore, there is some degree of correlation between the variables. On the one hand, we'd like to conclude that there is this relationship in the population. On the other hand, perhaps there really is no correlation in the population, but by chance we obtained frequencies that poorly represent this. The above translate into our null and alternative hypotheses. In the two-way chi square, H_0 is that category membership on one variable is independent of (not correlated with) category membership on the other variable. If the sample data look correlated, this is due to sampling error. H_a is that category membership on the two variables in the population is dependent (correlated).

TABLE 15.2   An Example of Observed Frequencies When Personality Type and Heart Attacks Are Perfectly Dependent

		Personality Type	
		Type A	Type B
Health	Heart Attack	$f_o = 40$	$f_o = 0$
	No Heart Attack	$f_o = 0$	$f_o = 40$

TABLE 15.3 Observed Frequencies as a Function of Personality Type and Health

		Personality Type		
		Type A	*Type B*	
Health	**Heart Attack**	$f_o = 25$	$f_o = 10$	row total = 35
	No Heart Attack	$f_o = 5$	$f_o = 40$	row total = 45
		column total = 30	column total = 50	total = 80 $N = 80$

Computing the Expected Frequencies in the Two-Way Chi Square

As usual, expected frequencies are based on the model described by H_0, so here we compute the f_e in each category based on the idea that the variables are independent. To see how to do this, consult Table 15.3 above. First compute the total of the observed frequencies in each *column* and in each *row*. Also, compute the total of all frequencies, which equals N. (*Note:* The sum of the row totals should equal the sum of the column totals, which equals N.)

Now compute the expected frequency in each cell. We'll begin with the logic—and the long way—of doing this. Each expected frequency is based on the probability of a participant falling into the cell if the variables are independent. First, let's compute the probability of someone being in the cell of heart attack and Type A. Out of 80 people in the study, 35 reported having had a heart attack (the row total). Thus, the probability of someone reporting a heart attack is 35/80, or .438. Similarly, the probability of someone being Type A is 30 (the column total) out of 80, or 30/80, which is .375. We want to know the probability of someone being Type A *and* reporting a heart attack. The probability of having two independent events occur simultaneously equals the probability of one event multiplied times the probability of the other. Multiplying the probability of a heart attack (.438) times the probability of being Type A (.375) gives .164. Thus, the probability of someone falling into the cell for a heart attack and Type A is .164 if the two variables are independent. Therefore, out of 80 participants, we expect .164 times 80, or 13.125 people, to be in this cell. So, the expected frequency for this cell is $f_e = 13.125$.

Luckily, there is a shortcut for calculating each f_e. Above, we multiplied 35/80 times 30/80 and then multiplied the answer times 80. The 35 is the total f_o of the *row* that contains the cell, 30 is the total f_o of the *column* that contains the cell, and 80 is the total N of the study. Using these components, we have

THE COMPUTATIONAL FORMULA FOR COMPUTING THE EXPECTED FREQUENCY IN A CELL OF A TWO-WAY CHI SQUARE IS

$$f_e = \frac{(\text{Cell's row total } f_o)(\text{Cell's column total } f_o)}{N}$$

For each cell, multiply the total observed frequencies for the row containing the cell times the total observed frequencies for the column containing the cell, and then divide by the N of the study.

Table 15.4 shows the completed computations of f_e for our study. To check your work, confirm that the sum of the f_es in each column or row equals the column or row total.

If H_0 is true and the variables are independent, then each observed frequency should equal its expected frequency. However, the larger the difference between each f_o and f_e, the less likely it is that the data represent variables that are independent. And, the larger the difference between each f_o and f_e, the larger the value of χ^2_{obt}.

Computing the Two-Way Chi Square

Compute the two-way χ^2_{obt} using the same formula used in the one-way design, which is

$$\chi^2_{obt} = \Sigma \left(\frac{(f_o - f_e)^2}{f_e} \right)$$

With the data in Table 15.4 we have

$$\chi^2_{obt} = \left(\frac{(25 - 13.125)^2}{13.125} \right) + \left(\frac{(10 - 21.875)^2}{21.875} \right) + \left(\frac{(5 - 16.875)^2}{16.875} \right)$$
$$+ \left(\frac{(40 - 28.125)^2}{28.125} \right)$$

In the numerator of each fraction is the squared quantity of the observed frequency minus the expected frequency for a cell, and in the denominator is the expected frequency for that cell. Solving each fraction gives

$$\chi^2_{obt} = 10.74 + 6.45 + 8.36 + 5.01$$

so

$$\chi^2_{obt} = 30.56$$

TABLE 15.4   Diagram Containing f_o and f_e for Each Cell

Each f_e equals the row total times the column total, divided by N.

		Personality Type		
		Type A	*Type B*	
Health	**Heart Attack**	$f_o = 25$ $f_e = 13.125$ (35)(30)/80	$f_o = 10$ $f_e = 21.875$ (35)(50)/80	row total = 35
	No Heart Attack	$f_o = 5$ $f_e = 16.875$ (45)(30)/80	$f_o = 40$ $f_e = 28.125$ (45)(50)/80	row total = 45
		column total = 30	column total = 50	total = 80

Although this is a rather large value, such answers are possible.

To evaluate χ^2_{obt}, compare it to the appropriate χ^2_{crit}. First, determine the degrees of freedom.

THE DEGREES OF FREEDOM IN A TWO-WAY CHI SQUARE EQUAL

$$df = (\text{Number of rows} - 1)(\text{Number of columns} - 1)$$

For our study, df is $(2 - 1)(2 - 1)$, or 1. Find the critical value of χ^2 in Table 7 in Appendix B. At $\alpha = .05$ and $df = 1$, the χ^2_{crit} is 3.84.

Our χ^2_{obt} of 30.56 is larger than χ^2_{crit}, so the obtained χ^2 is significant. When the two-way χ^2_{obt} is significant, the observed frequencies are unlikely to represent frequencies from variables that are independent. Therefore, we reject H_0 that the variables are independent and accept the alternative hypothesis: We are confident that the sample represents frequencies from two variables that are dependent in the population. In other words, we conclude that there is a significant correlation such that the frequency of having or not having a heart attack depends on the frequency of being Type A or Type B (and vice versa). Report the results as

$$\chi^2(1) = 30.56, p < .05$$

If χ^2_{obt} is not larger than the critical value, do not reject H_0. Then, we cannot say whether these variables are independent or not.

> *REMEMBER* A significant *two-way* χ^2 indicates that the sample data are likely to represent two variables that are dependent (or correlated) in the population.

Additional Procedures in the Two-Way Chi Square

When you find a significant two-way χ^2_{obt}, there are two procedures to apply to further describe the data: graph the data, and describe the strength of the relationship.

Graphing the Two-Way Chi Square Graph the data in a two-way chi square in the same way that we graphed a two-way interaction in the previous chapter, except that here create a *bar graph*. Frequency is plotted along the Y axis, and one of the nominal variables is plotted along the X axis. The other variable is indicated within the body of the graph. Figure 15.3 shows a bar graph for the heart attack study. It is interpreted in the same way that you interpreted the table of frequencies: Whether there is a high or low frequency of people having or not having a heart attack depends on whether we're talking about Type A or Type B personalities.

Describing the Relationship in a Two-Way Chi Square A significant two-way chi square indicates that there is a significant correlation between the two variables. To determine the size of this correlation, compute one of two new correlation coefficients, either the *phi coefficient*, or the *contingency coefficient*.

FIGURE 15.3 Frequency of heart attacks and personality type

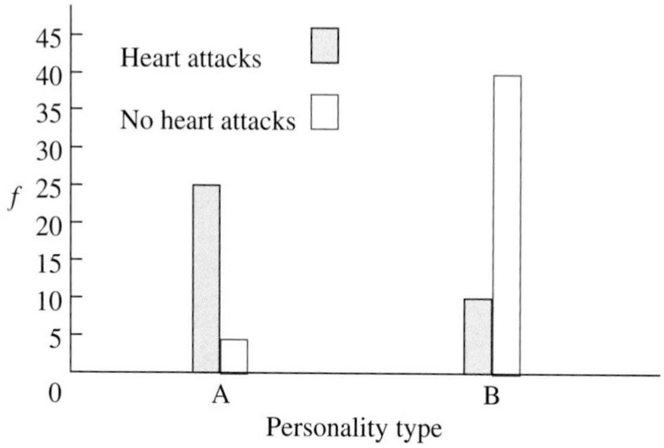

If you have performed a 2 × 2 chi square and it is significant, compute the correlation coefficient known as the **phi coefficient.** The symbol for the phi coefficient is φ, and its value can be between 0 and +1. Think of phi as comparing your data to the previous ideal situations when the variables are or are not dependent. A value of 0 indicates that the data are not dependent, producing a pattern such as shown back in Table 15.1. The larger the value of phi, however, the closer the data come to being perfectly dependent, like the pattern shown back in Table 15.2.

THE COMPUTATIONAL FORMULA FOR THE PHI COEFFICIENT IS

$$\phi = \sqrt{\frac{\chi^2_{obt}}{N}}$$

N equals the total number of participants in the study.

For the heart attack study, χ^2_{obt} was 30.56 and N was 80, so

$$\phi = \sqrt{\frac{\chi^2_{obt}}{N}} = \sqrt{\frac{30.56}{80}} = \sqrt{.382} = .62$$

Thus, on a scale of 0 to +1, where +1 indicates perfect dependence, the correlation is .62 between the frequency of heart attacks and the frequency of personality types.

But remember, the best way to describe a relationship is to think *squared correlation coefficient* and compute the proportion of variance accounted for. If you didn't take the square root in the above formula, you have ϕ^2 (phi squared). This is analogous to r^2 or η^2, indicating how much more accurately we can predict scores by using the relationship. Above, $\phi^2 = .38$, so we are 38% more accurate in predicting the frequency of heart attacks/no heart attacks when we know personality type (or vice versa).

The other correlation coefficient is the **contingency coefficient,** symbolized by C, which is used to describe a significant two-way chi square that is *not* a 2 × 2 design (it's a 2 × 3, a 3 × 3, etc.).

> *THE COMPUTATIONAL FORMULA FOR THE CONTINGENCY COEFFICIENT IS*
>
> $$C = \sqrt{\frac{\chi^2_{obt}}{N + \chi^2_{obt}}}$$

N is the number of participants in the study. Interpret C in the same way you interpret ϕ. Likewise, C^2 is analogous to ϕ^2.

NONPARAMETRIC PROCEDURES FOR RANKED DATA

In addition to chi square, we have other nonparametric procedures that are used with rank-ordered (ordinal) scores. You obtain ranked scores in a study for one of two reasons. First, sometimes you'll directly measure participants using ranked scores (where you directly assign participants a score of 1st, 2nd, etc.). Second, sometimes you'll initially measure interval or ratio scores, but they violate the assumptions of parametric procedures by not being normally distributed or not having homogeneous variance. Then you transform these scores to ranks (the highest raw score is ranked 1, the next highest score is ranked 2, and so on). Either way, you then compute one of the following nonparametric inferential statistics to determine whether there are significant differences between the conditions of your independent variable.

The Logic of Nonparametric Procedures for Ranked Data

Instead of computing the mean of each condition in the experiment, with nonparametric procedures we add the ranked scores in each condition and examine each sum of ranks. The symbol for a sum of ranks is ΣR. (First, always handle tied ranks as described in Chapter 7.) Then we compare the observed sum of ranks to an expected sum of ranks. To see the logic of this, say we have the following ranked scores:

Group 1	*Group 2*
1	2
4	3
5	6
8	7
$\Sigma R = 18$	$\Sigma R = 18$

Here, there is no difference between the groups, with each group containing both high and low ranks. When the high and low ranks are distributed equally between the two groups, the sums of ranks are equal (here, ΣR is 18 in each group). Because there is no difference between these two samples, they appear to represent the same population that contains both low ranks and high ranks. The null hypothesis always states that the populations are the same, so the fact that each ΣR is 18 supports the H_0 that we have the same population of ranks for each condition. Turning this around, we could have first determined the *expected sum of ranks* in each condition when H_0 is true (it would have been 18 here). Then, if the actual *observed sum of ranks* equals the expected, we would have evidence that H_0 is true.

But say the data had turned out differently, as here:

Group 1	Group 2
1	5
2	6
3	7
4	8

$$\Sigma R = 10 \qquad \Sigma R = 26$$

Group 1 contains all of the low ranks, and Group 2 contains all of the high ranks. Because these samples are different, they may represent two different populations. The alternative hypothesis is always that the populations are different, so here H_a says that one population contains predominantly low ranks and the other contains predominantly high ranks. Notice that when our data are consistent with H_a, the *observed* sum of ranks in each sample is different from the *expected* sum of ranks produced when H_0 is true. (Here, each ΣR is not equal to 18.)

Thus, the observed sum of ranks in each condition should equal the expected sum if H_0 is true, but the observed sum will *not* equal the expected sum if H_a is true. But there is another reason that each observed sum may not equal the expected sum: It may be that H_0 is true, but the data reflect sampling error in representing this. The larger the difference between the expected and observed sum of ranks, however, the less likely it is that this difference is due to sampling error, and the more likely it is that each sample represents a different population.

In each of the following procedures, we compute a statistic that measures the difference between the expected and the observed sum of ranks. If we can then reject H_0 and accept H_a, we are confident that the reason the observed sum is different from the expected sum is that the samples represent different populations. And, if the ranks reflect underlying interval or ratio scores, a significant difference in ranks indicates that the raw scores also differ significantly.

Choosing a Nonparametric Procedure

Each of the major parametric procedures found in previous chapters has a corresponding nonparametric procedure for ranked data. Your first task is to know which nonparametric procedure to choose for your type of research design. Table 15.5 shows the name of the nonparametric version of each parametric procedure we have discussed. The steps in calculating these nonparametric tests are described in the following sections.

TABLE 15.5 Parametric Procedures and Their Nonparametric Counterparts

Type of Design	Parametric Test	Nonparametric Test
Two independent samples	Independent-samples t-test	Mann-Whitney U or rank sums test
Two related samples	Related-samples t-test	Wilcoxon T test
Three or more independent samples	Between-subjects ANOVA (Post hoc test: protected t-test)	Kruskal-Wallis H test (Post hoc test: rank sums test)
Three or more repeated-measures samples	Within-subjects ANOVA (Post hoc test: Tukey's HSD)	Friedman χ^2 test (Post hoc test: Nemenyi's test)

Tests for Two Independent Samples: The Mann-Whitney U Test and the Rank Sums Test

There are two nonparametric procedures that are analogous to the t-test for two independent samples: the Mann-Whitney U test and the rank sums test. Both are used to test for significant differences between ranked scores measured under two conditions of an independent variable. Which test we use depends on the n in each condition.

The Mann-Whitney U Test   Perform the **Mann-Whitney U test** when the n in each condition is equal to or less than 20 and there are two independent samples of ranks. For example, say we measure the reaction times of two groups of people to different visual symbols, printed in either black ink or red ink. A raw score population of reaction times tends to be highly positively skewed, so we cannot perform the t-test. Therefore, we convert the reaction time scores to ranks. Say that our n in each condition is 5 (but we can perform this procedure when the ns are not equal). Table 15.6 gives the reaction times (measured in milliseconds) and their corresponding ranks.

TABLE 15.6 Ranked Data from Two Independent Samples

Red Symbols		Black Symbols	
Reaction Time	Ranked Score	Reaction Time	Ranked Score
540	2	760	7
480	1	890	8
600	5	1105	10
590	3	595	4
605	6	940	9
$\Sigma R = 17$		$\Sigma R = 38$	
$n = 5$		$n = 5$	

To perform the Mann-Whitney U test, do the following.

1. *Assign ranks to all scores in the experiment.* As shown in Table 15.6, assign the rank of 1 to the lowest score in the experiment, regardless of which group it is in. Assign the rank of 2 to the second-lowest score, and so on.

2. *Compute the sum of the ranks for each group.* Compute ΣR for each group, and note its n, the number of scores in the group.

3. *Compute two versions of the Mann-Whitney U.* First, compute U_1 for Group 1, using the formula

$$U_1 = (n_1)(n_2) + \frac{n_1(n_1 + 1)}{2} - \Sigma R_1$$

where n_1 is the n of Group 1, n_2 is the n of Group 2, and ΣR_1 is the sum of ranks from Group 1. Let's call the red symbol condition Group 1, so from Table 15.6, we have

$$U_1 = (5)(5) + \frac{5(5 + 1)}{2} - 17 = 40 - 17 = 23.0$$

Now compute U_2 for Group 2, using the formula

$$U_2 = (n_1)(n_2) + \frac{n_2(n_2 + 1)}{2} - \Sigma R_2$$

(*Note:* Here, we subtract the sum of ranks for Group 2.) Our black symbol condition is Group 2, so

$$U_2 = (5)(5) + \frac{5(5 + 1)}{2} - 38 = 40 - 38 = 2.0$$

4. *Determine the Mann-Whitney* U_{obt}. In a two-tailed test the value of U_{obt} equals the smaller of U_1 or U_2. In the example $U_1 = 23.0$ and $U_2 = 2.0$, so $U_{obt} = 2.0$. In a one-tailed test we predict that one of the groups has the *larger* sum of ranks. The corresponding value of U_1 or U_2 from that group becomes U_{obt}.

5. *Find the critical value of* U *in Table 8 of Appendix B entitled "Critical Values of the Mann-Whitney U."* Choose the table for either a two-tailed or a one-tailed test. Then locate U_{crit} using n_1 and n_2. For our example, with a two-tailed test and $n_1 = 5$ and $n_2 = 5$, the U_{crit} is 2.0.

6. *Compare* U_{obt} *to* U_{crit}. WATCH OUT! Unlike any statistic we've discussed, the U_{obt} is significant if it is *equal to or less than* U_{crit}. (This is because the *smaller* the U_{obt}, the more likely it is that the group represents a distribution of ranks that is different from the distribution represented by the other group.)

> **REMEMBER** The *Mann-Whitney* U_{obt} is significant if it is *less than or equal to* the critical value of U.

In the example, $U_{obt} = 2.0$ and $U_{crit} = 2.0$, so the samples of ranked scores differ significantly, representing different populations of ranks. Because the ranks reflect reaction time scores, the samples of reaction times also differ significantly and represent different populations ($p < .05$.)

7. *To describe the effect size, compute eta squared.* If U_{obt} is significant, then ignore the rule about the ns and reanalyze the data using the following rank sums test to get to η^2.

The Rank Sums Test   Perform the **rank sums test** when you have two independent samples of ranks and *either n* is greater than 20. To illustrate the calculations, we'll violate this rule and use the data from the previous reaction time study.

To perform the rank sums test, do the following.

1. *Assign ranks to the scores in the experiment.* As in Table 15.6, rank-order all scores in the experiment.

2. *Choose one group and compute the sum of the ranks.* Compute ΣR for one group, and note n, the number of scores in the group.

3. *Compute the expected sum of ranks (ΣR_{exp}) for the chosen group.* Use the formula

$$\Sigma R_{exp} = \frac{n(N + 1)}{2}$$

where n is the n of the chosen group and N is the total N of the study. We'll compute ΣR_{exp} for the red symbol group, which had $n = 5$ (N is 10). Filling in the formula, we have

$$\Sigma R_{exp} = \frac{n_1(N + 1)}{2} = \frac{5(10 + 1)}{2} = \frac{55}{2} = 27.5$$

Thus, $\Sigma R_{exp} = 27.5$.

4. *Compute the rank sums statistic, symbolized by z_{obt}.* Use the formula

$$z_{obt} = \frac{\Sigma R - \Sigma R_{exp}}{\sqrt{\dfrac{(n_1)(n_2)(N + 1)}{12}}}$$

where ΣR is the sum of the ranks for the chosen group, ΣR_{exp} is the expected sum of ranks for the chosen group, n_1 and n_2 are the ns of the two groups, and N is the total N of the study.

For our example, $\Sigma R = 17$ so

$$z_{obt} = \frac{\Sigma R - \Sigma R_{exp}}{\sqrt{\dfrac{(n_1)(n_2)(N + 1)}{12}}} = \frac{17 - 27.5}{\sqrt{\dfrac{(5)(5)(10 + 1)}{12}}}$$

$$z_{obt} = \frac{-10.5}{\sqrt{22.92}} = \frac{-10.5}{4.79} = -2.19$$

so

$$z_{obt} = -2.19$$

5. *Find the critical value of z in the z-tables (Table 1 in Appendix B).* At $\alpha = .05$, the two-tailed $z_{crit} = \pm 1.96$. (If we had predicted that the sum of ranks of the chosen group would be either only greater than or only less than the expected sum of ranks, then we would use the one-tailed value of either $+1.645$ or -1.645.)

6. *Compare z_{obt} to z_{crit}.* If the absolute value of z_{obt} is *larger* than z_{crit}, there is a significant difference between the samples. In our example $z_{obt} = -2.19$ and $z_{crit} = \pm 1.96$. Therefore, we conclude that the samples of ranked scores—as well as the underlying samples of reaction times—differ significantly ($p < .05$).

7. *Describe a significant relationship using eta squared.* Here eta squared is analogous to r_{pb}^2 (discussed in Chapter 12). Use the formula

$$\eta^2 = \frac{(z_{obt})^2}{N - 1}$$

where z_{obt} is computed in the above rank sums test and N is the total number of participants.

In the example, z_{obt} is -2.19 and N is 10, so we have $(2.19)^2/9$, or .53. Thus, the color of the symbols accounts for .53 of the variance in the ranks. Because the ranks reflect reaction time scores, *approximately* 53% of the differences in reaction time scores are associated with the color of the symbol.

The Wilcoxon *T* Test for Two Related Samples

Perform the **Wilcoxon *T* test** when you have *related samples* of ranked data. Recall that related samples occur when you match samples or have repeated measures. For example, say we perform a study similar to the previous reaction time study, but this time we measure the reaction times of the *same* participants to both the red and black symbols. Table 15.7 gives the data we might obtain.

To compute the Wilcoxon T_{obt}:

1. *Determine the difference score for each pair of scores.* Subtract the score in one condition from the score in the other for each pair. It makes no difference which score is subtracted from which, but subtract the scores the same way for all pairs.

2. *Determine the N of the nonzero difference scores.* Ignore any difference scores equal to zero, and count the number of the other difference scores. In our study there is one difference of zero (for participant 10), so $N = 9$.

3. *Assign ranks to the nonzero difference scores.* Ignore the sign ($+$ or $-$) of each difference. Assign the rank of 1 to the smallest difference, the rank of 2 to the second-smallest difference, and so on. Record the ranked scores in a column.

4. *Separate the ranks, using the sign of the difference scores.* Create two columns of ranks, labeled "$R-$" and "$R+$." The $R-$ column contains the ranks assigned to negative differences in step 3 above. The $R+$ column contains the ranks assigned to positive differences.

5. *Compute the sums of ranks for the positive and negative difference scores.* Compute ΣR for the column labeled "$R+$," and for the column labeled "$R-$."

TABLE 15.7 Data for the Wilcoxon Test for Two Related Samples

Participant	Reaction Time to Red Symbols	Reaction Time to Black Symbols	Difference	Ranked Scores	R−	R+
1	540	760	− 220	6	6	
2	580	710	− 130	4	4	
3	600	1105	− 505	9	9	
4	680	880	− 200	5	5	
5	430	500	− 70	3	3	
6	740	990	− 250	7	7	
7	600	1050	− 450	8	8	
8	690	640	+ 50	2		2
9	605	595	+ 10	1		1
10	520	520	0			
			$N = 9$		$\Sigma R = 42$	$\Sigma R = 3$

6. *Determine the Wilcoxon* T_{obt}. In the two-tailed test the Wilcoxon T_{obt} equals the *smallest* ΣR. In the example the smallest ΣR equals 3, so $T_{obt} = 3$. In the one-tailed test we predict whether most differences are positive or negative, depending on our experimental hypotheses. Thus, we predict whether R+ or R− contains the smaller ΣR, and the one we predict is smallest is T_{obt}. (If we predicted that red symbols would produce the largest reaction time scores, given the way we subtracted, we would predict that ΣR for the $R-$ column would be smaller, so T_{obt} would be 42.)

7. *Find the critical value of* T *in Table 9 of Appendix B, entitled "Critical Values of the Wilcoxon* T*."* Find T_{crit} for the appropriate α and N, the number of nonzero difference scores. In our study, $N = 9$, and $\alpha = .05$, so T_{crit} is 5.0.

8. *Compare* T_{obt} *to* T_{crit}. Again, watch out: T_{obt} is significant if it is *equal to or less than* T_{crit}. (The critical value is the largest value that our smallest ΣR can be and still reflect a significant difference.)

   REMEMBER The *Wilcoxon* T_{obt} is significant if it is *less than or equal to* the critical value of *T*.

In the example, for a two-tailed test, the T_{obt} of 3.0 is less than the T_{crit} of 5.0, so we have a significant difference. Therefore, we conclude that each sample represents a different distribution of ranks and thus a different population of reaction time scores ($p < .05$).

There is no way to compute η^2 for this procedure.

The Kruskal-Wallis *H* Test

The **Kruskal-Wallis *H* Test** is analogous to a one-way, between-subjects ANOVA for ranks. It assumes the study involves one factor involving at least *three* conditions, and each is tested using *independent samples* with at least five participants in each sample. The null hypothesis is that all conditions represent the same population of ranks.

As an example, let's explore the relationship between the independent variable of a golfer's height and the dependent variable of the distance he or she hits the ball. We will test three groups of novice golfers, classified as either short, medium, or tall. We will measure the distance each person drives the ball in meters. However, say that we cannot assume that the distance scores have homogeneous variance, so we dare not perform ANOVA. Instead, we rank the scores and perform the Kruskal-Wallis *H* test. The data are shown in Table 15.8.

To compute the Kruskal-Wallis *H*:

1. *Assign ranks, using all scores in the experiment.* Assign the rank of 1 to the lowest score in the experiment, the rank of 2 to the second-lowest score, and so on.

2. *Compute the sum of the ranks in each condition.* Compute the ΣR in each column. Also note the *n* in each condition.

3. *Compute the sum of squares between groups* (SS_{bn}). Use the formula

$$SS_{bn} = \frac{(\Sigma R_1)^2}{n_1} + \frac{(\Sigma R_2)^2}{n_2} + \cdots + \frac{(\Sigma R_k)^2}{n_k}$$

For our example,

$$SS_{bn} = \frac{(21)^2}{5} + \frac{(35)^2}{5} + \frac{(64)^2}{5} = 88.2 + 245 + 819.2$$

so

$$SS_{bn} = 1152.4.$$

4. *Compute* H_{obt}. Use the formula

$$H_{obt} = \left(\frac{12}{N(N + 1)}\right)(SS_{bn}) - 3(N + 1)$$

TABLE 15.8   Data for the Kruskal-Wallis *H* Test

	Height				
Short		**Medium**		**Tall**	
Score	*Rank*	*Score*	*Rank*	*Score*	*Rank*
10	2	24	3	68	14
28	6	27	5	71	15
26	4	35	7	57	10
39	8	44	9	60	12
6	1	58	11	62	13
$\Sigma R_1 = 21$		$\Sigma R_2 = 35$		$\Sigma R_3 = 64$	
$n_1 = 5$		$n_2 = 5$		$n_3 = 5$	$N = 15$

where N is the total N of the study, and SS_{bn} is computed as above.
In the example

$$H_{obt} = \left(\frac{12}{15(15 + 1)}\right)(1152.4) - 3(15 + 1) = (.05)(1152.4) - 48$$

$$H_{obt} = 57.62 - 48$$

so

$$H_{obt} = 9.62$$

5. *Find the critical value of* H *in the* χ^2 *tables* (Table 7 in Appendix B). Values of H have the same sampling distribution as χ^2. The degrees of freedom are

$$df = k - 1$$

where k is the number of levels in the factor.
In the example, k is 3, so for $\alpha = .05$ and $df = 2$, χ^2_{crit} is 5.99.

6. *Compare the obtained value of* H *to the critical value of* χ^2. The H_{obt} is significant if it is *larger* than the critical value. Above, the H_{obt} of 9.62 is larger than the χ^2_{crit} of 5.99, so it is significant. This means that at least two samples represent different populations of ranks. Because the distance participants hit the ball underlies each rank, we conclude that at least two of the populations of distances for short, medium, and tall golfers are not the same ($p < .05$).

7. *Perform post hoc comparisons using the rank sums test.* When H_{obt} is significant, determine which specific conditions differ by performing the rank sums test on every pair of conditions. This is analogous to Fisher's protected t-test (discussed in Chapter 13), and it is used regardless of the n in each group. For each pair, treat the two conditions being compared as if they comprised the entire study: re-rank the scores using only the two conditions being compared and then perform the previous rank sums test.

In the example, comparing short versus medium golfers produces a z_{obt} of 1.36, comparing short with tall golfers produces a z_{obt} of 2.62, and comparing medium versus tall golfers produces a z_{obt} of 2.40. With $\alpha = .05$, from the z-tables z_{crit} is ±1.96. Therefore, the scores of short and medium participants are not significantly different, but they both differ significantly from those in the tall condition. We conclude that tall golfers produce one population of distances that is different from the population for short and medium golfers.

8. *If* H$_{obt}$ *is significant, compute eta squared.* Use the formula

$$\eta^2 = \frac{H_{obt}}{N - 1}$$

where H_{obt} is computed in the Kruskal-Wallis test and N is the total number of participants. Above, $H_{obt} = 9.62$ and $N = 15$, so $\eta^2 = 9.62/14$, or .69. Therefore, the variable of a player's height accounts for approximately 69% of the variance in the distance scores.

The Friedman χ^2 Test

The **Friedman χ^2 test** is analogous to a one-way, within-subjects ANOVA for ranks. It assumes that the study involves one factor having at least *three* levels, and that the samples in each are *related* (because of either *matching* or *repeated measures*). If there are only three levels of the factor, there must be at least ten participants in the study. If there are only four levels of the factor, there must be at least five participants.

As an example say that we consider the three teaching styles of Dr. Highman, Dr. Shyman, and Dr. Whyman. A sample of students who have taken courses from all three instructors is repeatedly measured, with each student rank-ordering the three instructors. Table 15.9 shows the data.

To perform the Friedman χ^2 test:

1. Assign ranks within the scores of each participant. If the scores are not already ranks, assign the rank of 1 to the lowest score received by Participant 1, assign the rank of 2 to the second-lowest score received by Participant 1, and so on. Repeat the process for each participant.

2. Compute the sum of the ranks in each condition. Find ΣR in each column.

3. Compute the sum of squares between groups (SS_{bn}). Use the formula

$$SS_{bn} = (\Sigma R_1)^2 + (\Sigma R_2)^2 + \cdots + (\Sigma R_k)^2$$

In the example

$$SS_{bn} = (12)^2 + (23)^2 + (25)^2$$

so

$$SS_{bn} = 1298$$

4. Compute the Friedman χ^2 statistic. Use the formula

$$\chi^2_{obt} = \left(\frac{12}{(k)(N)(k+1)} \right)(SS_{bn}) - 3(N)(k+1)$$

TABLE 15.9 Data for the Friedman Test

	Rankings for Three Instructors		
Participant	*Dr. Highman*	*Dr. Shyman*	*Dr. Whyman*
1	1	2	3
2	1	3	2
3	1	2	3
4	1	3	2
5	2	1	3
6	1	3	2
7	1	2	3
8	1	3	2
9	1	3	2
10	2	1	3
$N = 10$	$\Sigma R_1 = 12$	$\Sigma R_2 = 23$	$\Sigma R_3 = 25$

where N is the number of participants and k is the number of levels of the factor.

In the example

$$\chi^2_{obt} = \left(\frac{12}{(3)(10)(3 + 1)}\right)(1298) - 3(10)(3 + 1)$$

$$\chi^2_{obt} = (.10)(1298) - 120 = 129.8 - 120$$

so

$$\chi^2_{obt} = 9.80$$

5. *Find the critical value of χ^2 in the χ^2-tables* (Table 7 in Appendix B). The degrees of freedom are

$$df = k - 1$$

where k is the number of levels in the factor.

For the example, $k = 3$, so for $df = 2$ and $\alpha = .05$, the critical value is 5.99.

6. *Compare χ^2_{obt} to the critical value of χ^2.* If χ^2_{obt} is larger than χ^2_{crit}, the results are significant. Our χ^2_{obt} of 9.80 is larger than the χ^2_{crit} of 5.99, so our results are significant. Thus, we conclude that at least two of the samples represent different populations ($p < .05$).

7. *When the χ^2_{obt} is significant, perform post hoc comparisons using **Nemenyi's procedure.*** This procedure is analogous to Tukey's *HSD* procedure (in Chapter 13). Compute a value that is the *critical difference.* Any two conditions that differ by more than this critical difference are significantly different. To perform Nemenyi's procedure, follow these steps.

a. *Compute the critical difference.* Use the formula

$$\text{Critical difference} = \sqrt{\left(\frac{k(k + 1)}{6(N)}\right)(\chi^2_{crit})}$$

where k is the number of levels of the factor, N is the number of participants (or rows), and χ^2_{crit} is the critical value used to test the Friedman χ^2.

In the example $\chi^2_{crit} = 5.99$, $k = 3$, and $N = 10$, so

$$\text{Critical difference} = \sqrt{\left(\frac{k(k + 1)}{6(N)}\right)(\chi^2_{crit})} = \sqrt{\left(\frac{3(3 + 1)}{6(10)}\right)(5.99)}$$

$$\text{Critical difference} = \sqrt{(.2)(5.99)} = \sqrt{1.198} = 1.09$$

Critical difference is ± 1.09.

b. *Compute the mean rank for each condition.* For each condition divide the sum of ranks (ΣR) by the number of participants. In the example the sums of ranks are 12, 23, and 25 in the three conditions, and N is 10. Therefore, the mean ranks are 1.2, 2.3, and 2.5 for Highman, Shyman, and Whyman, respectively.

c. *Compute the differences between all pairs of mean ranks.* Subtract each mean rank from the other mean ranks. Any absolute difference between two means that is greater than the critical difference indicates that the two conditions differ significantly. In the example the differences between the mean ranks for Dr. Highman and the other two instructors are 1.10 and 1.30, respectively, and the difference between Shyman and Whyman is .20. The critical difference is 1.09, so only Dr. Highman's ranking is significantly different from those of the other two instructors. Thus, we conclude that if the entire population were to rank the three instructors, Dr. Highman would be ranked superior to the other two instructors!

8. *Describe a significant relationship using eta squared.* Use the formula

$$\eta^2 = \frac{\chi^2_{obt}}{(N)(k) - 1}$$

where χ^2_{obt} is computed in the Friedman χ^2 test, N is the number of participants, and k is the number of levels of the factor. For the example

$$\eta^2 = \frac{\chi^2_{obt}}{(N)(k) - 1} = \frac{9.80}{(10)(3) - 1} = \frac{9.80}{30 - 1} = .34$$

Thus, the instructor variable accounts for 34% of the variability in rankings.

PUTTING IT ALL TOGETHER

Congratulations! You have read an entire statistics book and that's an accomplishment! You should be proud of the sophisticated level of your knowledge because you are now familiar with the vast majority of statistical procedures used in psychology and other behavioral sciences. Even if you someday go to graduate school, you'll find that there is little in the way of basics for you to learn.

CHAPTER SUMMARY

1. *Nonparametric procedures* are used when data do not meet the assumptions of parametric procedures. Nonparametric procedures are inherently less powerful than parametric procedures.

2. *Chi square* (χ^2) is used with one or more nominal (categorical) variables, and the data are the frequencies with which participants fall into each category.

3. The *one-way* χ^2 determines whether the observed frequencies fit the model described by H_0. A significant χ^2_{obt} indicates that the observed frequencies are unlikely to represent the distribution of frequencies in the population described by H_0.

4. In the *two-way* χ^2, H_0 states that the frequency of participants falling into each category of one variable is independent of their frequency of falling into each category of the other variable. A significant χ^2_{obt} indicates that the observed frequencies are unlikely to represent variables that are independent in the population. Instead, we conclude that the two variables are dependent, or correlated.

5. In a significant 2×2 chi square, the strength of the relationship is described by the *phi correlation coefficient* (ϕ). In a significant two-way chi square that is not

a 2 × 2, the strength of the relationship is described by the *contingency coefficient* (C). The larger these coefficients are, the closer the variables are to being perfectly dependent, or correlated. Squaring ϕ or C gives the proportion of variance accounted for, which indicates how much more accurately the frequencies of category membership on one variable can be predicted by knowing category membership on the other variable.

6. There are two nonparametric versions of the independent-samples *t*-test for ranks. The *Mann-Whitney* U *test* is performed when the *n* in each condition is less than 20. The *rank sums test* is performed when the *n* in either condition is greater than 20.

7. The *Wilcoxon* T *test* is the nonparametric equivalent of the related-samples *t*-test for ranks.

8. The *Kruskal-Wallis* H *test* is the nonparametric equivalent of the one-way, between-subjects ANOVA for ranks. The rank sums test is the post hoc test for identifying the specific conditions that differ.

9. The *Friedman* χ^2 *test* is the nonparametric equivalent of the one-way, within-subjects ANOVA for ranks. *Nemenyi's test* is the post hoc test for identifying the specific conditions that differ.

10. *Eta squared* describes the relationship found in experiments involving ranked data.

KEY TERMS: Can You Define the Following?

f_o f_e χ^2_{obt} χ^2_{crit} ϕ ϕ^2 C C^2

chi square procedure *404*
contingency coefficient *416*
expected frequency *406*
Friedman chi square test *426*
goodness of fit test *405*
Kruskal-Wallis *H* test *423*
Mann-Whitney *U* test *419*
Nemenyi's procedure *427*

nonparametric statistics *403*
observed frequency *405*
one-way chi square *404*
phi coefficient *416*
rank sums test *421*
test of independence *411*
two-way chi square *410*
Wilcoxon *T* test *422*

REVIEW QUESTIONS

(Answers for odd-numbered questions are in Appendix C.)

1. What do all nonparametric procedures have in common with all parametric procedures?

2. (a) Which variable in an experiment determines whether to use parametric or nonparametric procedures? (b) When should you turn to nonparametric procedures?

3. (a) With which two scales of measurement do you use nonparametric procedures? (b) What two things can be "wrong" with interval/ratio scores that ultimately lead you to use nonparametric procedures for ranked data?

4. (a) Why, if possible, should a researcher design a study so that the data meet the assumptions of a parametric procedure? (b) Why shouldn't you use parametric procedures for data that clearly violate their assumptions?

5. (a) When do you use the chi square? (b) When do you use the one-way chi square? (c) When do you use the two-way chi square?

6. (a) What is the symbol for observed frequency? What does it mean? (b) What is the symbol for expected frequency? What does it mean?

7. What does a significant one-way chi square indicate?

8. What does a significant two-way chi square indicate?

9. (a) What is the phi coefficient, and when is it used? (b) What does the squared phi coefficient indicate? (c) What is the contingency coefficient, and when is it used? (d) What does the squared contingency coefficient indicate?

10. What is the nonparametric version of each of the following? (a) A one-way, between-subjects ANOVA (b) An independent-samples t-test ($n < 20$) (c) A related-samples t-test (d) An independent-samples t-test ($n > 20$) (e) A one-way, within-subjects ANOVA (f) Fisher's protected t-test (g) Tukey's HSD test

APPLICATION QUESTIONS

11. In the general population, the distribution of political party affiliation is 30% Republican, 55% Democratic, and 15% other. To determine whether this distribution is also found among the elderly, in a sample of 100 senior citizens, we find 18 Republicans, 64 Democrats, and 18 other. (a) What are H_0 and H_a? (b) What is f_e for each group? (c) Compute χ^2_{obt}. (d) With $\alpha = .05$, what do you conclude about party affiliation in the population of senior citizens?

12. A survey finds that, given the choice, 34 females prefer males much taller than themselves, and 55 females prefer males only slightly taller than themselves. (a) What are H_0 and H_a? (b) With $\alpha = .05$, what would you conclude about the preference of females in the population? (c) Describe how you would graph these results.

13. Foofy counts the students who like Professor Demented and those who like Professor Randomsampler. She then performs a one-way χ^2 to determine if there is a significant difference between the frequency with which students like each professor. (a) Why is this approach incorrect? (b) How should she analyze the data?

14. The following data reflect the frequency with which people voted in the last election and were satisfied with the officials elected:

		Satisfied	
		Yes	*No*
Voted	*Yes*	48	35
	No	33	52

(a) What are H_0 and H_a? (b) What is f_e in each cell? (c) Compute χ^2_{obt}. (d) With $\alpha = .05$, what do you conclude about the correlation between these variables? (e) How consistent is this relationship?

15. A study determines the frequency of the different political party affiliations for male and female senior citizens. The following data are obtained:

Affiliation

		Republican	Democrat	Other
Gender	**Male**	18	43	14
	Female	39	23	18

(a) What are H_0 and H_a? (b) What is f_e in each cell? (c) Compute χ^2_{obt}. (d) With $\alpha = .05$, what do you conclude about gender and party affiliation in the population of senior citizens? (e) How consistent is this relationship?

16. Select the statistical procedure to use in each of the following: (a) A study of the effects of a new pain reliever on rankings of the emotional content of words describing pain. A randomly selected group of people is tested before and after administration of the drug. (b) A study of the effects of eight different colors of spaghetti sauce on tastiness scores. A different random sample of people tastes each color of sauce, and then the tastiness scores are ranked. (c) A study of the effects of increasing amounts of alcohol consumption on reaction-time scores. The scores are ranked, and the same group of participants is tested after 1, 3, and 5 drinks. (d) A study of two levels of the variable of family income. Two random samples of scores are used to rank-order the percentage of the family's income that was spent on clothing last year.

17. What is the basic logic underlying the testing of H_0 in all nonparametric procedures for ranked data?

18. We wish to compare the attitude scores of people when tested in the morning to their scores when tested in the afternoon. From a morning and an afternoon attitude test, we obtain the following interval data. We do not have homogeneous variance. With $\alpha = .05$, determine if there is a significant difference in scores as a function of testing times.

Morning	Afternoon
14	36
18	31
20	19
28	48
3	10
34	49
20	20
24	29

19. A study compares the maturity level of a group of students who have completed statistics to a group of students who have not. Maturity scores for college

students tend to be skewed. For the following interval scores, answer the questions below.

Nonstatistics	Statistics
43	51
52	58
65	72
23	81
31	92
36	64

(a) Do the groups differ significantly ($\alpha = .05$)? (b) What do you conclude about maturity scores you expect to find in the population of students who have taken statistics and in the population that hasn't?

20. A therapist evaluates the progress of a sample in a new treatment program after one month, after two months, and again after three months. Such progress data don't have homogeneous variance. (a) What statistical procedure should be used to analyze the data? Why? (b) What is the first thing the therapist must do? (c) If the results are significant, what should the therapist then do? (d) Ultimately, what will the therapist be able to identify?

21. An investigator evaluated the effectiveness of a therapy on three types of patients. She collected the following improvement ratings. (In the population these data form highly skewed distributions.)

Depressed	Manic	Schizophrenic
16	7	13
11	9	6
12	6	10
20	4	15
21	8	9

(a) Which procedure should be used to analyze these data? Why? (b) What should the investigator do first to the data? (c) If the results are significant, what should she do next? (d) Ultimately, what conclusions can be drawn from this study?

22. A research article indicates that the Friedman test was significant ($p < .01$). (a) What does this test indicate about the design of the study? (b) What does it indicate about the raw scores? (c) What two procedures do you also expect to be reported? (d) What will you conclude about the relationship?

23. A research article indicates that the Wilcoxon T test was significant ($p < .05$). (a) What does this test indicate about the design of the study? (b) What does it indicate about the raw scores? (c) What will you conclude about the relationship here?

24. Thinking back on the previous few chapters, what three aspects of your independent variable(s) and one aspect of your dependent variable determine the specific inferential procedure to perform in a particular experiment?

25. To study nonverbal communication, you show participants a picture of a person either smiling, frowning, or smirking. For each, you ask them to indicate whether the pictured person was either happy or sad. (a) What are the factor(s) and level(s) in this design, and how will you analyze the results? (b) What potential flaw is built into the study in terms of the statistics you must use with such data? (c) When would this flaw be a concern? (d) How can you eliminate the flaw?

26. If a researcher summarizes scores using the mode and computes a chi square, how has he or she measured the dependent variable?

SUMMARY OF FORMULAS

A. SUMMARY OF CHI SQUARE FORMULAS

1. *The computational formula for chi square is*

$$\chi^2_{obt} = \Sigma\left(\frac{(f_o - f_e)^2}{f_e}\right)$$

where f_o is the observed frequency in a cell and f_e is the expected frequency in a cell.

a. Computing expected frequency

   (1) *In a one-way chi square, when testing an H_0 of no difference, the computational formula for each expected frequency is*

$$f_e \text{ in each category} = \frac{N}{k}$$

   where N is the total N in the study and k is the number of categories.

   (2) *In a two-way chi square the computational formula for finding the expected frequency in each cell is*

$$f_e = \frac{(\text{Cell's row total } f_o)(\text{Cell's column total } f_o)}{N}$$

b. Critical values of χ^2 are found in Table 7 of Appendix B.

   (1) *In a one-way chi square, the degrees of freedom is*

$$df = k - 1$$

   where k is the number of categories in the variable.

   (2) *In a two-way chi square, the degrees of freedom is*

$$df = (\text{Number of rows} - 1)(\text{Number of columns} - 1)$$

2. *The computational formula for the phi coefficient is*

$$\phi = \sqrt{\frac{\chi^2_{obt}}{N}}$$

where N is the total number of subjects in the study.

3. *The computational formula for the contingency coefficient* (C) *is*

$$C = \sqrt{\frac{\chi^2_{obt}}{N + \chi^2_{obt}}}$$

where N is the total number of subjects in the study.

B. SUMMARY OF NONPARAMETRIC FORMULAS

1. *For two independent samples*
   a. *Mann-Whitney* U: For two independent samples when both ns are less than or equal to 20, the computational formula is

$$U_1 = (n_1)(n_2) + \frac{n_1(n_1 + 1)}{2} - \Sigma R_1$$

and

$$U_2 = (n_1)(n_2) + \frac{n_2(n_2 + 1)}{2} - \Sigma R_2$$

where n_1 and n_2 are the ns of the groups. After ranks are assigned based on all scores, ΣR_1 is the sum of ranks in Group 1, and ΣR_2 is the sum of ranks in Group 2. In a two-tailed test U_{obt} equals the *smaller* of U_1 or U_2. In a one-tailed test the value of U_1 or U_2 from the group predicted to have the largest sum of ranks is U_{obt}. Critical values of U are found in Table 8 of Appendix B. U_{obt} is significant if it is *equal to or less than* the critical value.
   b. *Rank sums test:* For two independent samples when either n is greater than 20, the computational formula is

$$z_{obt} = \frac{\Sigma R - \Sigma R_{exp}}{\sqrt{\frac{(n_1)(n_2)(N + 1)}{12}}}$$

Where n_1 and n_2 are the ns of the two groups, and N is the total N. After ranks are assigned based on all scores, ΣR is the sum of the ranks for the chosen group. ΣR_{exp} is the expected sum of ranks for the chosen group, found using the formula

$$\Sigma R_{exp} = \frac{n(N + 1)}{2}$$

where n is the n of the chosen group. Critical values of z are found in Table 1 of Appendix B.

  c. *Eta squared is computed using the formula*

$$\eta^2 = \frac{(z_{obt})^2}{N - 1}$$

2. *Wilcoxon* T: *For two related samples the computational formula is*

$$T_{obt} = \Sigma R$$

After the difference scores are found and assigned ranks, in the two-tailed test ΣR is the smaller of the sum of ranks for the positive difference scores or the sum of ranks for the negative difference scores. In the one-tailed test ΣR is the sum of ranks that is predicted to be the smallest. Critical values of T are found in Table 9 of Appendix B, where N is the number of nonzero difference scores. T is significant if it is *equal to or less than* the critical value.

3. *Kruskal-Wallis* H *test: For three or more independent samples, the computational formula is*

$$H_{obt} = \left(\frac{12}{N(N + 1)}\right)(SS_{bn}) - 3(N + 1)$$

where N is the total number of participants. After ranks are assigned using all scores, SS_{bn} is found using the formula

$$SS_{bn} = \frac{(\Sigma R_1)^2}{n_1} + \frac{(\Sigma R_2)^2}{n_2} + \cdots + \frac{(\Sigma R_k)^2}{n_k}$$

where each n is the number of scores in a level, each ΣR is the sum of ranks for that level, and k is the number of levels of the factor.

  Critical values of H are found in Table 7 of Appendix B, for $df = k - 1$, where k is the number of levels in the factor.
  a. When H_{obt} is significant, post hoc comparisons are performed using the rank sums test, regardless of the size of n.
  b. Eta squared is computed using the formula

$$\eta^2 = \frac{H_{obt}}{N - 1}$$

4. *Friedman* χ^2 *test: For three or more repeated measures samples, the computational formula is*

$$\chi^2_{obt} = \left(\frac{12}{(k)(N)(k + 1)}\right)(SS_{bn}) - 3(N)(k + 1)$$

where N is the total number of participants and k is the number of levels of the factor. After ranks are assigned within the scores of each participant, SS_{bn} is found using the formula

$$SS_{bn} = (\Sigma R_1)^2 + (\Sigma R_2)^2 + \cdots + (\Sigma R_k)^2$$

where each $(\Sigma R)^2$ is the squared sum of ranks for a level. Critical values of χ^2 are found in Table 7 of Appendix B, for $df = k - 1$, where k is the number of levels in the factor.

a. When the Friedman χ^2 is significant, post hoc comparisons are performed using Nemenyi's procedure.
   (1) Compute the critical difference using the formula

   $$\text{Critical difference} = \sqrt{\left(\frac{k(k+1)}{6(N)}\right)(\chi^2_{\text{crit}})}$$

   where k is the number of levels of the factor and N is the number of participants. χ^2_{crit} is the critical value of χ^2 for the appropriate α at $df = k - 1$.
   (2) Compute the mean rank in each condition as $\Sigma R/n$.
   (3) Any two mean ranks that differ by more than the critical difference are significantly different.
b. Eta squared is found using the formula

   $$\eta^2 = \frac{\chi^2_{\text{obt}}}{(N)(k) - 1}$$

ADDITIONAL STATISTICAL FORMULAS

A.1: COMPUTING PERCENTILES

This section shows how to calculate either the percentile of a particular score, or the score at a particular percentile, as discussed in Chapter 3. To understand these formulas, you must first understand how to create grouped frequency distributions.

CREATING GROUPED FREQUENCY DISTRIBUTIONS

In a grouped distribution, different scores are grouped together, and then the total f, $rel.$ f, or cf of each group is reported. For example, say that we measured the level of anxiety exhibited by 25 participants, obtaining the following scores:

03	4	4	18	4	28	26	41	5	40	4	6	5
18	22	3	17	12	26	4	20	8	15	38	36	

First, determine the number of scores the data span (their "range"). You can count them on your fingers, or you can calculate the number spanned between any two scores using this formula:

Number of scores = (High score − Low score) + 1

Thus, there is a span of 39 values between 41 and 3, inclusive.

Next, decide how many scores to put into each group, with the same range of scores in each. You can operate as if the sample contained a wider range of scores than was actually in the data. For example, we'll operate as if these scores are from 0 to 44, spanning 45 scores, inclusive. This allows nine groups, each spanning 5 scores, resulting in the grouped distribution shown in Table A.1.

The group labeled "0–4" contains the scores 0, 1, 2, 3, and 4, while "5–9" contains 5 through 9, and so on. Each group is called a **class interval,** and the number of scores spanned by an interval is called the **interval size.** Here, the interval size is 5, so each group includes five scores. Choose an interval size that is easy to work with (such as 2, 5, 10, or 20), and that results in between 8 and 18 intervals. Also, an interval size that is an odd number is preferable, because later we'll use the middle score of the interval and an even number produces a cumbersome score containing a fraction, but an odd number does not.

Notice several things about the score column in Table A.1. First, each interval is labeled with the low score on the left. Second, the low score in each interval is a whole-number multiple of the interval size of 5. Third, every class interval is the same size. (Even though the highest score in the data is only 41, we have the complete interval of 40–44.) Finally, the intervals are arranged so that higher scores are located toward the top of the column.

To complete the table, find the f for each class interval by summing the individual frequencies of all scores in the group. In the example data there were no scores of 0, 1, or 2, but there were two 3s and five 4s. Thus, the 0–4 interval has a total f of 7. For the 5–9 interval, there were two 5s, one 6, no 7s, one 8, and no 9s, so the 5–9 interval has a total f of 4. And so on.

TABLE A.1 Grouped Distribution
Showing *f, rel. f,* and *cf* for Each
Group of Anxiety Scores

*The column on the left identifies the lowest
and highest score in each class interval.*

Anxiety Scores	f	rel. f	cf
40–44	2	.08	25
35–39	2	.08	23
30–34	0	.00	21
25–29	3	.12	21
20–24	2	.08	18
15–19	4	.16	16
10–14	1	.04	12
5– 9	4	.16	11
0– 4	7	.28	7
	Total: 25	1.00	

Compute the relative frequency for each interval by dividing the *f* for the interval by *N*. Remember, *N* is the total number of raw scores (here, 25), not the number of class intervals. Thus, for the 0–4 interval, *rel. f* equals 7/25, or .28.

Compute the cumulative frequency for each interval by counting the number of scores that are at or below the *highest* score in the interval. Begin with the lowest interval. There are 7 scores at 4 or below, so the *cf* for interval 0–4 is 7. Next, *f* is 4 for the scores between 5 and 9, and adding the 7 scores below the interval produces a *cf* of 11 for the interval 5–9. And so on.

Real versus Apparent Limits

What if one of the scores in the above example were 4.6? This score seems too large for the 0–4 interval, but too small for the 5–9 interval. To allow for such scores, we consider the "real limits" of each interval. These are different from the upper and lower numbers of each interval seen in the frequency table, which are called the *apparent upper limit* and the *apparent lower limit,* respectively. As in Table A.2, the apparent limits for each interval imply corresponding real limits. Thus, for example, the interval having the apparent limits of 40–44 actually contains any score between the real limits of 39.5 and 44.5.

Note that (1) each real limit is halfway between the lower apparent limit of one interval and the upper apparent limit of the interval below it, and (2) the lower real limit of one interval is always the same number as the upper real limit of the interval below it. Thus, 4.5 is halfway between 4 and 5, so 4.5 is the lower real limit of the 5–9 interval and the upper real limit of the 0–4 interval. Also, the difference between the lower real limit and the upper real limit equals the interval size ($9.5 - 4.5 = 5$).

TABLE A.2 Real and Apparent Limits

The apparent limits in the column on the left
imply the real limits in the column on the right.

Apparent Limits (Lower–Upper)	Imply	Real Limits (Lower–Upper)
40–44	→	39.5–44.5
35–39	→	34.5–39.5
30–34	→	29.5–34.5
25–29	→	24.5–29.5
20–24	→	19.5–24.5
15–19	→	14.5–19.5
10–14	→	9.5–14.5
5– 9	→	4.5– 9.5
0– 4	→	−0.5– 4.5

Real limits eliminate the gaps between intervals, so now a score such as 4.6 falls into the interval 5–9 because it falls between 4.5 and 9.5. If scores equal a real limit (such as two scores of 4.5), put half in the lower interval (between − 0.5 and 4.5) and half in the upper interval (4.5–9.5). If one such score is left over, flip a coin to pick the interval.

The principle of real limits also applies to ungrouped data. Implicitly, each individual score is a class interval with an interval size of 1. Thus, when a score in an ungrouped distribution is labeled 6, this is both the upper and the lower *apparent* limits. However, the lower *real* limit for this interval is 5.5, and the upper *real* limit is 6.5.

Graphing Grouped Distributions

Grouped distributions are graphed in the same way as ungrouped distributions, *except* that the X axis is labeled differently. To graph simple frequency or relative frequency, label the X axis using the *midpoint* of each class interval. To find the midpoint, multiply .5 times the interval size, and add the result to the lower real limit. Above, the interval size was 5, which multiplied times .5 is 2.5. For the 0–4 interval, the lower real limit was −.5. Adding 2.5 to −.5 yields 2. Thus, the score of 2 on the X axis identifies the class interval of 0–4. Similarly, for the 5–9 interval, 2.5 plus 4.5 is 7, so this interval is identified using 7.

As usual, for nominal or ordinal scores create a bar graph, and for interval or ratio scores create a histogram or polygon. Figure A.1 presents a histogram and polygon for the grouped distribution from Table A.1. The height of each data point or bar corresponds to the total simple frequency of all scores in the class interval. Plot a relative frequency distribution in the same way, except that the Y axis is labeled in increments between 0 and 1.

Figure A.2 presents the cumulative frequency polygon for the preceding data. With a grouped cumulative frequency distribution, the X axis is labeled using the *upper real limit* of each interval. Thus, the 0–4 interval is represented at 4.5 on the X axis, and the 5–9 interval is at 9.5. Then each data point is the *cf* for a group.

FIGURE A.1   Grouped frequency polygon and histogram

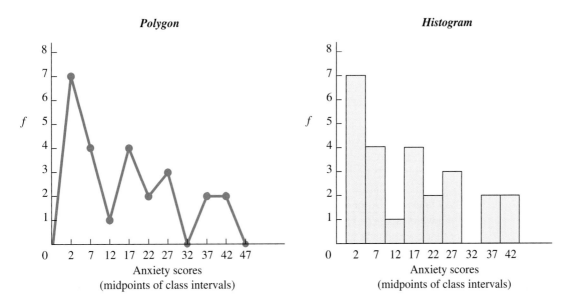

FIGURE A.2   Grouped cumulative frequency polygon

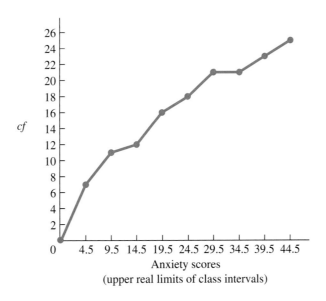

DETERMINING THE SCORE AT A GIVEN PERCENTILE

Percentiles are computed from a cumulative frequency distribution. Here's a new example: Say that we measure the number of minutes required for a rat to find the end of a maze. The ungrouped cumulative frequency distribution for these data is presented in Table A.3.

TABLE A.3 Cumulative Frequency Distribution of Maze-Running Times for Laboratory Rats

Score	f	cf
5	1	10
4	1	9
3	2	8
2	3	6
1	3	3
	$N = 10$	

Say that we seek the score at the 50th percentile, asking "50% of the scores are at or below which score?" To find the score at a particular percentile, find the score that has a *cf* that corresponds to that particular percentage of *N*. Here, we are looking for the score with a *cf* that is 50% of *N*. Because *N* is 10, the score at the 50th percentile is the score having a *cf* of 5. But, the score of 1 has a *cf* of only 3, and the score of 2 has a *cf* of 6. Therefore, the score having a *cf* of 5 is somewhere between 1 and 2.

To compute a percentile, treat the scores as if they were from a continuous variable that allows decimals. Then look at the real limits. For the scores of 1 and 2, we see

Scores	f	cf
1.5–2.5	3	6
.5–1.5	3	3

Because the score we seek has a *cf* of 5, the score must be above 1.5 (which has a *cf* of only 3), so the score is in the interval 1.5–2.5. Thus, we'll proceed into this interval far enough beyond 1.5 to accumulate a *cf* of 5. We assume that the frequency in an interval is evenly spread throughout the interval, so that, for example, if we go to a score that is halfway between the upper and lower limits, we accumulate one-half of the frequency in the interval. Conversely, if we accumulate one-half of the frequency in an interval, we're at the score that is halfway between the upper and lower limits. Above, the score we seek has a *cf* of 5, so we want the score above 1.5 that increases the *cf* by 2. If we went to a score of 2.5, we would accumulate an additional *f* of 3, increasing the *cf* by 3, which is too much. We want an *f* of 2 out of the 3, so we want two-thirds of the total frequency in the interval. To accumulate two-thirds of the frequency in the interval, we go to the score that is two-thirds of the way between the lower and upper limits. To find the score that is two-thirds of the way between 1.5 and 2.5, multiply two-thirds, or .667, times the interval size of 1, which gives .667. Then adding .667 to 1.5 takes us to the score of 2.17. Thus, 2.17 is two-thirds of the way through this interval, so it has a *cf* of 5. Therefore, 2.17 is at the 50th percentile, so 50% of the rats completed the maze in 2.17 minutes or less.

Luckily, there's a formula that accomplishes all of the above at once.

THE FORMULA FOR FINDING THE SCORE AT A GIVEN PERCENTILE IS

$$\text{Score} = \text{LRL} + \left(\frac{\text{Target } cf - cf \text{ below interval}}{f \text{ within interval}} \right)(\text{Interval size})$$

The formula requires the following:

1. Target *cf:* The cumulative frequency of the score you seek. To find it, transform the percentile into a proportion and then multiply it by *N*. The interval containing this *cf* contains the score you seek. (In the example the target *cf* is 5.)

2. LRL: The lower real limit of the interval that contains the score you seek. (In the example it is 1.5.)

3. *cf* below interval: The cumulative frequency for the interval below the interval containing the score you seek. (In the example it is 3.)

4. *f* within interval: The frequency in the interval that contains the score. (In the example it is 3.)

5. Interval size: The interval size used to create the frequency distribution. (Above, it is 1.)

Putting these numbers into the above formula gives

$$\text{Score} = 1.5 + \left(\frac{5 - 3}{3} \right)(1)$$

In the fraction, subtracting $5 - 3$ gives 2/3, which is .667. So

$$\text{Score} = 1.5 + (.667)(1)$$

After multiplying,

$$\text{Score} = 1.5 + .667$$

So finally,

$$\text{Score} = 2.17$$

Again, the score at the 50th percentile in these data is 2.17.

Although we had an interval size of 1, you can use this formula for any interval size.

Finding a Percentile for a Given Score

You can also work from the opposite direction when you have a score in mind and wish to determine its percentile. For example, say in the rat data back in Table A.3, we seek the percentile for the score of 4. First, we'll find the *cf* of the score within the interval, and then add the *cf* below the interval. Then we determine the percent of scores that are at or below the score.

You accomplish this using the following formula.

THE FORMULA FOR FINDING THE PERCENTILE OF A GIVEN SCORE IS

$$\text{Percentile} = \left(\frac{cf \text{ below interval} + \left(\dfrac{\text{Score} - \text{LRL}}{\text{Interval size}} \right)\left(\begin{array}{c} f \text{ within} \\ \text{interval} \end{array} \right)}{N} \right)(100)$$

This formula requires the following:

1. Score: The score for which you are computing the percentile. (Here, it is 4.)
2. *cf* below interval: The cumulative frequency of the interval below the interval containing the score. (In the example it is 8.)
3. LRL: The lower real limit of the interval containing the score. (Here, it is 3.5.)
4. *f* within interval: The frequency in the interval containing the score. (Here, it is 1.)
5. Interval size: The interval size used to create the grouped distribution. (Here, it is 1.)
6. *N:* The total number of scores in the sample. (Here, $N = 10$.)

Putting these numbers into the above formula gives

$$\text{Percentile} = \left(\frac{8 + \left(\dfrac{4.0 - 3.5}{1} \right)(1)}{10} \right)(100)$$

In the numerator 4.0 minus 3.5, divided by 1 is .5, so

$$\text{Percentile} = \left(\frac{8 + (.5)(1)}{10} \right)(100)$$

Multiplying .5 by 1 gives

$$\text{Percentile} = \left(\frac{8 + .5}{10} \right)(100)$$

After adding,

$$\text{Percentile} = \left(\frac{8.5}{10} \right)(100)$$

and after dividing,

$$\text{Percentile} = (.85)(100)$$

Finally, the answer is

$$\text{Percentile} = 85$$

Thus, the score of 4.0 is at the 85th percentile.

APPLICATION QUESTIONS

(Answers for odd-numbered questions are in Appendix C.)

1. Organize the scores below into an ungrouped distribution showing simple frequency, cumulative frequency, and relative frequency.

49	52	47	52	52	47	49	47	50
51	50	49	50	50	50	53	51	49

(a) What is the percentile for the score of 51? (b) What score is at the 50th percentile?

2. A group of students received the following grades on a test of typing ability. Using an interval size of 5, group the scores and construct a table that shows simple, relative, and cumulative frequency. The highest apparent limit is 95.

76	66	80	82	76	80	84	86	80	86
85	87	74	90	92	87	91	94	94	91
94	93	57	82	76	76	82	90	87	91
66	80	57	66	74	76	80	84	94	66

(a) Find the score that corresponds to the 70th percentile. (b) What is the percentile for a score of 91?

3. Below are the weights (in pounds) of 28 high school students. Using an interval size of 4, group the scores and construct a table showing simple, relative, and cumulative frequency. The lowest apparent limit is 100.

122	117	116	114	110	109	107
105	103	102	129	126	123	123
122	122	119	118	117	112	108
117	117	126	123	118	113	112

(a) What is the percentile for a student who weighs 117 pounds? (b) What weight corresponds to the 80th percentile?

A.2: PERFORMING LINEAR INTERPOLATION

This part presents the procedures for linear interpolation of z-scores as discussed in Chapter 6, and of values of t_{crit} discussed in Chapter 11.

INTERPOLATING FROM THE z-TABLES

You interpolate to find an exact proportion not shown in the z-table or when dealing with a z-score that has three decimal places (carry all computations to four decimal places).

Finding an Unknown z-Score

Say that we seek a z-score that corresponds to exactly .45 (.4500) of the curve between the mean and z. First, from the z-tables, identify the two bracketing proportions that are above and below the target proportion. Note their corresponding z-scores. For .4500, the bracketing proportions are .4505 at $z = 1.6500$ and .4495 at $z = 1.6400$. Arrange the values this way:

	Known Proportion under Curve	*Unknown z-score*
Upper bracket	.4505	1.6500
Target	.4500	?
Lower bracket	.4495	1.6400

Because the "known" target proportion is bracketed by .4505 and .4495, the "unknown" target z-score falls between 1.6500 and 1.6400.

First, deal with the known side. The target of .4500 is halfway between .4495 and .4505. That is, the difference between the lower known proportion and the target proportion is one-half of the difference between the two known proportions. We assume that the z-score corresponding to .4500 is also halfway between the two bracketing z-scores of 1.6400 and 1.6500. The difference between these z-scores is .010, and one-half of that is .005. To go to halfway between 1.6400 and 1.6500, we add .005 to 1.6400. Thus, a z-score of 1.6450 corresponds to .4500 of the curve between the mean and z.

The answer will not always be as obvious as in this example, so use the following steps.

Step 1: Determine the difference between the upper and lower known brackets. In the example .4505 − .4495 = .0010. This is the total distance between the two proportions.

Step 2: Determine the difference between the known target and the lower known bracket. Above, .4500 − .4495 = .0005.

Step 3: Form a fraction with the answer from step 2 as the numerator and the answer from step 1 as the denominator. Above, the fraction is .0005/.0010 = .5. Thus, .4500 is one-half of the distance from .4495 to .4505.

Step 4: Find the difference between the two brackets in the unknown column. Above, 1.6600 − 1.6400 = .010. This is the total distance between the two z-scores that bracket the unknown target z-score.

Step 5: Multiply the answer in step 3 by the answer in step 4. Above, (.5)(.010) = .005. The unknown target z-score is .005 larger than the lower bracketing z-score.

Step 6: Add the answer in step 5 to the lower bracketing z-score. Above, .005 + 1.640 = 1.645. Thus, .4500 of the normal curve lies between the mean and $z = 1.645$.

Finding an Unknown Proportion

Apply the above steps to find an unknown proportion for a known three-decimal z-score. For example, say we seek the proportion between the mean and a z of 1.382.

From the z-tables the upper and lower brackets around this z are 1.390 and 1.380. Arrange the z-scores and corresponding proportions as shown below.

	Known z-score	Unknown Proportion under Curve
Upper bracket	1.390	.4177
Target	1.382	?
Lower bracket	1.380	.4162

To find the target proportion, use the preceding steps.

Step 1: $1.390 - 1.380 = .010$
This is the total difference between the known bracketing z-scores.
Step 2: $1.382 - 1.380 = .002$
This is the distance between the lower known bracketing z-score and the target z-score.
Step 3: $\dfrac{.002}{.010} = .20$
This is the proportion of the distance that the target z-score lies from the lower bracket. A z of 1.382 is .20 of the distance between 1.380 and 1.390.
Step 4: $.4177 - .4162 = .0015$
The total distance between the brackets of .4177 and .4162 in the unknown column is .0015.
Step 5: $(0.20)(0.0015) = .0003$
Thus, .20 of the distance separating the bracketing proportions in the unknown column is .0003.
Step 6: $.4162 + .0003 = .4165$
Increasing the lower proportion in the unknown column by .0003 takes us to the point corresponding to .20 of the distance between the bracketing proportions. This point is .4165, which is the proportion that corresponds to $z = 1.382$.

INTERPOLATING CRITICAL VALUES

Sometimes you must interpolate between the critical values in a table. Apply the same steps described above, except now use degrees of freedom and critical values.

For example, say that we seek the t_{crit} corresponding to 35 df (with $\alpha = .05$, two-tailed test). The t-tables have values only for 30 df and 40 df, giving the following:

	Known df	Unknown Critical Value
Upper bracket	30	2.042
Target	35	?
Lower bracket	40	2.021

Because 35 *df* is halfway between 30 *df* and 40 *df*, the corresponding critical value is halfway between 2.042 and 2.021. Following the steps described for z-scores, we have

Step 1: $40 - 30 = 10$
This is the total distance between the known bracketing *df*s.
Step 2: $35 - 30 = 5$
Notice a change here: This is the distance between the *upper* bracketing *df* and the target *df*.
Step 3: $\dfrac{5}{10} = .50$
This is the proportion of the distance that the target *df* lies from the upper known bracket. Thus, the *df* of 35 is .50 of the distance from 30 to 40.
Step 4: $2.042 - 2.021 = .021$
The total distance between the bracketing critical values of 2.042 and 2.021 in the unknown column is .021.

The *df* of 35 is .50 of the distance between the bracketing *df*s, so the target critical value is .50 of the distance between 2.042 and 2.021, or .50 of .021.
Step 5: $(.50)(.021) = .0105$
Thus, .50 of the distance between the bracketing critical values is .0105. Because critical values *decrease* as *df* increases, we are going from 30 *df* to 35 *df*, so subtract .0105 from the larger value, 2.042.
Step 6: $2.042 - .0105 = 2.0315$
Thus, $t = 2.0315$ is the critical value for 35 *df* at $\alpha = .05$ for a two-tailed test.
The same logic can be applied to find critical values for any other statistic.

APPLICATION QUESTIONS

(Answers for odd-numbered questions are in Appendix C.)

1. What is the z-score you must score above to be in the top 25% of scores?
2. Foofy obtains a z-score of 1.909. What proportion of scores are between her score and the mean?
3. For $\alpha = .05$, what is the two-tailed t_{crit} for $df = 50$?
4. For $\alpha = .05$, what is the two-tailed t_{crit} for $df = 55$?

A.3: ADDITIONAL FORMULAS FOR COMPUTING PROBABILITY

This part extends the discussion of computing probability found in Chapter 9.

COMPUTING THE PROBABILITY OF EQUALLY LIKELY EVENTS

When nature has no bias that favors one event over another, the events are *equally likely*.

THE FORMULA FOR COMPUTING PROBABILITY WHEN EVENTS ARE EQUALLY LIKELY IS

$$p(\text{event}) = \frac{\text{Number of outcomes that satisfy event}}{\text{Total number of possible outcomes}}$$

The numerator is the number of possible outcomes that satisfy the event we are describing. When flipping a coin, for example, there is one outcome that satisfies a head. In the denominator is the total number of possible outcomes. With a coin, either a head or a tail can occur. Therefore, the probability of a head is 1/2, or .5.

Likewise, we might define the event as drawing a king from a deck of cards. There are four kings in a deck, and any one would satisfy us. With a total of 52 possible outcomes, the probability of randomly drawing a king on one draw is 4/52, or .0769.

In the real world, raffle tickets are sometimes sold one for a dollar and sometimes sold three for a dollar. Many people think they have a better chance of winning when everyone gets three tickets for a dollar. They're wrong. Say that 100 people each buy one ticket. Then each person's probability of winning equals 1/100, or .01. However, if 100 people each buy 3 tickets for a dollar, then each person's probability of winning equals 3/300. But, 3/300 equals 1/100, so each person still has a probability of winning equal to .01.

The above formula is rather tedious when the event being described is a complex sequence of alternatives. Instead, we use the following shortcut formulas.

THE MULTIPLICATION RULE

When computing the probability of complex events, sometimes we are "satisfied" only if several events occur. Use the multiplication rule when the word "and" links the events that must all occur to be satisfied. *The following multiplication rule can be used only with independent events.* (For dependent events, a different, more complex rule is needed.)

THE MULTIPLICATION RULE FOR INDEPENDENT EVENTS IS

$$p(A \text{ and } B) = p(A) \times p(B)$$

This says that the probability of several independent events is equal to their individual probabilities multiplied together. Thus, the probability of having both A and B occur is equal to the probability of A multiplied times the probability of B. (If there were three events, then all three probabilities would be multiplied together, and so on.)

The multiplication rule is appropriate when describing a *series* of independent events. Say that we seek the probability of obtaining 3 heads on 3 coin tosses. We're actually asking, "What is the probability of obtaining a head *and* then a head *and* then a head?" Using the multiplication rule, the answer is

$$p(\text{head}) \times p(\text{head}) \times p(\text{head}) = .5 \times .5 \times .5 = .125$$

Also, use the multiplication rule when two or more independent events occur *simultaneously*. For example, the probability of drawing the king of hearts can be restated as the probability of drawing a king *and* a heart simultaneously. With 4 kings, the probability of drawing a king is 4/52, or .0769. With 13 hearts, the probability of drawing a heart is 13/52, or .25. The probability of drawing a king and a heart is (.0769 × .25), which is .0192.

THE ADDITION RULE

Sometimes we seek any *one* of a number of outcomes that may occur. Use the addition rule when the word "or" links the events that will satisfy us. For example, if we will be satisfied by either A *or* B, then we seek $p(A$ or $B)$. There are two versions of the addition rule, however, depending on whether these are mutually exclusive or mutually inclusive events. **Mutually exclusive events** cannot occur together: The occurrence of one event prohibits, or excludes, the occurrence of another. Heads and tails, for example, are mutually exclusive on any *one* flip of a coin. Conversely, **mutually inclusive events** can occur together. For example, drawing a king from a deck is mutually inclusive with drawing a heart, because we can draw the king of hearts.

> *THE ADDITION RULE FOR MUTUALLY EXCLUSIVE EVENTS IS*
>
> $$p(A \text{ or } B) = p(A) + p(B)$$

Here the probability of having either A or B occur is equal to the probability of A plus the probability of B. For example, the probability of randomly drawing a queen or a king equals the probability of a king (4/52 or .0769) plus the probability of a queen (also .0769). Thus, $p(\text{king or queen}) = .0769 + .0769 = .1538$.

When events are mutually *inclusive,* you may obtain A, or B, or A and B simultaneously. To see how this plays havoc with the computations, say that we seek the probability of drawing either a king *or* a heart in one draw. We *might* think that with 4 kings and 13 hearts, there are a total of 17 cards that will satisfy us—right? Wrong! There are only 16. The problem is that we counted the king of hearts twice, once as a king and once as a heart. To correct this, we must subtract the "extra" king of hearts.

> *THE ADDITION RULE FOR MUTUALLY INCLUSIVE EVENTS IS*
>
> $$p(A \text{ or } B) = p(A) + p(B) - [p(A) \times p(B)]$$

This says that the probability of any one of several mutually inclusive events is equal to the sum of the probabilities of the individual events *minus* the probability of the events' occurring simultaneously (minus the probability of A and B). Compute the probability of A and B using the multiplication rule, where $p(A \text{ and } B) = p(A) \times p(B)$. For example, the probability of a king is 4/52, or .0769, and the probability of a heart is 13/52, or .25. The probability of a king and a heart is 1/52, or .0192. Therefore,

$$p(\text{king or heart}) = .0769 + .25 - .0192 = .3077$$

You can combine the addition and multiplication rules. For example, what is the probability of drawing either the jack of diamonds *or* the king of spades on one draw, *and then* drawing either the 5 *or* the 6 of diamonds on a second draw? In symbols, this is

$$p[(A \text{ or } B) \text{ and } (C \text{ or } D)]$$

Because these events are all mutually exclusive, we have

$$p[(A \text{ or } B) \text{ and } (C \text{ or } D)] = [p(A) + p(B)] \times [p(C) + p(D)]$$

If we're sampling with replacement, the answer is .00148. If we're sampling without replacement, the answer is .00151.

THE BINOMIAL EXPANSION

Sometimes we seek the probability of getting a subset of outcomes out of a larger series of tries. For example, we might seek the probability of seeing 1 head out of 3 coin tosses, In such cases, we use the formula called the **binomial expansion.** A "binomial" situation exists when one of two possible outcomes occurs on each occasion, and the two outcomes are mutually exclusive. In statistical terms we find the probability of a *combination* of N events taken r at a time. We'll use the symbol p_C to stand for the probability of the particular combination that satisfies us.

THE FORMULA FOR THE BINOMIAL EXPANSION IS

$$p_C = \left(\frac{N!}{r!(N-r)!} \right)(p^r)(q^{N-r})$$

Let's find the probability of obtaining 1 head in 3 tries. Then N is the total number of tries or occasions, and r is the number of events that satisfy us, so $N = 3$ and $r = 1$. The p is the probability of the desired event, and we raise it to the r power (multiply it times itself r times). Here, heads is the desired event, so $p = .5$. With $r = 1$, we have $.5^1$. The q is the probability of the event that is not desired, and it is raised to the $N - r$ power. Tails is the undesirable event, so $q = .5$. Because $N - r$ equals 2, we have $.5^2$. Thus, we have

$$p_C = \left(\frac{3!}{1!(3-1)!} \right)(.5^1)(.5^2)$$

The exclamation point (!) is the symbol for *factorial,* meaning you multiply the number times all whole numbers less than it down to 1. Thus, 3! equals 3 times 2 times 1, or 6.

The quantity 1! is (1)(1), or 1, and the quantity $(3 - 1)!$ is (2)!, which is (2)(1), or 2. Now

$$p_C = \left(\frac{6}{1(2)}\right)(.5^1)(.5^2)$$

Any number raised to the first power is that number, so $.5^1$ equals .5. (In a different problem, if you had to raise p or q to the zero power, the answer would be 1.) Because $.5^2$ is .25, we have

$$p_C = \left(\frac{6}{1(2)}\right)(.5)(.25)$$

And then

$$p_C = 3(.125)$$

So $p_C = .375$: The probability of obtaining precisely 1 head (and 2 tails) in 3 coin tosses is .375.

You can also use the binomial expansion when classifying events as either "yes" or "no." For example, say we want the probability of showing a 2 on 4 out of 6 rolls of one die. The desired 2 is the "yes," and we want it to happen 4 times, so $r = 4$. Its probability on any single roll is p, which is 1/6, or .167. Any other number on the die is a "no," the probability of which is q, which equals 5/6, or .83. Thus,

$$p_C = \left(\frac{N!}{r!(N - r)!}\right)(p^r)(q^{N-r}) = \left(\frac{6!}{4!(6 - 4)!}\right)(.167^4)(.83^2)$$

which becomes

$$p_C = \left(\frac{720}{24(2)}\right)(.00078)(.689)$$

so

$$p_C = \left(\frac{720}{48}\right)(.00054)$$

Thus,

$$p_C = 15(.00054) = .0081$$

so the probability of rolling a die 6 times and showing a two on 4 of the rolls equals .0081.

APPLICATION QUESTIONS

(Answers for odd-numbered questions are in Appendix C.)

1. (a) When you state a question in terms of the probability of this "and" that, what mathematical procedure do you employ? (b) When the question is in terms of this "or" that, what do you do? (c) When you phrase a question using "or," what characteristics of the events must you consider?

2. Which of the following events are mutually inclusive, and which are mutually exclusive? (a) Being male or female; (b) being sunny and rainy; (c) being tall and weighing a lot; (d) being age 16 and being a registered voter.

3. What is the probability of: (a) Getting a 6 when rolling a die? (b) Selecting a diamond from a deck of cards? (c) Guessing the answer to a four-choice multiple choice question? (d) Selecting the ace of diamonds twice in a row when sampling without replacement?

4. Foofy chooses as her pick in the million dollar lottery the numbers 1, 2, 3, 4, and 5, to be selected in any order out of 50 possible numbers. Poindexter says that these numbers are much less likely than, say, the numbers 7, 18, 23, 31, and 49. Who has the greater probability of winning the lottery?

5. Researchers have found that for every 100 people, 34 have an IQ above 116 and the rest are below 116, and 40 are introverted, 35 are extroverted, and 25 are in-between. (a) What is the probability of randomly selecting two people with an IQ above 116? (b) What is the probability of selecting either an introverted or an extroverted person? (c) What is the probability of selecting someone with an IQ above 116 who is introverted? (d) What is the probability of selecting either someone with an IQ above 116 or someone who is introverted? (e) What is the probability of selecting someone in-between introverted and extroverted, and then selecting either someone who has an IQ above 116 or who is introverted?

6. We seek the probability of obtaining 3 heads in a row with three tosses. (a) Determine the probability by making a fraction of the total number of ways 3 heads can occur and the total number of possible combinations of heads and tails. (b) Determine the probability using the multiplication rule.

7. (a) When do you use the binomial expansion? (b) Out of 5 coin tosses, what is the probability of obtaining 4 heads? (c) What is the probability of obtaining only 1 head in 5 coin tosses? (d) Why is the answer in part c the same as in part b?

8. When rolling dice, what is the probability of each of the following? (a) Getting a 4 or a 5 rolling 1 die; (b) getting a 4 twice in a row rolling 1 die; (c) getting a 5 on only 1 die when rolling 2 dice at once; (d) getting three 1s in 5 rolls of 1 die.

A.4: THE ONE-WAY, WITHIN-SUBJECTS ANALYSIS OF VARIANCE

This section contains formulas for the one-way, within-subjects ANOVA discussed in Chapter 13. This ANOVA is similar to the two-way ANOVA discussed in Chapter 14, so read that chapter first.

ASSUMPTIONS OF THE WITHIN-SUBJECTS ANOVA

In a within-subjects ANOVA, either the same participants are measured repeatedly or different participants are matched under all levels of one factor. The other assumptions here are (1) the dependent variable is a ratio or interval variable, (2) the populations are normally distributed, and (3) the population variances are homogeneous.

LOGIC OF THE ONE-WAY, WITHIN-SUBJECTS ANOVA

As an example, say that we're interested in whether a person's form of dress influences how comfortable he or she feels in a social setting. On three consecutive days we ask each participant to act as a "greeter" for other people participating in a different experiment. On the first day participants dress casually, on the second day they dress semiformally, and on the third day they dress formally. We test the very unpowerful N of 5. At the end of each day, participants complete a questionnaire measuring the dependent variable of their comfort level while greeting people. Labeling the independent variable of type of dress as factor A, the layout of the study is shown in Design Diagram A.1.

To describe the relationship that is present, we'll find the mean of each level (column) under factor A. As usual, we test whether the means from the levels represent different μs. Therefore, the hypotheses are the same as in a between-subjects design.

H_0: $\mu_1 = \mu_2 = \mu_3$

H_a: Not all μs are equal

ELEMENTS OF THE WITHIN-SUBJECTS ANOVA

Notice in the design diagram that this one-way ANOVA can be viewed as a two-way ANOVA: Factor A (the columns) is one factor, and the different subjects (the rows) are a second factor, here with five levels. The interaction is between subjects and type of dress.

In Chapters 13 and 14 we computed F_{obt} by dividing by the mean square within groups (MS_{wn}). This was an estimate of the error variance (σ^2_{error}), the inherent variability in the population. We computed MS_{wn} using the differences between the scores in each *cell* and the mean of the cell. However, in the design diagram each cell contains

DESIGN DIAGRAM A.1   One-Way Repeated-Measures Study of the Factor of Type of Dress

Each X represents a participant's score on the dependent variable of comfort level.

		Factor A: Type of Dress		
		Level A_1: *Casual*	**Level A_2:** *Semiformal*	**Level A_3:** *Formal*
	Subject 1	X	X	X
	Subject 2	X	X	X
Subjects Factor	*Subject 3*	X	X	X
	Subject 4	X	X	X
	Subject 5	$\overline{X}$	X	X
		$\overline{X}_{A1}$	$\overline{X}_{A2}$	$\overline{X}_{A3}$

only one score. Therefore, the mean of each cell *is* the score in the cell, and the differences within a cell are always zero. Obviously, we cannot compute MS_{wn} in the usual way.

Instead, the mean square for the interaction between factor A and subjects (abbreviated $MS_{A \times subs}$) reflects the inherent variability of scores. Recall that an interaction indicates that the effect of one factor changes as the levels of the other factor change. It is because of the inherent variability among subjects that the effect of type of dress will change as we change the "levels" of which participant we test. Therefore, $MS_{A \times subs}$ is our estimate of the error variance, and it is used as the denominator of the F-ratio. (If the study involved matching, each triplet of matched participants would provide the scores in each row, and the $MS_{A \times subs}$ here would still show the inherent variability among the scores.)

As usual, MS_A describes the difference between the means in factor A, and it estimates the variability due to error plus the variability due to treatment. Thus, the F-ratio here is

$$\textbf{Sample} \qquad\qquad \textbf{Estimates} \qquad \textbf{Population}$$

$$F_{obt} = \frac{MS_A}{MS_{A \times subs}} \qquad \begin{array}{c} \rightarrow \\ \rightarrow \end{array} \qquad \frac{\sigma^2_{error} + \sigma^2_{treat}}{\sigma^2_{error}}$$

If H_0 is true and all μs are equal, then both the numerator and the denominator will contain only σ^2_{error}, so F_{obt} will equal 1. However, the larger the F_{obt}, the less likely it is that the means for the levels of factor A represent one population μ. If F_{obt} is significant, then at least two of the means represent different μs.

COMPUTING THE ONE-WAY, WITHIN-SUBJECTS ANOVA

Say that we obtained these data:

Factor A: Type of Dress

Participants		Level A_1: Casual	Level A_2: Semiformal	Level A_3: Formal	
	Subject 1	4	9	1	$\Sigma X_{sub} = 14$
	Subject 2	6	12	3	$\Sigma X_{sub} = 21$
	Subject 3	8	4	4	$\Sigma X_{sub} = 16$
	Subject 4	2	8	5	$\Sigma X_{sub} = 15$
	Subject 5	10	7	2	$\Sigma X_{sub} = 19$

$\Sigma X = 30$	$\Sigma X = 40$	$\Sigma X = 15$	Total: $\Sigma X_{tot} = 30 + 40 + 15 = 85$
$\Sigma X^2 = 220$	$\Sigma X^2 = 354$	$\Sigma X^2 = 55$	$\Sigma X^2_{tot} = 220 + 354 + 55 = 629$
$n_1 = 5$	$n_2 = 5$	$n_3 = 5$	$N = 15$
$\overline{X}_1 = 5$	$\overline{X}_2 = 8$	$\overline{X}_3 = 3$	$k = 3$

The first step is to compute the ΣX, the $\overline{X}$, and the ΣX^2 for each level of factor A (each column). Then compute ΣX_{tot} and ΣX^2_{tot}. Also, compute ΣX_{sub}, which is the ΣX for each subject's scores (each row). Notice that the ns and N are based on the number of *scores,* not the number of participants.

Then follow these steps.

Step 1 Compute the total sum of squares (SS_{tot}).

THE COMPUTATIONAL FORMULA FOR THE TOTAL SUMS OF SQUARES IS

$$SS_{tot} = \Sigma X^2_{tot} - \left(\frac{(\Sigma X_{tot})^2}{N} \right)$$

From the example data we have

$$SS_{tot} = 629 - \left(\frac{85^2}{15} \right)$$

$$SS_{tot} = 629 - 481.67$$

$$SS_{tot} = 147.33$$

Note that the quantity $(\Sigma X_{tot})^2/N$ is the *correction* in the following computations. (Here, the correction is 481.67.)

Step 2 Compute the sum of squares for the column factor, factor A (SS_A).

THE COMPUTATIONAL FORMULA FOR THE SUM OF SQUARES BETWEEN GROUPS FOR FACTOR A IS

$$SS_A = \Sigma \left(\frac{(\text{Sum of scores in the column})^2}{n \text{ of scores in the column}} \right) - \left(\frac{(\Sigma X_{tot})^2}{N} \right)$$

Find ΣX in each level (column) of factor A, square the sum, and divide by the n of the level. After doing this for all levels, add the results together and subtract the correction. In the example

$$SS_A = \left(\frac{(30)^2}{5} + \frac{(40)^2}{5} + \frac{(15)^2}{5} \right) - 481.67$$

$$SS_A = 545 - 481.67$$

$$SS_A = 63.33$$

Step 3 Find the sum of squares for the row factor, for subjects (SS_{subs}).

THE COMPUTATIONAL FORMULA FOR THE SUM OF SQUARES FOR SUBJECTS IS

$$SS_{subs} = \frac{(\Sigma X_{sub1})^2 + (\Sigma X_{sub2})^2 + \cdots + (\Sigma X_n)^2}{k} - \frac{(\Sigma X_{tot})^2}{N}$$

Take the sum for each subject (ΣX_{sub}) and square it. Then add the squared sums together. Next, divide by k, where k is the number of levels of factor A. Finally, subtract the correction.

In the example,

$$SS_{subs} = \frac{(14)^2 + (21)^2 + (16)^2 + (15)^2 + (19)^2}{3} - 481.67$$

$$SS_{subs} = 493 - 481.67$$

$$SS_{subs} = 11.33$$

Step 4 Find the sum of squares for the interaction ($SS_{A \times subs}$). To do this, subtract the sums of squares for the other factors from the total.

THE COMPUTATIONAL FORMULA FOR THE INTERACTION OF FACTOR A BY SUBJECTS IS

$$SS_{A \times subs} = SS_{tot} - SS_A - SS_{subs}$$

In the example

$$SS_{A \times subs} = 147.33 - 63.33 - 11.33$$

$$SS_{A \times subs} = 72.67$$

Step 5 Determine the degrees of freedom.

THE DEGREES OF FREEDOM BETWEEN GROUPS FOR FACTOR A IS

$$df_A = k_A - 1$$

k_A is the number of levels of factor A. (In the example $k_A = 3$, so df_A is 2.)

THE DEGREES OF FREEDOM FOR THE INTERACTION IS

$$df_{A \times subs} = (k_A - 1)(k_{subs} - 1)$$

k_A is the number of levels of factor A, and k_{subs} is the number of subjects. In the example there are three levels of factor A and five subjects, so $df_{A \times subs} = (2)(4) = 8$.

Compute df_{subs} and df_{tot} to check the above df. The $df_{subs} = k_{subs} - 1$, where k_{subs} is the number of subjects. The $df_{tot} = N - 1$, where N is the total number of *scores* in the experiment. The df_{tot} is also equal to the sum of all other dfs.

Step 6 Place the sum of squares and the dfs in the summary table. For the example:

Summary Table of One-Way Within-Subjects ANOVA

Source	*Sum of Squares*	df	*Mean Square*	F
Subjects	11.33	4		
Factor A (dress)	63.33	2	MS_A	F_A
Interaction				
(A × subjects)	72.67	8	$MS_{A \times subs}$	
Total	147.33	14		

Because there is only one factor of interest here (type of dress), we will find the F_{obt} only for factor A.

Step 7 Find the mean squares for factor A and the interaction.

THE MEAN SQUARE FOR FACTOR A IS

$$MS_A = \frac{SS_A}{df_A}$$

In our example

$$MS_A = \frac{SS_A}{df_A} = \frac{63.33}{2} = 31.67$$

THE MEAN SQUARE FOR THE INTERACTION BETWEEN FACTOR A AND SUBJECTS IS

$$MS_{A \times subs} = \frac{SS_{A \times subs}}{df_{A \times subs}}$$

In the example

$$MS_{A \times subs} = \frac{SS_{A \times subs}}{df_{A \times subs}} = \frac{72.67}{8} = 9.08$$

Step 8 Find F_{obt}.

THE WITHIN-SUBJECTS F-RATIO IS

$$F_{obt} = \frac{MS_A}{MS_{A \times subs}}$$

In the example

$$F_{obt} = \frac{MS_A}{MS_{A \times subs}} = \frac{31.67}{9.08} = 3.49$$

The finished summary table is

Source	Sum of Squares	df	Mean Square	F
Subjects	11.33	4		
Factor A (dress)	63.33	2	31.67	3.49
Interaction				
(A × subjects)	72.67	8	9.08	
Total	147.33	14		

Step 9 Find the critical value of F in Table 5 of Appendix B. Use df_A as the degrees of freedom between groups and $df_{A \times subs}$ as the degrees of freedom within groups. In the example for $\alpha = .05$, $df_A = 2$, and $df_{A \times subs} = 8$, the F_{crit} is 4.46.

INTERPRETING THE WITHIN-SUBJECTS *F*

Interpret the above F_{obt} in exactly the same way you would a between-subjects F_{obt}. Because F_{obt} in the above example is *not* larger than F_{crit}, it is not significant. Thus, we do not have evidence that the means from at least two levels of type of dress represent different populations of comfort scores. Had F_{obt} been significant, it would indicate that at least two of the level means differ significantly. Then, for post hoc comparisons, graphing, eta squared, and confidence intervals, follow the procedures discussed in Chapter 13. However, in any of those formulas, in place of the term MS_{wn} use $MS_{A \times subs}$.

Note: You've seen that the related-samples *t*-test in Chapter 12 is more powerful than the independent-samples *t*-test because the variability in the scores is less. For the same reason, a within-subjects ANOVA is more powerful than a between-subjects ANOVA for the same data. The within-subjects ANOVA deletes some variability in the raw scores by separating (and then ignoring) the sum of squares for the subjects factor. By removing the differences due to subjects from the calculations, the $MS_{A \times subs}$ is smaller than the MS_{wn} would be in a between-subjects ANOVA. Therefore, F_{obt} is larger and more likely to be significant, so we have greater power. The results in the above example were not significant because of the relatively small N, given the amount of variability in the scores. However, this design was still more powerful—more likely to produce significant results—than a comparable between-subjects design.

APPLICATION QUESTIONS

(Answers for odd-numbered questions are in Appendix C.)

1. You read in a research report that the repeated measures factor for a person's weight gain led to a decrease in his or her mood. (a) What does this tell you about the design? (b) What does it tell you about the results?

2. Which of these relationships suggest using a repeated-measures design?
(a) Examining the improvement in language ability as children grow older.
(b) Measuring participants' reaction when the experimenter surprises them by unexpectedly shouting, under three levels of volume of shouting. (c) Comparing the dating strategies of males and females. (d) Comparing memory ability under the conditions of participants' consuming different amounts of alcoholic beverages.

3. In a study on the influence of practice on performing a task requiring eye–hand coordination, we test people with no practice, after 1 hour of practice, and again after 2 hours of practice. We obtain the following data, with higher scores indicating better performance. (a) What are H_0 and H_a? (b) Complete the ANOVA summary table (c) With $\alpha = .05$, what do you conclude about F_{obt}? (d) Perform the appropriate post hoc comparisons. (e) What is the effect size in this study? (f) What should you conclude about this relationship?

Amount of Practice

Subjects	None	1 Hour	2 Hours
S1	4	3	6
S2	3	5	5
S3	1	4	3
S4	3	4	6
S5	1	5	6
S6	2	6	7
S7	2	4	5
S8	1	3	8

4. You conduct a study in which you measure 21 students' degree of positive attitude toward statistics at 4 equally spaced intervals during the semester. The mean score for each level is as follows: time 1, 62.50; time 2, 64.68; time 3, 69.32; time 4, 72.00. You obtain the following sums of squares:

Source	Sum of Squares	df	Mean Square	F
Subjects	402.79			
Factor A	189.30			
A × subjects	688.32			
Total	1280.41			

(a) What are H_0 and H_a? (b) Complete the ANOVA summary table (c) With $\alpha = .05$, what do you conclude about F_{obt}? (d) Perform the appropriate post hoc comparisons. (e) What is the effect size in this study? (f) What should you conclude about this relationship?

A.5: THE TWO-WAY, WITHIN-SUBJECTS ANALYSIS OF VARIANCE

The following shows the calculations for the two-way, within-subjects ANOVA discussed in Chapter 14.

Recall that sometimes an experiment involves related samples because we've either repeatedly measured the same participants under all conditions of a factor, or matched different participants on a variable. When you have two factors that both involve related samples, perform the **two-way, within-subjects ANOVA.** For example, say that we're studying the influence on creativity of two factors: the time of day people are tested (morning or evening) and their level of motivation (low or high). We might design this study using repeated measures on both factors. The same three participants are tested four times: twice in the morning and twice in the evening, and for each, once with low motivation and again with high motivation. Table A.4 shows example data from this 2×2 within-subjects design, with three scores per cell.

TABLE A.4 Data from 2×2 Within-Subjects Design: Both Factors Are Repeated-Measures Factors

Each participant was tested in all four cells of the study.

		Factor A: Time of Test		
Factor B: Motivation		A_1: *Morning*	A_2: *Evening*	
B_1: Low	*Subject 1*	8	18	
	Subject 2	12	17	
	Subject 3	13	15	
		$\overline{X} = 11.00$	$\overline{X} = 16.70$	$\overline{X} = 13.85$
		$\Sigma X = 33$	$\Sigma X = 50$	$\Sigma X = 83$
		$\Sigma X^2 = 377$	$\Sigma X^2 = 838$	$n = 6$
		$n = 3$	$n = 3$	
B_2: High	*Subject 1*	9	6	
	Subject 2	10	8	
	Subject 3	17	4	
		$\overline{X} = 12.00$	$\overline{X} = 6.00$	$\overline{X} = 9.00$
		$\Sigma X = 36$	$\Sigma X = 18$	$\Sigma X = 54$
		$\Sigma X^2 = 470$	$\Sigma X^2 = 116$	$n = 6$
		$n = 3$	$n = 3$	
		$\Sigma X = 69$	$\Sigma X = 68$	$\Sigma X_{total} = 137$
		$n = 6$	$n = 6$	$\Sigma X_{total}^2 = 1801$
		$\overline{X} = 11.50$	$\overline{X} = 11.33$	$N = 12$
				$k_A = 2$
				$k_B = 2$

Although the calculations here are different than in previous ANOVAs, the logic is the same. Collapsing across motivation level, examine the main effect means for time of day (comparing 11.50 versus 11.33). Then collapsing across time of day, examine the main effect means for motivation level (13.85 versus 9.00). Then, without collapsing, examine the interaction between time of day and motivation (comparing the cell means of 11.00, 16.70, 12.00, and 6.00). For any significant F_{obt}, perform post hoc tests if needed, compute η^2 and confidence intervals, and graph the effect.

CALCULATING THE TWO-WAY, WITHIN-SUBJECTS ANOVA

Step 1 In each cell compute the sum of scores (ΣX), the sum of the squared scores, (ΣX^2), n, and the mean (the interaction means). Determine k_A, the number of levels of factor A, and for each column compute ΣX, n, and the mean (the main effect means of factor A). Determine k_B, the number of levels of factor B, and for each row compute ΣX, n, and the mean (the main effect means of factor B).

Step 2 Also, determine

$$\Sigma X_{total} = 69 + 68 = 137$$

$$\Sigma X^2_{total} = 377 + 838 + 470 + 116 = 1801$$

$$N = 3 + 3 + 3 + 3 = 12$$

Create a table in which you collapse across factor B, as in Table A.5. Create another table in which you collapse across factor A, as in Table A.6. (*Note:* The ΣX_{sub} for each subject must be the same in each table.)

TABLE A.5 A × Subject Table after Collapsing across Factor B

	Factor A		
	A_1	A_2	ΣX_{sub}
Subject 1	17	24	41
Subject 2	22	25	47
Subject 3	30	19	49

TABLE A.6 B × Subject Table after Collapsing across Factor A

	Factor B		
	B_1	B_2	ΣX_{sub}
Subject 1	26	15	41
Subject 2	29	18	47
Subject 3	28	21	49

Step 3 Compute the correction term:

$$\text{Correction term} = \left(\frac{(\Sigma X_{total})^2}{N}\right) = \frac{137^2}{12} = 1564.08$$

Step 4 As you perform the following calculations, create the analysis of variance summary table shown in Table A.7.

Step 5 Compute the total sum of squares:

$$SS_{tot} = \Sigma X_{total}^2 - \text{Step 3}$$

$$SS_{tot} = 1801 - 1564.08 = 236.92$$

Step 6 Compute the sum of squares for the column factor A:

$$SS_A = \Sigma\left(\frac{(\text{Sum of scores in each column})^2}{n \text{ of scores in the column}}\right) - \text{Step 3}$$

$$SS_A = \left(\frac{(69)^2}{6} + \frac{(68)^2}{6}\right) - 1564.08 = .09$$

Step 7 Compute the sum of squares for the row factor B:

$$SS_B = \Sigma\left(\frac{(\text{Sum of scores in each row})^2}{n \text{ of scores in the row}}\right) - \text{Step 3}$$

$$SS_B = \left(\frac{(83)^2}{6} + \frac{(54)^2}{6}\right) - 1564.08 = 70.09$$

Step 8 Compute the total sum of squares between groups (not reported in summary table):

$$SS_{bn} = \Sigma\left(\frac{(\text{Sum of in each cell})^2}{n \text{ of scores in the cell}}\right) - \text{Step 3}$$

$$SS_{bn} = \left(\frac{(33)^2}{3} + \frac{(50)^2}{3} + \frac{(36)^2}{3} + \frac{(18)^2}{3}\right) - 1564.08$$

$$SS_{bn} = 172.25$$

TABLE A.7 Summary Table of Two-Way, Within-Subjects ANOVA

Source	Sum of Squares	df	Mean Square	F
Factor				
A	.09	1	.09	.004
B	70.09	1	70.09	52.70
A × B	102.07	1	102.07	23.52
Subjects				
A × S	44.66	2	22.33	
B × S	2.66	2	1.33	
A × B × S	8.68	2	4.34	
Total	236.92	11		

Step 9 Compute the sum of squares for the A $\times$ B interaction:

$$SS_{A \times B} = SS_{bn} - SS_A - SS_B$$

$$SS_{A \times B} = \text{Step 8} - \text{Step 6} - \text{Step 7}$$

$$SS_{A \times B} = 172.25 - .09 - 70.09 = 102.07$$

Step 10 Compute the sum of squares for subjects (not reported in summary table):

$$SS_{subs} = \frac{(\Sigma X_{sub1})^2 + (\Sigma X_{sub2})^2 \ldots + (\Sigma X_n)^2}{(k_A)(k_B)} - \text{Step 3}$$

$$SS_{subs} = \frac{(41)^2 + (47)^2 + (49)^2}{(2)(2)} - 1564.08$$

$$SS_{subs} = 8.67$$

Step 11 Compute the sum of squares for the A $\times$ S interaction (using Table A.5):

$$SS_{A \times S} = \Sigma \frac{(\text{Sum of each A} \times \text{Subject score})^2}{k_B} - \text{Step 3} - SS_A - SS_{subs}$$

$$SS_{A \times S} = \Sigma \frac{(\text{Sum of each A} \times \text{Subject score})^2}{k_B} - \text{Step 3} - \text{Step 6} - \text{Step 10}$$

$$SS_{A \times S} = \frac{(17)^2 + (24)^2 + (22)^2 + (25)^2 + (30)^2 + (19)^2}{2} - 1564.08 - .09 - 8.67$$

$$SS_{A \times S} = 44.66$$

Step 12 Compute the sum of squares for the B $\times$ S interaction (using Table A.6):

$$SS_{B \times S} = \Sigma \frac{(\text{Sum of each B} \times \text{Subject score})^2}{k_A} - \text{Step 3} - SS_B - SS_{subs}$$

$$SS_{B \times S} = \Sigma \frac{(\text{Sum of each B} \times \text{Subject score})^2}{k_A} - \text{Step 3} - \text{Step 7} - \text{Step 10}$$

$$SS_{B \times S} = \frac{(26)^2 + (15)^2 + (29)^2 + (18)^2 + (28)^2 + (21)^2}{2} - 1564.08 -$$

$$70.09 - 8.67$$

$$SS_{B \times S} = 2.66$$

Step 13 Compute the sum of squares for the A $\times$ B $\times$ S interaction:

$$SS_{A \times B \times S} = SS_{tot} - SS_A - SS_B - SS_{A \times B} - SS_{subs} - SS_{A \times S} - SS_{B \times S}$$

$$SS_{A \times B \times S} = \text{Step 5} - \text{Step 6} - \text{Step 7} - \text{Step 9} - \text{Step 10} - \text{Step 11} - \text{Step 12}$$

$$SS_{A \times B \times S} = 236.92 - .09 - 70.09 - 102.07 - 8.67 - 44.66 - 2.66$$

$$SS_{A \times B \times S} = 8.68$$

Step 14 Compute the degrees of freedom:
(a) Factor A:

$$df_A = k_A - 1$$
$$df_A = 2 - 1 = 2$$

(b) Factor B:

$$df_B = k_B - 1$$
$$df_B = 2 - 1 = 1$$

(c) A × B interaction:

$$df_{A \times B} = (df_A)(df_B)$$
$$df_{A \times B} = (1)(1) = 1$$

(d) Subjects:

$$df_S = \text{Number of subjects} - 1$$
$$df_S = 3 - 1 = 2$$

(e) A × Subjects interaction:

$$df_{A \times S} = (df_A)(df_S)$$
$$df_{A \times S} = (1)(2) = 2$$

(f) B × Subjects interaction:

$$df_{B \times S} = (df_B)(df_S)$$
$$df_{B \times S} = (1)(2) = 2$$

(g) A × B × Subjects interaction:

$$df_{A \times B \times S} = (df_A)(df_B)(df_S)$$
$$df_{A \times B \times S} = (1)(1)(2) = 2$$

(h) Total:

$$df_{tot} = N - 1$$
$$df_{tot} = 12 - 1 = 11$$

Step 15 Compute the mean square for factor A:

$$MS_A = \frac{SS_A}{df_A}$$

$$MS_A = \frac{\text{Step 6}}{\text{Step 14.a}}$$

$$MS_A = \frac{.09}{1} = .09$$

Step 16 Compute the mean square for factor B:

$$MS_B = \frac{SS_B}{df_B}$$

$$MS_B = \frac{\text{Step 7}}{\text{Step 14.b}}$$

$$MS_B = \frac{70.09}{1} = 70.09$$

Step 17 Compute the mean square for the A $\times$ B interaction:

$$MS_{A \times B} = \frac{SS_{A \times B}}{df_{A \times B}}$$

$$MS_{A \times B} = \frac{\text{Step 9}}{\text{Step 14.c}}$$

$$MS_{A \times B} = \frac{102.07}{1} = 102.07$$

Step 18 Compute the mean square for the A $\times$ S interaction:

$$MS_{A \times S} = \frac{SS_{A \times S}}{df_{A \times S}}$$

$$MS_{A \times S} = \frac{\text{Step 11}}{\text{Step 14.e}}$$

$$MS_{A \times S} = \frac{44.66}{2} = 22.33$$

Step 19 Compute the mean square for the B $\times$ S interaction:

$$MS_{B \times S} = \frac{SS_{B \times S}}{df_{B \times S}}$$

$$MS_{B \times S} = \frac{\text{Step 12}}{\text{Step 14.f}}$$

$$MS_{B \times S} = \frac{2.66}{2} = 1.33$$

Step 20 Compute the mean square for the A $\times$ B $\times$ S interaction:

$$MS_{A \times B \times S} = \frac{SS_{A \times B \times S}}{df_{A \times B \times S}}$$

$$MS_{A \times B \times S} = \frac{\text{Step 13}}{\text{Step 14.g}}$$

$$MS_{A \times B \times S} = \frac{8.68}{2} = 4.34$$

Step 21 Compute the F for the main effect of factor A:

$$F_A = \frac{MS_A}{MS_{A \times S}}$$

$$F_A = \frac{\text{Step } 15}{\text{Step } 18}$$

$$F_A = \frac{.09}{22.33} = .004$$

Step 22 Compute the F for the main effect of factor B:

$$F_B = \frac{MS_B}{MS_{B \times S}}$$

$$F_B = \frac{\text{Step } 16}{\text{Step } 19}$$

$$F_B = \frac{70.09}{1.33} = 52.70$$

Step 23 Compute the F for the A $\times$ B interaction:

$$F_{A \times B} = \frac{MS_{A \times B}}{MS_{A \times B \times S}}$$

$$F_{A \times B} = \frac{\text{Step } 17}{\text{Step } 20}$$

$$F_{A \times B} = \frac{102.07}{4.34} = 23.52$$

Step 24 For each F above, find the appropriate critical value in Table 5 in Appendix B, using as degrees of freedom:

> For factor A: df_A is the df between, and $df_{A \times S}$ is the df within. Above, for $\alpha = .05$ and $df_A = 1$, and $df_{A \times S} = 2$, F_{crit} is 18.51, so F_{obt} of .004 is not significant.
>
> For factor B: df_B is the df between, and $df_{B \times S}$ is the df within. Above, for $\alpha = .05$ and $df_B = 1$, and $df_{B \times S} = 2$, the F_{crit} is 18.51, so F_{obt} of 52.70 is significant.
>
> For A $\times$ B: $df_{A \times B}$ is the df between, and $df_{A \times B \times S}$ is the df within. Above, for $\alpha = .05$ and $df_{A \times B} = 1$ and $df_{A \times B \times S} = 2$, the F_{crit} is 18.51, so F_{obt} of 23.52 is significant.

Step 25 For each significant F with more than two levels, compute Tukey's HSD using the formula:

$$HSD = (q_k)\left(\sqrt{\frac{\text{Denominator in } F \text{ ratio}}{n}}\right)$$

where "denominator in F ratio" is the MS used as the denominator when calculating F_{obt}, and n is the number of scores that each mean being compared is based on.

For the interaction find q_k using the *adjusted k* as described in Chapter 14.

Step 26 For each significant F compute η^2 using the formula:

$$\eta^2 = \frac{\text{Sum of squares for the effect}}{SS_{\text{tot}}}$$

where "sum of squares for the effect" is the sum of squares used in calculating the numerator of the F_{obt}, whether SS_A, SS_B or $SS_{A \times B}$. The SS_{tot} is the total sum of squares in the ANOVA.

Step 27 Compute the confidence interval for the μ represented by the mean of any level or cell using the formula:

$$\left(\sqrt{\frac{MS_{\text{wn}}}{n}} \right)(-t_{\text{crit}}) + \overline{X} \le \mu \le \left(\sqrt{\frac{MS_{\text{wn}}}{n}} \right)(+t_{\text{crit}}) + \overline{X}$$

where MS_{wn} is the denominator used in computing F_{obt}, $\overline{X}$ is the mean of the level or cell being described, n is the number of scores the mean is based on, and t_{crit} is the two-tailed critical value from Table 2 in Appendix B, using as df the df used in computing the denominator of the F_{obt}.

APPLICATION QUESTIONS

(Answers to odd-numbered questions are in Appendix C.)

1. You measure the dependent variable of participants' hypnotic suggestibility as a function of whether they meditate before being tested, and whether they were shown a film containing a low, medium, or high amount of fantasy. The same participants are tested under all conditions. Perform all appropriate statistical analyses, and determine what you should conclude about this study.

Amount of Fantasy

	Low	Medium	High
Meditation	5	7	9
	6	5	8
	2	6	10
	2	9	10
	5	5	10
No Meditation	10	2	5
	10	5	6
	9	4	5
	10	3	7
	10	2	6

2. You study whether alcohol affects performing a simple eye–hand coordination task and whether the time of year the alcohol is consumed affects performance. Each participant performed the task either before drinking 0 or 3 drinks, and each was tested during the summer and during the winter. With $n = 3$ in each cell the following cell means and sums of squares were obtained.

Drinks Prior to Task Performance

		A_1: 0 Drinks	A_2: 3 Drinks
Time of Year	B1: Summer	16	6
	B2: Winter	11	12

Summary Table

Source	Sum of Squares	df	Mean Square	F
Factor				
A	90.75	____	____	____
B	6.75	____	____	____
A × B	47.50	____	____	____
Subjects				
A × S	8.00	____	____	
B × S	2.00	____	____	
A × B × S	4.25	____	____	
Total	236.92	____	(not computed)	

(a) Complete the ANOVA summary table. (b) With $\alpha = .05$, what do you conclude about each F_{obt}? (c) Perform the appropriate post hoc comparisons. What do you conclude about the relationships in this study? (d) Determine the effect size where appropriate and interpret it.

A.6: THE TWO-WAY, MIXED-DESIGN ANALYSIS OF VARIANCE

The following shows the calculations for the two-way, mixed-design ANOVA discussed in Chapter 14.

If you "mix" a design, with one factor a within-subjects factor (involving related samples) and the other factor a between-subjects factor (involving independent samples), then perform the **two-way, mixed-design ANOVA.** For example, say that we are again interested in the influence of the time of day people are tested (morning or evening) and whether they have low or high motivation. But there is reason to believe that one's overall motivation level is rather permanent and cannot be effectively manipulated. Therefore, we'll study two separate (independent) samples, one having low motivation and one having high motivation. In each group the same three participants will be tested twice in the repeated-measures factor of time of day of testing (morning or evening). Table A.8 shows example data from this 2×2 design, but note, for the formulas presented here:

Diagram the study differently than previous designs. The *row* factor is now factor A and is the between-subjects factor. The *column* factor is factor B and is the within-subjects factor.

TABLE A.8   Data from Two-Way, Mixed Design

Morning versus evening testing is the within-subjects, column factor B, and low versus high motivation level is the between-subjects, row factor A.

		Factor B: Time of Test		
		B_1: Morning	B_2: Evening	ΣX_{sub}
Factor A: Motivation	**Subject 1**	3	10	13
A_1: Low	**Subject 2**	5	16	21
	Subject 3	7	13	20
		$\overline{X} = 5.00$ $\Sigma X = 15$ $\Sigma X^2 = 83$ $n = 3$	$\overline{X} = 13.00$ $\Sigma X = 39$ $\Sigma X^2 = 525$ $n = 3$	$\overline{X} = 9.00$ $\Sigma X = 54$ $n = 6$
	Subject 4	8	7	15
A_2: High	**Subject 5**	6	7	13
	Subject 6	4	4	8
		$\overline{X} = 6.00$ $\Sigma X = 18$ $\Sigma X^2 = 116$ $n = 3$	$\overline{X} = 6.00$ $\Sigma X = 18$ $\Sigma X^2 = 114$ $n = 3$	$\overline{X} = 6.00$ $\Sigma X = 36$ $n = 6$
		$\Sigma X = 33$ $n = 6$ $\overline{X} = 5.50$	$\Sigma X = 57$ $n = 6$ $\overline{X} = 12.50$	$\Sigma X_{total} = 90$ $\Sigma X^2_{total} = 838$ $N = 12$ $k_A = 2$ $k_B = 2$

Step 1 In each cell compute the sum of scores (ΣX), the sum of the squared scores (ΣX^2), n, and the mean (the interaction means). Determine k_A, the number of levels of factor A, and for each row compute ΣX, n, and the mean (the main effect means of factor A). Determine k_B, the number of levels of factor B, and for each column compute ΣX, n, and the mean (the main effect means of factor B).

Also, calculate the sum of the scores obtained by each participant (ΣX_{sub}).

Step 2 Determine

$$\Sigma X_{total} = 54 + 36 = 90$$

$$\Sigma X^2_{total} = 83 + 525 + 116 + 114 = 838$$

$$N = 3 + 3 + 3 + 3 = 12$$

TABLE A.9 Summary Table of Two-Way, Mixed-Design ANOVA

Source	Sum of Squares	df	Mean Square	F
Between groups				
Factor A	27.00	1	27.00	3.38
Error between	32.00	4	8.00	
Within groups				
Factor B	48.00	1	48.00	24.00
A × B interaction	48.00	1	48.00	24.00
Error within	8.00	4	2.00	
Total	163.00	11		

Step 3 Compute the correction term:

$$\text{Correction term} = \left(\frac{(\Sigma X_{\text{total}})^2}{N}\right) = \frac{90^2}{12} = 675$$

Step 4 As you perform the following calculations, create the analysis of variance summary table shown in Table A.9. (*Note:* Components of the between-subjects, factor A are placed together, and components of the within-subjects, factor B and the interaction are placed together.)

Computing the ANOVA will again be different, but as usual, by collapsing vertically across the motivation factor, we examine the main effect means for time of test (comparing 5.50 to 12.50). Then collapsing across time of test, we examine the main effect means for motivation (9.00 versus 6.00). Then without collapsing, we examine the interaction between time of test and motivation (comparing the cell means of 5.00, 13.00, 6.00, and 6.00). For any significant F_{obt}, perform post hoc tests if needed, compute η^2 and confidence intervals, and graph the effect.

CALCULATING THE TWO-WAY, MIXED-DESIGN ANOVA

Step 5 Compute the total sum of squares:

$$SS_{\text{tot}} = \Sigma X_{\text{total}}^2 - \text{Step 3}$$

$$SS_{\text{tot}} = 838 - 675 = 163$$

Step 6 Compute the sum of squares for subjects (not reported in summary table):

$$SS_{\text{subs}} = \frac{(\Sigma X_{\text{sub1}})^2 + (\Sigma X_{\text{sub2}})^2 \ldots + (\Sigma X_n)^2}{k_B} - \text{Step 3}$$

$$SS_{\text{subs}} = \frac{(13)^2 + (21)^2 + (20)^2 + (15)^2 + (13)^2 + (8)^2}{2} - 675$$

$$SS_{\text{subs}} = 59$$

Step 7 Compute the sum of squares for the between-subjects, row factor A:

$$SS_A = \Sigma\left(\frac{(\text{Sum of scores in each row})^2}{n \text{ of scores in the row}}\right) - \text{Step 3}$$

$$SS_A = \left(\frac{(54)^2}{6} + \frac{(36)^2}{6}\right) - 675 = 27$$

Step 8 Compute the sum of squares for the within-subjects, column factor B:

$$SS_B = \Sigma\left(\frac{(\text{Sum of scores in each column})^2}{n \text{ of scores in the column}}\right) - \text{Step 3}$$

$$SS_B = \left(\frac{(33)^2}{6} + \frac{(57)^2}{6}\right) - 675 = 48$$

Step 9 Compute the sum of squares for error between subjects:

$$SS_{e:bn} = SS_{subs} - SS_A$$

$$SS_{e:bn} = \text{Step 6} - \text{Step 7}$$

$$SS_{e:bn} = 59 - 27 = 32$$

Step 10 Compute the total sum of squares between groups (not reported in summary table):

$$SS_{bn} = \Sigma\left(\frac{(\text{Sum of scores in each cell})^2}{n \text{ of scores in the cell}}\right) - \text{Step 3}$$

$$SS_{bn} = \left(\frac{(15)^2}{3} + \frac{(39)^2}{3} + \frac{(18)^2}{3} + \frac{(18)^2}{3}\right) - 675$$

$$SS_{bn} = 123$$

Step 11 Compute the sum of squares for the A $\times$ B interaction:

$$SS_{A\times B} = SS_{bn} - SS_A - SS_B$$

$$SS_{A\times B} = \text{Step 10} - \text{Step 7} - \text{Step 8}$$

$$SS_{A\times B} = 123 - 27 - 48 = 48$$

Step 12 Compute the sum of squares for error within subjects:

$$SS_{e:wn} = SS_{tot} - SS_{subs} - SS_B - SS_{A\times B}$$

$$SS_{e:wn} = \text{Step 5} - \text{Step 6} - \text{Step 8} - \text{Step 11}$$

$$SS_{e:wn} = 163 - 59 - 48 - 48 = 8$$

Step 13 Compute the degrees of freedom:
(a) Factor A:

$$df_A = k_A - 1$$

$$df_A = 2 - 1 = 1$$

(b) Factor B:

$$df_B = k_B - 1$$
$$df_B = 2 - 1 = 1$$

(c) A $\times$ B interaction:

$$df_{A \times B} = (df_A)(df_B)$$
$$df_{A \times B} = (\text{Step 13.a})(\text{Step 13.b})$$
$$df_{A \times B} = (1)(1) = 1$$

(d) Error between groups:

$$df_{e:bn} = (k_A)(n - 1)$$
$$df_{e:bn} = (2)(3 - 1) = 4$$

(e) Error within subjects:

$$df_{e:wn} = (k_B - 1)(k_A)(n - 1)$$
$$df_{e:wn} = (2 - 1)(2)(3 - 1) = 4$$

(f) Total:

$$df_{tot} = N - 1$$
$$df_{tot} = 12 - 1 = 11$$

Step 14 Compute the mean square for factor A:

$$MS_A = \frac{SS_A}{df_A}$$

$$MS_A = \frac{\text{Step 7}}{\text{Step 13.a}}$$

$$MS_A = \frac{27}{1} = 27$$

Step 15 Compute the mean square for factor B:

$$MS_B = \frac{SS_B}{df_B}$$

$$MS_B = \frac{\text{Step 8}}{\text{Step 13.b}}$$

$$MS_B = \frac{48}{1} = 48$$

Step 16 Compute the mean square for the A $\times$ B interaction:

$$MS_{A \times B} = \frac{SS_{A \times B}}{df_{A \times B}}$$

$$MS_{A \times B} = \frac{\text{Step 11}}{\text{Step 13.c}}$$

$$MS_{A \times B} = \frac{48}{1} = 48$$

Step 17 Compute the mean square for error between groups:

$$MS_{e:bn} = \frac{SS_{e:bn}}{df_{e:bn}}$$

$$MS_{e:bn} = \frac{\text{Step 9}}{\text{Step 13.d}}$$

$$MS_{e:bn} = \frac{32}{4} = 8$$

Step 18 Compute the mean square for error within subjects:

$$MS_{e:wn} = \frac{SS_{e:wn}}{df_{e:wn}}$$

$$MS_{e:wn} = \frac{\text{Step 12}}{\text{Step 13.e}}$$

$$MS_{e:wn} = \frac{8}{4} = 2$$

Step 19 Compute the F for the main effect of A:

$$F_A = \frac{MS_A}{MS_{e:bn}}$$

$$F_A = \frac{\text{Step 14}}{\text{Step 17}}$$

$$F_A = \frac{27}{8} = 3.38$$

Step 20 Compute the F for the main effect of B:

$$F_B = \frac{MS_B}{MS_{e:wn}}$$

$$F_B = \frac{\text{Step 15}}{\text{Step 18}}$$

$$F_B = \frac{48}{2} = 24$$

Step 21 Compute the F for the A $\times$ B interaction:

$$F_{A \times B} = \frac{MS_{A \times B}}{MS_{e:wn}}$$

$$F_{A \times B} = \frac{\text{Step 16}}{\text{Step 18}}$$

$$F_{A \times B} = \frac{48}{2} = 24$$

Step 22 For each F above, find the appropriate critical value in Table 5 in Appendix B, using as degrees of freedom:

For factor A: df_A is the df between, and $df_{e:bn}$ is the df within. Above, for $\alpha = .05$ and $df_A = 1$, and $df_{e:bn} = 4$, the F_{crit} is 7.71, so the main effect of factor A is not significant.

For factor B: df_B is the df between, and $df_{e:wn}$ is the df within. Above, for $\alpha = .05$ and $df_B = 1$, and $df_{e:wn} = 4$ the F_{crit} is 7.71, so the main effect of factor B is significant.

For A $\times$ B: $df_{A \times B}$ is the df between, and $df_{e:wn}$ is the df within. Above, for $\alpha = .05$ and $df_{A \times B} = 1$ and $df_{e:wn} = 4$, the F_{crit} is 7.71, so the interaction effect is significant.

Step 23 For each significant F with more than two levels, compute Tukey's *HSD* using the formula in step 25 in the previous section describing the two-way, within-subjects ANOVA.

Step 24 For each significant F, compute eta squared using the formula given in step 26 in the previous section for the two-way, within-subjects ANOVA.

Step 25 Compute the confidence interval for the μ represented by the mean of any level or cell using the formula given in step 27 in the previous section for the two-way, within-subjects ANOVA.

APPLICATION QUESTIONS

(Answers to odd-numbered questions are in Appendix C.)

1. You measure the dependent variable of participants' hypnotic suggestibility as a function of whether they meditate before being tested, and whether they were shown a film containing a low, medium, or high amount of fantasy. The meditation factor is between subjects, the fantasy-level factor is repeated measures.

Amount of Fantasy

	Low	*Medium*	*High*
Meditation	5	7	9
	6	5	8
	2	6	10
	2	9	10
	5	5	10
No Meditation	10	2	5
	10	5	6
	9	4	5
	10	3	7
	10	2	6

(a) Perform the appropriate statistical analysis, and determine what you should conclude about this study.

2. A researcher studies the influence of four doses of a new drug to reduce depression in adult women who either have the AIDs virus (are HIV+) or do not have it (are HIV−). Dosage is a repeated-measures factor, and HIV status is a between-subjects factor. With $n = 3$ in each cell the following overall mean mood improvement scores were obtained.

Factor B: Dose of Antidepressant

		B_1: Control	B_2: Low	B_3: Med.	B_4: High
Factor A: *HIV Status*	A_1: *HIV−*	4	5	13	17
	A_2: *HIV+*	3	6	12	19

Summary Table

Source	Sum of Squares	df	Mean Square	F
Between groups				
Factor A	21.00	___	___	___
Error between	20.50	___	___	___
Within groups				
Factor B	67.75	___	___	___
A × B interaction	30.00	___	___	___
Error within	34.50	___	___	
Total	173.75	___		

(a) Complete the ANOVA summary table. (b) With $\alpha = .05$ what do you conclude about each F_{obt}? (c) Perform the appropriate post hoc comparisons. What do you conclude about the relationships in this study? (d) Determine the effect size where appropriate. What does it indicate about the observed effects?

STATISTICAL TABLES

STATISTICAL TABLES

TABLE 1   Proportions of Area under the Standard Normal Curve: The *z*-Tables

Column (A) lists *z*-score values. Column (B) lists the proportion of the area between the mean and the *z*-score value. Column (C) lists the proportion of the area beyond the *z*-score in the tail of the distribution. (*Note:* Because the normal distribution is symmetrical, areas for negative *z*-scores are the same as those for positive *z*-scores.)

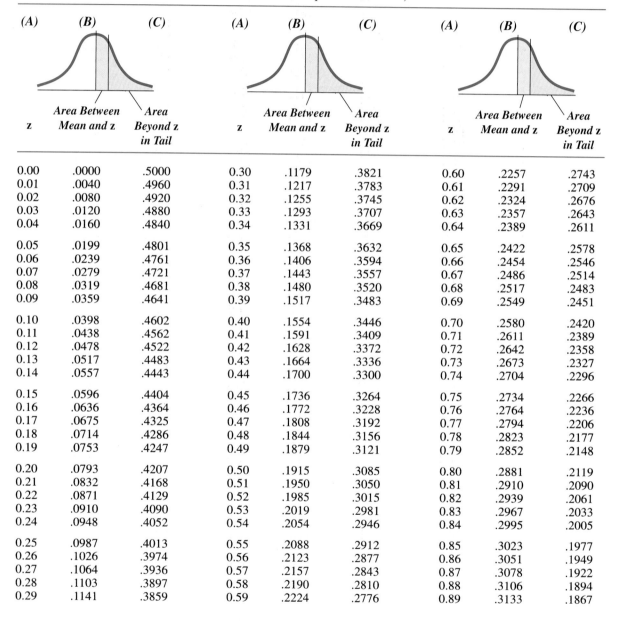

(A) z	*(B)* Area Between Mean and z	*(C)* Area Beyond z in Tail	*(A)* z	*(B)* Area Between Mean and z	*(C)* Area Beyond z in Tail	*(A)* z	*(B)* Area Between Mean and z	*(C)* Area Beyond z in Tail
0.00	.0000	.5000	0.30	.1179	.3821	0.60	.2257	.2743
0.01	.0040	.4960	0.31	.1217	.3783	0.61	.2291	.2709
0.02	.0080	.4920	0.32	.1255	.3745	0.62	.2324	.2676
0.03	.0120	.4880	0.33	.1293	.3707	0.63	.2357	.2643
0.04	.0160	.4840	0.34	.1331	.3669	0.64	.2389	.2611
0.05	.0199	.4801	0.35	.1368	.3632	0.65	.2422	.2578
0.06	.0239	.4761	0.36	.1406	.3594	0.66	.2454	.2546
0.07	.0279	.4721	0.37	.1443	.3557	0.67	.2486	.2514
0.08	.0319	.4681	0.38	.1480	.3520	0.68	.2517	.2483
0.09	.0359	.4641	0.39	.1517	.3483	0.69	.2549	.2451
0.10	.0398	.4602	0.40	.1554	.3446	0.70	.2580	.2420
0.11	.0438	.4562	0.41	.1591	.3409	0.71	.2611	.2389
0.12	.0478	.4522	0.42	.1628	.3372	0.72	.2642	.2358
0.13	.0517	.4483	0.43	.1664	.3336	0.73	.2673	.2327
0.14	.0557	.4443	0.44	.1700	.3300	0.74	.2704	.2296
0.15	.0596	.4404	0.45	.1736	.3264	0.75	.2734	.2266
0.16	.0636	.4364	0.46	.1772	.3228	0.76	.2764	.2236
0.17	.0675	.4325	0.47	.1808	.3192	0.77	.2794	.2206
0.18	.0714	.4286	0.48	.1844	.3156	0.78	.2823	.2177
0.19	.0753	.4247	0.49	.1879	.3121	0.79	.2852	.2148
0.20	.0793	.4207	0.50	.1915	.3085	0.80	.2881	.2119
0.21	.0832	.4168	0.51	.1950	.3050	0.81	.2910	.2090
0.22	.0871	.4129	0.52	.1985	.3015	0.82	.2939	.2061
0.23	.0910	.4090	0.53	.2019	.2981	0.83	.2967	.2033
0.24	.0948	.4052	0.54	.2054	.2946	0.84	.2995	.2005
0.25	.0987	.4013	0.55	.2088	.2912	0.85	.3023	.1977
0.26	.1026	.3974	0.56	.2123	.2877	0.86	.3051	.1949
0.27	.1064	.3936	0.57	.2157	.2843	0.87	.3078	.1922
0.28	.1103	.3897	0.58	.2190	.2810	0.88	.3106	.1894
0.29	.1141	.3859	0.59	.2224	.2776	0.89	.3133	.1867

TABLE 1 (CONT.) Proportions of Area under the Standard Normal Curve: The z-Tables

(A) z	(B) Area Between Mean and z	(C) Area Beyond z in Tail	(A) z	(B) Area Between Mean and z	(C) Area Beyond z in Tail	(A) z	(B) Area Between Mean and z	(C) Area Beyond z in Tail
0.90	.3159	.1841	1.25	.3944	.1056	1.60	.4452	.0548
0.91	.3186	.1814	1.26	.3962	.1038	1.61	.4463	.0537
0.92	.3212	.1788	1.27	.3980	.1020	1.62	.4474	.0526
0.93	.3238	.1762	1.28	.3997	.1003	1.63	.4484	.0516
0.94	.3264	.1736	1.29	.4015	.0985	1.64	.4495	.0505
0.95	.3289	.1711	1.30	.4032	.0968	1.65	.4505	.0495
0.96	.3315	.1685	1.31	.4049	.0951	1.66	.4515	.0485
0.97	.3340	.1660	1.32	.4066	.0934	1.67	.4525	.0475
0.98	.3365	.1635	1.33	.4082	.0918	1.68	.4535	.0465
0.99	.3389	.1611	1.34	.4099	.0901	1.69	.4545	.0455
1.00	.3413	.1587	1.35	.4115	.0885	1.70	.4554	.0446
1.01	.3438	.1562	1.36	.4131	.0869	1.71	.4564	.0436
1.02	.3461	.1539	1.37	.4147	.0853	1.72	.4573	.0427
1.03	.3485	.1515	1.38	.4162	.0838	1.73	.4582	.0418
1.04	.3508	.1492	1.39	.4177	.0823	1.74	.4591	.0409
1.05	.3531	.1469	1.40	.4192	.0808	1.75	.4599	.0401
1.06	.3554	.1446	1.41	.4207	.0793	1.76	.4608	.0392
1.07	.3577	.1423	1.42	.4222	.0778	1.77	.4616	.0384
1.08	.3599	.1401	1.43	.4236	.0764	1.78	.4625	.0375
1.09	.3621	.1379	1.44	.4251	.0749	1.79	.4633	.0367
1.10	.3643	.1357	1.45	.4265	.0735	1.80	.4641	.0359
1.11	.3665	.1335	1.46	.4279	.0721	1.81	.4649	.0351
1.12	.3686	.1314	1.47	.4292	.0708	1.82	.4656	.0344
1.13	.3708	.1292	1.48	.4306	.0694	1.83	.4664	.0336
1.14	.3729	.1271	1.49	.4319	.0681	1.84	.4671	.0329
1.15	.3749	.1251	1.50	.4332	.0668	1.85	.4678	.0322
1.16	.3770	.1230	1.51	.4345	.0655	1.86	.4686	.0314
1.17	.3790	.1210	1.52	.4357	.0643	1.87	.4693	.0307
1.18	.3810	.1190	1.53	.4370	.0630	1.88	.4699	.0301
1.19	.3830	.1170	1.54	.4382	.0618	1.89	.4706	.0294
1.20	.3849	.1151	1.55	.4394	.0606	1.90	.4713	.0287
1.21	.3869	.1131	1.56	.4406	.0594	1.91	.4719	.0281
1.22	.3888	.1112	1.57	.4418	.0582	1.92	.4726	.0274
1.23	.3907	.1093	1.58	.4429	.0571	1.93	.4732	.0268
1.24	.3925	.1075	1.59	.4441	.0559	1.94	.4738	.0262

TABLE 1 (CONT.)   Proportions of Area under the Standard Normal Curve: The z-Tables

(A) z	(B) Area Between Mean and z	(C) Area Beyond z in Tail	(A) z	(B) Area Between Mean and z	(C) Area Beyond z in Tail	(A) z	(B) Area Between Mean and z	(C) Area Beyond z in Tail
1.95	.4744	.0256	2.30	.4893	.0107	2.65	.4960	.0040
1.96	.4750	.0250	2.31	.4896	.0104	2.66	.4961	.0039
1.97	.4756	.0244	2.32	.4898	.0102	2.67	.4962	.0038
1.98	.4761	.0239	2.33	.4901	.0099	2.68	.4963	.0037
1.99	.4767	.0233	2.34	.4904	.0096	2.69	.4964	.0036
2.00	.4772	.0228	2.35	.4906	.0094	2.70	.4965	.0035
2.01	.4778	.0222	2.36	.4909	.0091	2.71	.4966	.0034
2.02	.4783	.0217	2.37	.4911	.0089	2.72	.4967	.0033
2.03	.4788	.0212	2.38	.4913	.0087	2.73	.4968	.0032
2.04	.4793	.0207	2.39	.4916	.0084	2.74	.4969	.0031
2.05	.4798	.0202	2.40	.4918	.0082	2.75	.4970	.0030
2.06	.4803	.0197	2.41	.4920	.0080	2.76	.4971	.0029
2.07	.4808	.0192	2.42	.4922	.0078	2.77	.4972	.0028
2.08	.4812	.0188	2.43	.4925	.0075	2.78	.4973	.0027
2.09	.4817	.0183	2.44	.4927	.0073	2.79	.4974	.0026
2.10	.4821	.0179	2.45	.4929	.0071	2.80	.4974	.0026
2.11	.4826	.0174	2.46	.4931	.0069	2.81	.4975	.0025
2.12	.4830	.0170	2.47	.4932	.0068	2.82	.4976	.0024
2.13	.4834	.0166	2.48	.4934	.0066	2.83	.4977	.0023
2.14	.4838	.0162	2.49	.4936	.0064	2.84	.4977	.0023
2.15	.4842	.0158	2.50	.4938	.0062	2.85	.4978	.0022
2.16	.4846	.0154	2.51	.4940	.0060	2.86	.4979	.0021
2.17	.4850	.0150	2.52	.4941	.0059	2.87	.4979	.0021
2.18	.4854	.0146	2.53	.4943	.0057	2.88	.4980	.0020
2.19	.4857	.0143	2.54	.4945	.0055	2.89	.4981	.0019
2.20	.4861	.0139	2.55	.4946	.0054	2.90	.4981	.0019
2.21	.4864	.0136	2.56	.4948	.0052	2.91	.4982	.0018
2.22	.4868	.0132	2.57	.4949	.0051	2.92	.4982	.0018
2.23	.4871	.0129	2.58	.4951	.0049	2.93	.4983	.0017
2.24	.4875	.0125	2.59	.4952	.0048	2.94	.4984	.0016
2.25	.4878	.0122	2.60	.4953	.0047	2.95	.4984	.0016
2.26	.4881	.0119	2.61	.4955	.0045	2.96	.4985	.0015
2.27	.4884	.0116	2.62	.4956	.0044	2.97	.4985	.0015
2.28	.4887	.0113	2.63	.4957	.0043	2.98	.4986	.0014
2.29	.4890	.0110	2.64	.4959	.0041	2.99	.4986	.0014

TABLE 1 (CONT.) Proportions of Area under the Standard Normal Curve: The z-Tables

(A) z	(B) Area Between Mean and z	(C) Area Beyond z in Tail	(A) z	(B) Area Between Mean and z	(C) Area Beyond z in Tail	(A) z	(B) Area Between Mean and z	(C) Area Beyond z in Tail
3.00	.4987	.0013	3.12	.4991	.0009	3.24	.4994	.0006
3.01	.4987	.0013	3.13	.4991	.0009	3.25	.4994	.0006
3.02	.4987	.0013	3.14	.4992	.0008	3.30	.4995	.0005
3.03	.4988	.0012	3.15	.4992	.0008	3.35	.4996	.0004
3.04	.4988	.0012	3.16	.4992	.0008	3.40	.4997	.0003
3.05	.4989	.0011	3.17	.4992	.0008	3.45	.4997	.0003
3.06	.4989	.0011	3.18	.4993	.0007	3.50	.4998	.0002
3.07	.4989	.0011	3.19	.4993	.0007	3.60	.4998	.0002
3.08	.4990	.0010	3.20	.4993	.0007	3.70	.4999	.0001
3.09	.4990	.0010	3.21	.4993	.0007	3.80	.4999	.0001
3.10	.4990	.0010	3.22	.4994	.0006	3.90	.49995	.00005
3.11	.4991	.0009	3.23	.4994	.0006	4.00	.49997	.00003

TABLE 2 Critical Values of *t:* The *t*-Tables

(*Note:* Values of $-t_{crit}$ = values of $+t_{crit}$.)

	Two-Tailed Test				One-Tailed Test		

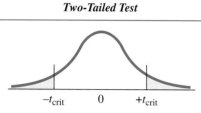

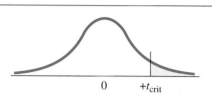

	Alpha Level				*Alpha Level*	
df	α = .05	α = .01		*df*	α = .05	α = .01
1	12.706	63.657		1	6.314	31.821
2	4.303	9.925		2	2.920	6.965
3	3.182	5.841		3	2.353	4.541
4	2.776	4.604		4	2.132	3.747
5	2.571	4.032		5	2.015	3.365
6	2.447	3.707		6	1.943	3.143
7	2.365	3.499		7	1.895	2.998
8	2.306	3.355		8	1.860	2.896
9	2.262	3.250		9	1.833	2.821
10	2.228	3.169		10	1.812	2.764
11	2.201	3.106		11	1.796	2.718
12	2.179	3.055		12	1.782	2.681
13	2.160	3.012		13	1.771	2.650
14	2.145	2.977		14	1.761	2.624
15	2.131	2.947		15	1.753	2.602
16	2.120	2.921		16	1.746	2.583
17	2.110	2.898		17	1.740	2.567
18	2.101	2.878		18	1.734	2.552
19	2.093	2.861		19	1.729	2.539
20	2.086	2.845		20	1.725	2.528
21	2.080	2.831		21	1.721	2.518
22	2.074	2.819		22	1.717	2.508
23	2.069	2.807		23	1.714	2.500
24	2.064	2.797		24	1.711	2.492
25	2.060	2.787		25	1.708	2.485
26	2.056	2.779		26	1.706	2.479
27	2.052	2.771		27	1.703	2.473
28	2.048	2.763		28	1.701	2.467
29	2.045	2.756		29	1.699	2.462
30	2.042	2.750		30	1.697	2.457
40	2.021	2.704		40	1.684	2.423
60	2.000	2.660		60	1.671	2.390
120	1.980	2.617		120	1.658	2.358
∞	1.960	2.576		∞	1.645	2.326

TABLE 3 Critical Values of the Pearson Correlation Coefficient and the Point-Biserial Correlation Coefficient: The r and r_{pb} Tables

	Two-Tailed Test			*One-Tailed Test*	

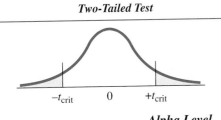

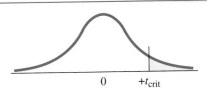

	Alpha Level			*Alpha Level*	
df (no. of pairs − 2)	$\alpha = .05$	$\alpha = .01$	*df (no. of pairs − 2)*	$\alpha = .05$	$\alpha = .01$
1	.997	.9999	1	.988	.9995
2	.950	.990	2	.900	.980
3	.878	.959	3	.805	.934
4	.811	.917	4	.729	.882
5	.754	.874	5	.669	.833
6	.707	.834	6	.622	.789
7	.666	.798	7	.582	.750
8	.632	.765	8	.549	.716
9	.602	.735	9	.521	.685
10	.576	.708	10	.497	.658
11	.553	.684	11	.476	.634
12	.532	.661	12	.458	.612
13	.514	.641	13	.441	.592
14	.497	.623	14	.426	.574
15	.482	.606	15	.412	.558
16	.468	.590	16	.400	.542
17	.456	.575	17	.389	.528
18	.444	.561	18	.378	.516
19	.433	.549	19	.369	.503
20	.423	.537	20	.360	.492
21	.413	.526	21	.352	.482
22	.404	.515	22	.344	.472
23	.396	.505	23	.337	.462
24	.388	.496	24	.330	.453
25	.381	.487	25	.323	.445
26	.374	.479	26	.317	.437
27	.367	.471	27	.311	.430
28	.361	.463	28	.306	.423
29	.355	.456	29	.301	.416
30	.349	.449	30	.296	.409
35	.325	.418	35	.275	.381
40	.304	.393	40	.257	.358
45	.288	.372	45	.243	.338
50	.273	.354	50	.231	.322
60	.250	.325	60	.211	.295
70	.232	.302	70	.195	.274
80	.217	.283	80	.183	.256
90	.205	.267	90	.173	.242
100	.195	.254	100	.164	.230

From Table IV of R. A. Fisher and F. Yates, *Statistical Tables for Biological, Agricultural and Medical Research*, 6th ed. (London: Longman Group Ltd., 1974). Reprinted by permission of Pearson Education Limited.

TABLE 4   Critical Values of the Spearman Rank-Order Correlation Coefficient: The r_s-Tables

To interpolate the critical value for an N not given, find the critical values for the N above and below your N, add them together, and then divide the sum by 2. When N is greater than 30, transform r_s to a z-score using the formula $z_{obt} = (r_s)(\sqrt{N-1})$. For $\alpha = .05$, the two-tailed $z_{crit} = \pm 1.96$ and the one-tailed $z_{crit} = 1.645$.

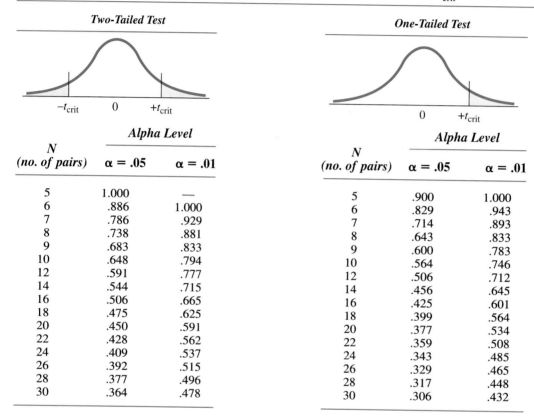

Two-Tailed Test				*One-Tailed Test*		
	Alpha Level				*Alpha Level*	
N (no. of pairs)	$\alpha = .05$	$\alpha = .01$		*N* (no. of pairs)	$\alpha = .05$	$\alpha = .01$
5	1.000	—		5	.900	1.000
6	.886	1.000		6	.829	.943
7	.786	.929		7	.714	.893
8	.738	.881		8	.643	.833
9	.683	.833		9	.600	.783
10	.648	.794		10	.564	.746
12	.591	.777		12	.506	.712
14	.544	.715		14	.456	.645
16	.506	.665		16	.425	.601
18	.475	.625		18	.399	.564
20	.450	.591		20	.377	.534
22	.428	.562		22	.359	.508
24	.409	.537		24	.343	.485
26	.392	.515		26	.329	.465
28	.377	.496		28	.317	.448
30	.364	.478		30	.306	.432

From E. G. Olds (1949), "The 5 Percent Significance Levels of Sums of Squares of Rank Differences and a Correction," *Annals of Math Statistics*, 20, pp. 117–118; and E. G. Olds (1938), "Distribution of Sums of Squares of Rank Differences for Small Numbers of Individuals," *Annals of Math Statistics*, 9, pp. 133–148. Reprinted with permission of the Institute of Mathematical Statistics.

TABLE 5 Critical Values of *F:* The *F*-Tables

Critical values for $\alpha = .05$ are in **dark numbers.**
Critical values for $\alpha = .01$ are in light numbers.

Degrees of Freedom Within Groups (degrees of freedom in denominator of F-ratio)	α	Degrees of Freedom Between Groups (degrees of freedom in numerator of F-ratio)														
		1	*2*	*3*	*4*	*5*	*6*	*7*	*8*	*9*	*10*	*11*	*12*	*14*	*16*	*20*
1	.05	**161**	**200**	**216**	**225**	**230**	**234**	**237**	**239**	**241**	**242**	**243**	**244**	**245**	**246**	**248**
	.01	4,052	4,999	5,403	5,625	5,764	5,859	5,928	5,981	6,022	6,056	6,082	6,106	6,142	6,169	6,208
2	.05	**18.51**	**19.00**	**19.16**	**19.25**	**19.30**	**19.33**	**19.36**	**19.37**	**19.38**	**19.39**	**19.40**	**19.41**	**19.42**	**19.43**	**19.44**
	.01	98.49	99.00	99.17	99.25	99.30	99.33	99.34	99.36	99.38	99.40	99.41	99.42	99.43	99.44	99.45
3	.05	**10.13**	**9.55**	**9.28**	**9.12**	**9.01**	**8.94**	**8.88**	**8.84**	**8.81**	**8.78**	**8.76**	**8.74**	**8.71**	**8.69**	**8.66**
	.01	34.12	30.82	29.46	28.71	28.24	27.91	27.67	27.49	27.34	27.23	27.13	27.05	26.92	26.83	26.69
4	.05	**7.71**	**6.94**	**6.59**	**6.39**	**6.26**	**6.16**	**6.09**	**6.04**	**6.00**	**5.96**	**5.93**	**5.91**	**5.87**	**5.84**	**5.80**
	.01	21.20	18.00	16.69	15.98	15.52	15.21	14.98	14.80	14.66	14.54	14.45	14.37	14.24	14.15	14.02
5	.05	**6.61**	**5.79**	**5.41**	**5.19**	**5.05**	**4.95**	**4.88**	**4.82**	**4.78**	**4.74**	**4.70**	**4.68**	**4.64**	**4.60**	**4.56**
	.01	16.26	13.27	12.06	11.39	10.97	10.67	10.45	10.27	10.15	10.05	9.96	9.89	9.77	9.68	9.55
6	.05	**5.99**	**5.14**	**4.76**	**4.53**	**4.39**	**4.28**	**4.21**	**4.15**	**4.10**	**4.06**	**4.03**	**4.00**	**3.96**	**3.92**	**3.87**
	.01	13.74	10.92	9.78	9.15	8.75	8.47	8.26	8.10	7.98	7.87	7.79	7.72	7.60	7.52	7.39
7	.05	**5.59**	**4.47**	**4.35**	**4.12**	**3.97**	**3.87**	**3.79**	**3.73**	**3.68**	**3.63**	**3.60**	**3.57**	**3.52**	**3.49**	**3.44**
	.01	12.25	9.55	8.45	7.85	7.46	7.19	7.00	6.84	6.71	6.62	6.54	6.47	6.35	6.27	6.15
8	.05	**5.32**	**4.46**	**4.07**	**3.84**	**3.69**	**3.58**	**3.50**	**3.44**	**3.39**	**3.34**	**3.31**	**3.28**	**3.23**	**3.20**	**3.15**
	.01	11.26	8.65	7.59	7.01	6.63	6.37	6.19	6.03	5.91	5.82	5.74	5.67	5.56	5.48	5.36
9	.05	**5.12**	**4.26**	**3.86**	**3.63**	**3.48**	**3.37**	**3.29**	**3.23**	**3.18**	**3.13**	**3.10**	**3.07**	**3.02**	**2.98**	**2.93**
	.01	10.56	8.02	6.99	6.42	6.06	5.80	5.62	5.47	5.35	5.26	5.18	5.11	5.00	4.92	4.80
10	.05	**4.96**	**4.10**	**3.71**	**3.48**	**3.33**	**3.22**	**3.14**	**3.07**	**3.02**	**2.97**	**2.94**	**2.91**	**2.86**	**2.82**	**2.77**
	.01	10.04	7.56	6.55	5.99	5.64	5.39	5.21	5.06	4.95	4.85	4.78	4.71	4.60	4.52	4.41
11	.05	**4.84**	**3.98**	**3.59**	**3.36**	**3.20**	**3.09**	**3.01**	**2.95**	**2.90**	**2.86**	**2.82**	**2.79**	**2.74**	**2.70**	**2.65**
	.01	9.65	7.20	6.22	5.67	5.32	5.07	4.88	4.74	4.63	4.54	4.46	4.40	4.29	4.21	4.10
12	.05	**4.75**	**3.88**	**3.49**	**3.26**	**3.11**	**3.00**	**2.92**	**2.85**	**2.80**	**2.76**	**2.72**	**2.69**	**2.64**	**2.60**	**2.54**
	.01	9.33	6.93	5.95	5.41	5.06	4.82	4.65	4.50	4.39	4.30	4.22	4.16	4.05	3.98	3.86
13	.05	**4.67**	**3.80**	**3.41**	**3.18**	**3.02**	**2.92**	**2.84**	**2.77**	**2.72**	**2.67**	**2.63**	**2.60**	**2.55**	**2.51**	**2.46**
	.01	9.07	6.70	5.74	5.20	4.86	4.62	4.44	4.30	4.19	4.10	4.02	3.96	3.85	3.78	3.67
14	.05	**4.60**	**3.74**	**3.34**	**3.11**	**2.96**	**2.85**	**2.77**	**2.70**	**2.65**	**2.60**	**2.56**	**2.53**	**2.48**	**2.44**	**2.39**
	.01	8.86	6.51	5.56	5.03	4.69	4.46	4.28	4.14	4.03	3.94	3.86	3.80	3.70	3.62	3.51
15	.05	**4.54**	**3.68**	**3.29**	**3.06**	**2.90**	**2.79**	**2.70**	**2.64**	**2.59**	**2.55**	**2.51**	**2.48**	**2.43**	**2.39**	**2.33**
	.01	8.68	6.36	5.42	4.89	4.56	4.32	4.14	4.00	3.89	3.80	3.73	3.67	3.56	3.48	3.36
16	.05	**4.49**	**3.63**	**3.24**	**3.01**	**2.85**	**2.74**	**2.66**	**2.59**	**2.54**	**2.49**	**2.45**	**2.42**	**2.37**	**2.33**	**2.28**
	.01	8.53	6.23	5.29	4.77	4.44	4.20	4.03	3.89	3.78	3.69	3.61	3.55	3.45	3.37	3.25

TABLE 5 (CONT.) Critical Values of *F:* The *F*-Tables

Degrees of Freedom Within Groups (degrees of freedom in denominator of **F**-ratio)	α	1	2	3	4	5	6	7	8	9	10	11	12	14	16	20
							Degrees of Freedom Between Groups (degrees of freedom in numerator of **F**-ratio)									
17	.05	4.45	3.59	3.20	2.96	2.81	2.70	2.62	2.55	2.50	2.45	2.41	2.38	2.33	2.29	2.23
	.01	8.40	6.11	5.18	4.67	4.34	4.10	3.93	3.79	3.68	3.59	3.52	3.45	3.35	3.27	3.16
18	.05	4.41	3.55	3.16	2.93	2.77	2.66	2.58	2.51	2.46	2.41	2.37	2.34	2.29	2.25	2.19
	.01	8.28	6.01	5.09	4.58	4.25	4.01	3.85	3.71	3.60	3.51	3.44	3.37	3.27	3.19	3.07
19	.05	4.38	3.52	3.13	2.90	2.74	2.63	2.55	2.48	2.43	2.38	2.34	2.31	2.26	2.21	2.15
	.01	8.18	5.93	5.01	4.50	4.17	3.94	3.77	3.63	3.52	3.43	3.36	3.30	3.19	3.12	3.00
20	.05	4.35	3.49	3.10	2.87	2.71	2.60	2.52	2.45	2.40	2.35	2.31	2.28	2.23	2.18	2.12
	.01	8.10	5.85	4.94	4.43	4.10	3.87	3.71	3.56	3.45	3.37	3.30	3.23	3.13	3.05	2.94
21	.05	4.32	3.47	3.07	2.84	2.68	2.57	2.49	2.42	2.37	2.32	2.28	2.25	2.20	2.15	2.09
	.01	8.02	5.78	4.87	4.37	4.04	3.81	3.65	3.51	3.40	3.31	3.24	3.17	3.07	2.99	2.88
22	.05	4.30	3.44	3.05	2.82	2.66	2.55	2.47	2.40	2.35	2.30	2.26	2.23	2.18	2.13	2.07
	.01	7.94	5.72	4.82	4.31	3.99	3.76	3.59	3.45	3.35	3.26	3.18	3.12	3.02	2.94	2.83
23	.05	4.28	3.42	3.03	2.80	2.64	2.53	2.45	2.38	2.32	2.28	2.24	2.20	2.14	2.10	2.04
	.01	7.88	5.66	4.76	4.26	3.94	3.71	3.54	3.41	3.30	3.21	3.14	3.07	2.97	2.89	2.78
24	.05	4.26	3.40	3.01	2.78	2.62	2.51	2.43	2.36	2.30	2.26	2.22	2.18	2.13	2.09	2.02
	.01	7.82	5.61	4.72	4.22	3.90	3.67	3.50	3.36	3.25	3.17	3.09	3.03	2.93	2.85	2.74
25	.05	4.24	3.38	2.99	2.76	2.60	2.49	2.41	2.34	2.28	2.24	2.20	2.16	2.11	2.06	2.00
	.01	7.77	5.57	4.68	4.18	3.86	3.63	3.46	3.32	3.21	3.13	3.05	2.99	2.89	2.81	2.70
26	.05	4.22	3.37	2.98	2.74	2.59	2.47	2.39	2.32	2.27	2.22	2.18	2.15	2.10	2.05	1.99
	.01	7.72	5.53	4.64	4.14	3.82	3.59	3.42	3.29	3.17	3.09	3.02	2.96	2.86	2.77	2.66
27	.05	4.21	3.35	2.96	2.73	2.57	2.46	2.37	2.30	2.25	2.20	2.16	2.13	2.08	2.03	1.97
	.01	7.68	5.49	4.60	4.11	3.79	3.56	3.39	3.26	3.14	3.06	2.98	2.93	2.83	2.74	2.63
28	.05	4.20	3.34	2.95	2.71	2.56	2.44	2.36	2.29	2.24	2.19	2.15	2.12	2.06	2.02	1.96
	.01	7.64	5.45	4.57	4.07	3.76	3.53	3.36	3.23	3.11	3.03	2.95	2.90	2.80	2.71	2.60
29	.05	4.18	3.33	2.93	2.70	2.54	2.43	2.35	2.28	2.22	2.18	2.14	2.10	2.05	2.00	1.94
	.01	7.60	5.42	4.54	4.04	3.73	3.50	3.33	3.20	3.08	3.00	2.92	2.87	2.77	2.68	2.57
30	.05	4.17	3.32	2.92	2.69	2.53	2.42	2.34	2.27	2.21	2.16	2.12	2.09	2.04	1.99	1.93
	.01	7.56	5.39	4.51	4.02	3.70	3.47	3.30	3.17	3.06	2.98	2.90	2.84	2.74	2.66	2.55
32	.05	4.15	3.30	2.90	2.67	2.51	2.40	2.32	2.25	2.19	2.14	2.10	2.07	2.02	1.97	1.91
	.01	7.50	5.34	4.46	3.97	3.66	3.42	3.25	3.12	3.01	2.94	2.86	2.80	2.70	2.62	2.51
34	.05	4.13	3.28	2.88	2.65	2.49	2.38	2.30	2.23	2.17	2.12	2.08	2.05	2.00	1.95	1.89
	.01	7.44	5.29	4.42	3.93	3.61	3.38	3.21	3.08	2.97	2.89	2.82	2.76	2.66	2.58	2.47
36	.05	4.11	3.26	2.86	2.63	2.48	2.36	2.28	2.21	2.15	2.10	2.06	2.03	1.98	1.93	1.87
	.01	7.39	5.25	4.38	3.89	3.58	3.35	3.18	3.04	2.94	2.86	2.78	2.72	2.62	2.54	2.43
38	.05	4.10	3.25	2.85	2.62	2.46	2.35	2.26	2.19	2.14	2.09	2.05	2.02	1.96	1.92	1.85
	.01	7.35	5.21	4.34	3.86	3.54	3.32	3.15	3.02	2.91	2.82	2.75	2.69	2.59	2.51	2.40
40	.05	4.08	3.23	2.84	2.61	2.45	2.34	2.25	2.18	2.12	2.07	2.04	2.00	1.95	1.90	1.84
	.01	7.31	5.18	4.31	3.83	3.51	3.29	3.12	2.99	2.88	2.80	2.73	2.66	2.56	2.49	2.37
42	.05	4.07	3.22	2.83	2.59	2.44	2.32	2.24	2.17	2.11	2.06	2.02	1.99	1.94	1.89	1.82
	.01	7.27	5.15	4.29	3.80	3.49	3.26	3.10	2.96	2.86	2.77	2.70	2.64	2.54	2.46	2.35

TABLE 5 (CONT.)   Critical Values of *F:* The *F*-Tables

Degrees of Freedom Within Groups (degrees of freedom in denominator of **F**-ratio)	α	*1*	*2*	*3*	*4*	*5*	*6*	*7*	*8*	*9*	*10*	*11*	*12*	*14*	*16*	*20*
44	.05	4.06	3.21	2.82	2.58	2.43	2.31	2.23	2.16	2.10	2.05	2.01	1.98	1.92	1.88	1.81
	.01	7.24	5.12	4.26	3.78	3.46	3.24	3.07	2.94	2.84	2.75	2.68	2.62	2.52	2.44	2.32
46	.05	4.05	3.20	2.81	2.57	2.42	2.30	2.22	2.14	2.09	2.04	2.00	1.97	1.91	1.87	1.80
	.01	7.21	5.10	4.24	3.76	3.44	3.22	3.05	2.92	2.82	2.73	2.66	2.60	2.50	2.42	2.30
48	.05	4.04	3.19	2.80	2.56	2.41	2.30	2.21	2.14	2.08	2.03	1.99	1.96	1.90	1.86	1.79
	.01	7.19	5.08	4.22	3.74	3.42	3.20	3.04	2.90	2.80	2.71	2.64	2.58	2.48	2.40	2.28
50	.05	4.03	3.18	2.79	2.56	2.40	2.29	2.20	2.13	2.07	2.02	1.98	1.95	1.90	1.85	1.78
	.01	7.17	5.06	4.20	3.72	3.41	3.18	3.02	2.88	2.78	2.70	2.62	2.56	2.46	2.39	2.26
55	.05	4.02	3.17	2.78	2.54	2.38	2.27	2.18	2.11	2.05	2.00	1.97	1.93	1.88	1.83	1.76
	.01	7.12	5.01	4.16	3.68	3.37	3.15	2.98	2.85	2.75	2.66	2.59	2.53	2.43	2.35	2.23
60	.05	4.00	3.15	2.76	2.52	2.37	2.25	2.17	2.10	2.04	1.99	1.95	1.92	1.86	1.81	1.75
	.01	7.08	4.98	4.13	3.65	3.34	3.12	2.95	2.82	2.72	2.63	2.56	2.50	2.40	2.32	2.20
65	.05	3.99	3.14	2.75	2.51	2.36	2.24	2.15	2.08	2.02	1.98	1.94	1.90	1.85	1.80	1.73
	.01	7.04	4.95	4.10	3.62	3.31	3.09	2.93	2.79	2.70	2.61	2.54	2.47	2.37	2.30	2.18
70	.05	3.98	3.13	2.74	2.50	2.35	2.23	2.14	2.07	2.01	1.97	1.93	1.89	1.84	1.79	1.72
	.01	7.01	4.92	4.08	3.60	3.29	3.07	2.91	2.77	2.67	2.59	2.51	2.45	2.35	2.28	2.15
80	.05	3.96	3.11	2.72	2.48	2.33	2.21	2.12	2.05	1.99	1.95	1.91	1.88	1.82	1.77	1.70
	.01	6.96	4.88	4.04	3.56	3.25	3.04	2.87	2.74	2.64	2.55	2.48	2.41	2.32	2.24	2.11
100	.05	3.94	3.09	2.70	2.46	2.30	2.19	2.10	2.03	1.97	1.92	1.88	1.85	1.79	1.75	1.68
	.01	6.90	4.82	3.98	3.51	3.20	2.99	2.82	2.69	2.59	2.51	2.43	2.36	2.26	2.19	2.06
125	.05	3.92	3.07	2.68	2.44	2.29	2.17	2.08	2.01	1.95	1.90	1.86	1.83	1.77	1.72	1.65
	.01	6.84	4.78	3.94	3.47	3.17	2.95	2.79	2.65	2.56	2.47	2.40	2.33	2.23	2.15	2.03
150	.05	3.91	3.06	2.67	2.43	2.27	2.16	2.07	2.00	1.94	1.89	1.85	1.82	1.76	1.71	1.64
	.01	6.81	4.75	3.91	3.44	3.14	2.92	2.76	2.62	2.53	2.44	2.37	2.30	2.20	2.12	2.00
200	.05	3.89	3.04	2.65	2.41	2.26	2.14	2.05	1.98	1.92	1.87	1.83	1.80	1.74	1.69	1.62
	.01	6.76	4.71	3.88	3.41	3.11	2.90	2.73	2.60	2.50	2.41	2.34	2.28	2.17	2.09	1.97
400	.05	3.86	3.02	2.62	2.39	2.23	2.12	2.03	1.96	1.90	1.85	1.81	1.78	1.72	1.67	1.60
	.01	6.70	4.66	3.83	3.36	3.06	2.85	2.69	2.55	2.46	2.37	2.29	2.23	2.12	2.04	1.92
1000	.05	3.85	3.00	2.61	2.38	2.22	2.10	2.02	1.95	1.89	1.84	1.80	1.76	1.70	1.65	1.58
	.01	6.66	4.62	3.80	3.34	3.04	2.82	2.66	2.53	2.43	2.34	2.26	2.20	2.09	2.01	1.89
∞	.05	3.84	2.99	2.60	2.37	2.21	2.09	2.01	1.94	1.88	1.83	1.79	1.75	1.69	1.64	1.57
	.01	6.64	4.60	3.78	3.32	3.02	2.80	2.64	2.51	2.41	2.32	2.24	2.18	2.07	1.99	1.87

*Degrees of Freedom Between Groups (degrees of freedom in numerator of **F**-ratio)*

STATISTICAL TABLES

Reprinted by permission from *Statistical Methods*, 8th edition by G. Snedecor and W. Cochran. © 1989 by The Iowa State University Press, Ames, Iowa.

TABLE 6 Values of Studentized Range Statistic, q_k

For a one-way ANOVA, or a comparison of the means from a main effect, the value of k is the number of means in the factor.

To compare the means from an interaction, find the appropriate design (or number of cell means) in the table below and obtain the adjusted value of k. Then use adjusted k as k to find the value of q_k.

Values of Adjusted k

Design of Study	Number of Cell Means in Study	Adjusted Value of k
2 × 2	4	3
2 × 3	6	5
2 × 4	8	6
3 × 3	9	7
3 × 4	12	8
4 × 4	16	10
4 × 5	20	12

Values of q_k for $\alpha = .05$ are **dark numbers** and for $\alpha = .01$ are light numbers.

Degrees of Freedom Within Groups (degrees of freedom in denominator of F-ratio)	α	2	3	4	5	6	7	8	9	10	11	12
						k = Number of Means Being Compared						
1	.05	**18.00**	**27.00**	**32.80**	**37.10**	**40.40**	**43.10**	**45.40**	**47.40**	**49.10**	**50.60**	**52.00**
	.01	90.00	135.00	164.00	186.00	202.00	216.00	227.00	237.00	246.00	253.00	260.00
2	.05	**6.09**	**8.30**	**9.80**	**10.90**	**11.70**	**12.40**	**13.00**	**13.50**	**14.00**	**14.40**	**14.70**
	.01	14.00	19.00	22.30	24.70	26.60	28.20	29.50	30.70	31.70	32.60	33.40
3	.05	**4.50**	**5.91**	**6.82**	**7.50**	**8.04**	**8.48**	**8.85**	**9.18**	**9.46**	**9.72**	**9.95**
	.01	8.26	10.60	12.20	13.30	14.20	15.00	15.60	16.20	16.70	17.10	17.50
4	.05	**3.93**	**5.04**	**5.76**	**6.29**	**6.71**	**7.05**	**7.35**	**7.60**	**7.83**	**8.03**	**8.21**
	.01	6.51	8.12	9.17	9.96	10.60	11.10	11.50	11.90	12.30	12.60	12.80
5	.05	**3.64**	**4.60**	**5.22**	**5.67**	**6.03**	**6.33**	**6.58**	**6.80**	**6.99**	**7.17**	**7.32**
	.01	5.70	6.97	7.80	8.42	8.91	9.32	9.67	9.97	10.20	10.50	10.70
6	.05	**3.46**	**4.34**	**4.90**	**5.31**	**5.63**	**5.89**	**6.12**	**6.32**	**6.49**	**6.65**	**6.79**
	.01	5.24	6.33	7.03	7.56	7.97	8.32	8.61	8.87	9.10	9.30	9.49
7	.05	**3.34**	**4.16**	**4.69**	**5.06**	**5.36**	**5.61**	**5.82**	**6.00**	**6.16**	**6.30**	**6.43**
	.01	4.95	5.92	6.54	7.01	7.37	7.68	7.94	8.17	8.37	8.55	8.71
8	.05	**3.26**	**4.04**	**4.53**	**4.89**	**5.17**	**5.40**	**5.60**	**5.77**	**5.92**	**6.05**	**6.18**
	.01	4.74	5.63	6.20	6.63	6.96	7.24	7.47	7.68	7.87	8.03	8.18
9	.05	**3.20**	**3.95**	**4.42**	**4.76**	**5.02**	**5.24**	**5.43**	**5.60**	**5.74**	**5.87**	**5.98**
	.01	4.60	5.43	5.96	6.35	6.66	6.91	7.13	7.32	7.49	7.65	7.78

TABLE 6 (CONT.)   Values of Studentized Range Statistic, q_k

Degrees of Freedom Within Groups (degrees of freedom in denominator of F-ratio)	α	2	3	4	5	6	7	8	9	10	11	12
						k = *Number of Means Being Compared*						
10	.05	3.15	3.88	4.33	4.65	4.91	5.12	5.30	5.46	5.60	5.72	5.83
	.01	4.48	5.27	5.77	6.14	6.43	6.67	6.87	7.05	7.21	7.36	7.48
11	.05	3.11	3.82	4.26	4.57	4.82	5.03	5.20	5.35	5.49	5.61	5.71
	.01	4.39	5.14	5.62	5.97	6.25	6.48	6.67	6.84	6.99	7.13	7.26
12	.05	3.08	3.77	4.20	4.51	4.75	4.95	5.12	5.27	5.40	5.51	5.62
	.01	4.32	5.04	5.50	5.84	6.10	6.32	6.51	6.67	6.81	6.94	7.06
13	.05	3.06	3.73	4.15	4.45	4.69	4.88	5.05	5.19	5.32	5.43	5.53
	.01	4.26	4.96	5.40	5.73	5.98	6.19	6.37	6.53	6.67	6.79	6.90
14	.05	3.03	3.70	4.11	4.41	4.64	4.83	4.99	5.13	5.25	5.36	5.46
	.01	4.21	4.89	5.32	5.63	5.88	6.08	6.26	6.41	6.54	6.66	6.77
16	.05	3.00	3.65	4.05	4.33	4.56	4.74	4.90	5.03	5.15	5.26	5.35
	.01	4.13	4.78	5.19	5.49	5.72	5.92	6.08	6.22	6.35	6.46	6.56
18	.05	2.97	3.61	4.00	4.28	4.49	4.67	4.82	4.96	5.07	5.17	5.27
	.01	4.07	4.70	5.09	5.38	5.60	5.79	5.94	6.08	6.20	6.31	6.41
20	.05	2.95	3.58	3.96	4.23	4.45	4.62	4.77	4.90	5.01	5.11	5.20
	.01	4.02	4.64	5.02	5.29	5.51	5.69	5.84	5.97	6.09	6.19	6.29
24	.05	2.92	3.53	3.90	4.17	4.37	4.54	4.68	4.81	4.92	5.01	5.10
	.01	3.96	4.54	4.91	5.17	5.37	5.54	5.69	5.81	5.92	6.02	6.11
30	.05	2.89	3.49	3.84	4.10	4.30	4.46	4.60	4.72	4.83	4.92	5.00
	.01	3.89	4.45	4.80	5.05	5.24	5.40	5.54	5.56	5.76	5.85	5.93
40	.05	2.86	3.44	3.79	4.04	4.23	4.39	4.52	4.63	4.74	4.82	4.91
	.01	3.82	4.37	4.70	4.93	5.11	5.27	5.39	5.50	5.60	5.69	5.77
60	.05	2.83	3.40	3.74	3.98	4.16	4.31	4.44	4.55	4.65	4.73	4.81
	.01	3.76	4.28	4.60	4.82	4.99	5.13	5.25	5.36	5.45	5.53	5.60
120	.05	2.80	3.36	3.69	3.92	4.10	4.24	4.36	4.48	4.56	4.64	4.72
	.01	3.70	4.20	4.50	4.71	4.87	5.01	5.12	5.21	5.30	5.38	5.44
∞	.05	2.77	3.31	3.63	3.86	4.03	4.17	4.29	4.39	4.47	4.55	4.62
	.01	3.64	4.12	4.40	4.60	4.76	4.88	4.99	5.08	5.16	5.23	5.29

From B. J. Winer, *Statistical Principles in Experimental Design,* McGraw-Hill, 1962; abridged from H. L. Harter, D. S. Clemm, and E. H. Guthrie, "The probability integrals of the range and of the studentized range," WADC Tech. Rep., 58–484, Vol. 2, 1959, Wright Air Development Center, Table II.2, pp. 243–281. Reproduced by permission of the McGraw-Hill Companies, Inc.

STATISTICAL TABLES

TABLE 7 Critical Values of Chi Square: The χ^2-Tables

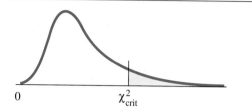

	Alpha Level	
df	$\alpha = .05$	$\alpha = .01$
1	3.84	6.64
2	5.99	9.21
3	7.81	11.34
4	9.49	13.28
5	11.07	15.09
6	12.59	16.81
7	14.07	18.48
8	15.51	20.09
9	16.92	21.67
10	18.31	23.21
11	19.68	24.72
12	21.03	26.22
13	22.36	27.69
14	23.68	29.14
15	25.00	30.58
16	26.30	32.00
17	27.59	33.41
18	28.87	34.80
19	30.14	36.19
20	31.41	37.57
21	32.67	38.93
22	33.92	40.29
23	35.17	41.64
24	36.42	42.98
25	37.65	44.31
26	38.88	45.64
27	40.11	46.96
28	41.34	48.28
29	42.56	49.59
30	43.77	50.89
40	55.76	63.69
50	67.50	76.15
60	79.08	88.38
70	90.53	100.42

From Table IV of R. A. Fisher and F. Yates, *Statistical Tables for Biological, Agricultural and Medical Research*, 6th ed. (London: Longman Group Ltd., 1974). Reprinted by permission of Pearson Education Limited.

TABLE 8   Critical Values of the Mann-Whitney U

To be significant, the U_{obt} must be equal to or *less than* the critical value. (Dashes in the table indicate that no decision is possible.) Critical values for $\alpha = .05$ are **dark numbers** and for $\alpha = .01$ are light numbers.

Two-Tailed Test

n_2 *(Number of Scores in Group 2)*	α	n_1 *(Number of Scores in Group 1)*								
		1	*2*	*3*	*4*	*5*	*6*	*7*	*8*	*9*
1	**.05**	—	—	—	—	—	—	—	—	—
	.01	—	—	—	—	—	—	—	—	—
2	**.05**	—	—	—	—	—	—	—	**0**	**0**
	.01	—	—	—	—	—	—	—	—	—
3	**.05**	—	—	—	—	**0**	**1**	**1**	**2**	**2**
	.01	—	—	—	—	—	—	—	—	0
4	**.05**	—	—	—	**0**	**1**	**2**	**3**	**4**	**4**
	.01	—	—	—	—	—	0	0	1	1
5	**.05**	—	—	**0**	**1**	**2**	**3**	**5**	**6**	**7**
	.01	—	—	—	—	0	1	1	2	3
6	**.05**	—	—	**1**	**2**	**3**	**5**	**6**	**8**	**10**
	.01	—	—	—	0	1	2	3	4	5
7	**.05**	—	—	**1**	**3**	**5**	**6**	**8**	**10**	**12**
	.01	—	—	—	0	1	3	4	6	7
8	**.05**	—	**0**	**2**	**4**	**6**	**8**	**10**	**13**	**15**
	.01	—	—	—	1	2	4	6	7	9
9	**.05**	—	**0**	**2**	**4**	**7**	**10**	**12**	**15**	**17**
	.01	—	—	0	1	3	5	7	9	11
10	**.05**	—	**0**	**3**	**5**	**8**	**11**	**14**	**17**	**20**
	.01	—	—	0	2	4	6	9	11	13
11	**.05**	—	**0**	**3**	**6**	**9**	**13**	**16**	**19**	**23**
	.01	—	—	0	2	5	7	10	13	16
12	**.05**	—	**1**	**4**	**7**	**11**	**14**	**18**	**22**	**26**
	.01	—	—	1	3	6	9	12	15	18
13	**.05**	—	**1**	**4**	**8**	**12**	**16**	**20**	**24**	**28**
	.01	—	—	1	3	7	10	13	17	20
14	**.05**	—	**1**	**5**	**9**	**13**	**17**	**22**	**26**	**31**
	.01	—	—	1	4	7	11	15	18	22
15	**.05**	—	**1**	**5**	**10**	**14**	**19**	**24**	**29**	**34**
	.01	—	—	2	5	8	12	16	20	24
16	**.05**	—	**1**	**6**	**11**	**15**	**21**	**26**	**31**	**37**
	.01	—	—	2	5	9	13	18	22	27
17	**.05**	—	**2**	**6**	**11**	**17**	**22**	**28**	**34**	**39**
	.01	—	—	2	6	10	15	19	24	29
18	**.05**	—	**2**	**7**	**12**	**18**	**24**	**30**	**36**	**42**
	.01	—	—	2	6	11	16	21	26	31
19	**.05**	—	**2**	**7**	**13**	**19**	**25**	**32**	**38**	**45**
	.01	—	0	3	7	12	17	22	28	33
20	**.05**	—	**2**	**8**	**13**	**20**	**27**	**34**	**41**	**48**
	.01	—	0	3	8	13	18	24	30	36

TABLE 8 (CONT.)   Critical Values of the Mann-Whitney U

Two-Tailed Test

n_1 *(Number of Scores in Group 1)*

10	11	12	13	14	15	16	17	18	19	20
—	—	—	—	—	—	—	—	—	—	—
—	—	—	—	—	—	—	—	—	—	—
0	**0**	**1**	**1**	**1**	**1**	**1**	**2**	**2**	**2**	**2**
—	—	—	—	—	—	—	—	—	0	0
3	**3**	**4**	**4**	**5**	**5**	**6**	**6**	**7**	**7**	**8**
0	0	1	1	1	2	2	2	2	3	3
5	**6**	**7**	**8**	**9**	**10**	**11**	**11**	**12**	**13**	**13**
2	2	3	3	4	5	5	6	6	7	8
8	**9**	**11**	**12**	**13**	**14**	**15**	**17**	**18**	**19**	**20**
4	5	6	7	7	8	9	10	11	12	13
11	**13**	**14**	**16**	**17**	**19**	**21**	**22**	**24**	**25**	**27**
6	7	9	10	11	12	13	15	16	17	18
14	**16**	**18**	**20**	**22**	**24**	**26**	**28**	**30**	**32**	**34**
9	10	12	13	15	16	18	19	21	22	24
17	**19**	**22**	**24**	**26**	**29**	**31**	**34**	**36**	**38**	**41**
11	13	15	17	18	20	22	24	26	28	30
20	**23**	**26**	**28**	**31**	**34**	**37**	**39**	**42**	**45**	**48**
13	16	18	20	22	24	27	29	31	33	36
23	**26**	**29**	**33**	**36**	**39**	**42**	**45**	**48**	**52**	**55**
16	18	21	24	26	29	31	34	37	39	42
26	**30**	**33**	**37**	**40**	**44**	**47**	**51**	**55**	**58**	**62**
18	21	24	27	30	33	36	39	42	45	48
29	**33**	**37**	**41**	**45**	**49**	**53**	**57**	**61**	**65**	**69**
21	24	27	31	34	37	41	44	47	51	54
33	**37**	**41**	**45**	**50**	**54**	**59**	**63**	**67**	**72**	**76**
24	27	31	34	38	42	45	49	53	56	60
36	**40**	**45**	**50**	**55**	**59**	**64**	**67**	**74**	**78**	**83**
26	30	34	38	42	46	50	54	58	63	67
39	**44**	**49**	**54**	**59**	**64**	**70**	**75**	**80**	**85**	**90**
29	33	37	42	46	51	55	60	64	69	73
42	**47**	**53**	**59**	**64**	**70**	**75**	**81**	**86**	**92**	**98**
31	36	41	45	50	55	60	65	70	74	79
45	**51**	**57**	**63**	**67**	**75**	**81**	**87**	**93**	**99**	**105**
34	39	44	49	54	60	65	70	75	81	86
48	**55**	**61**	**67**	**74**	**80**	**86**	**93**	**99**	**106**	**112**
37	42	47	53	58	64	70	75	81	87	92
52	**58**	**65**	**72**	**78**	**85**	**92**	**99**	**106**	**113**	**119**
39	45	51	56	63	69	74	81	87	93	99
55	**62**	**69**	**76**	**83**	**90**	**98**	**105**	**112**	**119**	**127**
42	48	54	60	67	73	79	86	92	99	105

TABLE 8 (CONT.)   Critical Values of the Mann-Whitney *U*

One-Tailed Test

n₂ *(Number of Scores in Group 2)*	α	*1*	*2*	*3*	*4*	*5*	*6*	*7*	*8*	*9*
1	.05	—	—	—	—	—	—	—	—	—
	.01	—	—	—	—	—	—	—	—	—
2	.05	—	—	—	—	0	0	0	1	1
	.01	—	—	—	—	—	—	—	—	—
3	.05	—	—	0	0	1	2	2	3	3
	.01	—	—	—	—	—	—	0	0	1
4	.05	—	—	0	1	2	3	4	5	6
	.01	—	—	—	—	0	1	1	2	3
5	.05	—	0	1	2	4	5	6	8	9
	.01	—	—	—	0	1	2	3	4	5
6	.05	—	0	2	3	5	7	8	10	12
	.01	—	—	—	1	2	3	4	6	7
7	.05	—	0	2	4	6	8	11	13	15
	.01	—	—	0	1	3	4	6	7	9
8	.05	—	1	3	5	8	10	13	15	18
	.01	—	—	0	2	4	6	7	9	11
9	.05	—	1	3	6	9	12	15	18	21
	.01	—	—	1	3	5	7	9	11	14
10	.05	—	1	4	7	11	14	17	20	24
	.01	—	—	1	3	6	8	11	13	16
11	.05	—	1	5	8	12	16	19	23	27
	.01	—	—	1	4	7	9	12	15	18
12	.05	—	2	5	9	13	17	21	26	30
	.01	—	—	2	5	8	11	14	17	21
13	.05	—	2	6	10	15	19	24	28	33
	.01	—	0	2	5	9	12	16	20	23
14	.05	—	2	7	11	16	21	26	31	36
	.01	—	0	2	6	10	13	17	22	26
15	.05	—	3	7	12	18	23	28	33	39
	.01	—	0	3	7	11	15	19	24	28
16	.05	—	3	8	14	19	25	30	36	42
	.01	—	0	3	7	12	16	21	26	31
17	.05	—	3	9	15	20	26	33	39	45
	.01	—	0	4	8	13	18	23	28	33
18	.05	—	4	9	16	22	28	35	41	48
	.01	—	0	4	9	14	19	24	30	36
19	.05	0	4	10	17	23	30	37	44	51
	.01	—	1	4	9	15	20	26	32	38
20	.05	0	4	11	18	25	32	39	47	54
	.01	—	1	5	10	16	22	28	34	40

TABLE 8 (CONT.)   Critical Values of the Mann-Whitney U

One-Tailed Test

n_1 *(Number of scores in Group 1)*

10	11	12	13	14	15	16	17	18	19	20
—	—	—	—	—	—	—	—	—	**0**	**0**
—	—	—	—	—	—	—	—	—	—	—
1	**1**	**2**	**2**	**2**	**3**	**3**	**3**	**4**	**4**	**4**
—	—	—	0	0	0	0	0	0	1	1
4	**5**	**5**	**6**	**7**	**7**	**8**	**9**	**9**	**10**	**11**
1	1	2	2	2	3	3	4	4	4	5
7	**8**	**9**	**10**	**11**	**12**	**14**	**15**	**16**	**17**	**18**
3	4	5	5	6	7	7	8	9	9	10
11	**12**	**13**	**15**	**16**	**18**	**19**	**20**	**22**	**23**	**25**
6	7	8	9	10	11	12	13	14	15	16
14	**16**	**17**	**19**	**21**	**23**	**25**	**26**	**28**	**30**	**32**
8	9	11	12	13	15	16	18	19	20	22
17	**19**	**21**	**24**	**26**	**28**	**30**	**33**	**35**	**37**	**39**
11	12	14	16	17	19	21	23	24	26	28
20	**23**	**26**	**28**	**31**	**33**	**36**	**39**	**41**	**44**	**47**
13	15	17	20	22	24	26	28	30	32	34
24	**27**	**30**	**33**	**36**	**39**	**42**	**45**	**48**	**51**	**54**
16	18	21	23	26	28	31	33	36	38	40
27	**31**	**34**	**37**	**41**	**44**	**48**	**51**	**55**	**58**	**62**
19	22	24	27	30	33	36	38	41	44	47
31	**34**	**38**	**42**	**46**	**50**	**54**	**57**	**61**	**65**	**69**
22	25	28	31	34	37	41	44	47	50	53
34	**38**	**42**	**47**	**51**	**55**	**60**	**64**	**68**	**72**	**77**
24	28	31	35	38	42	46	49	53	56	60
37	**42**	**47**	**51**	**56**	**61**	**65**	**70**	**75**	**80**	**84**
27	31	35	39	43	47	51	55	59	63	67
41	**46**	**51**	**56**	**61**	**66**	**71**	**77**	**82**	**87**	**92**
30	34	38	43	47	51	56	60	65	69	73
44	**50**	**55**	**61**	**66**	**72**	**77**	**83**	**88**	**94**	**100**
33	37	42	47	51	56	61	66	70	75	80
48	**54**	**60**	**65**	**71**	**77**	**83**	**89**	**95**	**101**	**107**
36	41	46	51	56	61	66	71	76	82	87
51	**57**	**64**	**70**	**77**	**83**	**89**	**96**	**102**	**109**	**115**
38	44	49	55	60	66	71	77	82	88	93
55	**61**	**68**	**75**	**82**	**88**	**95**	**102**	**109**	**116**	**123**
41	47	53	59	65	70	76	82	88	94	100
58	**65**	**72**	**80**	**87**	**94**	**101**	**109**	**116**	**123**	**130**
44	50	56	63	69	75	82	88	94	101	107
62	**69**	**77**	**84**	**92**	**100**	**107**	**115**	**123**	**130**	**138**
47	53	60	67	73	80	87	93	100	107	114

From the *Bulletin of the Institute of Educational Research*, 1, No. 2, Indiana University, with permission of the publishers.

TABLE 9 Critical Values of the Wilcoxon T

To be significant, the T_{obt} must be equal to or *less than* the critical value. (Dashes in the table indicate that no decision is possible.) In the table N is the number of nonzero differences that occurred when T_{obt} was calculated.

Two-Tailed Test

N	$\alpha = .05$	$\alpha = .01$	N	$\alpha = .05$	$\alpha = .01$
5	—	—	28	116	91
6	0	—	29	126	100
7	2	—	30	137	109
8	3	0	31	147	118
9	5	1	32	159	128
10	8	3	33	170	138
11	10	5	34	182	148
12	13	7	35	195	159
13	17	9	36	208	171
14	21	12	37	221	182
15	25	15	38	235	194
16	29	19	39	249	207
17	34	23	40	264	220
18	40	27	41	279	233
19	46	32	42	294	247
20	52	37	43	310	261
21	58	42	44	327	276
22	65	48	45	343	291
23	73	54	46	361	307
24	81	61	47	378	322
25	89	68	48	396	339
26	98	75	49	415	355
27	107	83	50	434	373

TABLE 9 (CONT.)   Critical Values of the Wilcoxon *T*

One-Tailed Test

N	$\alpha = .05$	$\alpha = .01$	N	$\alpha = .05$	$\alpha = .01$
5	0	—	28	130	101
6	2	—	29	140	110
7	3	0	30	151	120
8	5	1	31	163	130
9	8	3	32	175	140
10	10	5	33	187	151
11	13	7	34	200	162
12	17	9	35	213	173
13	21	12	36	227	185
14	25	15	37	241	198
15	30	19	38	256	211
16	35	23	39	271	224
17	41	27	40	286	238
18	47	32	41	302	252
19	53	37	42	319	266
20	60	43	43	336	281
21	67	49	44	353	296
22	75	55	45	371	312
23	83	62	46	389	328
24	91	69	47	407	345
25	100	76	48	426	362
26	110	84	49	446	379
27	119	92	50	466	397

From F. Wilcoxon and R. A. Wilcox, *Some Rapid Approximate Statistical Procedures,* New York: Lederle Laboratories, 1964. Reproduced with the permission of the American Cyanamid Company.

ANSWERS TO ODD-NUMBERED QUESTIONS

Chapter 1

1. To conduct research and to understand the research of others.

3. Because this is a language course and you must memorize a language.

5. (a) To two more decimal places than were in the original scores.

   (b) If the number in the third decimal place is 5 or greater, round up the number in the second decimal place. If the number in the third decimal place is less than 5, round down by not changing the number in the second decimal place.

7. Perform squaring and taking a square root first, then multiplication and division, and then addition and subtraction.

9. It is the "dot" placed on a graph when plotting a pair of X and Y scores.

11. A proportion is a decimal indicating a fraction of the total. To transform a number to a proportion, divide the number by the total.

13. (a) $5/15 = .33$ (b) $10/50 = .20$
    (c) $1/1000 = .001$

15. (a) 33%   (b) 20%   (c) .1%

17. (a) 13.75   (b) 10.04   (c) 10.05   (d) .08
    (e) 1.00

19. $Q = (8 + -2)(64 + 4) = (6)(68) = 408$

21. $D = (-3.25)(3) = -9.75$

23. (a) $(.60)40 = 24$; $(.60)35 = 21$; $(.60)60 = 36$
    (b) $(.60)135 = 81$;
    (c) $115/135 = 85$, multiplied by 100 is 85%

25. (a) Space the labels to reflect the actual distance between the scores.

    (b) So that they don't give a misleading impression.

Chapter 2

1. A relationship exists when certain scores on one variable are associated with certain scores on the other variable, and as the scores on one variable change, the scores on the other variable tend to change in a consistent fashion.

3. The design of the study and the scale of measurement used.

5. The independent variable is the overall variable the researcher is interested in; the conditions are the specific amounts or categories of the independent variable under which participants are tested.

7. It is a method of selecting a sample in which every score in the population has an equal chance of being selected.

9. They are used to organize, summarize, and describe the characteristics of sample scores.

11. (a) A statistic describes a characteristic of a sample of scores. A parameter describes a characteristic of a population of scores.

    (b) Statistics use letters from the English alphabet. Parameters use letters from the Greek alphabet.

13. The problem is that a statistical analysis cannot prove anything.

15. Her sample may not be representative of all college students. Perhaps she selected those few students who prefer sauerkraut juice.

17. Because of individual differences and external influences, not everyone who obtains a certain X score will obtain the same Y score, so there will be inconsistency in the relationship.

19. Samples A (Y scores increase) and D (Y scores increase then decrease).

21. Study A and Study C. In each, as the scores on one variable change, the scores on the other variable change in a consistent fashion.

23. Because each relationship suggests that in nature, as the amount of X changes, Y also changes.

25.

Variable	Qualitative or Quantitative	Continuous, Discrete or Dichotomous	Type of Measurement Scale
gender	qualitative	dichotomous	nominal
academic major	qualitative	discrete	nominal
number of minutes before and after an event	quantitative	continuous	interval
restaurant ratings (best, next best, etc.)	quantitative	discrete	ordinal
speed	quantitative	continuous	ratio
number of dollars in your pocket	quantitative	discrete	ratio
position in line	quantitative	discrete	ordinal
change in weight	quantitative	continuous	interval

Chapter 3

1. (a) N is the number of scores in a sample.
   (b) f is frequency, the number of times a score occurs.
   (c) *rel. f* is relative frequency, the proportion of time a score occurs.
   (d) *cf* is cumulative frequency, the number of times scores at or below a score occur.
3. (a) A histogram has a bar above each score; a polygon has datapoints above the scores that are connected by straight lines.
   (b) Histograms are used with a few different interval or ratio scores, polygons are used with a wide range of interval/ratio scores.
5. (a) Relative frequency (the proportion of time a score occurs) may be easier to interpret than simple frequency (the number of times a score occurs).
   (b) Percentile (the proportion of scores at or below a score) may be easier to interpret than cumulative frequency (the number of scores at or below a score).
7. A negatively skewed distribution has only one tail at the extreme low scores; a positively skewed distribution has only one tail at the extreme high scores.
9. The graph showed the relationship where, as scores on the X variable change, scores on the Y variable also

change. A frequency distribution shows the relationship where, as X scores change, their frequency (shown on Y) also changes.
11. It means that the score is either a high or low extreme score that occurs relatively infrequently.
13. (a) The middle IQ score has the highest frequency in a symmetrical distribution; the higher and lower scores have lower frequencies, and the highest and lowest scores have a relatively very low frequency.
   (b) The agility scores form a symmetrical distribution containing two distinct "humps" where there are two scores that occur more frequently than the surrounding scores.
   (c) The memory scores form an asymmetrical distribution in which there are some very infrequent, extremely low scores, but there are not correspondingly infrequent high scores.
15. It indicates that the test was difficult for the class, because most often the scores are low or middle scores, and seldom are there high scores.
17. (a) bar graph   (b) polygon   (c) bar graph
   (d) histogram
19. (a) 35% of the sample scored at or below the score.
   (b) The score occurred 40% of the time.
   (c) It is one of the highest and least frequent scores.
   (d) It is one of the lowest and least frequent scores.
   (e) 50 participants had either your score or one below it.
   (f) 60% of the area under the curve and thus 60% of the distribution is to the left of (below) your score.
21. (a) 70, 72, 60, 85, 45.
   (b) Because .20 of the curve is to the left of 60, it's at the 20th percentile.
   (c) With .50 of the curve to the left of 70, .50 of the sample is below 70.
   (d) With .50 of the curve below 70, and .20 of the curve below 60, then $.50 - .20 = .30$ of the curve is between 60 and 70.
   (e) .20.
   (f) With .30 of the scores between 70 and 80, and .50 of the curve below 70, a total of $.30 + .50 = .80$ of scores are below 80, so it's at the 80th percentile.
23.

Score	f	rel. f	cf
53	1	.06	18
52	3	.17	17
51	2	.11	14
50	5	.28	12
49	4	.22	7
48	0	.00	3
47	3	.17	3

25. _____

Score	f	rel. f	cf
16	5	.33	15
15	1	.07	10
14	0	.00	9
13	2	.13	9
12	3	.20	7
11	4	.27	4

Chapter 4

1. It indicates where on a variable most scores tend to be located.

3. The mode is the most frequently occurring score, used with nominal scores.

5. The mean is the average score—the mathematical center of a distribution, used with symmetrical distributions of interval or ratio scores.

7. Because here the mean is not near most of the scores.

9. Deviations convey (1) whether a score is above or below the mean, and (2) how far the score is from the mean.

11. (a) $\Sigma X = 638, N = 11, \overline{X} = 58$
    (b) The mode is 58.

13. $\Sigma X = 460, N = 20, \overline{X} = 23.00$

15. (a) Mean
    (b) Median (these ratio scores are skewed)
    (c) Mode (this is a nominal variable)
    (d) Median (this is an ordinal variable)

17. (a) The person with -5; it is farthest below the mean.
    (b) The person with -5; it is in the tail where the lowest-frequency scores occur.
    (c) The person with 0; this score equals the mean, which is the highest-frequency score.
    (d) The person with $+3$; it is farthest above the mean.

19. She is correct _unless_ the variable is something on which it is undesirable to have a high score. Then, being below the mean with a negative deviation is best.

21. Mean errors do not change until there has been 5 hours of sleep deprivation. Mean errors then increase as a function of increasing sleep deprivation.

23. (a) Line graph; income on Y axis, age on X axis; find median income per age group (income is skewed).
    (b) Bar graph; positive votes on Y axis, presence or absence of a wildlife refuge on X axis; find mean number of votes if normally distributed.
    (c) Line graph; running speed on Y axis, amount of carbohydrates consumed on X axis; find mean running speed if normally distributed.
    (d) Bar graph; alcohol abuse on Y axis, ethnic group on X axis; find mean rate of alcohol abuse per group if normally distributed.

25. (a) The means for Conditions 1, 2, and 3 are 15, 12, and 9, respectively.

(b)
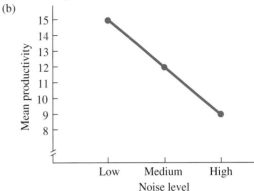

(c)
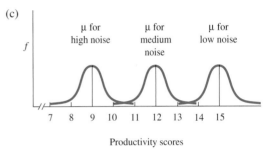

(d) Apparently the relationship is that as noise level increases, the typical productivity score decreases from around 15 to around 12 to around 9.

Chapter 5

1. (a) The distribution's shape, its central tendency, and its variability.
   (b) It is needed for a complete description of the data, indicating how spread out scores are and how accurately the mean summarizes them.

3. (a) The range is the distance between the highest and lowest scores in a distribution.
   (b) Because it includes only the most extreme and often least-frequent scores, so it does not summarize most of the differences in a distribution.
   (c) With nominal or ordinal scores or with interval/ratio scores that cannot be accurately described by other measures.

5. (a) Variance is the average of the squared deviations around the mean.
   (b) Variance equals the squared standard deviation, and the standard deviation equals the square root of the variance.

7. Because a sample value too often tends to be smaller than the population value. The unbiased estimates of the population involve the quantity $N - 1$, resulting in a slightly larger estimate.

9. (a) Range $= 9 - 0 = 9$, so the scores spanned 9 different scores.
   (b) Because $\Sigma X = 100$, $\Sigma X^2 = 668$, and $N = 20$, $S_X^2 = (668 - 500)/20 = 8.40$. The average squared deviation of creativity scores from the mean is 8.40.
   (c) Because $S_X = \sqrt{8.4} = 2.90$, the average amount individual creativity scores differed from the mean is 2.90.

11. About 160 people. The score of 2.90 is one standard deviation below the mean of 5 $(5 - 2.90 = 2.10)$. Since a total of 50% of all scores are below the mean and about 34% of the scores are between 2.10 and the mean, $50\% - 34\%$, or 16%, of the scores are below the score of 2.10. And 16% of 1000 is $(.16)(1000) = 160$.

13. (a) Because the sample tends to be normally distributed, the population should be normal too.
    (b) Because $\overline{X} = 1297/17 = 76.29$, we would estimate the μ to be 76.29.
    (c) The estimated population variance is $(99,223 - 98,953.47)/16 = 16.85$.
    (d) The estimated standard deviation is $\sqrt{16.85} = 4.10$.
    (e) Between 72.19 $(76.29 - 4.10)$ and 80.39 $(76.29 + 4.10)$.

15. (a) Guchi. Because his standard deviation is larger, his scores are spread out around the mean, so he tends to be a more inconsistent student.
    (b) Pluto, because his scores are closer to the mean of 60, so it more accurately describes all of his scores.
    (c) Pluto, because we predict each will score at his mean score, and Pluto's individual scores tend to be closer to his mean than Guchi's are to his mean.
    (d) Guchi, because his scores vary more widely above and below 60.

17. Predict the mean of 65 for each student. "Average error" is variance, so your error will be $S_X^2 = 6^2 = 36$.

19. She is computing the proportion of variance in exam scores accounted for by the relationship with study time.

21. (a) Compute the mean and sample standard deviation in each condition.
    (b) Changing conditions A, B, C changes dependent scores from around 11.00 to 32.75 to 48.00, respectively.
    (c) The S_X for the three conditions are .71, 1.09, and .71, respectively. These show little spread, so participants scored very consistently within each condition.

23. A large proportion: The overall range of scores is between 10 and 49, so without using the relationship

there is much error. Within the conditions, scores are close to each $\overline{X}$, so using the relationship reduces the error considerably.

25. (a) For conditions 1, 2, and 3, we'd expect μs of about 13.33, 8.33, and 5.67, respectively.
    (b) Somewhat inconsistently, because based on s_X we'd expect a σ_X of 4.51, 2.52, and 3.06, respectively.

Chapter 6

1. (a) A z-score indicates the distance, measured in standard deviation units, that a score is above or below the mean.
   (b) z-scores can be used to interpret scores from any normal distribution of interval or ratio scores.

3. It is the distribution that results after transforming a distribution of raw scores into z-scores.

5. Because z-scores standardize or equate different distributions so that they can be compared.

7. (a) It is our model of the perfect normal z-distribution.
   (b) It is used as a model of any normal distribution of raw scores after being transformed to z-scores.
   (c) The raw scores should be at least approximately normally distributed, they should be from a continuous interval or ratio variable, and the sample should be relatively large.

9. (a) That it is normally distributed, that its μ equals the μ of the raw score population, and that its standard deviation (the standard error of the mean) equals the raw score population's standard deviation divided by the square root of N.
   (b) Because it indicates the characteristics of any sampling distribution, without our having to actually measure all possible sample means.

11. (a) Convert the raw score to z, use z with the z-tables to find the proportion of the area under the appropriate part of the normal curve, and that proportion is the *rel. f*, or use it to determine percentile.
    (b) In column B or C of the z-tables, find the specified *rel. f* or the *rel. f* converted from the percentile, identify the corresponding z at the proportion, transform the z into its raw score, and that score is the cut-off score.
    (c) Compute the standard error of the mean, transform the sample mean into a z-score, follow the steps in part above.

13. (a) He should consider the size of each class' standard deviation.
    (b) Small. This will give him a large positive z-score, placing him at the top of his class.
    (c) Large. Then he will have a small negative z and be close to the mean.

15. $\Sigma X = 103$, $\Sigma X^2 = 931$, and $N = 12$, so $S_X = 1.98$ and $\overline{X} = 8.58$.
  (a) For $X = 10$, $z = (10 - 8.58)/1.98 = +.72$.
  (b) For $X = 6$, $z = (6 - 8.58)/1.98 = -1.30$.
17. (a) $z = +1.0$ (b) $z = -2.8$
  (c) $z = -.70$ (d) $z = -2.0$
19. (a) .4706 (b) .0107 (c) $.3944 + .4970 = .8914$
  (d) $.0250 + .0250 = .05$
21. From the z-table the 25th percentile is at approximately $z = -.67$. The cutoff score is then $X = (-.67)(10) + 75 = 68.3$.
23. For City A her salary has a z of $(27,000 - 50,000)/15,000 = -1.53$. For City B her salary has a z of $(12,000 - 14,000)/1000 = -2.0$. City A is the better offer, because her income will be closer to the average cost of living in that city.
25. Convert $\overline{X}$ to a z-score. First, $\sigma_{\overline{X}}$ equals $6/\sqrt{50}$, or $.849$. Then $z = (18 - 19.4)/.849 = -1.65$. From the z-tables, $.0495$ of the curve is below this score. Out of 1000 samples you would expect $(.0495)(1000) = 49.5$ sample means to be below 18.
27. (a) $z = (60 - 56)/8 = .50$, so $.1915$ of the curve is between 60 and 56, plus $.50$ of the curve below the mean gives a total of $.6915$ or 69.15% of the curve is expected to be below 60.
  (b) $z = (54 - 56)/8 = -.25$, so $.0987$ of the curve is between 54 and 56, plus $.50$ of the curve that is above the mean for a total of $.5987$ or 59.87% scoring above 54.
  (c) The approximate upper .20 of the curve $(.2005)$ is above $z = +.84$ so the corresponding raw score is $X = (+.84)(8) + 56 = 62.72$.
29. (a) Compute that $\overline{X} = 68.90$ and $S_X = 13.693$; then 65 has a $z = (65 - 68.90)/13.693 = -.28$; from the z-tables, $.3897$ of the curve is below this, and $(.3897)(200) = 77.94$, so about 78 more people should score below 65.
  (b) $z = (70 - 68.90)/13.693 = +.08$; from the z-tables, $.4681$ of the curve is above this, and $(.4681)(200) = 93.62$, so about 94 more people should score above 70.
  (c) If the data are not normally distributed, the normal curve is not a very accurate model for our expectations.

Chapter 7

1. (a) In experiments the researcher manipulates one variable and measures participants on another variable; in correlational studies the researcher measures participants on two variables.

  (b) In experiments the researcher computes the mean of the dependent (Y) scores for each condition of the independent variable (each X); in correlational studies the researcher examines the relationship over all X-Y pairs by computing a correlation coefficient.
3. You don't necessarily know which variable occurred first, nor have you controlled other variables that might cause scores to change.
5. (a) A scatterplot is a graph of the individual data points formed from a set of X-Y pairs.
  (b) A regression line is the summary straight line that best fits through the scatterplot.
7. (a) As the X scores increase, the Y scores tend to increase.
  (b) As the X scores increase, the Y scores tend to decrease.
  (c) As the X scores increase, the Y scores do not only increase or only decrease.
9. (a) The scatterplot has a circular or horizontal elliptical shape.
  (b) The variability in Y at each X is equal to the overall variability in all Y scores in the data.
  (c) The Y scores are not close to the regression line.
  (d) Knowing X does not improve accuracy in predicting Y.
11. (a) ρ stands for the Pearson correlation coefficient in the population.
  (b) ρ is estimated from an r calculated on a random sample.
  (c) ρ indicates the strength and type of linear relationship found between X and Y scores in the population.
13. He is drawing the causal inference that more people cause fewer bears, but it may be the number of hunters, or the amount of pesticides used, or the noise level associated with more people.
15. (a) With $r = -.73$, the scatterplot is skinnier.
  (b) With $r = -.73$, there is less variability in Y at each X.
  (c) With $r = -.73$, the Y scores hug the regression line more closely.
  (d) No. He thought a positive r was better than a negative r. Consider the absolute value.
17. Disagree. Exceptionally smart people will produce a *restricted range* of IQ scores and grade averages. With an unrestricted range, the r would be larger.
19. (a) In correlational research there is no independent or dependent variable.
  (b) Either variable can be X or Y, depending on which the researcher views as the *given* variable.
21. Compute r_{pb}. For those with degrees, $\overline{Y}_2 = 8.6$; for those without degrees, $\overline{Y}_1 = 5.2$; $S_Y = 3.208$, $p = .50$, and $q = .50$. $r_{pb} = (1.06)(.50) = .53$. Comparing those without degrees and those with degrees, this is a posi-

tive linear relationship with an intermediate degree of association.

23. Compute r. $\Sigma X = 38$; $\Sigma X^2 = 212$; $(\Sigma X)^2 = 1444$; $\Sigma Y = 68$; $\Sigma Y^2 = 552$; $(\Sigma Y)^2 = 4624$, $\Sigma XY = 317$, and $N = 9$. $r = (2853 - 2584)/\sqrt{(464)(344)} = +.67$. This is a strong positive linear relationship, so a nurse's "burnout" score will allow reasonably accurate prediction of her absenteeism.

25. Compute r_s: $\Sigma D^2 = 312$; $r = 1 - (1872/990) = -.89$. This is a very strong negative relationship, so that the most dominant consistently weigh the most, and the less dominant weigh less.

Chapter 8

1. It is the line that summarizes a scatterplot by, on average, passing through the center of the Y scores at each X.

3. Y' is the predicted Y score for a given X, computed from the regression equation.

5. (a) The Y intercept is the value of Y when the regression line crosses the Y axis.
   (b) The slope indicates the direction and degree the regression line is slanted.

7. (a) The standard error of the estimate.
   (b) It is a standard deviation, indicating the "average" amount that the Y scores deviate from their corresponding values of Y'.
   (c) It indicates the "average" amount that the actual scores differ from the predicted Y' scores, so it is the "average" error.

9. $S_{Y'}$ is inversely related to the absolute value of r. Because a smaller $S_{Y'}$ indicates the Y scores are closer to the regression line (and Y') at each X, which is what happens with a stronger relationship (a larger r).

11. (a) r^2 is the coefficient of determination, or the proportion of variance in Y that is accounted for by the relationship with X.
    (b) r^2 indicates the proportional improvement in accuracy when using the relationship with X to predict Y scores, compared to using the overall mean of Y to predict Y scores.

13. They use the SAT scores of college-bound students as X scores in the regression equation to obtain a predicted Y' of the student's college grade average. If the predicted average is high enough, the student is admitted to the college.

15. The researcher measured several X variables and then correlated them with one Y variable, and used the Xs to predict Y.

17. (a) Foofy. The positive r indicates that the higher the statistics grade, the higher the test score.

(b) The relationship does not account for 83% of the variance (and $S_{Y'}$ is rather large), so predictions based on this relationship will not be very accurate.

19. (a) He should use multiple correlation and multiple regression, simultaneously considering a person's concentration and visualization abilities when predicting memory ability.
    (b) With a multiple r of $+.67$, r^2 is .45: he will be 45% more accurate in predicting memory ability by considering concentration and visualization abilities than if these predictors were not considered.

21. (a) Compute r: $\Sigma X = 45$, $\Sigma X^2 = 259$, $(\Sigma X)^2 = 2025$, $\Sigma Y = 89$, $\Sigma Y^2 = 887$, $(\Sigma Y)^2 = 7921$, $\Sigma XY = 460$, and $N = 10$, so $r = (4600 - 4005)/\sqrt{(565)(949)} = +.81$.
    (b) $b = (4600 - 4005)/565 = +1.05$ and $a = 8.9 - (1.05)(4.5) = 4.18$, so $Y' = (+1.05)X + 4.18$.
    (c) Using the regression equation, for people with an attraction score of 9, the predicted anxiety score is $Y' = (+1.05)9 + 4.18 = 13.63$.
    (d) Compute $S_{Y'}$: $S_Y = 3.081$, so $S_{Y'} = (3.081)\sqrt{1 - .81^2} = 1.81$. The "average error" is 1.81 when using Y' to predict anxiety scores.

23. Square each coefficient: $.20^2 = .04$, so knowing the relationship and students' class rankings allows you to be 4% more accurate in predicting their studiousness scores. Using the relationship with gender also accounts for 4% of the variance in studiousness scores.

25. (a) The size of the correlation coefficient indirectly indicates this, but the standard error of the estimate most directly communicates how much better (or worse) than predicted she's likely to perform.
    (b) Not very useful: Squaring a small correlation coefficient produces a small proportion of variance accounted for.

Chapter 9

1. (a) It is the expected relative frequency of the event.
   (b) The relative frequency of the event in the population.

3. (a) Sampling with replacement is replacing the individuals or events from a sample back into the population before another sample is selected.
   (b) Sampling without replacement is not replacing the individuals or events from a sample before another is selected.
   (c) Over successive samples, sampling without replacement increases the probability of an event, because there are fewer events that can occur; with replacement, each probability remains constant.

5. Either the sample poorly represents that population, or it represents some other population.

7. It indicates whether or not the sample's z-score (and the sample $\overline{X}$) lies in the region of rejection.

9. No. A child's gender is an independent event, so the probability that the child will be a boy is still .5.

11. The p of a hurricane is $160/200 = .80$. The uncle is looking at an unrepresentative sample over the past 13 years. Poindexter uses the gambler's fallacy, failing to realize that p is based on the long run, and so in the next few years there may not be a hurricane.

13. (a) Dependent: You are less likely to golf in rain, snow, hurricanes, and so on.
    (b) The answer depends on the amount of money or credit you have. If you are rich, the events are independent; if you are poor, they are probably dependent.
    (c) Dependent: Weight loss depends on calories consumed.
    (d) Independent: Your chances of winning are the same, whether you use the same or different numbers.

15. (a) $z = (27 - 43)/8 = -2.0$; $p = .0228$
    (b) $z = (51 - 43)/8 = +1.0$; $p = .1587$
    (c) $z = (42 - 43)/8 = -.125 = -.13$; $z = (44 - 43)/8 = +.125 = +.13$; $p = .0517 + .0517 = .1034$
    (d) $z = (33 - 43)/8 = -1.25$; $z = (49 - 43)/8 = +.75$; $p = .1056 + .2266 = .3322$

17. Transform 24 to z: $\sigma_{\overline{X}} = 12/\sqrt{30} = 2.19$; $z = (24 - 18)/2.19 = +2.74$; $p = .0031$.

19. (a) Chance should not produce a sample that is very different from and thus unlikely to come from the population, so we reject that it does.
    (b) Samples different from the population are likely to occur, so we accept that the sample represents this population.

21. (a) 100% of the time we'll conclude the coin is not fair and .008 of the time chance produces the result and we'll be wrong, so the p that we're wrong this time is .008.
    (b) The p that chance would not produce the result, which is $p = .992$.

23. No. With a $z = +2.74$, this mean falls beyond the critical value of 1.96. It is too unlikely to be accepted as representing this population.

25. (a) The $\overline{X} = 321/9 = 35.67$; $\sigma_{\overline{X}} = 5/\sqrt{9}, = 1.67$. Then $z = (35.67 - 30)/1.67 = +3.40$. With a critical value of ± 1.96, conclude that the football players do not represent this population.
    (b) Football players, as represented by your sample, form a population different from non–football players, having a μ of about 35.67.

27. (a) For Fred's sample, $\mu = 26$, and for Ethel's, $\mu = 18$.

(b) The population with $\mu = 26$ is most likely to produce a sample with $\overline{X} = 26$, and the population with $\mu = 18$ is most likely to produce a sample with $\overline{X} = 18$.

Chapter 10

1. (a) Sampling error is the difference between a statistic and the parameter it represents; it occurs by luck in drawing a sample.
   (b) A sample may (1) poorly represent one population because of sampling error, or (2) represent some other population.

3. (a) α stands for the criterion probability; it determines the size of the region of rejection, and it is the theoretical probability of a Type I error.
   (b) The smaller the α, the larger the absolute value of z_{crit}, and the larger z_{obt} must be to be significant.

5. They describe the predicted relationship that may or may not be demonstrated in an experiment.

7. Use a two-tailed test when predicting a relationship but not the direction that scores will change. Use a one-tailed test when predicting the direction the scores will change.

9. (a) They are more powerful than nonparametric procedures.
   (b) They are robust, so violating the assumptions somewhat results in a small error when estimating the probability of a Type 1 error.
   (c) The probability of a Type I error will be much larger than α.

11. (a) Power is the probability of not making a Type II error.
    (b) So we can detect relationships when they exist and thus learn something about nature.
    (c) When results are not significant, we worry if we missed a real relationship.
    (d) In a one-tailed test the critical value is smaller than in a two-tailed test; so the obtained value is more likely to be significant.

13. (a) The experiment will demonstrate that changing the independent variable from a week other than finals week to finals week increases the dependent variable of amount of pizza consumed; the experiment will not demonstrate an increase.
    (b) The experiment will demonstrate that changing the independent variable from not performing breathing exercises to performing them changes the dependent variable of blood pressure; the experiment will not demonstrate a change.
    (c) The experiment will demonstrate that changing the independent variable by increasing hormone levels

changes the dependent variable of pain sensitivity; the experiment will not demonstrate a change.

(d) The experiment will demonstrate that changing the independent variable by increasing amount of light will decrease the dependent variable of frequency of dreams; the experiment will not demonstrate a decrease.

15. In a real relationship, there is something in nature that ties different X scores to different Y scores. Sampling error produces scores that by chance pair up to look like a relationship.

17. (a) Use a two-tailed test because we do not predict the direction that scores will change.

(b) $H_0: \mu = 50, H_a: \mu \neq 50$

(c) $\sigma_{\bar{X}} = 12/\sqrt{49} = 1.71$; $z_{obt} = (54.63 - 50)/1.71 = +2.71$

(d) $z_{crit} = \pm 1.96$

(e) Yes, because z_{obt} is beyond z_{crit}, the results are significant: Changing from the condition of no music to the condition of music results in test scores' changing from a μ of 50 to a μ of around 54.63.

19. (a) The probability of a Type I error is $p < .05$. The error would be concluding that music influences scores when really it does not.

(b) By rejecting H_0, there is no chance of making a Type II error. It would be concluding that music does not influence scores when really it does.

21. She is incorrect about Type I errors, because the total size of the region of rejection (which is α) is the same regardless of whether a one- or two-tailed test is used; α is also the probability of making a Type I error, so it is equally likely using either type of test.

23. (a) She is correct; that is what $p < .0001$ indicates.

(b) She is incorrect. In both studies the researchers decided the results were unlikely to reflect sampling error from the H_0 population; they merely defined unlikely differently.

(c) The probability of a Type I error is less in Study B.

25. This study seeks to prove the null hypothesis, seeking to reject H_a and accept H_0 (which cannot be done.) At best, both hypotheses will be retained, and failing to reject H_0 does not mean it's true.

27. (a) The researcher decided that the difference between the scores for Brand X and other brands is too large to have resulted by chance if there wasn't a real difference between them.

(b) The $p < .44$ indicates an α of .44, so the probability is .44 that the researcher made a Type I error. This p is far too large for us to accept the conclusion.

Chapter 11

1. (a) The t-test and the z-test.

(b) Compute z if the standard deviation of the raw score population (σ_X) is known; compute t if σ_X is estimated by s_X.

(c) That we have one random sample of interval or ratio dependent scores, and the scores are approximately normally distributed.

3. (a) $s_{\bar{X}}$ is the estimated standard error of the mean; $\sigma_{\bar{X}}$ is the true standard error of the mean.

(b) Both are used as a standard deviation to locate a sample mean on the sampling distribution of means.

5. Determine if the coefficient is significant by comparing it to the appropriate critical value; if the coefficient is significant, compute the regression equation and graph it, compute the proportion of variance accounted for, and interpret the relationship psychologically.

7. To describe the relationship and interpret it psychologically.

9. (a) Power is the probability of rejecting H_0 when it is false (not making a Type II error).

(b) When a result is not significant.

(c) Because then we may have made a Type II error.

(d) When designing a study.

11. (a) $H_0: \mu = 68.5; H_a: \mu \neq 68.5$

(b) $s_X^2 = 130.5; s_{\bar{X}} = \sqrt{130.5/10} = 3.61$; $t_{obt} = (78.5 - 68.5)/3.61 = +2.77$

(c) With $df = 9, t_{crit} = \pm 2.262$.

(d) Using this book rather than other books produces a significant improvement in exam scores: $t_{obt}(9) = 2.77, p < .05$.

(e) $(3.61)(-2.262) + 78.5 \leq \mu \leq (3.61)(+2.262) + 78.5 = 70.33 \leq \mu \leq 86.67$

13. (a) $H_0: \mu = 50; H_a: \mu \neq 50$.

(b) $t_{obt} = (53.25 - 50)/8.44 = +.39$

(c) For $df = 7, t_{crit} = \pm 2.365$

(d) $t(7) = +.39, p > .05$.

(e) The results are not significant, so do not compute the confidence interval.

(f) She has no evidence that strong arguments change people's attitudes toward this issue.

15. Disagree. Everything Poindexter said was meaningless, because he failed to first perform significance testing to eliminate the possibility that his correlation was merely a fluke resulting from sampling error.

17. (a) $H_0: \rho = 0; H_a: \rho \neq 0$.

(b) With $df = 70, r_{crit} = \pm .232$

(c) $r(70) = +.38, p < .05$ (and even $< .01$)

(d) The correlation is significant, so he should conclude that the relationship exists in the population, and he should estimate that ρ is approximately $+.38$.

(e) The regression equation and r^2 should be computed.

19. (a) r_{pb}

(b) $H_0: \rho_{pb} = 0; H_a: \rho_{pb} \neq 0$.

(c) For $df = 40$, $r_{crit} = \pm.304$

(d) The r_{pb} is significant, so she expects the ρ_{pb} to be approximately .33. She should expect it to be a positive relationship only if left-handers are assigned a lower score than right-handers on the variable of handedness.

(e) $(r_{pb})^2 = .11$. The relationship accounts for only 11% of the variance in personality scores, so the results are not very useful.

21. (a) Math majors will all score high and close together, restricting the range of this variable.

(b) Having only 3 puns restricts the range of humor scores between 0 and 3.

(c) Increase his N.

23. The df of 80 is .33 of the distance between the df at 60 and 120, so the target t_{crit} is .33 of the distance from 2.000 to 1.980: $2.000 - 1.980 = .020$, so $(.020)(.33) = .0066$, and thus $2.000 - .0066$ equals the target t_{crit} of 1.993.

25. (a) We must first believe that it is a real relationship, which is what significant indicates.

(b) Significant means only that we believe that the relationship exists in the population; a significant relationship is unimportant if it accounts for little of the variance.

Chapter 12

1. (a) The independent-samples t-test and the related-samples t-test.

(b) Whether the scientist created independent samples or related samples.

3. Create a related-samples design if possible, because the related-samples t-test is more powerful.

5. (a) $s_{\bar{X}_1 - \bar{X}_2}$ is the standard error of the difference—the standard deviation of the sampling distribution of differences between means from independent samples.

(b) $s_{\bar{D}}$ is the standard error of the mean difference, the standard deviation of the sampling distribution of $\bar{D}$ from related samples.

(c) n is the number of scores in each condition; N is the number of scores in the experiment.

7. It indicates a range of values of μ_D, one of which $\bar{D}$ is likely to represent.

9. The independent-samples t-test, the related- (dependent-) samples t-test, the confidence interval for $\mu_1 - \mu_2$, the confidence interval for μ_D, and the effect size (r_{pb}^2).

11. She should graph the results, compute the appropriate confidence interval, and compute the effect size.

13. (a) H_0: $\mu_1 - \mu_2 = 0$; H_a: $\mu_1 - \mu_2 \neq 0$.

(b) $s_{pool}^2 = 23.695$; $s_{\bar{X}_1 - \bar{X}_2} = 1.78$; $t_{obt} = (43 - 39)/1.78 = +2.25$

(c) With $df = (15 - 1) + (15 - 1) = 28$, $t_{crit} = +2.048$.

(d) The results are significant: In the population, hot baths (with μ about 43) produce different relaxation scores than cold baths (with μ about 39).

(e) $(1.78)(-2.0480) + 4 \leq \mu_1 - \mu_2 \leq (1.78)(+2.048) + 4 = .35 \leq \mu_1 - \mu_2 \leq 7.65$

(f) $r_{pb}^2 = (2.25)^2/[(2.25)^2 + 28] = .15$, so bath temperatures do not have a very large effect.

(g) Label the X axis as bath temperature; label the Y axis as mean relaxation score; plot the data point for cold baths at a Y of 39 and for hot baths at a Y of 43; connect the data points with a straight line.

15. (a) She should retain H_0, because in her one-tailed test the signs of t_{obt} and t_{crit} are different.

(b) She probably did not subtract her sample means in the same way that she subtracted the μs in her hypotheses.

17. (a) H_0: $\mu_D = 0$; H_a: $\mu_D \neq 0$.

(b) $t_{obt} = (2.63 - 0)/.75 = +3.51$

(c) With $df = 7$, $t_{crit} = \pm 2.365$, so $t(7) = +3.51$, $p < .05$.

(d) $.86 \leq \mu_D \leq 4.40$

(e) The $\bar{X}$ of 15.5, the $\bar{X}$ of 18.13.

(f) $r_{pb}^2 = (3.51)^2/[(3.51)^2 + 7] = .64$; they are on average about 64% more accurate.

(g) People exposed to high amounts of sunshine exhibit a significantly higher well-being score than when exposed to lower amounts, with the μ of the difference scores between .86 and 4.40.

19. (a) H_0: $\mu_D \leq 0$; H_a: $\mu_D > 0$.

(b) $\bar{D} = 1.2$, $s_D^2 = 1.289$, $s_{\bar{D}} = .359$; $t_{obt} = (1.2 - 0)/.359 = +3.34$

(c) With $df = 9$, $t_{crit} = +1.833$

(d) The results are significant. In the population, children exhibit more aggressive acts after watching the show (with μ about 3.9), than they do before the show (with μ about 2.7).

(e) $(.359)(-2.262) + 1.2 \leq \mu_D \leq (.359)(+2.262) + 1.2 = .39 \leq \mu_D \leq 2.01$

(f) $r_{pb}^2 = (3.34)^2/[(3.34)^2 + 9] = .55$; so violence on television is an important variable to consider here.

21. You cannot test the same people first when they're males and then again when they're females.

23. (a) Two-tailed.

(b) H_0: $\mu_1 - \mu_2 = 0$, H_a: $\mu_1 - \mu_2 \neq 0$

(c) $\bar{X}_1 = 11.5$, $s_1^2 = 4.72$; $\bar{X}_2 = 14.1$, $s_2^2 = 5.86$, $s_{\bar{X}_1 - \bar{X}_2} = 1.03$, $t_{obt} = (11.5 - 14.1)/1.03 = -2.52$. With $df = 18$, $t_{crit} = \pm 2.101$, so t_{obt} is significant.

(d) $(1.03)(-2.101) + -2.6 \leq \mu_1 - \mu_2 \leq (1.03)(+2.101) + -2.6 = -4.76 \leq \mu_1 - \mu_2 \leq -.44$

(e) Police who've taken this course are more successful at solving disputes than police who have not taken it. The μ for the police with the course is around 14.1, and the μ for police without the course is around 11.5. The absolute difference between these μs will be between 4.76 and .44.

(f) $r_{ph}^2 = .26$; taking the course is somewhat important.

25. Conduct a repeated-measures study; alter the training to make a bigger difference in test participants more consistently; increase N.

Chapter 13

1. (a) Analysis of variance.
   (b) A study that contains one independent variable.
   (c) An independent variable.
   (d) A condition of the independent variable.
   (e) Another name for a level.
   (f) All samples are independent.
   (g) All samples are related either through a repeated-measures or matched-samples design.

3. Because the hypotheses require more than two levels, or because it's easy to obtain additional information.

5. (a) It is the probability of making a Type I error after comparing all possible pairs of means in an experiment.
   (b) Multiple t-tests result in an experiment-wise error rate larger than alpha, but performing ANOVA and then post hoc tests keeps the experiment-wise error rate equal to alpha.

7. (a) When F_{obt} is significant and k is greater than 2. The F_{obt} indicates only that two or more sample means differ significantly; post hoc tests determine which levels differ significantly.
   (b) When F_{obt} is not significant or when $k = 2$.

9. (a) Both describe the effect size, or the proportion of variance in dependent scores accounted for by changing the levels of the independent variable.
   (b) η^2 describes the effect size for a factor having any number of levels, r_{pb}^2 is for an independent variable having two levels.

11. The researcher measured participants on more than one dependent variable in each condition of the independent variable.

13. (a) H_0: $\mu_1 = \mu_2 = \mu_3 = \mu_4$
    (b) H_a: not all μs are equal.
    (c) H_0 is that a relationship is not represented; H_a is that one is.

15. (a) The MS_{bn} is less than the MS_{wn}; either term is a poor estimate of σ_{error}^2 and H_0 is assumed to be true.
    (b) He made a computational error—F_{obt} cannot be a negative number.

17. (a) For a relationship to be potentially important, we must first believe that it's a real relationship.

(b) Significant indicates the sample relationship is unlikely to occur if there is not a real relationship in the population.
   (c) The relationship is unimportant if it accounts for little of the variance.

19. (a) This is a pretest-posttest design, comparing the weights of one group before and after they dieted.
    (b) A within-subjects design.

21. (a)

Source	Sum of Squares	df	Mean Square	F
Between	134.80	3	44.93	17.08
Within	42.00	16	2.63	
Total	176.80	19		

(b) With $df = 3$ and 16, $F_{crit} = 3.24$, so F_{obt} is significant, $p < .05$.
   (c) For $k = 4$ and $df_{wn} = 16$, $q_k = 4.05$, so $HSD = (4.05)$ $(\sqrt{2.63/5}) = 2.94$: $\overline{X}_4 = 4.4, \overline{X}_6 = 10.8, \overline{X}_8 = 9.40$, $\overline{X}_{10} = 5.8$. Only ages 4 and 10 and ages 6 and 8 do not differ significantly.
   (d) Because $\eta^2 = 134.8/176.8 = .76$, this relationship accounts for 76% of the variance, so it's a very important relationship.
   (e) Label the X axis as the factor of age and the Y axis as the mean creativity score. Plot the mean score for each condition, and connect adjacent data points with straight lines.

23. The one-way between-subjects ANOVA, the protected t-test, Tukey's HSD test, the confidence interval for μ using ANOVA, eta squared, and the F_{max} test.

Chapter 14

1. (a) She can use either a t-test or a one-way ANOVA.
   (b) She can use either a two-way, between-subjects ANOVA; a two-way, within-subjects ANOVA; or a two-way, mixed-design ANOVA.
   (c) Whether both factors are tested using independent samples, both factors are tested using related samples (usually with repeated measures), or one factor involves related samples.

3. To examine the interaction between two independent variables, or for the efficiency of simultaneously studying multiple factors.

5. (a) A main effect mean is based on scores in a level of one factor while collapsing across the other factor. A cell mean is the mean of scores from a particular

combination of a level of factor A with a level of factor B.

(b) That changing the levels of the factor produced one or more significant differences among the level means.

(c) That the effect of changing one factor depends on the level of the other factor present.

7. (a) A confounded comparison involves two cells that differ along more than one factor. It occurs with cells that are diagonally positioned in a study's diagram.

(b) An unconfounded comparison involves two cells that differ along only one factor. It occurs with means within the same column or within the same row of a diagram.

(c) Because we cannot determine which factor produced the difference.

9. (a) H_0 is that the μs represented by the level means from factor A are all equal; H_a is that not all μs are equal.

(b) H_0 is that the μs represented by the level means from factor B are all equal; H_a is that they are not all equal.

(c) H_0 is that the μs represented by the cell means do not form an interaction; H_a is that they do form an interaction.

11. With three or more factors, the interaction is virtually uninterpretable. Yet, if significant, it contradicts the conclusions for any main effects, and so the interpretation of the study is based on this confusing interaction.

13. (a) By maximizing the differences between the main effect means or the cells of the interaction, minimizing the variability of scores in each cell, and maximizing n.

(b) The post hoc comparisons.

15. *Study 1:* For A, means are 7 and 9; for B, means are 3 and 13. Apparently there are effects for A and B but not for A $\times$ B.

Study 2: For A, means are 7.5 and 7.5; for B, means are 7.5 and 7.5. There is no effect for A or B but there is an effect for A $\times$ B.

Study 3: For A, means are 8 and 8; for B, means are 11 and 5. There is no effect for A, but there are effects for B and A $\times$ B.

17. Perform Tukey's post hoc comparisons on each main effect and the interaction, graph each main effect and interaction and compute its η^2; where appropriate, compute confidence intervals for the μ represented by a cell or level mean.

19. Only the main effect for difficulty level is significant.

21. (a) For low reward $\overline{X} = 8$; for medium $\overline{X} = 10$; and for high $\overline{X} = 12$. It appears that as reward increases, performance increases.

(b) For low practice $\overline{X} = 7$; for medium $\overline{X} = 8$; for high $\overline{X} = 15$. It appears that increasing practice increases performance.

(c) Yes: How the scores change with increasing reward depends on the level of practice, and vice versa.

(d) By comparing the three means within each column and the three means within each row.

23. Amount of practice is most influential in determining and predicting a participant's performance, size of reward has roughly one-half as much influence, and the interaction has minimal influence.

25. (a)

Source	Sum of Squares	df	Mean Square	F
Between groups				
Factor A	7.20	1	7.20	1.19
Factor B	115.20	1	115.20	19.04
Interaction	105.80	1	105.80	17.49
Within groups	96.80	16	6.05	
Total	325.00			

For each factor, $df = 1$ and 16, so $F_{crit} = 4.49$: factor B and the interaction are significant, $p < .05$.

(b) For factor A, $\overline{X}_1 = 8.9$, $\overline{X}_2 = 10.1$; for factor B, $\overline{X}_1 = 11.9$, $\overline{X}_2 = 7.1$; for the interaction, $\overline{X}_{A_1B_1} = 9.0$, $\overline{X}_{A_1B_2} = 8.8$, $\overline{X}_{A_2B_1} = 14.8$, $\overline{X}_{A_2B_2} = 5.4$.

(c) Because factor A is not significant and factor B contains only two levels, such tests are unnecessary. For A $\times$ B, *adjusted* $k = 3$, so $q_k = 3.65$, $HSD = (3.65)(\sqrt{6.05/5}) = 4.02$; the only significant differences are between males and females tested by a male, and between females tested by a male and females tested by a female.

(d) Conclude that a relationship exists between gender and test scores when testing is done by a male, and that male versus female experimenters produce a relationship when testing females, $p < .05$.

(e) For B, $\eta^2 = 115.2/325 = .35$; for A $\times$ B, $\eta^2 = 105.8/325 = .33$.

Chapter 15

1. Both types of procedures test whether, due to sampling error, the data poorly represent the absence of the predicted relationship in the population.

3. (a) Either nominal or ordinal scores.

(b) They may form very nonnormal distributions, or their populations may not have homogeneous variance, so they are transformed to ranks.

5. (a) When the data consist of the frequency that participants fall into each category of one or more variables.

(b) When categorizing participants along only one variable.

(c) When simultaneously categorizing participants along two variables.

7. That the sample frequencies are unlikely to represent the distribution of frequencies in the population described by H_0.

9. (a) It is the correlation coefficient between the two variables in a significant 2×2 chi square design.

(b) ϕ^2 indicates the improvement in predicting participants' category membership on one variable by knowing their category membership on the other variable.

(c) C is the correlation coefficient between the two variables in a significant two-way chi square that is not a 2×2 design.

(d) C^2 indicates the improvement in predicting participants' category membership on one variable by knowing their category membership on the other variable.

11. (a) H_0: The elderly population is 30% Republican, 55% Democrat, and 15% other; H_a: Affiliations in the elderly population are not distributed this way.

(b) For Republicans, $f_e = (.30)(100) = 30$; for Democrats, $f_e = (.55)(100) = 55$; and for others, $f_e = (.15)(100) = 15$.

(c) $\chi^2_{obt} = 4.80 + 1.47 + .60 = 6.87$

(d) For $df = 2$, $\chi^2_{crit} = 5.99$, so the results are significant: Party membership in the population of senior citizens is different from party membership in the general population, and it is distributed as in our samples, $p < .05$.

13. (a) The frequency with which students dislike each professor also must be included.

(b) She can perform a separate one-way χ^2 on the data for each professor to test for a difference between the frequency for "like" and "dislike," or she can perform a two-way χ^2 to determine if whether students like or dislike one professor is correlated with whether they like or dislike the other professor.

15. (a) H_0: Gender and political party affiliation are independent in the population; H_a: Gender and political party affiliation are dependent in the population.

(b) For males, Republican $f_e = (75)(57)/155 = 27.58$, Democrat $f_e = (75)(66)/155 = 31.94$, and other $f_e = (75)(32)/155 = 15.48$. For females, Republican $f_e = (80)(57)/155 = 29.42$, Democrat $f_e = (80)(66)/155 = 34.06$, and other $f_e = (80)(32)/155 = 16.52$.

(c) $\chi^2_{obt} = 3.33 + 3.83 + .14 + 3.12 + 3.59 + .133 = 14.14$

(d) With $df = 2$, $\chi^2_{crit} = 5.99$, so the results are significant: In the population, frequency of political party affiliation depends on gender, $p < .05$.

(e) $C = \sqrt{14.14/(155 + 14.14)} = .29$, indicating a somewhat consistent relationship.

17. If the sample is perfectly representative of the distribution of ranks described by H_0, then the sum of the ranks in a group should equal the expected sum of the ranks. The greater the difference between the observed and the expected sums of ranks, the less likely that H_0 is true. When the statistic is significant, the observed ranks are too unlikely for us to accept as representing the distribution of ranks described by H_0.

19. (a) Yes. Because these are independent groups, perform the Mann-Whitney test. $U_1 = 32$ and $U_2 = 4$; therefore, $U_{obt} = 4$. $U_{crit} = 5$, so the two groups of ranks differ significantly, as do the groups of underlying maturity scores, $p < .05$.

(b) Return to the raw scores: For students who have not taken statistics, $\overline{X} = 41.67$, so you would expect μ to be around 41.67. For statistics students, $\overline{X} = 69.67$, so you would expect their μ to be around 69.67.

21. (a) She should use the Kruskal-Wallis H test, because this is a nonparametric one-way, between-subjects design.

(b) She should assign ranks to the 20 scores, assigning a 1 to the lowest score in the study, a 2 to the next lowest, and so on.

(c) She should perform the post hoc comparisons: For each possible pair of conditions, she should rerank the scores and perform the rank sums test.

(d) She will determine which types of patients have significantly different improvement ratings.

23. (a) The design involved a within-subjects factor with two conditions.

(b) The raw scores were ordinal scores.

(c) That the ranks in one group were significantly higher or lower than those in the other group.

25. (a) One factor is the pictured facial expression having three categories, and participants' categorizing each picture as happy or sad is a second factor; counting

the number of participants falling into a category produces a two-way chi square design.

(b) The flaw is that the nonparametric chi square is not a powerful procedure.

(c) If you did not obtain a significant result.

(d) Measure the amount of sadness a participant sees using an interval/ratio scale and analyze using a one-way ANOVA.

Appendix A: Additional Statistical Formulas

Section A.1: Computing Percentiles

1.

Score	f	rel. f	cf
53	1	.05	18
52	3	.17	17
51	2	.11	14
50	5	.28	12
49	4	.22	7
48	0	.00	3
47	3	.17	3

(a) The score of 51 is at the 72nd percentile.

(b) The score at the 50th percentile is

$$\text{Score} = 49.5 + \left(\frac{9-7}{5}\right)(1) = 49.90$$

3.

Score	f	rel. f	cf
128–131	1	.04	28
124–127	2	.07	27
120–123	6	.21	25
116–119	8	.29	19
112–115	4	.14	11
108–111	3	.11	7
104–107	2	.07	4
100–103	2	.07	2

(a) Percentile $= \left(\dfrac{11 + \dfrac{117 - 115.5}{4}(8)}{28}\right)(100) =$

$\left(\dfrac{11 + .375(8)}{28}\right)(100) = \left(\dfrac{11 + 3}{28}\right)(100) =$

50th percentile

(b) Score $= 119.5 + \left(\dfrac{22.4 - 19}{6}\right)(4) = 119.5 +$

.567(4)

Score $= 119.5 + 2.268 = 121.768 = 121.77$

Section A.2: Performing Linear Interpolation

1. The target z-score is between $z = .670$ at .2514 of the curve and $z = .680$ at .2483. With .2500 at .0014/.0031 of the distance between .2514 and .2483, the corresponding z-score is .00452 above .67, at .67452.

3. The df of 50 is bracketed by $df = 40$ with $t_{crit} = 2.021$, and $df = 60$ with $t_{crit} = 2.000$. Because 50 is at .5 of the distance between 40 and 60, the target t_{crit} is .5 of the .021 between the brackets, which is 2.0105.

Section A.3: Additional Formulas for Computing Probability

1. (a) With "and" multiply the individual probabilities times each other.

(b) With "or" add the individual probabilities together.

(c) Consider whether the events are mutually inclusive or mutually exclusive.

3. (a) $p = 1/6 = .167$

(b) $p = 13/52 = .25$

(c) $p = 1/4 = .25$

(d) $p = 0$. After selecting the ace the first time, it could not be drawn again.

5. (a) The probability is the same as that of first selecting one such person and then selecting another. The $p(\text{above } 116) = .34$, so $p(\text{two people above } 116) = (.34)(.34) = .1156$.

(b) These are mutually exclusive events, so with $p(\text{introverted}) = .40$ and $p(\text{extroverted}) = .35$, $p(\text{introverted or extroverted}) = .40 + .35 = .75$.

(c) With $p(\text{above } 116) = .34$ and $p(\text{introverted}) = .40$, $p(\text{above } 116 \text{ and introverted}) = (.34)(.40) = .136$.

(d) These are mutually inclusive events, so with $p(\text{above } 116) = .34$, $p(\text{introverted}) = .40$, and $p(\text{above } 116 \text{ and introverted}) = .136$, $p(\text{above } 116 \text{ or introverted}) = (.34 + .40) - .136 = .604$.

(e) The $p(\text{in-between}) = .25$, and from part d, $p(\text{above } 116 \text{ or introverted}) = .604$. Therefore, $p(\text{in-between and then above } 116 \text{ or introverted}) = (.25)(.604) = .151$.

7. (a) Use the binomial expansion when you seek the probability of obtaining a sequence of events in which each event involves one of two mutually exclusive possibilities.

(b) $p(4 \text{ heads}) = (5!/4!(1))(.5^4)(.5^1) = (120/24)(.03125) = .15625$.

(c) $p(1 \text{ head}) = (5!/(1!(4!)))(.5^1)(.5^4) = (120/24)(.03125) = .15625$.

(d) Obtaining only 1 head out of 5 tosses is equivalent to obtaining 4 tails; since $p(4 \text{ tails}) = p(4 \text{ heads})$, the answer in (c) is the same as in (b).

Section A.4: The One-Way, Within-Subjects
Analysis of Variance

1. (a) It tells you that the researcher tracked participants' weight gain at different times and, at each, measured their mood.
   (b) On some occasions when participants' weight increased, their mood significantly decreased.
3. (a) H_0: $\mu_1 = \mu_2 = \mu_3$; H_a: Not all μs are equal.
   (b) $SS_{tot} = 477 - 392.04$; $SS_A = 475.125 - 392.04$; and $SS_{subs} = 1205/3 - 392.04$

Source	Sum of Squares	df	Mean Square	F
Subjects	9.63	7		
Factor A	53.08	2	26.54	16.69
A × Subjects	22.25	14	1.59	
Total	84.96	23		

(c) With $df_A = 2$ and $df_{A \times subs} = 14$, the F_{crit} is 3.74. The F_{obt} is significant.
(d) The $q_k = 3.70$ and $HSD = 1.65$. The means for zero, one, and two hours are 2.13, 4.25, and 5.75, respectively. Significant differences occurred between zero and one hour and between zero and two hours, but not between one and two hours.
(e) Eta squared $(\eta^2) = 53.08/84.96 = .62$.
(f) The variable of amount of practice is important in determining performance scores, but although 1 or 2 hours of practice significantly improved performance compared to no practice, 2 hours was not significantly better than 1 hour.

Section A.5: The Two-Way, Within-Subjects
Analysis of Variance

1.

Factor B: Amount of Fantasy

Factor A		B_1: Low	B_2: Medium	B_3: High	
	Sub 1	5	7	9	
	Sub 2	6	5	8	
A_1: Meditation	Sub 3	2	6	10	
	Sub 4	2	9	10	
	Sub 5	5	5	10	
		$\overline{X} = 4$	$\overline{X} = 6.4$	$\overline{X} = 9.4$	$\overline{X} = 6.6$
		$\Sigma X = 20$	$\Sigma X = 32$	$\Sigma X = 47$	$\Sigma X = 99$
		$\Sigma X^2 = 94$	$\Sigma X^2 = 216$	$\Sigma X^2 = 445$	$n = 15$
		$n = 5$	$n = 5$	$n = 5$	
	Sub 1	10	2	5	
	Sub 2	10	5	6	
A_2: No Meditation	Sub 3	9	4	5	
	Sub 4	10	3	7	
	Sub 5	10	2	6	
		$\overline{X} = 9.8$	$\overline{X} = 3.2$	$\overline{X} = 5.8$	$\overline{X} = 6.09$
		$\Sigma X = 49$	$\Sigma X = 16$	$\Sigma X = 29$	$\Sigma X = 94$
		$\Sigma X^2 = 481$	$\Sigma X^2 = 58$	$\Sigma X^2 = 171$	$n = 15$
		$n = 5$	$n = 5$	$n = 5$	
		$\Sigma X = 69$	$\Sigma X = 48$	$\Sigma X = 76$	$\Sigma X_{total} = 193$
		$\overline{X} = 6.9$	$\overline{X} = 4.8$	$\overline{X} = 7.6$	$\Sigma X^2_{total} = 1465$
		$n = 10$	$n = 10$	$n = 10$	
			$N = 30$	$k_A = 2$	$k_B = 3$

A × Subject Table after Collapsing across Factor B:

Factor A

	A_1	A_2	A_2	ΣX_{sub}
Subject 1	15	9	14	38
Subject 2	16	10	14	40
Subject 3	11	10	15	36
Subject 4	12	12	17	41
Subject 5	15	7	16	38

B × Subject Table after Collapsing across Factor A:

Factor B

	B_1	B_2	ΣX_{sub}
Subject 1	21	17	38
Subject 2	19	21	40
Subject 3	18	18	36
Subject 4	21	20	41
Subject 5	20	18	38

$$\text{Correction term} = \left(\frac{(\Sigma X_{\text{total}})^2}{N}\right) = \frac{193^2}{30} = 1241.63$$

$$SS_{\text{tot}} = 1465 - 1241.63 = 223.37$$

$$SS_A = \left(\frac{(69)^2 + (68)^2 + (68)^2}{10}\right) - 1241.63 = 42.47$$

$$SS_B = \left(\frac{(99)^2 + (94)^2}{15}\right) - 1241.63 = .84$$

$$SS_{\text{bn}} = \left(\frac{(33)^2 + (50)^2 + (36)^2 + (18)^2 + (36)^2 + (18)^2}{5}\right) - 1241.63 = 184.57$$

$$SS_{A\times B} = 184.57 - 42.47 - .84 = 141.26$$

$$SS_{\text{subs}} = \frac{(38)^2 + (40)^2 + (36)^2 + (41)^2 + (38)^2}{(2)(3)} - 1241.63$$

$$SS_{\text{subs}} = 2.54$$

$$SS_{A\times S} = \frac{(15)^2 + (9)^2 + (14)^2 + (16)^2 + (10)^2 + (14)^2 + (11)^2 + (10)^2}{2} +$$
$$\frac{(15)^2 + (12)^2 + (12)^2 + (17)^2 + (15)^2 + (7)^2 + (16)^2}{2} -$$
$$1241.63 - 42.47 - 2.54$$

$$SS_{A\times S} = 16.86$$

$$SS_{B\times S} = \frac{(21)^2 + (17)^2 + (19)^2 + (21)^2 + (18)^2 + (18)^2 + (21)^2 + (20)^2}{2} +$$
$$\frac{(20)^2 + (18)^2}{3} - 1241.63 - .84 - 2.54 = 3.32$$

$$SS_{A\times B\times S} = 223.37 - 42.47 - .84 - 141.26 - $$
$$2.54 - 16.86 - 3.32 = 16.08$$

Source	Sum of Squares	df	Mean Square	F
Factor				
A	42.47	2	21.35	10.12
B	.84	1	.84	1.01
A × B	141.26	2	70.63	35.14
Subjects				
A × S	16.86	8	2.11	
B × S	3.32	4	.83	
A × B × S	16.08	8	2.01	
Total	223.37	29		

For $\alpha = .05$ and $df_A = 2$, and $df_{A\times S} = 8$, $F_{\text{crit}} = 4.46$, so A is significant. For $df_B = 1$, and $df_{B\times S} = 4$, $F_{\text{crit}} = 7.71$, so B is not significant. For $df_{A\times B} = 2$ and $df_{A\times B\times S} = 8$, $F_{\text{crit}} = 4.46$, so A × B is significant.

For factor A, $k = 3$ and $df = 8$, so $q_k = 4.04$. $HSD = (4.04)(\sqrt{2.11/10}) = (4.04)(0.46) = 1.86$. All levels differ significantly. For the interaction, $k = 5$ and $df = 8$, so $q_k = 4.89$. $HSD = (4.89)(\sqrt{2.01/5}) = (4.89)(0.63) = 3.1$. Meditation and no meditation differ at each level of fantasy. With meditation, low versus high differ; with no meditation, low versus medium and low versus high differ.

For factor A, $\eta^2 = 42.47/223.37 = .19$. For $A \times B$, $\eta^2 = 141.26/223.37 = .63$.

Section A.6: The Two-Way, Mixed-Design Analysis of Variance

1. (a)

Level of Fantasy: Factor A

Factor A Meditation		B_1: Low	B_2: Medium	B_3: High	ΣX_{sub}
	Sub 1	5	7	9	21
	Sub 2	6	5	8	19
A_1:	Sub 3	2	6	10	18
Meditation	Sub 4	2	9	10	21
	Sub 5	5	5	10	20
		$\overline{X} = 4$	$\overline{X} = 6.4$	$\overline{X} = 9.4$	$\overline{X} = 6.6$
		$\Sigma X = 20$	$\Sigma X = 32$	$\Sigma X = 47$	$\Sigma X = 99$
		$\Sigma X^2 = 94$	$\Sigma X^2 = 216$	$\Sigma X^2 = 445$	$n = 15$
		$n = 5$	$n = 5$	$n = 5$	
	Sub 1	10	2	5	17
	Sub 2	10	5	6	21
A_2:	Sub 3	9	4	5	18
No Meditation	Sub 4	10	3	7	20
	Sub 5	10	2	6	18
		$\overline{X} = 9.8$	$\overline{X} = 3.2$	$\overline{X} = 5.8$	$\overline{X} = 6.09$
		$\Sigma X = 49$	$\Sigma X = 16$	$\Sigma X = 29$	$\Sigma X = 94$
		$\Sigma X^2 = 481$	$\Sigma X^2 = 58$	$\Sigma X^2 = 171$	$n = 15$
		$n = 5$	$n = 5$	$n = 5$	
		$\Sigma X = 69$	$\Sigma X = 48$	$\Sigma X = 76$	$\Sigma X_{total} = 193$
		$\overline{X} = 6.9$	$\overline{X} = 4.8$	$\overline{X} = 7.6$	$\Sigma X^2_{total} = 1465$
		$n = 10$	$n = 10$	$n = 10$	
		$N = 30$	$k_A = 2$	$k_B = 3$	

Correction term $= \left(\dfrac{193^2}{30} \right) = 1241.63$

$SS_{tot} = \Sigma X^2_{total} - \text{step 3} = 1465 - 1241.63 = 223.37$

$$SS_{subs} = \frac{(21)^2 + (19)^2 + (18)^2 + (21)^2 + (20)^2 + (17)^2 + (21)^2}{3} +$$

$$\frac{(18)^2 + (20)^2 + (18)^2}{3} - 1241.63 = 6.70$$

$$SS_A = \left(\frac{(99)^2 + (94)^2}{15}\right) - 1241.63 = .84$$

$$SS_B = \left(\frac{(69)^2 + (48)^2 + (76)^2}{10}\right) - 1241.63 = 42.47$$

$$SS_{e:bn} = 6.70 - .84 = 5.86$$

$$SS_{bn} = \left(\frac{(20)^2 + (32)^2 + (47)^2 + (49)^2 + (16)^2 + (29)^2}{5}\right) - 1241.63 = 184.57$$

$$SS_{A \times B} = 184.57 - .84 - 42.47 = 141.26$$

$$SS_{e:wn} = 223.37 - 6.70 - 42.47 - 141.26 = 32.94$$

Source	Sum of Squares	df	Mean Square	F
Between groups				
A (meditation)	.84	1	.84	1.15
Error between	5.86	8	.73	
Within groups				
B (fantasy)	42.47	2	21.24	10.31
A × B	141.26	2	70.63	34.29
Error within	32.94	16	2.06	
Total	223.37	29		

For $\alpha = .05$ and $df_A = 1$, and $df_{e:bn} = 8$, $F_{crit} = 5.32$, so A is not significant. For $df_B = 2$ and $df_{e:wn} = 16$, $F_{crit} = 3.63$, so B is significant. For $df_{A \times B} = 2$ and $df_{e:wn} = 16$, $F_{crit} = 3.63$, so A × B is significant.

For the B main effect $k = 3$ and the $df = 12$, so $q_k = 3.65$. $HSD = (3.65)(\sqrt{2.06/10}) = (3.65)(0.45) = 1.66$. Only low versus medium and medium versus high differ significantly. For the interaction $k = 5$ and $df = 16$, so $q_k = 4.33$. $HSD = (4.33)(\sqrt{2.06/5}) = (4.33)(0.64) = 2.78$. There is a significant difference between meditation versus no meditation for each fantasy level. With meditation, only low and medium fantasy don't differ. With no meditation, only medium and high fantasy don't differ.

For the fantasy main effect $\eta^2 = 42.47/223.37 = .19$. For the interaction $\eta^2 = 141.26/223.37 = .63$.

GLOSSARY

Alpha The Greek letter α, which symbolizes the criterion, the size of the region of rejection of a sampling distribution, and the theoretical probability of making a Type I error

Alternative hypothesis The statistical hypothesis describing the population parameters that the sample data represent if the predicted relationship does exist; symbolized by H_a

Analysis of variance The parametric procedure for determining whether significant differences exist in an experiment containing two or more sample means; abbreviated ANOVA

ANOVA Abbreviation of analysis of variance

As a function of A way to describe a relationship using the format "changes in Y as a function of changes in X"

Bar graph A graph in which a free-standing vertical bar is centered over each score on the X axis; used with nominal or ordinal scores

Beta The Greek letter β, which symbolizes the theoretical probability of making a Type II error

Between-subjects ANOVA The type of ANOVA that is performed when a study involves between-subjects factors

Between-subjects factor An independent variable that is studied using independent samples in all conditions

Bimodal distribution A symmetrical frequency polygon with two distinct humps where there are relatively high-frequency scores and with center scores that have the same frequency

Binomial expansion The mathematical formula for computing the probability of obtaining a specified number of outcomes in some total number of tries

Cell In a two-way ANOVA, the combination of one level of one factor with one level of the other factor

Central limit theorem A statistical principle that defines the mean, standard deviation, and shape of a theoretical sampling distribution

χ^2-distribution The sampling distribution of all possible values of χ^2 that occur when the samples represent the distribution of frequencies described by the null hypothesis

Chi square procedure The nonparametric inferential procedure for testing whether the frequencies of category membership in the sample represent the predicted frequencies in the population

Class interval The name for each group of scores in a grouped frequency distribution

Coefficient of alienation The proportion of variance not accounted for by a relationship; computed by subtracting the squared correlation coefficient from 1

Coefficient of determination The proportion of variance accounted for by a relationship; computed by squaring the correlation coefficient

Collapsing In a two-way ANOVA, averaging together all scores from all levels of one factor in order to calculate the main effect means for the other factor

Complete factorial design A two-way ANOVA design in which all levels of one factor are combined with all levels of the other factor

Condition An amount or category of the independent variable that creates the specific situation under which subjects' scores on the dependent variable are measured

Confidence interval for a single μ A range of values of μ, one of which is likely to be represented by the sample mean

Confidence interval for μ_D A range of values of μ_D, one of which is likely to be represented by the sample mean $(\overline{D})$ in a related-samples t-test

Confidence interval for the difference between two μs A range of differences between two population μs, one of which is likely to be represented by the difference between the two sample means

Confounded comparison In a two-way ANOVA, a comparison of two cells that differ along more than one factor

Contingency coefficient The statistic that describes the strength of the relationship in a two-way chi square when there are more than two categories for either variable; symbolized by C

515

Continuous scale   A measurement scale that allows for fractional amounts of the variable being measured

Correlation coefficient   A number that describes the type and the strength of the relationship present in a set of data

Correlational study   A procedure in which subjects' scores on two variables are measured, without manipulation of either variable, to determine whether they form a relationship

Criterion   The probability that defines whether a sample is too unlikely to have occurred by chance and thus is unrepresentative of a particular population

Criterion variable   The variable in a relationship whose unknown scores are predicted through use of the known scores on the predictor variable

Critical value   The value of the sample statistic that marks the edge of the region of rejection in a sampling distribution; values that fall beyond it lie in the region of rejection

Cumulative frequency   The frequency of the scores at or below a particular score; symbolized by cf

Cumulative frequency distribution   A distribution of scores organized to show the frequency of the scores at or below each score

Curvilinear relationship   See *Nonlinear relationship*

Data point   A dot plotted on a graph to represent a pair of X and Y scores

Degree of association   See *Strength of a relationship*

Degrees of freedom   The number of scores in a sample that are free to vary, and thus the number that is used to calculate an estimate of the population variability; symbolized by df

Dependent events   Events for which the probability of one is influenced by the occurrence of the other

Dependent samples   See *Related samples*

Dependent variable   In an experiment, the variable that is measured under each condition of the independent variable

Descriptive statistics   Procedures for organizing and summarizing data so that the important characteristics can be described and communicated

Deviation   The distance that separates a score from the mean and thus indicates how much the score differs from the mean

Dichotomous variable   A discrete variable that has only two possible amounts or categories

Discrete scale   A measurement scale that allows for measurement only in whole-number amounts

Distribution   An organized set of data

Effect size   The proportion of variance accounted for in an experiment, which indicates how consistently differences in the dependent scores are "caused" by changes in the independent variable

Empirical   Obtaining knowledge through observation

Empirical probability distribution   A probability distribution based on observations of the relative frequency of events

Error variance   The inherent variability within a population, estimated in ANOVA by the mean square within groups

Estimated population standard deviation   The unbiased estimate of the population standard deviation calculated from sample data using degrees of freedom ($N - 1$); symbolized by s_X

Estimated population variance   The unbiased estimate of the population variance calculated from sample data using degrees of freedom ($N - 1$); symbolized by s_X^2

Estimated standard error of the mean   An estimate of the standard deviation of the sampling distribution of means, used in calculating the one-sample t-test; symbolized by $s_{\bar{X}}$

Eta   The correlation coefficient used to describe a linear or nonlinear relationship containing two or more levels of a factor; symbolized by η

Eta squared   The proportion of variance in the dependent variable that is accounted for by changing the levels of a factor, and thus the measurement of effect size; symbolized by η^2

Expected frequency   In chi square, the frequency expected in a category if the sample data perfectly represent the distribution of frequencies in the population described by the null hypothesis; symbolized by f_e

Experiment   A research procedure in which one variable is actively changed or manipulated, the scores on another variable are measured, and all other variables are kept constant, to determine whether there is a relationship

Experimental hypotheses   Two statements made before a study is begun, describing the predicted relationship that may or may not be demonstrated by the study

Experiment-wise error rate   The probability of making a Type I error when comparing all means in an experiment

Extreme scores   The scores that are relatively far above and below the middle score of any distribution

Factor   In ANOVA, an independent variable

F-distribution   The sampling distribution of all possible values of F that occur when the null hypothesis is true and all conditions represent one population μ

Fisher's protected *t*-test The post hoc procedure performed with ANOVA to compare means from a factor in which all levels do not have equal n

***F*-ratio** In ANOVA, the ratio of the mean square between groups to the mean square within groups

Frequency The number of times each score occurs within a set of data; also called simple frequency; symbolized by f

Frequency polygon A graph that shows interval or ratio scores (X axis) and their frequencies (Y axis), using data points connected by straight lines

Friedman χ^2-test The nonparametric version of the one-way, repeated-measures ANOVA for ranked scores

***F* statistic** In ANOVA, the statistic used to compare all sample means for a factor to determine whether two or more sample means represent different population means; equal to the F-ratio

Goodness of fit test A name for the one-way chi square, because it tests how "good" the "fit" is between the data and H_0

Grouped distribution A distribution formed by combining different scores to make small groups whose total frequencies, relative frequencies, or cumulative frequencies can then be manageably reported

Heterogeneity of variance A characteristic of data describing populations represented by samples in a study that do not have the same variance

Heteroscedasticity An unequal spread of Y scores around the regression line (that is, around the values of Y')

Histogram A graph similar to a bar graph but with adjacent bars touching, used to plot the frequency distribution of a small range of interval or ratio scores

Homogeneity of variance A characteristic of data describing populations represented by samples in a study that have the same variance

Homoscedasticity An equal spread of Y scores around the regression line and around the values of Y'

Incomplete factorial design A two-way ANOVA design in which not all levels of the two factors are combined

Independent events Events for which the probability of one is not influenced by the occurrence of the other

Independent samples Samples created by selecting each participant for one sample, without regard to the participants selected for any other sample

Independent variable In an experiment, a variable that is changed or manipulated by the experimenter; a variable hypothesized to cause a change in the dependent variable

Individual differences Variations in individuals' traits, backgrounds, genetic makeup, etc., that influence their behavior in a given situation and thus the strength of a relationship

Inferential statistics Procedures for determining whether sample data represent a particular relationship in the population

Interaction effect The effect produced by the manipulation of two independent variables such that the influence of changing the levels of one factor depends on which level of the other factor is present

Interval estimation A way to estimate a population parameter by describing an interval within which the population parameter is expected to fall

Interval scale A measurement scale in which each score indicates an actual amount and there is an equal unit of measurement between consecutive scores, but in which zero is simply another point on the scale (not zero amount)

Interval size The number of values spanned by each class interval in a grouped frequency distribution

Kruskal-Wallis *H* test The nonparametric version of the one-way, between-subjects ANOVA for ranked scores

Level In ANOVA, each condition of the factor (independent variable); also called treatment

Linear regression The procedure for describing the best-fitting straight line that summarizes a linear relationship

Linear regression equation The equation that defines the straight line summarizing a linear relationship by describing the value of Y' at each X

Linear regression line The straight line that summarizes the scatterplot of a linear relationship by, on average, passing through the center of all Y scores

Linear relationship A correlation between the X scores and Y scores in a set of data in which the Y scores tend to change in only one direction as the X scores increase, forming a slanted straight regression line on a scatterplot

Line graph A graph of an experiment when the independent variable is an interval or ratio variable; plotted by connecting the data points with straight lines

Main effect In a two-way ANOVA, the effect on the dependent scores of changing the levels of one factor; found by collapsing over the other factor

Mann-Whitney *U* test The nonparametric version of the independent samples *t*-test for ranked scores when n is less than or equal to 20

Matched-samples design An experiment in which each participant in one sample is matched on an extraneous variable with a participant in the other sample

Mean The score located at the mathematical center of a distribution

Mean square In ANOVA, an estimated population variance, symbolized by MS

Mean square between groups In ANOVA, the variability in scores that occurs between the levels in a factor or the cells in an interaction

Mean square within groups In ANOVA, the variability in scores that occurs in the conditions, or cells; also known as the error term

Measure of central tendency A score that summarizes the location of a distribution on a variable by indicating where the center of the distribution tends to be located

Measures of variability Measures that summarize the extent to which scores in a distribution differ from one another

Median The score located at the 50th percentile; symbolized by Mdn

Mode The most frequently occurring score in a sample

Multiple correlation The correlation that describes the relationship between multiple predictor (X) variables and one criterion (Y) variable

Multiple regression The procedure for simultaneously using multiple predictor (X) variables to predict scores on one criterion (Y) variable

Negative linear relationship A linear relationship in which the Y scores tend to decrease as the X scores increase

Negatively skewed distribution A frequency polygon with low-frequency, extreme low scores but without corresponding low-frequency, extreme high ones, so that its only pronounced tail is in the direction of the lower scores

Nemenyi's procedure The post hoc procedure performed with the Friedman χ^2-test

Nominal scale A measurement scale in which each score is used simply for identification and does not indicate an amount

Nonlinear relationship A relationship in which the Y scores change their direction of change as the X scores change; also called a curvilinear relationship

Nonparametric statistics Inferential procedures that do not require stringent assumptions about the parameters of the raw score population represented by the sample data; usually used with scores most appropriately described by the median or the mode

Nonsignificant Describes results that are considered likely to result from chance sampling error when the predicted relationship does not exist; it indicates failure to reject the null hypothesis

Normal curve The symmetrical, bell-shaped curve produced by graphing a normal distribution

Normal distribution A set of scores in which the middle score has the highest frequency, and proceeding toward higher or lower scores the frequencies at first decrease slightly, but then decrease drastically, with the highest and lowest scores having very low frequency

Null hypothesis The statistical hypothesis describing the population parameters that the sample data represent if the predicted relationship does not exist; symbolized by H_0

Observed frequency In chi square, the frequency with which participants fall into a category of a variable; symbolized by f_o

One-sample t-test The parametric procedure used to test the null hypothesis for a one-sample experiment when the standard deviation of the raw score population must be estimated

One-tailed test The test used to evaluate a statistical hypothesis that predicts that scores will only increase or only decrease

One-way ANOVA The analysis of variance performed when an experiment has only one independent variable

One-way chi square The chi square procedure for testing whether the sample frequencies of category membership on one variable represent the predicted distribution of frequencies in the population

Ordinal scale A measurement scale in which scores indicate rank order

Parameter See *Population parameter*

Parametric statistics Inferential procedures that require certain assumptions about the parameters of the raw score population represented by the sample data; usually used with scores most appropriately described by the mean

Participants The individuals who are measured in a sample

Pearson correlation coefficient The correlation coefficient that describes the linear relationship between two interval or ratio variables; symbolized by r

Percent A proportion multiplied times 100

Percentile The percentage of all scores in the sample that are at or below a particular score

Phi coefficient The statistic that describes the strength of the relationship in a two-way chi square when there are only two categories for each variable; symbolized by ϕ

Point-biserial correlation coefficient The correlation coefficient that describes the linear relationship between scores from one continuous interval or ratio variable and one dichotomous variable; symbolized by r_{pb}

Point estimation A way to estimate a population parameter by describing a point on the variable at which the population parameter is expected to fall

Pooled variance The weighted average of the sample variances in a two-sample experiment; symbolized by s^2_{pool}

Population The infinitely large group of all possible scores that would be obtained if the behavior of every individual of interest in a particular situation could be measured

Population parameter A number that describes a characteristic of a population of scores, symbolized by a letter from the Greek alphabet; also called a parameter

Population standard deviation The square root of the population variance, or the square root of the average squared deviation of scores around the population mean; symbolized by σ_X

Population variance The average squared deviation of scores around the population mean; symbolized by σ_X^2

Positive linear relationship A linear relationship in which the Y scores tend to increase as the X scores increase

Positively skewed distribution A frequency polygon with low-frequency, extreme high scores but without corresponding low-frequency, extreme low ones, so that its only pronounced tail is in the direction of the higher scores

Post hoc comparisons In ANOVA, statistical procedures used to compare all possible pairs of sample means in a significant effect, to determine which means differ significantly from each other

Power The probability that a statistical test will detect a true relationship and allow the rejection of a false null hypothesis

Predicted Y score In linear regression, the best prediction of the Y scores at a particular X, based on the linear relationship summarized by the regression line; symbolized by Y'

Predictor variable The variable for which known scores in a relationship are used to predict unknown scores on another variable

Probability A mathematical statement indicating the likelihood that an event will occur when a particular population is randomly sampled; symbolized by p

Probability distribution The probability of every possible event in a population, derived from the relative frequency of every possible event in that population

Proportion A decimal number between 0 and 1 that indicates a fraction of a total

Proportion of the area under the curve The proportion of the total area beneath the normal curve at certain scores, which represents the relative frequency of those scores

Proportion of variance accounted for The proportion of the error in predicting scores that is eliminated when, instead of using the mean of Y, we use the relationship with the X variable to predict Y scores; the proportional improvement in predicting Y scores thus achieved

Qualitative variable A variable that reflects a quality or category

Quantitative variable A variable that reflects a quantity or amount

Random sampling A method of selecting samples so that all members of the population have the same chance of being selected for a sample

Range The distance between the highest and lowest scores in a set of data

Rank sums test The nonparametric version of the independent-samples t-test for ranked scores when n is greater than 20; also, the post hoc procedure performed with the Kruskal-Wallis H test

Ratio scale A measurement scale in which each score indicates an actual amount, there is an equal unit of measurement, and there is a true zero

Rectangular distribution A symmetrical frequency polygon shaped like a rectangle; it has no discernible tails because its extreme scores do not have relatively low frequencies

Region of rejection That portion of a sampling distribution containing values considered too unlikely to occur by chance, found in the tail or tails of the distribution

Regression line The line drawn through the long dimension of a scatterplot that best fits the center of the scatterplot, thereby visually summarizing the scatterplot and indicating the type of relationship that is present

Related samples Samples created by matching each participant in one sample with a participant in the other sample or by repeatedly measuring the same participant under all conditions; also called dependent samples

Relationship A correlation between two variables whereby a change in one variable is accompanied by a consistent change in the other

Relative frequency The proportion of time a score occurs in a distribution, which is equal to the proportion of the total number of scores that the score's simple frequency represents; symbolized by $rel.\ f$

Relative frequency distribution A distribution of scores, organized to show the proportion of time each score occurs in a set of data

Relative standing A description of a particular score derived from a systematic evaluation of the score using the characteristics of the sample or population in which it occurs

Repeated-measures design A related-samples design in which the same subjects are measured repeatedly under all conditions of an independent variable

Representative sample A sample whose characteristics accurately reflect those of the population

Research design The way in which a study is laid out so as to demonstrate a relationship

Restriction of range In correlation, improper limitation of the range of scores obtained on one or both variables, leading to an underestimate of the strength of the relationship between the two variables

Robust procedure A procedure that results in only a negligible amount of error in estimating the probability of a Type I error, even if the assumptions of the procedure are not perfectly met; describes parametric procedures

Sample A relatively small subset of a population, intended to represent the population; a subset of the complete group of scores found in any particular situation

Sample standard deviation The square root of the sample variance or the square root of the average squared deviation of sample scores around the sample mean; symbolized by S_X

Sample statistic A number that describes a characteristic of a sample of scores, symbolized by a letter from the English alphabet; also called a statistic

Sample variance The average squared deviation of a sample of scores around the sample mean; symbolized by S_X^2

Sampling distribution of a correlation coefficient A frequency distribution showing all possible values of the coefficient that occur when samples of a particular size are drawn from a population whose correlation coefficient is zero

Sampling distribution of differences between the means A frequency distribution showing all possible differences between two means that occur when two independent samples of a particular size are drawn from the population of scores described by the null hypothesis

Sampling distribution of mean differences A frequency distribution showing all possible mean differences that occur when the difference scores from two related samples of a particular size are drawn from the population of difference scores described by the null hypothesis

Sampling distribution of means A frequency distribution showing all possible sample means that occur when samples of a particular size are drawn from the raw score population described by the null hypothesis

Sampling error The variation, due to random chance, between a sample statistic and the population parameter it represents

Sampling with replacement A sampling procedure in which previously selected individuals or events are returned to the population before any additional samples are selected

Sampling without replacement A sampling procedure in which previously selected individuals or events are not returned to the population before additional samples are selected

Scatterplot A graph of the individual data points from a set of X-Y pairs

Semi-interquartile range The average distance between the median and the scores at the 25th and 75th percentiles (the quartiles), used to describe highly skewed distributions

Significant Describes results that are too unlikely to accept as resulting from chance sampling error when the predicted relationship does not exist; it indicates rejection of the null hypothesis

Simple frequency distribution A distribution of scores, organized to show the number of times each score occurs in a set of data

Skewed distribution A frequency polygon similar in shape to a normal distribution except that it is not symmetrical and it has only one pronounced tail

Slope A number that indicates how much a linear regression line slants and in which direction it slants; used in computing predicted Y scores; symbolized by b

Spearman rank-order correlation coefficient The correlation coefficient that describes the linear relationship between pairs of ranked scores; symbolized by r_s

Squared sum of X A result calculated by adding all scores and then squaring their sum; symbolized by $(\Sigma X)^2$

Standard error of the difference The estimated standard deviation of the sampling distribution of differences between the means of independent samples in a two-sample experiment; symbolized by $s_{\bar{X}_1 - \bar{X}_2}$

Standard error of the estimate A standard deviation indicating the amount that the actual Y scores in a sample differ from, or are spread out around, their corresponding Y′ scores; symbolized by $S_{Y'}$

Standard error of the mean The standard deviation of the sampling distribution of means; used in the z-test (symbolized by $\sigma_{\bar{X}}$) and estimated in the one-sample t-test (symbolized by $s_{\bar{X}}$)

Standard error of the mean difference The standard deviation of the sampling distribution of mean differences between related samples in a two-sample experiment; symbolized by $s_{\bar{D}}$

Standard normal curve A theoretical perfect normal curve, which serves as a model of the perfect normal z-distribution

Standard scores See z-score

Statistic See *Sample statistic*

Statistical hypotheses Two statements (H_0 and H_a) that describe the population parameters the sample statistics will represent if the predicted relationship exists or does not exist

Statistical notation The standardized code for the mathematical operations performed in formulas, for the order operations are performed, and for the answers obtained

Strength of a relationship The extent to which one value of Y within a relationship is consistently associated with one and only one value of X; also called the degree of association

Subjects See *Participants*

Sum of squares The sum of the squared deviations of a set of scores around a statistic

Sum of the deviations around the mean The sum of all differences between the scores and the mean; symbolized as $\Sigma(X - \overline{X})$

Sum of the squared Xs A result calculated by squaring each score in a sample and adding the squared scores; symbolized by ΣX^2

Sum of X The sum of the scores in a sample; symbolized by ΣX

Tail (of a distribution) The far-left or far-right portion of a frequency polygon, containing the relatively low-frequency, extreme scores

t-distribution The sampling distribution of all possible values of *t* that occur when samples of a particular size represent the raw score population(s) described by the null hypothesis

Test of independence A name for the two-way chi square, because it tests whether the frequencies in the categories of one variable are independent of the categories of the other variable

Theoretical probability distribution A probability distribution based on a theoretical model of the relative frequencies of events in a population

Tied rank The situation that occurs when two subjects in a sample receive the same rank-order score on a variable

Total area under the curve The area beneath the normal curve, which represents the total frequency of all scores

Transformation A systematic mathematical procedure for converting a set of scores into a different but equivalent set of scores

Treatments The conditions of the independent variable; also called levels

Treatment effect The result of changing the conditions of an independent variable so that different populations of scores having different μs are produced

Treatment variance In ANOVA, the variability between scores from different populations that would be created by the different levels of a factor

t-test for independent samples The parametric procedure used for significance testing of sample means from two independent samples

t-test for related samples The parametric procedure used for significance testing of sample means from two related (dependent) samples

Tukey's *HSD* multiple comparisons test The post hoc procedure performed with ANOVA to compare means from a factor in which all levels have equal *n*

Two-tailed test The test used to evaluate a statistical hypothesis that predicts a relationship but not whether scores will increase or decrease

Two-way ANOVA The parametric inferential procedure performed when an experiment contains two independent variables

Two-way, between-subjects ANOVA The parametric inferential procedure performed when both factors are between-subjects factors

Two-way chi square The chi square procedure for testing whether, in the population, frequency of category membership on one variable is independent of frequency of category membership on the other variable

Two-way design An experiment in which there are two independent variables

Two-way interaction In a two-way ANOVA, the combination of the levels of one factor with the levels of the other factor

Two-way, mixed-design ANOVA The parametric inferential procedure performed when the design involves one within-subjects factor and one between-subjects factor

Two-way, within-subjects ANOVA The parametric inferential procedure performed when both factors are within-subjects factors

Type I error A statistical decision-making error in which a large amount of sampling error causes rejection of the null hypothesis when the null hypothesis is true (that is, when the predicted relationship does not exist)

Type II error A statistical decision-making error in which the closeness of the sample statistic to the population parameter described by the null hypothesis causes the null hypothesis to be retained when it is false (that is, when the predicted relationship does exist)

Type of relationship The form of the correlation between the *X* scores and the *Y* scores in a set of data, determined by the overall direction in which the *Y* scores change as the *X* scores change

Unconfounded comparisons In a two-way ANOVA, comparisons between cells that differ along only one factor

Unimodal distribution A distribution whose frequency polygon has only one hump and thus has only one score qualifying as the mode

Variable Anything that, when measured, can produce two or more different scores

Variance A measure of the variability of the scores in a set of data, computed as the average of the squared deviations of the scores around the mean

Variance between groups   In ANOVA, the differences in scores that occur between participants who are in different conditions or populations

Variance of Y scores around Y'   In regression, the average squared deviation between the actual Y scores and corresponding predicted Y' scores, symbolized by $S_{Y'}$

Variance within groups   In ANOVA, the inherent differences in scores that occur among participants who are in the same condition or population

Wilcoxon T test   The nonparametric version of the related-samples t-test for ranked scores

Within-subjects ANOVA   The type of ANOVA performed when a study involves within-subjects factors

Within-subjects factor   The type of factor created when an independent variable is studied using related samples in all conditions because subjects are either matched or repeatedly measured

Y intercept   The value of Y at the point where the linear regression line intercepts the Y axis; used in computing predicted Y scores; symbolized by a

z-distribution   The distribution of z-scores produced by transforming all raw scores in a distribution into z-scores

z-score   The statistic that describes the location of a raw score in terms of its distance from the mean when measured in standard deviation units; symbolized by z; also known as a standard score because it allows comparison of scores on different kinds of variables by equating, or standardizing, the distributions

z-test   The parametric procedure used to test the null hypothesis for a single-sample experiment when the true standard deviation of the raw score population is known

INDEX

List of Symbols

Chapter 3

N	number of scores in the data
f	frequency
cf	cumulative frequency
$rel. f$	relative frequency

Chapter 4

X	scores
Y	scores
K	constant
ΣX	sum of X
Mdn	median
$\overline{X}$	sample mean of Xs
$X - \overline{X}$	deviation
μ	mu; population mean
$\Sigma(X - \overline{X})$	sum of deviations around the mean

Chapter 5

ΣX^2	sum of squared Xs
$(\Sigma X)^2$	squared sum of Xs
S_X	sample standard deviation
S_X^2	sample variance
σ_X	population standard deviation
σ_X^2	population variance
s_X	estimated population standard deviation
s_X^2	estimated population variance
df	degrees of freedom

Chapter 6

$\pm$	plus or minus
z	z-score
$\sigma_{\overline{X}}$	standard error of the mean

Chapter 7

$\overline{Y}$	sample mean of Ys
ΣY	sum of Ys

ΣY^2	sum of squared Ys
$(\Sigma Y)^2$	squared sum of Ys
ΣXY	sum of cross products of X and Y
D	difference score
r	Pearson correlation coefficient
r_s	Spearman correlation coefficient
r_{pb}	point-biserial correlation coefficient
ρ	rho; population correlation coefficient

Chapter 8

Y'	Y prime; predicted value of Y
$S_{Y'}^2$	variance of the Y scores around Y'
$S_{Y'}$	standard error of the estimate
b	slope of the regression line
a	Y-intercept of the regression line
r^2	coefficient of determination
$1 - r^2$	coefficient of alienation

Chapter 9

p	probability
$p(A)$	probability of event A

Chapter 10

$>$	greater than
$<$	less than
$\geq$	greater than or equal to
$\leq$	less than or equal to
$\neq$	not equal to
H_a	alternative hypothesis
H_0	null hypothesis
z_{obt}	obtained value of z-test
z_{crit}	critical value of z-test
α	alpha; theoretical probability of a Type I error
β	beta; theoretical probability of a Type II error
$1 - \beta$	power

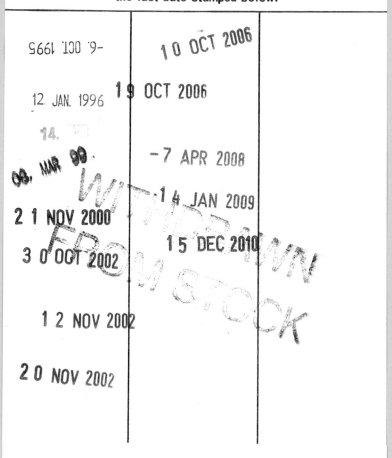